LEARNING LEGAL SKILLS

LEARNING LEGAL SKILLS

Third Edition

Marie Fox

Christine Bell

BLACKSTONE
PRESS LIMITED

First published in Great Britain 1991 by Blackstone Press Limited,
Aldine Place, London W12 8AA. Telephone 0181-740 2277
www.blackstonepress.com

First edition 1991
Reprinted 1992
Reprinted 1993
Second edition 1994
Third edition 1999

ISBN: 1 85431 766 0

British Library Cataloguing in Publication Data
A CIP catalogue record for this book is available from the British Library

Typeset by Style Photosetting Limited, Mayfield, East Sussex
Printed by Bell & Bain Limited, Glasgow

Contents

Preface

This new edition has benefited from the many comments we received on the first and second editions from students, colleagues and reviewers. We would like to thank them for their help and to invite further assistance.

This edition is shaped by those comments and also by a continually changing legal landscape. One of the most significant changes in the last year has been the introduction of a radical package of Constitutional reform. Devolution and incorporation of the European Convention on Human Rights into domestic law will affect both law-making and the interpretation of laws. Accordingly we have taken still greater account of European and international matters. Traditional notions of judicial interpretation have for many years now been affected by the integration of European Community Law into the UK legal system. Incorporation of the European Convention on Human Rights in the Human Rights Act 1998 will also have an impact on traditional legal skills. A second area of considerable change since the last edition concerns Access to Justice, and the materials on this topic aim at providing an overview of the ongoing changes in this context.

All chapters have been updated and many changed substantially, in some cases completely. We wish to thank the secretarial staff at Belfast and Manchester, especially Michelle Cassidy and Shirley Tiffany; our colleagues, especially Claire Archbold, Michael Gunn, Colin Harvey, Tamara Hervey, Stephen Livingstone, Martin Loughlin, Clare McGlynn, Jean McHale, John Morison, John Stannard and Noel Whitty. Our thanks are also due to the staff at Blackstone Press, especially Paula Doolan, Jo Herbert, Alistair MacQueen and Heather Saward. Finally, our special thanks are due to Simon Lee. This text evolved out of our joint teaching on a course in *Legal Reasoning* at Queens. Although pressures of time meant that he could not be involved with this edition, the book continues to bear his imprint — in particular his input to the overall concept of the project, the material which he contributed to earlier editions and his vision of how to make law a lively and interesting subject in the classroom and beyond.

As with the last edition, the only criticisms which we have not accepted are those which would turn this into a different kind of book, an introduction to the (usually English) legal system, of which there are already many excellent examples. In particular we urge readers to consult Blackstone's companion volume, Holland & Webb's *Learning Legal Rules*, for a wealth of detail about traditional approaches to legal interpretation and the important study skill of acquiring familiarity with the support which libraries and information technology can provide. Those who seek a detailed but up-to-date and accessible survey of the legal system should consult SH Bailey and MJ Gunn, *Smith & Bailey on The Modern English Legal System*, 3rd edition, London, Sweet & Maxwell (1996).

This book serves a different purpose; although its concerns overlap with those of Holland & Webb and Bailey & Gunn. *Learning Legal Skills* is a book to use in lectures, seminars and tutorials, as well as in private study, in order to develop vital skills and an understanding of the different perspectives from which law can be approached as a challenging university discipline. This is an exciting time for students commencing their studies in law; the legal landscape they will learn about is constantly changing and evolving. We hope that the skills in this book will equip the student for challenges in law still to emerge or fully take shape, while simultaneously providing transferable skills to deal with other challenges in their lives and careers.

Marie Fox, Manchester
Christine Bell, Belfast
April 1999

Preface to the Second Edition

This new edition has benefited from many critical comments on our first attempt by students, teachers and reviewers. We would like to thank them for their help and to invite further such assistance.

This edition accordingly takes much more account of European and international matters. We have also become more confident in using literature as an aid to the development of legal skills. All chapters have been updated and many have been changed substantially, in some cases completely. This is particularly true of Chapter 5 on Negotiation for which we are indebted to Christine Bell, and of Chapter 10 on Putting It All Together. We wish to thank Christine Bell, who was solely responsible for Chapter 5, Michelle Cassidy and also Mike Redmayne for his suggestions on Chapter 4. Our thanks are also due to the staff at Blackstone Press, especially Alistair MacQueen, Heather Saward and Mandy Preece.

The only criticisms which we have not accepted are those which would turn this into a different kind of book, an introduction to the (usually English) legal system, of which there are already many excellent examples. In particular we urge readers to consult Blackstone's companion volume, Holland & Webb's *Learning Legal Rules*, for a wealth of detail about traditional approaches to legal interpretation and the important study skill of acquiring familiarity with the support which libraries and information technology can provide. Those who seek a detailed but up-to-date and accessible survey of the legal system should consult Joshua Rozenberg's *In Search of Justice*, Hodder and Stoughton, 1994.

This book serves a different purpose although its concerns overlap with those of Holland & Webb and Rozenberg. *Learning Legal Skills* is a book to use in lectures, seminars and tutorials, as well as in private study, in order to develop vital skills and an understanding of the different perspectives from which law can be approached as a challenging university discipline.

Simon Lee, Belfast
Marie Fox, Manchester
June 1994

Preface to the First Edition

Studying law should be exciting, challenging and rigorous. Too often, however, it has the reputation of being boring and mechanical. We offer this book to those studying law for the first time in the hope that it will help confirm the former view and give the lie to the latter. The materials are based on our teaching of law students at The Queen's University of Belfast. We hope that the book will complement other courses, both for law students and for students throughout the Arts and Social Sciences who may be taking a law option. Since we reject the idea that studying law is a matter of memorising rules, it makes sense to structure the book around the *skills* which are fundamental to law. The materials can be used as the basis of a first-year course, or an intensive introductory course in the first few weeks, or to develop skills throughout a three-or four-year course. We would welcome suggestions from teachers and students alike as to ways in which we could improve upon this start. We would like to thank our students and colleagues for their help and especially Jenny Greenaway, Karen Agnew and Nancy Bowman.

Simon Lee
Marie Fox

Acknowledgements

We wish to thank the Incorporated Council of Law Reporting for England and Wales for their permission to use extracts from the legal cases which appear in the text. In addition the authors and publishers would like to thank the following for permission to reproduce copyright material:

Aldershot, Dartmouth: C Bell & J Morison, *Tall Stories? Reading Law and Literature* (1996)

Allen & Unwin *Law & the Sexes: Explorations in Feminist Jurisprudence* (1990)

Arrow Books: C Hardy, *The Age of Unreason* (1990)

Bantam Books: W Ury, *Getting Past No: Negotiating your way from Confrontation to Cooperation* (1993)

Basil Blackwell Ltd: R Nozick, *Anarchy, State and Utopia* (1974); P Fitzpatrick & A Hunt *Critical Legal Studies* (1987); P Thomas (ed) *Tomorrow's Lawyers* (1992)

Blackstone Press Ltd: M Hyam, *Advocacy Skills* (1990); A Halpern, *Negotiating Skills* (1992); C Walker, *Justice in Error* (1993); D Bean (ed) *Law Reform for All* (1996)

Butterworths: Z Bankowski, 'The Jury and Reality' in M Findlay and P Duff (eds), *The Jury Under Attack* (1988); J W Harris, *Legal Philosophies* (1994); C McGlynn, *The Woman Lawyer: Making the Difference* (1998)

Carswell: A Hutchinson, *Dwelling on the Threshold* (1988)

Cavendish: S Sheldon and M Thomson (eds) *Feminist Perspectives on Health Care Law* (1998)

Chatto and Windus: H Kennedy, *Eve was Framed: Women and British Justice* (1992)

Clarendon Press: A Ogus and C E Veljanovski (eds) *Readings in the Economics of Law and Regulation* (1984); S Parker and C Sampford (eds) *Legal Ethics and Legal Practice* (1995); P Craig and G de Burca, *EC Law: Text, Cases and Materials* (1998)

Columbia University Press: J Rawls, *Political Liberalism* (1993)

Cornell University Press: M Minnow, *Making All the Difference: Inclusion, Exclusion and American law* (1990)

Department of Education and Employment: J Bell and J Johnstone, *General Transferable Skills in the Law Curriculum* (1998)

Faber and Faber Ltd: S Lee, *Judging Judges* (1989)

Fontana: R Dworkin, *Law's Empire* (1996); J A G Griffith, *The Politics of the Judiciary* (1997)

Frances Pinter: F Zemans (ed) *Perspectives on Legal Aid* (1979)

Gower: S Livingstone and J Morison (eds) *Law, Society and Change* (1990)

Harper Collins: R Dworkin, *Life's Dominion: An Argument about Abortion and Euthanasia* (1993)

Hart Publishing: M Hunt, *Using Human Rights in English Courts* (1997)

Institute of Economic Affairs: C Veljanovski, *The Economics of Law* (1992)

Macmillan: T Campbell, *Justice* (1988); *McLibel: Burger Culture on Trial* (1997)

Martin Robertson: P Morris, R White and P Lewis, *Social Needs and Legal Action* (1973)

Open University Press: J Morison and P Leith, *The Barrister's World and the Nature of Law* (1992); M Cain and C Harrington (eds) *Lawyers in a postmodern world* (1994)

Oxford University Press: B Jowett, *The Dialogues of Plato, Vol 1* (1953); P Devlin, *The Enforcement of Morals* (1965); H L A Hart, *Law, Liberty and Morality* (1963); J Rawls, *A Theory of Justice* (1971); S Lee, *Law and Morals* (1986); T Nagel, *What Does It All Mean?* (1987); D Pannick, *Advocates* (1992); H Steiner & P Alston *International Human Rights in Context: Law, Politics, Morals* (1996); J Eekelaar & J Bell (eds) *Oxford Essays in Jurisprudence* (3rd Series) (1987); L Goldstein (ed) *Precedent in Law* (1987); M Zander, *A Matter of Justice* (1989); J Jackson and S Doran, *Judge Without Jury: Diplock Trials in the Adversary System* (1995)

Oyez: S Pollock, *Legal Aid — The First Twenty-Five Years* (1975)

Pantheon Books: D Kairys (ed) *The Politics of Law* (1984)

Penguin Books, A Dershowitz, *Reversal of Fortune: Inside the von Bulow case* (1991); R Fisher, W Ury with B Patton *Getting to Yes: Negotiating Agreement without Giving In* (1991); S Turow, *Presumed Innocent* (1987)

Pluto: I Grogg-Spall & P Ireland, *The Critical Lawyer's Handbook* (1992); K O'Donovan, *Family Law Matters* (1993)

Princeton University Press: J Frank, *Courts on Trial* (1973)

Program on Negotiation at Harvard Law School: J W Breslin & J Rubin, *Negotiation Theory and Practice* (1991)

Routledge: Z Bankowski and G Mungham, *Images of Law* (1976); J Radcliffe-Richards, *The Sceptical Feminist* (1980); D Fuss, *Human: All Too Human* (1996)

Sweet & Maxwell: L Neville-Brown and T Kennedy, *The Court of Justice of the European Communities* (1994)

The Stationery Office: C Archbold, C White, P McKee, L Spence, B Murtagh and M McWilliams *Divorce in Northern Ireland* (1999)

Touchstone: A M Dershowitz, *Reasonable Doubts: The Criminal Justice System and the O.J. Simpson Case* (1996)

Ulster Quaker Service Committee: *Prospects for Restorative Justice in Northern Ireland* (1996)

Vintage: T Morrison and C Brodsky Lacour (eds) *Birth of a Nationhood: Gaze Script and Spectacle in the O.J. Simpson Case* (1997)

Weidenfeld and Nicolson Ltd: J Mortimer, *Clinging to the Wreckage* (1982); W Twining and D Miers, *How to Do Things with Rules* (3rd edn) (1991); M Zander, *The Law-Making Process,* (1995)

Journals:
Civil Justice Quarterly, Feminist Legal Studies, International Journal of the Sociology of Law, Journal of Law and Society, Law and Critique, Law Quarterly Review, Legal Action, Liverpool Law Review, Michigan Law Review, Modern Law Review, New Law Journal, New Mexico Law Review, Stanford Law Review, Statute Law Review, Student Law, Trouble & Strife, University of California, Los Angeles, Law Review, University of California, Los Angeles, Women's Law Journal, University of Toronto Law Journal, Yale Law Report.

We would also like to thank the Criminal Cases Review Commission, the Commission for Racial Equality and the Northern Ireland Commission for Racial Equality, The Lord Chancellor's Department, H.M.S.O., the Law Commission for England and Wales, the Council of Europe, and the United Nations and Uncaged Campaigns.

Chapter 1

Introduction

SKILLS

Which skills do lawyers need to cultivate? Close the book and jot down a list of the skills which *you* think are most relevant.
  Our list of legal skills would include the following abilities:

1. To make, apply and criticise precise distinctions.
2. To separate rapidly the relevant from the irrelevant.
3. To think logically.
4. To think critically.
5. To research.
6. To plan.
7. To communicate, to argue fluently, concisely and persuasively, both orally and on paper.
8. To concentrate, working with speed and stamina.
9. To use the above skills to evaluate knowledge.
10. To use those skills to analyse and solve problems.
11. To work independently with initiative and self confidence.
12. To work co-operatively, to lead and to support with sensitivity.

Those are not only the skills which law firms seek in their recruits but, more importantly, are the skills which any liberal Arts degree ought to cultivate. The knowledge to which the student should apply those skills is perhaps really a matter for other substantive law courses, but might be summarised as including:

1. How law is made.
2. What the roles and functions of the law might be.
3. What the social, political, economic and other contexts are in which the law operates.

4. What the moral, economic, and other concepts are by which the law is criticised.

5. What the law is in chosen subjects, i.e.:

   (a) to understand basic concepts;
   (b) to know where to look for detail;
   (c) to know how to apply (a) and (b);
   (d) to know how (a) and (b) could be criticised;
   (e) to know the likely developments in (a) and (b).

You now have two lists of skills: yours and ours. Are the skills exclusively 'legal', or would development of these skills be valuable for other walks of life? Compare your account with the Lord Chancellor's Advisory Committee on Legal Education and Conduct (ACLEC), *First Report on Legal Education and Training* (April 1996).

B. Requirements and aims of the system of legal education and training

2.3 [One] way of approaching a statement of our goals is to list the *general aims* of legal education and training. The Ormerod Report (para. 100) provided a fairly detailed analysis of the characteristics of professional work generally, and of the requirements for work as a barrister and solicitor:

> 'the professional lawyer requires a sufficiently general and broad-based education to enable him to adapt himself successfully to new and different situations as his career develops; an adequate knowledge of the more important branches of the law and its principles; the ability to handle fact, both analytically and synthetically, and to apply the law to situations of fact; and the capacity to work, not only with clients, but also with experts in different disciplines. He must also acquire the professional skills and techniques which are essential to practice, and a grasp of the ethos of the profession; he must also cultivate a critical approach to existing law, an appreciation of its social consequences, and an interest in, and positive attitude to, appropriate development and change.'

2.4 While this provides a good starting point, a modern statement has to take account not only of the changing shape of legal services and higher and professional education, but also of new research on higher education and the professions in general, and on legal education in particular. In the light of these writings and the responses to our consultation papers, we offer the following necessarily superficial general statement of what legal education and training should aim to achieve:

   ● Intellectual integrity and independence of mind. This requires a high degree of self-motivation, an ability to think critically for oneself beyond conventional attitudes and understanding and to undertake self-directed learning to be 'reflective', in the sense of being self-aware and self-critical; to be committed to truthfulness, to be open to other viewpoints, to be able to formulate and evaluate alternative possibilities, and to give comprehensible reasons for what one is doing or saying. These abilities and other transferable intellectual skills are usually developed by *degree-level education*;

● Core knowledge. This means a proper knowledge of the general principles, nature and development of law and of the analytical and conceptual skills required by lawyers. These abilities are normally developed through a *degree in law* or the equivalent;

● Contextual knowledge. This involves an appreciation of the law's social, economic, political, philosophical, moral and cultural contexts. This appreciation may be acquired in part by the study of legal subjects in a law degree in their relevant contexts, or by taking a non-law or mixed degree which provides these perspectives;

● Legal values. This means a commitment to the rule of law, to justice, fairness and high ethical standards, to acquiring and improving professional skills, to representing clients without fear or favour, to promoting equality of opportunity, and to ensuring that adequate legal services are provided to those who cannot afford to pay for them. These values are acquired not only *throughout the legal educational process* but also over time through *socialisation* within the legal professions;

● Professional skills. This means learning to act like a lawyer, and involves a combination of knowing how to conduct oneself in various practice settings, and also carrying out those forms of practice. These skills are normally acquired through *vocational courses and in-service training*.

Still more recently the subject of general transferable skills within the law curriculum has been addressed in a report produced for the Department of Education and Employment:

John Bell and Jennifer Johnstone, *General Transferable Skills in the Law Curriculum: Report of a DfEE funded Discipline Network Project* (1998)

. . .

2. General transferable skills should be seen primarily as a language through which students are enabled to articulate aspects of their achievements in their law studies and beyond which are appropriate both to legal practice and to other fields of employment. They are not an optional extra matter to

be studied, but specific attention needs to be given to them so that students are able to recognise the skills they are developing and to articulate their achievements. The ability to transfer such skills to new contexts is a distinctive attribute which needs to be fostered as well as the skills themselves, e.g. by exercises which encourage students to apply their skills to new situations . . .

1.   Definition of General Transferable Skills

This project proposes to define general transferable skills as abilities not confined to the learning or application of a specific subject. We are aware that there is a large literature on general transferable skills, much of which produces very varied lists of what should be included under this heading. We have drawn on that literature and tried to reduce it to certain manageable ideas which are both usable within the law curriculum and meet the current national agendas of key skills and graduateness.

In this Report, 'general transferable skills' have been identified as the following:

Communication: the ability to present and communicate in written and oral form and to use language appropriately in complex argument;
Problem-solving: the ability to identify and analyse practical issues arising in a situation and to offer a practical solution, making effective use of time and resources available;
Teamwork: the ability to establish working relations with others, to interact effectively, and to promote productive cooperation;
Autonomy and Personal Skills: the ability to act independently, to deal with the unexpected, to reflect on one's own actions and to accept and provide constructive feedback;
Information Technology: the ability to use IT tools and develop that use by integrating it into their own work;
Numeracy: the ability to make use of numerical and statistical information as part of an argument or in a report;
Intellectual Skills: the ability to analyse, think critically, evaluate and synthesise information.

1.1   Legal Skills and General Transferable Skills

Much work has been done in law to identify and develop certain competences among students as specifically legal skills e.g. the DRAIN skills (drafting, research, advocacy, interviewing and advising, and negotiation) in the vocational courses. Though often taught rather narrowly as peculiarly legal skills, they are obviously capable of much wider application. For example, advocacy and negotiation skills are relevant in many professions. While some legal skills training does have broader application, some of the skills developed are very specific to the context of legal professional practice, e.g. legal drafting. Given this background, there is thus typically a distinction between legal skills and general transferable skills, though one must also recognise the overlap between these categories . . .

2.1 The ideals of liberal education

Liberal education has traditionally concerned itself with broadening horizons and facilitating individual personal development. Liberal education achieves its objectives both through the curriculum and through the broader range of learning experiences which are part of life in a university setting, e.g. in societies, union activities, argument with fellow students, and so on. Liberal education is not preparation for any specific job, but a preparation for a critical, aware and responsible appreciation of what is happening in the world both at work and outside.

Understood in a narrow way, there is a distinction between *operational skills* required for the world of work and *academic skills* developed within higher education. The former are said to aim to achieve effect, utility and are basically strategic; the latter are critical and concerned with establishing a rational argument and are not necessarily going to achieve improved production or commercial advantage. Such a distinction is often also made between the values of the vocational stage and the academic stage of legal education. But the distinction is too sharply drawn. Harvey and Mason suggest that the desirability of graduates in employment lies in their *transformation potential*, rather than in their specific knowledge. The skills identified for the workplace are the critical and imaginative skills that are precisely those cherished by the liberal education tradition. The degree of preparation needed to make use of them in a specific occupational setting will be different from vocational to academic stages, but there is no need to exaggerate the distinction between academic and operational or vocational skills. After all, the flexibility of the employment market and the changes in skill demands make it clear that specific preparation for immediate employment has limited value, since the workplace will change and the individual must adapt accordingly.

The issue of broader skills development is reflected in the ACLEC *First Report on Legal Education and Training* of April 1996 [the above report] . . . which emphasises the role of legal education (as a whole) as a liberal discipline and an excellent preparation for many high-level careers (para. 2.2). Legal education at all stages must be able to equip students to move to a number of different exit points, not just becoming a barrister and solicitor. Indeed, what is involved in being a barrister or solicitor is likely to undergo radical change in the course of a career in any case. General transferable skills offer a focus for the promotion of the generic outcomes described which will provide a variety of exit points.

Questions:
1.   Are the aims of liberal education in general in conflict with the notion of inculcating (a) specifically legal skills and (b) general transferable skills?

2.   If you are studying for a Single Honours degree in law, do you think you would benefit from studying other disciplines?

3. If you are studying law as part of another degree programme, how, if at all, do you think the other subjects you study influence your understanding of the law?

In comparing these lists of legal skills, and thinking about the objectives of legal education, you should think critically about what skills are desirable, and, in particular the purpose of inculcating such skills. For example, one American legal scholar has criticised some of our listed skills, and indeed the very process of 'thinking like a lawyer', in the following manner:

M Minow, *Making All the Difference: Inclusion, Exclusion and American Law,* New York, Cornell University Press, (1990), pp. 1–2.

> The children's television show *Sesame Street* instructs with animation, skits and songs. One song asks, 'Which one of these things is not like the others?'. The screen depicts a group of items, perhaps a chair, a table, a cat, and a bed. By asking young viewers to pick out the items that do not belong with the rest of the group, the song helps them sharpen their vocabulary, perception, and analysis of objects in the world.
>
> I often tell people that if you master this *Sesame Street* episode, you have started to think like a lawyer. For much of legal reasoning demands familiarity with legal terms, practice in perceiving problems through categories, and acceptance of the consequences assigned to particular legal categories . . . Legal analysis is a process of perceiving and selecting traits of a given conflict and analogizing and distinguishing prior decisions. Legal rules announced in statutes and in judicial opinions provide definitions and categories; legal precedents appearing in prior court judgments provide constellations of fact patterns and competing normative rules that allow advocates to fit a new case to the rule — or to an exception. And the basic method of legal analysis requires simplifying the problem to focus on a few traits rather than the full complexity of the situation, and to use those traits for the comparison with both the governing rule and the precedents that could apply . . .
>
> This extract is continued in Chapter 10 at pp. 353–6.

When you read the section on discrimination in Chapter 10 you should reflect upon how far modes of legal analysis help or hinder finding a solution to problems of discrimination. Moreover, as Minow makes clear, our possession of traits she lists like gender, colour, class etc., also affect how we view the world (and law). A further academic perspective on 'thinking like a lawyer' is offered in the following extract by Joseph Singer on the aims of legal education:

J W Singer, 'Persuasion' *Michigan Law Review* (1989), vol. 87, pp. 2442–58.

> Law professors spend most of their time teaching — or at least practising — the art of persuasion. We do this by exposing students to a wide array of argumentative moves and countermoves in the context of real world disputes. Law students react to this training with deep ambivalence. On the one hand,

'thinking like a lawyer' has a broadening effect: addressing real cases from the standpoint of both sides teaches students that the questions they thought were easy are actually hard. No claim or interest or right appears to be absolute. Understanding the reasons why this is so, and why we might want to protect competing interests, helps students develop expertise in argumentative tactics. Moreover, by teaching our students to recognise the complex and contradictory nature of our values, legal education at its best clarifies the value choices we must make in governing social relations. This process may be empowering . . .

On the other hand, legal reasoning often appears narrow: the professor may reject out of hand an argument that appears perfectly sensible, even compelling, to a lay person. Law professors have special professional knowledge of what kinds of arguments will have a chance of working in legal settings. At the same time, they may have serious disagreements about this, as well as about which arguments are worth attempting even if they are unlikely to succeed. This cultural knowledge of the profession and the legal system cannot be reduced to a formula. Since everyone believes that some existing laws are wrong or unwise, everyone has the experience of wanting to argue for some result, but being told that the argument is out of bounds, or that it has no chance of success. Students are constantly surprised and frustrated by this process. They are also often confused about what it means to say that an argument will not work. Does it mean that their position is morally wrong or unjust, or does it simply mean that decisionmakers — the people in power — have a professional or personal ideology that rejects the position, and that the argument is unlikely to persuade them to change their minds?

Legal training creates a sense of conflict between the realisation that one can argue for and against anything, and the realisation that there are significant — even overwhelming — professional and social constraints on what counts as acceptable arguments in particular contexts. Judges decide cases somehow, even though they know how to argue both for and against the results they reach — results which are often quite predictable. There may be a professional consensus that a particular law reform proposal is unlikely to persuade those who have the power to make the decision. But the fact that there is a consensus among a significant number of lawyers that an argument is out of bounds does not necessarily mean that it *should* be out of bounds. Lawyers may be experts in knowing which arguments are likely to work in particular contexts, but we are not necessarily experts in knowing which arguments *ought* to work.

Question:
1. Do you think that legal education does limit or constrain the way in which you approach or discuss issues in class?

PERSPECTIVES

It follows from the contentions of Minnow and Singer that the study of law should ideally expose you to many different views of law, life, humanity and society. The point has been made by analogy to art:

S Lee, 'Changing the Province of Jurisprudence', Inaugural lecture delivered at
Queen's University, Belfast (1990).

Monet's studies of the Cathedral at Rouen present different images of their
subjects. One of my Yale professors, Dean Calabresi, once coauthored an
article on law which was subtitled 'one view of the cathedral'. Each analysis
of law gives us one view of the cathedral of law. It can do no more. It cannot
paint the cathedral of law from all angles. At different times, the view from
the same place is different. Each picture tells us something about the
cathedral but also something about the painter and his or her vantage points.
Monet produced thirty studies of the cathedral at Rouen. Many are on display
at Boston, in an exhibition which is moving to London later this year. Each
study adds something, it builds on Monet's experience, as well as reflecting
the different light and shade from the different time of day.

I have developed the analogy and said that what we need is to paint the
picture of law from all manner of perspectives and from inside the cathedral.
Different painters will represent reality differently. We all need to know the
context, something about religion, something about architecture and the
history thereof, before we can understand the cathedral.

On the analogy to Monet, there is nothing wrong, and everything right, in
legal philosophers and other academic lawyers returning again and again to
the same theme. It is sometimes the thirtieth study which captures the
imagination. We can try out different techniques. Remember that Monet
exhibited at a place other than the traditional salon, rather like writing in the
press rather than the unread law reviews. Remember that he got out of the
studio and genuinely *studied* his subjects in their natural habitat before
polishing up his impressions in what we could call the library.

We need to offer many studies, in different media, so our task is to paint
a picture, or as Monet and I would prefer to call the outcome, to create a
series of studies. But Legal Impressionism has more to learn from its artistic
forebears. A sense of dynamism, of movement, of time, shines through
Monet's work, as it should through that of legal scholars, for the law is
always in flux, as demonstrated recently by Eastern Europe.

Moreover, understanding and appreciation do not always come from the
most accurate, realistic representation. Monet developed a new way of
depicting reality. This involved new techniques of brush strokes and tones.
Dramatists, purveyors of fiction, film producers, television playwrights and
others have developed all manner of techniques for representing truth about
law in an unconventional way.

Questions:
1.   Do you agree with the thrust of the analogy?

2.   As with all the extracts in this book, can you summarise the message in a
single sentence?

3.   Is *your* picture of law equally as valid as the picture painted by your tutor?
Can we evaluate competing visions? Students often claim that one opinion is as

good as another on moral or legal issues, as if a toddler's first picture is as artistically meritorious as a Picasso painting (which they might also claim to be true). Do you agree with respect to morality, law and art?

4. Which perspectives on law do you expect to find in your college studies? We will start with a list of possible, plausible answers: middle-class, male, conservative . . .

A TRADITIONAL LEGAL PERSPECTIVE

The traditional view of law (sometimes referred to as a 'black-letter' approach) is to regard law as a set of legal rules derived from cases and statutes, which are applied by a judge who acts as a neutral and impartial referee seeking to resolve a dispute. Although such a definition of law is necessarily limited and does not seem to accord with the reality of law, it has nevertheless been remarkably pervasive. In the following extract a Canadian Supreme court judge considers this image of the traditional judge, and how it is increasingly untenable. (For another, and more substantive, example of a traditional or 'black-letter' approach to law, see the extract from Glanville Williams, at pp. 239–42 of Chapter 7.)

B McLachlin (Justice of the Supreme Court of Canada), 'The Role of Judges in Modern Commonwealth Society', *Law Quarterly Review* (1994), vol. 110, pp. 260–269, at pp. 260–263.

We all possess a certain image of a judge. He is old, male, and wears pin-stripe trousers. He decides only what is necessary, says only what is necessary, and on no account ever talks to the press. He is respected and revered. His word is, literally and figuratively, the law, eternal, majestic. Even those of us who do not fit naturally into the traditional image tend to grow into it. The truth cannot be avoided. We judges like the old image. We cling to it. And why not? It brings comfort, the comfort of knowing one is right, at least pending the verdict of the Court of Appeal, although most of us have learned to rationalise that as well. It brings security, the security of knowing what to do and when to do it. And it brings gratification, the gratification of knowing we are important and appreciated. As Lord Hewart is said to have put it to the guests at the Lord Mayor of London's banquet in 1936:

'His Majesty's judges are satisfied with the almost universal admiration in which they are held.'

In similar vein Lord Devlin suggested in 1979 that:

'The English judiciary is popularly treated as a national institution . . . and tends to be admired to excess.'

In similar vein also can be cited the story of Sir George Jessel MR, who upon learning that Lord Selborne LC proposed to begin an address to the Queen with the words 'We, Your Majesty's judges, conscious as we are of our manifold defects,' is said to have objected strongly, saying 'I am not conscious of manifold defects, and if I were I should not be fit to sit on the bench.'

But wait a minute. What is this I'm hearing? What is this I'm reading? Is this the world I thought I knew? Not too long ago I picked up a copy of *The Spectator*, and was shocked to stumble on an article entitled 'The Judge is a Bastard', followed closely by a second entitled 'The Era of the Blabbing Judge.' In my own country, Canada, journalists have declared open season on judges. Not a week goes by, it seems, that one does not read some commentary critical of the judiciary. And the criticism is not confined to the journalists. While for the most part they prove unsubstantiated, public complaints about the judiciary are on the increase. This is not the world we judges thought we knew, comfortable and secure. What, we are driven to ask, is happening?

The prolific English lawyer and writer, John Mortimer, speaks of 'a general decrease in the awe and wonder with which the population looks at its established institutions,' an attitude from which the courts are not exempted. He puts it this way:

'Many years ago, when I first took up the law, proceedings in court were shrouded in myth. In those days the country at large believed that trials invariably came to the right conclusion, that police officers told nothing but the truth, and that judges were miraculously conceived and were born unencumbered with the usual human luggage of preconceived ideas, kneejerk reactions, prejudice, failures of the imagination, inability to admit mistakes or pure bloody-mindedness.

These myths have now, no doubt to the regret of many members of the legal profession, gone the way of witchcraft and the Flat Earth Society. Trials have, despite energetic whitewashing by appeal tribunals, been shown to have gone horribly wrong. Police evidence is now taken by juries with large helpings of salt. And the pronouncements of some judges, before and since retirement, have gone beyond endearing eccentricity to give some cause for alarm.'

Changes in the work of judges

There was a time, not so long ago, when the main job of judges was to resolve disputes. The whole common law is predicated on this notion. Two parties find themselves in a disagreement. They cannot resolve it. So they go to a judge for a decision. Parliament made the laws. The judge applied them to the case. That was the entire story, or almost.

Resolving disputes is still the primary and most fundamental task of the judiciary. But for some time now, it has been recognised that the matter is not so simple. In the course of resolving disputes, common law judges interpreted and inevitably, incrementally, with the aid of the doctrine of precedent or *stare decisis*, changed the law. The common law thus came to recognize that while dispute resolution was the primary task of the judge, the judge played a secondary role of lawmaker, or at least, law-developer. In the latter part of the twentieth century, the lawmaking role of the judge in Commonwealth countries has dramatically expanded. Judicial lawmaking is no longer always confined to small, incremental changes. Increasingly, it is invading the domain of social policy, formerly the exclusive right of Parliament and the legislatures.

From different standpoints or perspectives various different criticisms of this traditional view have been put forward:

ONE FEMINIST CRITIQUE

C MacKinnon, Graduation Address to Yale Law School,
Yale Law Report (1989).

I want to talk with you about the nature of law in terms of some of the qualities shared by law in the academy and law in the world, and about what it means to hold the power of law in your hands. Law is written by the more powerful. You know that. But there is more. Law *is* words in power; it is written by power. Its power is not unlimited but it is real . . .
Women, compared with men, have been historically deprived of the franchise, and still are deprived of income and adequate means of material survival and are systematically allocated to disrespected work. Women are deprived of physical security through targeting for sexual assaults in settings that range from the intimate to the anonymous. Women are used in denigrating entertainment, bought and sold on street corners for sexual use and abuse, and deprived of reproductive control. Women's authentic voice has been silenced, our culture taken away, our contributions often stolen when they have been recognised at all, and when not recognised, erased. Women of colour are intensively subjected to these denigrations, abuses, and humiliations that afflict all women.
This is what it means to say that power takes a male form, and that powerlessness takes a female form . . .
Law in the academy and in the world actively collaborates in this situation through excluding women's points of view from the public realm and by denying women equal access to justice under law — for example, by excluding harms that happen particularly to women from the legal definition of harm at all. Law collaborates by depriving women of credibility through the institutionalised belief that we are likely to lie about sexual assault, and by legally defining sexual assault from the point of view of the perpetrator. Law collaborates through the active protection of some forms of abuse of women, such as pornography, through affirmative guarantees to men of individual rights called, in this case, speech. Law collaborates through the elimination of the right to abortion for women who are least able to get access

to it by depriving them of government funding and, of course, the law is working on eliminating that right for all other women as well. Law also actively collaborates in women's status by defining sex inequality under law so that one virtually already has to have sex equality before the law recognises your right to demand it.

Power's latest myth in this area is that the problem of inequality between women and men has been solved. Because now a few women can become lawyers, we all have sex equality. Yet 44 per cent of women are still victims of rape and attempted rape, at least once in our lives; 85 per cent of us are sexually harassed; 38 per cent of us are sexually abused as children; a quarter to a third of us are battered in our homes. Women still make around half the average male wage. Thousands and thousands of women are still being bought and sold on street corners as and for sex. Pornographers still traffick us and our children, making ten billion dollars a year. We are told that sex inequality is over, when some proud mothers must, statistically, sit here at graduation next to their batterers; when some excited graduates must sit a row or two away from their rapists, relieved to be leaving their sexual harassers, trying not to think about those who molested them as children, who may also be celebrating this moment with them. Women especially must live with a division between what we know and what can be publicly acknowledged, between what we know and what the law will tell us back is true.

I want to talk about some of the professional pressure that helps account for how those who have law's power in their hands have not changed this, and have not yet made it unnecessary to speak about such atrocities on joyful occasions like this one. I have identified three strategies for comfort, three deep mechanisms that, both with law in school and law in the world, conspire to keep situations like women's in place. They are the avoidance of accountability, the aspiration to risklessness and the assumption of immortality. I want to challenge you, the graduates, to resist these pressures.

By avoidance of accountability I mean: you may have noticed in the legal academy a tendency to treat ideas as if they are just ideas, as if one can choose among them without consequence, as if they have no part in shaping or sharing power. You may also have noticed the use of neutrality as a norm and the way it hides its standards, obscures its reference point, and does not produce fairness but rather derails accountability for the point of view being taken by presenting itself as no point of view at all. You may have observed, and learned to engage in, devil's advocacy: 'Nobody really thinks this, certainly not me, but let me ram this particular point down your throat'. You may have noticed hypothetical reasoning, the 'as if' form, when law is not practical nor is life lived in the hypothetical. There are also ethical norms in law that purport to protect the client from the lawyer, but as often protect the lawyer from accountability to the client. As to the practice of law, you may have heard that everyone has a right to counsel. The less-asked question is whether everyone has a right to counsel by *you*. I urge you to see through these devices and hold yourself accountable including for the uses to which you are put.

Question:
1. Do you agree with MacKinnon that the problem of inequality between women and men has yet to be solved?

In the context of the legal profession consider the following figures:

Table 7.1: Number of women judges in 1998 and 1989

	Women bar.sol		Total women	Men bar.sol		Total men	% women 1998	% women 1999
Lords of Appeal in Ordinary (House of Lords)	–	–	–	12	–	12	0%	0%
Lords Justices of Appeal (Court of Appeal)	1	–	1	34	–	34	3%	4% (1 woman)
High Court Judges	7	–	7	89	1	90	7%	1% (1 woman)
Circuit Judges	25	5	30	446	71	517	5%	4% (17 women)
Recorders	65	4	69	722	71	793	8%	5% (38 women)
Assistant Recorders	43	18	61	240	53	293	17%	5% (25 women)
Ass. Recorders in Training	12	3	15	66	7	73	17%	–
District Judges	1	37	38	3	296	299	11%	4% (7 women)
Deputy District Judges	5	69	74	11	612	623	11%	–
Stipendiary Magistrates	12	2	14	26	51	77	15%	13%
Total			308			2811	10%	

[Table from C McGlynn, *The Woman Lawyer: Making the difference*, London, Butterworths, (1998), p. 173.]

(See also Chapter 7 at pp. 247–8 for discussion of female judges.)

2. When you have finished reading this book, you should consider whether you agree with MacKinnon that law actively collaborates in women's powerlessness by excluding women's point of view and denying women equal access to justice under the law.

ONE BLACK CRITIQUE

Pretoria Trial 1962
Nelson Mandela was charged on two counts: inciting African workers to strike
(the March of 1961 stay-at-home); and leaving South Africa without a valid
travel document. The trial opened on 22 October 1962.

Your Worship, I have elected to conduct my own defence. I want to apply for
Your Worship's recusal from this case. It is true that an African who is
charged in a court of law enjoys, on the surface, the same rights and
privileges as an accused who is white in so far as the conduct of this trial is
concerned. He is governed by the same rules of procedure and evidence as
apply to a white accused. But it would be grossly inaccurate to conclude from
this fact that an African consequently enjoys equality before the
law . . .

The white man makes all the laws, he drags us before his courts and
accuses us, and he sits in judgment over us.

It is fit and proper to raise the question sharply, what is this rigid colour
bar in the administration of justice? Why is it that in this courtroom I face a
white magistrate, I am confronted by a white prosecutor, and escorted into
the dock by a white orderly? Can anyone honestly and seriously suggest that
in this type of atmosphere the scales of justice are evenly balanced?

. . . the real purpose of this rigid colour bar is to ensure that the justice
dispensed by the courts should conform to the policy of the country, however
much that policy might be in conflict with the norms of justice accepted in
judiciaries throughout the civilised world.

I feel oppressed by the atmosphere of white domination that lurks all
around in this courtroom. Somehow this atmosphere calls to mind the
inhuman injustices caused to my people outside this courtroom by this same
white domination.

It reminds me that I am voteless because there is a Parliament in the
country that is white-controlled. I am without land because the white minority
has taken a lion's share of my country and forced me to occupy poverty-
stricken Reserves, over-populated and over-stocked. We are ravaged by
starvation and disease . . .

I am aware that in many cases of this nature in the past, South African
courts have upheld the right of the African people to work for democratic
changes. Some of our judicial officers have even openly criticised the policy
which refuses to acknowledge that all men are born free and equal, and
fearlessly condemned the denial of the opportunities of our people.

But such exceptions exist in spite of, not because of, the grotesque system
of justice that has been built up in this country. These exceptions furnish yet
another proof that even among the country's whites there are honest men
whose sense of fairness and justice revolts against the cruelty perpetrated by
their own white brothers on our people.

The existence of genuine democratic values among some of the country's
whites in the judiciary, however slender they may be, is welcomed by me.

But I have no illusions about the significance of this fact, healthy a sign as it might be. Such honest and upright whites are few and they have certainly not succeeded in convincing the vast majority of the rest of the white population that white supremacy leads to dangers and disaster.

However, it would be a hopeless commander who relied for his victories on the few soldiers in the enemy camp who sympathise with his cause. A competent general pins his faith on the superior striking power he commands and on the justness of his cause which he must pursue uncompromisingly to the bitter end.

I hate race discrimination most intensely and in all its manifestations. I have fought it all through my life; I fight it now, and will do so until the end of my days. Even although I now happen to be tried by one whose opinion I hold in high esteem, I detest most violently the set-up that surrounds me here. It makes me feel that I am a black man in a white man's court. This should not be. I should feel perfectly at ease and at home with the assurance that I am being tried by a fellow South African who does not regard me as an inferior, entitled to a special type of justice.

This is not the type of atmosphere most conducive to feelings of security and confidence in the impartiality of a court.

Questions:
1.   Can a white-dominated or male-dominated legal system be fair to blacks or women respectively?

2.   Although Mandela insists that he is not racist, does the thrust of this speech amount to racism? Define racism.

Given Nelson Mandela's criticism of the legal regime in South Africa in 1962 (above), do you think he would feel equally uncomfortable in the UK's legal system today? Javoid offers the following account of how our criminal justice system is perceived by black defendants:

M Javoid, 'Racism in the system', *Legal Action*, March 1994, p. 8.

We have seen an enormous resurgence of the view that the criminal justice system is 'colour-blind' and that the gross disparity between the incarceration rates of black people and their proportion in the population is due to their disproportionate criminality . . . The effectiveness of any criminal administration system has to be judged not only by the likelihood of the guilty being convicted and the innocent acquitted, but also by measuring the treatment that is afforded to the vulnerable, oppressed and poor. As the Institute of Race Relations told the Royal Commission [on Criminal Justice]: 'The prism of race offers a unique perspective through which to expose and evaluate the underlying failure of the criminal justice system as a whole'.

By that yardstick, we have a system that is not only in a state of crisis but which appears actively to accommodate and facilitate racial prejudice. A wealth of research is now available which substantiates the prevalence of both direct and indirect discrimination on the part of every agency and at every stage of the process. Relevant findings include:

— Black people (irrespective of their age or socio-economic status) are more likely to be stopped and searched by the police.
— Afro-Caribbeans, in particular, are much less likely to be cautioned or otherwise diverted from the courts; and more likely to be arrested.
— Afro-Caribbeans are more likely to face more serious charges for the same substantive offence.
— Black people are more likely to be subjected to 'pro-active policing', leading to more cases of the police looking for evidence to implicate black suspects and fewer involving independent witnesses. Also, Afro-Caribbeans are more likely to be charged with victimless crimes (e.g. motoring offences, drunkenness and possession of drugs).
— Black people are more likely than whites to be remanded in custody. Their over-representation in the remand population is even greater than among convicted prisoners. A much higher proportion of cases go to the Crown Court as a result of committal by magistrates than from choice by the defendant. Magistrates closely following CPS recommendations are more likely to make such committals in the case of Afro-Caribbeans.
— Afro-Caribbeans (and Asians between the ages of 21 and 25) are more likely to be tried in a Crown Court.
— Black people are far more likely to receive custodial sentences (Roger Hood in his study of a number of Crown Courts in the West Midlands was of the view that the greater probability stood at around 16%) and for longer periods.
— Black people are less likely to receive probation decisions.

A separate study on the issue carried out for the Royal Commission on Criminal Justice found indirect discrimination was 'pervasive and significant' and a 'discriminatory chain reaction' operating against black people. This does not exclude the judiciary which, as Roger Hood has shown, is the final link in the discriminatory process that is most likely to lead the black defendant inexorably into custody. The prison statistics alone must cause alarm. The proportion of black prisoners has been steadily increasing from 12.6% in 1985 to 16% in 1992 compared with the 5.5% in the general population. Among male prisoners, 15% are from racial minorities, among women the figure is 26% (mid-1992). The over-representation of black women in prison, even when foreign resident black women are excluded, stands at 13%.

The issue of racism in the criminal justice system has recently been the focus of public attention following the inquiry into the racially-motivated murder of black teenager Stephen Lawrence in 1993. The police were accused of incompetence and racism in the handling of the crime. The Macpherson Inquiry published their report in February 1999. Can you find it on the Internet? For a website setting out some of the allegations made in the case see www.carf.demon.co.uk/feat17.html.

As the following table demonstrates, there are no ethnic minority judges in the senior ranks of the judiciary.

Table 7.2: Number of ethnic minority judges in 1997 and 1994

	No. of ethnic minority judges [1997]	Total	1994 (number)
Lords of Appeal in Ordinary	–	0%	–
Lords Justice of Appeal	–	0%	–
High Court Judges	–	0%	–
Circuit Judges	6	558 (1.1%)	4
Recorders	14	929 (1.5%)	11
Assistant Recorders	9	323 (2.8%)	8
District Judges	3	335 (0.9%)	1
Deputy District Judges	13	697 (1.9%)	7
Total	45	2842 (1.6%)	31

[Table from C McGlynn, *The Woman Lawyer: Making the difference*, London, Butterworths, (1998), p. 174.]

Such under-representation is also apparent in the lower ranks of the legal profession, and at the point of access to it:

'Trainee lawyers suffer discrimination', *Legal Action*, May 1994, p. 8.

Widespread race and class discrimination in the legal profession has been revealed by major investigations of barristers and solicitors' training courses and of recruitment of trainee lawyers. The results of a two year survey of 4,000 law students carried out for the Law Society by the Policy Studies Institute were described as 'shocking' by Law Society President Roger Pannone.

— While white students have a 44 per cent success rate of winning places on the solicitors' Legal Practice Course, that of black students was just 12 per cent.
— Getting training contracts is even more difficult for black students: only 7 per cent succeeded, compared with 47 per cent of whites.

Findings of the Barrow Committee Report on equal opportunities on the Bar course are equally damning. Black and ethnic minority students were three times as likely as white students to fail the Bar vocational course. Black students are significantly less likely to gain a pupillage prior to completion of the vocational course.

Both enquiries found a strong bias in favour of students who had attended 'old' universities — particularly Oxford and Cambridge. Black students are especially disadvantaged by this bias as the vast majority gain law degrees at the new universities or former polytechnics. While only 22 per cent of such students got training places, the success rate of Oxbridge students was 88 per cent.

Questions:
1. Do you think that the student body in your Law Faculty reflects the multi-cultural society of the United Kingdom?

2. To what extent does discrimination against black people in the legal system result from their under-representation amongst legal officials? (See also Chapter 7, pp. 247–8.)

3. Do you think the legal profession may be more resistant to change than other professions or occupations with regard to recruitment and promotion of black people? If so, why?

4. Do you think there is a peculiarly black perspective on law, in the way that women may arguably perceive it differently from men? For example, would a black woman have a different experience of and perception of law than a white woman or a white man?

FEMINIST, BLACK AND CLASS PERSPECTIVES ON LAW

H Kennedy, *Eve was Framed: Women and British Justice*, London, Chatto & Windus (1992), pp. 25–31.

Given the nature of our legal system and the history of its development, it is hardly surprising that women have special problems in our courtrooms.

Until comparatively recently women played no part at all in the construction and content of the law, and even now their role in lawmaking is barely significant . . .

The nineteenth century saw a revolutionary change in women's status, brought about (as is always the case), not by the generous bequest of the powerful, but by the pressure of women's demands. The Married Women's Property Acts of 1870 and 1882 were historic victories, allowing married women a legal identity and removing in part their invisibility. But the task of pulling the weight of this legal monolith into the late twentieth century, when people have very different roles and expectations, seems Herculean, especially when well nigh all of the powerful positions within the law are held by the kind of men who explode with laughter or implode with rage at the very mention of gender bias. Most legislation and case law nowadays has the semblance of neutrality, and some legislative changes are designed to improve the position of women, but the letter of the law can too easily become a cloak for the reality.

Discriminatory practices surface with regularity in many areas of the law. In the Family Courts, despite enormous improvements, there is still too little value placed on the woman's contribution to the family over the years. The courts are often ignorant of the kinds of jobs and salaries available to women, the costs of child-care and the particular employment problems of the displaced homemaker. I recently attended some judicial training sessions in the USA in which a group of judges were asked to put the value on a bag of groceries. Few were able to do so. It would be interesting to run a similar experiment in this country.

When I did my stint at family work I saw decisions being made about custody in which women were penalised if they had left the matrimonial home, leaving children behind, even when they did so to escape abuse. This was particularly true if a woman had found a boyfriend. It was the same test which had been applied over a century before to Annie Besant, the pioneer of contraception, who was prosecuted for publishing pamphlets on family planning in 1877. Her sexual politics were seen as a sign of her unsuitability as a mother, and she too suffered the slings of courtroom bias, by being denied custody of her daughter.

Women have problems in obtaining realistic damages for personal injuries, because awards are so closely tied to wage earning and those who work in the home often receive ridiculously low sums: the real economic value of housework is never explored . . .

In many areas of the law women still suffer from antiquated views. Most of the time it is quite unconscious, and therefore hard to challenge. In this book I have concentrated on the criminal justice system, partly because it is the area in which I have now practised, woman and girl, for nearly twenty years, but also because, affecting as it does the liberty of the subject, it is an area of the law which needs to be addressed with the greatest urgency.

The web of prejudice, privilege and misinformation that affects women is, of course, compounded for the poor. The experience of women is a paradigm of that which faces any person, male or female, who is not part of the dominant culture. There is no conspiracy. Often the assumptions arise simply from a lack of insight into the lives lived by people of a different class. A woman who practises in the field of child-care says that over the years, whenever judges have expressed concern about working mothers not spending enough time with their children, she has always made the simple comparison with children who are sent to boarding school. She says that the discomfort can be tangible . . .

If any single category of human being is unaccustomed to being treated as inferior or subordinate, it is a white, male, British judge. In broad terms, four out of five full-time professional judges are still products of public schools and of Oxford and Cambridge. Very occasionally the less privileged have joined the ranks, and that number is slowly growing. It is barely possible to mention the narrow background of the judiciary now without some fellow jumping up and informing you that his father was a coalman or at the very least a mere doctor. Products of the grammar schools will become somewhat thicker on the ground as the beneficiaries of expanded university education in the 1960s progress through the Bar. The retirement age for judges has only just been reduced to 70. The average age of judges in this country is between 60 and 65, which coincides with the time when most other people are retiring. In March 1991, according to statistics presented by the Lord Chancellor's Department, only one judge out of 550 was black. One Lord Justice, two High Court judges and nineteen circuit judges were female.

Being told that you may be unfair, even unconsciously, is not something any of us welcome. The Lord Chancellor, Lord Mackay, who is sensitive to these issues, tells a story about his days as a lecturer at Edinburgh University when he was required to mark a register of student attendance. For the most part he would call out the names of students, but on a number of occasions he marked off the name of the one black student without calling it out, partly because he was well aware of the student's presence but also because he was hesitant about the pronunciation. The student challenged him about it and Lord Mackay was wretched to think he had been hurtful to a student whom he liked and regarded well. It must be emphasised that there are many decent judges who are keen to take on board new learning and who think deeply about the power and authority they wield.

The law mirrors society with all its imperfections and it therefore reflects the subordination of women, even today. But holding up a mirror can never be its sole function. The law affects as well as reflects, and all of those involved in the administration of justice have a special obligation to reject society's irrational prejudices. The law is symbolic, playing an important role in the internalising of ideas about what is right and natural. If the men of law say sexily dressed women have it coming to them, they reinforce that view in the man on the street. The law constructs beliefs about roles of men and women in the home and at work which feed back into generally held attitudes about women.

True justice is about more than refereeing between two sides. It is about breathing life into the rules so that no side is at a disadvantage because of sex or race or any of the other impediments which deny justice.

It is no answer to make a simple call for equal treatment. Dealing equally with those who are unequal creates more inequality. Justice is obtained by giving a fair and unbiased appraisal of each person and situation, without relying on preconceived notions, whether the defendant is black or white, male or female. Justice recognises the tension between the ideal of equality and the reality of people's lives. There are those who claim that the true classical symbol of Justice has her wearing a blindfold of impartiality, but I prefer the image of an all-seeing goddess, as she appears above the Central Criminal Court at the Old Bailey.

One famous case which appears to suggest that different standpoints really do have an impact on observers' views regarding the guilt or innocence of the defendant was the criminal trial of O J Simpson. In 1994 Simpson, a famous ex-footballer and actor, was charged with the murder of his white estranged wife and her friend. In this case the lawyers — Simpson's expensively-assembled 'dream team' — were widely castigated for 'playing the race-card' to a predominantly black jury which ultimately acquitted Simpson. As one commentator stated, 'Within a month of the murders of Nicole Brown Simpson and Ronald Goldman, it was relatively clear that African Americans as a group and whites as a group had different views on whether or not O J Simpson was guilty. Polls by USA Today, CNN and Gallup showed that sixty per cent of black Americans believed him to be innocent of the murder charges filed against him while sixty-eight per cent of white Americans believed him to be guilty.' (CK Wingate, 'Forward', *Hastings Women's Law Journal* (1995) Vol. 6, pp. 121–133, at p. 126). Moreover, the allegations that Simpson had murdered his wife, whom he had previously been convicted of abusing, meant that the trial also had an important gender dimension. As Wingate points out 'Women's groups have understandably been enraged and energized by the trial and [not guilty] verdict' (*op. cit.* at p. 129).

A M Dershowitz, *Reasonable Doubts: The Criminal Justice System and the O.J. Simpson Case*, New York, Touchstone (1996), pp. 115 (footnotes omitted):

What about the gender of the jurors and the domestic violence evidence? Commentators have concluded that 'race must have trumped gender in the jurors' minds'. The prosecution made an appeal to the jurors — of whom ten out of twelve were female — to sympathize with Nicole Brown, especially by introducing evidence of her past domestic abuse at the hands of O.J. Simpson. The defence, in turn, introduced to the jury — nine of whose members were black — evidence of racially motivated evidence tampering, perjury, and constitutional violations in the investigation and prosecution of the killings. If the defense's appeal was more effective, many have concluded, it must be because the racial basis of the jurors outweighed the strength of their identification with battered women.

'That women — black or white — with presumably so much in common could see the verdict so differently suggested that the racial wall was higher and thicker than anyone had imagined. The 'not guilty' verdict suggests that the women on the jury identified more with the racial issues raised by the defense than with the issues of domestic violence outlined by the prosecution.'

These analysts seem to be assuming that the black jurors on the Simpson jury somehow had their powers of reason swamped by their racial identities, or that identification with the defendant and racial solidarity must have motivated the verdict regardless of evidence. But race and gender may have affected the juror's deliberations in more subtle, and less overt, ways.

First, commentators who argue that 'race trumps gender' may be correct in the sense that race makes much more of a difference in many black jurors' perceptions and beliefs than gender does. Under the cultural-experience explanation of juror 'biases', this makes perfect sense. The everyday experiences of blacks and whites are far more different than are those of men and women of the same race. From day to day, men and women of the same race associate with each other and with many of the same people. Although their experiences and beliefs do differ, they also overlap a great deal. By contrast blacks and whites are almost fully isolated from each other in many parts of our society. They live in different worlds, whereas men and women with the same racial and socioeconomic characteristics inhabit pretty much the same world. So it is no wonder that black jurors bring radically different perceptions into the jury room, which in jury research show up as more pronounced differences across race than across gender.

Many black women find that racism is a more pronounced force in their lives than sexism:

> 'While to many black women sexism pales in the face of racism, white women, unburdened by race in a predominantly white society, are freer to focus on sexism. But that often leaves them perplexed when black women break ranks, maybe even to their own detriment, as when many women sided with Clarence Thomas and vilified Anita Hill in his confirmation hearings for the Supreme Court.'

Donna Franklin . . . suggests that black women may choose to identify with a black male defendant rather than a white female victim because racism has prevented black women from being in an economic position to pursue feminism. She states:

> 'The black woman's envy of the white women was that they had a man taking care of them. Black women never had that luxury. We have been deprived of a provider by the system. We wish we could sit in the suburbs and write *The Feminine Mystique*. That's why black women and white women have always been apart. We can't move to the next level until we have those first needs met.'

Aside from these dramatic cultural differences, the second reason why race may have trumped gender as a perceptual prism had to do with different evidence in this case that played into race-determined beliefs, as opposed to gender-determined beliefs. Some jurors may have recognized that the evidence of police misconduct was more directly relevant to doubts about Simpson's guilt or innocence than was the evidence of alleged abuse. Women may be more sensitive to domestic violence issues than men, but that does not mean they will easily be fooled into believing that domestic violence is predictive of spousal murder. Indeed, one scholar has suggested that they might have been able to resist such a ploy with fewer misgivings than men:

> 'The fact that there were women on the jury is very important, because they were able to assess the kind of card Marcia Clark (the lead prosecutor) was playing on them . . . Is it just a leap of justice to say he finally killed? . . . I think this jury showed that although you had good reasons to think somebody may be pushed to kill if they had battered before, this is not enough to prove that they actually did. I think the jury showed great ability to distance themselves from any personal prejudice.'

Even this recognition, however, may have been influenced by the relative importance of race and gender in the jurors' world-views.

Questions:
1. Do you think this extract overemphasises identification on the basis of race while downplaying gender differences? Will race always play a larger role than gender in influencing jurors' beliefs? (For further discussion of the factors which impact on jury decision-making, see Chapter 9; for discussion of the case by a black woman see P Williams in T Morrison and C Brodsky Lacour, *Birth of a Nationhood: gaze, script and spectacle in the O.J. Simpson case*, New York, Vintage (1997); and for an interesting discussion by a mixed race woman on the whole issue of standpoint and racial categories see J Floyd, 'The Other Box: Intersectionality and the O.J. Simpson Trial', *Hastings Women's Law Journal* (1995) vol. 6, pp 241–274.)

2. Do you think the outcome of the Simpson case really depended on the tactics employed by prosecution and defence as this extract suggests? (For further discussion of trial tactics see Chapter 6.)

3. Note that Alan Dershowitz was a member of O J Simpson's defence team. Do you think his positioning as a participant in the trial has influenced his account?

A POSTMODERN PERSPECTIVE

One problem in considering feminist, black and class perspectives, which all pose a challenge to the traditional view of law, is that such approaches can tend to assume that all women, or blacks, or those who are economically disempowered think in the same way. Such 'essentialism' is in turn challenged by postmodern theory which emphasises fragmentation and diversity, and challenges the notion of society being structured by divisions like class, gender or nationality which can explain deep-rooted structures of oppression. Postmodernism also provides an important challenge and corrective to some varieties of feminism.

S Jackson, 'The Amazing Deconstructing Woman', *Trouble & Strife*, 25 Winter 1992, pp. 25–31 at pp. 26–27.

What is postmodernism?
First we need to clear up some confusion over the term 'postmodernism'. There are at least three senses in which it is used . . .
    First postmodernism refers to an artistic and architectural style which borrows from and reassembles elements of past styles.
    Secondly it refers to the notion that we are living in a postmodern world. There are different variants of this 'postmodernity' thesis, suggesting for example that we are living in a post-industrial age, that capitalism has become less organized, that new technologies and new working practices have radically altered the relations between classes, or that social divisions

are now based around the sphere of consumption rather than production. The overall picture is of a more fragmented and fluid society.

The third sense of the term . . . refers to a body of theory which is also sometimes called poststructuralism. The word postmodernism is now more frequently used since it carries with it some of the ideas of the second usage — that old certainties have gone and therefore a new mode of theorizing is appropriate.

The structuralism to which this theory is 'post', and from which it often takes its point of departure, concerns ideas about the structures underlying all human language and culture: for example Sausure's structural linguistics. It is also 'post' another form of structural explanation, marxism . . .

The modernism to which this body of theory is 'post', and from which it distances itself, is usually defined in relation to ideas which emerged from the 18th century, in the period known as the Enlightenment. This is a useful starting point since most postmodernists define their project in opposition to what they identify as Enlightenment thought, questioning ideas about language, the self, and truth which derive from that period. The basic tenets of postmodernism can be thus outlined as follows:

1. Language does not simply *transmit* thoughts or meaning. Thought and meaning are *constructed through* language, and there can be no meaning outside language. Meaning is also, for all these theorists, in some way relational. A word, for example, means something only in relation to other words. Meaning is never fixed. Nothing has a stable, unambiguous meaning. Hence the word 'woman' does not of itself mean anything. It is defined in relation to its opposite 'man' (which also has no fixed meaning) and means different things in different contexts. It can even refer to a man, as in the derogatory phrase 'old woman'.

2. There is no fixed, unitary, rational subject. There is no essential self which exists outside culture and language. Subjectivity is constituted through language and culture and is fragmented and always in process. There is no place from 'outside' language and culture from which we can 'know' anything (including ourselves). Our identities and knowledges of the world are products of the way in which we are positioned (or position ourselves) within knowledge and culture. (This is referred to as 'de-centring the subject'.) Our own experience as women cannot therefore be taken as an unproblematic starting point for feminist theory and politics, because that experience has no given meaning, because there is no experience outside language and culture. For example, doing housework for a man can (theoretically) be 'experienced' as a labour of love *or* as exploitative drudgery, depending on whether it is understood in terms of a discourse of traditional femininity or a feminist discourse.

3. There is no possibility of objective scientific 'truth' which exists out there waiting to be discovered. Knowledges are 'discursive constructs'. This idea comes from Michel Foucault, for whom discourses (ways of thinking and talking about the world) produce objects of knowledge, rather than describing pre-existing objects. (There is, in any case, no objective 'knower' standing

outside the culture which produces her; nor is there a transparent language in which to convey some absolute truth. Knowledges and discourses can be deconstructed — taken apart — in such a way as to reveal that they are not universal truths but rather discourses constructed from particular positions. This leads to the sceptical dismissal of grand theoretical 'metanarratives', like marxism, which purport to explain the social world. At its most extreme this scepticism implies a denial of *any* material reality.

On the basis of these propositions, postmodernists oppose all forms of 'essentialism', any perspectives which posit social groups or social structures (like 'women' or 'patriarchy') as natural objects which exist independently of our understandings of them. Feminist postmodernists, for example, contest essentialist conceptualisations of 'women': the idea that women exist as a natural category. They seek to 'deconstruct' gender categories, to reveal the ways in which they have been culturally constructed, to demonstrate that they are 'regulatory fictions' rather than natural facts.

The idea of deconstruction derives from the work of Jacques Derrida. In general it means looking closely at any text, argument or assumption in order to reveal the inconsistences and paradoxes which underpin it. Hence statements which define what women are, can be shown to contain contradictory assumptions. For example, we are told that femininity is 'natural' and yet women are constantly exhorted to work hard at producing femininity. This suggests that 'femininity' is not natural but rather the product of specific discourses which define it. For Foucauldians there is also the issue of power: the power inevitably at play in the production and deployment of discourse. Knowledge and power are inextricably linked (often the form 'knowledge/power' is used to convey this), hence Judith Butler's conceptualisation of gender as a *regulatory* fiction.

For a discussion of postmodern legal theory, see pp. 254–6.

Questions:
1.   Does acceptance of the insights of postmodernism make it impossible to speak in terms of law (or particular laws) having a negative impact upon women (or men) as a group? For example, would it be possible to argue in postmodern terms that the way our current law on rape is structured adversely affects *all* women?

2.   In abandoning the notion that it is possible to speak on behalf of monolithic constituencies (like 'woman' or 'the working class'), is postmodernism an apolitical theory which lacks the transformative power of meta-theories like feminism or Marxism?

STUDENT PERSPECTIVES

To date in this chapter we have focused on the issue of perspectives and how certain perspectives may be excluded in law and by the legal profession. What about the position of female and minority students in law schools? Can any of you empathise with the following student perspectives?

D Kennedy, 'Legal Education and the Reproduction of Hierarchy', *Journal of Legal Education* (1982) vol. 32, pp. 591–615 at p. 605.

There is a subtle message conveyed in student/teacher relations. Teachers are overwhelmingly white, male, and middle class, and most (by no means all) black and women law teachers give the impression of thorough assimilation to that style or of insecurity and unhappiness. Students who are women or black or working class find out something important about the professional universe from the first day of class: that it is not even nominally pluralist in cultural terms. The teacher sets the tone — a white, male, middle-class tone. Students adapt. They do so partly out of fear, partly out of hope of gain, partly out of genuine admiration for their role models. But the line between adaptation to the intellectual and skills content of legal education and adaptation to the white, male, middle-class cultural style is a fine one, easily lost sight of. While students quickly understand that there is diversity among their fellow students and that the faculty is not really homogeneous in terms of character, background, or opinions, the classroom itself becomes more rather than less uniform as legal education progresses.

D A Bell, 'The Law Student As Slave', (1982) *Student Law* 18

There is an understandable concern among law students that all of the work, sacrifice and trauma that is law school will provide no more than the barrier of a bar exam and no job opportunities.

There is no need to quote you the gruesome statistics. In legal education, as in most other aspects of our society, the principles of the free market simply do not work. There are many forces that push undergraduates toward law school: the truly awful job prospects in the traditional liberal and fine arts graduate programs, the desire for independence offered by professional status, the flexibility offered by law for those who have no specific career goals, and even — in some cases — idealism.

Beginning in the late 1960s, all of these motivations caused law school applications to soar. During the years of economic growth in the 1970s most of the thousands of new lawyers were able to find law-related work. But as the flood of graduates remained steady in the face of downturn in the country's economic fortunes, jobs in law have become harder and harder to find.

In reaction — and not surprisingly — law students have tended to become more conformist, more supportive of the status quo, more determined to accept rather than challenge. The protest/reform era of a decade ago has almost vanished from our halls. It has been replaced by a fierce and often inhumane competitiveness that manifests itself not simply in better class attendance and more filled seats in the library, but in taking liberties with exam rules and paper requirements, and even stealing or defacing library books so as to gain an advantage over class mates.

K C Worden, 'A Student Polemic', *New Mexico Law Review* (1986) vol. 16, pp. 573–588 at pp. 572–574.

Students possess an important perspective on the state of legal education and present an enormous amount of potential political power. Too often, however, that power is never acknowledged, mobilized, or valued. For too long, students have been insignificant actors in the politics of legal education; for too long, we have been excluded from the forum of law review publication as a means of expression, communication, and debate about the politics of being a law student.

Progressive and innovative renovations in legal education are beginning to take place . . . As students, we cannot passively wait for 'it' to happen 'for'/'to' us. We must not let ourselves be lulled into limiting our political struggles to those 'out of the real world'. The image of student apathy and cynicism must not rise to thwart the efforts of those on the 'cutting edge' of legal education.We must make known to faculties and administrations that such progressive efforts are necessary and beneficial to law students, law schools, and the legal profession in general.

More importantly, we must also be willing to forge ahead on our own. We must challenge, on a daily basis, the myriad ways in which law schools serve to alienate, indoctrinate, and debilitate students. Law school need not be the most degrading and anaesthetizing experience of our lives. It's *our* tuition dollars, *our* careers, and *our* intellectual and emotional investments that are at stake. We are the 'grassroots' of the law schools; we must take part in the struggle against the reproduction of hierarchy fostered by our institutions. If we wait for the renovations and 'student empowerment' to be handed down to us from the professorial powers above (no matter how progressive those powers may be) we will only further entrench and legitimate the ultimate systemic powerlessness of students. Passivity on our part will imply that we are not only disinterested, but that we ourselves consider students powerless and insignificant members of the law school community. This can be a dangerously self-fulfilling prophecy.

Questions:
1.   Do you recognise the picture which Bell paints of law students? Has conformism replaced idealism? What impact, if any, might this have on the provision of legal services? (See Chapter 9.)

2.   Does Worden's view have more validity because it is written by a student?

Consider the following extracts from law students in the United Kingdom:

C Bell and D Keaney, 'Teaching Justice? An Experiment in Group Work and Peer Assessment', *The Liverpool Law Review* (1995) vol. XVII, pp. 47–68, at pp. 51–2.

As a third year student in a four year law degree one dilemma I face is the question of which subjects best prepare me for my future.

With aspirations of practising, this was heightened by my experience of a summer job in legal practice where knowledge of cases and materials was of little help in dealing with real people and their problems. The law degree on which I study attempts to balance the emphasis on black-letter subjects with a series of more socially oriented and jurisprudential courses. These address the theoretical questions underlying substantive law and in my opinion are an advancement in legal education. However, from a student perspective, it seems that often the more a course delves into underlying theoretical issues, the more complex and abstract its content becomes and the more difficult it becomes. With black-letter courses, students have a body of law in the form of statutes or case notes to refer to and memorise. By contrast jurisprudence courses pose questions to which students do not easily have answers. Even when they do have answers they can find them difficult to communicate effectively because of the complexity of subject matter. As a result, there is often student bias towards black-letter subjects such as contract and tort, which are additionally advantaged by the student perception that as core subjects they are more closely related to practice. Teaching of 'justice' issues, must overcome these biases, and make its case for relevance to the students.

Critical Legal Groups, 'A "Discussion" With Students', *Law and Critique* (1990) vol. I, pp. 120–6, at pp. 123–4.

What do you think of the current attempts at critical legal education? Do you think it is possible, or desirable, or important to get away from the sorts of hierarchical relations and effects Duncan Kennedy [at p. 26 above] talks about?

We accept much of Duncan Kennedy's analysis of how traditional legal education is both a training in subordination and a training for subordination. 'Black letter' doctrinal teaching trains law students to accept not only the notion of law as a complex set of neutral impartial rules but also as a set of legitimate hierarchies of authority — the teacher substituting for the judge as the high priest of truth. This is a training in and for subordination to law, judges and the courts and involves an ultimate 'castration' of all critical thought — a denial and repression of politics. We must, as critical lawyers, seek in every possible way to 'subvert' this dominant tradition — to 'subvert' the law school if you like and to put at the centre of legal education (as with legal practice) the questions of Whose law? Whose values? Whose hierarchy?

What, as a law student, do you think you are learning? Should there be law degrees at all?

As law students we are offered two distinct 'realities'. First, a number of legal facts coupled with an adeptness at playing legal games and, secondly, an overt or subliminal internalisation of a bourgeois individualistic approach to society, an unquestioning impression that equality means being subject to the law. As to the latter question, any degree presupposes a meritocracy and to this extent we could argue there should be no degrees at all. However, given the present climate, it is important to have access to a three year study of law in an academic environment. It contains the possibility and space to explore a critical approach, although, if these opportunities are not treated seriously, a law degree merely produces students destined to become nothing more than an alternative police force.

Do you think 'academic freedom' is important or 'meaningful' in faculties of law? Does it matter to students?

Obviously the quality of our education is an important issue for students. When academic freedom is directly restricted by right wing state control, our access to a full critical education has been forced two or twenty steps backwards, depending on the particular academic in question. However, we are aware that academic teaching is dominated by bourgeois idealogy and that academic freedom is often not taken seriously. Academic freedom may serve as a guise for promoting reactionary ideologies and so called liberal or even radical educators may in reality act as 'soldiers with typewriters'.

For further student perspectives on law see C McGlynn, *The Woman Lawyer: Making the difference,* London, Butterworths, (1998) Chapter 1.

Questions:
1.   What ideologies do you think are promoted by the legal education you receive?

2.   What input do you have to the law curriculum within your Faculty? Does a 'critical legal group' exist within your law school, or have you thought about forming one? (For more information see I Grigg-Spall and P Ireland (eds) *The Critical Lawyers Handbook*, London, Pluto (1992) Chapter 4, or the CLC website at www.nclg.org.uk.)

THE WHOLE PICTURE

To obtain a whole picture of law, both in the law school and society it is essential to seek to understand law from various standpoints. But what *is* law? Malcolm Wood has argued that it is a rich tapestry rather than an Impressionist study:

M Wood 'EC 1992: Free Market Framework or Grand Design' in S Livingstone and J Morison (eds), *Law, Society and Change,* London, Gower (1990), p. 185.

Law is a proliferating tapestry of tradition, custom, usage, convention, principle, policy, precedent, by law, rule, order, statute, decision, directive, regulation and treaty. Law's strands flow inexorably into morality, politics, economics, ideology, history, philosophy, religion and society. Yet the dominant ideology of law is that it is discrete, known and certain. A phenomenon capable of being isolated, ascertained and acted upon. Law is therefore a paradox.

Law is but one weapon in a massive political arsenal where the possible may be achieved by a combination of forces, actions and inactivity. Such forces include repression, covert practices, media manipulation, censorship, educational socialisation, economic intervention, social, health and employment policies, nationalism, corporatism and law. As a weapon, law has certain inherent advantages or defects, depending upon the situation. Law requires validity, publicity and external review. Law is relatively inflexible, has inherent time delays built into its adaptive and adjudicative systems, and often fails to restore ongoing relations.

Law depoliticises political decisions. Such decisions, having been enacted and promulgated according to defined criteria, somehow transcend politics and ostensibly acquire a valued neutral identity. Such decisions become part of the body of law which supposedly governs both rulers and ruled alike and, which is interpreted by officials seen as being above politics. This ideology, known as the rule of law, carries an important psychological message and gives both authority and prestige to the elements of law, even where single decisions may be individually unpopular.

On its own, law can be persuasive and illuminating but, ultimately, it is impotent. History is littered with ancient legal codes, charters and statutes which now exist without jurisdiction. UK law is sprinkled with anachronisms that are neither obeyed nor enforced but, without desuetude, are nonetheless law — albeit in hibernation. Some modern statutes can be described as largely symbolic and, for a variety of reasons, fail to modify human behaviour to their dictates. Most laws contain an inherent uncertainty which is not simply a peripheral issue but which can go right to the core of meaning, whilst all laws contain concepts whose flexibility of interpretation defy precise construction.

Ultimately, law is simply an abstract theoretical maze, it requires the technical and organisational resources of legal institutions to complete the circle of validity, effectiveness and jurisdiction. When these forces are allied together there is an assumption that law can confront and overcome social mores.

Wood offers many suggestions about law's forms, techniques and purposes. Our concern in this chapter has been to open your eyes to the huge range of perspectives from which people paint pictures of law or, more prosaically, from which they answer the question: 'What is law?'.

You have now begun to think about 'law' and 'legal skills'. But what do we mean by 'learning'?

C Hardy, *The Age of Unreason,* Arrow Books Ltd (1990).

Learning is *not* just knowing the answers. That is *Mastermind* learning at its best, rote learning at its most boring, and conditioned response at its most basic. It does not help you to change or to grow, it does not move the wheel.

Learning is *not* the same as study, nor the same as training. It is bigger than both. It is a cast of mind, a habit of life, a way of thinking about things, a way of growing.

Learning is *not* measured by examinations, which usually only test the Theory stage, but only by a growing experience, an experience understood and tested.

Learning is *not* automatic, it requires energy, thought, courage and support. It is easy to give up on it, to relax and to rest on one's experience, but that is to cease to grow.

Learning is *not* finding out what other people already know, but is solving our own problems for our own purposes, by questioning, thinking and testing until the solution is a new part of our life.

Chapter 2

Precedent

In the United Kingdom, historically, it has been left to the judges to develop what is called the 'common' law through their judgments in particular cases. Although much of the common law has now been superseded by statute (see Chapter 3), even where there is a statute, there will also probably be cases interpreting that Act of Parliament. So this chapter asks you to consider how you should read such judgments and how the legal system should use them. Begin by answering these questions.

Questions
1.   What is the point of a long judicial opinion or judgment? Why not just give the result?

2.   How should you note judgments? What should you be looking for when you read a case?

Neither question is easily answered but you might well begin your legal studies by ensuring that when you read a case you understand:

(a)   the facts;
(b)   the issues;
(c)   the decision;
(d)   the reasons for the decision.

THE DOCTRINE OF PRECEDENT

When a case is decided on the basis of an earlier case, we call that a *precedent*. The word 'precedent' is used in everyday life to mean much the same thing as it does in law. What do people mean when they say:

'that would create a precedent', or

'there is no precedent for that', or
'this was an unprecedented event'?

Lawyers have traditionally been taught that the essential ruling on law in a case is the *ratio decidendi* (Latin for reason for the decision) and that the rest of the judgment is *obiter dicta* (incidental comments). The most common formulation of the *ratio decidendi* is that it is a ruling expressly or impliedly given by a judge which is sufficient to settle a point of law put in issue by the parties' arguments in a case, being a point on which a ruling was necessary to his or her justification (or one of his or her alternative justifications) of the decisions in the case. (See R Cross and J W Harris, *Precedent in English Law*, Oxford University Press, 4th edn, 1991, p. 72.) Then they are told that the doctrine of *precedent* or *stare decisis* (stand by earlier decisions) requires judges to follow the ratio of decisions which are binding on them, which are principally those emanating from a loftier place in the court hierarchy.

Judges do not have to follow a precedent if they can *distinguish* the facts of the earlier cases from their own. (For further discussion of the interpretation of facts and the process of distinguishing them see Chapter 4.) Sometimes they can overrule a precedent (e.g. if they are sitting in a superior court in the hierarchy of courts). The following table gives a much simplified indication of the hierarchy of courts). It should be noted that with the increasing significance of European Community law (see pp. 110–127) and the incorporation into British law of the European Convention on Human Rights (see pp. 102–9) it is increasingly artificial to depict the English court system in isolation from other supranational legal systems.

[*Court structure*]

CIVIL JURISDICTION

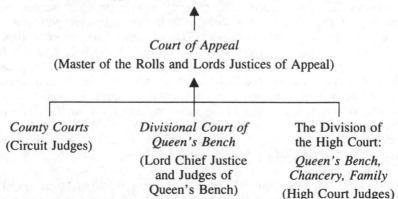

House of Lords (Judicial Committee)
(Lords of Appeal in Ordinary also called Law Lords)

↑

Court of Appeal
(Master of the Rolls and Lords Justices of Appeal)

↑

County Courts	*Divisional Court of*	The Division of
(Circuit Judges)	*Queen's Bench*	the High Court:
	(Lord Chief Justice	*Queen's Bench,*
	and Judges of	*Chancery, Family*
	Queen's Bench)	(High Court Judges)

CRIMINAL JURISDICTION

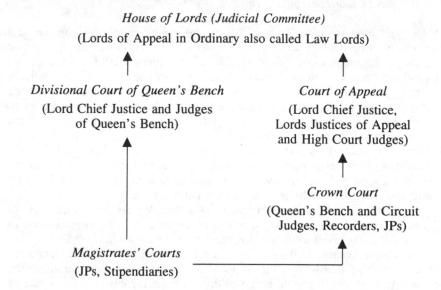

House of Lords (Judicial Committee)
(Lords of Appeal in Ordinary also called Law Lords)

Divisional Court of Queen's Bench
(Lord Chief Justice and Judges
of Queen's Bench)

Court of Appeal
(Lord Chief Justice,
Lords Justices of Appeal
and High Court Judges)

Crown Court
(Queen's Bench and Circuit
Judges, Recorders, JPs)

Magistrates' Courts
(JPs, Stipendiaries)

The basic 'rules' of precedent are summed up in the following extract:

J W Harris, *Legal Philosophies*, 2nd edn, London, Butterworths (1997), p. 171.

In England, the House of Lords is not bound by its own decisions, though it will not depart from them merely because they are 'wrong' [see below]. All inferior courts and tribunals are bound by decisions of the House of Lords. The Court of Appeal is bound by its own decisions, with certain exceptions mentioned below. All courts below the Court of Appeal are bound by its decisions. Divisional courts, when hearing appeals from magistrates' courts by way of case stated, are bound by their own decisions, with the same exceptions as those applicable to the Court of Appeal; and inferior courts and tribunals are bound by decisions of divisional courts. Judges of the High Court are not strictly bound by each other's decisions, but will not depart from them unless convinced that they were mistaken; and divisional courts exercising merely supervisory (as distinct from appellate) jurisdiction are nowadays regarded as being in the same position *vis à vis* their own prior decisions as judges of the High Court. In relation to all these rules, 'decision' refers to the *ratio decidendi* of a case. Where there is more than one *ratio decidendi*, each is binding.

Since 1966, when the Judicial Committee of the House of Lords issued the following *Practice Statement*, the House of Lords has been free to depart from its own previous decisions in certain circumstances:

Practice Statement (Judicial Precedent) [1966] 1 WLR 1234.

Lord Gardiner QC:

> Their Lordships regard the use of precedent as an indispensable foundation on which to decide what is the law and its application to individual cases. It provides at least some degree of certainty upon which individuals can rely in the conduct of their affairs, as well as a basis for orderly development of legal rules.
>
> Their Lordships nevertheless recognise that too rigid adherence to precedent may lead to injustice in a particular case and also unduly restrict the proper development of the law. They propose therefore to modify their present practice and, while treating former decisions of this House as normally binding, to depart from a previous decision when it appears right to do so.
>
> In this connection they will bear in mind the danger of disturbing retrospectively the basis on which contracts, settlements of property and fiscal arrangements have been entered into and also the especial need for certainty as the criminal law.
>
> This announcement is not intended to affect the use of precedent elsewhere than in this House.

The following additional explanatory note was issued to the press by the House of Lords contemporaneously with the *Practice Statement*:

M Zander, *The Law-Making Process*, 4th edn, London, Weidenfeld and Nicolson (1995) pp. 192–3

> Since the House of Lords decided the English case of *London Street Tramways* (sic) v *London County Council* in 1898, the House has considered themselves bound to follow their own decisions, except where a decision has been given per incuriam in disregard of a statutory provision or another decision binding on them.
>
> The statement made is one of great importance, although it should not be supposed that there will frequently be cases in which the House thinks it right not to follow their own precedent. An example of a case in which the House might think it right to depart from a precedent is where they consider that the earlier decision was influenced by the existence of conditions which no longer prevail, and that in modern conditions the law ought to be different.
>
> One consequence of this change is of major importance. The relaxation of the rule of judicial precedent will enable the House of Lords to pay greater attention to judicial decisions reached in the superior courts of the Commonwealth, where they differ from earlier decisions of the House of Lords. That would be of great help in the development of our own Law. The superior courts of many other countries are not rigidly bound by their own decisions and the change in practice of the House of Lords will bring us more into line with them.

Questions:
1.   Why do you think that the 1996 *Practice Statement* was issued?

2.   J W Harris, *Legal Philosophies* (see above) at p. 172, estimates that from 1966 to the beginning of 1997 there have only been nine occasions on which the House of Lords has unequivocally exercised its power under the *Practice Statement.* What factors do you think account for the reticence of the Law Lords to depart from their own earlier decision?

3.   Should the House of Lords be more prepared to use its power under the *Practice Statement*?

4.   Should the Court of Appeal have a similar power to depart from its own previous decisions?

J W Harris, *Legal Philosophies* (see above), at p. 174 (footnotes omitted).

Is there any sound reason for holding that intermediate appellate courts should be bound by their own decisions to any greater extent than final appellate courts are? Most academic commentators on the position of the English Court of Appeal have answered that question in the negative. Where there is extant an erroneous Court of Appeal ruling it would (they maintain) save the trouble and expense of an appeal to the House of Lords if the Court of Appeal could overrule itself. The contrary view, which was vigorously re-asserted by the House of Lords in *Davis* v *Johnson* [[1979] AC 264], is that finality would be gravely threatened if the Court of Appeal were not strictly bound by its own decisions. Since the Court of Appeal sits in panels of only three (sometimes only two), it could easily happen that a point might be ruled one way in case A, another in case B, and the view accepted in case A be re-inserted in case C, and so on. Accordingly, in *Davis* v *Johnson* the House of Lords insisted that the only exceptions to the rule that the Court of Appeal is bound by its own decisions are the three enunciated by Lord Greene MR in *Young* v *Bristol Aeroplane Co. Ltd* [[1944] KB 718]: first, where there are two conflicting decisions of the Court of Appeal; second where a decision of the Court of Appeal cannot stand with a decision of the House of Lords; third, where a decision of the Court of Appeal was made *per incuriam.*

This formula is repeated frequently. However, the second exception has been extended to instances in which a prior decision of the House of Lords was 'misunderstood' in an earlier Court of Appeal case; and the *per incuriam* exception has been said to include, not merely instances where some relevant authority was overlooked, but also 'rare and exceptional cases; in which a decision of the Court of Appeal involved a 'manifest slip or error'. There are, furthermore, occasional invocations of exceptions other than the three listed in *Young's* case.

Question:
1.   Are you convinced by the arguments put forward by Harris concerning why the Court of Appeal is in a different position from the House of Lords as far as departing from its own previous decisions is concerned?

Martha Minnow, who used the analogy between the process of legal reasoning and *Sesame Street's* 'Which one of these things is not like the others' (see Chapter 1 at p. 6) illustrates how precedent works in practice in relation to negligence claims, and suggests that its application is not always simple, but involves complex choices.

M Minnow, *Making All the Difference: Inclusion, Exclusion and American Law*, New York, Cornell University Press (1990), p. 2.

The categories of negligence and cause might seem infinitely malleable. Certainly, in the abstract, we could debate a variety of duties people may owe to one another when driving cars; we could also identify an infinite chain of causes and effects, preceding the births of the drivers and extending long into the future. But legal analysis contracts such discussions by sharpening the definitions and by referring back to precedents: prior judicial decisions ruling on the meanings of negligence and causation in similar contexts. The lawyers turn to these precedents to engage directly in a *Sesame Street* analysis: which of the precedents does the current case resemble? Is it like the prior decision declaring it nonnegligent conduct for a driver cruising at the legal speed to fail to slow down at the intersection? Or does it more comfortably belong with the case declaring it negligent conduct for the driver to fail to slow down at the intersection when it was raining? Legal analysis is a process of perceiving and selecting traits of a given conflict, and analogizing and distinguishing prior decisions. Legal rules announced in statutes and in judicial opinions provide definitions and categories; legal precedents appearing in prior court judgments provide constellations of fact patterns and competing normative rules that allow advocates to fit a new case to the rule — or to an exception. And the basic method of legal analysis requires simplifying the problem to focus on a few traits rather than the full complexity of the situation, and to use those traits for the comparison with both the governing rule and the precedents that could apply.

The following extract discusses further techniques of reasoning from precedent.

W Twining and D Miers, *How To Do Things With Rules*, 3rd edn, London, Weidenfeld and Nicolson (1991), pp. 301–4.

Precedent techniques are techniques of reasoning about how prior cases should be interpreted. They are typically used in the context of justifying a particular result in a case, or in persuading others to come to a particular conclusion, or in supporting formulations of legal doctrine in the process of exposition or in making certain kinds of predictions. It has long been recognised that a variety of techniques is involved in interpreting cases, but it was Karl Llewellyn [see further Chapter 7 at p. 245] who first attempted an extensive examination of this aspect of legal reasoning. His somewhat rough and ready list of sixty-four techniques of following and avoiding precedent decisions suggests that even in England the explicit doctrine and tacit conventions of precedent are not necessarily as restrictive an influence on legal developments as is commonly suggested by formalistic discussions of the subject. Within the armoury of techniques available to courts in dealing with precedents, there are many devices for creating law within the frame-work of authority.

From the standpoint of the advocate [see further Chapter 6], prior cases are potentially favourable, adverse, or neutral, and it is from this standpoint that we can most easily see the way in which these techniques of reasoning are employed. Where the advocate is faced with an adverse precedent he has a number of choices open to him. He may, for example, argue that the precedent was rightly decided but is distinguishable on its facts or on the issue of law it raised. On the other hand, where the cases are analogous, the advocate may use a number of techniques to argue that the precedent was wrongly decided or is of weak authority by suggesting, for example:

(a)   that the precedent involved a faulty interpretation of other prior cases;
(b)   that the precedent was a decision given *per incuriam*, that is, in ignorance of a binding statutory or judicial authority;
(c)   that the precedent has been subsequently overruled or doubted by other judges;
(d)   that the precedent is reconcilable with prior or subsequent decisions.

These primary techniques are employed quite commonly to avoid prior cases, but in addition there are various secondary techniques for weakening their precedent value, for example, by arguing;

(e)   that the deciding court was of low authority;
(f)   that the scope of the decision is unclear;
(g)   that the reasoning other than from authority is weak;
(h)   that the deciding court was particularly influenced by special con-siderations;
(i)   that social conditions have changed;
(j)   that the report of the precedent is unreliable;
(k)   that the decision has been criticised by academic writers.

This is by no means a comprehensive list, nor are the techniques of equal weight. A precedent can be favourable either in its result or in its reasoning or both, and there are similarly supplementary ways in which additional weight can be attached to a decision, for example by emphasising the high reputation of the judges in the prior case or the fact of its subsequent approval . . .

Advocates, however, are not the only participants in the legal process who seek to persuade others to accept a particular line of reasoning. Together with their primary task of justifying their decisions, judges too may try to persuade their colleagues that a particular legal solution to a dispute is the one to be adopted [see further Chapter 7]. Where a judge is espousing a currently unpopular result, he must rely heavily on his powers of persuasion, and he may employ a number of rhetorical devices to bolster and protect his case. Some of the devices have been indicated earlier, but we should stress that while some precedent techniques can be isolated, they tend to overlap and fuse into one another and operate cumulatively, so that their effect can best be appreciated by reading a judgment as a whole.

READING JUDGMENTS

As an introduction to the process of reading and interpreting cases we reproduce the following judgments interrupting the text with our comments. Try to see the kinds of questions which more experienced readers of cases would be asking themselves. That is the best way to learn the skill of understanding judgments. Then try to write a summary (or headnote) or using our structure: facts, issues, decision, reasons for decision.

Re B (Baby Alexandra) [1981] 1 WLR 1421, CA.

Templeman LJ
   This is a very poignantly sad case.

   [Why begin in this way? Is this an *obiter dictum?* Whom is Templeman LJ addressing? The parents? What is 'irrelevant' for a student may be much appreciated by another audience, the parties in court.]

   Although we sit in public,

[Should the court sit in private?]

   for reasons which I think will be obvious to everybody in court, and if not will be obvious in the course of this judgment, it would be lamentable if the names of the parents or the child concerned were revealed in any way to the general public.

[What about freedom of information?]

   The press and people who frequent these courts are usually very helpful in referring to names by initials, and this is particularly important in this case where nothing ought to be leaked out to identify those concerned with the case. It concerns a little

[Would the case have ever come to court if the intestinal blockage had developed in, say, a 5 year old? Should we treat newly born babies differently? Is it relevant that she is little?]

   girl

[Does her sex matter?]

   who was born on 28 July 1981. She was born suffering from Down's Syndrome,

[Does her particular mental and physical disability matter? Would the 'ratio' of this judgment also apply to those suffering from, say, cystic fibrosis?]

which means that she will be a mongol. She was also born with an intestinal blockage which will be fatal unless it is operated upon. When the parents were informed of the condition of the child they took the view that it would be unkind to this child to operate upon her, and that the best thing to do was for her not to have the operation, in which case she would die within a few days. During those few days she could be kept from pain and suffering by sedation. They took the view that would be the kindest thing in the interests of the child. They so informed the doctors at the hospital, and refused to consent to the operation taking place. It is agreed on all hands that the parents came to that decision with great sorrow. It was a firm decision: they genuinely believed that it was in the best interest of this child. At the same time, it is of course impossible for parents in the unfortunate position of these parents to be certain that their present view should prevail. The shock to caring parents finding that they have given birth to a child who is a mongol is very great indeed, and therefore while great weight ought to be given to the views of the parents they are not views which necessarily must prevail.

[Do you agree? What does it mean to give the views 'great weight' and then decide the exact opposite?]

What happened then was that the doctors being informed that the parents would not consent to the operation contacted the local authority

[Should the doctors have just let the child die?]

who very properly made the child a ward of court and asked the judge to give care and control to the local authority and to authorise them to direct that the operation be carried out, and the judge did so direct. But when the child was moved from the hospital where it was born to another hospital for the purposes of the operation a difference of medical opinion developed. The surgeon who was to perform the operation was informed that the parents objected. In a statement he said that when the child was referred to him for the operation he decided he wished to speak to the parents of the child personally and he spoke to them on the telephone and they stated that in view of the fact that the child was mongoloid they did not wish to have the operation performed. He further stated:

'I decided therefore to respect the wishes of the parents and not to perform the operation, a decision which would, I believe (after about 20 years in the medical profession), be taken by the great majority of surgeons faced with a similar situation.'

[Should this surgeon be prosecuted for contempt of court in refusing to carry out a court order?]

Therefore the local authority came back to the judge. The parents were served in due course and appeared and made their submissions to the judge, and in addition inquiries were made and it was discovered that the surgeon in the hospital where the child was born and another surgeon in a neighbouring hospital were prepared and advised that the operation should be carried out. So there is a difference of medical opinion.

This morning the judge was asked to decide whether to continue his order that the operation should be performed or whether to revoke that order, and the position now is stark.'

[How did the judge decide? Are cases usually resolved on appeal in the afternoon of the earlier decision? Why allow delays of years elsewhere in the legal system? See Chapter 9.]

The evidence, as I have said, is that if this little girl does not have this operation she will die within a matter of days. If she has the operation there is a possibility that she will suffer heart trouble as a result and that she may die within two or three months. But if she has the operation and is successful, she has Down's syndrome, she is mongoloid, and the present evidence is that her life expectancy is short, about 20 to 30 years.

[Would the result have been different if the expectancy was 20 to 30 hours, or days, or weeks? Should that make a difference?]

The parents say that no one can tell what will be the life of a mongoloid child who survives during that 20 or 30 years, but one thing is certain. She will be very handicapped mentally and physically and no one can expect that she will have anything like a normal existence. They make that point not because of the difficulties which will be occasioned to them but in the child's interest. This is not a case in which the court is concerned with whether arrangements could or could not be made for the care of this child if she lives, during the next 20 or 30 years; the local authority is confident that the parents having for good reason decided that it is in the child's best interests that the operation should not be performed, nevertheless good adoption arrangements could be made and that in so far as any mongol child can be provided with a happy life then such a happy life can be provided.

[So what if good adoption arrangements could not be made?]

The question which this court has to determine is whether it is in the interests of this child to be allowed to die within the next week or to have the operation in which case if she lives she will be a mongoloid child, but no one can say to what extent her mental or physical defects will be apparent.

[Is this the issue?]

No one can say whether she will suffer or whether she will be happy in part. On the other hand the probability is that she will not be a cabbage as it is called when people's faculties are entirely destroyed. On the other hand it is certain that she will be very severely mentally and physically handicapped.

On behalf of the parents Mr Gray has submitted very movingly, if I may say so, that this is a case where nature has made its own arrangements to terminate a life which would not be fruitful and nature should not be interfered with. He has also submitted that in this kind of decision the views of responsible and caring parents, as these are, should be respected, and that their decision that it is better for the child to be allowed to die should be respected.

[Why?]

Fortunately or unfortunately, in this particular case the decision no longer lies with the parents or with the doctors, but lies with the court.

[Why? Why are judges entrusted with the decision? Why not a specially created commission of experts? Who would count as an expert for this purpose?]

It is a decision which of course must be made in the light of the evidence and views expressed by the parents and the doctors,

[But what does this mean?]

but at the end of the day it devolves on this court in this particular instance to decide whether the life of this child is demonstrably going to be so awful that in effect the child must be condemned to die, or whether the life of this child is still so imponderable that it would be wrong for her to be condemned to die.

[Is 'demonstrably awful' a test which could be used to resolve future cases?]

There may be cases, I know not, of severe proved damage where the future is so certain and where the life of the child is so bound to be full of pain and suffering that the court might be driven to a different conclusion,

[Is this part of the ruling or is the judge speculating on possible future cases? If so, could later judges ignore such speculation?]

but in the present case the choice which lies before the court is this: whether to allow an operation to take place which may result in the child living for 20 or 30 years as a mongoloid or whether (and I think this must be brutally the result) to terminate the life of a mongoloid child because she also has an intestinal complaint.

[Is this the issue? Is the judge repeating himself?]

Faced with that choice I have no doubt that it is the duty of this court to decide that the child must live.

[Is this the decision?]

The judge was much affected by the reasons given by the parents and came to the conclusion that their wishes ought to be respected.

[Why? Are we told? Should we be told? How would you find out?]

In my judgment he erred in that the duty of the court is to decide whether it is in the interests of the child that an operation should take place.

[Is this the key part of the judgment or *ratio decidendi*?]

The evidence in this case only goes to show that if the operation takes place and is successful then the child may live the normal span of a mongoloid child with the handicaps and effects and life of a mongol child, and it is not for this court to say that life of that description ought to be extinguished.

Accordingly the appeal must be allowed and the local authority must be authorised themselves to authorise and direct the operation to be carried out on the little girl.

[What if the doctor still refuses?]

Dunn LJ
I agree, and as we are differing from the view expressed by the judge

[Again, why are we not given the lower judge's judgment?]

I would say a few words of my own. I have great sympathy for the parents in the agonising decision to which they came. As they put it themselves, 'God or nature has given the child a way out.' But the child now being a ward of court, although due weight must be given to the decision of the parents which everybody accepts was an entirely responsible one, doing what they considered was the best, the fact of the matter is that this court now has to make the decision.

[Why?]

It cannot hide behind the decision of the parents or the decision of the doctors; and in making the decision this court's first and paramount consideration is the welfare of this unhappy little baby.

[Is this the same as Templeman LJ's test?]

One of the difficulties in the case is that there is no prognosis as to the child's future, except that as a mongol her expectation of life is confined to 20 to 30 years. We were told that no reliable prognosis can be made until probably she is about two years old. That in itself leads me to the route by which the court should make its decision, because there is no evidence that this child's short life is likely to be an intolerable one.

[Can you think of what would count as evidence of an intolerable life?]

There is no evidence at all as to the quality of life which the child may expect. As Mr Turcan on behalf of the Official Solicitor said, the child should be put into the same position as any other mongol child and must be given the chance to live an existence. I accept that way of putting it.

I agree with Templeman LJ that the court must step in to preserve this mongol baby's life. I would allow the appeal and I agree with the order proposed by Templeman LJ.

[If he agrees with the other judge, why add his own, potentially different, explanation?]

Questions:
1. What, if anything, surprises you about these judgments?

2. Did you notice that no other cases are mentioned by the judges? (That's our answer to question 1.) Why not?

3.   If there had been time to find them and if there had been any relevant cases from other countries, should the court have been made aware of them? Is it now easier than it was back in 1981 to track down precedents from other jurisdictions? How would you go about doing so?

4.   Supposing that there had been an earlier UK case, let's call it *Re A,* in which a Down's Syndrome baby with a similar condition and intestinal blockage but with a life expectancy of 20–30 *weeks* rather than years, had been allowed to die with the approval of the Court of Appeal, should the court in our case have followed that earlier decision?

5.   If there had been no *Re A* but the same problem (20–30 *weeks'* life expectancy) emerges after *Re B* in a case we will call *Re C,* should the court in *Re C* follow the decision in *Re B*?

6.   One of the points we want you to think about is whether judges should follow precedents or get round them if they disagree with them? List the advantages and disadvantages of following earlier decisions.

7.   If *you* were a judge, would you try to get round a decision you did not want to follow? Does that suggest (a) that all judges do this, and/or (b) that you would not be a good judge?

8.   Why do you think that this case was not appealed to the House of Lords?

9.   Is it relevant if you are deciding a future case, say *Re C,* to note that *Re B* was decided in a hurry? Do appellate judges normally give judgments immediately? How can you find out their practice?

10.   What, if anything, equips a judge to take such awesome decisions of life and death?

11.   If you have difficulty in imagining how this judgment would be used as a precedent, there have in fact been further cases. Consider the following factual extract from the real (as opposed to our hypothetical *Re C,* in question 5 above) case. See if you can annotate this case with comments similar to ours in the previous case.

Re C [1989] 2 All ER 782, CA.

Lord Donaldson MR

I have most regrettably to start with one fundamental and inescapable fact. Baby C is dying and nothing that the court can do, nothing that the doctors can do and nothing known to medical science can alter that fact . . .

C was born prematurely on 23 December 1988. She is now 16 weeks old. At birth she was found to be afflicted with with a much more serious type of condition than the usual type of hydrocephalus. There was not merely a blockage of cerebral spinal fluid within the brain, but as a result the brain structure itself was poorly formed. Her progress since then and further examinations have revealed how badly she has been affected . . . The essential problem was what treatment should be given in the best interests of C if, as sooner or later was inevitable, she suffered some infection or illness over and above the handicaps from which she was already suffering . . .

Dr W [the physician in charge of C] had raised the question of what he should do if the time came when it proved impossible to feed C through a syringe, in itself a procedure fraught with difficulty. Should he set up an intravenous drip? If C developed a terminal respiratory infection should she be given antibiotics? All these were legitimate and difficult questions, given the sad but fundamental truth that C was dying and the only question was how soon this would happen. Faced with these problems, the judge invited the intervention of the Official Solicitor, who asked one of the nation's foremost paediatricians to examine C and to make recommendations . . . The professor reported as follows and I read from the report:

. . . [C's] appearance is of a tiny baby. Although she is 16 weeks old, she is the size of a 4 week baby apart from her head, which is unusually large by way of being tall and thin — squashed because of sleeping on her side. She lies quiet until handled and then cries as if irritated. Her eyes move wildly in an uncoordinated way and she does not appear to see . . . my impression was that she did not hear or had very poor hearing. She holds her limbs in a stiff flexed position. More detailed examination suggested that she had generalised spasticity of all her limbs as a result of the brain damage. She sometimes can be pacified by stroking her face. She does not smile and does not respond in any other way. The only certain evidence of her feeling or appreciating events is the report of her quietening when her face is stroked. Thus she does not have the developmental skills and abilities of a normal new born baby. It is inconceivable that appreciable skills will develop, bearing in mind that she has made no progress during the past four months. She has severe brain damage. She is very thin and has not gained weight despite devoted nursing care [at the hospital]. She is receiving regular small doses of the sedative Chloral. If she does not receive this she cries 'as if in pain', though the carers are unsure where the pain originates. I do not believe that there is any treatment which will alter the ultimate prognosis which appears to be hopeless . . . In the event of her acquiring a serious infection, or being unable to take feeds normally by mouth I do not think it would be correct to give antibiotics, to set up intravenous fusions or nasal-gastric feeding regimes. Such action would be prolonging a life which has no future and which appears to be unhappy for her.

Questions:
1. Given these facts, how useful do you think the case of *Re B* was as a precedent for the Court of Appeal judges in *Re C*?

2. If you had been a judge in the Court of Appeal how would you have decided the case in the light of *Re B*? What are the relevant differences between *C* and *B*? (Now read the full reported judgment to find out how the Court did decide. In it are there any other relevant factual differences between *B* and *C*?)

Re J [1990] 3 All ER 930, CA.

Lord Donaldson MR
Baby J has suffered almost every conceivable misfortune. He was a very
premature baby, born after 27 weeks' gestation on 28 May 1990. He weighed
only 1.1 kg (2.5 lb) at birth. He was not breathing. Almost immediately he
was placed on a ventilator and given antibiotics to counteract an infection.
He was put on a drip. His pulse rate frequently became very low and for ten
days it was touch and go whether he survived. One month later, on 28 June,
the doctors were able to take him off the ventilator, but he was, and still is,
a very sick and handicapped baby. There followed recurrent convulsions and
episodes when he stopped breathing (apnoea). As a result he was oxygen
dependent until early August. At the end of August the doctors thought he
could be allowed to go home, although the prognosis was gloomy in the
extreme. Four days later, on 1 September 1990, he had to be readmitted to
hospital because he had choked and become cyanosed.

The subsequent history of J has been traumatic both for him, his parents
and those professionally involved in caring for him. On 3 September it was
noted that J had become cyanosed when he cried. On 5 September he
collapsed suddenly and was again cyanosed. He was without a pulse, but was
resuscitated. Two days later he again collapsed and had to be put on a
ventilator. Between then and 23 September he was continuously on a
ventilator. During that period four attempts were made to wean him from it.
The first three failed because he suffered fits which interfered with the
efficiency of the ventilator and on one occasion the doctors had to paralyse
him in order to make his oxygen level safe. Since 23 September J has been
breathing independently and in some ways his condition has slightly improved. However this improvement is from a base line which can only be
described as abysmally low.

Needless to say the doctors have been concerned to discover what are
likely to be J's long-term disabilities. As a result it is clear that he has
suffered very severe brain damage due to shortage of oxen and impaired
blood supply around the time of his birth. This is no one's fault, but stems
from his prematurity. Ultrasound scans of his brain were conducted on 22
August and 10 September. They showed a large area of fluid-filled cavities
where there ought to have been brain tissue. The body is incapable of making
this good. Of the three neo-natalogists who have been concerned with his
care, the most optimistic is Dr W. His view is that J is likely to develop
serious spastic quadriplegia, that is to say paralysis of both his arms and legs.
It is debatable whether he will ever be able to sit up or to hold his head
upright. J appears to be blind, although there is a possibility that some degree
of sight may return. He is likely to be deaf. He may be able to make sounds
which reflect his mood, but he is unlikely ever to be able to speak, even to
the extent of saying 'Mum' or 'Dad'. It is highly unlikely that he will develop
even limited intellectual abilities. Most unfortunately of all, there is a
likelihood that he will be able to feel pain to the same extent as a normal
baby, because pain is a very basic response. It is possible that he may achieve

the ability to smile and to cry. Finally, as one might expect, his life expectancy has been considerably reduced at most into his late teens, but even Dr W would expect him to die long before then . . .

The problem which has now to be faced by all concerned is what is to be done if J suffers another collapse. This may occur at any time, but is not inevitable . . . On 11 October Scott Baker J made an order authorising the hospital to treat J within the parameters of the opinion expressed by Dr W in his report of 4 October 1990, subject to amendments . . . made in the course of his oral evidence. This opinion, as amended and explained in the course of the hearing before this court, was as follows:

24 I am of the opinion that it would not be in [J's] best interests to reventilate him [using a ventilation machine] in the event of his stopping breathing, unless to do so seems appropriate to the doctors caring for him given the prevailing clinical situation. However, I think it would be reasonable to suck out his airway to remove any plug of mucous or milk and to give oxygen by his face mask.

25 If he developed a chest infection I would recommend treatment with antibiotics and maintenance of hydration, but not prolonged [manual] ventilation.

The Official Solicitor has appealed against this decision . . . [Counsel for the Official Solicitor's] first, or absolutist, submission is that a court is never justified in withholding consent to treatment which could enable a child to survive a life-threatening condition, whatever the pain or other side-effects inherent in the treatment and whatever the quality of life which it would experience thereafter. In making this submission he distinguished a case such as that of *Re C* . . .

Counsel for the Official Solicitor then turns to the decision of the Supreme Court of British Columbia in *Re Superintendendent of Family and Child Service and Dawson* (1983) 145 (3d) 610 . . . There the issue was whether a severely brain damaged child should be subjected to a relatively simple kind of surgical treatment which would assure the continuation of his life, or whether, as the parents considered was in the child's best interests, consent to the operation should be refused with a view to the child being allowed to die in the near future with dignity rather than to continue a life of suffering. Counsel for the Official Solicitor relies on the first paragraph of the judgment of McKenzie J, but I think that paragraph read in isolation is capable of being misleading. The full quotation is (145 DLR (3d) 610 at 620–621):

I do not think that it lies within the prerogative of any parent or of this court to look down upon a disadvantaged person and judge the quality of that person's life to be so low as not to be deserving of continuance. The matter was well put in an American decision (*Re Weberlist* (1974) 360 NYS 2d 783 at 787), where Justice Ashe said: 'There is a strident cry in America to terminate the lives of *other* people — deemed physically or mentally defective . . . Assuredly, one test of a civilization is its concern

with the suvival of the 'unfittest', a reversal of Darwin's formulation . . .
In this case, the court must decide what its ward would choose, if he were
in a position to make a sound judgment'. This last sentence puts it right.
It is not appropriate for an external decision maker to apply his standards
of what constitutes a liveable life and exercise the right to impose death if
that standard is not met in his estimation. The decision can only be made
in the context of the disabled person viewing the worthwhileness or
otherwise of his life in its own context as a disabled person — and in that
context he would not compare his life with that of a person enjoying
normal advantages. He would know nothing of a normal person's life
having never experienced it.

I am in complete agreement with McKenzie J that the starting point is not
what might have been, but what is. He was considering the best interests of
a severely handicapped child, not of a normal child, and the latter's feelings
and interests were irrelevant. I am also in complete agreement with his
implied assertion of the vast importance of the sanctity of human life. I cavil
mildly, although it is a very important point, with his use of the phrase 'the
right to impose death'. No such right exists in the court or the parents. What
is in issue in these cases is not a right to impose death, but a right to choose
a course of action which will fail to avert death. The choice is that of the
patient, if of full age and capacity, the choice is that of the parents or court
if, by reason of his age, the child cannot make the choice and it is a choice
which must be made solely *on behalf* of the child and in what the court or
the parents conscientiously believe to be in his best interests. In my view the
last sentence of the passage which I have quoted from the judge's judgment
shows that he was rejecting a particular comparison as a basis for decision
rather than denying that there was a balancing exercise to be performed. I do
not therefore think that this decision supports the absolutist approach which
I would in any event unhesitatingly reject. In real life there are presumptions,
strong presumptions and almost overwhelming presumptions, but there are
few, if any, absolutes.

I turn, therefore, to the alternative submission of counsel for the Official
Solicitor that a court is only justified in withholding consent to treatment
which could enable a child to survive a life-threatening condition if it is
certain that the quality of the child's subsequent life would be 'intolerable to
the child', 'bound to be full of pain and suffering' and 'demonstrably so awful
that in effect the child must be condemned to die'. As I have already
mentioned, this submission owes much to the decision of this court in *Re B*.
It is I think, important to remember the facts of that case and what was in
issue . . . *Re B* seems to me to come very near to being a binding authority
for the proposition that there is a balancing exercise to be performed in
assessing the course to be adopted in the best interests of the child. Even if
it is not, I have no doubt that this should be, and is, the law.

This brings me face to face with the problem of formulating the critical
equation. In truth it cannot be done with mathematical or any precision. There
is without doubt a very strong presumption in favour of a course of action

which will prolong life, but, even excepting the 'cabbage' case to which special considerations may well apply, it is not irrebuttable. As this court recognised in *Re B*, account has to be taken of the pain and suffering and quality of life which the child will experience if life is prolonged. Account has also to be taken of the pain and suffering involved in the proposed treatment. *Re B* was probably not a borderline case and I do not think we are bound to, or should treat Templeman LJ's use of the words 'demonstrably so awful' or Dunn LJ's use of the word 'intolerable' as providing a quasi-statutory yardstick.

For my part I prefer the formulation of Ashe J in *Re Weberlist* (1974) 360 NYS 2d 783 at 787 as explained by McKenzie J in the passage from his judgment in *Dawson's* case (1983) 145 DLR (3d) 610 at 620–621 which I have quoted, although it is probably merely another way of expressing the same concept. We know that the instinct and desire for survival is very strong. We all believe in and assert the sanctity of human life. As explained, this formulation takes account of this and also underlines the need to avoid looking at the problem from the point of view of the decider, but instead requires him to look at it from the assumed point of view of the patient. This gives effect, as it should, to the fact that even very severely handicapped people find a quality of life rewarding which to the unhandicapped may seem manifestly intolerable. People have an amazing adaptability. But in the end there will be cases in which the answer must be that it is not in the interests of the child to subject it to treatment which will cause increased suffering and produce no commensurate benefit, giving the fullest possible weight to the child's and mankind's desire to survive . . .

The doctors were unanimous in recommending that there should be no mechanical reventilation in the event of his stopping breathing, subject only to the qualifications injected by Dr W and accepted by the judge that in the event of a chest infection short term manual ventilation would be justified and that in the event of the child stopping breathing the provisional decision to abstain from mechanical ventilation could and should be revised, if this seemed appropriate to the doctors caring for him in the prevailing clinical situation . . .

The basis of the doctors' recommendations, approved by the judge, was that mechanical ventilation is in itself an invasive procedure which, together with its essential accompaniments, such as the introduction of a naso-gastric tube, drips which have to be resited and constant blood sampling, would cause the child distress. Furthermore, the procedures involve taking active measures which carry their own hazards, not only to life but in terms of causing even greater brain damage. This had to be balanced against what could possibly be achieved by the adoption of such active treatment. The chances of preserving the child's life might be improved, although even this was not certain and account had to be taken of the extremely poor quality of life at present enjoyed by the child, the fact that he had already been ventilated for exceptionally long periods, the unfavourable prognosis with or without ventilation and a recognition that if the question of reventilation ever arose, his situation would have deteriorated still further.

I can detect no error in the judge's approach and in principle would affirm his decision.

Questions:

1. Why was *J* a more difficult case than *C*?

2. Do you agree with one or both of the Official Solicitor's arguments in *J* that:

    (a) judges could never authorise such a course of (in)activity and
    (b) even if they could, it would not be appropriate in this case?

3. What was the status as precedent of the Canadian case cited in the judgment? Can you find this case in your law-library or on Lexis? On the facts does it differ in any relevant respect from *Re B*?

4. Do you agree with Lord Donaldson MR's interpretation of *Re B*? How far was it binding upon him?

5. Suppose a child K is born with similar disabilities to J but would not experience pain, or would not be paralysed, or was not blind or deaf: would the decision in *J* still bind a High Court judge? Which aspects of J's medical condition were really decisive? Would the case of *J* only be of use as a 'precedent' where all of those features are present in a child?

6. Who do you think is best-placed to decide these types of cases? Is it really possible for whoever decides to perform the 'substituted judgment' test which Lord Donaldson approves and which seems to involve the decider placing herself in the shoes of the disabled neonate?

7. What was the *ratio decidendi* of *Re J*? Does reading *Re J* change your opinion of what the *ratio* of *Re B* was?

Re T (a minor) (wardship: medical treatment) [1997] 1 All ER 906, CA.

Butler-Sloss LJ
C was born on 10 April 1995 suffering from biliary atresia, a life-threatening liver defect. The unanimous medical prognosis is that he will not live beyond the age of two to two and a half without a liver transplantation. It is equally the unanimous clinical opinion of the consultants that it is in his interests to undergo the operation when a donor liver becomes available. The parents, who were trained as health care professionals and are both experienced in the care of young sick children do not want the operation to take place. The main issue before the judge and on appeal before this court is whether the court should overrule the decision of the parents and consent to the operation. It arises as a specific issue in respect of which the court is asked to exercise its inherent jurisdiction.

The background to this tragic and deeply worrying case is as follows. The parents are not married but have a stable relationship. They decided to apply for jobs in a distant Commonwealth country (country AB) . . . and remain there now. The mother gave evidence to Connell J in the proceedings, the subject of this appeal, by video link.

Once C's liver defect was diagnosed the medical advice at the local hospital was for him to undergo an operation called 'Kasai' with the hope that this would improve his condition. The parents agreed and he underwent the operation at the age of three and a half weeks but the outcome was unsuccessful. The mother's view of the proposed liver transplantation operation has been much influenced by the circumstances of the 'Kasai' operation and the pain and distress caused to the baby both by it and by the consequential treatment. She and the father came to the conclusion, having sought medical advice, that if the 'Kasai' operation proved unsuccessful, they would not wish their baby to undergo major transplant surgery . . .

The mother did not consent to the carrying out of the [proposed] operation. Dr A made it clear to the mother that it was in the best interests of C that the operation be carried out and could not accept the mother's reasons for refusing to consent. Inevitably, the relationship between Dr A and the mother became strained. Dr A told the mother that the hospital would seek legal advice if the mother did not consent. The mother obtained a second opinion from a consultant paediatrician, Dr P at hospital Y, another centre of liver transplant operations . . . He and his team strongly urged the mother to consent to the offer of transplantation at hospital X, but said that if she and the father after further consideration did not consent, that decision should be respected . . .

On 17 July 1996 the local authority sought the leave of the court to commence proceedings under the provisions of s. 100(3) of the Children Act 1989 . . .

At the substantive hearing of the application of the local authority . . . [i]n their reports and in their oral evidence the three doctors were unanimous that the prospects of success were good and that this operation was in the best interests of the child . . .

The local authority in their originating summons sought the answers to three specific questions: (1) whether it was in the best interests of C to undergo surgery for a liver transplantation; (2) for permission to be granted to perform the surgery notwithstanding the refusal of the mother to consent, and (3) for the child to be returned to the jurisdiction for the purpose of such surgery. They were neutral before the judge and the proposed surgery was strongly advocated by the guardian ad litem . . .

[Connell J] answered the three questions posed by the local authority in the affirmative and directed the return of the mother with C to the jurisdiction within 21 days in order to undergo the surgery for liver transplantation . . .

A line of cases from 1981 has, in my opinion, clearly established the approach of the court to these most difficult and anxious questions. In *Re B (a minor)* . . . [t]his court allowed the appeal and held that the question for the court was whether it was in the best interests of the child that she should have the operation and not whether the wishes of the parents should be respected . . .

The House of Lords in *Re B (a minor) (wardship: sterilisation)* [1987] 2 All ER 206, [1988] AC 199 held that a court exercising wardship jurisdiction, when reaching a decision on an application to authorise an operation for sterilisation of the ward, was concerned with only one primary and paramount consideration, the welfare of the child.

This court in *Re J (a minor) (wardship: medical treatment)* considered the future medical management of a severely brain-damaged premature baby with a considerably shortened life expectancy. Lord Donaldson MR said . . .

'As this court recognised in *Re B*, account has to be taken of the pain and suffering and quality of life which the child will experience if life is prolonged. Account has also to be taken of the pain and suffering involved in the proposed treatment itself . . . But in the end there will be cases in which the answer must be that it is not in the interests of the child to subject it to treatment which will cause increased suffering and produce no commensurate benefit, giving the fullest possible weight to the child's and mankind's desire to survive.'

In *Re Z (a minor) (freedom of publication)* . . . Bingham MR said ([1995] 4 All ER 961 at 968):

'I would for my part accept without reservation that the decision of a devoted and responsible parent should be treated with respect. It should certainly not be disregarded or lightly set aside. But the role of the court is to exercise an independent and objective judgment . . . '

From the decisions to which I have referred which bind this court, it is clear that when an application under the inherent jurisdiction is made to the court the welfare of the child is the paramount consideration. The consent or refusal of consent of the parents is an important consideration to weight in the balancing exercise to be carried out by the judge. In that context, the extent to which the court will have regard to the view of the parent will depend upon the court's assessment of that view. But as Bingham MR said in *Re Z*, the court decided and in doing so may overrule the decision of a reasonable parent . . .

The mother certainly told the judge that she recognised her son had only a short time to live if no operation was performed. She was focusing, it seems to me, on the present peaceful life of the child who had the chance to spend the rest of his short life without the pain, stress and upset of intrusive surgery against the future with the operation and treatment taking place. That is an alternative point of view to that to which the judge came and with some hesitation. I doubt that he was right to deem the mother to be unreasonable in her assessment of the broader perspective of whether this operation should be carried out. But in any event, the reasonableness of the mother was not the primary issue. This mother and this child are one for the purpose of this unusual case and the decision of the court to consent to the operation jointly affects the mother and son and it also affects the father. The welfare of this child depends upon his mother. The practical considerations of her ability to cope with supporting the child in the face of her belief that this course is not right for him, the requirement to return probably for a long period to this country, either to leave the father behind and lose his support or to require him to give up his present job and seek one in England were not put by the judge into the balance when he made his decision.

In *Re W* (*a minor*) (*medical treatment*) [1992] 4 All ER 627, [1993] Fam 64, a case about the medical treatment of a girl of 16 suffering from anorexia nervosa, Lord Donaldson MR said that there were two purposes to seeking consent, clinical and legal:

'The clinical purpose stems from the fact that in many instances the co-operation of the patient and the patient's faith or at least confidence in the efficacy of the treatment is a major factor contributing to the treatment's success.' (See [1992] 4 All ER 627 at 633, Fam 64 at 76.)

That passage applies, in my judgement, with equal force to the need for the confidence and the commitment to the proposed treatment by the principal carer on the unusual facts of this case. Unlike the intestinal obstruction of the Down's Syndrome baby which could be cured by a simple operation, C's problems require complicated surgery and many years of special care from the mother.

The reservations of Dr P, to which he held despite concessions he made in his evidence, remain of great significance and importance. His view that the decision of a loving, caring mother should be respected, ought to be given great weight, and are reinforced by the Fact Sheet 10 provided by hospital X. The alternative of the court giving the consent and passing back the responsibility for the parental care to the mother and expecting her to provide the commitment to the child after the operation is carried out in the face of her opposition is in itself fraught with danger for the child. She will have to comply with the court order, return to this country and present the child to one of the hospitals. How will the mother cope? Can her professionalism overcome her view that her son should not be subjected to this distressing procedure? Will she break down? How will the child be affected by the conflict with which the mother may have to cope? What happens if the treatment is partially successful and another transplant is needed? . . .

The welfare of the child is the paramount consideration and I recognise the 'very strong presumption in favour of a course of action which will prolong life' and the inevitable consequences for the child of not giving consent. But to prolong life, as Lord Donaldson MR recognised in somewhat different circumstances, is not the sole objective of the court and to require it at the expense of other considerations may not be in a child's best interests. I would stress that, on the most unusual facts of this case with the enormous significance of the close attachment between the mother and baby, the court is not concerned with the reasonableness of the mother's refusal to consent but with the consequences of that refusal and whether it is in the best interests of C for this court in effect to direct the mother to take on this total commitment where she does not agree with the course proposed . . .

I would allow this appeal and would answer the three questions posed in the originating summons in the negative and would set aside the orders of the judge.

Waite LJ

I agree. The law's insistence that the welfare of a child shall be paramount is easily stated and universally applauded, but the present case illustrates, poignantly and dramatically, the difficulties that are encountered when trying to put it into practice . . . The parents' opposition is partly instinctive and (being based on their own awareness of the procedures involved) partly practical. It has sufficient cogency to have led one of the principal medical experts in the field of this operation to say that his team would decline to operate without the mother's committed support.

What is the court to do in such a situation? It is not an occasion — even in an age preoccupied with 'rights' — to talk of the rights of a child, or the rights of a parent, or the rights of the court. The cases cited by Butler-Sloss LJ are uncompromising in their assertion that the sole yardstick must be the need to give effect to the demands of paramountcy for the welfare of the child . . .

All these cases depend on their own facts and render generalisations — tempting though they may be to the legal or social analyst — wholly out of place. It can only be said safely that there is a scale, at one end of which lies the clear case where parental opposition to medical intervention is prompted by scruple or dogma of a kind which is patently irreconcilable with principles of child health and welfare widely accepted by the generality of mankind; and that at the other end lie highly problematic cases where there is genuine scope for a difference of view between parent and judge. In both situations it is the duty of the judge to allow the court's own opinion to prevail in the perceived paramount interests of the child concerned, but in cases at the latter end of the scale, there must be a likelihood (though never of course a certainty) that the greater the scope for genuine debate between one view and another the stronger will be the inclination of the court to be influenced by a reflection that in the last analysis the best interests of every child include an expectation that difficult decisions affecting the length of its life will be taken for it by the parent to whom its care has been entrusted by nature.

Questions:

1.   Is this decision in line with the earlier cases decided above?

2.   In what ways did the facts in this case differ from those decided above?

3.   To what extent do you think that the judge was influenced by the fact that the parents in this case were trained health professionals? Should this have been influential?

4.   How significant do you think it was that the earlier operation on this child was unsuccessful?

5. Were the judges in this case really concerned with the best interests of the child, or were they more concerned with the best interests of the carer? Can these best interests be separated?

6. Was Waite LJ right to distinguish this case from those 'prompted by scruple or dogma of a kind which is patently irreconcilable with principles of child health and welfare widely accepted by the generality of mankind'? What sort of cases do you think he had in mind? (See M Fox and J McHale, 'In whose Best Interests?' *Modern Law Review* (1997) vol. 60, pp. 700–709.)

Re C (a minor) (medical treatment) [1998] 1 FCR 1.

Sir Stephen Brown P

Little C (as I shall call her) was born on 3 July 1996. She is now 16 months of age. She suffers from a dreadful fatal disease, spinal muscular atrophy, type 1. It is known in short as SMA 1. This is a tragic case. She came into hospital first in March 1997. She then weighed $7\frac{1}{4}$ kilograms. She now weighs only $5\frac{1}{2}$ kilograms. When she came into hospital in March 1997 she remained for only a few days and was then allowed to go home, but she came back in July 1997, and briefly stayed in hospital. She went with her parents to Israel in October 1997 and was there for 2 weeks. When she was there, she was put on ventilation, and returned as an emergency case to this country. She has been in hospital in intensive care since that time and is on ventilation. This is known as intermittent positive pressure ventilation which is designed to support her own breathing.

She is seriously disabled. The disease means that she is seriously emaciated. She has little movement of her feet and no other movement in her legs. She does not have what is termed anti-gravity movement in her arms, and is on what the doctor responsible for her care terms as a 'no chance' situation. That is a phrase which appears in a publication of the Royal College of Paediatrics and Child Health issued in September 1997 entitled 'Withholding or Withdrawing Lifesaving Treatment in Children, a Framework for Practice'. It defines the 'no chance' situation as 'where the child has such severe disease that life-sustaining treatment simply delays death without significant alleviation of suffering. Medical treatment in this situation may thus be deemed inappropriate . . .'

The doctor, a consultant paediatric neurologist, having the responsibility for the care of C considers that this is a grave case within that bracket and is so grave that it is not in her best interests that she should be further ventilated, and if and when ventilation is withdrawn it should not be reinstituted in the event of a further respiratory arrest. The doctor's view is that such treatment would be futile, it would not improve her quality of life and would subject her to further suffering without conferring any benefit. It is the inevitable and dreadfully sad feature of this disease that the life expectancy is very short indeed. Not many children survive one year of life in this condition. There are some exceptional cases where it may go to 18 months or perhaps even a little longer. This little child is now 16 months and is in a desperately serious condition. Nevertheless, she is conscious and is able to recognise her parents and is able to smile. She can move her hands laterally, that is not in an anti-gravity way. But she has grave difficulties clearly and the future is very bleak indeed.

The doctors having her care — Dr H is responsible, with other doctors who have also been concerned — have come to the conclusion that it is not in the best interests of this little child that she should continue on indefinite ventilation which would produce increasing distress and would inevitably involve a tracheotomy operation under anaesthetic which might of itself give rise to epilepsy, but that she should be taken off ventilation at this stage and if she were then, as they believe is highly probable, to suffer a further respiratory relapse it would be against her interests to seek to place her back on ventilation or indeed to engage in resuscitative treatment.

This is a serious situation for doctors to contend with. It is a dreadful situation for the parents to have to face. The parents of C are highly responsible religious orthodox Jews. They love their child. They have other children. They cannot bring themselves to face what seems to be the inevitable future for this little child. They visit her and see a reaction which is a favourable reaction in her face towards them. They do not believe that it is within their religious tenets to contemplate the possibility of indirectly shortening life, even if that is not the purpose of the course which the doctors believe to be appropriate in order to spare her further suffering. Accordingly, they have not been able to consent to the proposed course of treatment which the doctors have recommended . . . they believe that they should be able to be assured that should she suffer further respiratory relapse or arrest she should be replaced on to ventilation. The doctors are unable to contemplate undertaking such a course of treatment in the best interests of the child . . .

The hospital authority has applied to this court to exercise its inherent jurisdiction and to approve the course which the doctors wish to follow.

An originating summons was therefore issued last week by the hospital trust and, as drawn, it sought an order that in C's best interests the plaintiff's servants or agents be permitted to withdraw ventilation of C and be permitted not thereafter to resuscitate C in the event of C suffering respiratory arrest without the consent of the first or second defendant, being the mother and the father.

The case has been presented and argued on the basis that the court has power to exercise its inherent jurisdiction in a case such as this and that it is established by the evidence as being in the best interests of the child. The order sought would be in these terms:

> 'There be leave to treat the minor, C, as advised by Dr H, such treatment to include the withdrawal of artificial ventilation and non-resuscitation in the event of a respiratory arrest and palliative care to ease her suffering and permit her life to end peacefully and with dignity, such treatment being in C's best interests . . .'

It is quite clear from the authorities, and is stated perhaps most aptly in the leading case of *Re J (A Minor)* . . . and more specifically in the course of the judgment of Lord Donaldson MR, what is the position of the court in relation to treatment proposed by doctors. At 27 and 173 respectively Lord Donaldson said this:

'It is trite law but in general a doctor is not entitled to treat a patient without the consent of someone who is authorised to give that consent. However, consent by itself creates no obligation to treat, it is merely a key which unlocks a door'.

Questions:

1.   Given that Sir Stephen Brown seems to indicate that the legal position was already settled, why do you think that this case was litigated at all? How did the facts in this case differ from the previous decisions?

2.   Should parents be able to compel doctors to undertake the treatment which they deem appropriate for their children if they pay for their treatment?

3.   How should the religious beliefs of the parents and the best interests of the child be reconciled in cases such as this? (See further, Chapter 10 at pp. 373–85.)

JUDICIAL REVIEW

A particularly interesting area for examining precedent is that of administrative law and judicial review. The process of judicial review may be invoked, where the applicant feels aggrieved by the decision of some public body. She is not technically appealing against that decision, but simply invoking:

the inherent supervisory jurisdiction of the High Court to *review* the conduct of persons or bodes purporting to exercise public functions, to ensure that they remain within the confines of their legal (usually statutory) powers (*intra vires*), and do not stray beyond the limits of that authority (*ultra vires*); and also to ensure that duties owed by them to the public are duly performed. (B L Jones and K Thompson, *Garner's Administrative Law*, 8th edn, London, Butterworths, 1996, at p. 152.)

The following cases raise questions about the scope of judicial review, the role of the court when faced with conflicting precedents and the power of courts to avoid precedents that lead logically to consequences which the judges to not agree with. The cases have two parts: a first part which deals with the statutory interpretation of a Prison Rule in order to consider whether a decision was properly taken under a prison rule, or whether the prison rule itself was properly made, and a second part which discusses whether in principle legal remedies (whether judicial review, damages or recognition of civil rights) should be given to prisoners. It is with this second aspect that we are most concerned, although for the sake of coherence, aspects of the first part of the decision are given. The statutory interpretation aspects deal with a skill which will be further considered in Chapter 3, so do not worry too much about them at this stage. You may want to re-read these cases after reading Chapter 3.

In the first case, the applicant Mr King, was ordered to forfeit 14 days' remission of his prison sentence after a hypodermic needle was found in his cell (which he shared with three other prisoners). Rule 47(7) of the Prison Rules 1964 state that: 'A Prisoner shall be guilty of an offence against discipline if he . . . (7) has in his cell or room or in his possession any unauthorised article, or attempts to obtain such an article . . .' King argued that the Prison Governor had misapplied this rule, in finding that King had possessed the needle merely by virtue of its presence in his cell, without proving that King knew of its presence. King asked the Court to review the Prison Governor's decision to take away remission. The Court had to first consider whether there were grounds for judicial review, by deciding whether the Prison Governor had erred in how he had applied Prison Rule 47(7) which dealt with possession of unauthorised articles. The court then had to decide whether there was any jurisdiction in the High Court to order judicial review on the application of Mr King, or in other words, whether this was a decision which could properly be judicially reviewed.

R v *Deputy Governor of Camphill Prison, ex parte King* [1985] QB 735, CA.

Griffiths LJ
I agree that the governor misconstrued rule 47(7) of the Prison Rules 1964. The primary meaning of 'has' is given in the *Shorter Oxford English Dictionary* as to hold in hand, or in possession; to hold or possess as property, or as something at one's disposal. This is the meaning I attach to the word 'has' in rule 47(7), which means that to be guilty of an offence the prisoner must be exercising some degree of control over the unauthorised article in his cell and it is not sufficient merely to 'know' of the presence of the article. This construction brings the offence into line with all the other offences against discipline set out in rule 47 as requiring a real degree of personal guilt, or mens rea. And it is the meaning that would naturally have attached to the rule when it was first drafted in the days when each prisoner occupied a single cell. If in the case of a prisoner in sole occupation of a cell an unauthorised article comes to light on a cell search it is not difficult to then draw the inference that it is in his possession or under his control. I sympathise with the difficulty of a prison governor when faced with the discovery of an unauthorised article in a cell in multiple occupation, it may be more difficult to know whether the article is in the joint possession of all the prisoners or whether one or more are the guilty parties. However, with the governor's knowledge of the personalities with whom he is dealing I suspect that he will usually be left in no doubt as to the truth of the matter . . .

I cannot, therefore, agree with the construction placed upon rule 47(7) by the deputy prison governor. Nevertheless, despite the powerful judgment of Kerr LJ in the Divisional Court I am firmly of opinion that the court should not extend the boundaries of judicial review to embrace the decisions of prison governors.

The Court of Appeal, now with the approval of the House of Lords, has already extended judicial review to the disciplinary proceedings of the board of visitors. I see the force of the argument that it is a necessary logical extension of the jurisdiction that it should also embrace disciplinary proceedings before the governor, who is adjudicating upon the same code of discipline albeit with lesser powers of punishment, and who also derives his authority to do so from the same statutory instrument, namely, the Prison Rules 1964.

I see also that the governor can be said to fit into the language used by Lord Diplock when considering the scope of judicial review in *O'Reilly* v *Mackman* [1983] 2 AC 277, although it is right to stress that it is unlikely that Lord Diplock had in mind the particular problem with which the court is now faced when drafting that speech.

We have also been pressed by Mr Sedley with the absurdity of the court declaring that it has no power to correct a decision based upon a misconstruction of rule 47(7) by the governor but yet would have power to intervene upon the same misconstruction by the board of visitors.

But the common law of England has not always developed upon strictly logical lines, and where logic leads down a path that is beset with practical difficulties the courts have not been frightened to turn aside and seek the pragmatic solution that will best serve the needs of society.

I can think of no more difficult task in contemporary society than that of managing and maintaining discipline in our seriously overcrowded prisons, nor a task more dependent upon the personal authority of the incumbent. I am convinced that we should make it very much more difficult to carry out that task if the authority of the governor is undermined by the prospect of every disciplinary award being the subject of potential challenge in the courts. I say 'every disciplinary award' because if judicial review is to be available I cannot see how it could be restricted to cases of loss of remission as was suggested at one point in the argument. I appreciate that if the jurisdiction was extended to include governors' awards the court, in its discretion, would refuse to entertain frivolous and unmeritorious applications, but that would not stop the applications being made, and until the court had given its ruling a question mark would hang over the governor's award and to that extent, and I think a serious extent, his authority would be undermined. Nor would it be an easy matter to winnow out all the unmeritorious applications, and I have little doubt that many would squeeze through the net only to be exposed as a result of a full hearing.

I wish I could find a logical way in which to distinguish between governors and boards of visitors, but I have not been able to do so and I think at the end of the day I must content myself by pointing to some of the differences that justify a different approach.

Although both the board of visitors and the governors are administering the same disciplinary code the adjudication process is necessarily very different. The board of visitors are entirely independent. In all probability they do not know the prisoner, or, if they do, not nearly as well as the governor. They are dealing with more serious offences than the governor and their powers of punishment are very much greater. More formality will attend their proceedings and they have a discretion to allow legal representation; whereas the speed with which a governor is required to deal with matters under the disciplinary code — see rule 48(4) — shows that legal representation before a governor cannot have been contemplated. The proceedings before a board of visitors is closely analogous to a hearing before a court, whereas the hearing before a governor is more analogous to coming before a commanding officer or headmaster. Judicial review goes to review the decision of an inferior court but not to review that of the commanding officer or headmaster.

If a governor was a law unto himself it would be a powerful reason for having judicial review available to curb any excess or abuse of his powers. But the governor is not a law unto himself, he is appointed by and responsible to the Secretary of State for the Home Department, and Parliament has placed a special responsibility upon the Secretary of State to supervise governors and other prison officers to ensure that they discharge their duties properly and to report annually to Parliament on the state of the prisons including all punishments inflicted therein: see Prison Act 1952, sections 4 and 5, which set out the duties of the prison commissioners now vested in the Secretary of State, and in particular section 4(2):

'The prison commissioners, by themselves or their officers, shall visit all prisons and examine the state of buildings, the conduct of officers, the treatment and conduct of prisoners and all other matters concerning the management of prisons and shall ensure that the provisions of this Act and of any rules made under this Act are duly complied with.'

In these circumstances the court should, in the first instance, be prepared to assume that the Secretary of State will discharge the duty placed upon him by Parliament to ensure that the prison governor is doing his job properly. If it is shown that the Minister is not discharging this duty and allowing a prison governor to disregard the prison rules then judicial review will go to correct that situation by requiring the Minister to perform his statutory duty. I regard this as the route by which the court in the present case could legitimately have been called upon to construe rule 47(7). If the prisoner had petitioned the Secretary of State and made clear that his complaint was that he had lost remission because the governor had wrongly construed the rule it would have been the duty of the Secretary of State to consider the construction of the rule. If the Secretary of State had then misconstrued the rule and thus rejected the petition it would then have been open to the prisoner to seek judicial review of the Secretary of State's decision on the ground that he had rejected his petition because he had misdirected himself in law.

Thus it seems to me there is a route open to a prisoner to seek redress from the court if he suffers injustice as a result of the misconstruction of the prison rules without having to resort to extending judicial review to the decisions of prison governors. I am therefore satisfied that no substantial injustice will be suffered by prisoners in refusing to extend judicial review to governors' decisions which is a factor that naturally weighs very heavily with me in deciding that judicial review should not be so extended.

I see very little, if any, real advantage to prisoners and grievous difficulties being created for governors by the undermining of their authority in the prisons they administer if we were now to extend judicial review to the disciplinary decisions of prison governors. I would follow the steps of Megaw LJ in the *St Germain* case [1979] QB 425, 448 and decline to do so. Accordingly, I would dismiss this appeal.

Questions:
1. What was the ratio of the case?

2. What was the legal basis for the finding?

3. Should the courts be free to ignore precedent and decide upon pragmatic grounds as Lord Justice Griffiths suggests?

In the following case, the House of Lords had to decide whether to overrule *ex parte King*. (In the meantime an inconsistent judgment had been given in the Northern Ireland Court of Appeal in *R* v *Governor of the Maze Prison, ex parte McKiernan* (1985) 6 NIJB 6). Having decided that (as in *ex parte King*) there were grounds for a successful judicial review, the Court had to address the policy arguments in *ex parte King*, in particular the argument that the decisions of prison governors should not be subject to judicial review.

Leech v *Deputy Governor of Parkhurst Prison* [1988] 1 AC 533, HL.

Lord Bridge of Harwich.
My Lords, these two appeals raise the important question whether the court has jurisdiction to entertain an application for judicial review of an adjudication by a prison governor on a charge against a prisoner of a disciplinary offence and an award of punishment for the offence under the Prison Rules 1964. The Court of Appeal in *R* v *Deputy Governor of Camphill Prison, ex parte King* [1985] QB 735 held that there was no such jurisdiction. But the Court of Appeal in Northern Ireland took the opposite view in accepting jurisdiction to review a governor's adjudication and award under the corresponding rules applicable in Northern Ireland: *R* v *Governor of The Maze Prison, ex parte McKiernan* (1985) 6 NIJB 6. This is the conflict which must be resolved . . .
    Mr Laws held out the prospect, as one which should make our judicial blood run cold, that opening the door to judicial review of governors' awards would make it impossible to resist an invasion by what he called 'the tentacles of the law' of many other departments of prison administration. My Lords, I decline to express an opinion on any of the illustrations advanced in support of this part of the argument. In a matter of jurisdiction it cannot be right to draw lines on a purely defensive basis and determine that the court has no jurisdiction over one matter which it ought properly to entertain for fear that acceptance of jurisdiction may set a precedent which will make it difficult to decline jurisdiction over other matters which it ought not to entertain. Historically the development of the law in accordance with coherent and consistent principles has all too often been impeded, in diverse areas of the law besides that of judicial review, by the court's fear that unless

an arbitrary boundary is drawn it will be inundated by a flood of unmeritorious claims. If there are other circumstances beyond those arising from a governor's disciplinary award where the jurisdiction of the court may be invoked to remedy some injustice alleged to have been suffered by a prisoner consequent upon an abuse of power by those who administer the prison system, I am content to leave those claims for decision as they arise with every confidence in the court's ability to protect itself from abuse by declining jurisdiction where no proper basis to establish jurisdiction is shown or by the exercise of discretion to refuse a discretionary remedy for claims within jurisdiction but without substance.

What must on the other hand be of great concern to your Lordships is the fear so strongly voiced by three judges of the eminence and experience of Lawton, Griffiths and Browne-Wilkinson LJJ that for the court to assume direct supervision in judicial review proceedings of governors' disciplinary awards would by itself undermine the governor's authority and seriously aggravate the already difficult task of maintaining order and discipline in prisons. I recognise that there are some situations where, as Griffiths LJ points out, the law's experience justifies it in preferring a pragmatic to a strictly logical solution of a particular problem. Whether that approach is permissible here depends, I think, on two balancing considerations. First, quite apart from any reliance on section 4(2) of the Act of 1952, has the prisoner, who complains of a legally invalid adjudication and award against him by the governor, an adequate remedy available by way of petition to the Secretary of State, followed by judicial review as may be necessary of the Secretary of State's decision on his petition? Secondly, to the extent that the remedy falls short of adequacy, can the court's fear of the effect of granting a direct judicial remedy afford a legitimate 'public policy' reason to deny jurisdiction?

One manifest inadequacy of the remedy by petition is the absence of any power in the Secretary of State to quash the adjudication. This may seem of minor significance. If the award has been remitted, it may perhaps be of little consequence that the adjudication of guilt has not been set aside. But when the prisoner's record shows merely that the punishment awarded for an offence has been remitted by the Secretary of State, those who have to take account of the record, as for example when the prisoner's eligibility for parole is under consideration, will not know, in a case such as that of Leech, that the proceedings leading to the award were wholly invalid and it is at least possible that the record may operate to his prejudice. This is a lacuna in the rules which can readily be cured by amendment and it is very desirable that it should be. If the Secretary of State had power to quash the adjudication as well as power to remit the award, it would be difficult to suppose that the court, as a matter of discretion, would be likely to grant judicial review to a prisoner who had not petitioned the Secretary of State, save in a case of urgency where the prisoner's release was imminent but would be delayed by loss of remission ordered by the disputed award.

In a case such as *King's* case where the ground of challenge to the governor's award was an alleged misconstruction of the prison rule under which the prisoner was charged, it is apparent that, subject to any question of urgency, the court can just as well adjudicate on the point at issue by judicial review of the Secretary of State's decision on the petition as by judicial review of the award itself. But such a case is likely to be exceptional. Most challenges are likely to relate to the conduct of the proceedings by the governor, as in the instant case of Prevot. In such a case I do not see how a petition to the Secretary of State can possibly provide an adequate remedy. Save perhaps in a case that is taken up by a member of Parliament, the matter will come before a civil servant in the Home Office who will consider on the one hand the prisoner's petition, on the other hand the relevant records and reports supplied by the governor. If those disclose an issue of fact, I hope it is not unduly cynical to suppose that in the majority of cases the civil servant is likely simply to accept the governor's account. But even if he wishes to resolve any issue of fact in a judicial way, he probably lacks the experience and certainly lacks the procedural machinery, including the power to require evidence on oath, enabling him to do so. If the court's jurisdiction is limited to considering an application for judicial review of the Secretary of State's decision on a prisoner's petition, the court will have to accept the Secretary of State's findings as a barrier to prevent the use of its own procedure and powers to ascertain the facts on which the validity of the governor's adjudication essentially depends. This cannot be an adequate substitute for judicial review of the award itself.

Can it then be right for the court to refuse jurisdiction to afford what seems prima facie to be both the appropriate and the necessary remedy on the ground of 'public policy'? My Lords, with every respect to the views expressed in *King's* case as to the consequences which the acceptance of jurisdiction will bring in its train, I have to point out that they are based on subjective judicial impression. In the nature of the case they can have no foundation in previous experience. No one can predict the consequences with any certainty. It may be a virtual certainty that a number of trouble makers will take every opportunity to exploit and abuse the jurisdiction. But that is only one side of the coin. On the other side it can hardly be doubted that governors and deputy governors dealing with offences against discipline may occasionally fall short of the standards of fairness which are called for in the performance of any judicial function. Nothing, I believe, is so likely to generate unrest among ordinary prisoners as a sense that they have been treated unfairly and have no effective means of redress. If a prisoner has a genuine grievance arising from disciplinary proceedings unfairly conducted, his right to petition a faceless authority in Whitehall for a remedy will not be of much comfort to him. Thus, I believe, it is at least possible that any damage to prison discipline that may result from frivolous and vexatious applications for judicial review may be substantially offset by the advantages which access to the court will provide for the proper ventilation of genuine grievances and perhaps also that the availability of the court's supervisory role may have the effect on the conduct of judicial proceedings by governors which it appears to have had in the case of boards of visitors of enhancing the standards of fairness observed. I acknowledge that the views which I express are no less speculative than those expressed in *King's* case. Time alone will show which is right. But I am firmly of the opinion that, if the social consequences of the availability of judicial review to supervise governors' disciplinary awards are so detrimental to the proper functioning of the prison system as *King's* case predicts, it lies in the province of the legislature not of the judiciary to exclude the court's jurisdiction.

In *R* v *Deputy Governor of Parkhurst Prison and others, Ex parte Hague*, [1991] 1 WRL 340 (HL), the House of Lords confirmed that 'the availability of judicial review as a means of questioning the legality of action purportedly taken in pursuance of the prison rules is a beneficial and necessary jurisdiction which cannot properly be circumscribed by considerations of public policy of expediency in relation to prison administration' (per Lord Bridge at 345). In a later case, a prisoner who was exploring whether to undertake civil litigation became concerned that his correspondence with his solicitor was being subjected to censorship under the Prison Rules 1964. He applied for judicial review and sought to quash to the Prison Governor's power under Rule 33(3) to censor a prisoner's correspondence, insofar as it included letters between a prisoner and his legal advisor concerning legal proceedings not yet begun. He argued that Rule 33(3) was beyond the scope (or *ultra vires*) of section 47(1) of the Prison Act 1952 which provides that:

The Secretary of State may make rules for the regulation and management of prisons, remand centres, detention centres and youth custody centres respectively, and for the classification, treatment, employment, discipline and control of persons required to be detained therein.

Again look for the two parts of the judgment, the first part dealing with the *ultra vires* question, and the second addressing the question of principle.

R v *Secretary of State for the Home Department, ex parte Leech (No. 2)* [1994] QB 198, CA.

Steyn LJ
The ultra vires question
It is important not to lose sight of the precise nature of the question to be answered. The question is simply one of vires: is rule 33(3) of the Rules of 1964 within the scope of the rule-making power which was conferred by section 47(1) of the Act of 1952? Nobody suggests that section 47(1) expressly authorises the making of a rule such as rule 33(3). The question is whether section 47 by necessary implication authorises the making of a rule of the width and scope of rule 33(3). The power is concisely and simply expressed in section 47(1) as the power to 'make rules for the regulation and management of prisons'. Given that the matter to be considered is whether these words by necessary implication authorised the making of rule 33(3), it is necessary to examine in the first place the scope of rule 33(3).

The extent of the discretion under rule 33(3)

The question is in what circumstances the discretion under rule 33(3) of the Rules of 1964 may be exercised in respect of letters passing between a solicitor and client. It is plain that rule 33(3) draws a distinction between (a) the power of prison authorities to read and examine letters and (b) the power to stop letters. Rule 33(3) creates an unrestricted power to read or examine 'every letter'. On the other hand, the power to stop a letter is qualified by the purpose for which it may be exercised 'on the ground than its contents are objectionable or that it is of inordinate length'. If the governor or an officer deputed by him forms the view on reasonable grounds that the contents are objectionable or that the letter is of inordinate length the discretion to stop the letter may be exercised. The meaning of the words 'inordinate length' is clear. But an issue arose as to the meaning of the word 'objectionable'.

Mr Fitzgerald helpfully referred us to the legislative history of rule 33(3). And it is clear that a provision for reading a prisoner's correspondence and stopping it, has existed since 1898: see rule 76 of the Prison Rules 1899 rule 52 of the Prison Rules 1933 and rule 75 of the Prison Rules 1949. The concept of objectionability was therefore first introduced at a time when the curtailment of prisoners' rights was far greater than it is today. In any event, the word objectionable is in its ordinary sense of wide import. Prima facie it means unacceptable. And it is important to bear in mind that rule 33(3) applies alike to a prisoner's ordinary correspondence and to a prisoner's correspondence with solicitors. Moreover, the word 'objectionable' must be read in context. It is difficult to avoid the conclusion that anything which in the view of the prison authorities constitutes a disciplinary offence under rule 47 of the Rules of 1964 could be regarded as objectionable. And when the Rules of 1964 were promulgated the making of false and malicious allegations against an officer, or the repeated making of groundless complaints, were disciplinary offences. When those two disciplinary offences were abolished such conduct did not necessarily cease to be objectionable within the meaning of rule 33(3).

Mr Jay submitted that both the power to read and examine letters and to stop letters are only intended to enable the prison authorities to take action, where there are no extant legal proceedings, in order 'to satisfy themselves that it is, in fact, bona fide legal correspondence'. This submission does not distinguish between the two powers. It cannot be squared with the generality of the language which creates an unrestricted right to read and examine letters. It cannot be squared with the language which creates a qualified but wide power to stop correspondence on the ground of objectionability or prolixity. In our view Mr Jay's submission on the interpretation of rule 33(3) is unsustainable.

The extent of civil rights of prisoners

It is now necessary to examine the impact of rule 33(3) on the civil rights of prisoners. This seems to us an important inquiry since, in relation to rule-making powers alleged to arise by necessary implication, it can fairly be said that the more fundamental the right interfered with, and the more drastic the interference, the more difficult becomes the implication. It is an axiom of our law that a convicted prisoner, in spite of his imprisonment, retains all civil rights which are not taken away expressly or by necessary implication: see *Raymond* v *Honey* [1983] 1 AC 1, 10 *per* Lord Wilberforce. The present case is concerned with civil rights in respect of correspondence. An ordinary citizen has a prima facie right which protects the confidentiality of letters sent by or to him. That right is not dependent on the existence of a right of property. It derives from the law of confidentiality . . . It is obvious, however, that a power to regulate prisons must include a power to make some rules about prisoners' correspondence. By necessary implication section 47(1) of the Act of 1952 confers a power of rule-making which may limit a prisoner's general civil rights in respect of the confidentiality of correspondence.

In ascending order of importance, in the context of this case, the next relevant civil right is based on the general duty of solicitors to keep confidential all communications between themselves and their clients. This is a rule founded on principles of equity, and binds third parties who knowingly receive the communication in breach of confidence. On the other hand, such rights and duties are not peculiar to the relationship of solicitor and client. They extend to the relationship of all professional men and their clients: see *Parry-Jones* v *Law Society* [1969] 1 Ch 1, 6–7. There is a presumption against statutory interference with vested common law rights. That must entail a presumption against a statute authorising interference with vested common law right by subordinate legislation. But we incline to the view that it is not unreasonable to interpret section 47(1) of the Act of 1952 as authorising by necessary implication some interference with this general right of confidentiality in accordance with the terms of rule 33(3) of the Rules of 1964.

Now we turn to a principle of greater importance. It is a principle of our law that every citizen has a right of unimpeded access to a court. In *Raymond* v *Honey* [1983] 1 AC 1, 13, Lord Wilberforce described it as a 'basic right'. Even in our unwritten constitution it must rank as a constitutional right. In *Raymond* v *Honey*, Lord Wilberforce said that there was nothing in the Prison Act 1952 that conferred power to 'interfere' with this right or to 'hinder' its exercise. Lord Wilberforce said that rules which did not comply with that principle would be ultra vires. Lord Elwyn-Jones and Lord Russell of Killowen agreed with Lord Wilberforce. It is true that Lord Wilberforce held that the rules, properly construed, were not ultra vires. But that does not affect the importance of his observations. Lord Bridge of Harwich held that the rules in question in that case were ultra vires. He agreed with Lord Wilberforce on the basic principle. But he went further than Lord Wilberforce and said that a citizen's right to unimpeded access could only be taken away by express enactment. Lord Lowry agreed with both Lord Wilberforce and Lord Bridge. It seems to us that Lord Wilberforce's observations rank as the ratio decidendi of the case, and we accept that such rights can as a matter of legal principle be taken away by necessary implication.

Equally clearly established is the important principle that a prisoner's unimpeded right of access to a solicitor for the purpose of receiving advice and assistance in connection with the possible institution of civil proceedings in the courts forms an inseparable part of the right of access to the courts themselves. The principle was laid down by the European Court of Human Rights in *Golder* v *United Kingdom*, [1975] 1 EHRR 524 . . .

It follows that section 47(1) of the Act of 1952 does not authorise the making of any rule which creates an impediment to the free flow of communications between a solicitor and a client about contemplated legal proceedings . . .

In our judgment section 47(1) must be interpreted as conferring by necessary implication a power to make rules to achieve the stated objectives. We are satisfied that this implied power is wide enough to comprehend rules permitting the examining and reading of correspondence passing between a prisoner and his solicitor in order to ascertain whether it is in truth bona fide correspondence between a prisoner and a solicitor and to stop letters which fail such scrutiny. But it is a rule in much wider terms that needs to be justified: in particular the difference in the powers governing actual and contemplated litigation must be justified.

Questions:
1. Do you agree with Lord Bridge in 'Leech 1' that any possible damage to prison discipline will be outweighed by the advantages of allowing access to the courts for prisoners who have genuine grievances?

2. Can the two *Leech* cases be reconciled with *King*?

3. Has the Constitutional right of access to a court been affected by the enactment of the Human Rights Act 1998?

Martin Loughlin has argued that these cases illustrate a shift from a notion of powers as a basis for decision making to a notion of rights as the basis of decision making:

M Loughlin, 'Rights Discourse and Public Law Thought in the United Kingdom' in G Anderson, *Rights and Democracy: Essays in UK-Canadian Constitution*, London, Blackstone Press, (1999), Chapter 9, pp. 209–10.

The significance of this shift from powers to rights may be highlighted in a number of fields which have been the subject of developments in judicial review. Consider, for example, the case of prisoners. Until the late 1970s, the courts refused to extend judicial review beyond the walls of the prison. Jurisdiction was vested in the Home Secretary and, in the words of Lord Denning MR: 'If the courts were to entertain actions by disgruntled prisoners, the governor's life would be made intolerable. The discipline of the prison would be undermined.' With the growth of judicial oversight since then, there has occurred not only an extension of jurisdiction but also the emergence of a different form of legal discourse. Further, the courts are not only embracing a more rationalistic language but also are proceeding to apply it from a different premiss; that is, rather than focusing on the sovereign power of

Parliament, the judiciary are undertaking review from the starting point of the individual as a bearer of rights. Rather than asking whether the prison authorities have exceeded their statutory powers, the judiciary, recognizing that they are 'the ultimate custodians of the liberties of the subject, whatever his status', commence from the premiss that 'a convicted prisoner . . . retains all those civil rights which are not taken away expressly or by necessary implication'.

The tensions which have been thrown up as a result of this change in the mode of judicial discourse may be illustrated by comparing the judgments of the Court of Appeal in *King* with those of the House of Lords in *Leech* on the issue of whether their supervisory jurisdiction extended to governors' disciplinary hearings. In the former, Griffiths LJ articulates the traditional approach in expressing the view that: 'the common law of England has not always developed upon strictly logical lines, and where logic leads down a path that is beset with practical difficulties the courts have not been frightened to turn aside and seek the pragmatic solution that will best serve the needs of society.' In the latter, Lord Bridge comes down clearly on the side of principle: 'Historically the development of the law in accordance with coherent and consistent principles has all too often been impeded . . . by the court's fear that unless an arbitrary boundary is drawn it will be inundated by a flood of unmeritorious claims.' If, then, the social consequences of judicial intervention turn out to be disastrous for the proper functioning of the prison system, Lord Bridge holds that it is for the legislature and not the judiciary to exclude the court's jurisdiction. Similar shifts may be seen in the differing approaches adopted by the Divisional Court and Court of Appeal in *Leech (No. 2)*. Here, while the lower court dismissed a challenge to the vires of Prison Rule 33(3) in so far as it purported to authorise governors to intercept communications between prisoners and their legal advisers, the Court of Appeal struck down the Rule, essentially by adopting a presumption against the statutory interference with fundamental common law rights.

What in effect is happening is that the courts are rapidly developing a jurisprudence of fundamental rights in public law.

Question:
1.   In a democracy, is it justifiable for judges to arrogate to themselves such wide powers? How does the decision in *Leech* square with Ronald Dworkin's theory of adjudication (see Chapter 7)? For further reading on these cases and prison law generally, see S Livingstone & T Owen, *Prison Law*, (2nd ed), *Oxford University Press*, (1999).

2.   Did the court in these cases overrule their previous decisions, or did they distinguish them?

3.   Do judges change the law? If so, what is the relationship between the role of the judiciary and Parliament?

THE PROBLEM OF BAD PRECEDENTS

Often a court will face a dilemma over how it is to deal with a line of precedent. In Chapter 7 at p. 237, we look at the House of Lords judgment in the case of

R v *R*. This case concerned whether rape of a wife by her husband from whom she had separated was unlawful. The common law starting point was considered to be a statement in the eighteenth century by Sir Matthew Hale, a Chief Justice of England that: 'The husband cannot be guilty of a rape committed by himself upon his lawful wife, for by their mutual matrimonial consent and contract the wife hath given herself up in this kind unto her husband, which she cannot retract.' It was considered that this marital rape exemption was preserved under Section 1(1) Sexual Offences (Amendment) Act 1976, and in particular its use of the word 'unlawful' which was said to mean outside marriage. This section provides:

a man commits rape if — (a) he has unlawful sexual intercourse with a woman who at the time of the intercourse does not consent to it; and (b) at the time he knows that she does not consent to the intercourse or he is reckless as to whether she consents to it . . .

Consider here Lord Lane's judgment in the Court of Appeal decision, where he is considering the different approaches which the Court might take to the prior cases and also the interpretation of the word 'unlawful', and the different results which that will lead to.

R v *R* [1991] 2 All ER 257 at 263–265 (CA)

Lord Lane
[The possible solutions] may be summarised as follows:
(1) *The literal solution*
The 1976 Act by defining rape as it did as including the word 'unlawful' made it clear that the husband's immunity is preserved, there being no other meaning for the word [unlawful] except 'outside the bounds of matrimony'. It is not legitimate to treat the word as surplusage when there is a proper meaning which can be ascribed to it.
(2) *The compromise solution*
The word 'unlawful' is to be construed in such a way as to leave intact the exceptions to the husband's immunity which have been engrafted onto Hale CJ's proposition from the decision in *R* v *Clarke* onwards and is also to be construed so as to allow further exceptions as the occasion may arise.
(3) *The radical solution*
Hale CJ's proposition is based on a fiction and moreover a fiction which is inconsistent with the proper relationship between husband and wife today . . . it is repugnant and illogical in that it permits a husband to be punished for treating his wife with violence in the course of rape but not for the rape itself which is an aggravated and vicious form of violence . . .
  The drawbacks are these. The first solution requires the word 'unlawful' to be given what is said to be its true effect. That would mean that the husband's immunity would remain impaired so long as the marriage subsisted. The effect would be to overrule [prior decisions] which have engrafted exceptions onto Hale CJ's proposition. It is hard to believe that Parliament intended that

result. If it was intended to preserve the exceptions which existed at the time the 1976 Act came into force, it would have been easy to say so.

The second or compromise solution adopts what is, so to speak, the open-ended interpretation of the 1976 Act and would permit further exceptions to be engrafted onto Hale CJ's proposition. In particular, an exception in circumstances such as those in the instant case where the wife has withdrawn from cohabitation so as to make it clear that she wishes to bring to an end matrimonial relationships. There would be formidable difficulties of definition and interpretation . . .

The third or radical solution is said to disregard statutory provisions of the 1976 Act and, even if it does not do that, it is said that it goes beyond the legitimate bounds of judge-made law and trespasses on the province of Parliament. In other words, the abolition of a rule of such long standing, despite its emasculation by later decisions, is a task for the legislature and not the courts.

Questions:
1. Which solution do you prefer and why? Was your reasoning primarily legal or moral? Does your answer lead you to a different position from what you feel should be the just or moral solution to the case?

2. You should now read for yourself the remainder of the Court of Appeal decision and that of the House of Lords. Which of the three approaches did the Courts take?

Having read some judgments for yourself, now consider the following:

N MacCormick, 'Why Cases have Rationes and what these are' L Goldstein (ed), *Precedent in Law*, Oxford, Oxford University Press (1987), pp. 157–158, 170.

The greatest difficulty in the way of a clear understanding of any doctrine of precedent and thus of any kind of case-law is the controversial quality of the *ratio decidendi*. It is a disputed question whether there is any such thing as *a* or *the ratio* in a given case; it is disputed whether or not there is a *ratio* to be found authoritatively within a given opinion, or whether the so-called *ratio* is simply some proposition of law which a later court or courts find it expedient to ascribe to an earlier decision as the ground of that decision which may then be used to help justify some later decision — perhaps even under the guise of its being that which necessitates the granting of the given later decision. An extreme version of this view would presumably be that the *ratio* of a case is whatever it is at any time authoritatively said to be authority for, and thus no one single proposition over time. Although the term *ratio* seems in ordinary legal usage to refer to some single proposition or principle of law, this apparent referentiality of the term is an illusion, and the category '*ratio*' is no more than one of what Julius Stone has called 'categories of illusory reference'. These are systematically misleading forms of expression which convey an illusion of reference and thus of legal stability and certainty while the legal reality is one of change.

What this indicates is that in addition to doctrines of precedent, that is, doctrines of positive law telling us what authority is to be ascribed to judicial precedents, we also have to have theories of precedent. For without some theoretical understanding of precedents and of such key concepts as that of *ratio decidendi* we cannot in fact implement any legal doctrine of precedent. As usual, the question is not whether to have or to do without a theory; it is only whether or not to have an articulate, well thought out and, preferably, correct theory or to rest content with an implicit, inarticulate, and quite probably incorrect one.

We can consider theories of precedent as tending from the more or less strict or formalistic to the more or less sceptical end of a spectrum. At the formalistic end are those which represent the *ratio* as relatively fixed and determinate or at least determinable; at the sceptical end are those which treat the term as having only illusory reference and thus as signifying whatever its current user wishes. The theory for which I shall argue in this paper is a relatively strict or formalistic one, for I see no great difficulty in showing why and how the sound and justifiable decisions of a legal dispute must proceed on the basis of a reasonably firm and determinate ruling as to the applicable law. Such a ruling is, in my view, properly to be understood as the *ratio* of the decision.

For avoidance of doubt, I ought to add that this formalistic view of the *ratio* by no means necessitates any sort of adherence to or advocacy of a strict or strong doctrine of binding precedent. For reasons which will also appear, it seems wise to me to treat precedents, and especially single precedents, as revisable rather than fixed and binding for all purposes. Case-law ought to be somewhat flexible and open-ended over time. So precedents are best treated as more or less highly persuasive rather than absolutely binding. But that is not to say that there no determinate propositions in respect of which they are well treated as persuasive, and can in appropriate situations be held binding. There are; and these are what (I submit) have been given the technical name of *rationes decidendi* . . .

A *ratio decidendi* is a ruling expressly or impliedly given by a judge which is sufficient to settle a point of law put in issue by the parties' arguments in a case, being a point on which a ruling was necessary to his justification (or one of his alternative justifications) of the decision above in the case.

Questions:
1.   MacCormick has suggested a definition of the term *ratio decidendi*. What do you understand by the following terms: *obiter dicta,* precedent, binding, persuasive, follow, distinguish, overrule, *stare decisis,* common law, discretion?

2.   How influential are non-binding comments by judges for the development of the common law?

3.   In the light of the cases you have read in this Chapter and your answers to the questions we have posed, what is the status of the rules of precedent and

statutory interpretation? If there are 'rules', can they be changed just by judges changing their minds?

4. Can you draft a concise account of precedent? Bear in mind that such a summary should not only explain what is most important in a judgment but also when that *has* to be followed and when it is persuasive. Students sometimes think the work is done once they have established a broad or narrow understanding of the *ratio decidendi.* But it may be easy to determine the ratio and much more difficult to decide whether to follow it or not.

In the next Chapter we will consider the legal skill of Statutory Interpretation, but remember as a line of cases develops around the meaning of a word or phrase in a statute, you will use the skills from this Chapter as well.

Chapter 3

Interpreting Statutes

Imagine that a Victorian statute declares 'No vehicles should be allowed in parks', that you are an appellate judge in the millenium, and that the following people are appealing against their convictions:

(a)   Ahmed who was pushing a pram in a park.
(b)   Bernadette who was skateboarding in a park.
(c)   Catherine who was flying a stunt plane over a park at a height of 25 metres.
(d)   Daniel who was driving a hovercraft over a park at a height of 2.5 centimetres.
(e)   Esther who rides a bicycle through a university's 'science park' which has sought to provide an alternative to vehicles through a network of 'travelators' (horizontal escalators or moving walkways).

APPROACHES TO STATUTORY INTERPRETATION

How would you decide? You will already be conscious of the need to look at the problems from alternative perspectives (what are the best arguments for the defence, the prosecution, the park-keepers, the public?) and to establish whether the facts are sufficient (does it matter whether there is a baby or shopping in the pram?) What is most important for this chapter is to consider how you set about interpreting words in the statute such as 'vehicles', 'in' and 'parks'.

In our experience, most students instinctively adopt one of two 'rules' of statutory interpretation, and can be easily encouraged into also using a third. One way in which to resolve the five cases is to determine the literal meaning of the key words. Students sometimes merely assert that they know the 'true' meaning. Others refer to dictionaries (but which one?) This approach is obviously called the literal or plain meaning doctrine.

Another line of thought is to reject the literal method either because it yields no clear result or one absurd result. Students might then look for an interpretation which offers a fair result. The 'golden rule' is not to interpret a statute in such a way as to lead to absurd consequences.

The first kind of student might criticise the second, however, by claiming that the latter is making up the law as she goes along. How would you respond to that critique? One answer is to say 'So what?' Another is to say that when Parliament passed the statute, they would not have wanted it to be interpreted so as to result in an absurdity.

The counter to that leads us on to a third possibility. If we are interested in Parliament's wishes, why not find out what they intended, what 'mischief' the statute was designed to frustrate or more positively what purposes it was meant to serve? Hence the 'mischief' or 'purposive' rule.

All three canons of statutory interpretation (literal, golden, purposive) are *themselves* susceptible to a variety of interpretations. There is considerable doubt as to the relationship between them (e.g. should you ever use the purposive rule if the literal rule gives a single clear answer, or only to resolve ambiguities?). There are many helpful hints on how to apply them (e.g. statutory presumptions). There is a vigorous debate on their respective advantages and disadvantages.

The *application* of any such rules is easier said than done. For example, here is the text of part of the US Constitution's 14th Amendment:

. . . no state shall deny any person the 'equal protection of the laws'.

Question:
Does that prohibit discrimination in favour of Blacks, a previously disadvantaged group?

Or again, here are some of the articles of the European Convention on Human Rights:

European Convention on Human Rights.

Article 3:
No one shall be subjected to torture or to inhuman or degrading treatment or punishment.

Article 6:
   (1)   In the determination of his civil rights and obligations or of any criminal charge against him, everyone is entitled to a fair and public hearing within a reasonable time by an independent and impartial tribunal established by law . . .
   (2)   Everyone charged with a criminal offence shall be presumed innocent until proved guilty according to law.
   (3)   Everyone charged with a criminal offence has the following minimum rights:

(a)   to be informed promptly, in a language which he understands and in detail, of the nature and cause of the accusation against him;

(b)   to have adequate time and facilities for the preparation of his defence;

(c)   to defend himself in person or through legal assistance of his own choosing or, if he has not sufficient means to pay for legal assistance, to be given it free when the interests of justice so require;

(d)   to examine or have examined witnesses against him and to obtain the attendance and examination of witnesses on his behalf under the same conditions as witnesses against him;

(e)   to have the free assistance of an interpreter if he cannot understand or speak the language used in court.

Article 8:

(1)   Everyone has the right to respect for his private and family life, his home and his correspondence.

(2)   There shall be no interference by a public authority with the exercise of this right except such as is in accordance with the law and is necessary in a democratic society in the interests of national security, public safety or the economic well-being of the country, for the prevention of disorder or crime, for the protection of health or morals, or for the protection of the rights and freedoms of others.

Article 9:

(1)   Everyone has the right to freedom of thought, conscience and religion: this right includes freedom to change his religion or belief, and freedom, either alone or in community with others and in public or private, to manifest his religion or belief, in worship, teaching, practice and observance.

(2)   Freedom to manifest one's religion or beliefs shall be subject only to such limitations as are necessary in a democratic society in the interests of public safety, for the protection of public order, health or morals, or for the protection of the rights and freedoms of others.

Article 10:

(1)   Everyone has the right to freedom of expression. This right shall include freedom to hold opinions and to receive and impart information and ideas without interference by public authority and regardless of frontiers. This Article shall not prevent States from requiring the licensing of broadcasting, television or cinema enterprises.

(2)   The exercise of these freedoms, since it carries with it duties and responsibilities, may be subject to such formalities, conditions, restrictions or penalties as are prescribed by law and are necessary in a democratic society in the interests of national security, territorial integrity or public safety, for the prevention of disorder or crime, for the protection of health or morals, for the protection of the reputation or the rights of others, for preventing the disclosure of information received in confidence, or for maintaining the authority and impartiality of the judiciary.

Article 12:
Men and women of marriageable age have the right to marry and to found a family, according to national laws governing the exercise of this right.

Article 14:
The enjoyment of the rights and freedoms set forth in this Convention shall be secured without discrimination on any ground such as sex, race, colour, language, religion, political or other opinion, national or social origin, association with a national minority, property, birth or other status.

Question:
1. Do you think that the ECHR allows (a) the compulsory sterilisation of mentally disabled people; (b) a law prohibiting the publication of books which blaspheme against the Christian religion; (c) a law prohibiting the marriage of transexuals?

Contrary to popular belief, legal drafting is sometimes deliberately vague or ambiguous.

The following is an extract from The Agreement reached on Good Friday 1998 by the British and Irish Governments and the political parties to the talks in the Northern Ireland Peace Process.

The 'Good Friday' Agreement, 1998

1. The participants endorse the commitment made by the British and Irish Governments that, in a new British-Irish Agreement replacing the Anglo-Irish Agreement, they will:
    . . .
    (ii) recognise that it is for the people of the island of Ireland alone, by agreement between the two parts respectively and without external impediment, to exercise their right of self-determination on the basis of consent, freely and concurrently given, North and South, to bring about a united Ireland, if that is their wish, accepting that this right must be achieved and exercised with and subject to the agreement and consent of a majority of the people of Northern Ireland . . .

Questions:
1. What if people in the South of Ireland wish to have a United Ireland and the people of Northern Ireland do not?

2. Is there one right of self-determination for people in the North and another for people in the South? Or is there one 'right of self-determination' for the 'people of the island of Ireland alone'?

3. Why do you think that The Agreement was worded in a way that suggests that self-determination is to be determined by the people of the 'island of Ireland' while in effect giving the North of Ireland a veto on any decision made by the South?

Compare Article 1(1) of both the United Nations International Covenants on Economic, Social and Cultural Rights (1966), and Civil and Political Rights (1996) which grants a right of self-determination:

All peoples have the right of self-determination. By virtue of that right they freely determine their political status and freely pursue their economic, social and cultural development.

Question:
1. Who are the 'peoples'? Are they the whole peoples of a territory? Are they a group within the territory? What is the territory in question? Does The Agreement conform with these international provisions? Are these provisions of law clear?

INTERPRETING RACE RELATIONS LEGISLATION

By now, we hope that you will appreciate some of the challenges which lie ahead in statutory interpretation. Let's now study another judgment from the most famous English judge of recent vintage, Lord Denning. Read his opinion, which is set out in full, noting the way he resolves the meaning of the statute.

Mandla v *Lee* [1982] 3 All ER 1108, CA.

How far can Sikhs in England insist on wearing their turbans? A turban is their distinctive headgear. They do not cut their hair but plait it under their turbans. Some of them feel so strongly about it that when they are motor cyclists, they do not wear crash helmets: and when they are barristers they do not wear wigs.

Sewa Singh Mandla, the first plaintiff, is Sikh and rightly proud of it. He is a solicitor of the Supreme Court, practising in Birmingham. In 1978 he applied to send his son Gurinder, the second plaintiff, to a private school in Birmingham called the Park Grove School. The boy was then aged 13. The school was very suitable for him. It had a high reputation. It took boys of all races. There were 305 boys altogether. Over 200 were English, but there were many others. Five were Sikhs, 34 Hindus, 16 Persians, 6 Negroes, 7 Chinese, and about 15 from European countries.

Mr Mandla took his son to see the headmaster. Both he and his son were wearing their turbans. The headmaster felt that it might give rise to difficulties if the boy wore his turban in school. He asked the father: 'Will you consent to his removing his turban and cutting his hair?' The father said: 'No. That is completely out of the question.' The headmaster said that he would think about it. Then on July 24, 1978, he wrote:

'Thank you for bringing your son to see me. As I promised, I have given much thought to the problem and I have reluctantly come to the conclusion that on balance it would be unwise to relax the school rules with regard to uniform at the moment. I do not see any way in which it would be possible to reconcile the two conflicting requirements. May I wish you well in your efforts to promote harmony and peace, and I hope you find a suitable school for your son without difficulty'.

Mr Mandla did find another school for his son where he is allowed to wear his turban. So all is now well with them. But Mr Mandla reported the headmaster to the Commission for Racial Equality. They took the matter up with the headmaster. On September 19, 1978, he wrote this letter:

'To make my position quite clear, the boy was not rejected because he was a Sikh since we do not make racial distinctions and we have several Sikhs in the school. It was the turban that was rejected, and I believe your Acts cover people, not clothes.'

The commission, however, did not let the matter rest. They pursued the headmaster relentlessly. They interviewed him. They demanded information from him. Eventually they decided to assist Mr Mandla in legal proceedings against him. With their assistance in money and advice Mr Mandla issued proceedings against the headmaster of the school in the Birmingham County Court. He claimed damage limited to £500 and a declaration that the defendants had committed an act of unlawful discrimination. The judge heard the case for five days in February and June 1980, with many witnesses and much arguments. The judge dismissed the claim.

The Commission for Racial Equality — in Mr Mandla's name — appeal to this court. The headmaster appeared before us in person. He has not the means to instruct counsel and solicitors. He put his case moderately and with restraint. He has himself done much research in the India Office Library and elsewhere. It must have taken him many hours and many days. Now we have to consider what it all comes to.

[Note that Lord Denning seems hostile to the CRE's role in this case. Note also that the headmaster picked up the legal skills of interpretation and advocacy.]

The Law
The case raises this point of great interest: what is a 'racial group' within the Race Relations Act 1976? If the Sikhs are a 'racial group', no one is allowed to discriminate against any of their members in the important fields of education and employment and so forth. No matter whether the discrimination is direct or indirect, it is unlawful. But if they are not a 'racial group' discrimination is perfectly lawful. So everything depends on whether they are a 'racial group' or not.

The statute in section 3(1) contains a definition of a 'racial group'. It means a 'group of persons defined by reference to colour, race, nationality or ethnic or national origins'. That definition is very carefully framed. Most interesting is that it does not include religion or politics or culture.

[Note that in Northern Ireland it is unlawful to discriminate on grounds of religion or political opinion. Should the law be harmonised?]

You can discriminate for or against Roman Catholics as much as you like without being in breach of the law. You can discriminate for or against Communists as much as you please, without being in breach of the law. You can discriminate for or against the 'hippies' as much as you like, without being in breach of the law. But you must not discriminate against a man because of his colour or of his race or of his nationality, or of 'his ethnic or national origins'.

It is not suggested that the Sikhs are a group defined by reference to colour or race or nationality. Nor was much stress laid on national origins. But it is said — most persuasively by Mr Irvine — that the Sikhs are a group of persons 'defined by reference to ethnic origins'. It is so important that I will consider each word of that phrase.

'Ethnic'

The word 'ethnic' is derived from the Greek word which meant simply 'heathen'.

[Note that Lord Denning first looks at etymology].

It was used by the 72 Palestinian Jews who translated the Old Testament from Hebrew into Greek (in the Septuagint). They used it to denote the non-Israelitish nations, that is, the Gentiles. When the word 'ethnic' was first used in England, it was used to denote peoples who were not Christian or Jewish. This was the meaning attached to it in the great *Oxford English Dictionary* itself in 1890.

But in 1934 in the *Concise Oxford Dictionary* it was given an entirely different meaning. It was given as: 'pertaining to race, ethnological'. And 'ethnological' was given as meaning: 'corresponding to a division of races'. That is the meaning which I — acquiring my vocabulary in 1934 —

[at the age of 22?]

have always myself attached to the word 'ethnic'.

[Always? can't the meaning change?]

It is, to my mind, the correct meaning.

[Correct? on whose authority?]

It means 'pertaining to race'.

But then in 1972 there was appended a second supplement of the *Oxford English Dictionary.*

[Why the emphasis on Oxford dictionaries?]

It gives a very much wider meaning than that which I am used to. It was relied upon by Mr Irvine:

'Also, pertaining to or having common racial, cultural, religious, or linguistic characteristics, especially designating a racial *or other group* within a larger system; hence (US colloquial), foreign, exotic'.

As an example of this new meaning, the second supplement refers to a book by Huxley & Haddon called 'We Europeans' (1935). It mentions 'the non-committal term *ethnic group*' and refers to the 'special type of reference to the Jews gives a clue to the meaning of ethnic'.

Why are 'the Jews' given as the best known example of 'ethnic grouping'? What is their special characteristic which distinguishes them from non-Jews? To my mind it is a racial characteristic. The *Shorter Oxford Dictionary* describes a Jew as 'a person of Hebrew race'. Some help too can be found in our law books, especially from *Clayton* v *Ramsden* [1942] Ch 1; [1943] AC 320 and *In re Tuck's Settlement Trusts* [1978] Ch 49. If a man desires that his daughter should marry 'a Jew' and cuts her out of his will if she should marry a man who is not 'a Jew', he will find that the court will hold the condition void for uncertainty. It may mean a man of the Jewish faith. Even if he was a convert from Christianity, he would be of the Jewish faith. Or it may mean a man of Jewish parentage, even though he may be a convert to Christianity. It may suffice if his grandfather was a Jew and his grandmother was not. The Jewish blood may have become very thin by intermarriage with Christians, but still many would call him 'a Jew'. All this leads me to think that, when it is said of the Jews that they are an 'ethnic group', it means that the group as a whole share a common characteristic which is a racial characteristic. It is that they are descended, however remotely from a Jewish ancestor. When we spoke of the 'Jewish regiments' which were formed and fought so well during the war, we had in mind those who were of Jewish descent or parentage. When Hitler and the Nazis so fiendishly exterminated 'the Jews', it was because of their racial characteristics and not because of their religion.

There is nothing in their culture or language to mark out Jews in England from others. The Jews in England share all of these characteristics equally with the rest of us. Apart from religion, the one characteristic which is different is a racial characteristic.

'Origins'

The statute uses the word 'ethnic' in the context of 'origins'. This carries the same thought. I turn once again to the *Shorter Oxford Dictionary*. Where the word 'origin' is used of a person it means 'descent, parentage'. I turn also to the speech of Lord Cross of Chelsea in *Ealing London Borough Council* v *Race Relations Board* [1972] AC 342, 365:

'To me it suggests a connection subsisting at the time of birth . . . The connection will normally arise because the parents or one of the parents of the individual in question are or is identified by descent'.

So the word 'origins' connotes a group which has a common racial characteristic.

'Ethnic Origins'

If I am right in thinking that the phrase 'ethnic origins' denotes a group with a common racial characteristic, the question arises — why is it used at all? The answer is given by Lord Cross of Chelsea in the *Ealing London Borough Council* case [1972] AC 342, 366:

'The reason why the words 'ethnic or national origins' were added to the words 'racial grounds' which alone appear in the long title was, I imagine, to prevent argument over the exact meaning of the word 'race'.

[Imagine? Why not find out?]

In other words, there might be much argument as to whether one group or other was of the same 'race' as another: but there was thought to be less as to whether it was a different 'ethnic group'.

'Racial Group'
This brings me back to the definition in the statute of a 'racial group'. It means 'a group of persons defined by reference to colour, race, nationality or ethnic or national origins'.

The word 'defined' shows that the group must be distinguished from another group by some definable characteristic. English, Scots or Welsh football teams are to be distinguished by their national origins. The Scottish clans are not distinguishable from one another either by their ethnic or national origins: only by their clannish or tribal differences. French Canadians are distinguished from other Canadians by their ethnic or national origins. Jews are not to be distinguished by their national origins. The wandering Jew has no nation. He is a wanderer over the face of the earth.

[What does this mean?]

The one definable characteristic of the Jews is a racial characteristic.

[But do not Israel's Jews, for example, share the racial characteristics — whatever that means — of other Semites including Arabs?]

I have no doubt that, in using the words 'ethnic origins', Parliament had in mind primarily the Jews. There must be no discrimination against the Jews in England. Anti-semitism must not be allowed. It has produced great evils elsewhere. It must not be allowed here.

[Is this the mischief which the Act was designed to prevent?]

But the words 'ethnic origins' have a wider significance than the Jews. The question before us today is whether they include the Sikhs.

The Sikhs
The word 'Sikh' is derived from the Sanskrit 'Shishya', which means 'disciple'. Sikhs are the disciples or followers of Guru Nanak, who was born on April 5, 1469. There are about 14 million Sikhs, most of whom live in the part of the Punjab which is in India. Before the partition of the province in 1947 half of them lived in that portion which is now Pakistan: but on the partition most of them moved across into India. There was tragic loss of life.

There is no difference in language which distinguishes the Sikhs from the other peoples in India. They speak Punjabi or Hindi or Urdu, or whatever the vernacular may be. There is no difference in blood which distinguishes them either.

[What does this mean?]

The people of India are largely the product of successive invasions that have swept into the country. They have intermingled to such an extent that it is impossible now to separate one strain from the other. The Sikhs do not recognise any distinction of race between them and the other peoples of India. They freely receive converts from Hinduism — or vice versa. Not only from outside, but even within the same family. The outstanding distinction between the Sikhs and the other peoples of India is in their religion Sikhism, and its accompanying culture.

This is so marked that Dr Ballard, who is a lecturer in race relations in the University of Leeds, thought it was an ethnic difference. But, if you study his evidence, it is plain that he was using the word 'ethnic' in a special sense of his own. For him it did not signify any racial characteristic at all. These are some illuminating passages from his evidence:

'Sikhs, most obviously, are not a race in biological terms. Their origins are extremely diverse, probably more diverse than us English . . . I think they are a classic example of an ethnic group because of their distinctive cultural traditions . . . We are busy coining lots of new words here. I think ethnicity is the proper word to coin . . .'

The evidence shows that the Sikhs as a community originate from the teaching of Guru Nanak. About the 15th century he founded the religious sect. There were a series of gurus who followed Nanak, but the tenth and last is most important. Early in the 19th century he instituted major social and cultural reforms and turnèd the Sikhs into a community. He laid down the rules by which the hair was not to be cut and it was to be covered by a turban. By adopting this uniform, Sikhs made their communal affiliation very clear, both to each other and to outsiders. But they remained at bottom a religious sect.

It is sometimes suggested that the Sikhs are physically a different people. But that is not so. In an important book on 'The People of Asia' (1977), p. 327, Professor Bowles of Syracuse University, New York, says:

'The differences [between Muslims, Sikhs and Hindus] are mainly cultural, not biological. Much has been written about the tallness . . . the excellent physique of the Sikhs, qualities often attributed to their well-balanced vegetarian diet. In part this may be true, but the Sikhs are matched in physique by several other Punjab populations — meat-eating as well as vegetarian, Muslims as well as Hindus. Some of the neighbouring Pathan tribesmen are even taller. The Sikh physique is probably due to the fact that many have entered professions that have given them an economic advantage over their compatriots, Indians or Pakistanis. A correlation between nutrition and physique holds throughout the entire subcontinent . . . but it may be more noticeable in Punjab, where there is such a variety of merchants and traders . . .'

On all this evidence, it is plain to me that the Sikhs, as a group cannot be distinguished from others in the Punjab by reference to any racial character-istic whatever. They are only to be distinguished by their religion and culture. That is not an ethnic difference at all.

Conclusion

I have dealt with the evidence at length: because of the differences on the point in the lower courts and tribunals. In our present case the evidence has been more fully canvassed than ever before. It has been most well and carefully considered by Judge Gosling here. I agree with his conclusion that Sikhs are not a racial group. They cannot be defined by reference to their ethnic or national origins. No doubt they are a distinct community, just as many other religious and cultural communities. But that is not good enough. It does not enable them to complain of discrimination against them.

You must remember that it is perfectly lawful to discriminate against groups of people to whom you object — so long as they are not a racial group. You can discriminate against the Moonies or the Skinheads or any other group which you dislike or to which you take objection. No matter whether your objection to them is reasonable or unreasonable, you can discriminate against them — without being in breach of the law.

No doubt the Sikhs are very different from some of those groups. They are a fine community upholding the highest standards, but they are not a 'racial group'. So it is not unlawful to discriminate against them. Even though the discrimination may be unfair or unreasonable, there is nothing unlawful in it.

In our present case the headmaster did not discriminate against the Sikhs at all. He has five Sikh boys in his school already. All he has done is to say that, when the boy attends school, he must wear the school uniform and not wear a turban. They make no objection. Mr Mandla is, I expect, strictly orthodox. He feels so strongly that he insists on his son wearing his turban at all times. But that feeling does not mean that the headmaster was at fault in any way. *He was not unfair or unreasonable.* It is for him to run his school in the way he feels best. He was not guilty of any discrimination against the Sikhs, direct or indirect.

I cannot pass from this case without expressing some regret that the Commission for Racial Equality thought it right to take up this case against the headmaster. It must be very difficult for educational establishments in this country to keep a proper balance between the various pupils who seek entry. The statutes relating to race discrimination and sex discrimination are difficult enough to understand and apply anyway. They should not be used so as to interfere with the discretion of schools and colleges in the proper management of their affairs.

In the circumstances I need say nothing as to the contentions about the word 'can' or 'justifiable' in the statute. They do not arise.

I would dismiss the appeal.

Questions:
1. The other two members of the Court of Appeal agreed with Lord Denning that Sikhs did not constitute an ethnic group for the purposes of this legislation. For our purposes, however, what is most important is the way in which they set about interpreting the statute. In the following passage, does Oliver LJ adopt the same approach as Lord Denning?

. . . The discussion before us, therefore, has centred — and, in my judgment, rightly centred — upon the word 'ethnic'. A glance at the dictionary is sufficient to show both that this is a term of very uncertain meaning and that the sense in which the word is used has altered considerably with the passage of time so that it is now long removed from that borne by the Greek from which it is derived.

[So there, Lord Denning?]

For my part, I doubt whether one can obtain anything but the most general assistance from dictionaries.

[Do you agree?]

We have to construe an Act of Parliament and it is permissible and indeed essential to construe the words used in the light of what the legislature was obviously seeking to achieve.

[In which case, why not look at the record of Parliamentary debates? See further pp. 92–102 below.]

The one thing that must surely be clear is that Parliament cannot have intended

[Can a disparate group intend anything?]

to create (as it did in this Act) a criminal offence which involves an extensive etymological research before any member of the public can determine whether he is offending or not.

[Is this sentence self-contradictory?]

The word must, I infer, have been used in its popularly accepted meaning; but, having said that, one is faced with the difficulty of discovering what the popularly accepted meaning is. Mr Irvine submits that it imports no more than a state of being united by common features such as language, race, culture, religion, literature and habit of life. No one aspect is necessarily essential — one has to look at the matter in the round and ask whether the combination of features which one finds constitutes an identifiable 'community' in the loose sense of the word.

[Did Parliament 'intend' a 'loose' interpretation?]

If it does then a member of that community is a member of an ethnic group. Here, he points out, the Sikhs display a large number of common features. They have a common religion; they have common customs, such as the wearing of turban and the comb; they have a common language, for most of them hail from the Punjab and speak Punjabi; a substantial proportion is literate in a script (Gurmukhi), whilst not peculiar to the Sikhs, is read by many more Sikhs than Hindus; and there is, so the evidence shows, a Sikh literature.

There appear to me to be a number of difficulties about this. In the first place, it is evident that their customs, whilst widespread, are by no means common to all Sikhs. A substantial proportion do not assume the turban — and, indeed, the evidence shows that there are two sects within Sikhism with differing customs and, to some extent, differing philosophies. The proportion of all Sikhs literate in the Gurmukhi script is small, and it is read by a much smaller number of Hindus, both men and women, who nevertheless form a sizeable minority of Gurmukhi readers. Moreover, Mr Irvine's test of an ethnic group would, it seems to me, be equally applicable to any number of organisations, religious, political or social. Furthermore, one must not lose sight of the terms of the definition. What the statute directs us to look for is not membership of an ethnic group but membership of a group which (that is the group, not the individual) is defined by reference to its ethnic 'origins'. Mr Irvine may be right in saying that 'ethnic' as a word on its own, embraces more than a merely racial concept — why otherwise, he asks, does the legislature use the word as an alternative to 'racial' or 'national'? — and I would accept that it embraces, perhaps, notions of cultural or linguistic community. Nevertheless, in its popular meaning, it does, in my judgment, involve essentially a racial concept — the concept of something with which the members of the group are born; some fixed or inherited characteristic. I do not believe that the man in the street would apply the word 'ethnic' to a characteristic which the propositus could assume or reject as a matter of choice.

[Do people in streets use the term 'ethnic' at all? If so, how does Oliver LJ know their usage? Why not take evidence on popular usage?]

No one, for instance, in ordinary speech, would describe a member of the Church of England or the Conservative Party as a member of an ethnic group.

2.   What about Kerr LJ? Does he agree with Lord Denning?

As the title of the Act indicates, its object was to outlaw discrimination against anyone on the ground of their race. However 'race' is an elusive term. Some scientists and social anthropologists deny that it has any meaning. But it clearly has a meaning for Parliament and ordinary people.

[So, is the term literally meaningless or full of different meanings?]

. . .

Parliament must accept responsibility for the difficulties which this word [ethnic] has created for the courts.

[Was it a smart move on the part of Parliament to let judges resolve the issue and be lumbered with criticism?]

3.   Should the judges be considering *Parliament's* view? If so, how?

4.   Would you expect the House of Lords to have agreed with the Court of Appeal? Explain your hunch (which is articulating your implicit theory of adjudication).

5.   The Law Lords unanimously took a different line from the Court of Appeal, defining ethnic groups in such a way as to include Sikhs. Can you guess how

they defined ethnic (bearing in mind not only their wish to include Sikhs but also to exclude the groups Lord Denning mentioned, such as Moonies and skinheads)? Once you have tried this exercise for yourself, you should track down the House of Lords judgment in the law library. (How?)

6. How convincing do you find Lord Fraser's 'solution' to the question of what an ethnic group is:

Lord Fraser in *Mandla* v *Lee* (1983), HL.

> For a group to constitute an ethnic group in the sense of the 1976 Act, it must, in my opinion, regard itself and be regarded by others, as a distinct community by virtue of certain characteristics. Some of these characteristics are essential; others are not essential but one or more of them will commonly be found and will help to distinguish the group from the surrounding community. The conditions which appear to me to be essential are these: (a) a long shared history, which it keeps alive; (b) a cultural tradition of its own, including family and social customs and manners, often but not necessarily associated with religious observance. In addition to those two essential characteristics the following characteristics are, in my opinion, relevant; (c) either a common geographical origin, or descent from a small number of common ancestors; (d) a common language, not necessarily peculiar to the group; (e) a common literature peculiar to the group; (f) a common religion different from that of neighbouring groups or from the general community surrounding it; (g) being a minority or being an oppressed or a dominant group within a larger community, for example, a conquered people (say, the inhabitants of England shortly after the Norman conquest) and their conquerors might both be ethnic groups.

To what extent do you think that Lord Fraser's definition was binding on the courts/tribunal which had to decide the following cases?

Commission for Racial Equality v *Dutton* [1989] 2 WLR 17, CA.

Nicholls LJ
   One weekend, after the defendant had been at the Cat and Mutton for about 18 months, some 15 or so caravans parked opposite the public house on London Fields, illegally, about 150 yards away. On Sunday morning some of these 'travellers' came into the Cat and Mutton. The defendant refused to serve one of them on the ground he was from the site. There was an incident. The defendant then put up handwritten signs in the windows of the door of the Cat and Mutton: 'Sorry, no travellers'. Since then he has had no more trouble with 'travellers'.
   In June 1985 a local resident, who does not use the Cat and Mutton, brought these signs to the attention of the Commission for Racial Equality. The commission took the view that the signs discriminated against gipsies. After correspondence this action was brought by the commission, in the

exercise of its functions under section 63. The commission seeks a declaration that by displaying the signs the defendant has contravened section 29 of the Race Relations Act 1976 and an injunction restraining him from continuing to display the signs . . .

Taking the judge's assessment of the witnesses fully into account, and with all respect to the judge, I am unable to agree with his conclusion on what have been called the *Mandla* conditions when applied, not to the larger, amorphous group of 'travellers' or 'gipsies', colloquially so-called, but to 'gipsies' in the primary, narrower sense of that word. On the evidence it is clear that such gipsies are a minority, with a long-shared history and a common geographical origin. They are a people who originated in northern India. They migrated thence to Europe through Persia in medieval times. They have certain, albeit limited, customs of their own, regarding cooking and the manner of washing. They have a distinctive, traditional style of dressing, with heavy jewellery worn by the women, although this dress is not worn all the time. They also furnish their caravans in a distinctive manner. They have a language or dialect, known as 'pogadi chib', spoken by English gipsies (Romany chals) and Welsh gipsies (Kale) which consists of up to one-fifth of Romany words in place of English words. They do not have a common religion, nor a peculiar, common literature of their own, but they have a repertoire of folktales and music passed on from one generation to the next. No doubt, after all the centuries which have passed since the first gipsies left the Punjab, gipsies are no longer derived from what, in biological terms, is a common racial stock, but that of itself does not prevent them from being a racial group as widely defined in the Act.

I come now to the part of the case which has caused me most difficulty. Gipsies prefer to be called 'travellers' as they think that term is less derogatory. This might suggest a wish to lose their separate, distinctive identity so far as the general public is concerned. Half or more of them now live in houses, like most other people. Have gipsies now lost their separate, group identity, so that they are no longer a community recognisable by ethnic origins within the meaning of the Act? The judge held that they had. This is a finding of fact.

Nevertheless, with respect to the judge, I do not think that there was before him any evidence justifying his conclusion that gipsies have been absorbed into a larger group, if by that he meant that substantially all gipsies have been so absorbed. The fact that some have been so absorbed and are indistinguishable from any ordinary member of the public, is not sufficient in itself to establish loss of what Richardson J, in *King-Ansell* v *Police* [1979] 2 NZLR 531, 543, referred to as 'an historically determined social identity in [the group's] own eyes and in the eyes of those outside the group'. There was some evidence to the contrary from Mr Mercer, on whose testimony the judge expressed no adverse comment. He gave evidence that 'we know who are members of our community' and that 'we know we are different'. In my view the evidence was sufficient to establish that, despite their long presence in England, gipsies have not merged wholly in the population, as have the Saxons and the Danes, and altogether lost their separate identity. They, or many of them, have retained a separateness, a self-awareness, of still being gipsies.

I feel less constrained than otherwise I would to depart from the judge's conclusions on this point because of the importance attached by him to the meaning borne by the word 'gipsy' in the Highways Act 1959 and the Caravan Sites Act 1968. He said:

'Although the Highways Act 1959 and the Caravan Sites Act 1968 are statutory examples of the use of the word 'gipsy' the meaning given to the word in those Acts does have great weight in my mind. If you find a word defined in a definition section of one Act of Parliament and defined by the Divisional Court on another use of the same word in another statute it would be difficult to say: well when you are looking at the Race Relations Act 1976 you must have a wholly and totally different meaning attached to it. I consider, agreeing as I do with the Divisional Court in *Mills* v *Cooper* [1967] 2 QB 459, that it would be impossible to discover if any person or any body of persons were members of the Romany race or true gipsies. It is not difficult to discover whether they are leading a nomadic life, whether they are travelling from place to place with no fixed abode and no fixed employment. But having ascertained these matters one might justifiably come to the conclusion that they being travellers were not clearly gipsies. As I say I do not think one can be a gipsy or a non-gipsy in one statute and not in another.'

In my view those two statutes do not materially assist in the present case, and the judge misdirected himself on this point. The present case is quite different from *Mills* v *Cooper*. In the present case the issue is not which of two or more meanings of the word 'gipsy' is to be preferred in the context of a particular statute or document. The question is whether there is an identifiable group of persons, traditionally called 'gipsies', who are defined by reference to ethnic origins. That is essentially a question of fact, to be determined on the evidence, applying the approach set out in *Mandla (Sewa Singh)* v *Dowell Lee* [1983] 2 AC 548. On that question the definition of 'gipsy' used in the Caravan Sites Act 1968, and the meaning of the word 'gipsy' in the Highways Act 1959 as interpreted in *Mills* v *Cooper*, are of little assistance, if any. Furthermore the difficulty, mentioned in *Mills* v *Cooper*, at pp. 467, 468, of determining today whether a person is of 'the Romany race' or is of 'pure Romany descent' or 'Romany origin', seems to have led the judge into thinking that that difficulty constituted an obstacle to the commission's success in the present case. But that is not so. The material provision in the Act of 1976 is concerned with ethnic origins, and 'ethnic' is not used in that Act in a strictly biological or racial sense. That was decided in *Mandla (Sewa Singh)* v *Dowell Lee* [1983] 2 AC 548.

In my view, accepting the judge's doubts about the evidence of Dr Kenrick and Dr Acton, the evidence was still sufficient to establish that gipsies are an identifiable group of persons defined by reference to ethnic origins within the meaning of the Act.

In Northern Ireland there was no race discrimination legislation in place until 1996. Campaigners, noting that it had taken the test case of *Dutton* to establish that travellers were protected under British race legislation, lobbied for travellers to be specifically mentioned in any comparable legislation covering Northern Ireland. This was seen as important given the existence of an ethnically indigenous group of Irish Travellers who face discrimination within Northern Ireland. Section 5 of the Race Relations (NI) Order 1997 included the following:

Meaning of 'Racial grounds' 'racial group' etc.

5.—(2)   In this Order 'racial grounds'—

(a)   includes the grounds of belonging to the Irish Traveller community, that is to say the community of people commonly so called who are identified (both by themselves and by others) as people with a shared history, culture and traditions including, historically, a nomadic way of life on the island of Ireland; and

(b)   does not include the grounds of religious belief or political opinion.

(3)   In this Order 'racial group'—

(a)   includes the Irish Traveller community;

(b)   does not include a group of persons defined by reference to religious belief or political opinion.

Crown Suppliers (Property Services Agency) v *Dawkins* [1991] ICR 583, EAT.

Tucker J

This is an appeal from a decision of the industrial tribunal held at London (South) on 16 and 17 January 1989, given on 28 March 1989. It was a majority decision that the applicant's claim of racial discrimination was made out. The grounds of appeal are that the tribunal was wrong in law to have held that Rastafarians are an ethnic group.

. . .

Applying [Lord Fraser's] tests to Rastafarians, we ask whether they possess any of the characteristics of a race? We very much doubt whether the majority of Rastafarians can claim that they are of group descent, though some of them may be. Their geographical origin is Jamaica. We doubt whether they can be said to have a group history. Lord Templeman held that the Sikhs qualified as a group defined by ethnic origins because they constitute a separate and distinct community derived from racial characteristics. But in our judgment, Rastafarians cannot be so described. There is in our view insufficient to distinguish them from the rest of the Afro-Caribbean community so as to render them a separate group defined by reference to ethnic origins. They are a religious sect and no more. In any event returning to Lord Fraser's test, we are unable to agree with the majority of the industrial tribunal that Rastafarians have a long shared history. It cannot reasonably be said that a movement which goes back for only 60 years, i.e. within the living memory of many people, can claim to be long in existence. Its history, in the judgment of the majority, is insufficiently sustained. The fact that the movement has maintained itself and still exists is insufficient. We have no hesitation in disagreeing with the conclusion of the majority of the industrial tribunal on this point, because first we do not regard it as a finding of fact, and secondly, even if it were we would regard it as a finding which no reasonable tribunal could make, and therefore perverse.

So far as Lord Fraser's second essential test is concerned, that of a cultural tradition of its own, our view is that Rastafarians are a group with very little structure, no apparent organisation and having customs and practices which have evolved in a somewhat haphazard way. Nevertheless, notwithstanding these reservations and placing them in the context of a formerly enslaved people striving for an identity, there may be a sufficient cultural tradition to satisfy the test, and we are not prepared to disagree with the finding of the tribunal on this point.

These are the views of the majority of the members of the appeal tribunal. One member dissents from them. On the basis of a book '"One Love" Rastafari: History, Doctrine and Livity' by Jah Bones (not referred to in argument before us) he is of the view that Rastafarians have a sufficiently long shared history to fulfil the test. In addition he would hold that they are more than a religious sect. However, by a majority, we allow the appeal for the reasons which we have expressed.

Appeal allowed.

Questions:
1.   Do you agree with the outcomes in these cases? How far were the decisions determined by the case of *Mandla* v *Lee*? Can the distinctions made between Sikhs, gipsies and Rastafarians really stand up to scrutiny?

2.   How consistent with these cases was the decision in *Nyazi* v *Rymans* Ltd (EAT 10 May 1988, unreported) which upheld an industrial tribunal's decision that several characteristics of ethnicity identified by Lord Fraser in *Mandla* were missing in the case of Muslims; because, for example, 'Muslims include people of many nations and colours, who speak many languages and whose only common denominator is religion and religious culture'? See discussion in Chapter 10 at pp. 356–60.

3.   Would a Scottish person count as a member of a 'distinctive ethnic group' under the Race Relations Act? In two cases in Industrial Tribunals it has been found that an Irish person in Britain could be so regarded: *Bryans* v *Northumberland College and others* (Case No. 36674/94 unreported) and *McAuley* v *Auto Alloys* (Case No. 62824/93 unreported). A case of alleged discrimination against a Scottish person is at present underway.

The following extract from the *Daily Mail* discusses the *McAuley* case:

Who's Taking the Mickey?, Anthony Doran and John Woodcock *Daily Mail*, 8 June 1994, p. 1

A storm erupted last night over a £6000 compensation award to an Irishman tormented by jokes at work. MPs denounced it as 'political correctness gone mad'. They said it could open the floodgates to claims from every conceivable minority, costing employers millions. Machinist Trevor McAuley, 36, told an industrial tribunal that the daily abuse ruined his work and affected his family life. He did not mind Irish jokes but drew the line at being called a 'typical thick Paddy' . . . Tory MP Sir Paul Beresford a New Zealander of Irish origin said the CRE had a serious job to do but was 'running a high risk of discrediting itself'.

'This is crazy. Where will it stop?' he asked. 'Will it cover the Scots when they're south of the border and the English when they're in Scotland?'

[Mr McAuley's boss, Dan Taylor said:]

'We're reaching the stage where no one dares say anything about anyone else for fear of upsetting some pressure group or vested interest. What about Yorkshiremen having a laugh at the expense of Lancastrians and vice-versa? People poke fund at Brummies, Cockneys and Scots, almost any geographical group you care to name. There are jokes about Poles and virtually every other race, and Jewish people thrive on poking fun at themselves. When does a joke become a racial issue. . .'

But CRE chairman Herman Ouseley said:

'We know from regular complaints that Irish people suffer this abuse day after day. We hope they will be able to use this result to secure a change in attitude on the part of their employers. It is intolerable that anyone should have to suffer this kind of treatment.'

Dave Murphy, of the Action Group for Irish Youth, said:

'This is a significant breakthrough for the Irish community in Britain. It illustrates how constant derogatory remarks can affect a person's self-esteem, confidence and health and even lead to an Irish person losing their job.'

Question:
1. Would 'Yorkshiremen, Lancastrians, Brummies, and Cockneys' be covered by the legislation?

The first decision given under the Race Relations (NI) Order 1997 was in favour of an employee of English origin against his employer for not affording him sufficient protection from racial harassment by his colleagues on the grounds of his national origin. In response, the Commission for Racial Equality for Northern Ireland commented that 'the case showed that racism is not just about skin colour and that racism, contrary to popular belief, exists throughout Northern Ireland' (Press Release: Tuesday 14 April, 1998). *Robins* v *Norfil Ltd*, 14 April 1998.

AIDS TO INTERPRETATION

The race discrimination cases show that what begins as an apparently simple task of interpreting a statute soon requires the skills of handling precedent which were outlined in the previous chapter. By the time of the gypsy or traveller cases, lawyers are interpreting both the statute and the growing line of precedents. One of the issues which runs through the cases is what legislators 'intended'. However, this raises the problem of how we decide what Parliament intended. Is it to be judged solely from the words they enacted, or should judges look at the debates which led to that enactment?

In the case of *Pepper* v *Hart* [1992] 3 WLR 1049, HL, the House of Lords, overruling earlier judgments, decided that it was permissible in certain circumstances to look at Hansard, the verbatim record of proceedings in Parliament, to determine how to interpret a statute.

Pepper v *Hart* [1992] 3 WLR 1049, HL.

Lord Browne-Wilkinson
1. *Should the rule prohibiting references to Parliamentary material be relaxed?*
Under present law, there is a general rule that reference to Parliamentary material as an aid to statutory construction is not permissible ('the exclusionary rule'): *Davis* v *Johnson* [1979] AC 264 and *Hadmor Productions Ltd* v *Hamilton* [1983] 1 AC 191. This rule did not always apply but was judge made. Thus, in *Ash* v *Abdy* (1678) 3 Swans. 664 Lord Nottingham took judicial notice of his own experience when introducing the Bill in the House of Lords. The exclusionary rule was probably first stated by Willes J in *Millar* v *Taylor* (1769) 4 Burr. 2303, 2332. However, the case of *In re Mew and Thorne* (1862) 31 LJ Bank. 87 shows that even in the middle of the last century the rule was not absolute: in that case Lord Westbury LC in construing an Act had regard to its Parliamentary history and drew an inference as to Parliament's intention in passing the legislation from the making of an amendment striking out certain words.

The exclusionary rule was later extended so as to prohibit the court from looking even at reports made by commissioners on which legislation was based: *Salkeld* v *Johnson* (1848) 2 Exch. 256, 273. This rule has now been relaxed so as to permit reports of commissioners, including law commissioners, and white papers to be looked at for the purpose solely of ascertaining the mischief which the statute is intended to cure but not for the purpose of discovering the meaning of the words used by Parliament to effect such cure: *Eastman Photographic Materials Co. Ltd* v *Comptroller-General of Patents, Designs and Trademarks* [1898] AC 571 and *Assam Railways and Trading Co. Ltd* v *Commissioners of Inland Revenue* [1935] AC 445, 457–458. Indeed, in *Reg.* v *Secretary of State for Transport, Ex parte Factortame Ltd* [1990] 2 AC 85 your Lordships' House went further than this and had regard to a Law Commission report not only for the purpose of ascertaining the mischief but also for the purpose of drawing an inference as to Parliamentary intention from the fact that Parliament had not expressly implemented one of the Law Commission's recommendations.
. . .

My Lords, I have come to the conclusion that, as a matter of law, there are sound reasons for making a limited modification to the existing rule (subject to strict safeguards) unless there are constitutional or practical reasons which outweigh them. In my judgment, subject to the questions of the privileges of the House of Commons, reference to Parliamentary material should be permitted as an aid to the construction of legislation which is ambiguous or obscure or the literal meaning of which leads to an absurdity. Even in such cases references in court to Parliamentary material should only be permitted where such material clearly discloses the mischief aimed at or the legislative intention lying behind the ambiguous or obscure words. In the case of statements made in Parliament, as at present advised I cannot foresee that any statement other than the statement of the minister or other promoter of the Bill is likely to meet these criteria.

I accept Mr. Lester's submissions, but my main reason for reaching this conclusion is based on principle. Statute law consists of the words that Parliament has enacted. It is for the courts to construe those words and it is the court's duty in so doing to give effect to the intention of Parliament in using those words. It is an inescapable fact that, despite all the care taken in passing legislation some statutory provisions when applied to the circumstances under consideration in any specific case are found to be ambiguous. One of the reasons for such ambiguity is that the members of the legislature in enacting the statutory provision may have been told what result those words are intended to achieve. Faced with a given set of words which are capable of conveying that meaning it is not surprising if the words are accepted as having that meaning. Parliament never intends to enact an ambiguity. Contrast with that the position of the courts. The courts are faced simply with a set of words which are in fact capable of bearing two meanings. The courts are ignorant of the underlying Parliamentary purpose. Unless something in other parts of the legislation discloses such purpose, the courts are forced to adopt one of the two possible meanings using highly technical rules of construction. In many, I suspect most, cases references to Parliamentary materials will not throw any light on the matter. But in a few cases it may emerge that the very question was considered by Parliament in passing the legislation. Why in such a case should the courts blind themselves to a clear indication of what Parliament intended in using those words? The court cannot attach a meaning to words which they cannot bear, but if the words are capable of bearing more than one meaning why should not Parliament's true intention be enforced rather than thwarted?

The *Pepper* v *Hart* rule has now been applied in many cases. In the case of *McKay* v *NIPSA* (below), for example, the Fair Employment Tribunal, and then the Court of Appeal in Northern Ireland, had to decide the scope of the term 'political belief or opinion' in the Fair Employment Act 1976 (as amended). In the course of doing this they considered whether the rule in *Pepper* v *Hart* enabled them to look at the Parliamentary record, and then whether that helped them to interpret the phrase in question. Fair employment discrimination provisions were enacted against a background of civil rights lobbying which focused on discrimination against the Catholic/Nationalist community in Northern Ireland. The case illustrates potential advantages and disadvantages of the *Pepper* v *Hart* ruling.

In this case Brendan McKay alleged that he had been the victim of discrimination on the basis of his political opinions when he was not appointed to a job because he was a member of a trade union — 'NIPSA Broad Left' — which espoused left wing politics, and was opposed to what the 'broad left' regarded as the right wing approach and tendencies of the leadership of NIPSA. The Fair Employment Tribunal found that the term 'political opinion' was obscure, and having considered the legislative history, decided that the term did not cover McKay's opinions, as it was only intended to cover opinions related to religion and 'Protestant'/'Catholic' politics in Northern Ireland. Now read the following extract from the Northern Ireland Court of Appeal:

Brendan McKay v *Northern Ireland Public Service Alliance* ([1994] NILR 103, at p. 111), NICA Hutton, LCJ.

In *Pepper* v *Hart* [1993] 1 All ER 42 at 69d Lord Browne-Wilkinson (with whose judgment the majority of the House of Lords agreed) stated:

'I therefore reach the conclusion, subject to any question of parliamentary privilege, that the exclusionary rule should be relaxed so as to permit reference to parliamentary materials where: (a) legislation is ambiguous or obscure, or leads to an absurdity; (b) the material relied on consists of one or more statements by a minister or other promoter of the Bill together if necessary with such other parliamentary material as is necessary to understand such statements and their effect; (c) the statements relied on are clear. Further than this, I would not at present go.'

Therefore, in considering whether the tribunal was entitled to refer to the debate in *Hansard* as an aid to the construction of the term 'political opinion', the first question to be considered is whether the legislation is ambiguous or obscure, or leads to an absurdity. It is only if this question is answered in the affirmative that the court or the tribunal is entitled to consider what was said by the Minister promoting the Bill.

In my opinion the term 'political opinion' is not ambiguous or obscure, nor do I think that the ordinary natural meaning of the words leads to absurdity. I consider that the term has a meaning which is recognised and used both in legal documents and in every day speech. Section 19(1) of the Northern Ireland Constitution Act 1973 provides:

'19(1)   It shall be unlawful for a Minister of the Crown, a member of the Northern Ireland Executive or other person appointed under section 8 above, the Post Office and any authority or body listed in Schedule 2 to the Parliamentary Commissioner Act 1967, Schedule 1 to the Parliamentary Commissioner for Complaints Act (Northern Ireland) 1969 to discriminate, or aid, induce or incite another to discriminate, in the discharge of functions relating to Northern Ireland against any person or class of persons on the ground of religious belief or political opinion.'

Article 14 of the European Convention for the Protection of Human Rights and Fundamental Freedoms states:

'The enjoyment of the rights and freedoms set forth in this Convention shall be secured without discrimination on any ground such as sex, race, colour, language, religion, political or other opinion, national or social origin, association with a national minority, property, birth or other status.'

Article 26 of the International Covenant on Civil and Political Rights states:

'All persons are equal before the law and are entitled without any discrimination to the equal protection of the law. In this respect, the law shall prohibit any discrimination and guarantee to all persons equal and effective protection against discrimination on any ground such as race, colour, sex, language, religion, political or other opinion, national or social origin, property, birth or other status.'

The International Labour Organisation Convention concerning Discrimination in respect of Employment and Occupation defines 'discrimination' to include:

'any discrimination, exclusion or preference made on the basis of race, colour, sex, religion, political opinion, national extraction or social origin, which has the effect of nullifying or impairing equality of opportunity or treatment in employment or occupation.'

Cases can arise not infrequently where it may be difficult for a court or tribunal to decide whether a statutory provision applies to the facts of a particular case. It may also be difficult to define with precision the exact boundary where a term ceases to apply to a particular set of facts or circumstances. But that is not a reason why a court or tribunal should hold that the words in the statutory provision are obscure and that a special or restricted meaning should be given to them.

. . .

I also consider that the tribunal erred in its opinion that it accorded entirely with common sense to hold that the term 'political opinion' in the 1976 Act had to be construed on the basis that it must display 'some connection or correlation between religion and politics in Northern Ireland', with the implication that it was contrary to common sense to hold that 'political opinion' in the Act needed no connection with religious belief.

Arguments can be advanced in support of, and in opposition to, the proposition that it is right that discrimination on the ground of political opinion should be made unlawful in private employment. I express no opinion on the merits of those arguments or on which argument should prevail. But I consider that there is substance in both arguments and, bearing in mind (inter alia) the provisions in the Conventions to which I have referred above, I think that the argument in favour of the proposition cannot be dismissed as contrary to common sense.

Therefore I consider that as the relevant statutory provision is not ambiguous or obscure and does not lead to absurdity, it was not permissible for the tribunal to refer to the debate in Hansard. But, even if it had been permissible to refer to Hansard, I consider it to be abundantly clear, with all respect to the tribunal, that the words of the Minister of State in the debate did not make it clear that the words 'political opinion' were to be connected or linked with 'religious belief'. In my opinion the reverse is the case. It is correct that in the debate as reported in *Hansard* at p. 304 the Minister of State used the words cited by the tribunal in its decision:

> 'Our reason for including these words is this. Because of the correlation between religion and politics in Northern Ireland, we envisage that employers could, in effect, avoid their responsibility by discriminating on a political base while at the same time suggesting or implying that they were discriminating on a religious base. One must catch the two. Otherwise one would be played off against the other.'

In the debate the Standing Committee was considering an amendment moved by Mr Enoch Powell MP to leave out the words 'or political opinion' from Clause 16(1)(a), and Mr Powell stated at col. 303:

> 'In Clause 16(1)(a), in addition to religious belief, we find an alternative, namely, the words "or political opinion". It is important that the committee should focus its attention upon those words and decide whether they are necessary or helpful in securing the prevention of discrimination on religious grounds . . .
>
> **Mr Powell:** "I am sure that if an employer in an area threatened with nationalisation was confronted with two prospective employees, one of whom was a known advocate of the nationalisation of that firm among others, that person would fare less well in selection compared with somebody who was a known advocate of and believer in the private enterprise system. But I form no view on what I happen to believe was the legislation placed before the House. I find it very difficult to imagine that such political views, intentions and attitudes on the part of an applicant for a job are irrelevant to his suitability for a job."
>
> I was not thinking of what we suppose is the old style, when landlords evicted tenants who did not vote for their candidate. I was thinking more of the fact that the very atmosphere in this country — certainly within some industries and some areas — is permeated by political difference. It is common knowledge that it is bound favourably or otherwise to influence the prospects of individuals in certain employments. I certainly was not conscious of announcing anything which would be in the least degree surprising or out of line with people's experience.

I am sorry that I was diverted just as I was closing. I hope that the right hon. Gentleman has seized the major point which is being put to him. I am sure that he has. I put it to him not wishing to wreck his Bill but wishing to eliminate from it elements which could bring about its failure — a failure which in some respects my hon. Friends and I fear, but which could make that failure more likely.''

Mr Orme: ''I take the argument fully. As I explained to the Committee, the purpose of the clause is to show that religious discrimination under the guise of political discrimination is wrong, and one should obviously catch the other. But the Bill also deals with political discrimination in its own right in this definition. I am sure that neither my hon. Friends nor the Opposition would be opposed to that. I am amazed at the strength of the argument that the right hon. Gentleman has made, as it were, in defence. He said 'It is all right not to discriminate in the public sector, but it is quite in order to discriminate in the private sector'. That is the sort of argument that my hon. Friends find it very difficult to countenance or to follow.

There will not necessarily be a greater number of cases under the clause. But discrimination between members of the SDLP and the Alliance Party, or between UPNI members and Ulster Unionists, on the basis of their political affiliation, will be caught by the Bill.''

Therefore, it is quite clear that, faced with the points raised by Mr Powell and Mr Biggs-Davison, the Minister ultimately stated in express terms 'the Bill also deals with political discrimination in its own right in this definition'.

Therefore, even if, under the principle stated in *Pepper* v *Hart*, the tribunal had been entitled to look at the parliamentary material before it, that material provided no support for the tribunal's conclusion that in construing the 1976 Act political opinion must be linked with religious belief . . .

Mr Beattie, who appeared for the respondent on the hearing of the appeal, did not seek to support the reasoning of the tribunal and informed the court that the points relied on by the tribunal in its decision had not been raised by him at the hearing before the tribunal. However, Mr Beattie advanced a different argument in support of the tribunal's decision, which was that although discrimination on the ground of 'political opinion' referred to in the 1976 Act did not need to be linked to religious belief, nevertheless having regard to the context of the Act which related solely to Northern Ireland, discrimination on the ground of 'political opinion' was only unlawful if it related to 'political opinion' in respect of political matters relating solely to the political affairs of Northern Ireland. Therefore Mr Beattie contended that discrimination on the ground of political opinion relating to the Unionist/ Nationalist divide was unlawful, but that discrimination relating to the Conservative/Socialist divide or to the left wing/right wing divide of the Labour Party was not unlawful.

Although the 1976 Act extends only to Northern Ireland, I can see no valid ground upon which to confine the term 'political opinion' to the Unionist/ Nationalist divide. As in other parts of the United Kingdom, the citizens of Northern Ireland can hold political opinions in relation to political matters relating to Conservatism and Socialism. To confine the term 'political opinion' to Unionist/Nationalist politics would be to read words of restriction into the Act which it does not contain. Moreover, if it had been the intention of Parliament to restrict the term 'political opinion' to Unionist/Nationalist politics it would have been simple for Parliament to have inserted words into the Act to make this clear.

It would appear that the decision of the tribunal that the term 'political opinion' could not apply to the present case was influenced to some extent by its concern about the difficulty of the decision which would face it on the facts of this case in deciding whether the appellant had been discriminated against on the ground of 'political opinion'. Whilst I express no opinion whatever on the effect of the section in relation to the facts of this case, it is apparent that when the tribunal resumes its hearing of the case it will be desirable for it to consider the effect of section 37(3) of the 1976 Act which provides:

> 'Parts III and IV (which includes section 16 and 17), so far as they relate to discrimination on the ground of religious belief, shall not apply to or in relation to any employment or occupation, other than one mentioned in subsection (1), where the essential nature of the job requires it to be done by a person holding, or not holding, a particular religious belief; nor, so far as they relate to discrimination on the ground of political opinion, shall they apply to or in relation to an employment or occupation where the essential nature of the job requires it to be done by a person holding, or not holding, a particular political opinion.'

I would allow this appeal and I would answer each question in the case stated in the affirmative.

Questions:

1. Did the Court of Appeal consider it permissible to look into evidence of the legislators' intent?

2. What did it find after looking at such intent?

3. Is the phrase 'political opinion' unclear? Do you agree with the interpretation of the legislative history?

4. Note section 57(2), (3) of the Fair Employment Act 1976 (as amended).

> (2)   In this Act references to a person's religious belief or political opinion include references to his supposed religious belief or political opinion and to the absence or supposed absence of any, or any particular, religious belief or political opinion.
> (3)   In this Act any reference to a person's political opinion does not include an opinion which consists of or includes approval or acceptance of the use of violence for political ends connected with Northern Irish affairs (including the use of violence for the purpose of putting the public or any section of the public in fear).

Given that 'political opinion' has a specific meaning under the legislation, does this change your view on whether the phrase is unclear?

5. Would a Muslim person be protected under the Fair Employment legislation?

6. To what extent does the rule in *Pepper* v *Hart* provide an aid to statutory interpretation? Read the following extract which summarises the arguments for and against looking at statutory intent. It was written by one of the leading counsel in the case, Lord Lester QC.

Lord Lester of Herne Hill QC, '*Pepper* v *Hart* Revisited', *Statute Law Review*, 1994, vol. 15, pp. 10–22, at pp. 11–22.

When I was a graduate student at Harvard Law School in 1960 I followed a fascinating course on 'The Legal Process' by Professors Henry M Hart and Albert M Sacks. It dramatically changed my approach to the legal process and indeed to the practice of law. I vividly remember the discussion of the British rule of total exclusion, forbidding counsel and court alike from referring to material drawn from internal legislative history. It described the English cases as a 'true wasteland of legalism'; quoting from TS Eliot

'What are the roots that clutch, what branches grow
Out of this stony rubbish? Son of man,
You cannot say, or guess, for you know only
A heap of broken images, where the sun beats,
And the dead tree gives no shelter, the cricket no relief,
And the dry stone no sound of water.'

The authors of those provocative and critical legal materials asked whether there was a connection between what they described as the frequent arid quality of English judgments and the English courts' refusal to consider honest, direct evidence of purpose. They also asked this interesting question, to which I could find no ready answer: 'What would you do as Counsel in a case before the House of Lords if you knew of illuminating material which you were forbidden to quote in argument? Might you not at least find a way to let their Lordships know where the material could be found?' I remember reading and discussing this material as a student and feeling uncomfortable with what even then was clearly an unsatisfactory situation. Little did I think that, more than thirty years later, it would be my task to seek to persuade their Lordships to abandon the ancient exclusionary rule. . . .

The main arguments in favour of abolishing the absolute prohibition against any reference to the parliamentary record as an extrinsic aid to statutory interpretation can be summarized in this way:

1. The purpose of using the parliamentary record is to help give better informed effect to the legislative outcome of parliamentary proceedings. It is therefore irrational for the courts to maintain an absolute rule depriving

themselves of access to potentially relevant evidence or information for this purpose. Why, in Lord Denning's words, should judges grope about in the dark searching for the meaning of an Act, when they can so easily switch on the light?

2.   The history of a statute, including the parliamentary debates, may be relevant to determine the meaning of legislation where a provision is ambiguous or obscure, or where the ordinary meaning is manifestly absurd or unreasonable.

3.   The parliamentary record may be of real assistance to the court—

(a)   by showing that Parliament has considered and suggested an answer to the issue of interpretation before the court;

(b)   by showing the object and purpose of the legislation and the mischief which the Act was designed to remedy;

(c)   by explaining the reason for some obscurity or ambiguity in the wording of the legislation; and

(d)   by providing direct evidence for the origins, background, and historical context to the legislation.

4.   Where a statutory provision has been enacted following an authoritative ministerial statement as to the understanding by the Executive of its meaning and effect, such a statement may provide important evidence about the object and purpose of the provision and the intention of Parliament in agreeing to its enactment, and may create reasonable expectations among Members of Parliament and those affected by the legislation.

5.   The courts do not consider themselves confined exclusively by the text for the purposes of interpreting the statute. There is no basis in principle or logic for them to be willing to have regard to extrinsic aids in White Papers etc. while rigidly excluding any recourse to parliamentary debates.

6.   A purposive approach to interpretation requires the courts to construe legislation in accordance with its purposes. It is therefore illogical to hold that courts are entitled to read a report to determine the mischief sought to be remedied but must ignore it when considering the statute.

The main arguments against any alteration in the rule were summarized by the New Zealand Law Commission as follows:

(1)   The text of the statute as enacted is the law; those affected by the statute should be able to rely on the text passed by the House, assented to by the Crown and appearing in the statute book.

(2)   Use of the material may involve an improper, even an unconstitutional examination of the proceedings of Parliament.

(3)   The parliamentary material may be unreliable and may indeed be created to support a particular interpretation.

(4)   The parliamentary material is not likely to help since the issue in dispute may not have been anticipated.

(5)   The process may cause delay and increase the cost of litigation.

There is, of course, force in each of these points but the Law Commission of New Zealand concluded that they do not lead to the conclusion that the material cannot or should not be used in appropriate cases. Of course, the text of a statute is sacred but where there is real controversy about what it means, so that the statutory language cannot itself be relied upon, courts should not be confined exclusively to the text for the purposes of interpretation.

Judicial use of the parliamentary material does not alter the constitutional relationships between Parliament, the Executive, and the Judiciary or the nature of the judicial process of statutory interpretation. This is because it does not mean that the courts must become in Lord Wilberforce's words 'a reflecting mirror of what some other interpretation agency may do'. It is for the courts to determine whether to consider parliamentary materials and to decide what weight and value to attach to them. It is for the courts to exercise their judgment in determining the relevance of the material and its evidential weight. It is for the courts to ensure that there is no unnecessary recourse to Hansard in litigation. Moreover, the record of parliamentary debates is no less accessible than White Papers etc., and as regards accessibility, this can be facilitated in various practical ways.

The argument based on delay and the increased cost of litigation applies to the use of any extrinsic aids to statutory interpretation. It is only the rare case which might call for a comprehensive reference to legislative history. In most cases the reference to Hansard need be no more extensive than to passages of an official report or a White Paper. And the courts have ample powers to deter the parties from unnecessarily referring to parliamentary history, including the power to award the payment of costs unreasonably incurred in this way.

In the end the majority of the House of Lords came down unequivocally in favour of altering the rule but with effective safeguards against the misuse of the parliamentary record as an aid to interpretation . . .

We also made it clear in our submissions to the Appellate Committee that a rule permitting recourse to the parliamentary record does not and should not mean that the courts are bound by any statement of parliamentary opinion outside a statute as to what the statute means. An Act of Parliament takes effect only through the language in which its principles and rules are expressed and through their proper interpretation by the courts. If, for example, a Minister chooses to put an administratively convenient gloss upon statutory language in the course of the parliamentary debates, without proposing any amendment to the statutory language itself, the courts can and no doubt will continue to insist upon applying the well-known constitutional principles of judicial interpretation protecting basic human rights and freedoms. For this purpose they will continue to have recourse to the important extrinsic aid to statutory interpretation contained in the European Convention on Human Rights and the International Covenant on Civil and Political Rights. Nor will the courts permit ministers to interfere with basic rights and freedoms on the basis of what Ministers say in Parliament.

Parliament could and should assist the courts in their task by incorporating the rights and freedoms guaranteed by these international instruments into

United Kingdom law, and by enacting legislation prescribing the circumstances and the extent to which extrinsic materials can be of assistance in the
interpretation of statutes and subordinate legislation. Parliament should also
ensure that the text of legislation is well drafted and that the legislation is
readily accessible to the public.

The lamentable record of inaction by successive governments and Parliaments in this area suggests that *Pepper* v *Hart* will not lead them to create a
better system of preparing, enacting, publicizing, and explaining legislation.
Inadequately aided by the legislative and executive branches, the judiciary
and the legal profession will have to do their best to make sense of what is
written in statutes and, where necessary, of what has been said during or
outside parliamentary debates, so as to give proper effect to the often
defective handiwork of our sovereign Parliament. Meanwhile, it would be
better for Members of Parliament to consider how to use their vital powers
and privileges so as to promote the rule of law, rather than complaining that
the courts have decided to pay attention to what is said, as well as to what is
done, in Parliament.

Questions:
1.   Lord Lester notes two influences of particular interest to us. First, he
acknowledges the impact of his legal education at Harvard. Second, he
considers that the courts have been influenced by European and Commonwealth
developments. We would urge students to bear both these explanations of the
dynamism of the law in mind, not simply for statutory interpretation but across
the legal system as a whole. How you are inspired as students can make a
difference. So can developments abroad.

2.   Turning to the particular issue, who has the better of the arguments about
the wisdom of referring to Hansard?

3.   There is a dispute between the judges in the case and between the
commentators/counsel as to whether the result will be efficient or too costly.
(See Chapter 8 on Critical Skills.) Are there any circumstances in which you
can envisage reference to Hansard being restricted in the future?

HUMAN RIGHTS AND EUROPEAN COMMUNITY LAW: THE
CHANGING RULES OF STATUTORY INTERPRETATION

One of the arguments against looking at documents which evidence statutory
intent is the idea that Parliament is sovereign — that is that its laws are supreme
and take precedence over other legal standards. In *Pepper* v *Hart* the Attorney-
General had submitted that '[i]f statements by Ministers as to the intent or effect
of an Act were allowed to prevail, this would contravene the constitutional rule
that Parliament is ''sovereign only in respect of what it expresses by the words
used in the legislation it has passed''.'. Increasingly, however, this doctrine of
sovereignty of Parliament is coming under attack from another front — that of
the international obligations undertaken by the government, for example
through membership of the European Union, with the legal obligations imposed

by that, and signing of International Treaties, such as Human Rights Conventions. In the extract above, Lord Lester made reference to these obligations and mentioned the need to 'incorporate' them into domestic law. Since that time, the Labour Government has incorporated the European Convention on Human Rights and Fundamental Freedoms into domestic legislation in the Human Rights Act 1998. (You can find the Act at the following website: http:///www.hmso.gov.uk/acts/acts1998.htm.)

In a White Paper the Government put the case for incorporation:

Rights Brought Home: The Human Rights Bill, October 1997, Cm 3782 (http://www.official-documents.co.uk/document/hoffice/rights/rights.htm).

The Case for Incorporation

1.14 The effect of non-incorporation on the British people is very practical one. The rights, [in the European Convention on Human Rights] originally developed with major help from the United Kingdom Government, are no longer seen as British rights. And enforcing them takes too long and costs too much. It takes on average five years to get an action into the European Court of Human Rights once all domestic remedies have been exhausted; and it costs an average of £30,000. Bringing these rights home will mean that the British people will be able to argue for their rights in the British courts — without this inordinate delay and cost. It will also mean that the rights will be brought much more fully into the jurisprudence of the courts throughout the United Kingdom, and there will be another distinct benefit. British judges will be enabled to make a distinctively British contribution to the development of the jurisprudence of human rights in Europe.

1.15 Moreover, in the Government's view, the approach which the United Kingdom has so far adopted towards the Convention does not sufficiently reflect its importance and has not stood the test of time.

1.16 The most obvious proof of this lies in the number of cases in which the European Commission and Court have found that there have been violations of the Convention rights in the United Kingdom. The causes vary. The Government recognises that interpretations of the rights guaranteed under the Convention have developed over the years, reflecting changes in society and attitudes. Sometimes United Kingdom laws have proved to be inherently at odds with the Convention rights. On other occasions, although the law has been satisfactory, something has been done which our courts have held to be lawful by the United Kingdom standards but which breaches the Convention. In other cases again, there has simply been no framework within which the compatibility with the Convention rights of an executive act or decision can be tested in the British courts: these courts can of course review the exercise of executive discretion, but they can do so only on the basis of what is lawful or unlawful according to the law in the United Kingdom as it stands. It is plainly unsatisfactory that someone should be the victim of a breach of the Convention standards by the State yet cannot bring any case at all in the British courts, simply because British law does not recognise the right in the same terms as one contained in the Convention.

1.17   For individuals, and for those advising them, the road to Strasbourg is long and hard. Even when they get there, the Convention enforcement machinery is subject to long delays. This might be convenient for a Government which was half-hearted about the Convention and the right of individuals to apply under it, since it postpones the moment at which changes in domestic law or practice must be made. But it is not in keeping with the importance which this Government attaches to the observance of basic human rights.

Bringing Rights Home

1.18   We therefore believe that the time has come to enable people to enforce their Convention rights against the State in British courts, rather than having to incur the delays and expense which are involved in taking a case to the European Human Rights Commission and Court in Strasbourg and which may altogether deter some people from pursuing their rights. Enabling courts in the United Kingdom to rule on the application of the Convention will also help to influence the development of case law on the Convention by the European Court of Human Rights on the basis of familiarity with our laws and customs and of sensitivity to practices and procedures in the United Kingdom. Our courts' decisions will provide the European Court with a useful source of information and reasoning for its own decisions. United Kingdom judges have a very high reputation internationally, but the fact that they do not deal in the same concepts as the European Court of Human Rights limits the extent to which their judgments can be drawn upon and followed. Enabling the Convention rights to be judged by British courts will also lead to closer scrutiny of the human rights implications of new legislation and new policies. If legislation is enacted which is incompatible with the Convention, a ruling by the domestic courts to that effect will be much more direct and immediate than a ruling from the European Court of Human Rights. The Government of the day, and Parliament, will want to minimise the risk of that happening.

1.19   Our aim is a straightforward one. It is to make more directly accessible the rights which the British people already enjoy under the Convention. In other words, to bring those rights home.

When the Human Rights Act comes into force in the near future, it will put a new onus on judges to interpret statutes where possible so that they are in accordance with the rights laid out in the European Convention on Human Rights and Fundamental Freedoms.

The Human Rights Act 1998

Interpretation of Legislation

3.—1(1)   So far as it is possible to do so, primary legislation and subordinate legislation must be read and given effect in a way which is compatible with the Convention rights.

(2)   This section—
(a)   applies to primary legislation and subordinate legislation whenever enacted;
(b)   does not affect the validity, continuing operation or enforcement of any incompatible primary legislation; and
(c)   does not affect the validity, continuing operation or enforcement of any incompatible subordinate legislation if (disregarding any possibility of revocation) primary legislation prevents removal of the incompatibility.

4.—(1)   Subsection (2) applies in any proceedings in which a court determines whether provision of primary legislation is compatible with a Convention right.
(2)   If the court is satisfied that the provision is incompatible with a Convention right, it may make a declaration of that incompatibility.
(3)   Subsection (4) applies in any proceedings in which a court determines whether a provision of subordinate legislation, made in the exercise of a power conferred by primary legislation, is compatible with a Convention right.
(4)   If the court is satisfied—
(a)   that the provision is incompatible with a Convention right, and
(b)   that (disregarding any possibility of revocation) the primary legislation concerned prevents removal of the incompatibility.
It may make a declaration of that incompatibility.
(5)   in this section 'court' means—
(a)   the House of Lords;
(b)   the Judicial Committee of the Privy Council;
(c)   The Courts-Martial Appeal Court;
(d)   in Scotland, the High Court of Justiciary sitting otherwise than as a trial court or the Court of Session;
(e)   in England and Wales or Northern Ireland, the High Court or the Court of Appeal.
(6)   A declaration under this section ('a declaration of incompatibility')—
(a)   does not affect the validity, continuing operation or enforcement of the provision in respect of which it is given; and
(b)   is not binding on the parties to the proceedings in which it is made
. . .

10.—(2)   If a Minister of the Crown considers that, there are compelling reasons for proceeding under this section, he may by order make such amendments to the legislation as he considers necessary to remove incompatibility.

In other words, where possible, legislation is to be interpreted so as to conform with obligations under the European Convention on Human Rights, and where this is not possible, the Court must make a declaration of incompatibility with the Convention. Where such a declaration is made a Minister can amend the law without waiting for Parliament to produce a new law, so as to make it compatible (see s. 10 of the Human Rights Act 1998). However, there is still some ambiguity over exactly how the interpretative process will take place: as section 3 states, '*So far as it is possible to do so* primary legislation and subordinate legislation must be read and given effect in a way which is compatible with the Convention rights' (emphasis added). It is likely that early cases under the new Act will debate what this means, and under *Pepper* v *Hart* it is likely that documents such as the White Paper will be examined to see what Parliament meant by the phrase 'so far as it is possible to do so'.

On that matter the White Paper states:

2.7 The Bill provides for legislation — both Acts of Parliament and secondary legislation — to be interpreted so far as possible so as to be compatible with the Convention. This goes far beyond the present rule which enables the courts to take the Convention into account in resolving any ambiguity in a legislative provision. The courts will be required to interpret legislation so as to uphold the Convention rights unless the legislation itself is so clearly incompatible with the Convention that it is impossible to do so.

2.8 This 'rule of construction' is to apply to past as well as to future legislation. To the extent that it affects the meaning of a legislative provision, the courts will not be bound by previous interpretations. They will be able to build a new body of case law, taking into account the Convention rights.

So, interestingly (and confusingly!) this would suggest that in cases where there is a possible Convention-compatible interpretation of a statute, and a possible incompatible interpretation, the compatible interpretation is to be used, whether or not the statute is ambiguous. Therefore, in this situation it will not now be necessary to resort to *Pepper* v *Hart* to decide how to resolve an ambiguity.

However, the matter is even more complicated. The European Convention on Human Rights is *itself* a legal document which has already been interpreted by the European Commission on Human Rights and the European Court of Human Rights. Therefore, to what extent are UK courts to apply the Convention not just by looking at its language, but by looking at how the European Court has interpreted the Convention in its cases?

Section 2 of the Human Rights Act provides:

2.—(1) A court or tribunal determining a question which has arisen under this Act in connection with a Convention right must take into account any—

(a) judgment, decision, declaration or advisory opinion of the European Court of Human Rights,

(b) opinion of the Commission given in a report adopted under Article 31 of the Convention, or in connection with Article 26 or 27(2) of the Convention, or

(c) decision of the Commission, or

(d) decision of the Committee of Ministers taken under Article 46 of the Convention, whenever made or given, so far as, in the opinion of the court or tribunal, it is relevant to the proceedings in which that question has arisen.

(2)   Evidence of any judgment, decision, declaration or opinion of which account may have to be taken under this section is to be given in proceedings before any court or tribunal in such manner as may be provided by rules.

Question:
1.   What does it mean to 'take account' of a relevant decision? How persuasive do you think an ECHR decision will be?

Domestic courts are only to take such decisions into account when 'in [their] opinion, it is relevant to the proceedings'. How is the Court to decide what is relevant? Should they consider the international nature of the court or commission whose decision they are examining and how that might have affected its approach? International tribunals, for example, traditionally have given a degree of latitude to the domestic law of member states, as they are wary of stepping on the toes of national Parliaments. The European Court of Human Rights has adopted some interpretative guidelines for its own decision making. Two of the more important ones are, the doctrine of 'proportionality' (any restriction of rights must be proportionate to the legitimate aim pursued) and the 'margin of appreciation' doctrine, under which signatory States are allowed some leeway in the application of Convention rights, reflecting the fact that national authorities may be better placed to determine the most appropriate action in a given case, and also have to apply international standards within their own political and cultural context. Should a national court follow these interpretative guidelines?

In a recent book, Murray Hunt has argued that even without incorporation international obligations (particularly those imposed through membership of the European Community) have radically changed how judges approached statutory interpretation:

M Hunt, *Using Human Rights Law in English Courts*, Oxford, Hart Publishing (1997), at pp. 13–15.

4.   The International Treaty Presumption

According to the traditional, most expansive account of parliamentary sovereignty, the interpretation of statutes is a straightforward matter of discovering and applying Parliament's historical intention when enacting the relevant legislation. In reality, of course, Parliament's 'intention' is seldom discoverable by any linguistic or factual inquiry, but is constructed by the courts against a background set of assumptions rooted in the common law.

In carrying out their inevitably interpretive function, courts in practice achieve a degree of entrenchment for common law values by deploying presumptions of statutory interpretation of varying strengths. One of the best known examples is the presumption that, in the absence of clear language to the contrary, Parliament did not intend to impose retrospective criminal liability.

Since, as was seen in the previous section, the values recognised by the common law include some of those protected in international law, it would be surprising if unincorporated international law were treated as wholly irrelevant by the courts whenever Parliament had legislated in the same field. In practice, the apparent purity of the dualist position has often been compromised by the courts when interpreting statutes, and, as with the more familiar domestic qualifications of pure sovereignty theory in favour of common law values, the main vehicle for this compromise has been a presumption of statutory interpretation, based on Parliament's presumed intention when enacting the statute in question. Notwithstanding the frequently uncompromising judicial statements of the dualist position, including the refusal even to have regard to the relevant international obligation when construing implementing legislation, a rule of construction gradually emerged, to the effect that where legislation is passed to implement an international treaty, it is to be presumed that Parliament intended to fulfil its international obligations.

In *Salomon* v *Commissioners of Customs and Excise* [1987] 2 QB 116, for example, there arose a question of construction of a statute which was clearly based on an international convention but which neither included that convention as a schedule nor made any express reference to it. Diplock LJ began impeccably, reciting the received dualist wisdom that an international treaty is irrelevant to any issue in domestic courts so long as no legislative steps have been taken to fulfil the obligations thus incurred. Even when implementing legislation has been enacted, he held, if its terms are clear and unambiguous they must be given effect by the courts whether or not they fulfil the treaty obligations, because Parliament's sovereign power extends to breaking treaties, for which the only remedy lies elsewhere than in domestic courts. This much is standard dualist dogma, but Diplock LJ went on to add an important qualification. Any ambiguity in the terms of the implementing legislation, he said, triggered a presumption that Parliament does not intend to act in breach of international law, including specific treaty obligations, and the treaty itself therefore became relevant to the exercise in construction. In choosing between the possible meanings of the ambiguous legislation, the presumption required the court to prefer the meaning which was consonant with the treaty obligations. In addition, it was said to be no obstacle to such use being made of a treaty to resolve statutory ambiguities or obscurities that the statute itself made no mention of the convention which it was its purpose to implement. It was sufficient if that intention was apparent from extrinsic evidence such as a comparison between the subject matter of the statute and the treaty.

After *Salomon*, then, it was clear that resort to a convention as an aid to interpretation of a statute was permissible on two conditions being satisfied: first, that the terms of the legislation were not clear but were 'ambiguous', in the sense of being reasonably capable of more than one meaning; and, second, that there was cogent extrinsic evidence that the enactment was intended to fulfil obligations under a particular convention. The case was soon being cited as authority for the legitimacy of judicial resort to unincorporated conventions, notwithstanding the dualist stance to which the courts were theoretically committed.

. . .

In this way, judges have contrived to give practical effect to a hybrid of the monist and dualist approaches when interpreting domestic law, whilst at the same time maintaining at the theoretical level a commitment to a dualist stance towards international treaties underpinned by the sovereignty of Parliament, which could be invoked to preclude reference to such international law as and when convenient.

These qualifications of dualistic purity mean that in practice the stance of English courts towards international legal norms is much more of a compromise between monism and dualism than is commonly supposed. Moreover, each of these qualifications of the pure dualist position has been expanded in significant ways in recent years, in a development which, it will be argued, reveals both to be particular manifestations of a more general interpretive principle that English courts ought to interpret and apply domestic law consistently with the UK's international obligations. First, there has been an important shift in the courts' approach to the question of the domestic status of customary international law, towards a greater receptiveness. Second, in a judicial development which is clearly not unrelated to the first, there has been a gradual relaxation of the conditions for the application of the treaty presumption, resulting in a considerable enhancement of its strength and a correspondingly greater degree of domestic protection for the values contained in international treaties. The inevitable effect of the combination of these trends has been to render domestic law more permeable by international standards. (See further, special issue of the *Journal of Law and Society*, vol. 26(1), 1999, on 'Human Rights: Changing the Culture'.

The judgments in the legal battle over the extradition of General Augosto Pinochet of Chile for crimes of genocide, murder on a large scale, torture and the taking of hostages, show the extent to which international law can influence and impact on domestic law. In November 1998 the House of Lords ruled in a three to two decision that he could be extradited to Spain. International law standards played a significant role in reaching this conclusion (*R v Bartle and the Commissioner of Police for the Metropolis and others, ex Parte Pinochet*; *R v Evans and another and the Commissioner of Police for the Metropolis and others, ex Parte Pinochet*, [1998] 4 All ER 897, HL). The judgment is a complicated one. It uses skills of statutory interpretation with regard to several different statutes and also interpretation of common law standards. There is extensive discussion of how international law shapes both domestic standards and common law standards. Incidentally, it is interesting to note that the judgment was set aside because one of the Law Lords — Lord Hoffman — was a member of the board of Amnesty International's Charitable Trust. Amnesty International legal teams had submitted what is known as an *amicus* (friend of the court) brief arguing for extradition. We will go on to consider who the judges are, what influences them, and how they make decisions in Chapter 7. This second judgment *In re Pinochet* (oral judgment, 17 December 1998, written reasons, 15 January 1999) and the new judgment dated 24 March 1999 can be found at the House of Lords' website at www.parliament.the-stationery-office.co.uk/pa/ld/ldjudinf.htm, where House of Lords' judgments are posted within two hours of delivery. Try looking it up. You should continue to monitor this site for recent House of Lords cases.

European Community law provides a good example of judicial attempts to develop statutory interpretation techniques which harmonise domestic law and European Community law. It illustrates some of the techniques of statutory interpretation which may come to be used when applying the Human Rights Act 1998. Such developments in traditional notions of statutory interpretation cannot be ignored by lawyers or law students.

The following case provides an example of how the Courts combine interpretation of supra-national legal standards with their interpretation of domestic standards, and reach a result which is quite different to that which they would have reached had they looked at domestic standards alone (although it can still be said to be consistent with those standards). In this case, the Courts had to consider whether sex discrimination law, which was designed to provide for equality between men and women, could protect transsexuals. In doing so the Court had to harmonise the wording of the Sex Discrimination Act 1975 with the provisions of the European Equal Treatment Directive 1976 as interpreted by the European Court of Justice. European law provides, in cases such as this, that domestic law must be construed consistently with the Directive in order to achieve the purpose of the Directive, if such a construction is possible. This meant taking into account a decision of the ECJ called *P v S* where it had been decided that the Directive *did* protect transsexuals. (Extracts from *P v S* can be found in Chapter 10 pp. 360–64, where you can look at some of the arguments the ECJ used.)

The facts of the case were that the applicant was a biological male who started work with the employers and several years later announced her change of gender identity from male to female. After this announcement she was subjected to prolonged and serious harassment and ostracism by a very small minority of her male colleagues. This led to her becoming ill and having to leave work, and later to her attempting suicide. Although the management had known of the harassment, they had not taken any steps to remedy the situation. She took the case to an industrial tribunal [now employment tribunal] alleging sex discrimination. The industrial tribunal found for her and the employers appealed to the Employment Appeal Tribunal. Now read that judgment.

Chessington World of Adventures Ltd v Reed [1998] ICR 97, EAT.

The appeal
The following issues raised by the parties fall to be determined in this appeal: (1) whether the Sex Discrimination Act 1975 applies in a case where the complainant relies upon less favourable treatment following notice of intention to undergo gender reassignment.
. . .

First issue

The Sex Discrimination Act 1975 provides by section 1:

'(1)   A person discriminates against a woman in any circumstances relevant for the purposes of any provision of this Act if — (a) on the ground of her sex he treats her less favourably than he treats or would treat a man . . .'

Section 2(1) provides:

'Section 1, and the provisions of Parts II and III relating to sex discrimination against women, are to be read as applying equally to the treatment of men, and for that purpose shall have effect with such modifications as are requisite.'

Section 5 provides:

'. . . (2) In this Act — 'woman' includes a female of any age, and 'man' includes a male of any age. (3) A comparison of the cases of persons of different sex . . . under section 1(1) or 3(1) must be such that the relevant circumstances in the one case are the same, or not materially different, in the other.'

Section 6(2) provides:

'It is unlawful for a person, in the case of a woman employed by him at an establishment in Great Britain, to discriminate against her — . . . (b) by . . . subjecting her to any other detriment.'

The Equal Treatment Directive, Council Directive 76/207/EEC (OJ 1976 L 39, p. 40), provides by article 5(1):

'Application of the principle of equal treatment with regard to working conditions, including the conditions governing dismissal, means that men and women shall be guaranteed the same conditions without discrimination on grounds of sex.'

It is common ground that, since the employers are not an emanation of the state, the applicant cannot rely directly on the Directive. However, it is equally clear that the Sex Discrimination Act 1975 must be construed consistently with the Directive in order to achieve the purpose of the Directive, if such a construction is possible: see *Marleasing SA* v *La Comercial Internacional de Alimentación SA* [1990] ECR I-4135.

Mr Bowers submitted, however, that it is not permissible to distort the meaning of the statute. In this connection he relies, first, upon the House of Lords' approach in *Duke* v *Reliance Systems Ltd* [1988] ICR 339. There the issue was whether a private employer's policy whereby the normal retirement age for women was 60 and men 65 constituted unlawful discrimination contrary to the Act of 1975 against the female appellant who was dismissed shortly after her sixtieth birthday. The House of Lords dismissed the appeal on the grounds that the employer's retirement policy was 'provision in relation to . . . retirement' within the meaning of section 6(4) and therefore the dismissal was saved from being unlawful by virtue of that subsection.

During the course of giving the leading speech, Lord Templeman observed, at p. 352f, that the Sex Discrimination Act 1975 was not intended to give effect to Directive 76/207/EEC, and that the words of section 6(4) could not be distorted in order to enforce against an individual a Directive which has no direct effect between individuals, as construed by the European Court of Justice in *Marshall* v *Southampton and South West Hampshire Area Health Authority (Teaching)* (Case 152/84) [1986] ICR 335.

More recently, in *MacMillan* v *Edinburgh Voluntary Organisations Council* [1995] IRLR 536 the Employment Appeal Tribunal sitting in Scotland (Mummery J presiding) held that an industrial tribunal had correctly held that the Act of 1975, when construed in accordance with Directive 76/207/EEC, did not allow an award of compensation for unintentional indirect discrimination. It held that the clear words of section 65(1)(b) and section 66(3) could not be construed to accord with the provisions of the Directive. There was no ambiguity in the language of the statute: it was not permissible, in the guise of interpretation, to distort the language for the purpose of making the provision conform to the Directive.

Both *Duke* v *Reliance Systems Ltd* [1988] ICR 339 and *MacMillan* v *Edinburgh Voluntary Organisations Council* [1995] IRLR 536 were clear cases in which the remedy sought was specifically excluded by the wording of the Act. Can it be said that the case of a transsexual, who experienced different treatment before and after notification of an intention to undergo gender reassignment, is excluded from the protection of the Act?

We begin with the position under Directive 76/207/EEC. In *P* v *S* (Case C-13/94) [1996] ICR 795 the applicant, who was employed in an educational establishment by a local authority which was accepted to be an emanation of the state, informed the employer of an intention to undergo gender reassignment. After undergoing preliminary surgical procedures the applicant was given notice of dismissal and brought a complaint of unlawful sex discrimination before an industrial tribunal. The matter was referred to the Court of Justice for a preliminary ruling on the question whether the dismissal of a transsexual for a reason related to gender reassignment was precluded by article 5(1) of the Directive. That question was answered in the affirmative. The court said, at p. 814, paras 20 and 21:

'20. Accordingly, the scope of Directive 76/207/EEC cannot be confined simply to discrimination based on the fact that a person is of one or other sex. In view of its purpose and the nature of the rights which it seeks to safeguard, the scope of the Directive is also such as to apply to discrimination arising, as in this case, from the gender reassignment of the person concerned.

21. Such discrimination is based, essentially if not exclusively, on the sex of the person concerned. Where a person is dismissed on the ground

that he or she intends to undergo, or has undergone, gender reassignment, he or she is treated unfavourably by comparison with persons of the sex to which he or she was deemed to belong before undergoing gender reassignment.'

The question raised under the first issue in this appeal, therefore, is whether the Sex Discrimination Act 1975 may be read consistently with the purpose of Directive 76/207/EEC as interpreted in *P* v *S* without doing impermissible violence to language.

Mr Bowers submits not. He submits that the basis of the Act is a comparison between a person of one sex and an actual or hypothetical member of the opposite sex. Less favourable treatment of a man than a woman has recently been emphasised in the Court of Appeal decision in *Smith* v *Safeway plc* [1996] ICR 868. Mr Bowers contends that the industrial tribunal simply applied the reasoning in *P* v *S* (Case C-13/94) [1996] ICR 795 to the Act, without considering the difference in language between the statute and the Directive. In particular, he submits that the structure of section 1(1)(a) and the reference to a comparison of the cases of different sex in section 5(3) make clear that there must be a comparison between persons of different biological sexes. Conversely, the Directive lays down no requirement for a comparison between one case and another; it contains no definition of man and woman; the only question is one of causation, not comparison. Further, the applicant has remained a biological male throughout. Mr Bowers relies on the family case of *Corbett* v *Corbett (orse Ashley)* [1971] P 83, in which a marriage between a person born a biological male, who subsequently underwent a sex change operation, and a male was declared void. In reaching that conclusion Ormrod J stated, at p. 107: 'Marriage is a relationship which depends on sex and not on gender'.

Further, we have taken note of the ruling of the European Court of Human Rights in *X, Y and Z* v *United Kingdom, The Times*, 23 April 1997, to the effect that the United Kingdom's refusal to register a post-operative transsexual as the father of a child born to a female partner by artificial insemination by a donor was not a denial of the respect of the applicant's family and private life as guaranteed by Article 8 of the Convention for the Protection of Human Rights and Fundamental Freedoms (1953) (Cmd 8969).

Ms Rose first submits that there is no clear language in the Act of 1975 to exclude the case of a transsexual: cf *Duke* v *Reliance Systems Ltd* [1988] ICR 339 and *MacMillan* v *Edinburgh Voluntary Organisations Council* [1995] IRLR 536. We accept that submission. She distinguishes the test for establishing a person's 'legal sex' in the context of marriage. Again, we accept that distinction. A biological test is necessary in relation to marriage where heterosexual intercourse plays an essential part. That necessity does not arise in relation to the Act of 1975.

We are also reminded of the course of events in *Webb* v *EMO Air Cargo (UK) Ltd (No. 2)* [1995] ICR 1021. When that case finally came before the House of Lords, following a reference to the Court of Justice, the House of Lords held that sections 1(1)(a) and 5(3) of the Act of 1975 were to be interpreted consistently with the ruling of the Court of Justice that it was discrimination on the grounds of sex contrary to Directive 76/207/EEC for an employer to dismiss a female employee who was pregnant in circumstances where no direct comparison could be made with a male employee.

Applying the same reasoning where, as in this case, the reason for the unfavourable treatment is sex based, that is a declared intention to undergo gender reassignment, there is no requirement for a male/female comparison to be made. In these circumstances we interpret the Sex Discrimination Act 1975 consistently with the ruling of the Court of Justice in *P* v *S* (Case C-13/94) [1996] ICR 795, and uphold the tribunal's finding on the first issue.

Questions
1.   Do you think the decision is consistent with the wording of the Sex Discrimination Act?

2.   Do you think the decision was a just one? (See further Chapter 8.)

Not only does the impact of European law mean that there are further layers of text to interpret but there are different approaches to interpretation.

L Neville-Brown & T Kennedy, *The Court of Justice of the European Communities*, 4th edn, London, Sweet & Maxwell (1994) pp. 299–322.

The methods of interpretation employed by the Court have added importance for British lawyers since they constitute the 'European way' which Lord Denning recognised the courts of England (and Scotland) should follow when called upon themselves to interpret Community law. In *Bulmer* v *Bollinger* [1974] Ch 401 at 425 Lord Denning declared:

'The (EC) treaty is quite unlike any of the enactments to which we have become accustomed . . . It lays down general principles. It expresses its aim and purposes. All in sentences of moderate length and commendable style. But it lacks precision. It uses words and phrases without defining what they mean. An English lawyer would look for an interpretation clause, but he would look in vain. There is none. All the way through the treaty there are gaps and lacunae. These have to be filled in by the judges, or by regulations or directives. It is the European way . . . Seeing these differences, what are the English courts to do when they are faced with a problem of interpretation? They must follow the European pattern. No longer must they argue about the precise grammatical sense. They must look to the purpose and intent . . . They must divine the spirit of the treaty and gain inspiration from it. If they find a gap, they must fill it as best they can . . . These are the principles, as I understand it, on which the European Court acts.' . . .

Interpretation of law is in no way an exact science but rather a judicial art. In the end, it is a matter of judicial instinct, and because the judge proceeds instinctively, the process cannot be reduced to a series of mechanical rules.

Writers sometimes refer to 'canons of interpretation', but it is better to think in terms of varying *approaches*: sometimes one approach is preferred, sometimes another, sometimes a combination of several; or one approach may be followed by another as a check upon the result achieved by the first.

The Court of Justice has no special methods of its own but uses those with which national courts are familiar. But the Court's use of traditional methods should not deceive us: the distinctive nature of Community law, when compared with national laws on the one hand and international law on the other, as well as the manner in which the Treaties are drafted, have led the Court to evolve its own style of interpretation. Moreover . . . the multilingual character of Community Law introduces an extra dimension not normally encountered in the courts of Member States. In addition, resort to comparative law is more common in the sense that the court may look to the national laws of the Member States for guidance . . .

In the exposition which follows, four methods of interpretation are discussed *seriatim*. These are the literal, historical, contextual and teleological. Although this order has a certain logic and accords broadly with the way in which the approaches to interpretation by national courts are traditionally presented, it would be quite wrong to assume that the methods are placed in descending order of importance. As will become apparent, the dominant approaches of the Court of Justice are the contextual and teleological.

Literal Interpretation
Every court must begin from the words of the text before it. If their meaning is plain, either in their ordinary connotation or in some special sense appropriate to the particular context, then for the national judge the task of interpretation is a light one and ends there. Usually, the same can be said for the Court of Justice, but exceptionally the Court may be led to disregard the plainest of wording in order to give effect to what it deems the overriding aims and objects of the Treaties. In other words the literal interpretation is displaced by the contextual or teleological approach, although the Court may speak rather in terms of looking to 'the spirit' of the text in question.

Case 22/70 *ERTA* [1971] ECR 263 provides a good example. The Commission sought the annulment of a Council discussion to co-ordinate the attitude to be adopted by the six Member States in certain international negotiations to revise the European Road Transport Agreement. The Council's defence included the plea that the discussion did not constitute an 'act' subject to annulment within the meaning of that term in Article 173 (now 230) EC: any such act was limited to the categories of regulation, directive or decision as enumerated in Article 189 (now 249). Despite the apparently exhaustive wording of Article 189 (now 249), the Court found against the Council on this plea, holding that the aim of Article 173 (now 230) was to subject to judicial review all measures taken by the institutions designed to have legal effect and declaring that 'It would be inconsistent with this objective to interpret the conditions under which the action is admissible so restrictively as to limit the availability of this procedure merely to the categories of measures referred to by Article 189 (now 249)' . . .

Historical Interpretation
By historical interpretation is usually meant the quest for the subjective intention of the original author of the text. It may also mean the discovery of the objective intention of the measure in question, to be deduced from its purpose at the date of enactment. The English so-called 'Mischief Rule' as laid down in *Heydon's Case* [(1584) Co Rep 7a] confined the English judge to the objective legislative intent, whereas in most Continental countries the judge may examine the *trauvaux préparatoires* (preparatory work) in pursuit of the subjective intention of the legislature . . . Historical interpretation in either sense is little used by the Court of Justice . . .

Contextual Interpretation
This method is extensively used by the Court in interpreting both the Treaties and Community legislation. It involves placing the provision in issue within its context and interpreting it in relation to other provisions of Community law. The Treaties, particularly the EC Treaty, set out a grand design or programme, and it is natural to stress the interrelationship of the individual provisions as component parts of the total scheme. Not seeing the wood for the trees is, for the Court, a cardinal sin. Hence, its judgments abound with references such as:

'the context of all the provisions establishing a common organisation of the market': Case 190/73 *Van Haaster* [1974] ECR 1123;
'the general scheme of the Treaty as a whole': Cases 2 and 3/62 *Gingerbread* case [1962] ECR 425;
'taking account of the fundamental nature, in the scheme of the Treaty, of the principles of freedom of movement and equality of treatment of workers': Case 152/73 *Sotgia* [1974] ECR 153;
'one must have regard to the whole scheme of the Treaty no less than to its specific provisions': Case 22/70 *ERTA* case [1971] ECR 263;
'the context of the Treaty': case 23/75 *Rey Soda* [1975] ECR 1279;
'the framework of Community law': Cases 90 and 91/63 *Dairy Products* case [1964] ECR 625; Case 6/64 *Costa* v *ENEL* [1964] ECR 585. . . .

Teleological Interpretation
The term teleological is applied to an interpretation which is based upon the purpose or object of the text facing the judge. This approach, which is increasingly favoured by the Court, is peculiarly appropriate in Community law where, as we have seen, the Treaties provide mainly a broad programme or design rather than a detailed blue-print. In setting forth the grand design the Treaties, both in their preambles and in certain Articles, express the objectives of the Communities in very general terms; in turn, these objectives are knit together by the underlying assumption that they will lead eventually to an economic and political union. Article 2 EC, as amended by the Maastricht Treaty, is a striking example with its declaration of intent that:

'The Community shall have as its task, by establishing a common market and an economic and monetary union and by implementing the common policies or activities referred to in Articles 3 and 3a (now 4), to promote throughout the Community a harmonious development of economic activities, sustainable and non-inflationary growth respecting the environment, a high degree of convergence of economic performance, a high level of employment and of social protection, the raising of the standard of living and quality of life, and economic and social cohesion and solidarity among Member States.'

. . .

This teleological approach is also extensively used in interpreting Community legislation. Thus, in Case 9/67 *Colditz* [1967] ECR 229, concerning certain social security regulations, the Court declared that

'the solution to this question . . . can only emerge from the interpretation of those regulations in the light of the objectives of the provisions of the Treaty (Articles 48 to 51)' (now 39–42).

. . .

The European Way
The separating out in this chapter of the various methods or approaches which the Court brings to its task of interpreting Community law should not mislead the reader into concluding that the Court operates in some mechanical way. As we have said, interpretation is an art in which the judicial instinct looms large. Frequently the Court uses a combination of methods, much as the artist blends the primary colours of his palette. A characteristic example is provided . . . by Case 6/72 *Continental Can* [1973] ECR 215 at 243 where the judgment states:

'In order to answer this question (whether Art. 86 [now 82] EC applies to changes in the structure of an undertaking) one has to go back to the spirit, general scheme and wording of Article 86 (now 82), as well as to the system and objectives of the Treaty'.

Literal, contextual and teleological approaches are here all mixed together to enable the Court to reach its landmark decision on the full scope of Article 86 (now 82).

Finally, over the four decades of its existence the Court has changed the emphasis of its methods, especially in interpreting the founding Treaties. The earlier reliance on literal interpretation has given place increasingly to the contextual and teleological approaches, approaches which befit a jurisdiction charged with a quasi-constitutional function as the guardian of the grand objectives laid down in the Treaties.

Pitfalls for the Common Lawyer
Non-civilian lawyers, be they English, Irish or Scottish, should beware of approaching Community law as if it were no different from their national law: they must heed the injunction of Lord Denning, with which we began this

chapter. In particular, they should not strain to apply to Community law the canons of interpretation which the common law judges have evolved over the centuries. It would be a salutary exercise for the English-speaking lawyer who has some French to make a practice of looking at the French as well as the English version of the text in issue.

P Craig and G de Burca, *EC Law: Text, Cases and Materials*, 2nd edition, Oxford, Clarendon Press (1998), at pp. 86–9.

Style of the court's judgments

The style of the Court of Justice's judgments contrasts considerably with the style and content of the opinions of the Advocate Generals. Article 33 of the Statute of the Court provides that judgments are to state the reasons on which they are based. But by way of contrast with the individual and less institutionally constrained opinion of the Advocates General, the Court's judgments are collegiate, representing the single and final ruling of all judges hearing the case. The fact that decisions may not often be unanimous and will require a vote is indicated by Article 15 of the Statute, which provides that decisions of the Court will be valid when an uneven number of its members is sitting in the deliberations. And since there are no dissents or separately concurring judgments, the divergent views of a number of different judges may have to be contained within the language of the judgment. This can sometimes result in obscurity or in a ruling which is ambiguous on matters of importance. Various explanations for the occasionally rather scanty reasoning or the less than thorough legal analysis of the Court's judgments are possible. Quite apart from the need to construct a single judgment when the judges are not fully in agreement, the Court does not always like to rule in detail on matters which are not strictly necessary for the decision in the case before it. Although the Advocate General's opinion will often consider exhaustively all the legal arguments which could be relevant to the case, the Court may prefer not to commit itself on a specific legal issue until another case arises where the resolution of that issue is directly necessary for it to give a decision. This approach by the Court can be seen in particular in its preliminary rulings under Article 234 (formerly 177) of the EC Treaty.

A further reason for the inelegance and not infrequent obscurity of the Court's judgments may be the fact that they are translated into all the official languages of the Community. Sentences in the judgments are often long, clumsy, and inadequately punctuated. The working language which the Court has adopted for its secret deliberations is French, but the 'language of the case' will depend on the kind of proceedings before the Court. In Article 234 (formerly 177) references, for example, the language of the case is that of the national court or tribunal from which the reference was sent, while in other cases the language will be that chosen by the applicant or that of the defendant Member State.

Role and methodology of the Court

The specific tasks to be performed by the Court are described in the Treaties. Its jurisdiction is set out therein, the main provisions being articles 226–243 of the EC Treaty (formerly Articles 169–186). The TEU [Treaty on European Union] enhanced the Court's jurisdiction under Article 228 (formerly Article 177) . . . However, it is Article 220 (previously Article 164), which has perhaps figured most prominently in the Court's shaping of its own sphere of influence. The Court has used this provision — imaginatively described as a 'pregnant formula' — to define its role very broadly. This Article provides that . . .

Article 164 (now 220) states that 'the Court of Justice shall ensure that in the interpretation and application of this Treaty, the law is observed' . . . [T]he Court has utilized this provision to extend its review jurisdiction to cover bodies which were not expressly subject to it, and to measures which were not listed in the Treaty. In the name of preserving 'the rule of law' in the Community, the Court has extended its functions beyond those expressly outlined in the Treaty under which it was established. Since the competence of the Community, and hence of its institutions, is an attributed competence, limited to what was given by the Treaty, the question of an inherent jurisdiction of the Court is problematic . . .

In the years of so-called institutional malaise or stagnation, the Court can be seen to have played a 'political' role through law, attempting to render the Treaty effective even when its provisions had not been implemented as required by the Community, and to render secondary legislation effective even when it had not been properly implemented by the Member States. It adopted an active part in the creation of the internal market through litigation which came before it, by the negative means of requiring the removal of national barriers to trade, at a time when progress towards completing the Single Market through positive legislative harmonization was hindered by institutional inaction.

The Court has achieved the 'hobbyhorse' status which it occupies amongst European lawyers as much on account of its reasoning and methodology as on account of the impact of its decisions. Its approach to interpretation is generally described as a purposive or teleological method, although not in the sense of seeking the purpose or aim of the authors of a text . . .

Rather than adopting a narrower historical-purposive approach, the Court tends to examine the whole context in which a particular provision is situated — which often involves looking at the preamble to the Treaties or to legislation — and it gives the interpretation most likely to further what the Court considers that provision in its context was aimed to achieve. Often this is very far from a literal interpretation of the Treaty or of the legislation in question, even to the extent of flying in the face of the express language, and this aspect of the Court's methodology has attracted a good deal of criticism . . .

Of course it is true that all constitutional courts engage in political issues, but given the unaccountability of courts, the real question . . . is the nature and origin of the 'unwritten' values which they promote, and the *extent* to which their decisions seem to depart from what their express powers under the constitution or Treaty establishing them would appear to allow. Perhaps more importantly, such Judicial decision-making requires full and thorough justification, whereas the reasoning of the ECJ tends to be . . . notriously thus.

The following case provides a good illustration of how the law in various national jurisdictions throughout Europe (as well as British football!) has been affected by European law. Try to identify the methods of interpretation used by the ECJ.

The facts of this case were as follows:

European football is organised in national federations or associations. They are all members of FIFA (the International Federation of Football Associations) which is divided into federations for each continent. The federation for Europe is UEFA.

Every professional footballer must be registered with his national association, and is entered as the present or former employee of a specific football club. According to FIFA regulations, a professional player could not leave his international association as long as he was bound by his contract and the rules of his national association, no matter how harsh they might be. The Belgian national association's rules provided in effect that the players could not be transferred without a 'transfer fee' being paid to the old club by the new club.

Bosman was a Belgian professional footballer, employed by RC Liège, under a contract expiring on 30 June 1990 at an average monthly salary of £2,400. In April 1990 he was offered a new contract for one season at the reduced monthly salary of £600. Having refused to agree these terms he was transfer listed with an asking price of £2,500,000. He was subsequently engaged by the French club, Dunkerque, and the two clubs agreed a temporary transfer fee of £24,000 for one year. The contract was subject to the condition that the transfer certificate be sent to the French Football Association.

Liège failed to effect the required transmission of the certificate to the FFA so that the contract did not take effect. Liège suspended Bosman, thus preventing him from playing for the 1990–1 season, as he had not signed up again with them.

In proceedings in the Belgian courts, Bosman sought an order restraining Liège and URBSFA [the Belgian football governing body] from impeding his engagement by a new club by requiring the payment of a transfer fee. Further parties, including UEFA, were later joined to the action. The Belgian court referred to the ECJ various questions on interpretation, *inter alia*, of Article 48 (now 39) EC on freedom of movement for workers. The relevant Treaty provision is as follows:

Article 39 (formerly 48) of the EC Treaty
1.   Freedom of movement of workers shall be secured within the Community.
2.   Such freedom of movement shall entail the abolition of any discrimination based on nationality between workers of the Member States as regards employment, remuneration and other conditions of work and employment.
3.   It shall entail the right, subject to limitations justified on grounds of public policy, public security or public health:

(a)   to accept offers of employment actually made;
(b)   to move freely within the territory of Member states for this purpose;
(c)   to stay in a Member State for the purpose of employment in accordance with the provisions governing the employment of nationals of that state laid down by law, regulation or administrative action;
(d)   to remain in the territory of a Member State after having been employed in that State, subject to conditions which shall be embodied in implementing regulations to be drawn up by the Commission.
4.   The provisions of this Article shall not apply to employment in the public service.

Essentially two issues were raised by the *Bosman* case — first, whether rules laid down by sporting associations under which in European matches which they organise, football clubs were permitted to field only a limited number of professional players who were nationals of other Member States, violated the provision; and secondly, whether the requirement that a transfer fee be paid to the player's previous club violated Article 48 (now 39) of the EC Treaty.

The ECJ found that the rule limiting the number of nationals from any one Member State who could participate was in breach of Article 48. The following extract considers the issue of whether the transfer fee system breached the Article:

Case C-415/93, *URBSFA* v *Jean-Marc Bosman* [1996] 1 CMLR 645, ECJ.

Application of Article 48 to rules laid down by sporting associations
69   It is necessary to consider certain arguments which have been put forward on the question of the application of Article 48 to rules laid down by sporting associations.

70   URBSFA argued that only the major European clubs may be regarded as undertakings, whereas clubs such as RC Liège carry on an economic activity only to a negligible extent. Furthermore, the question submitted by the national court on the transfer rules does not concern the employment relationships between players and clubs but the business relationships between clubs and the consequences of freedom to affiliate to a sporting federation. Article 48 of the Treaty is accordingly not applicable to a case such as that in issue in the main proceedings.

71   UEFA argued, *inter alia*, that the Community authorities have always respected the autonomy of sport, that it is extremely difficult to distinguish between the economic and the sporting aspects of football and that a decision of the Court concerning the situation of professional players might call in question the organisation of football as a whole. For that reason, even if Article 48 of the Treaty were to apply to professional players, a degree of flexibility would be essential because of the particular nature of the sport.

72   The German Government stressed, first, that in most cases a sport such as football is not an economic activity. It further submitted that sport in general has points of similarity with culture and pointed out that, under Article 128(1) of the EC Treaty, the Community must respect the national and regional diversity of the cultures of the Member States. Finally, referring to the freedom of association and autonomy enjoyed by sporting federations under national law, it concluded that, by virtue of the principle of subsidiarity, taken as a general principle, intervention by public, and particularly Community, authorities in this area must be confined to what is strictly necessary.

73   In response to those arguments, it is to be remembered that, having regard to the objectives of the Community, sport is subject to Community law only in so far as it constitutes an economic activity within the meaning of Article 2 of the Treaty (see Case 36/74 *Walrave* v *Union Cycliste Internationale* [1974] ECR 1405, paragraph 4). This applies to the activities of professional or semi-professional footballers, where they are in gainful employment or provide a remunerated service (see Case 13/76 *Donà* v *Mantero* [1976] ECR 1333, paragraph 12).

74   It is not necessary, for the purposes of the application of the Community provisions on freedom of movement for workers, for the employer to be an undertaking; all that is required is the existence of, or the intention to create, an employment relationship.

75   Application of Article 48 of the Treaty is not precluded by the fact that the transfer rules govern the business relationships between clubs rather than the employment relationships between clubs and players. The fact that the employing clubs must pay fees on recruiting a player from another club affects the players' opportunities for finding employment and the terms under which such employment is offered . . .

79   As regards the arguments based on the principle of freedom of association, it must be recognised that this principle, enshrined in Article 11 of the European Convention for the Protection of Human Rights and Fundamental Freedoms and resulting from the constitutional traditions common to the Member States, is one of the fundamental rights which, as the Court has consistently held and as is reaffirmed in the preamble to the Single European Act and in Article F(2) of the Treaty on European Union, are protected in the Community legal order.

80   However, the rules laid down by sporting associations to which the national court refers cannot be seen as necessary to ensure enjoyment of that freedom by those associations, by the clubs or by their players, nor can they be seen as an inevitable result thereof.

81   Finally, the principle of subsidiarity, as interpreted by the German Government to the effect that intervention by public authorities, and particularly Community authorities, in the area in question must be confined to what is strictly necessary, cannot lead to a situation in which the freedom of private

associations to adopt sporting rules restricts the exercise of rights conferred on individuals by the Treaty.

82   Once the objections concerning the application of Article 48 of the Treaty to sporting activities such as those of professional footballers are out of the way, it is to be remembered that, as the Court held in paragraph 17 of its judgment in *Walrave*, cited above, Article 48 not only applies to the action of public authorities but extends also to rules of any other nature aimed at regulating gainful employment in a collective manner.

83   The Court has held that the abolition as between Member States of obstacles to freedom of movement for persons and to freedom to provide services would be compromised if the abolition of State barriers could be neutralized by obstacles resulting from the exercise of their legal autonomy by associations or organisations not governed by public law (see *Walrave*, cited above, paragraph 18) . . .

Whether the situation envisaged by the national court is of a purely internal nature
88   UEFA considers that the disputes pending before the national court concern a purely internal Belgian situation which falls outside the ambit of Article 48 of the Treaty. They concern a Belgian player whose transfer fell through because of the conduct of a Belgian club and a Belgian association.

89   It is true that, according to consistent case-law (see, *inter alia*, Case 175/78 *Regina* v *Saunders* [1979] ECR 1129, paragraph 11; Case 180/83 *Moser* v *Land Baden-Würtemberg* [1984] ECR 2639, paragraph 15; Case C-332/90 *Steen* v *Deutsche Bundespost* [1992] ECR 1–341, paragraph 9; and Case C-19/92 *Kraus* v *Land-Baden-Wütemberg* [1993] ECR I-1663, paragraph 15), the provisions of the Treaty concerning the free movement of workers, and particularly Article 48, cannot be applied to situations which are wholly internal to a Member State, in other words where there is no factor connecting them to any of the situations envisaged by Community law.

90   However, it is clear from the findings of fact made by the national court that Mr Bosman had entered into a contract of employment with a club in another Member State with a view to exercising gainful employment in that State. By so doing, as he has rightly pointed out, he accepted an offer of employment actually made, within the meaning of Article 48(3)(a).

91   Since the situation in issue in the main proceedings cannot be classified as purely internal, the argument put forward by UEFA must be dismissed.

Existence of an obstacle to freedom of movement for workers
92   It is thus necessary to consider whether the transfer rules form an obstacle to freedom of movement for workers prohibited by Article 48 of the Treaty.

93   As the Court has repeatedly held, freedom of movement for workers is one of the fundamental principles of the Community and the Treaty

provisions guaranteeing that freedom have had direct effect since the end of the transitional period.

94   The Court has also held that the provisions of the Treaty relating to freedom of movement for persons are intended to facilitate the pursuit by Community citizens of occupational activities of all kinds throughout the Community, and preclude measures which might place Community citizens at a disadvantage when they wish to pursue an economic activity in the territory of another Member State (see Case 143/87 *Stanton* v *INASTI* [1988] ECR 3877, paragraph 13, and Case C-370/90 *The Queen* v *Immigration Appeal Tribunal and Surinder Singh* [1992] ECR 1–4265 paragraph 16).

95   In that context, nationals of Member States have in particular the right which they derive directly from the Treaty, to leave their country of origin to enter the territory of another Member State and reside there in order there to pursue an economic activity (see, *inter alia,* Case C-363/89 *Roux* v *Belgium* [1991] ECR 1–273, paragraph 9 . . .

96   Provisions which preclude or deter a national of a Member State from leaving his country of origin in order to exercise his right to freedom of movement therefore constitute an obstacle to that freedom even if they apply without regard to the nationality of the workers concerned (see also Case C-10/90 *Masgio* v *Bundesknappschaft* [1991] ECR 1–1119, paragraphs 18 and 19) . . .

98   It is true that the transfer rules in issue in the main proceedings apply also to transfers of players between clubs belonging to different national associations within the same Member State and that similar rules govern transfers between clubs belonging to the same national association.

99   However, as has been pointed out by Mr Bosman, by the Danish Government and by the Advocate General in points 209 and 210 of his Opinion, those rules are likely to restrict the freedom of movement of players who wish to pursue their activity in another Member State by preventing or deferring them from leaving the clubs to which they belong even after the expiry of their contracts of employment with those clubs.

100   Since they provide that a professional footballer may not pursue his activity with a new club established in another Member State unless it has paid his former club a transfer fee agreed upon between the two clubs or determined in accordance with the regulations of the sporting associations, the said rules constitute an obstacle to freedom of movement for workers.

103   It is sufficient to note that, although the rules in issue in the main proceedings apply also to transfer between clubs belonging to different national associations within the same Member State and are similar to those governing transfers between clubs belonging to the same national association, they still directly affect players' access to the employment market in other Member States and are thus capable of impeding freedom of movement for workers. They cannot, thus, be deemed comparable to the rules on selling arrangements for goods which in *Keck and Mithouard* [Cases C-267/91 and

C-268/91 [1993] ECR 1–6097] were held to fall outside the ambit of Article 30 of the Treaty (see also, with regard to freedom to provide services, Case C-384/93 *Alpine Investments* v *Minister van Financiën* [1995] ECR 1–1141, paragraphs 36 to 38).

104   Consequently, the transfer rules constitute an obstacle to freedom of movement for workers prohibited in principle by Article 48 of the Treaty. It could only be otherwise if those rules pursued a legitimate aim compatible with the Treaty and were justified by pressing reasons of public interest. But even if that were so, application of those rules would still have to be such as to ensure achievement of the aim in question and not go beyond what is necessary for that purpose (see, *inter alia, the judgment in* Kraus, cited above, paragraph 32, and Case C-55/94 *Gebhard* [1995] ECR 1–4165, paragraph 37).

Existence of justifications
105   First, URBSFA, UEFA and the French and Italian Governments have submitted that the transfer rules are justified by the need to maintain a financial and competitive balance between clubs and to support the search for talent and the training of young players.

106   In view of the considerable social importance of sporting activities and in particular football in the Community, the aims of maintaining a balance between clubs by preserving a certain degree of quality and uncertainty as to results and of encouraging the recruitment and training of young players must be accepted as legitimate.

107   As regards the first of those aims, Mr Bosman has rightly pointed out that the application of the transfer rules is not an adequate means of maintaining financial and competitive balance in the world of football. Those rules neither preclude the richest clubs from securing the services of the best players nor prevent the availability of financial resources from being a decisive factor in competitive sport, thus considerably altering the balance between clubs.

108   As regards the second aim, it must be accepted that the prospect of receiving transfer, development or training fees is indeed likely to encourage football clubs to seek new talent and train young players.

109   However, because it is impossible to predict the sporting future of young players with any certainty and because only a limited number of such players go on to play professionally, those fees are by nature contingent and uncertain and are in any event unrelated to the actual cost borne by clubs of training both future professional players and those who will never play professionally. The prospect of receiving such fees cannot, therefore, be either a decisive factor in encouraging recruitment and training of young players or an adequate means of financing such activities, particularly in the case of smaller clubs.

110   Furthermore, as the Advocate General has pointed out in point 226 et seq. of his Opinion, the same aims can be achieved at least as efficiently by other means which do not impede freedom of movement for workers.

111   It has also been argued that the transfer rules are necessary to safeguard the worldwide organisation of football.

112   However, the present proceedings concern application of those rules within the Community and not the relations between the national associations of the Member States and those of non-member countries. In any event, application of different rules to transfers between the clubs belonging to national associations within the Community and to transfers between such clubs and those affiliated to the national associations of non-member countries is unlikely to pose any particular difficulties. As is clear from paragraphs 22 and 23 above, the rules which have so far governed transfers within the national associations of certain Member States are different from those which apply at the international level.

113   Finally, the argument that the rules in question are necessary to compensate clubs for the expenses which they have had to incur in paying fees on recruiting their players cannot be accepted, since it seeks to justify the maintenance of obstacles to freedom of movement for workers simply on the grounds that such obstacles were able to exist in the past.

114   The answer to the first question must therefore be that Article 48 of the Treaty precludes the application of rules laid down by sporting associations, under which a professional footballer who is a national of one Member State may not, on the expiry of his contract with a club, be employed by a club of another Member State unless the latter club has paid to the former club a transfer, training or development fee.

On those grounds,

THE COURT,

in answer to the questions referred to it by the Court d'Appel, Liège, by judgment of 1 October 1993, hereby rules:

1.   Article 48 of the EEC Treaty precludes the application of rules laid down by sporting associations, under which a professional footballer who is a national of one Member State may not, on the expiry of his contract with a club, be employed by a club of another Member State unless the latter club has paid to the former club a transfer, training or development fee.

2.   Article 48 of the EEC Treaty precludes the application of rules laid down by sporting associations under which, in matches in competitions which they organize, football clubs may field only a limited number of professional players who are nationals of other Member States.

Questions:
1.   Do you agree with the ECJ's ruling that the transfer system breached Article 48 (now 39).

2.   Analyse the ECJ's interpretation of Article 48 (now 39) of the EC Treaty. How does it compare with interpretation in the English courts?

3. Is sport essentially an 'economic activity', appropriate for regulation by EC law? Does the ECJ's need to conceptualise Bosman's case as 'economic' affect the content or approach of the Court in its judgment?

4. Do you think that the ECJ gave sufficient weight to the justification arguments? (See P Morris, S Morrow and P Spink 'EC Law and Professional Football: Bosman and its Implications' (1996) vol. 59 *Modern Law Review* 87.)

5. Would the development of European Community law be aided if provision was made for judges of the ECJ to give dissenting opinions?

In this chapter we have sought to explore judicial approaches to interpreting statutes. It is becoming increasingly apparent that approaches to statutory interpretation must now be considered in the light of the United Kingdom's membership of two supranational legal orders — the European Union and the Council of Europe. To sum up your understanding of statutory interpretation write short answers to the following questions:

Questions:
1. How much scope for choice and creativity do judges (and lawyers) have in interpreting statutes? What does it mean to say that lawyers are wordsmiths?

2. To what extent (if at all) do you think that the United Kingdom's membership of the European Union has affected the approach of British judges to statutory interpretation?

3. How would you summarise the likely impact of the Human Rights Act 1998 on the process of statutory interpretation?

Chapter 4

Facts

The lists of skills with which we began this book include references to the identification and evaluation of facts. Yet law schools traditionally present their students with only the 'relevant' facts as stated in case headnotes. It is not until their experience in legal practice or other jobs that they will 'separate rapidly the relevant from the irrelevant' in a mass of facts. They may never be asked to reflect upon what *is* a 'fact'.

There are plausible reasons for the conventional practice and there are also many unsatisfactory explanations. In this chapter, we aim to stimulate interest among students and teachers alike in the skill of sifting 'facts'.

RELEVANCE OF FACTS

Legal actions begin with people's stories from which the lawyer distils the relevant facts. If the case goes to court, the judge will further condense the facts in the judgment. If the case is reported, a headnote will précis the facts again. But each stage of this process is problematic. How do we know what is 'relevant'?

Suppose that a court is asked to sterilise a 35 year-old, red-haired, mentally disabled woman whose mental age is 5 and who is involved in a sexual relationship with another mentally disabled patient at an institution under the care of the state. Is the fact that her hair is red relevant? What about her age (physical or mental)? You can read about such a case in *Re F* [1989] 2 All ER 545. Suppose that the judges have edited out a further fact, that her sexual partner is also involved in sexual relationships with five other patients at their institution? Is this relevant? Why might the judges have omitted the fact? Should the man be sterilised? Should all sexual conduct be prevented by the authorities?

Alan Dershowitz has compared the presentation of a legal case to the editing of a film.

A Dershowitz, *Reversal of Fortune: Inside the von Bulov case*, London, Penguin (1991), p. xxi.

A legal case is somewhat like a long unedited film containing thousands of frames, only a small portion of which ultimately appear on the screen as part of the finished product. The role of the legal system — police, prosecutor, defense lawyer, judge — is to edit the film for trial: to determine what is relevant for the jury to see, and what should end up on the cutting-room floor. How far back in time should the evidence go? How much detail should be included? Who should appear in supporting roles?

Questions:
1.   What influences a film-maker as to what to include or omit?

2.   Should a lawyer be influenced by different factors or give them different weight?

3.   Does it matter who the lawyer is, or should all the lawyers in a case present the same facts in the same way, in the interests of justice?

If it is 'facts' which are being edited, does this mean that lawyers decide cases on the basis not so much of 'the facts' as on a selective version of what happened? An American academic and judge, Jerome Frank, has been described as a 'fact-sceptic'.

Frank J, *Courts on Trial*, Princeton, New Jersey, Princeton University Press (1973), pp. 14–15, 20–22.

If you scrutinize a legal rule, you will see that it is a conditional statement referring to facts. Such a rule seems to say, in effect, 'If such and such a fact exists, then this or that legal consequence should follow'. It seems to say, for example, 'If a trustee for his own purposes, uses money he holds in trust, he must repay it'. Or, 'If a man, without provocation, kills another, the killer must be punished'. In other words, a legal rule directs that (if properly asked to do so) a court should attach knowable consequences to certain facts, if and whenever there are such facts. That is what is meant by the conventional statement, used in describing the decisional process, that courts apply legal rules to the facts of law-suits.

For convenience, let us symbolize a legal rule by the letter R, the facts of a case by the letter F, and the court's decision of that case by the letter D. We can then crudely schematize the conventional theory of how courts operate by saying

$$R \times F = D$$

In other words, according to the conventional theory, a decision is a product of an R and an F. If, as to any lawsuit, you know the R and the F, you should, then, know what the D will be.

In a simple, stable, society, most of the R's are moderately well stabilized. Which legal rules that society will enforce it is not difficult for men — or at any rate, for the lawyer, the professional court-man — to know in advance of any trial. In such a society, the R — one of the two factors in the $R \times F = D$ formula — is usually fixed.

In our society, however, with the rapid·changes brought about by modern life, many of the R's have become unstable. Accordingly, in our times, legal uncertainty — uncertainty about future decisions and therefore about legal rights — is generally ascribed to the indefiniteness of the R's. The increasing multiplicity of the rules, the conflicts between rules, and the flexibility of some of the rules, have arrested the attention of most legal thinkers. Those thinkers, perceiving the absence of rigidity in some rules, have assumed that the certainty or uncertainty of the D's, in the $R \times F = D$ equation, stems principally from the certainty or uncertainty of the R's.

That assumption leads to a grave miscomprehension of court-house government and to the neglect by most legal scholars of the more difficult part of the courts' undertaking. I refer to the courts' task with respect to the other factor in the $R \times F = D$ formula, the F. The courts, as we saw, are supposed to ascertain the facts in the disputes which become law suits. That is, a court is supposed to determine the actual, objective acts of the parties, to find out just what they did or did not do, before the law-suit began, so far as those facts bear on the compliance with, or the violation of, some legal rule. If there is uncertainty as to whether the court will find the true relevant facts — if it is uncertain whether the court's F will match the real, objective F — then what? Then, since the decision, the D, is presumably the joint product of an R and an F, the D is bound to be uncertain. To put it differently: No matter how certain the legal rules may be, the decisions remain at the mercy of the courts' fact-finding. If there is doubt about what a court, in a law-suit, will find were the facts, then there is at least equal doubt about its decision. . . .

The axiom or assumption that, in all or most trials, the truth will out, ignores, then, the several elements of subjectivity and chance. It ignores perjury and bias; ignores the false impression made on the judge or jury by the honest witness who seems untruthful because he is frightened in the court-room or because he is irascible or over-scrupulous or given to exaggeration. It ignores the mistaken witness who honestly and convincingly testifies that he remembers acts or conversations that happened quite differently than as he narrates them in court. It neglects, also, the dead or missing witness without whose testimony a crucial fact cannot be brought out, or an important opposing witness cannot be successfully contradicted. Finally it neglects the missing or destroyed letter, or receipt, or cancelled check.

Nor is it true that trial courts will be sure to detect lies or mistakes in testimony. That is clearly not so when a jury tries a case. Many experienced persons believe that of all the possible ways that could be devised to get at the falsity or truth of testimony, none could be conceived that would be more ineffective than trial by jury.

Judges, too, when they try cases without juries, are often fallible in getting at the true facts of a 'contested' case. Partly that is due to our faulty way of trying cases in which we hamstring the judge. But even with the best system that could be devised, there would be no way to ensure that the judge will know infallibly which witnesses are accurately reporting the facts. As yet we have no lie-detector for which all responsible psychologists will vouch and which most courts will regard as reliable. But even a perfect lie detector will not reveal mistakes in a witness' original observation of the facts to which he testifies, and probably will not disclose his mistakes due to his unconscious prejudices. . . .

The facts as they actually happened are therefore twice refracted first by the witnesses, and second by those who must 'find' the facts. The reactions of trial judges or juries to the testimony are shot through with subjectivity. Thus we have subjectivity piled on subjectivity. It is surely proper, then, to say that the facts as 'found' by a trial court are subjective.

When Jack Spratt, as a witness, testifies to a fact, he is merely stating his belief or opinion about that past fact. When he says, 'I saw McCarthy hit Schmidt', he means, 'I believe that is what happened'. When a trial judge or jury, after hearing that testimony, finds as a fact that McCarthy hit Schmidt, the finding means no more than the judge's or jury's belief that the belief of the witness Spratt is an honest belief, and that his belief accurately reflects what actually happened. A trial court's finding of fact is, then, at best, its belief or opinion about someone else's belief or opinion.

Question:
1. In what ways could the fact-finding facilities of the legal system be improved? (For further discussion of the role of juries see Chapter 9.)

A scholar has put the problems of facts in this way . . .

J D Jackson, 'Law's Truth, Lay Truth and Lawyers' Truth: The Representation of Evidence in Adversary Trials', *Law and Critique* (1992), vol. III, no. 1, pp. 29–49 at pp. 43–45 (references omitted).

More recently scholars have refined the notion that truth is reached by reliance on first-hand observation evidence and common sense generalisations, by recognising the importance of story-telling in adversarial trials. Bennett and Feldman in particular have argued that the American criminal trial is organised around story-telling. In their study of how cases are presented in criminal trials, they have argued that trial participants and jurors typically use stories to organise the evidence that is presented to them. The plausibility of a story is assessed by comparing the content of the story told with other stories which form the stock of social knowledge of the jury. They concede that jurors do not carry around a whole stock of substantive stories as concrete and detailed as the stories told in court but claim it is the implicit structures of stories which enable people to make comparisons. The plausibility of a story will thus depend on its structure as a whole and not on its truth in the sense of the extent to which it corresponds to reality.

The importance of stories is now generally accepted but there is argument over the relation between stories and the evidence in the case. To some, stories merely fill in gaps in the evidence. Others such as Bennett and Feldman see stories as more than just gap fillers but they still see a role for evidence. They see evidence as exercising some constraint over the possible stories that can emerge in a case.

. . .

Inspired by Bennett and Feldman's ideas of story-telling and imbued with the idea that the essence of trial proceedings is their oral nature, trial manuals now consider it important that lawyers tell a good story. Much attention is paid to the importance of developing an overall theory of the case, in selecting a theme to fit that theory and then in thinking how to present all the available data at the trial. The theory of the case is the best explanation of all the information to date which indicates that logically the claims made should succeed. Along with the development of a theory, a theme must be selected which goes beyond logic but is designed to influence the trier of fact to accept the theory. Manuals refer to themes based on moral generalisation, designed to show moral force is on the side of the advocate. But fictional accounts of constructing cases also refer to latent messages. The protagonist in Scott Turow's best-selling novel, *Presumed Innocent*, says that a trial lawyer always has a latent message to the jury, too prejudicial or improper to speak aloud, whether it is a racist appeal when black victims identify white defendants or the no big deal manner that is taken when a case is only an attempt.

The trial lawyer has an excellent opportunity of presenting his or her theory and theme in the opening speech and here it is often convenient to present the arguments in the form of a story. But the lawyer must then substantiate the claims made in dramatic form, and at this stage the emphasis switches from story-telling to drama. The bare scripts, the written statements of the various actors, have to be transformed into the action of a play, and to do this the lawyer will have available not only the actors or witnesses who made the statement but a whole host of other kinds of evidence — trial exhibits, original and copy documents, maps, photographs, tables, lists, drawings, plans, etc — all the visual props that go to make up the play. With all of this the advocate has to prepare a number of scenes to enact the events required to substantiate the claims made. The order of these events is often determined by convention, sometimes called the order of proof. So prosecutors in criminal trials will first depict the scene of the crime to establish that the crime has been committed and from this beginning they will depict the various scenes of investigation that led up to the incrimination of the accused, leading often at the end to a confession. In Turow's book, the state case began with the murder scene and the collection of physical evidence and proceeded with a slow, gradually accelerating demonstration of why the accused was the murderer. Of course, the advocate cannot conjure up these scenes alone. They have to be produced in the courtroom atmosphere with the aid of witnesses and other visual props. The play of the trial, the courtroom drama, will thus determine how successful the advocate is in constructing the scenes of his or her play.

The characterisation of courtroom interaction in terms of drama and theatre rather than in terms of stories helps to emphasise the importance of the visual over the oral. Evidence in criminal trials operates on two visual levels, what might be called the physical and the mental. The physical evidence some-times called the real evidence, consists of what triers see in the courtroom — the exhibits, the documents, the maps, photographs and the demeanour of the witnesses. The witness box represents the central stage for this evidence but the geography of the rest of the stage cannot be ignored. There is the elevated position of the judge and the demeaning position of the accused in the dock. There is also the position of the advocates and the way their relationship with witnesses and the judge is viewed. Much attention is given in trial manuals to the way counsel should deport themselves so as to convey an impression of competence and trust: know what your face is doing, be the honest guide, maintain your status, look at the jury when making a point, convey an impression of belief in the case, etc.

Questions:
1. How difficult does the substantive law and the law of evidence make it for defendants (or their lawyers) to convey their narratives to the jury?

2. When you read the extracts about the O.J. Simpson case (below) what do you think the latent messages (if any) to the jury were?

3. Would you agree with the proposition that a jury deciding a criminal case has three tasks: what to believe about the facts, what the law is, how to apply the latter to the former? If so, would you agree that 'the facts' themselves are the least important element in the first task, as compared with the perspectives (prejudices, bias?) of the jurors and their understanding of the catch-phrases of the law such as 'presumption of innocence' and 'proof beyond reasonable doubt'?

S Turow, *Presumed Innocent*, London, Penguin (1987), pp. 229–230.

Larren starts by telling the venire what the case is about. He has probably seen a thousand juries chosen during his career. His rapport is instantaneous: this big, good-looking black man, kind of funny, kind of smart. The white people take to him too, thinking, probably, they all should be like this. Nowhere in a trial is Larren's advantage to the defense likely to be greater than at this juncture. He is skilled in addressing juries, canny in divining hidden motivations, and committed to the foundation of his soul to the fundamental notions. The defendant is presumed innocent. Innocent. As you sit here you have gotta be thinking Mr Sabich didn't do it.
'I'm sorry, sir. In the first row, what is your name?'
'Mahalovich.'
'Mr Mahalovich. Did Mr Sabich commit the crime that he is charged with?'
Mahalovich, a stout middle-aged man who has his paper folded in his lap, shrugs.
'I wouldn't know, Judge.'
'Mr Mahalovich, you are excused. Ladies and gentlemen, let me tell you again what you are to presume. Mr Sabich is innocent. I am the judge. I am

telling you that. Presume he is innocent. When you sit there, I want you to look over and say to yourself, 'There sits an innocent man.'

It is possible to only pick up part of the whole story in any legal saga which is presented to us. If we rely on the judgment of Lord Denning MR in *Miller* v *Jackson* [1977] 3 All ER 338, CA for example, we would not know all the facts of that particular dispute between cricketers and their neighbours. (See W Twining, *Rethinking Evidence*, Oxford, Basil Blackwell (1990), pp. 235–277 or B Jackson, *Law, Fact and Narrative Coherence* (1989), pp. 94–97.) If a student relies on a digest, or the headnote to a case, there is even more room for a partial picture to be mistaken for the whole. One of the most important legal skills, then, is to respect the importance of the facts to any issue, to be sceptical of claims that this or that constitutes 'the facts' and to remember that the legal system has been embarrassed by many mistakes over many years in assessing 'the facts'.

Although the issue of facts is rarely considered in cases which you read at law school, which are generally appellate level cases where the facts are treated as settled and debates are about the applicable law, in most trials the disputed issue concerns the facts. When you go to court, try to estimate what percentage of cases turn on facts rather than law (though note also the difficulties in separating out issues of fact, law and morality — see the extract from John Jackson below at p. 158.)

CONTESTED FACTS

Two recent high profile trials in the United States have indicated the difficulties courts face in determining the facts of complex cases. First, the OJ Simpson case (which we considered briefly in Chapter 1 at pp. 20-23) demonstrated the difficulties juries face when dealing with disputed scientific evidence, especially when this is coupled with race and gender issues. Much of the 'factual' evidence depended on blood samples allegedly found at the scene of the crime. However, the defence case suggested that given the documented racism of the Los Angeles Police Department there must be at least a reasonable doubt concerning the evidence, since the police officers would have had opportunity to plant it.

A Ross, 'If the Genes Fit, How Do You Acquit? O.J. and Science' in T Morrison and C Brodsky Lacour (eds) *Birth of a Nationhood: Gaze, Script and Spectacle in the O.J. Simpson Case*, London, Vintage (1997), pp. 241–72, at pp. 256–9 (references omitted).

In recent years, genetic information has become a tool for decision making in a variety of legal fields — torts, criminal, trust, and estate law — and is increasingly used as a defence on grounds of genetic predisposition. Despite its promise of absolute precision and irrefutable truth — its 'aura of infallibility' as a Massachusetts Supreme Court decision put it — DNA evidence is commonly introduced in the form of quantified probability. For example, in the Simpson matter, the odds of some of the blood samples [found at the scene] matching any African American or Caucasian other than OJ were estimated as high as one in 170 million, and one in 6.8 billion Caucasians in the case of the genetic markers matching Nicole and Ron [the victims]. These astronomical odds, however much they varied from estimate to estimate (another put the Nicole odds, in the case of a particular blood sample, at one in twenty-one billion) conveyed the message that you 'can't argue' with such numbers. How could OJ possibly be innocent, given these odds? Such statistics carry the patina of irrefutable truth in a manner that tends to outweigh other kinds of evidence, like those supporting the motive in the murder charge by reference to the history of spousal abuse. Indeed, these odds were frequently cited in the courtroom of public opinion as overwhelming confirmation that science had proved OJ's guilt, and that the jury had disregarded science and, in Buckley's words, the whole of modern epistemology. These are false and perilous assumptions.

In a classic 1971 article, 'Trial by Mathematics' (long before DNA evidence became a controversial factor in legal adjudication), Lawrence Tribe summarised the problems raised by the practice of using statistical methods to resolve conflicting claims in lawsuits. Even if it were desirable for the legal system to defer to quantitative reasoning, Tribe asserts that statistical proofs 'decrease the likelihood of accurate outcomes' in trial. The impact of introducing statistical evidence to a jury's prior probability assessment of a defendant's guilt has a distorting effect, rendering an inference of guilt that is much greater than the evidence warrants. The hard, quantitative evidence will dwarf other 'soft variables' like impressionistic evidence, according to Tribe, and will indubitably warp the jurors' obligation to weigh all the evidence evenly. If the statistical assessment is introduced early, it is difficult for jurors not to focus on these over-impressive numbers, and hence the presumption of innocence is often thrown out before defendants have had their full say. So, too, the probability values attached to variables, such as estimating the risk of a frame-up, or an error in testimony, are something that only individual jurors can assign, and so, to give mathematical proofs full credence, each juror would have to be able to compute their own complex equations, involving hard and soft variables, to guarantee the accuracy of the outcomes. In addition, the authoritative weight of statistics harm the chances of a peer community's accepting a defendant's acquittal (in OJ's case, this community would presumably be his white neighbours in Brentwood and not downtown African Americans). Finally, Tribe argues that the use of statistics threatens to alter the entire character of the trial process itself, imposing standards unconvincing to the 'untutored contemporary intuition,' making the legal system appear 'even more alien and inhuman than it already does,' and undermining its responsibility to protecting the defendant's rights as a person.

Given its 'aura of infallibility,' many believe that the subsequent introduction of DNA evidence in the courts has only exacerbated these problems and has further eroded defendants' rights, especially when the defendant's resources are too meagre to muster counterevidence. OJ's privilege in this regard is truly exceptional, but it proved, nonetheless, *contra* Tribe, that a successful defence can be mounted against an overwhelming array of quantitative evidence. The larger flaw with Tribe's argument, however, is its assumption that quantitative evidence and reasoning arise at the outset from value-free knowledge. It is easy to conclude then that methodologies of scientific reasoning and the adversarial procedures of the legal system are difficult to reconcile. The one aims at isolating absolute truths that are irrefutable in any time or place, the other expresses the relationship between the individual and the state as defined by civil principles and rights that pledge respect for defendants as persons. As Marjorie Maguire Schultz puts it, 'science deals in particulars in order to determine generalisations, law deals in generalisations in order to determine particularities.' The legal process is supposed to resolve conflicts often involving the full coercive power of the state, in ways that protect individual rights and in accord with normative community values. The quantitative reasoning of science is not well suited to taking these values or rights into account. In times like the present, when civil rights and community values are under siege from social conservatives, scientific diagnoses in the service of law enforcement and legal adjudication have a particularly strong appeal to those swayed by right-wing ideas. Under these coercive circumstances, the trust in lay judgement, underpinned in part by a particularly American scepticism regarding the authority of experts, comes under fire.

But this acknowledged conflict between science's truth and the law's social wisdom assumes that the domain of science is indeed value-free, and sequestered from the social interests of those institutions in government and law and commerce that exercise their authority through the use of scientific knowledge or expertise. A large body of scholarly literature in science studies has challenged this view and has demonstrated that science is no less shaped by social interest than any other field of knowledge. The story about DNA profiling is no exception. It shows how the law enforcement system defines goals for researchers to deliver very particular kinds of knowledge. In a field largely created by the FBI, the direction of DNA forensic research has been wholly governed by the cliental needs of the Justice Department, while the vulnerability of its commercial and police laboratory environments has been fully exposed, and the infallibility of its scientific claims has been hotly contested. Indeed, the meaning of these claims is sufficiently contingent that the probative value of DNA evidence invariably has to be established in the courtroom through lengthy reviews of, or appeals to, the whole peer-review apparatus of scientific and legal literature, as was the case in the OJ trial. Scientific knowledge, as Sheila Jasanoff concludes in *Science at the Bar*, is not a simple ancillary to the legal process, waiting to be employed in the pursuit of truth. In many instances, it is highly provisional knowledge, while its authority emerges out of the courtroom battle to prove that the claims of one side's experts are more contingent than the claims of the other side's experts. *People* v *Simpson* was a dramatic demonstration of this process.

Questions:
1. What precisely does Ross object to about the manner in which DNA evidence was used in the OJ Simpson case?

2.   Is the thrust of the argument here that DNA evidence should never be used in a criminal case? Is this because the jury is unable to understand it or will be unduly influenced by it? (Note that some of the actual jurors contested press criticism that they disregarded or failed to understand the expert testimony.)

For a fuller discussion of the issues involved see D Balding and P Donnelly, 'The Prosecutor's Fallacy and DNA Evidence', *Criminal Law Review* (1994), pp. 711–721.

The next major US case to involve a televised trial which attracted world-wide attention was that of 19-year-old British au pair Louise Woodward, who was charged with murdering the infant for whom she was nanny in Boston, allegedly by shaking him too violently in order to quieten him. Again the difficulty of evaluating conflicting scientific evidence was a feature of this trial. Louise Woodward was initially convicted of murder by the jury, but the judge subsequently found her guilty only of manslaughter.

There follow some extracts relating to the medical evidence which were posted as daily highlights of the trial on the Internet:

Commonwealth v *Louise Woodward* (Commonwealth of Massachusetts, Superior Court, Criminal No. 97–0433).
[http://www.courttv.com/trials.woodward/week 2.html]

14 October 1997
Dr Lois Smith, the ophthalmologist who reviewed Matthew Eappen's eye examination and autopsy report, returned to the stand. She continued to maintain her belief that the infant's injuries could not have been caused by anything other than shaken baby impact syndrome. According to Smith, the force of the shaking and the impact with which the infant's head allegedly slammed against a hard surface was the equivalent of a truck hitting an infant in a baby carriage. Smith also said that injuries that caused Matthew's death were inflicted between minutes and hours before he was admitted to Children's Hospital in Boston.

During his cross-examination of Dr Smith, defense attorney Barry Scheck [who also defended OJ Simpson] suggested that a drawing of Matthew's eyes done at the time of his examination does not show the retinal haemorrhaging that Smith had said resulted from violent shaking. In a major concession, Smith admitted that if this drawing is correct, then her theory about the infant dying from shaken baby syndrome is wrong. However, Smith preferred to characterize the drawing as 'incomplete' rather than inaccurate . . .

Dr Stacey Linwood, Matthew Eappen's paediatrician, testified that Matthew seemed to be a normal, healthy baby with no unusual injuries. However, Linwood, who was the baby's doctor since he was two-weeks-old, said that Matthew suffered a subdural haematoma during birth. (A subdural haematoma is a mass of clotted blood that forms in brain tissue as a result of a broken blood vessel.) But, Linwood said, this injury was common among infants, and Matthew's subdural haematoma healed within a month after his birth. During cross-examination Linwood admitted that she had last examined

Matthew when he was six-months-old. (Matthew was eight-and-a-half months old when he died.) Linwood was not scheduled to examine the baby again until he was nine-months-old, and she said she did not know what he experienced between his last examination and the time of his death . . .

October 15
Dr Eli Newberger, a paediatrician who examined Matthew Eappen at Children's Hospital on the day of the alleged incident with defendant Louise Woodward, testified that he firmly believed that Matthew was a victim of shaken baby syndrome. Newberger said that the injuries the infant sustained were inflicted and that none of the injuries could have occurred accidentally.

'My opinion is that this child was violently shaken for a prolonged period,' Newberger said. 'This shaking was to such a violent degree that it would have required as much energy as an adult could muster, sustained over a period of time up to or exceeding a minute, possibly delivered in intervals.

According to Newberger, Matthew's [prognosis] was grim and he would have become comatose almost immediately after the infliction of his injuries.

'There was effectively no neurological function . . . I believe his [Matthew's] condition was irreversible,' Newberger told the jury. 'I believe that on February 9 [the day the infant was removed from life support] this child was brain dead as a result of neurological trauma. My opinion is that all of the injuries are attributable to child abuse.'

Defense attorney Barry Scheck challenged Newberger's theories during cross-examination. Dr Newberger refused to change his belief that the force needed to inflict Matthew Eappen's head injuries would be the equivalent of a child falling out of a second storey window onto concrete. Newberger said that Matthew's injuries occurred shortly before he arrived at the hospital.
However, Newberger did admit to Scheck that he is not an expert in radiology, ophthalmology, biomechanics. Much of the cross-examination exchange between Newberger and Scheck appeared confrontational, with Newberger at times accusing Scheck of distorting his testimony. And, despite his certainty that Matthew suffered from shaken baby syndrome, Newberger told Scheck that he would change his opinion if there was neuro-pathological evidence that the infant suffered from head injuries weeks before his February 4 incident with Woodward.
Then the mother of Matthew Eappen, Deborah Eappen, an ophthalmologist, took the stand . . . When Mrs Eappen saw Matthew in the hospital and examined his eyes with a special instrument, she saw extensive retinal haemorrhaging, a sign of shaken baby syndrome.

'I knew what that meant,' Mrs Eappen said. 'I was shocked . . . I couldn't believe it.'

The most emotional part of Deborah Eappen's testimony came when she described her son's five days in the hospital on life support and his last moments alive after being removed from life support.

'We [members of the Eappen family] all took turns holding Matthew,' she said. We played children's music, we lit my grandmother's candle, and we prayed . . . And then Matty died.'

Questions:

1.   Do you think that juries are capable of disregarding the emotional force of testimony like Deborah Eappen's, and simply evaluating the facts? Are judges? (For more on jury decision-making, see Chapter 9 at pp. 334–52.)

2.   Given the disagreement amongst medical experts about shaken baby syndrome, and their conflicting accounts as summarised above, do you think a jury is likely to be capable of evaluating the facts? (Note that, in this case also, some of the jurors themselves contested press criticism that they failed to understand the evidence when they convicted Woodward of second degree murder.)

3.   Do you think it represents (a) good tactics, (b) good ethics for a lawyer to question an expert witness aggressively? (For further discussion of Scheck as an advocate in this trial, see Chapter 6 at p. 202.)

The judge, in his summing-up in the case, dealt with the issue of conflicts in evidence, and the jury's role:

Commonwealth v *Louise Woodward* (Commonwealth of Massachusetts, Superior Court, Criminal No. 97–0433)
[http://www.courttv.com/trials.woodward/zobel.html].

Zobel J
Reduced to its appropriately bare essentials, this case turns on diametrically opposed theories of ultimate causation. Both sides agreed that Matthew Eappen died from massive intra-cranial bleeding. The prosecution's experts attributed the haemorrhage to a combination of extraordinarily violent shaking and overpowering contact with a hard flat surface, all occurring some time on February 4, 1997; the defense experts ascribed the haemorrhage to a 're-bleed' in a clot formed about three weeks earlier following a hitherto undetected injury.

The government buttressed the scientific evidence with testimony that the baby had been normal earlier in the day; that the Defendant had been the only adult in his presence throughout; and that she had admitted to police that she had been 'a little rough' with him when putting him on a bed, bathing him and placing him on the bathroom floor.

The defence relied for rejoinder entirely on the testimony of Defendant herself, who denied handling the child in an inappropriately vigorous manner, although she admitted that perhaps she had 'not been as gentle as I might have been' with Matthew.

Thus stripped of the jargon-filled overlay with which both sides filled the record, the issue for the jury's determination was simply: Did the government prove beyond a reasonable doubt that Matthew Eappen died because Defendant shook him and battered him against an unyielding object? Put another way: Did the defense evidence create a reasonable doubt that the death resulted from some other cause?

It is essential to understand that at no time was Defendant obliged to *prove* anything. The jurors were never required to choose between competing explanations. If the government's theory failed to win them over, beyond a reasonable doubt, their inquiry was complete; the defense's inability (if inability it was) to explain Matthew's injuries and their cause would make no difference.

The law never, in any way, demanded of Defendant that she provide a jury-satisfying answer to any question, whether medical (how old was the fatal haemorrhage?) or physical (what had Defendant done to Matthew?).

Questions:
1. Would the prosecution and defence have been able to avoid 'jargon-filled overlay' in this case?

2. Do you think that the fierce criticism of the juries in the Simpson and Woodward cases for allegedly misapplying or misunderstanding the facts, really stems from popular misunderstandings about the burden of proof in criminal trials, which is explained at the end of the extract from Judge Zobel's summing up?

Concerns raised by the issue of whether juries understand complex issues, such as the genetic and medical evidence presented in the Simpson and Woodward cases have been heightened by the exposure in recent years of a series of miscarriages of justice. As the following extract shows, facts can also fail to come to light due to deliberate suppression or fabrication of evidence (as well as disrupted scientific evidence).

C Walker and K Starmer (eds), *Justice in Error*, London, Blackstone Press (1993), pp. 2–13.

A miscarriage [of justice] occurs as follows: whenever individuals are treated by the State in breach of their rights; whenever individuals are treated adversely by the State to a disproportionate extent in comparison with the need to protect the rights of others; or whenever the rights of others are not properly protected or vindicated by State action against wrongdoers . . .

Since justice is applied by fallible, prejudiced human beings, miscarriages of justice are inevitable . . . The *Guildford Four* (Hill, Richardson, Conlon and Armstrong) were convicted of pub bombings on behalf of the IRA in Guildford and Woolwich. An appeal against conviction failed in 1977 despite the fact that other IRA defendants awaiting trial had by then claimed responsibility. However, other new evidence was eventually amassed which convinced the Home Secretary to order further investigations and a referral back to the Court of Appeal. Once it was discovered that detectives in the Surrey Police involved in the case had fabricated evidence and suppressed possible exculpatory evidence, the DPP decided not to contest the convictions, which were quashed in 1989. This outcome immediately prompted reconsideration of the *Maguire Seven* case. Suspicion first fell on the Maguire household when Gerard Conlon (one of the *Guildford Four*) made statements to the police that his aunt, Anne Maguire, had taught him to manufacture bombs. The police raided the house, and convictions were obtained mainly on the basis of forensic tests which were said to show traces of nitroglycerine. The Court of Appeal, on a reference back in 1990, grudgingly overturned the convictions because of the possibility that third parties had left the traces in the house and so caused innocent contamination (the non-disclosure of evidence was also a material irregularity in the case). However, the May Inquiry's Interim and Second Reports on the *Maguire* case more realistically cast doubt on whether the tests used and circumstantial evidence could in any event be taken to be conclusive proof of the knowing handling of explosives.

The next blow to confidence in the criminal justice system was the *Birmingham Six* case in 1991. The six (Hill, Hunter, McIlkenny, Power, Walker and Callaghan) had been convicted along with three others of bombings in two Birmingham pubs in 1974. The attacks had caused more deaths than any other IRA incident in Britain and were the signal for the passage of the Prevention of Terrorism Acts. The prosecution evidence rested upon three legs: confessions, which the accused claimed had been beaten out of them; forensic tests, which the accused claimed were inherently unreliable and had been performed unsatisfactorily by Dr Skuse; and highly circumstantial evidence, such as links to known Republicans, their movements and demeanour. After being refused leave to appeal in 1976, the six ploughed a furrow in the civil courts by way of a claim for damages for assault against the police and prison warders. However, their path was eventually blocked by the House of Lords as an abuse of process, since any civil victory would undermine the finality of their criminal conviction. Their focus then switched back to the criminal courts, and their new evidence was referred back to the Court of Appeal in 1988. The Court was then unpersuaded, but further revelations about the police fabrication of statements and new uncertainties about the quality of the forensic tests eventually resulted in their release in 1991. That outcome was swiftly followed by the establishment of the Royal Commission [on Criminal Justice].

The next Irish-related case of relevance is that of Judith Ward, who was convicted in 1974 for delivering the bombs which resulted in 12 deaths on an Army coach travelling along the M62 in Yorkshire. The conviction was once again undermined by the unreliability of the forensic evidence (Skuse's name appears once more) and of the confessions she made (though this time more because of her mental instability than because of police mistreatment of her). In the background were allegations of non-disclosure. Ward's case was referred to the Court of Appeal unilaterally by the Home Office, and she was released in 1992 after the prosecution declined to contest the matter. The Court's judgment was particularly censorious of the non-disclosure of evidence by named forensic scientists and prosecution counsel.

The final case arising from Irish terrorism concerns the *'Armagh Four'* — Latimer, Allen, Bell and Hegan. The four co-accused were members of the UDR who were convicted of the murder in Armagh city of Adrian Carroll, whom they believed to be active in the IRA. Their allegation of injustice arose from three main concerns. First, Latimer pointed to conflicting identification evidence and to oppressive treatment during his police interrogation. Further, it was shown that the police had tampered with the confessions by rewriting some notes, deleting references to requests to see solicitors and attaching false authentications. After referral back to the Court of Appeal in 1992, Allen, Bell and Hegan were all freed on the basis that the police had indeed tampered with the evidence, but Latimer's conviction was not overturned in the light of the identification evidence against him, his confirmation of his admission at the original trial in 1985 and the finding that he had lied to the court.

There are lastly various recently recognised miscarriages which do not relate to Irish terrorism. Most of these cases arise out of the business of the West Midlands Police Serious Crime Squad, whose activities have given rise to 91 complaints about beatings, the fabrication of evidence and denial of access to lawyers. Some of those affected have been released. An investigation into the conduct of the police resulted in the disbandment of the Squad in 1989 but no convictions. Another relevant case is that of the *Tottenham Three* (Silcott, Raghip and Braithwaite), who were convicted of the murder of PC Blakelock during the Broadwater Farm riot in 1985. On a referral back to the Court of Appeal in 1991, it was accepted that notes of the interview had been altered in the case of Silcott, that Raghip's confession was negated by his mental state and that Braithwaite had been unfairly denied a lawyer. Release after an even longer period of imprisonment was also ordered in the case of Kiszko. His conviction for murder was accepted as unsustainable in the light of the medical evidence that he was unable to produce the sperm found on the victim. The handling of this evidence by prosecution counsel also gave rise to concern . . .

Aside from these notorious cases, it is difficult to obtain a complete picture of the number of miscarriages produced overall. In a report in 1989, the organisation JUSTICE estimated that up to 15 defendants per year sentenced to four years or more on indictment have been wrongly convicted. Just over 1 per cent of those convicted on indictment fall into this sentencing band, so the total number of miscarriages in Crown Courts may be well over 1,000 per year, and no attempt has been made to estimate the rate in magistrates' courts where over 90 per cent of cases are heard. More recently, the Society of Prison Officers has estimated that there might be up to 700 innocent persons in prisons after conviction. Likewise, the Home Office has revealed that it receives about 700 to 800 petitions per year. Liberty has recently compiled a dossier of 163 cases which it intends to pursue.

Though they may be a small proportion of the total number of miscarriage cases, the Irish terrorism trials stick out as involving the most profound flaws and as being the most susceptible to error. The reasons for their prominence in this catalogue of cases are probably two-fold. First, special powers in the Prevention of Terrorism Act make abuses easier to commit and more difficult to detect . . . Secondly, miscarriages are in any event more likely because of the nature of these cases, regardless of whether draconian powers are invoked or not. In such prosecutions, the normal due process ideology of the criminal justice system is under pressure, and there is a tendency towards holding a grand 'State' trial. Considerations such as the primacy of the individual and the desire to stack the odds in favour of the innocent in part give way to conflicting goal-based rather than rights-based factors. The goals include the strategy of the criminalisation of terrorists — the policy of the condemnation of the motives and values held by the accused and their kind, together with the reinforcement of the legitimacy of the State. There is also the 'presentational' aspect — the desire to be seen to be taking effective action against terrorists. Even if the action is really worthless, it can still relieve public frustrations and fears. Hence, Lord Denning's comment in response to the *Guildford Four* case that even if the wrong people were convicted, 'the whole community would be satisfied'. These wider societal considerations may also explain why miscarriages seem so hard to remedy. The problem is not simply stubbornness, but that an acquittal becomes particularly costly to the State in terms of damage to its legitimacy and prestige. These same factors may apply to marginalised groups other than Irish Republicans — the black and deprived accused living on Broadwater Farm display many parallels.

The Royal Commission on Criminal Justice, The Runciman Commission, 1993, Cm 2263, was created in the aftermath of some of the cases described above. It concluded, by considering the kind of evidence that students and juries find most compelling, forensic evidence.

56.   It is our belief that, in cases involving scientific evidence, the pre-trial phase should be used to sort out and define as many scientific issues as possible and to consider where appropriate the best means of resolving (for example by further scientific tests) any matters that may be disputed. There will remain matters of disputed interpretation that can only be resolved by the jury. But the objective should be to ensure that, before the issues are presented to the jury, everything possible has been done to clarify the scientific evidence and to indentify the extent of agreement between the expert witnesses on matters of scientific fact and interpretation, or at least to narrow the differences between them.

57.   Of the contested cases covered by the Crown Court Study, a sizeable minority involved scientific evidence. Although participants differed in their assessments of the proportion of cases which involved such evidence, most estimates ranged between 30% and 40%: if these figures are broadly representative, this would mean that there may be some 10,000 or so cases a year in the Crown Court involving some form of scientific evidence. Participants agreed that where there was such evidence it was 'very important' in almost one half of the cases and 'fairly important' in over a third. In

about three-quarters of the total cases, it was not contested because there was no basis for any challenge. According to defence barristers, the evidence went unchallenged in two-thirds even of the 'very important' cases. But there was a defence challenge to the scientific evidence in about a quarter of the cases in which there was scientific evidence. On the basis that this would represent about a quarter of a third of all contested cases it would mean around 2,500 cases a year in the Crown Court. In two-thirds of the cases where there was a challenge, it took the form only of cross-examination of the prosecution expert. In the remainder, which would represent about 800 cases a year, there was both cross-examination and a defence expert was called or that expert's evidence was read to the court. But although a defence expert is called as a witness only relatively rarely, the defence may nevertheless have an expert to assist them both before the trial and during it. In the study by Stevenson, the author reported that although approximately two-thirds of the 34 defence lawyers in her sample had contested DNA evidence in court, expert witnesses had been called by the defence in only three cases.

. . .

59.   It seems to us that, in a minority of cases where the scientific evidence is contested, not enough is done to ensure that the case is properly prepared in a way that will ensure its clearest possible presentation before the jury. It is true that in the cases covered by the Crown Court Study, jurors themselves claimed to have understood the scientific evidence without much difficulty. But if scientific evidence is inaccurate, insufficiently understood, not disclosed, or misinterpreted, a major miscarriage of justice case may ensue with extremely serious consequences for the defendant. We believe therefore that it is very important that measures should be taken to improve the preparation of the minority of cases, however small in percentage terms, in which there is a risk of a miscarriage of justice if the judge, jury and counsel are not able fully to grasp the implications of the scientific evidence and the grounds on which it is disputed.

. . .

70.   We are told by forensic scientists and other expert witnesses that in their view the trial process was ill-suited to the objective presentation of expert evidence. The process of examination and cross-examination is, according to this view, sometimes exploited by skilful counsel in such a way as to give to the evidence a slant that is neither objective nor scientific. Some of the Forensic Science Service (FSS) respondents who participated in the study by Roberts and Wilmore were critical of the fact that counsel for the prosecution were sometimes ill-prepared and did not assist them in bringing out the salient aspects of their evidence. Some also expressed the view that defence lawyers frequently appeared to lack sufficient understanding of scientific evidence to enable them to subject it to adequate scrutiny or to highlight its limitations. We have already stated our firm belief that, where there is a dispute over the scientific evidence, expert witnesses must expect to have their evidence tested in examination and cross-examination in the same way as other witnesses. It cannot be said that, simply because it has been given by an expert, the evidence is necessarily correct or, indeed, credible. Serious

miscarriages of justice may occur if juries are too ready to believe expert evidence or because it is insufficiently tested in court. We believe that the overall aim in this area should be the objective presentation of expert evidence in a way which jurors who are not themselves experts can reasonably be expected to follow.

71. As part of this aim, we recommend that far more use is made of written summaries of such expert evidence as is not contested. All too often, expert evidence is given orally by witnesses in order, it would seem, to enhance the value of the evidence in the eyes of the jury. But where the defence have agreed the evidence, there should be no question of cross-examination and the attendance of the witness and his or her appearance in the box is unnecessary. We have been told that nevertheless some judges insist on the appearance of expert witnesses in such circumstances because they believe that this makes the trial more comprehensible to the jury. We do not, however, agree that such a course is necessary or justified. We therefore recommend that, where the expert evidence is agreed, it should be presented to the jury as clearly as possible, normally by written statement. It would be for counsel to speak to such a statement in their opening and closing speeches.

In the wake of the Runciman Report a new independent body — the Criminal Cases Review Commission — has been established under the Criminal Appeal Act 1995, to deal with alleged miscarriages of justice. After a year in operation it has been swamped with a huge number of applications and already has a backlog of 1000 cases. Over 30 cases have already been referred to the Court of Appeal. The first conviction to be overturned as a result of this process, interestingly was that of Danny McNamee who had been accused, among other things, of being responsible for the IRA's Hyde Park bomb.

Criminal Cases Review Commission, *Information Pack* (1997).

The Royal Commission's report was presented to Parliament in July 1993. It recommended the establishment of an independent body:

to consider suspected miscarriages of justice;

to arrange for their investigation where appropriate; and

to refer cases to the Court of Appeal where the investigation revealed matters that ought to be considered further by the courts.

The Criminal Appeal Act 1995 was subsequently passed, enabling the establishment of the Criminal Cases Review Commission as an executive Non-Departmental Public Body on 1 January 1997. The Commission started handling casework from 31 March 1997.

The Criminal Cases Review Commission has three further responsibilities:

The Court of Appeal may ask the Commission to help in settling an issue which it needs to resolve before it can decide a case;

The Home Secretary can ask the Commission for advice when he is considering advising Her Majesty the Queen to issue a Royal Pardon;

The Commission can refer cases to the Home Secretary where it feels a Royal Pardon should be considered . . .

Before putting time and money into a case, the Commission will need to believe that there is some prospect of discovering one of the following:

In reviews of convictions:
an argument;
or
evidence which was raised earlier in the proceedings;
or
some exceptional circumstances that justify referring the case without nay fresh arguments or evidence.

In reviews of sentences:
a legal argument;
or
information that was not raised earlier in the proceedings.

CONSTRUCTING FACTS

Some commentators have argued that the likelihood of miscarriages of justice has been increased by the abolition of the right to silence. The Criminal Justice and Public Order Act 1994 removed the 'right to silence' of those accused of criminal charges. As Stephen Greer explains in the following extract, the so-called 'right to silence' was actually a person's right not to have a negative inference drawn by the judge or jury from the fact that when accused, by police or in court, they remained silent.

S Greer, 'The Right to Silence: A Review of the Current Debate', *Modern Law Review* (1990) vol. 53, pp. 709–32, at p. 710.

To say that there is a right to silence in England and Wales does not merely mean that generally no legal obligation is imposed upon citizens to talk to the police or to give evidence in court. It implies in addition that no disadvantages should attach to a defendant's refusal to co-operate with the police or to testify. The 'right to silence', therefore, refers to the common law principles that normally tribunals of fact (juries and magistrates) should not be invited or encouraged to conclude, either by judges or prosecutors, that a defendant is guilty merely because he has refused to respond to allegations, particularly from the police, or has refused to testify in court in his own defence. This has been justified on the grounds that the prejudicial effect of such invitations is likely to outweigh the probative value of the silence itself.

The 1994 Act provided that negative inferences could be made. The right to silence was a well-known right as it made an indirect appearance on many TV police shows in the form of a police warning. More astute students may have noticed the change, on programmes such as *The Bill*, of the police warning to suspects from 'You have a right to remain silent, but anything which you do say may be taken down and used in evidence against you'; to the more complicated: 'You do not have to say anything, but I must caution you that if you do not mention when questioned something which you later rely on in court it may harm your defence. If you do say anything it may be given in evidence.'.

Questions:
1.   What reasons might there be for having a right not to have inferences drawn from silence when accused?

2.   What reasons, other than guilt, may a person have for remaining silent when accused of a crime?

3.   If inference can be made from silence, does this mean that silence is itself part of the evidence — a type of 'fact'?

Stephen Greer has identified four types of arguments for and against the 'right to silence': utilitarian abolitionism (UA), exchange abolitionism (EA), symbolic retentionism (SR), and instrumental retentionism (IR).

S Greer, 'The Right to Silence: A Review of the Current Debate' *op. cit.* at pp. 719, 722–5, 727.

Utilitarian Abolitionism
The utilitarian case for abolishing the right to silence . . . rests on Bentham's famous dictum: 'innocence claims the right of speaking, as guilt invokes the privilege of silence.' . . . The 'privilege against self incrimination' is seen by utilitarians as having no contribution to make either to the quest for the accurate outcome, or to the reduction or elimination of these extraneous considerations.

Exchange Abolitionism
. . . The basic assumption of exchange abolitionism is, that provided defendants' other legitimate interests are adequately protected, only the guilty will seek to hide behind silence in the police station. Therefore, unlike the [utilitarian abolitionists] the exchange abolitionists take defendants' right seriously. But unlike the retentionists they do not regard the right to silence as a right which the accused necessarily needs to have . . . The main weakness . . . in exchange abolitionism in general is the assumption that access to legal advice and other safeguards remove any legitimate reasons an innocent suspect might otherwise have had for preferring to remain silent in police custody . . . There are several flaws in the argument that this data implies that the right to silence should be abolished. First, while the evidence suggests that it is more likely that members of paramilitary organisations and

persistent serious offenders will remain silent in police custody than other types of suspect, it does not follow that any given suspect who does so will necessarily belong to one of these categories. Second, even if a given suspect has a serious criminal record or is charged with a serious offence, it should not be assumed that his or her only possible motive for staying silent on the instant occasion will be in order to evade just conviction. [There are] a large number of other reasons which might make any suspect reluctant to talk to the police . . . Any of these could just as easily apply to the suspect with a record charged with a serious offence which he or she did not in fact commit. Making silence in these circumstances potential evidence of guilt would create the risk that suspects would be convicted purely on account of their criminal record and/or the seriousness of the offence rather than solid evidence that they were guilty as charged.

Third, the proposed changes are likely to be ineffective against terrorists and professional criminals because a variety of other evasive tactics (e.g. false alibis) are already at their disposal and these may simply come to be used more widely with the right to silence gone. Finally, the Guildford Four and Birmingham Six cases amongst others strongly suggest that it was all too easy to obtain convictions against terrorist suspects in pre-PACE England and Wales even against those who were manifestly not guilty . . .

Symbolic Retentionism

It has been argued that the current debate about the right to silence is at least as much about its symbolic significance as it is about its practical value. The right to silence, it is said, has always been a touchstone against which broader criminal justice commitments have been tested . . . [Symbolic retentionists] would conclude that the attempt by the police to use the right to silence as a means of reasserting a sense of authority should be resisted in order to keep police power, in the broadest sense, within proper limits. Only a very pure form of symbolic retentionism would claim that the right to silence is *only* of symbolic importance. The strongest statements from this perspective so far tend to conclude that more empirical evidence is required before this verdict can be reached.

Instrumental Retentionism

The principal instrumental retentionist argument is that abolition of the right to silence would make it easier for the prosecution to establish guilt and that this, in its turn, is to increase the chances of innocent people being wrongly convicted with no obvious gains for law enforcement . . .

There are a number of legitimate reasons why an entirely innocent suspect may well be advised not to answer at least certain police questions. They may be in an emotional and highly suggestible state of mind. They may feel guilty when in fact they have not committed an offence. They may be ignorant of some vital fact which explains away otherwise suspicious circumstances. They may be confused and liable to make mistakes which could be interpreted as deliberate lies at the trial. They may forget important details which it would have been to their advantage to have remembered. They may use loose expressions unaware of the possible adverse interpretations which could be placed upon them at trial. They may not have heard or understood what the police interviewer said. They may be concerned that an early disclosure of their defence could be to their disadvantage. They may have given an explanation in the police car on the way to the police station which was not believed and thus prove reluctant to repeat it in the formal interview. Their silence may be an attempt to protect others or a reluctance to admit to having done something discreditable but not illegal. Some suspects may not want to be tricked into giving information about others because this could result in being stigmatised as an informer with all the dangers which this label carries particularly in Northern Ireland.

Section 34 of the Criminal Justice and Public Order Act 1994 permits the court or jury to draw inferences from an accused's failure to mention a fact later relied on in defence. Inferences cannot be drawn directly from the accused's refusal to answer questions or testify, but can only be drawn when an accused is relying on some fact which he failed to mention when questioned by the police but which he could reasonably have been expected to mention. Section 35 permits inferences to be drawn when an accused fails to testify or answer questions in court. Sections 36 and 37 deal with more specific circumstances. Section 36 permits inferences to be drawn from a refusal to answer questions relating to objects, substances or marks connected with the accused and section 37 permits inferences to be drawn from a refusal to answer questions relating to his presence in a place where an offence has been committed. Try looking up the provisions yourself and reading them in full.

The application of this rule means that silence can in effect amount to a 'fact' which may add up to a decision of guilty beyond all reasonable doubt. The following extract discusses the effect of the abrogation of the right to silence in cases under the equivalent Northern Irish provisions abolishing the right to silence (which have been in operation since 1988).

J D Jackson, 'Interpreting the Silence Provisions: The Northern Ireland Cases', *Criminal Law Review* [1995] p. 587, at p. 600.

As the Lord Chief Justice has said, before convicting, the court, having regard to the inferences (if any) which it draws under [Section 35], must always be satisfied that the Crown has discharged the burden of proving that the accused is guilty beyond reasonable doubt . . . [S]ection 35 do[es] not therefore alter the fundamental principle that the burden of proof rests on the Crown to prove guilt beyond reasonable doubt. But the common-sense approach [adopted in the cases] does ease the burden which the prosecution has to discharge as it has been assumed to permit the tribunal of fact in an appropriate case to draw a direct inference of guilt from the failure to testify on the basis that the accused was not prepared to assert his innocence on oath because he was not innocent. This would appear to allow the tribunal of fact to raise the prosecution case up to the standards of proof beyond reasonable doubt when the case standing alone cannot reach this standard.

Apart from the danger that such an approach risks flouting international standards of human rights, there is also the question whether common sense can ever dictate a direct inference of guilt from a failure to testify. It is difficult to see how a case which falls short of proof beyond reasonable doubt can be raised up to the standard of proof beyond reasonable doubt by the equivocal fact of an accused's failure to testify. The Criminal Law Revision Committee took the view that the stronger the evidence is, the more significant will be the accused's failure to give evidence. It may be that the stronger the case is, the harder it is to rebut. But no matter how strong the evidence, the court or jury is in a position to draw the 'proper' inference from silence only where it knows the reasons for silence. Without knowledge of the reason, it would only seem safe to draw an inference of guilt when the trier of fact is already convinced of guilt on the basis of existing proof beyond reasonable doubt. But the inference then becomes an *ex post facto* rationalisation of what the trier of fact is already convinced of and the provision becomes redundant. If the trier of fact has become convinced on the basis of lesser proof than this, then the provision is being used to do what in many cases it cannot do, namely provide the necessary evidence to bring the proof up to the standard.

The Northern Ireland provisions (found in Articles 3, 4, 5 and 6 of the Criminal Evidence (NI) Order 1988) were successfully challenged in the European Court of Human Rights as violating the defendant's right to a fair trial. While the challenge to the right to silence provisions alone failed, the Court found that the accused's right to a fair trial under Article 6 of the ECHR (see Chapter 3 at pp. 74–5) had been violated by the combined operation of the 'right to silence' provisions together with other emergency law provisions which denied access to a lawyer during questioning. The case indicates how the operation of negative inferences from silence operated as part of the fact finding. We have inserted some questions for you to consider while reading.

Murray v *United Kingdom* (App. No. 18731/91, (ECHR) 8 February 1996, 22 EHRR 29 at pp. 33–6).

The Facts

B.   The trial proceedings

17.   In May 1991 the applicant was tried by a single judge, the Lord Chief Justice of Northern Ireland, sitting without a jury, for the offences of conspiracy to murder, the unlawful imprisonment, with seven other people, of a certain Mr L and of belonging to a proscribed organisation, the Provisional Irish Republican Army (IRA).

18.   According to the Crown, Mr L had been a member of the IRA who had been providing information about their activities to the Royal Ulster Constabulary. On discovering that Mr L was an informer, the IRA tricked him into visiting a house in Belfast on 5 January 1990. He was falsely imprisoned in

one of the rear bedrooms of the house and interrogated by the IRA until the arrival of the police and the army at the house on 7 January 1990. It was also alleged by the Crown that there was a conspiracy to murder Mr L as punishment for being a police informer.

19.   In the course of the trial, evidence was given that when the police entered the house on 7 January, the applicant was seen by a police constable coming down a flight of stairs wearing a raincoat over his clothes and was arrested in the hall of the house.

[Does this amount to evidence of guilt?]

Mr L testified that he was forced under threat of being killed to make a taped confession to his captors that he was an informer. He further said that on the evening of 7 January he had heard scurrying and had been told to take off his blindfold, that he had done so and had opened the spare bedroom door. He had then seen the applicant standing at the stairs. The applicant had told him that the police were at the door and to go downstairs and watch television. While he was talking to him the applicant was pulling tape out of a cassette.

[Does this amount to evidence of guilt? Does L say how long the applicant had been there? Would your answer change if you were told that L was 'a man who is fully prepared to lie on oath to advance his own interests and is a man of no moral worth whatever'?]

On a search of the house by the police items of clothing of Mr L were subsequently found in the spare bedroom, whilst a tangled tape was discovered in the upstairs bedroom. The salvaged portions of the tape revealed a confession by Mr L that he had agreed to work for the police and had been paid for so doing. At no time, either on his arrest or during the trial proceedings, did the applicant give any explanation for his presence in the house.

20.   At the close of the prosecution case the trial judge, acting in accordance with Article 4 of the Order, called upon each of the eight accused to give evidence in their own defence. The trial judge informed them *inter alia*:

I am also required by law to tell you that if you refuse to come into the witness box to be sworn or if, after having been sworn, you refuse, without good reason, to answer any questions, then the court in deciding whether you are guilty or not guilty may take into account against you to the extent that it considers proper your refusal to give evidence or to answer any questions.

21.   Acting on the advice of his solicitor and counsel, the applicant chose not to give any evidence. No witnesses were called on his behalf. Counsel, with support from the evidence of a co-accused, DM, submitted, *inter alia*, that the applicant's presence in the house just before the police arrived was recent and innocent.

22.   On 8 May 1991 the applicant was found guilty of the offence of aiding
and abetting the unlawful imprisonment of Mr L and sentenced to eight years'
imprisonment. He was acquitted of the remaining charges.

23.   The trial judge rejected DM's evidence as untruthful. He considered
that:

> the surrounding facts, including the finding of the tangled tape in the
> bathroom with the broken cassette case, and the fact that, on entering the
> house some appreciable time after they arrived outside it and some
> appreciable time after they first knocked on the door, the police found
> Murray [the applicant] coming down the stairs at the time when all the
> other occupants of the house were in the living room, strongly confirm L's
> evidence that after the police knocked on the door Murray was upstairs
> pulling the tape out of the cassette.

[Does destruction of the tape amount to evidence of guilt of aiding and
abetting false imprisonment? Can you think of any innocent (as in 'not guilty'
of this offence) explanations for the applicant's actions?]

24.   In rejecting a submission by the applicant that Articles 4 and 6 of the
Order did not operate to permit the Court to draw an adverse inference against
him, where, at the end of the Crown case, there was a reasonably plausible
explanation for the accused's conduct consistent with his innocence, the trial
judge stated as follows:

> There can be debate as to the extent to which, before the making of the
> Criminal Evidence (Northern Ireland) Order 1988, a tribunal of fact in this
> jurisdiction was entitled to draw an adverse inference against an accused
> because he failed to give evidence on his own behalf, or to account for his
> presence at a particular place or to mention particular facts when ques-
> tioned by the police. But I consider that the purpose of Article 4 and of
> Articles 3 and 6 of the 1988 Order was to make it clear that, whatever was
> the effect of the previous legal rules, a judge trying a criminal case without
> a jury, or a jury in a criminal case, was entitled to apply common sense in
> drawing inferences against the accused in the circumstances specified in
> Article 4, and in Articles 3 and 6 . . .

> I think it is clear that the purpose of Article 4 is to permit the tribunal of
> fact to draw such inferences against the accused from his failure to give
> evidence in his own defence as common sense requires.

> The inference which it is proper to draw against an accused will vary from
> case to case depending on the particular circumstances of the case and, of
> course, the failure of the accused to give evidence on his own behalf does
> not in itself indicate guilt. Nor does the failure to mention particular facts
> when questioned or the failure to account for presence in a particular place
> in itself indicate guilt. But I consider that the intendment of . . . Article 4
> and Article 6 is to enable the tribunal of fact to exercise ordinary common
> sense in drawing inferences against an accused . . .

Therefore when I come to consider the case against the accused . . . I propose to draw such inferences against [him] under Article 4 and under Article 6 as ordinary common sense dictates.

[Is it obvious what ordinary common sense dictates? Does it make a difference that a judge rather than a jury is deciding the facts? (the trial took place in Northern Ireland's no jury 'Diplock' Courts. See further Chapter 9 at pp. 344–8).]

25.   In concluding that the applicant was guilty of the offence of aiding and abetting false imprisonment, the trial judge drew adverse inferences against the applicant under both Articles 4 and 6 of the Order. The judge stated that in the particular circumstances of the case he did not propose to draw inferences against the applicant under Article 3 of the Order. He stated furthermore:

I accept the submission of counsel for the accused that as demonstrated by his replies in cross-examination, L is a man who is fully prepared to lie on oath to advance his own interests and is a man of no moral worth whatever. I, therefore, accept the further submissions of counsel for the accused that, unless his evidence were confirmed by other evidence, a court should not act on his evidence, particularly against accused persons in a criminal trial . . .

I now turn to consider the fifth count charging the false imprisonment of L against the accused [the applicant]. For the reasons which I have already stated, I am satisfied that, as L described in his evidence, [the applicant] was at the top of the stairs pulling the tape out of the cassette after the police arrived outside the house.

I am also satisfied, for the reasons which I have already stated, that [the applicant] was in the house for longer than the short period described by his co-accused, [DM]. I am further satisfied that it is an irresistible inference that while he was in the house [the applicant] was in contact with the men holding L captive and that he knew that L was being held a captive. I also draw very strong inferences against [the applicant] under Article 6 of the 1988 Order by reason of his failure to give an account of his presence in the house when cautioned by the police on the evening of 7 January 1990 under Article 6, and I also draw very strong inferences against [the applicant] under Article 4 of the 1988 Order by reason of his refusal to give evidence in his own defence when called upon by the Court to do so.

Therefore I find [the applicant] guilty of aiding and abetting the false imprisonment of L because, knowing he was being held captive in the house, he was present in the house concurring in L being falsely imprisoned. As Vaughan, J stated in *R* v *Young* . . . [the applicant] was 'near enough to give [his] aid and to give [his] countenance and assistance'.

C.   *The appeal proceedings*

26.   The applicant appealed against conviction and sentence to the Court of Appeal in Northern Ireland. In a judgment of 7 July 1992, the court dismissed the applicant's appeal holding, *inter alia*:

... to suggest, with respect, that [the applicant] went into the house just as the police were arriving outside, immediately went upstairs, attempted to destroy a tape and then walked downstairs, and that this was the sum of his time and activity in the house defies common sense ...

We are satisfied that it can reasonably be inferred that [the applicant] knew before he came to the house that [L] was being held captive there. With this knowledge he assisted in the false imprisonment by directing the captive from the bedroom where he had been held and by giving him the directions and admonition [L] said. Accordingly [the applicant] aided and abetted the crime. We do not accept that [L] would have been free to leave the house, if the police and Army had been taken in by the pretence of the television watching and had departed without making any arrests. We have no doubt that [L] remained under restraint in the living room when the police were there and if they had left, he would have remained a prisoner to await the fate that his captors would determine.

We consider that there was a formidable case against [the applicant]. He was the only one of the accused whom [L] observed and identified as playing a positive part in the activities touching his captivity. L's evidence therefore called for an answer. No answer was forthcoming of any kind to the police or throughout the length of his trial. It was inevitable that the judge would draw 'very strong inferences' against him.

The Crown case deeply implicated [the applicant] in the false imprisonment of [L] ...

Questions:
1.   What appear to have been the facts in this case? How were they disputed by the witnesses called for Murray? How reliable was prosecution and defence witness evidence?

2.   What role did the accused's silence play in the finding of guilty?

3.   Make a note of the 'inferences' made by the trial judge and by the Court of Appeal? Are the inferences consistent with the evidence?

Now read the judgment given by the European Court of Human Rights:

Murray v *United Kingdom* (1996) 22 EHRR 29.

I.   *Alleged violation of Article 6 of the Convention*

40.   The applicant alleged that there had been a violation of the right to silence and the right not to incriminate oneself contrary to Article 6(1) and (2) of the Convention. He further complained that he was denied access to his solicitor in violation of Article 6(1) in conjunction with paragraph 3(c) of the Convention. The relevant provisions provide as follows:

1.   In the determination of . . . any criminal charge against him, everyone is entitled to a fair and public hearing within a reasonable time by an independent and impartial tribunal established by law . . .
2.   Everyone charged with a criminal offence shall be presumed innocent until proved guilty according to law.
3.   Everyone charged with a criminal offence has the following minimum rights:
. . .

(c)   to defend himself in person or through legal assistance of his own choosing or, if he has not sufficient means to pay for legal assistance, to be given it free when the interests of justice so require;

The Court will examine each of these allegations in turn.

A.   *Article 6(1) and (2): right to silence*

41.   In the submission of the applicant, the drawing of incriminating inferences against him under the Criminal Justice (Northern Ireland) Order 1988 ('the Order') violated Article 6(1) and (2) of the Convention. It amounted to an infringement of the right to silence, the right not to incriminate oneself and the principle that the prosecution bear the burden of proving the case without assistance from the accused.

He contended that a first, and most obvious element of the right to silence is the right to remain silent in the face of police questioning and not to have to testify against oneself at trial.
. . .

A second, equally essential element of the right to silence was that the exercise of the right by an accused would not be used as evidence against him in his trial. However, the trial judge drew very strong inferences, under Articles 4 and 6 of the Order, from his decision to remain silent under police questioning and during the trial. Indeed, it was clear from the trial judge's remarks and from the judgment of the Court of Appeal in his case that the inferences were an integral part of his decision to find him guilty.

Accordingly, he was severely and doubly penalised for choosing to remain silent: once for his silence under police interrogation and once for his failure to testify during the trial. To use against him silence under police questioning and his refusal to testify during trial amounted to subverting the presumption of innocence and the onus of proof resulting from that presumption: it is for the prosecution to prove the accused's guilt without any assistance from the latter being required.
. . .

44.   The Court must, confining its attention to the facts of the case, consider whether the drawing of inferences against the applicant under Articles 4 and 6 of the Order rendered the criminal proceedings against him — and especially his conviction — unfair within the meaning of Article 6 of the Convention. It is recalled in this context that no inference was drawn under Article 3 of the Order. It is not the Court's role to examine whether, in

general, the drawing of inferences under the scheme contained in the Order is compatible with the notion of a fair hearing under Article 6.

45.   Although not specifically mentioned in Article 6 of the Convention, there can be no doubt that the right to remain silent under police questioning and the privilege against self-incrimination are generally recognised international standards which lie at the heart of the notion of a fair procedure under Article 6. By providing the accused with protection against improper compulsion by the authorities these immunities contribute to avoiding miscarriages of justice and to securing the aim of Article 6.

46.   The Court does not consider that it is called upon to give an abstract analysis of the scope of these immunities and, in particular, of what constitutes in this context 'improper compulsion'. What is at stake in the present case is whether these immunities are absolute in the sense that the exercise by an accused of the right to silence cannot under any circumstances be used against him at trial or, alternatively, whether informing him in advance that, under certain conditions, his silence may be used, is always to be regarded as 'improper compulsion'.

47.   On the one hand, it is self-evident that is incompatible with the immunities under consideration to base a conviction solely or mainly on the accused's silence or on a refusal to answer questions or to give evidence himself. On the other hand, the Court deems it equally obvious that these immunities cannot and should not prevent that the accused's silence, in situations which clearly call for an explanation from him, be taken into account in assessing the persuasiveness of the evidence adduced by the prosecution.

 Wherever the line between these two extremes is to be drawn, it follows from this understanding of 'the right to silence' that the question whether the right is absolute must be answered in the negative.

 It cannot be said therefore that an accused's decision to remain silent throughout criminal proceedings should necessarily have no implications when the trial court seeks to evaluate the evidence against him. In particular, as the Government has pointed out, established international standards in this area, while providing for the right to silence and the privilege against self-incrimination, are silent on this point.

 Whether the drawing of adverse inferences from an accused's silence infringes Article 6 is a matter to be determined in the light of all the circumstances of the case, having particular regard to the situations where inferences may be drawn, the weight attached to them by the national courts in their assessment of the evidence and the degree of compulsion inherent in the situation.

. . .

55.   The applicant submitted that it was unfair to draw inferences under Article 6 of the Order from his silence at a time when he had not had the benefit of legal advice. In his view the question of access to a solicitor was inextricably entwined with that of the drawing of adverse inferences from

pre-trial silence under police questioning. In this context he emphasised that under the Order once an accused has remained silent a trap is set from which he cannot escape: if an accused chooses to give evidence or to call witnesses, he is, by reason of his prior silence, exposed to the risk of an Article 3 inference sufficient to bring about a conviction; on the other hand, if he maintains his silence inferences may be drawn against him under other provisions of the Order.

56.   The Court recalls that it must confine its attention to the facts of the present case. The reality of this case is that the applicant maintained silence right from the first questioning by the police to the end of his trial. It is not for the Court therefore to speculate on the question whether inferences would have been drawn under the Order had the applicant, at any moment after his interrogation, chosen to speak to the police or to give evidence at his trial or call witnesses. Nor should it speculate on the question whether it was the possibility of such inferences being drawn that explains why the applicant was advised by his solicitor to remain silent.

The Court then considered the effect of denial of access to a lawyer.

. . .

59.   The applicant submitted that he was denied access to a lawyer at a critical stage of the criminal proceedings against him. He pointed out that in Northern Ireland the initial phase of detention is of crucial importance in the context of the criminal proceedings as a whole because of the possibility of inferences being drawn under Articles 3, 4 and 6 of the Order.

He was in fact denied access to any legal advice for 48 hours. During that time Article 3 and Article 6 cautions had been administered without his having had the benefit of prior legal advice. He was interviewed on 12 occasions without a solicitor being present to represent his interests. When he was finally granted access to his solicitor he was advised to remain silent partly because he had maintained silence already during the interview and partly because the solicitor would not be permitted to remain during questioning. The silence which had already occurred prior to seeing his solicitor would have triggered the operation of both Articles 3 and 6 at any subsequent trial, even had he chosen to give an account to the police. Having regard to the very strong inferences which the trial judge drew under Articles 4 and 6 of the Order, the decision to deny him access to a solicitor unfairly prejudiced the rights of the defence and rendered the proceedings against him unfair contrary to Article 6(1) and (3)(c) of the Convention.

. . .

66.   The Court is of the opinion that the scheme contained in the Order is such that it is of paramount importance for the rights of the defence that an accused has access to a lawyer at the initial stages of police interrogation. It observes in this context that, under the Order, at the beginning of the police interrogation, an accused is confronted with a fundamental dilemma relating to his defence. If he chooses to remain silent, adverse inferences may be drawn against him in accordance with the provisions of the Order. On the other hand, if the accused opts to break his silence during the course of

interrogation, he runs the risk of prejudicing his defence without necessarily removing the possibility of inferences being drawn against him.

Under such conditions the concept of fairness enshrined in Article 6 requires that the accused has the benefit of the assistance of a lawyer already at the initial stages of police interrogation. To deny access to a lawyer for the first 48 hours of police questioning, in a situation where the rights of the defence may well be irretrievably prejudiced, is — whatever the justification for such denial — incompatible with the rights of the accused under Article 6.

Questions:
1.   What advice could the lawyer have given if he or she had had access to Murray during police questioning? (On the importance of such access, see Chapter 9.)

2.   What if the lawyer had advised the accused to stay silent? Can the accused's silence, based on legal advice, lead to a negative inference being drawn? Is this fair? Is it reliable?

THE INTERPRETATION OF FACTS

It is, however, important to note that it is not just in high profile cases or those in which miscarriages of justice have been exposed that the issue of fact-finding is important. Notwithstanding the importance of fact-finding to lawyers, John Jackson has argued that legal approaches to the process of fact-finding are fundamentally misconstrued:

J Jackson, 'Hart and the Concept of Fact' in P Ingram and P Leith (eds) *The Jurisprudence of Orthodoxy*, pp. 61–84, at pp. 63, 69, 70–2, 77, 79, 82 Routledge (1988) (references omitted).

[I]t will be argued that there is no safe haven of exclusively legal discourse which sits *sui generis* isolated from factual and moral discourse, but that to engage in legal discourse is to engage in both factual and moral discourse . . .

It is clear that Hart and certain other legal philosophers of the Oxford School have a particular concept of fact. Facts it seems are part of the world, and to the extent that there are different kinds of facts, so there are different parts of the world, be they 'brute' and 'institutional' parts, 'hard' parts and 'soft' parts, 'empirical' parts and 'non empirical' parts. This is a common usage of fact and it has found favour with a number of philosophers . . .

To view facts as items in the world is to subscribe to a theory of knowledge that has appealed to many philosophers and scientists since the seventeenth century, a theory that Popper has referred to as the 'bucket' theory of the mind. The starting-point of this theory is that before we can know or say anything about the world, we must first have had perceptions or sense-experiences. According to this view, our mind resembles a container or a kind of bucket in which these perceptions and knowledge accumulate. Perception and memory supply the basic data for reasoning and we can only go beyond the data of our senses and memory by relying on general principles of cause and effect which are known entirely from experience when we find that particular objects are conjoined with other objects . . .

In sum, the method can be characterised as one of elaborating principles by the method of induction and testing such principles by discovering to what extent matters that can be deduced from them correspond to the facts.

A number of basic assumptions follow from this method. First, it is assumed that there is a world of fact which exists 'out there' as part of reality independent of the human observer, and the task of the scientist is to discover as much of it as he can by comparing this reality with his own theories and hypotheses — what has been called the correspondence theory of truth. Second, it is assumed that although many conclusions can only be stated with probability, given time the complete truth is in principle capable of being revealed . . .

But the view that facts are part of the world has been increasingly challenged by philosophers during the course of this century . . . the facts that we find are not plucked out of reality ready made. They have to be stated and this requires language . . .

Once it is accepted that there is an important normative element in fact-finding, it can be argued that there is an important factual element in legal discourse. Despite the division of function between the judge as tribunal of law and the jury as tribunal of fact, there is not some neat dividing line by which fact can be separated from law. The jury does not hand the facts to the judge and let him get on with the job of applying the law to the facts . . .

[T]here is an important creative role for the fact-finder in any fact-finding enterprise, but at the end of the day it is open in most enquiries for him to say simply 'I cannot reach a conclusion within the prevailing paradigm' or alternatively 'a particular conclusion can be justified within the prevailing paradigm, but I don't want to commit myself to it.' The adjudicator on the other hand, is forced to come to a conclusion on guilt or innocence, liability or non-liability and in justifying his choice it is difficult to see how he can exclude moral justification.

Read the following analysis of two cases of battered women who killed their abusers as an example of how facts are constructed rather than 'plucked out of reality ready made':

D Nicolson, 'Telling Tales: Gender Discrimination, Gender Construction and Battered Women Who Kill', *Feminist Legal Studies* (1995) vol. III, pp. 185–206 at pp. 186–200 (footnotes omitted).

The stories of Sara Thornton and Kiranjit Ahluwalia are sufficiently similar to justify comparison. Both suffered numerous beatings and death threats from jealous and possessive husbands, although Kiranjit's ordeal lasted much longer, and included rape and sexual abuse. Both women killed their husbands following provocative conduct. Sara stabbed Malcolm after he had made wounding remarks, threatened to kill her and taunted her with her own helplessness. Kiranjit set Deepak alight a few hours after he had declared their marriage to be over, threatened to beat her and placed a hot iron against her face.

At both murder trials, their defences alleging no mens rea, provocation and diminished responsibility were rejected. On appeal, both appellants attacked the law on provocation, which requires that defendants actually lose their self-control — the subjective condition — and that a reasonable person sharing the defendant's age, sex and any other characteristic relevant to the type of provocation would have done so — the objective condition. In particular, both appeals alleged that the *Duffy* [[1949] 1 All ER 932] interpretation of the subjective condition, which required a 'sudden and temporary loss of self-control' and barred the defence whenever there is 'time for cooling' between provocation and the killing discriminates against battered women since they rarely act instantaneously following provocation, but after a 'slow burn' of fear and desperation.

But there the similarities between the two cases end. Whereas, in *Thornton* the Court of Appeal upheld the *Duffy* interpretation as authoritative and comprehensible to a jury, in *Ahluwalia* it subtly and surreptitiously rendered the law more amenable to battered women by holding, albeit *obiter*, that a 'cooling time' was no longer an absolute legal bar to the defence, merely evidence that self-control had not been suddenly lost. In addition, the *Ahluwalia* court also amended — again *obiter* — the objective condition of provocation so as to include the perspective of defendants suffering from so-called battered woman syndrome.

Both reforms are limited. Nevertheless, the *Ahluwalia* decision stands in stark contrast to the unsympathetic *Thornton* judgment which also tersely dismissed allegations that the trial judge had unfairly summarised conflicting evidence as to diminished responsibility, and that Sara's conviction was unsafe and unsatisfactory because her lawyers had not actively pursued a provocation defence. By contrast, Kiranjit Ahluwalia's appeal was upheld on the grounds of fresh evidence of diminished responsibility, notwithstanding contrary case law. At her retrial she was freed. Sara Thornton remains in jail. [NB Sara Thornton was eventually released in July 1995 pending appeal. The appeal against her murder conviction was successful and she did not return to prison. See p. 165.] . . .

The Court of Appeal's judgments of Sara Thornton and Kiranjit Ahluwalia as women emerge from its descriptions of 'the facts' of their cases. These 'facts' did not exist pre-packaged for judicial recital. 'Reality' is unbounded, multi-faceted, and subject to varying interpretations. Facts have to be selected, interpreted and communicated. This process is neither mechanical, nor neutral, but is aimed at persuading the reader of the logical and emotional force of the judge's decision in much the same way that advocates attempt to persuade courts . . .

The analysis of the *Thornton* and *Ahluwalia* judgments will endeavour to show how fact organisation and rhetoric were used to construct the two women at opposite ends of the scale of appropriate femininity, as having killed in very different circumstances, and hence as having differing claims to sympathetic treatment. In other words, the judicial description of 'the facts' were partial reconstructions of 'what really happened': partial in the sense that only part of the 'truth' was told; and partial in the sense of being biased . . .

The tone of the two stories are clearly set by their opening sentences. The detached listing of Sara Thornton's personal details anticipates the court's lack of sympathy for her. Throughout the judgment, Beldam LJ distanced himself from the emotive aspects of the case, baldly relating the 'facts' without comment and concentrating on action rather than understanding. This attempt at objectivity is markedly absent in the *Ahluwalia* judgment. Its opening words 'This is a tragic case . . . ' portend the sympathy for Kiranjit which pervades the judgment. But whereas Lord Taylor CJ openly stated his opinions, those of Beldam LJ are apparent from his description of Sara.

By commencing with a reference to her 'comfortable' upbringing and public school education, Beldam LJ provides a basis with which to contrast her downward spiral, through 'expulsion' from school, broken marriage, remarriage to an alcoholic and eventual conviction as a murderer. The intimation that Sara ungratefully threw away a promising start to life expanded into the more damning suggestion that she was responsible for her battered experience. Thus we are told that her previous husband drank and was violent, and that '[f]rom the start she realised that [Malcolm] was a heavy drinker and was jealous and possessive'. This echoes both the idea that sexual offence victims 'ask for it' and the equally absurd 'women who love too much' thesis, which portrays battered women as pathologically needing and even enjoying male violence . . .

Only the more negative characteristics of appropriate femininity were attributed to Sara. By fatuously commenting that Sara had 'several relationships with young men which did not work' and noting that she had moved in with Malcolm shortly after meeting him in a pub, Beldam LJ subtly suggests that Sara is promiscuous. Later he paraphrased Sara's reply to Malcolm's allegations that she had been selling her body as saying that 'she had only been trying to raise money for their business', thus leaving open the possibility that his allegations were true.

Sara was also portrayed as having rejected a woman's allotted domestic role. Her strenuous efforts to help Malcolm combat his alcoholism and to keep him alive were ignored. Instead we learn that while Malcolm was unemployed, Sara continued to work and attend a weekend conference where she 'seemed to be enjoying herself'. Her relationship with her daughter was left undeveloped and, when mentioned, was portrayed negatively . . .

The most striking and significant aspect of the judgment is that it drastically downplayed the single most important feature of the case: Sara's experience as a battered woman. Whereas, a total of 161 lines were devoted to describing 'the facts which led to the deceased's death', only five dealt directly with his violence and abusive behaviour. Moreover, their tone is so impassive as to completely understate Sara's pain and misery and their influence over her actions.

Thus, unlike in *Ahluwalia*, no mention was made of the size difference between Malcolm and Sara. Repeated and increasingly frequent violence over almost two years were reduced to describing Malcolm as being 'on occasions . . . violent in the home, breaking furniture and assaulting the appellant'. Only one specific incidence of 'serious assault' was mentioned. We learn that Malcolm was an alcoholic, but despite the leading of relevant expert evidence, not how this would have affected Sara.

By contrast, 41 out of 100 lines describing Kiranjit Ahluwalia's story were devoted to her 'many years of violence and humiliation'. Moreover, their description clearly indicates where Taylor LJ's sympathies lay. Deepak was described as 'a big man', Kiranjit as 'slight'. Her injuries and maltreatment were recounted in detail. She was described as being reduced to a 'state of humiliation and loss of self-esteem'. So affected was Lord Taylor CJ by Kiranjit's ordeal that he quoted from a letter in which she begged Deepak to return from his lover and made 'a number of self-denying promises of the most abject kind'.

However, this letter is also important because it illustrates Kiranjit's conformity with the attributes of passive femininity. From the judgment she appears as meek, obedient and submissive. Until the night she killed him, Kiranjit is shown as reacting passively and pathologically to Deepak's violence losing weight, showing 'signs of nervousness and distress' and twice attempting suicide.

The opening line of the judgment may have depicted Kiranjit's story as tragedy, but unlike Sara Thornton's it was not told in the classical dramaturgic tradition, in terms of which the tragedy stems from the protagonist's own character flaws. Kiranjit's tragedy was presented as that of a passive victim of harsh fate. Thus, although we learn of her comfortable middle class background, her biography was not traversed for signs of complicity in her own downfall. Instead, by noting that Kiranjit's studies were aborted due to being pressurised into an arranged marriage, Lord Taylor CJ implicitly traced the tragedy back to her culture rather than personal choice and reinforced the image of Kiranjit as passive victim.

Throughout the judgment the focus is on what was done to Kiranjit rather than on her own actions: her marriage was arranged, she suffered violence, etc. Even when she did act, her actions were described in the passive. Thus her marriage 'took place in Canada', her two sons 'were born' to her, 'The Croydon County Court granted her an injunction'.

The characteristic of passivity also emerges from the focus on Kiranjit's submissive role as mother and wife. Having detailed Deepak's violence and adultery, Lord Taylor CJ commented 'Despite all of this, the appellant wished to hold the marriage together, partly because of her sense of duty as a wife and partly for the sake of the children' . . .

Lord Taylor CJ's willingness to reserve the role of victim for Kiranjit is most striking in his cursory, two line treatment of evidence suggesting premeditation. A few days before setting alight Deepak, Kiranjit had bought petrol and caustic soda. Although she only used the former, only her intention to use the latter was mentioned. Regarding the petrol, the judge said: 'She had also bought a can of petrol . . .', thus rendering its purchase both innocent and subordinate to that of the caustic soda.

The suggestion of premeditation is further reduced by the story's narrative sequence. A chronological sequence, with conjugal violence being followed by the purchases, the provocation and then the killing would have suggested that, notwithstanding provocation, the killing flowed from a subsisting intention to take revenge. Instead, the purchases were mentioned in the form of a flashback during the description of Kiranjit's actions after Deepak's provocative action. Thus while brooding about her treatment, '[h]er mind turned to these substances'. The only relevance of the earlier purchases to this narrative is that it provided Kiranjit with the means to execute an intention formed in response to provocation . . .

Whereas in *Ahluwalia* potentially strong evidence of agency and rational planning was swept under the carpet, in *Thornton* the opposite occurred. Thus almost a quarter of the description of the facts covered the four days preceding the killing, and in particular a series of 'rows' between the Thorntons. The recounting of these 'rows' served three narrative functions.

First, their description suggested that Sara could give as good as she got. For example, when Malcolm threatened her with a guitar, she 'for her part' pointed a knife at him, called him a 'bastard' and threatened to kill him. The impression conveyed of two equal protagonists — eloquently conveyed by the phrase 'for her part' — is reinforced by the constant characterisation of Malcolm's threats and her responses as mere 'rows'.

Secondly, in recounting these 'rows' Beldam LJ was able to augment his picture of a woman who has rejected appropriate femininity by portraying Sara as uppity, rebellious and aggressive. Sara did not meekly crumble under Malcolm's threats; she armed herself, and retaliated with threats and bad language. After the penultimate 'row' with Malcolm, Sara is described as arranging for Luisa to leave the marital home, going out drinking with Martin and returning after him in a 'quarrelsome and arrogant' mood . . .

Finally, the concentration on the 'rows' was used to hint at a premeditated killing. Stripped of the context of marital violence, the tension built up by a narrative sequence in which 'row' follows 'row' and then climaxes with the killing carries with it the implication that the 'rows' were the cause of Sara's actions, not simply the last straw . . .

Thus far, by focusing on Sara Thornton's actions and intention prior to stabbing Malcolm, rather than on his violence and its effect on her, Beldam LJ has created the impression that, far from being reduced to mental abnormality or the end of her tether, Sara was angry and aggressive, but nevertheless in control. Indeed, she had decided to kill Malcolm. In comparison, by emphasising Deepak's violence and its effect on Kiranjit and by de-emphasising evidence of premeditation, Lord Taylor CJ has depicted her as passively borne along by events over which she had no control. These differing themes were subtly reinforced by the narrative style in which the two killings were recounted.

In *Ahluwalia*, the action was described in long, disjointed sentences containing a number of short clauses.

> Her mind turned to [the petrol and caustic soda] and some time after 2.30 am she got up, went downstairs, poured about two pints of the petrol into a bucket (to make it easier to throw), lit a candle on the gas cooker and carried these thing upstairs. She also took an oven glove for self-protection and a stick. She went to the deceased's bedroom, threw in some petrol, lit the stick from the candle and threw it into the room.

The impression created is of the action running headlong like a runaway train out of the control of its driver.

By contrast in *Thornton*, the description of the equivalent sequence of events was twice as long, largely due to its more deliberate pace. Quotations are preceded by colons rather than commas and qualifying phrases appear between commas rather than in brackets. Sentences are shorter and contain no more than two separate actions. Sentences and clauses are linked with conjunctives. The pace of the narrative is further slowed by ideas being spelt out in full and by the provision of the sort of detail omitted in *Ahluwalia*. For example, whereas Kiranjit 'took an oven glove for self-protection', Sara 'went into the kitchen and looked in the drawer for a truncheon, which the deceased kept there, so that she had some protection if he attacked her'. The differing narrative pace in the two judgments is best appreciated by contrasting the following passage with the above quotation from *Ahluwalia*.

> [S]he stood up in front of him holding the knife in her clenched hand over his stomach. She then brought it down towards him thinking he would ward it off. He did not do so and the knife entered his stomach. She did not mean to kill him or harm him in anyway. Her object in having the knife was merely to frighten him. She only brought the knife down slowly not quickly.

The narrative's slow motion quality implies a calm control, incompatible with provocation and not particularly supportive of diminished responsibility either . . .

Questions:

1.   Nicolson seems to imply that Sara Thornton was disadvantaged at her appeal by Lord Justice Beldam's attempts to distance himself from the emotive aspects of this case. Isn't this what judges are supposed to do? (See Chapter 7.)

2.   Can you think of other criminal cases (from your studies, or those which have been covered in the media) where gender stereotypes have impacted negatively upon female (or male) defendants?

3.   Is the thrust of this article that facts can never be presented or recounted in a manner which is neutral and objective? Does this analysis support the argument of John Jackson at pp. 131–33 above?

Read the following extract from the judgment of Lord Taylor, the Lord Chief Justice, when the Court of Appeal heard Sara Thornton's second appeal, and try to apply your own analysis of the facts along the lines of Nicolson's analysis.

R v *Thornton (No. 2)* [1996] 2 All ER 1023, CA.

Lord Taylor CJ
The appellant comes from a comfortable background, but from childhood onwards her life was punctuated by problems and unhappy incidents. She was asked to leave her boarding school. She twice had pregnancies which were terminated before meeting her first husband by whom she had one child, Luisa. She went abroad with that husband but left him in Venezuela because of his drinking and there was a divorce. She made a number of attempts at suicide by cutting her wrists, by cutting her throat and by overdose of drugs. In March 1981 she was admitted to a hospital for a period under the Mental Health Act 1959. She had a third abortion in 1983. It was common ground that this history was attributed to the fact that the appellant suffered and continues to suffer from a personality disorder, although after 1981 there appeared generally to be some improvement in her mental state.

She met the deceased, her second husband, in May 1987. Like her, he had been married before and he had a son, Martin, aged 18. The appellant and the deceased began living together in the autumn of 1987 and were married in August 1988. Even before the marriage, it was clear that the deceased had a serious drink problem. He underwent treatment for alcoholism but his condition and behaviour deteriorated in 1989. As a result the marriage was stormy. There were angry arguments when the deceased was drunk and he used violence to the appellant. In her evidence she described a number of assaults. It is unnecessary to specify all the incidents prior to the final weekend, but on about 20 May the appellant left the house (which was in their joint names) after the deceased had punched her in the face and knocked her out. She reported that incident to the police and the deceased was charged with assault. The case was pending at the time of his death. After the appellant left, the deceased's son, Martin, came to stay at the house. On 26 May the appellant and her daughter returned.

Matters came to a head between Saturday, 10 and Tuesday 13 June. On the Saturday, the appellant was attending a conference in Coventry in connection with her work. According to her, she learnt by telephone that the deceased had either assaulted Luisa or otherwise driven her from the home, so that she was in night-clothes at a taxi rank. Mrs Thomas, a friend and fellow employee of the appellant, gave evidence that the appellant said after the phone call 'I am going to kill him', adding that she was not prepared to lose everything. The appellant, in evidence, denied saying these things.

On 11 June she returned home accompanied by Mrs Thomas. The deceased had been drinking and there was an angry altercation. It continued after Mrs Thomas left. The deceased picked up a guitar and threatened to hit the appellant with it. She had a kitchen knife in her hand. According to Martin, she said 'You touch my daughter, you bastard, and I'll kill you', pointing the knife at the deceased and holding it in both hands. Martin claimed he had to take the knife from her. The appellant's account was that she had the knife in the normal course of preparing lunch, that she made no threat to kill the deceased and was not disarmed by Martin. On the same day, when the deceased was in the bath, the appellant gave him Mogadon tablets. Martin saw her administer two, but she crushed four more and concealed them amongst pieces of chicken she fed to the deceased. She then telephoned the doctor saying he had taken an overdose and was suicidal, which, as she admitted in evidence, was a deliberate lie. An ambulance and the police were called but the deceased refused to go to hospital. After they left there was an angry scene. The deceased threw a chair, which broke the glass in the kitchen door. The police were called again.

Still later on that day, the appellant spoke to Mrs Thomas on the telephone. According to the latter, the appellant talked of divorce, said she was not prepared to give everything up for the deceased and that she would set about forging some cheques. In evidence the appellant denied that account of the conversation.

Next day, 12 June, according to the appellant, the deceased said he wanted her and her daughter out of the house. He then went drinking. On his return, he was sick in the kitchen, he later burnt a hole in the armchair and he spent the night on the couch.

Tuesday, 13 June brought the fatal denouement. The deceased was again drunk. When he arrived home he noticed the appellant was not wearing her wedding ring. She said they did not have much of a marriage. He then threw his wedding ring into the garden. He abused the appellant, telling her to get out and take Luisa. Clothes were thrown out of the window. Luisa left. The appellant spoke to Mrs Thomas on the telephone, saying, 'I'm going to have to do what I said I'd do'. The appellant said in evidence that meant merely that she was going to leave. She wrote in lipstick on her bedroom mirror: 'Bastard Thornton, I hate you'. Later, she and Martin went out leaving the deceased dozing on the couch. Martin returned home first and went upstairs. The appellant got a taxi home. The taxi driver said she was arrogant and quarrelsome, which she denies.

Her account in evidence of what happened after that was that she found the deceased still lying on the couch. She went upstairs, changed into her night-clothes and came down again to persuade the deceased to come to bed. He insulted her, calling her a whore and alleging she had been selling her body. He wanted her out of the house and threatened to kill her. She went to the kitchen to calm down. She decided to try again to persuade him to come to bed, but looked for a truncheon retained from when he had been a policeman so as to protect herself if he became violent. Not finding the truncheon, she picked up a large kitchen knife. She returned to the deceased, who again threatened to kill her and called her a whore. She stood beside him, lifted the knife and then brought it down slowly. A post-mortem examination showed the single stab had entered just below the ribs and penetrated deeply through to the back of the ribcage. In evidence the appellant said she had not stabbed the deceased deliberately. She denied she did it because she was provoked or because she was mentally upset. Asked in cross-examination if it was an accident, she repeatedly said 'Yes'.

Martin who was upstairs when the appellant came home, had heard no quarrel or raised voices. What he did hear was the rattling of cutlery in the drawer, followed by a scream from his father. He went downstairs. The appellant said in a cold matter-of-fact tone: 'I've killed your father'. She telephoned for an ambulance and said: 'I've just killed my husband. I've stuck a six-inch carving knife in his belly on the left-hand side'. The ambulance and police came. To a police officer the appellant said: 'I've stabbed him with this carving knife'. Asked 'Have you tried to kill him?' she said 'I wanted to kill him'. When the emergency service were making efforts to save him the appellant said: 'I don't know why you are bothering, let him die'. Martin heard her say: 'Let the bastard die'. The police officer asked: 'Do you understand what you are saying?' She replied: 'Yes, I know exactly what I am saying. I sharpened up the knife so I could kill him. Do you know what he has done to me in the past?' Asked 'When did you sharpen the bread knife?' she replied:

'After I went to see him in there. I said are you coming to bed love and he told me to fuck off out and fuck some blokes to get some money, so I just walked into the kitchen, got the knife, sharpened it up and stuck it in his belly.'
Q. Did he beat you up tonight? A. No
Q. Did he threaten to? A. He would have.

Later, the appellant said to the police: 'I nearly did it on Sunday you know'. Whilst the police were at the house, the appellant behaved in a surprising, Mr Mansfield QC says bizarre, manner. She began to use the floor-mop, she talked about the washing, a meal, and wanting to tune the guitar. She wanted to take photographs of her husband and telephone the taxi for her handbag and cigarettes. She pinched a police officer's bottom, telling him he had 'a lovely bum'.

In her interviews with the police she said repeatedly she only intended to frighten her husband.

Questions:
1. How does Lord Taylor's construction of the facts and narrative sequence in this second appeal differ from those in Sara Thornton's earlier appeal as recounted by Nicolson above?

2. To what extent do you think this re-presentation of Thornton's story may have contributed to the Court's decision that the appeal should be allowed, on the grounds that fresh medical evidence of personality disorder and the fact that she suffered from 'battered wife syndrome' would have resulted in different directions to the jury?

For another excellent analysis of the way in which 'facts' may be presented in a biased or selective way (this time in the context of a health care decision on whether or not to authorise the sterilisation of a disabled adolescent), see R Lee and D Morgan, 'A Lesser Sacrifice: Sterilisation and the Mentally Handicapped Woman' in Lee and Morgan (eds) *Birthrights: Law and Ethics at the Beginning of Life*, London, Routledge, 1987.

Chapter 5

Negotiation

WHEN DO WE NEGOTIATE?

Before you read any further, to help put this chapter in the context of your own personal experience, try answering the following questions:

1. What is 'negotiation'?
2. What makes a good negotiator?
3. What is a 'good outcome' in a negotiation?

When you have worked through this chapter, reread what you have just written, and then modify it in light of what you have learnt.

Negotiation is something you have been doing all your life, whether you realised it or not. A baby soon learns that if it cries it will get food; as a teenager, you will have become skilled at negotiating how late you could stay out at night, where you could go and with whom. If working, you may have negotiated holidays, pay, or work conditions. If you have ever rented accommodation you may have negotiated the price, who will do repairs, who will pay what expenses, how much of a deposit to pay to cover possible damage, who will decide what 'damage' is, and how you evaluate its cost. In fact, every day you negotiate — what to have for tea, what programmes to watch on television, an essay deadline extension, or to reschedule a tutorial. Make a list of the negotiations you have done in the last week; you already have a well of experience from which to draw.

Often disputes which could end up in court are 'negotiated' before the dispute even reaches a solicitor. There are many ways of resolving disputes, which people may use depending on the nature of the dispute. For example, on the advice of organisations such as the Citizens' Advice Bureau or Consumer Advice, a person may have written letters, stating their case and demanding recompense. The person may have threatened legal action, they may have gone to an arbitration board, an ombudsman or a regulator (such as one of the independent watchdogs appointed to look after the interests of customers of privatised utilities such as gas and electricity). The person may have gone to a marriage guidance service such as 'Relate'; they may have consulted with a trade union. In many cases such action may lead to a satisfactory resolution of the dispute. It is often only after steps like these have been taken unsuccessfully that a person resorts to litigation.

Even when litigation is resorted to, negotiation is the prime method of reaching a resolution, and is a skill used daily by both solicitors and barristers. 95 per cent of High Court cases are settled before the inside of the court is ever reached. Consider the following discussion, which begins with a barrister's comparison of negotiation with litigation:

J Morison and P Leith, *The Barrister's World and the Nature of Law,* Milton Keynes, Open University Press (1992), pp. 122, 123.

'You use related skills . . . instead of persuading a judge or a jury . . . you're doing the same on your opposite number . . . I'm trying to persuade you that this is a very, very small case and there's nothing wrong with your guy. You're trying to persuade me that this is a big case. You have to be able to put it over to the other side in such a way that he is impressed.'

Negotiation and settlement is an important part of a civil practice. Barristers are often required to give opinions which will back up a position taken by a solicitor in a negotiation. The barrister may not be directly involved in all or even most of the settlements. However, there is still a large number of cases where barristers do play a very active role. As one fairly senior advocate put it, 'Ninety per cent of my work is settlement. You have to be a good settler as well as a good fighter'. Communicating with the opposition is a fairly basic step in running a case and one that is generally followed:

'You must always speak to the other counsel . . . we don't tell lies . . . he may have a good point which the judge is going to take on board and you're going to go down — you then say, "Give us some money and we will settle this thing".'

In addition to the informal practice of settling, negotiation or 'alternative dispute resolution' (being an alternative to a court process) is increasingly finding a formal place in different areas of legal practice. Processes of so-called 'alternative dispute resolution' include mediation, adjudication, private judging, conciliation and family mediation (see A Bevan, *Alternative Dispute Resolution,* London, Sweet & Maxwell, 1992, pp. 6–17). Contracts or collective agreements may stipulate that arbitration should take place if there is a dispute. In private international law, parties such as multi-national companies and governments have always favoured arbitration over courts; contracts between these parties often include a provision that any disputes will be resolved by arbitration. Why do you think this is? In the US a number of states with federal districts have developed compulsory but non-binding arbitration schemes which have to be used before litigation is allowed. It has even been argued that the court process itself is a form of negotiation: 'The advocate when presenting the lay client's case in court, is not presenting a list of logical facts. He or she is in constant social negotiation with the judge, the witness, the jury, the opposing advocate over what shall, in the trial, constitute the "facts".' (Morison and Leith, *op cit*, p. 191.)

PRACTISING SKILLS: WHAT IS NEGOTIATION?

All of the above examples illustrate the increasing use of negotiation skills for lawyers. Like any of the skills discussed in this book, some people already possess better negotiation skills than others. However, while natural ability will always be an advantage, each person can always improve their own skills. This chapter seeks to help you to improve your skills in two ways:

(a)   By becoming more self-conscious about your use of the skill. This involves becoming more aware of situations in which you are negotiating, and learning to analyse or reflect on your own approach or behaviour.

(b)   By practising your skills. This chapter has several 'games' which can be set up in class (or outside) for you to practise your skills in relative safety.

The following are some definitions of 'negotiation'.

Roger Fisher, 'Negotiating Power: Getting and Using Influence' in J W Breslin and J Z Rubin, *Negotiation Theory and Practice*, Cambridge, Massachusetts, Program on Negotiation at Harvard Law School (1991), pp. 127–140 at pp. 127–128.

It seems best to define 'negotiation' as including all cases in which two or more parties are communicating, each for the purpose of influencing the other's decision. Nothing seems to be gained by limiting the concept to formal negotiations taking place at a table, and much to be gained by defining the subject broadly. Many actions taken away from a table — ranging from making political speeches to building nuclear missiles — are taken for the purpose of 'sending a message' to affect decisions of the other side.

Ann Halpern, *Negotiating Skills*, London, Blackstone Press Ltd (1992), p. 2.

Negotiation is: a basic means of getting what you want from others. It is back and forth communication designed to reach an agreement when you and the other side have some interests that are shared and others that are opposed.

Carrie Menkel-Meadow, 'Toward Another View of Legal Negotiation: The Structure of Problem Solving', *UCLA Law Review* (1984), vol. 31 pp. 754–842 at p. 755.

When people negotiate they engage in a particular kind of social behaviour; they seek to do together what they cannot do alone. Those who negotiate are sometimes principals attempting to solve their own problems, or, more likely in legal negotiation, they are agents acting for clients, within the bounds of the law.

Albie M Davis, 'An Interview with Mary Parker Follett', in J W Breslin and J Z Rubin, *op cit*, pp. 13–26 at p. 14.

As conflict — difference — is here in the world, as we cannot avoid it, we should, I think, use it. Instead of condemning it, we should set it to work for us. Why not? What does the mechanical engineer do with friction? Of course his chief job is to eliminate friction, but it is true that he also capitalises friction. The transmission of power by belts depends on friction between the belt and the pulley. The friction between the driving wheel of the locomotive and the track is necessary to haul the train. All polishing is done by friction. The music of the violin we get by friction. We left the savage state when we discovered fire by friction. We talk of the friction of mind on mind as a good thing. So in business, too, we have to know when to try to eliminate friction and when to try to capitalise it, when to see what work we can make it do.

It is often suggested that there are three main strategies of negotiation: competitive or hard bargaining; co-operative or soft bargaining; and problem solving or principled bargaining. Hard bargaining is characterised by each side adopting a rigid position which is more extreme than the position they hope to settle for. Each side then concedes and counterconcedes very gradually until a midpoint between the positions is reached. This classically takes place in many personal injury disputes where an overly high opening bid is countered by an overly low counterbid, and settlement may ensue. Soft bargaining concentrates on the relationship between the bargainers rather than their demands. It is often used where there is a lot of trust between the parties and where preserving or improving the relationship between them is at least as important as the outcome of the negotiation. A good example is in the family settings where children and parents negotiate over time of coming home, or bed time. Positions adopted are flexible and concessions are made easily. Principled bargaining has been developed out of a dissatisfaction with the hard bargaining/soft bargaining choice. While many people feel that the hard bargaining approach is unsatisfactory, inefficient and risky to use, in many legal and business transactions soft bargaining is also inappropriate and if adopted against a hard bargainer will lead to a poor result. The choices between whether to use a competitive/hard strategy or a co-operative/soft strategy have been evaluated in the following way:

R Fisher and W Ury with B Patton, *Getting to Yes: Negotiating Agreement Without Giving In*, London, Penguin Books, 2nd edn (1991), p. 9.

Problem
Positional Bargaining: Which Game Should You Play?

Soft	**Hard**
Participants are friends	Participants are adversaries.
The goal is agreement.	The goal is victory.
Make concessions to cultivate the relationship.	Demand concessions as a condition of the relationship.
Be soft on the people and the problem.	Be hard on the problem and the people.
Trust others.	Distrust others.
Change your position easily.	Dig in to your position.
Make offers.	Make threats.
Disclose your bottom line.	Mislead as to your bottom line.
Accept one-sided losses to reach agreement.	Demand one-sided gains as the price of agreement.
Search for the single answer: the one *they* will accept.	Search for the single answer: the one *you* will accept.
Insist on agreement.	Insist on your position.
Try to avoid a contest of will.	Try to win a contest of will.
Yield to pressure.	Apply pressure.

Fisher, Ury and Patton suggest that instead of following one of these strategies, you 'change the game' to one of principled negotiation, which has four basic elements (*op cit*, pp. 10–12):

People: Separate the people from the problem.
Interests: Focus on interests, not positions.
Options: Generate a variety of possibilities before deciding what to do.
Criteria: Insist that the result be based on some objective standard.

The first point responds to the fact that human beings are not computers. We are creatures of strong emotions who often have radically different perceptions and have difficulty communicating clearly. Emotions typically become entangled with the objective merits of the problem. Taking positions just makes this worse because people's egos become identified with their positions. Hence, before working on the substantive problem, the 'people problem' should be disentangled from it and dealt with separately. Figuratively if not literally, the participants should come to see themselves as working side by side, attacking the problem, not each other. Hence the first proposition: *Separate the people from the problem.*

The second point is designed to overcome the drawback of focusing on people's stated positions when the object of a negotiation is to satisfy their underlying interests. A negotiating position often obscures what you really want. Compromising between positions is not likely to produce an agreement which will effectively take care of the human needs that led people to adopt those positions. The second basic element of the method is: *Focus on interest, not positions.*

The third point responds to the difficulty of designing optimal solutions while under pressure. Trying to decide in the presence of an adversary narrows your vision. Having a lot at stake inhibits creativity. So does searching for the one right solution. You can offset these constraints by setting aside a designated time within which to think up a wide range of possible solutions that advance shared interests and creatively reconcile differing interests. Hence the third basic point: Before trying to reach agreement; *invent options for mutual gain*.

Where interests are directly opposed, a negotiator may be able to obtain a favourable result simply by being stubborn. That method tends to reward intransigence and produce arbitrary results. However, you can counter such a negotiator by insisting that his single say-so is not enough and that the agreement must reflect some fair standard, independent of the naked will of either side. This does not mean insisting that the terms be based on the standard you select, but only that some fair standard such as market value, expert opinion, custom, or law determine the outcome. By discussing such criteria rather than what the parties are willing or unwilling to do, neither party need give in to the other; both can defer to a fair solution. Hence the fourth basic point: *Insist on using objective criteria*.

. . .

The four propositions of principled negotiation are relevant from the time you begin to think about negotiating until the time either an agreement is reached or you decide to break off the effort.

Try practising your own strategies by negotiating '*Rose* v *No Drama Insurance*' (the parts are at the end of this chapter). One person should take the part of solicitor for Ms Rose (p. 188 below), and the other should take the part of in-house lawyer for No Drama Insurance (p. 190 below). It is important at this stage that you *do not read the opposite part*, as for the role-play to work, it is necessary that you know your own side only. Both parts should refer to the medical report on p. 189. You should spend approximately half an hour preparing, and half an hour negotiating the exercise.

Questions:
1.   Did you reach agreement? If so, did you find it easy or difficult to reach agreement? What was your agreement? If you didn't reach agreement, why not?

2.   Did your partner have an identifiable strategy? Did you? Did your respective strategies change at all? If so, why? What did both of you lose or gain by adopting certain tactics? Did either of you make unilateral concessions?

3.   Did you discuss legitimate standards for reaching a settlement?

4.   How do you both feel about the outcome? Do you feel it was fair? Did your satisfaction change when you found out other people's outcomes?

Turn to p. 192 where some comparative court awards can be seen. Does this affect your satisfaction with your own outcome? Was your settlement result, or failure to settle a better course of action than if you had litigated and received a result such as this?

In personal injury cases, the negotiation is often essentially a 'zero sum game': a gain for one side is a loss for the other. In other types of dispute there are often a more varied set of interests with more scope for creative settlement.

WHAT IS A 'GOOD OUTCOME' IN NEGOTIATION?

One of the problems with question *4* above, is that often we are not sure of what constitutes a good outcome in a negotiation. Each person may have different reasons for feeling that an outcome was good or not. Look at the following markers of success in a negotiation — with which do you agree?

Not to feel cheated.	To feel that you got a fair deal.
To feel that you beat the other person down.	To get the most money possible.
To appear firm or tough.	To appear magnanimous or affable.
To reach agreement.	To reach an agreement with which your client is happy.
Not to compromise.	To compromise a little.
To extract concessions from the other side.	To make sure that they are more unhappy with it that you are.
To call their bluff.	To avoid criticism.
To avoid confrontation.	To be able to negotiate with this person again.

Often a 'good outcome' is one which is good on several different fronts, such as the result, fairness to both parties, ability to negotiate in the future. To achieve this, it is very important to prepare carefully and strategically before negotiating. Lawyers who would spend weeks preparing for a case will approach an offer of settlement with a 'let's see what they say' approach. Before you can begin a negotiation you should carefully assess and know your own position, and also try to anticipate the other side's. Having a sense of what a good negotiation result might look like before entering a negotiation can help your preparation. Consider the following criteria:

C Menkel-Meadow, *op cit*, p. 760 (footnotes omitted).

1.   Does the solution reflect the client's total set of 'real' needs, goals and objectives, in both the short and the long term?
2.   Does the solution reflect the other party's full set of 'real' needs, goals and objectives, in both the short and long term?
3.   Does the solution promote the relationship the client desires with the other party?
4.   Have the parties explored all the possible solutions that might either make each better off or one party better off with no adverse consequences to the other party?
5.   Has the solution been achieved at the lowest possible transaction costs relative to the desirability of the result?

6.   Is the solution achievable, or has it only raised more problems that need to be solved? Are the parties committed to the solution so it can be enforced without regret?

7.   Has the solution been achieved in a manner congruent with the client's desire to participate in and affect the negotiation?

8.   Is the solution 'fair' or 'just'? Have the parties considered the legitimacy of each other's claims and made any adjustments they feel are humanely or morally indicated?

While in negotiation, your negotiating power will also be strengthened by good *communication* between the parties. Good communication involves both active listening and responding. Think about what you are going to say to the other side — how will they perceive what you are going to say?

When negotiating, effective communication can become part of the solution to a problem in the following ways.

Effective communication can fulfil one of the other party's substative needs. Consider the following discussion:

S Goldberg, E Green and F Sander, 'Saying You're Sorry', in J W Breslin and J Z Rubin, *op cit*, pp. 141–144 at p. 141.

In my first year Contracts class, I wished to review various doctrines we had recently studied. I put the following:

In a long term instalment contract, seller promises buyer to deliver widgets at the rate of 1,000 a month. The first two deliveries are perfect. However, in the third month seller delivers only 900 widgets. Buyer becomes so incensed that he rejects deliveries and refuses to pay for the widgets already delivered.

After stating the problem, I asked, 'If you were Seller, what would you say?' What I was looking for was a discussion of the various common law theories which would force the buyer to pay for the widgets delivered and those which would throw Buyer into breach for cancelling the remaining deliveries. In short, I wanted the class to come up with the legal doctrines which would allow Seller to crush Buyer.

After asking the question, I looked around the room for a volunteer. As is so often the case with first year students, I found that they were all either writing in their notebooks or inspecting their shoes. There was, however, one eager face, that of an eight-year-old son of one of my students. It seems that he was suffering through Contracts due to his mother's sin of failing to find a sitter. Suddenly he raised his hand. Such behaviour, even from an eight-year-old, must be rewarded.

'OK.' I said, 'What would you say if you were the seller?'
'I'd say, "I'm Sorry".'

Many mediators have had one or more experiences in which an apology was the key to a settlement that might otherwise not have been attainable. At times, all the injured party wants is an admission by the other party that he or she did wrong; no more is necessary to achieve a settlement. At other times, an apology alone is insufficient to resolve a dispute, but will so reduce tension and ease the relationship between the parties that the issues separating them are resolved with dispatch.

Effective communication can persuade by 'reframing' issues.

W Ury, *Getting Past No: Negotiating Your Way From Confrontation To Cooperation*, New York, Bantam Books (1993), pp. 78, 80.

Remember the batting secret of the great home-run hitter, Sadahara Oh. Oh looked on the opposing pitcher as his *partner*, who with every pitch was serving up an *opportunity* for him to hit a home run. Oh changed the game by *reframing* the situation.

To change the negotiation game, you need to do the same thing. Do the opposite of what you may feel tempted to do. Treat your opponent like a partner. Instead of rejecting what your opponent says, accept it — and reframe it as an opportunity to talk about the problem.
. . .

Reframing works because every message is subject to interpretation. You have the *power of positive perception*, the ability to put a problem-solving frame around whatever the other side says. They will often go along with your reinterpretation . . . partly because they are surprised that you have not rejected their position and partly because they are eager to pursue their argument.

Because they are concentrating on the *outcome* of the negotiation, they may not even be aware that you have subtly changed the *process*. Instead of focusing on competing positions, you are figuring out how best to satisfy each side's interests. You don't need to ask the other side's permission. Just start to play the new game.

Reframing is one of the greatest powers you have at a negotiation. *The way to change the game is to change the frame.*

Consider the following effects of reframing communication (and compare this with the difference which a re-presentation of facts makes in Chapter 4):

M H Bazerman, 'Negotiator Judgment: A Critical Look at the Rationalist Assumption', in J W Breslin and J Z Rubin, *op cit,* pp. 197–209 at p. 198.

Tversky and Kahneman (1981) presented the following problem to a group of subjects:
    The US is preparing for the outbreak of an unusual . . . disease which is expected to kill 600 people. Two alternative programs are being considered. Which would you favour?

1. If Program A is adopted, 200 will be saved.
2. If Program B is adopted, there is a one-third probability that all will be saved and a two-thirds probability that none will be saved.

Of the 158 respondents, 76% chose Program A, while only 24% chose Program B. The prospect of being able to save 200 lives for certain was valued more highly by most of the subjects than a risky prospect of equal expected value. Thus, most subjects were risk-averse.

A second group of subjects received the same cover story and the following two choices:

1. If Program A is adopted, 400 people will die.
2. If Program B is adopted, there is a one-third probability that no-one will die and a two-thirds probability that 600 people will die.

Out of the 169 respondents in the second group, only 13% chose Program A, while 87% chose Program B. The prospect of 400 people dying was less acceptable to most of the subjects than a two-thirds probability that 600 would die. Thus, most subjects were risk-seeking.

Careful examination of two problems finds them to be *objectively* identical. However, changing the description of outcomes from lives saved (gains) to lives lost (losses) was sufficient to shift the majority of subjects from a risk-averse to a risk-seeking orientation.

Effective communication avoids escalation of antagonism.
Ury recommends a technique to achieve this which he calls 'going to the balcony'.

W Ury, *op cit*, pp. 37, 38.

O. Henry's story 'The Ransom of Red Chief' offers a fictional example of the power of not reacting. When their son was kidnapped, the parents chose not to respond to the kidnappers' demands. As time passed, the boy became such a burden to the kidnappers that they offered to pay the parents to take him back. The story illustrates the psychological game that depends on your reacting. By refusing to react, the parents thwarted the kidnappers' plans.

When you find yourself facing a difficult negotiation, you need to step back, collect your wits, and see the situation objectively. Imagine you are negotiating on a stage and then imagine yourself climbing onto a balcony overlooking the stage. The 'balcony' is a metaphor for a mental attitude of detachment. From the balcony you can calmly evaluate the conflict almost as if you were a third party. You can think constructively for both sides and look for a mutually satisfactory way to resolve the problem.

In the ancient Japanese art of swordsmanship, students were instructed to look at an opponent as if he were a far-off mountain. Musashi, the greatest samurai of all, called this a 'distanced view of close things'. Such is the view from the balcony.

Prepare for the second negotiation, called *Kramer* v *Kramer*. Solicitors for Mr Kramer will find their part on p. 189 and solicitors for Mrs Kramer will find their part on p. 191. Again do not look at the other part. Use the following questions to prepare. Preparation should take around 45 minutes, and negotiation 45 minutes. Consider:

What are the needs, objectives and interests of the people involved?
What issues of 'relationships' are present in the negotiation?
What possible solutions are there, depending on what the parties want, and what will satisfy legal obligations?
What legitimate standards do you have to refer to?
What are the communication issues?

Fisher, Ury and Patton also suggest that before entering any negotiation, you should consider what your *best alternative to a negotiated agreement* is (BATNA), i.e. what are 'the results you can obtain without negotiating' (*Getting to Yes: Negotiating Agreement Without Giving In, op cit,* p. 100). It is only by accurately evaluating what results you could obtain in the absence of an agreement that you can properly decide whether and when to enter an agreement. Think back to the negotiation exercise of *Rose* v *No Drama* and the question about whether your settlement was better than a possible in-court solution. Fisher and Ury's use of the BATNA would suggest that if it was not, you should have litigated. Likewise, if you failed to settle and the last offer on the table was better for you than an in-court settlement, then your decision to walk was the wrong one.

In a civil law dispute often the best alternative is to go to court and get a judgment. How good an alternative this is will depend on the strength of the case. In a family law case court may also be the best alternative, but any court judgment is still going to need an element of co-operation from each side in order to work.

The family law situation also raises the question of a gendered approach to negotiation. Do men and women perceive problems differently? Do they approach negotiation differently? It is often assumed that negotiation is a woman's natural sphere, and that women are natural conflict resolvers. Paradoxically, commentators have argued that women and minorities often do worse out of negotiation than when they go to court. Arguably, the negotiation process, being less formal, leaves more room for the subjective prejudices of negotiators to impact on the negotiation.

D Kolb and G Coolidge, 'Her Place at the Table: A Consideration of Gender Issues in Negotiation', in J W Breslin and J Z Rubin, *op cit*, pp. 261–277 at pp. 262–263 (references omitted).

There is a certain irony about trying to articulate a woman's voice in negotiation. Negotiation is often put forth as an alternative to violence and adversarial proceedings; it is an alternative which some argue reflects a feminine view of interaction. That is, it is better to talk than to fight, and to consider everybody's needs rather than pitting one party against the other in a win-lose contest. Further, advocates of negotiation and alternative forms of dispute resolution often espouse a model of negotiation that is based on problem-solving principles presumably designed to create outcomes that meet the interests and needs of all those involved, again a presumed feminine principle. If this is so, why should we care about articulating another voice? Presumably, if these authors are correct, that voice is already being heard and dominates much of the current prescriptive thinking about negotiation.

There are at least three reasons why the subject of an alternative voice in negotiation is not closed. First, our experience and those of others suggest that there are significant differences in the ways men and women are likely to approach negotiation and the styles they use in a search for agreement.

Although the research often yields contradictory conclusions, in every training situation in which we have been engaged, women come up and ask us to talk about the gender issues. The inference we draw from these interactions is that at least some women experience their gender as a factor in negotiation . . .

Secondly, there is evidence that in real negotiations (as opposed to simulations), women do not fare that well. In divorce mediation, for example, the settlements women received are inferior economically to those awarded in adjudication. In queries about salary negotiations, men report higher raises than women. If negotiation is a woman's place, we would expect women to excel, not be disadvantaged. There is a third reason why we need to focus on a woman's voice in negotiation: The prescriptions to get win-win outcomes in negotiation offer ambiguous advice to the negotiator, whether male or female. The advice to focus on interest, not positions and invent options for mutual gain emphasises the relational dimension of negotiation. There are indications, however that this advice is quite difficult for many to heed because it runs counter to prevailing cultural norms about the competitive and gaming aspect of negotiation.

Question:
1. In your attempts at negotiating have you perceived a male/female difference in approach? Which was more effective?

WHAT MAKES A GOOD NEGOTIATOR?

At the start of this book you considered what skills and qualities a lawyer should have. As lawyers are also negotiators it is useful to consider what skills and qualities a negotiator should have. Here are some suggestions:

A Halpern, *Negotiating Skills*, London, Blackstone Press Ltd (1992), pp. 8–10.

Successful negotiators tend to show a fair number of the qualities which are described here. To be successful you should aim to be: patient, willing to persevere, able to think on your feet, cool under pressure or under fire, inventive, creative, capable of changing and responding to a change in the pace of the negotiating meeting, capable of manipulating the proceedings so as to hide the true value to you of some or all of the issues which are on the table, self-confident, assertive, able to take and accept criticism, able to demonstrate good active listening skills, perceptive, able to exploit power, able to show self-control, able to take charge, analytical, persuasive, able to see the other side's point of view, flexible, slightly unpredictable, cautious, pleasant, tactful, reasonable, rational, realistic, ambitious, determined in the sense of having high goals, firm and resolute, able to show good business judgment, able to show that you can be unreasonable when necessary, able to show scepticism when necessary, able to feel comfortable with uncertainty and unemotional.

. . .

People who have been identified as generally not being very successful negotiators are those who: show eagerness to please, are rigid in their thinking, or are aggressive. Failing to prepare properly and so being unsure of the facts, the client's instructions and the law can completely undermine the position of a negotiator. Being inaccurate, slow to react or unable to think laterally or creatively will often lead to a poor result.

J Nyerges, 'Ten Commandments for a Negotiator', in J W Breslin and J Z Rubin, *op cit*, pp. 186–193 at pp. 186–187, 192–193.

The question of what makes a good negotiator continues to intrigue me. Based on my own observation and study I've developed my own 'Ten Commandments for a Negotiator'. Here they are:

1. You shall love and cherish your trade.
2. Be courageous. Accept your responsibilities gladly.
3. The eagle's eye must be yours: assess situations quickly.
4. Remember, there are no problems, only opportunities.
5. Be honest under all circumstances.
6. Love your opponent even if you receive something less than that in return.
7. Put yourself in the shoes of your opponent, but do not remain there too long.
8. Convert your opponent into your partner.
9. Do not act before you have found out your partner's aims.
10. Your partner is at least as intelligent as you are; but, you must have more will.

Question:
1. Try making a list of ten commandments for what amounts to a good negotiator.

EXAMPLES OF NEGOTIATION AS A PART OF THE LEGAL SYSTEM

1. CIVIL LAW

In his interim report 'Access to Justice', focusing on reform of the civil law, Lord Woolf considered the role of ADR and in particular whether it should be compulsory. The following extract lays out his discussion and recommendations, some of which were included in his final report.

'Access to Justice: Interim Report to the Lord Chancellor on the civil justice system in England and Wales', June 1995.

The Place of ADR in the civil justice system

1.   In recent years there has been, both in this country and overseas, a growth in alternative dispute resolution (ADR) and an increasing recognition of its contribution to the fair, appropriate and effective resolution of civil disputes. The fact that litigation is not the only means of achieving this aim, and may not in all cases be the best, is my main reason for including ADR in an Inquiry whose central focus is on improving access to justice through the courts. My second reason is to increase awareness still further, among the legal profession and the general public, of what ADR has to offer. Finally, it is also desirable to consider whether the various forms of ADR have any lessons to offer the courts in terms of practices and procedures.

2.   From the point of view of the Court Service, ADR has the obvious advantage of saving scarce judicial and other resources. More significantly, in my view, it offers a variety of benefits to litigants or potential litigants. ADR is usually cheaper than litigation, and often produces quicker results. In some cases the parties will want to avoid the publicity associated with court proceedings. It may also be more beneficial for them, especially if they are involved in a continuing personal or business relationship, to choose a form of dispute resolution that will enable them to work out a mutually acceptable solution rather than submit to a legally correct adjudication which at least one party would inevitably find disappointing.

3.   Despite these advantages I do not propose that ADR should be compulsory either as an alternative or as a preliminary to litigation. The prevalence of compulsory ADR in some United States jurisdictions is largely due to the lack of court resources for civil trials. Fortunately the problems in the civil justice system in this country, serious as they are, are not so great as to require a wholesale compulsory reference of civil proceedings to outside resolution.

4.   In any event, I do not think it would be right in principle to erode the citizen's existing entitlement to seek a remedy from the civil courts, in relation either to private rights or to the breach by a public body of its duties to the public as a whole. I do, however, believe that the courts can and should play an important part, which I shall consider in more detail later in this chapter, in providing information about the availability of ADR and encouraging its use in appropriate cases.

The scope of ADR

5.   The various forms of ADR include some which resemble litigation in that they follow a relatively formal procedure and produce decisions which are binding on the parties, while others offer a considerably more flexible approach. ADR is used effectively in a wide variety of disputes, ranging from neighbours' quarrels to international commercial actions. Schemes may be court-annexed or independent of the court system, and may be used either before legal proceedings have begun or in the course of litigation . . .

Forms of ADR

7.   *Arbitration* is governed by statute, has a long-established relationship with the courts, and results in a decision which is binding on the parties. It is used extensively for commercial disputes but there are also a number of trade arbitration schemes which deal with consumer claims in particular areas of business.

8.   *Administrative tribunals* are ultimately subordinate to the courts, and are not a form of ADR in the sense of an additional option available to the parties since their jurisdiction normally excludes that of the courts. They are, however, intended to provide a simpler, less formal and more accessible means of resolving certain types of disputes than through the normal court process.

9.   *Mini-trials*, which may be private or judicial, were developed in North America. They are presided over by a judicial figure or neutral adviser, and involve the abbreviated presentation of evidence by representatives of the parties who have authority to settle the dispute.

10.   *Ombudsmen* deal with complaints about a range of services in both the public and private sectors. The public or statutory ombudsmen include the Parliamentary Commissioner (in his various roles), the Local Government Commissioner and the Legal Services Ombudsman. Private ombudsmen cover a number of service industries, such as insurance, building societies, banking and estate agency. The ombudsmen have wide powers of investigation, and their recommendations need not be limited to what is strictly permitted as a matter of law. Complainants are not prevented by an ombudsman's decision from subsequently taking proceedings in the courts.

11.   *Mediation* is offered by a number of private and voluntary organisations. Unlike other forms of ADR it does not result in a determinative adjudication, but is perhaps best described as a form of facilitated negotiation where a neutral third party guides the parties to their own solution. Mediation can be used in a wide range of disputes, and in many cases produces an outcome which would not have been possible through the strict application of the law . . .

ADR and the courts

32.   It is to be hoped that most lawyers will regard it as their responsibility to be able fully to acquaint their clients with the options but, nonetheless, the courts must encourage their use. There is some evidence that ADR is less effective when the parties have not chosen for themselves to participate in it,

and that is another reason for not making it compulsory. There are also indications, however, that parties are often reluctant to make the first move towards a negotiated settlement or to suggest ADR, in case this is interpreted by their opponents as a sign of weakness. Legal advisers who are not themselves experienced in ADR often adopt a similar attitude and so the court itself, as a neutral third party, has an important role in pointing out what options are available.

33.   The Lord Chief Justice's and Vice-Chancellor's Practice Direction of 24 January 1995 requires the parties to lodge with the court, not later than two months before the date of trial, a pre-trial check-list which includes questions as to whether they have considered the possibility of using ADR to resolve the dispute or particular issues. In the court-managed system which I propose in this report . . . I suggest that at every case management conference and pre-trial review the parties should be required to state:

(a)   whether they have discussed the question of ADR;
(b)   if not, why not; and
(c)   if so, with what result.

34.   If ADR had not been discussed at all, the judge could suggest that the parties (who should be present at the hearing) might avoid substantial costs by this route. If ADR has been discussed but some obstacle encountered (e.g. that both parties are so confident of victory that they are fearful of ADR leading to compromise) then the judge may be able to offer some appropriate advice. In deciding on the future conduct of the case, he should also be able to take into account a litigant's unreasonable refusal to attempt ADR. That would arise, for example, if the litigant had insisted on resorting to the courts without first taking his case to a perfectly satisfactory ombudsman scheme which would almost certainly have been capable of resolving the dispute at no charge to the litigant. This approach would be entirely consistent with another recommendation of this report involving a radical departure from the present position: that a party's means should be taken into account by a procedural judge in deciding what court procedures are appropriate. I intend to consult further as to whether an unreasonable refusal to resort to ADR should be a relevant factor in deciding issues as to costs . . .

Recommendations

My main recommendations are as follows:

(1)   Developments abroad, particularly those in the United States, Australia and Canada, in relation to ADR should be monitored, the Judicial Studies Board giving as much assistance as is practicable in relation to this exercise.
(2)   The retail sector should be encouraged to develop private ombudsman schemes to cover consumer complaints similar to those which now exist in relation to service industries; the government should facilitate this.
(3)   The relationship between ombudsmen and the courts should be broadened, enabling issues to be referred by the ombudsman to the courts and the courts to the ombudsman with the consent of those involved.

(4)   The discretion of the public ombudsmen to investigate issues involving maladministration which could be raised before the courts should be extended.

(5)   In the review of legal aid, the funding of voluntary organisations providing mediation services should be considered.

(6)   The courts should encourage and facilitate mini-trials in appropriate cases and use of mini-trials should be tested on an experimental basis in a selected number of courts.

(7)   The courts should, where appropriate, consider taking advantage of bodies such as the City Disputes Panel, to give authoritative guidance on particular practices from those who have experience at the highest level.

(8)   Where there is a satisfactory alternative to the resolution of disputes in court, use of which would be an advantage to the litigants, then the courts should encourage the use of this alternative: for this purpose, the staff and the judiciary must be aware of the forms of ADR which exist and what can be achieved.

(9)   At the case management conference and pre-trial review the parties should be required to state whether the question of ADR has been discussed and, if not, why not.

(10)   In deciding on the future conduct of a case, the judge should be able to take into account the litigant's unreasonable refusal to attempt ADR.

(11)   The Lord Chancellor and the Court Service should treat it as one of their responsibilities to make the public aware of the possibilities which ADR offers.

(12)   Consideration should be given to the way in which members of the professions who are experienced in litigation and who retire at an early age, can be involved as 'civil magistrates' or otherwise, in support of the civil justice system.

Question:
1.   What are the potential advantages and disadvantages of the various types of ADR?

2.   Do you agree with Lord Woolf's contention that ADR should not formally be made a part of the civil justice system?

FAMILY LAW

Provision for mediation already exists in the area of family law. The Family Law Act 1996 made some provision for mediation upon marriage breakdown following an 'information meeting' or during a 'period of reflection and consideration' when counselling can also be an option. Section 3 of the Act states the conditions for a divorce order, and these include that the requirements for information meetings are satisfied. Section 5 provides that the order can only be made if one or both of the parties comply with various provisions, including that a period for reflection and consideration has ended, and that the party making the application for an order makes a declaration that 'having reflected on the breakdown', and 'having considered the requirements of this Part as to the parties' arrangements for the future', the 'applicant believes the marriage cannot be saved' (section 5(1)(d)). Section 7 provides in part:

Family Law Act 1996.

7.—(1)   Where a statement has been made, a period for the parties—

(a)   to reflect on whether the marriage can be saved and to have an opportunity to effect a reconciliation, and

(b)   to consider what arrangments should be made for the future,

must pass before an application for a divorce order or for a separation order may be made by reference to that statement.

(2)   That period is to be known as the period for reflection and consideration.

(3) The period for reflection and consideration is nine months beginning with the fourteenth day after the day on which the statement is received by the court.

. . .

(6)   A statement which is made before the first anniversary of any marriage to which it relates is ineffective for the purposes of any application for a divorce order.

Section 8 lays out the requirements regarding information meetings:

8.—(1)   The requirements about information meetings are as follows.

(2)   A party making a statement must (except in prescribed circumstances) have attended an information meeting not less than three months before making the statement.

. . .

(5)   Where one party has made a statement, the other party must (except in prescribed circumstances) attend an information meeting before—

(a)   making any application to the court—

(i)   with respect to a child of the family; or

(ii)   of a prescribed description relating to property or financial matters; or

(b)   contesting any such application.

(6)   In this section 'information meeting' means a meeting organised, in accordance with prescribed provisions for the purpose—

(a)   of providing, in accordance with prescribed provisions, relevant information to the party or parties attending about matters which may arise in connection with the provisions of, or made under, this Part or Part III; and

(b)   of giving the party or parties attending the information meeting the opportunity of having a meeting with a marriage counsellor and of encouraging that party or those parties to attend that meeting.

The following chart shows the process in simple terms:

From *Divorce in Northern Ireland: Unravelling the System*, HMSO, (forthcoming) by C Archbold, C White, P McKee, Spence B Murtagh and M McWilliams.

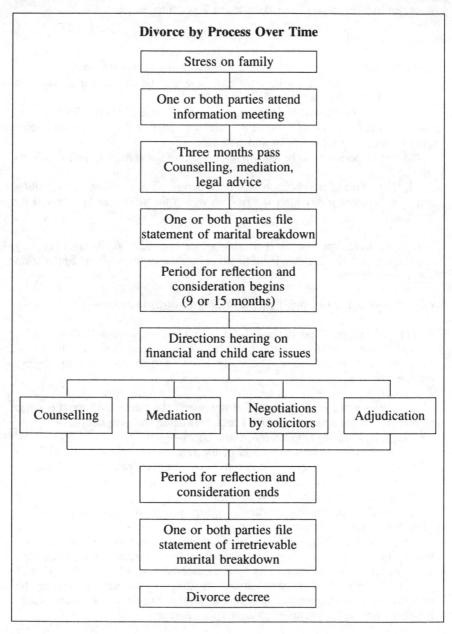

Questions:
1. Before full implementation of the Family Law Act 1996 (which may be in the year 2000) various aspects of the Act, including mediation, are being tested in a rolling programme of pilot projects; why do you think this is?

2. Do you think that negotiation is appropriate for all areas of law?

2. CRIMINAL LAW
It may seem that while negotiation is suitable for family and civil law, it is less suitable for criminal law. However, even in this area, the concept of 'plea bargaining' (reducing sentences in return for a guilty plea) has existed for a long time. More recently 'Restorative Justice' programmes are developing which attempt to view crime less as a violation of the state by an offender, and more as a breakdown of relationships between victim and offender which can be 'restored'. The following extract defines restorative justice and gives examples:

'Prospects for Restorative Justice in Northern Ireland', Quaker Service Committee, 1996

Definition of restorative justice
4.0   Given the wide range of practices which had been labelled Restorative Justice it was essential to develop a definition which could enable quantitative and qualitative data to be collected. Thus the definitions employed in this report are:

4.1   *Definition — Restorative justice is a dynamic attempt at reconciliation*
Restorative Justice is a response to a crime which invites and enables victims, offenders and the community to repair some of the injuries resulting from crime.

4.2   Restorative Justice can be defined as a set of processes which can take place within or outside of the formal criminal justice system which aim to make the victim central to the process of resolving the crime committed against them. The victim may be an individual, group of individuals or a community since crime is perceived as having both an individual and social dimensions of responsibility. The offenders are expected to accept accountability by assuming responsibility for their behaviour and taking subsequent action to repair harm done to the victim, directly or indirectly.

4.3   The focus of restorative justice is on problem solving, on liabilities and obligation and on the future i.e. planning what should be done to ameliorate some of the harm suffered. The emphasis throughout the process is on creating an environment in which voluntary dialogue may take place between the victim, offender and a third party (mediator/arbitrator).

4.4   Restitution may be used as a means of restoring both parties' (victim and offender) goal of reconciliation and restoration. Restoration in this context means return to the previous (enjoyed) undisturbed state of both victim and offender.

Practice methods

5.0   Restorative justice programmes have evolved in a range of practice methods, which include:

◆   Mediation — 'guided/structured communication' between the victim and offender implemented before, during or after (court) judgment.

◆   Reparation — in which the offender 'makes good' the damage created by his offence before, during or after (court) judgment. Reparation may be:

   ●   Direct — i.e. in which the offender repairs the damage he or she personally caused e.g. an act of vandalism in a park may be repaired by the actual offender under supervision.

   ●   Indirect i.e. in which the offender repairs the damage created by others e.g. an offender charged with criminal damage may clean graffiti on a park wall although there is no allegation or evidence that the offender was responsible for the specific graffiti.

◆   Compensation — in which the offender redresses the loss created by his offence before, during or after (court) judgment.

◆   Community Service — tasks undertaken and completed for the benefit of individuals or social institutions, as compensation for a crime may or may not be against the above individual or social institution. Community service can be undertaken informally or under a formal order of the court.

◆   Victim awareness education — in which offenders are confronted with the pain, loss and suffering caused directly or indirectly by their offending behaviour.

◆   Shaming and Reintegration — in which the offenders are confronted by the 'shame' associated pain and suffering caused to their 'supporters'; family, significant others, by having their victims outline their suffering in the presence of the offenders and their 'supporters'.

Question:

1.   Make a list comparing the strengths and weaknesses of advocacy and courts as compared to negotiation settlements as a way of resolving disputes.

Rose v No Drama Insurance Co. Ltd

Solicitor for Ms Rose

Rose v No Drama Insurance Co. Ltd

Ms Rose a nurse, d.o.b. 1/27/52, was involved in an accident in March 1997. She was driving with a seatbelt, when an on-coming car lost control and collided with the front of her car. Her car spun around but was not overturned or seriously mangled. Her driver's door and rear offside door were damaged and the repair bill to her car was under £900. Despite the fairly minimal damage Ms Rose claims that the impact was very severe. There appears to be little doubt that the other driver was at fault. Ms Rose has had ongoing injuries resulting from the accident. She is litigating against the insurers of the other driver, No Drama Insurance Company. You have received a doctor's report (see following page) which you have forwarded to the other side's lawyer. You are meeting with this solicitor and hope to settle the case to your advantage. You have jotted down the following figures as guidelines for damages: Ms Rose earns £200 net per week, with a few variations for overtime. She received her full pay for the first six months, and half pay for the next six months. She has just moved on to claiming invalidity benefit. As a general rule of thumb you calculate about £5,000–£6,000 per year for serious/bad pain and suffering. However, you have found a similiar case in which a man with similar symptoms lasting a year, and some permanent but not progressive sciatica received £10,000 general damages. Other awards have included money for housework and DIY in the future.

Kramer v Kramer
(designed by C Bell and C Archbold)

Solicitor representing Mr Kramer

Mr James Kramer is a 35 year old accountant and father of two children, Carie aged 9 and Jim aged 11. He has been married to Jean Kramer for 12 years. The marriage was a happy one at the start, but in the last couple of years it deteriorated and matters came to a head when James moved out of the matrimonial home five months ago. The couple do not see a reconciliation as realistic. James now lives with his mother and the children come to stay with him most Friday and Saturday nights. He has no formal maintenance agreement, but buys clothes and toys for the kids at the weekend, gives some money towards school trips, and most weekends also sends money home with the kids 'for mum' (usually around £60). He is fairly happy with the arrangement, but would like to 'see more of the kids' and in particular know when he can count on having them with him. He would like a formal joint custody arrangement where the kids reside half time with him. He has recently started to see someone else, but his main concern in developing that relationship is the kids' welfare and happiness. He has no immediate plans to set up a joint living arrangement with his new partner. When he has tried to discuss his wishes with Jean she has become very upset and matters have been left unresolved. James was very relieved when Jean agreed to a meeting of their solicitors to draw up an informal agreement as to their relationship in the future.

Ms Rose: Medical Report

Past History: Ms Rose is 47 years old, is trained as a nurse, and has worked for 17 years until the date of the accident, as a senior care assistant at Oldham Home for the Elderly, supervising two care assistants, with whose aid she looked after the needs of the elderly residents. In 1986 Ms Rose injured her back when lifting a patient, sustaining a lumbar disc lesion affecting the right leg. She attended an orthopaedic clinic in 1987, complaining of a nagging pain in her left leg which the attending consultant found difficult to assess, but from 1992 until the time of the accident she appears to have had relatively little trouble with her back. She has also had a history of anxiety and depression, attributable to a number of stressful situations in her domestic life.

History of the Injury: Ms Rose was the driver in a car, wearing a seat belt, when an on-coming vehicle lost control and collided with the front of her car. Ms Rose, while badly shocked by the collision, was not trapped in the car, nor did she suffer from any fractures or lacerations. However, due to her past conditions, her physical and psychiatric consequences went substantially beyond those which might have been expected. Within two days of the injury Ms Rose experienced pain in the back, radiating into the back of the leg. On the advice of her general practitioner she stayed in bed for two weeks, which relieved the symptoms, but they returned again after that period. In July 1997, she was admitted to hospital for a period of traction, remaining there for $3\frac{1}{2}$ weeks, when she was allowed home. During her time in hospital she suffered an ischaemic episode or minor stroke. This was not a true cerebral episode, but was a psychological or hysterical manifestation, and a consequence of her acute anxiety following the accident. On leaving hospital Ms Rose had physiotherapy for some six months. She was interviewed in December 1997, and discharged at the beginning of March 1998.

Present Complaints: Ms Rose still suffers from intermittent sciatic pain in her right leg and a certain amount of discomfort in her back. She describes the pain as tolerable in degree or mild, but at some periods she has complained of significant pain. Right leg raising is restricted, but this is not consistent with her ability to sit upright with legs extended on a couch, and it would appear that the limitation is caused by apprehension rather than real limitation. There is a pattern to her pain — certain things make it worse, such as stooping, standing too long or lifting, and she keeps it at bay with pain killers. Psychological troubles following from the psychological episode, are virtually a thing of the past. She has not returned to any type of work since the accident and has not made any serious attempt to find employment of any kind. At present she would not be fit for nursing duties which inevitably involve lifting and supporting of patients; however, she is fit for lighter duties.

Comment: I have advised Ms Rose not to return to her nursing duties for the indefinite future. I think that the likelihood is that her sciatic and back pain may not clear up sufficiently to enable her to return to work as a nurse, although she would be presently capable of working in other employment if lighter duties were involved. Although pre-existing injuries both physical and psychological were present, it is my opinion that their exacerbated presence is due to the recent injury. I estimate that her existing back injury would not have otherwise caused her problems in work until at least her mid fifties, if at all. Due to her level of function, I suggest that she needs to be re-evaluated at a later date in about nine months to one year.

Rose v No Drama Insurance Co. Ltd

Solicitor for No Drama Insurance Co. Ltd

Ms Rose a nurse, d.o.b. 1/27/52, was involved in an accident on 1 March 1997. She was driving with a seatbelt, when an on-coming car driven by your client's client, Mr Fleet, lost control and collided with the front of her car. Her car spun around but was not overturned or seriously mangled. Her driver's door and rear offside door were damaged and the repair bill to her car was under £900. Despite the fairly minimal damage Ms Rose claims that the impact was very severe. There appears to be little doubt that your client's client (a Mr Fleet) was at fault. Ms Rose has had ongoing injuries resulting from the accident. You have received a copy of the medical report dated 10 March 1998 (previous page), that you have received through Ms Rose's solicitor. You are meeting with this solicitor this afternoon, and hope to settle the case. You have jotted down the following figures as guidelines for damages: Ms Rose earns £200 net per week, with a few variations for overtime. She received her full pay for the first six months, and half pay for the next six months. She has just moved on to claiming invalidity benefit. As a general rule of thumb you calculate about £5,000–£6,000 per year for serious/bad pain and suffering. However, you have found a similiar case in which a man with similar symptoms lasting a year, and some permanent but not progressive sciatica received £10,000 general damages. Other awards have included money for housework and DIY in the future.

Kramer v Kramer

Solicitor representing Mrs Kramer

Mrs Jean Kramer is a 32 year old mother of two children, Carie aged 9 and Jim aged 11. She has been married to James Kramer, a 35 year old accountant, for 12 years. The marriage was a happy one at the start but in the last couple of years it deteriorated and matters came to a head when James moved out of the matrimonial home five months ago. The couple do not see a reconciliation as realistic. James now lives with his mother and the children stay with Jean, apart from some weekend nights when they go to James. There is no formal maintenance agreement (apart from the odd £40 passed to the kids when James is on a guilt trip). Jean is particularly worried about her financial situation. She pays the mortgage on the matrimonial home and also all bills and the children's expenses. Although she works part time in quite a well paid job, has flexible working hours and some choice over what days she works, she has been on sick leave for several months now due to the stress of her marriage break-up and the responsibilities it has left her with. Next month she must return to work or go onto half pay. Jean is resentful that James does not have any understanding of her financial difficulties, and is particularly upset at his attempts to 'buy the kids', by flaunting money for toys and luxuries which she cannot afford. She is also upset as she has heard rumours that James has a wealthy new girlfriend who is on the verge of moving him with him. Jean does not want James to have joint custody; indeed she would prefer not to have to work so that she can spend more time with the kids herself. However, she would need substantially more support from James to make ends meet even with her part time work. Whenever she begins to discuss her problems with James his lack of understanding makes her so furious that discussions break down almost straight away. Out of desperation she finally suggested to James that he meet with his solicitor to see if an informal agreement for maintenance payments could be drawn up. James agreed.

Note the following court awards:

In the Northern Irish case on which the facts of *Rose* v *No Drama* were based the judge found for the plaintiff, finding that the injury aggravated a pre-existing injury. The losses were calculated in 1993 as follows: sum to be refunded for benefits, £2,528; loss of earnings for approximately one year, £19,191, plus £20,000 for pain and injury; constituting a total of £41,719.

In *Skelson* v *Clwyd Health Authority* (2 November 1995, unreported) NLJ Digest 28 March 1997, p. 457, the following damages were awarded following a very painful back injury which left the plaintiff able to work with some pain, but unable to perform some tasks. General damages £14,000 for pain, suffering and loss of amenity; £9,000 (approximately 6 months' earnings); £6,290 for past housework, gardening and DIY costs; £32,760 for future housework and gardening (based on a multiplier of 18 on multiplicands of £600 per annum for housework, £520 per annum for ironing, £200 per annum for DIY and 35 weeks per annum at £10 per week for gardening); and £1,306.63 miscellaneous special damages.

Chapter 6

Advocacy

We saw in the previous chapter that we all unconsciously engage in negotiation in our everyday lives. This is equally true of advocacy — the skill which is the focus of this chapter. Advocacy, like negotiation, may therefore seem like a 'natural' skill.

However, although those who are naturally gifted with footballing skills may feel that football theory has little to offer them, even they will *watch* other skilful players in action and submit to *training* and *coaching*. Those who aspire to become good advocates can usefully observe good and bad advocates in action through visiting all levels of courts. They will soon find that basic communication skills, allied to the confident application of fact-finding and legal interpretation skills, form the foundation of good advocacy.

THE PRACTICE OF ADVOCACY

The role of advocacy has been undervalued in undergraduate legal education, although, together with negotiation, it is central to the practising lawyer's world:

J Morison and P Leith, *The Barrister's World and the Nature of Law*, Milton Keynes, Open University Press (1992), pp. 3–5.

We have lived through a century where, in the teaching and discussion of academic law, the role of the advocate has mostly been downplayed. As the training of the lawyer has moved from an apprenticeship system over to a university-based system, intending lawyers have found themselves more remote from the practice of law than ever before. In opposition to this, various forces and schools of thought (legal realism, clinical legal education and, most recently, Critical Legal Studies [see Chapter 7]) have tried to bring the horse of legal education to the water of practice. Unfortunately, the typical teacher of law has drunk elsewhere. Law, for most who teach law, has been seen to have life only in the law books on the library shelf, and to have authority only from the gradations of the printed word: case notes, legislation, law reports . . . Our view is that law is essentially rhetorical, rather than logical as many would have it. But rhetoric, exemplified and practised by the advocate, is about the dual facets of persuasion and information. Those who look to rhetoric as speechifying do not see that legal information and legal knowledge are as intimately connected to the rhetorical arts as is persuasion.

The more technical aspects of legal advocacy (how to address judges, the techniques of examination-in-chief and cross-examination, what questions would not be allowed etc) can be left to the vocational stage of legal training. The important skill to develop at undergraduate level is the technique of presenting a coherent and reasoned argument, based on your evaluation of the relevant facts. For our purposes, we follow Morison and Leith in defining advocacy as the art of rhetoric. This entails not only persuasion, but the marshalling of legal knowledge, and the construction of a reasoned argument.

M Hyam, *Advocacy Skills*, London, Blackstone Press Ltd (1990), pp. 5–6, 10.

At an early stage of preparation you must identify the argument which will be advanced in your speech, because it is a fundamental principle that effective speaking must be couched in the form of an argument. The word argument is here used to mean not only a connected series of statements or reasons intended to establish a position, but also to mean a theme or subject. The advantages of using the form of an argument are that, first it will provide you with a tool to cut into the amorphous mass of material with which you are confronted. For example, [in relation to] mitigation that you will be searching for an argument based on principle, and you will use the facts of the case to posit the argument. Secondly, as soon as the argument has been formulated the process of thinking out its logical sequence and bearings will greatly assist in the making of the groove in your mind. Thirdly, the logical sequence will be an aid to memory; and finally, the presentation of a flowing and coherent argument enables your hearers to understand what you are saying.

Once you have identified your argument, it should be constructed and developed by asking yourself intelligent questions, testing the validity of the argument, identifying weaknesses, silencing tacit objections and thinking how to present it with the maximum clarity . . .

Good advocacy depends on good preparation. It is necessary to prepare your case by taking both a general and specific view of it, so that you have clear in your mind not only what you have to prove or disprove, but also the way in which you are going to do it.

Rhetoric involves the selecting of relevant issues and formulation of narratives which help one's own (or client's) story, and then using that story to persuade the listener (or judge). In the legal context, Morison and Leith define it as 'the art of persuasion in a complex world'. They stress that aspiring barristers must do more than simply construct a clear argument:

J Morison and P Leith, *The Barrister's World, op cit*, pp. 192, 193 (references omitted).

Every piece of legal knowledge has the potential for confusion — from identifying the problem in the brief, developing strategy and, if necessary, presenting the case in a full court hearing . . . There is more to legal knowledge than simply telling a good (i.e. a coherent and consistent) story: that something else is the rhetorical element of selecting issues and negotiating and battling for facts which might help one's own story — all within the milieu of professional life. This is all to do with the construction of 'information', either in the court or before a case is initiated, or more generally from the interrelationships between the participants in the legal process. Furthermore, the information that is being constructed is, above all else, information that works within a given context and whose employment is closely determined by the pragmatic situation at hand . . . As Kuhn says in the context of scientific debate, in the end the force of scientific argument is 'only that of persuasion where "there is no standard higher than the assent of the relevant community" but what better criterion could there be?' In the legal context, the ruling of the court, the successful persuasion of a tribunal to a particular outlook, is itself constitutive of what is valid. Good legal information does not have to be 'true': it need only work . . .

[Storytelling (see further Chapter 4) and legal information] are both elements of the rhetorical constructional procedure which is the essence of applying legal knowledge. We can define the application of legal knowledge in fact, as the bringing together of narrative strategies and information construction . . .

[I]t is obvious from our interviews with barristers that the oral nature of the trial frequently gives rise to scenes and interpretations which cannot come from the more formal (but not necessarily non-narrative) use of paper advocacy. Observing barristers in action, for example, gives the lie to the 'golden rule' that can be found in most handbooks on advocacy and which was repeated by many barristers — that one should never ask a question to which the barrister does not know the answer. Though barristers all claim to be following this golden rule, it can easily be seen in many cross-examinations that they cannot follow it. An unexpected statement or a manner of answering a question by a witness which might lead to a whole new line of questioning (to which the barrister cannot know the answer) is marked by a silence of what seems several minutes as that barrister collects his wits, tries to keep a cool head and delves into the unknown. The manuals for the young barrister are explicit: they tell him or her at this point how important it is not so much as to raise an eyebrow in case the jury sees it. Notice that it does not have to be something which is *said* which leaves these openings, for it can be the intangible, non-verbalized signal which can only be seen or sensed and picked up through oral testimony.

And our informants frequently told us that it was important to have a judge who made some comment (either verbal or non-verbal) to show how the line of reasoning was being taken. The last thing our barristers wanted was the silent, static judge of the legal textbook. Without this feedback, their narratives would be cast, it seemed to them, into a void:

You have to have people on the bench who can read barristers and witnesses just as barristers can read the [other] barristers and witnesses. They [the judges] are missing part of what is going on in court; they are no longer part of the process.

Legal theorists have too often ignored the element of the spoken nature of introduced evidence, or the spoken nature of advocacy.

Questions:
1. In moots and mock trials, have you found the most difficult aspect to be the construction of arguments in advance, or thinking on your feet?

2. When you observe barristers in action to what extent do they have to think on their feet?

3. When you observe actual trials, how important do you think the advocate's body language and other non-verbal signals are?

As Hyam and Morison and Leith indicate, the skills of advocacy involve proper preparation and effective presentation of arguments — not just 'flowery speech'. On this view, there is a clear overlap, not only between advocacy and negotiation, but also advocacy and substantive law. Moreover, some barristers have suggested that advocacy is crucial in a democracy:

D Pannick, *Advocates*, Oxford, OUP (1992), pp. 7–11.

Acting in the interests of a client does not always promote the interests of society in general. Because he is paid to use his skills for causes which are at best dubious and may be positively dangerous, the advocate daily faces complex moral dilemmas. He must comply with a complex code of ethics which purports to reconcile his duties to his client with his duties to society . . .

[T]he barrister knows that there are limits to acceptable advocacy, problems concerning the extent to which he can and should act as mouthpiece of his (perhaps unscrupulous) client. He appreciates that there is a fine line between on the one hand, brilliant advocacy which focuses on the strength of his case and tugs at the emotions of the audience and, on the other hand, sharp practice and sham theatricals which mislead the court. He will often be uncertain where his duties to his client end and his obligations to society, and the court, begin . . .

[C]ourts recognize that for all its moral ambiguity, inherent contradictions, and plain absurdities, advocacy is central not only to our legal system but also to our way of life. Advocacy has, in its manifestation of freedom of expression, its protection of liberty, and its vital contribution to the rule of law, an essential morality which justifies its practice, excuses its excesses, and makes intolerable any society which lacks its presence. The advocate makes a valuable contribution to the maintenance of a society in which we have the protection that, whatever the allegations which may be made against us, the State can only punish or impose other detriments on us under the legal process by judging our conduct by reference to general rules laid down in advance and after hearing any points that can be made on our behalf. The role of the advocate is to ensure that in a legal system in which disputes are decided by rational debate, the viewpoints of those most affected are explained so that the court can properly decide where legal right lies. The advocate exemplifies the valuable principle that there is always another point of view, a different perspective, a contrary argument, of which account should be taken before judgement is delivered.

Indeed the principles of advocacy in our legal system have much to teach us about the more general values of reasoned debate, which are fundamental to the success, indeed the survival of a civilised society. Our culture is threatened by the decline of advocacy, that is the reluctance to present a case by means of persuasion, the refusal to listen to arguments for the other side, the resistance to considering the merits dispassionately, and the replacement of these methods of rational and objective debate and analysis by aggression and intolerance of all levels, domestic, national, and international.

There are, of course, many impediments to justice in our legal system, including the cost (inadequately met through current legal aid provision), the delay, and the complexity of the law. The maintenance of an independent profession of advocates, speaking on behalf of all litigants, cannot solve these difficulties. But it is important to appreciate the substantial contribution to justice made by the advocate. The essential principles of advocacy — a duty to act for any client, irrespective of the merits of his cause; an obligation to speak out on his behalf without fear or favour; and a legal immunity from action for what is said in court — are central to equality under the law . . .

Questions:
1.   Is Pannick guilty of overstating the importance of the services of legal professionals in a democracy? (See further Chapter 9 at pp. 331–4). Is advocacy really central to our way of life?

2.   Which other professions or ways of life involve advocacy? Can you think of any situations in which you have acted as an advocate? Is *legal* advocacy significantly different?

3.   Should advocates continue to be immune from prosecution for their performance in court? What are the arguments for and against?

For a rather different view of the significance of advocacy, consider the following extract from another celebrated barrister:

J Mortimer, *Clinging to the Wreckage*, London, Weidenfeld and Nicolson (1982), pp. 242, 243.

I have boasted, with no particular vanity, of being the best playwright ever to have defended a murderer at the Central Criminal Court. I have said this to the murderers I have defended. I doubt whether they have felt particularly encouraged. For them the Old Bailey is far removed from any sort of place of entertainment. I once congratulated a jury on having sat through what was undoubtedly the most boring case of the year, and the Judge was perfectly correct in his summing-up when he said, 'The sole purpose of the criminal law is not to amuse Mr Mortimer.'

And yet the practice of advocacy can only be a matter of deep interest to the writer whose daily obsession is with words. Standing to address a Jury, looking, as some have done, for a friend to support or an enemy to convert, the advocate tests the immediate effect of language. Like the actor he must lower or raise his voice to ensure attention. He must make his listeners feel that he is talking to them alone and yet he must seek for a combined response. In Court the right argument in the correct words may have the most obvious results; years of a man's or woman's life may depend on them. And in the theatre words have to prove themselves immediately, by solid laughter which unites an audience, or by that attentive silence when even the most bronchial listeners forget to cough, which is the greatest compliment that can be paid to the writer.

Oratory is no longer, as it was in classical times, or in the eighteenth century, considered an art. Most politicians' speeches are merely shrill assertions of their opponents' errors, and addresses in Court have become dull rehearsals of facts. It is as though we have become scared of our emotions and, if there are few calls now to the sense of freedom or natural justice, it may be because it's thought that such ideals would no longer interest an audience who, it is assumed, only care about wage differentials, law and order and 2p off the income tax. Alexander Herzen, who managed to preserve and develop his political beliefs during the gloomiest days of Czarist tyranny, said, 'You can waken them only by dreaming their dreams more clearly than they can dream them themselves, not by demonstrating their lives as geometrical theorems are demonstrated.' That, it seems to me, is a lesson which needs to be learnt, not only by the writer before his blank sheet of paper, but by everyone who gets up to make a speech.

And yet how many cases are won by advocacy? No doubt the answer is far, far fewer than the advocate cares to think. The facts of the matter are dealt to the barrister, like a hand at cards, or a bundle of inherited or acquired characteristics. At first glance he can tell if it is a rotten case or a winner and, although in the course of the argument he may persuade himself that a different result is possible, most cases turn out exactly as you had thought they would in the first half hour after undoing the tape and opening the brief. Clearly cases and hands at bridge can be lost, just as lives can be thrown away, by carelessness, over-confidence, letting in unnecessary evidence, failing to lead out trumps or not noticing when the queen went. And the consequences of defeat can be mitigated. Skill and persuasion, in the vast majority of cases, can go no further: we are stuck with the cards we are dealt and have to act out, as well as we can, the lives which we have been allotted. 'Everything is in other hands, Lucillius,' wrote Seneca the Stoic. 'Time alone is ours.'

Questions:
1.   Do you agree, from your observations in court, that very few cases are won by advocacy?
2.   Are the facts really as fixed as Mortimer suggests? (See Chapter 4.)

For a critical perspective on criminal advocacy and its standards consider the following:

Z Bankowski and G Mungham, *Images of Law*, London, Routledge & Kegan Paul (1976), p. 64.

> The emphasis on the importance of techniques in advocacy (i.e. the celebration of social skill rather than any insistence upon a detailed factual knowledge) is suggested in the following comments by solicitors:
>
> > 'Criminal advocacy is like criminal behaviour — in the sense that it is learnt.'
> > 'I think that the duty solicitor is a useful training ground for the young would-be advocate. Through it they can learn how to behave in court, because this is something that comes only by experience. You get the whole thing into you almost by a process of osmosis. You pick up the finer points of technique and it's this, rather than a detailed knowledge as such, that's really important in advocacy.'
>
> The difficulty of trying to establish any criteria for professional competence in the area of advocacy is borne out by the debate over the composition of the rota [for duty solicitors]. So far, the criteria for membership has gone through three phases: a 'free-for-all'; a restriction to two solicitors per firm; and finally granting access to all those who judge themselves to have 'substantial criminal court work experience'.

Question:
1. Can you think of any criteria for professional competence in advocacy?

THE ETHICS OF ADVOCACY

We saw in Chapter 4 that the role of the advocate could be crucial in challenging miscarriages of justice. One of the high profile cases discussed in Chapter 4 — the OJ Simpson case — raised similar concerns as the miscarriage of justice cases about popular and jury prejudice. In a book written subsequent to the case, US celebrity lawyer Alan Dershowitz, who was a member of the OJ Simpson 'dream team' of defence lawyers, discusses the different roles played by prosecution and defence witnesses.

A Dershowitz, *Reasonable Doubts: The Criminal Justice System and the OJ Simpson Case*, New York, Touchstone (1997), pp. 157, 166–7, 179–80.

> The role of defense lawyers and prosecutors in criminal cases is misunderstood by much of the public, including the well-informed public. Even many lawyers have little understanding of what advocates are expected to do in a hotly contested criminal trial . . .
> The most common complaint about lawyers — especially criminal defense lawyers — is that they distort the truth, and there is some sense in that

accusation. But . . . a criminal trial is anything but a pure search for truth. When defense lawyers represent guilty clients — as most do, most of the time — their responsibility is to try, by all fair and ethical means, to *prevent* the truth about their client's guilt from emerging. Failure to do so — failure or unwillingness to object to the truth on the ground that it was improperly obtained — is malpractice, which could get a defense lawyer disbarred and earn his client a new trial, at which he would be represented by a zealous defense lawyer willing and able to try to stop the truth from being proved.

Like it or not — and I like it — that is what our Constitution and our legal system require of defense counsel. Our legal system also permits the prosecutor to try to prevent certain truths from being proved, if the defense tries to prove them through hearsay or other improper evidence. But our legal system insists that the truth be suppressed exclusively by lawful and ethical means . . .

There is a general reason why prosecutors are more accepted than defense attorneys, and a particular reason why this was especially true in the Simpson case. In general, prosecutors wear the white hats: They stand for law and order; they represent the victims and the people or the state; they prosecute the guilty — at least most of the time; they are public servants; they are on the side of truth and the angels. Defense attorneys, on the other hand, generally represent guilty defendants. (And thank goodness for that. Would anyone want to live in a country where most defendants are innocent? Perhaps in Iran, Iraq or China, most people charged with crimes are innocent. Not so in this country, and it is the zealousness of the defense bar, among other factors that keeps it that way.) Defense attorneys are outsiders; they are perceived as obstructors of justice who invoke privileges, rights, and technicalities to exclude relevant evidence and to obscure the incriminating truth; if they are retained rather than appointed, they earn a profit from doing the devil's work.

Moreover, defense attorneys are supposed to be single-minded in their quest for acquittal by all legal and ethical means. They are not allowed to have any other agenda. They cannot put patriotism, good citizenship, religion, gender or racial solidarity, or commitment to any cause before the interests of their client. Nor is this a radical or modern notion. As a British barrister named Henry Brougham put it in 1820:

> An advocate, by the sacred duty which he owes his client, knows, in the discharge of that office, but one person in the world, that client and none other. To save that client by all expedient means — to protect that client at all hazards and costs to all others, and among others to himself, — is the highest and most unquestioned of his duties; and he must not regard the alarm, the suffering, the torment, the destructions which he may bring upon any other. Nay, separating even the duties of a patriot from those of an advocate, and casting them, if need be, to the wind, he must go on reckless of the consequences, if his fate it should happily be, to involve his country in confusion for his client's protection.

. . . A good defense attorney, especially one with a civil liberties perspective, could never win elective office because he or she must

occasionally represent very unpopular defendants — and sometimes even win
. . . Prosecutors, on the other hand are supposed to be good citizens. It is no
surprise, therefore that being a prosecutor is a stepping-stone to elective
office. The job of the prosecutor is to please the public. The job of the defense
attorney — whether he's a private lawyer or a public defender — is to win
for his client, without regard to what the public thinks. A defense attorney
must represent his client zealously within the bounds of law, whether the
client is guilty or innocent, popular or unpopular, rich or poor, male or
female, black or white. Since most defendants are guilty, and since an even
larger percentage are *assumed* to be guilty, defense attorneys will continue to
disappoint most of the public most of the time.

Questions:
1.   Do you agree with Dershowitz's characterisation of defence lawyers? Are
they really outsiders? Even if this is true of lawyers in the US, is it true of their
UK counterparts?

2.   Do you agree with Dershowitz's notion of what 'ethical' means? Does he
make any distinction between what is 'legal' and what is 'ethical'? (For a
contrary view see D Luban, *Lawyers and Justice: An Ethical Study*, New Jersey,
Princeton, 1988.)

3.   Are there any tactics which it would be unethical for an advocate to rely
upon? For example, is it ethical to rely on the right to silence? To question the
facts? To question whether the prosecution had *proved* the facts? To impugn the
authority of the court? (See the example of the Ceausescu trial used in the first
edition of this book at pp. 115–119.)

S Scheingold, 'The contradictions of radical law practice' in M Cain and C
Harrington (eds) *Lawyers in a postmodern world*, Buckingham, Open University
Press (1994), pp. 265–85, at pp. 266 (references omitted).

The standards of conventional advocacy that have been developed are rooted
in ostensibly contradictory principles of conduct. Lawyers are called upon to
combine neutrality with partisanship. On the one hand, the lawyer is to
maintain a studied detachment from the client's broader circumstances; on
the other, the lawyer is supposed to mount a highly partisan defence of the
client's legal interests — a defence which may include 'deception, obfusca-
tion, or delay' and worse.
     While appearing contradictory to the lay observer, this neutrality towards
both the most odious and meritorious of clients is to the legal mind a
precondition of effective partisan advocacy and is, therefore, essential to the
law. These principles of conventional legal ethics run counter to everyday
moral standards — amounting to 'an explicit refusal [by the lawyer] to be
bound by personal and social norms which he considers binding on others'.
Departures from lay morality serve the law, whose beneficent whole is greater
than the sum of its suspect tactical parts. More specifically, the procedural
standards which are at the heart of the legal enterprise have 'an inherent value

or legitimacy . . . which makes it possible for a lawyer to justify specific actions without reference to the consequences they are likely to promote'.

Both the prosecution and defence teams in the Simpson case were criticised for their tactics and ethics during the trial. Dershowitz's book is, in part, a rebuttal of the criticisms levelled at the defence. In the following extract, taken from a Web site on the Louise Woodward case (see Chapter 4 at pp. 137–40) Simpson himself phones in to a chatshow to defend another member of his defence team — Barry Scheck — who, as we have seen in Chapter 4, also acted as Woodward's lawyer.

Transcript of OJ Simpson Call on Defense Attorney Barry Scheck: Web address: http://www.courttv.com/trials/woodward/ojonscheck/jtml

O.J. Simpson Comments on Defense Lawyer Barry Scheck

During a court recess on October 17, Court TV anchor Carol Randolph spoke with O.J. Simpson. (Barry Scheck was part of Simpson's defense team during his criminal trial.) Simpson was responding to the many viewer comments about Scheck's style and tactics during the Woodward trial.

OCTOBER 17, 1997 AT 1:07 PM
O.J. Simpson called Court TV during the lunch break of Massachusetts v. Woodward, the trial of the 19-year-old au pair charged with murdering a baby. Below is the transcript of his live televised conversation with anchor Carol Randolph:

Carol Randolph:
There have been a lot of conversations today and throughout this trial about Barry Scheck and his very aggressive cross examination in the prosecution's case of many of the expert witnesses. Someone who knows first hand about Barry Scheck is our next caller who wanted to give an opinion about Barry Scheck, Mr. O.J. Simpson. Good morning Mr. Simpson. What is it that you want to add about Barry Scheck?

O.J. Simpson:
I find it curious that so many of your callers are calling in and your resident experts. I watched the case last week and this week before I go off to play golf and the comment that the general public seemed to have an attitude about Barry because of the outcome of my trial, I beg to differ with that. When I was in the courtroom I would read all the lawyers' letters. From day one, Barry, from the first appearance he made in court, got some very diverse letters, I would say 60/40 pro and con, pretty much like your callers have been, and most of the con towards Barry had to do with his, what I call Jewishness, and his style — I thought it was more rooted in maybe a certain animus towards his New York style Jewish style more than what he was actually doing in the courtroom.

When my trial was over I had one of my lawyers who was very against Barry presenting closing arguments because he felt that despite the length of the trial, Barry's style really didn't play to our jurors. But when the trial was over and the jury talked, almost unanimously, Barry was their favorite lawyer in that courtroom, and I think people are kind of overlooking it and using the result of my case as excuse to blame this controversy about Barry. I think it's more rooted in, possibly, in some people's animus toward that New York Jewish style, Brooklyn style, more than his ability. I don't know anyone in America, if they ever got in trouble that wouldn't want him on their defense team.

Carol Randolph:
Are you surprised that people would connect the outcome of your trial with Barry Scheck, or at least verbalize some animosity?

O.J. Simpson:
No not at all. Just about everything that happens — the El Nino out here in CA — is my fault. I think Barry Scheck is well respected. I spent some time with my entire defense team a few weeks ago celebrating the October 3 verdict in NY. I think the good that has come for Barry and many of those members of the entire defense team has far outweighed the negative that has come out. Once again, I want to stress from day one I would sit there in the courtroom and open all the lawyers' mail, and the reaction to Barry was immediate long before there was a verdict in my trial, and most of the reaction to him was to him and to his what I call his Jewishness and that New York style of his more so than the job he was doing in the courtroom.

Carol Randolph:
You also said that the jury said he was one of their favorites, did they say why?

O.J. Simpson:
I didn't read the jury books, but I saw them on TV. I think it was that fieriness of his; the fact that court can be boring. From last week and this week I've watched this trial because of Barry's involvement and it is boring. I was bored at times even in my trial, and Barry has a style that gets you interested immediately — like him or dislike him, he makes it a little more interesting in that courtroom. I believe unanimously every juror who spoke out after my trial — even on my defense team despite reservations about his style and how it played towards that jury — every member of that jury said that he was their favorite lawyer. And I think you'll be surprised when this trial is over and you poll that jury — one thing about Barry it won't be boring — I think he's always interesting.

Questions:
1. From your own observation of trials involving a jury, do you agree that jurors react to the personality of lawyers?

2. Do you agree with Simpson that the most important factor in attracting jury support for one's client is that the advocate should not be boring?

3. Can you think of any famous lawyers *you* would always want on your defence team?

As we seek to show through the above extracts, an undergraduate education ought to raise questions about the *ethics* of advocacy and ought to challenge students' preconceptions about the most successful methods of advocacy. Although we would encourage you to attend actual trials throughout your legal education, inevitably our notions of good advocacy are shaped by trial scenes from television, theatre and films. Indeed one aspect of the 'law and literature' movement (see Chapter 10 at pp. 409–11) involves considering how law is dealt with *in* literature. A trial is often used as a dramatic device — it creates the immediacy of a play within a play. Its popularity as a dramatic device brings us back to the notion of rhetoric and the 'drama of the courtroom'. Perhaps the most productive and enjoyable lesson is to watch films like *Music Box* in which an American advocate defends her father against accusations that he is a Nazi war criminal. Many other movies raise similar questions about the ethics of advocacy, such as *A Civil Action* and *The Accused*. But most drama, for obvious reasons, portrays the same kind of literally 'dramatic'; advocacy which distorts the diverse reality. There is little doubt that Shakespeare's *The Merchant of Venice* depicts the most famous fictional advocate of all time, Portia.

The Merchant of Venice, Act IV, Scene 1

Enter Portia as Balthazar, dressed like a Doctor of Laws.

DUKE:	You hear the learn'd Bellario, what he writes And here, I take it, is the doctor come. Give me your hand. Came you from old Bellario?
PORTIA	I did, my lord.
DUKE	Are you acquainted with the difference That holds this present question in court?
PORTIA	I am informed thoroughly of the cause Which is the merchant here?
DUKE	Antonio and old Shylock, both stand forth.
SHYLOCK	Shylock is my name.
PORTIA	Of a strange nature is the suit you follow, Yet in such rule that the Venetian law Cannot impugn you as you do proceed. (to Antonio) You stand within his danger, do you not?
ANTONIO	Ay, so he says.
PORTIA	Do you confess the bond?
ANTONIO	I do.
PORTIA	Then must the Jew be merciful.

SHYLOCK   On what compulsion must I? Tell me that.

PORTIA   The quality of mercy is not strained,
               It droppeth as the gentle rain from heaven
               Upon the place beneath. It is twice blest,
               It blesseth him that gives and him that takes.
               'Tis mightiest in the mightiest, it becomes
               The enthroned monarch better than his crown
               His sceptre shows the force of temporal power,
               The attribute to awe and majesty,
               Wherein doth sit the dread and fear of kings;
               But mercy is above this sceptred sway,
               It is enthroned in the hearts of kings,
               It is an attribute to God himself,
               And earthly power doth then show liketh God's
               When mercy seasons justice. Therefore, Jew,
               Though justice be thy plea, consider this:
               That in the course of justice none of us
               Should see salvation. We do pray for mercy,
               And that same prayer doth teach us all to render
               The deeds of mercy. I have spoke thus much
               To mitigate the justice of thy plea,
               Which if thou follow, this strict court of Venice
               Must needs give sentence 'gainst the merchant there.

SHYLOCK   My deeds upon my head! I crave the law,
               The penalty and forfeit of my bond.

PORTIA   Is he not able to discharge the money?

BASSANIO   Yes, here I tender it for him in the court
               Yea, twicc the sum. If that will not suffice,
               I will be bound to pay it ten times o'er
               On forfeit of my hands, my head, my heart.
               If this will not suffice, it must appear
               That malice bears down truth. And I beseech you,
               Wrest once the law to your authority,
               To do a great right, do a little wrong,
               And curb this cruel devil of his will.

PORTIA   It must not be. There is no power in Venice
               Can alter a decree established.
               'Twill be recorded for a precedent,
               And many an error by the same example
               Will rush into the state. It cannot be.

SHYLOCK   A Daniel come to judgement! Yea, a Daniel!
               O wise young judge, how I do honour thee!

PORTIA   I pray you let me look upon the bond.

SHYLOCK	Here 'tis, most reverend doctor, here it is.
PORTIA	Shylock, there's thrice the money offered thee.
SHYLOCK	An oath, an oath! I have an oath in heaven; Shall I lay perjury upon my soul? No, not for Venice!
PORTIA	Why, this bond is forfeit, And lawfully by this the Jew may claim A pound of flesh, to be by him cut off Nearest the merchant's heart. Be merciful, Take thrice thy money, bid me tear the bond.
SHYLOCK	When it is paid, according to the tenour. It doth appear you are a worthy judge, You know the law, your exposition Hath been most sound. I charge you by the law, Whereof you are a well-deserving pillar, Proceed to judgment. By my soul I swear There is no power in the tongue of man To alter me. I stay here on my bond.
ANTONIO	Most heartily I do beseech the court To give the judgment.
PORTIA	Why then, thus it is: You must prepare your bosom for his knife.
SHYLOCK	O, noble judge! O excellent young man!
PORTIA	For the intent and purpose of the law Hath full relation to the penalty, Which here appeareth due upon the bond.
SHYLOCK	'Tis very true. O wise and upright judge! How much more elder art thou than thy looks!
PORTIA	It is so. Are there balance here to weigh The flesh?
SHYLOCK	I have them ready.
PORTIA	Have by some surgeon, Shylock, on your charge, To stop his wounds, lest he do bleed to death.
SHYLOCK	Is it so nominated in the bond?
PORTIA	It is not so expressed, but what of that? 'Twere good you do so much for charity.
SHYLOCK	I cannot find it; 'tis not in the bond.
PORTIA	You, merchant, have you anything to say?

ANTONIO   But little. I am armed and well prepared.
             Give me your hand, Bassanio, fare you well.
             Grieve not that I am fallen to this for you,
             For herein, Fortune shows herself more kind
             Than is her custom; it is still her use
             To let the wretched man outlive his wealth
             To view with hollow eye and wrinkled brow
             An age of poverty, from which lingering penance
             Of such misery doth she cut me off.
             Commend me to your honourable wife,
             Tell her the process of Antonio's end,
             Say how I loved you, speak me fair in death,
             And when the tale is told, bid her be judge
             Whether Bassanio had not once a love.
             Repent but you that you shall lose your friend,
             And he repents not that he pays your debt,
             For if the Jew do cut but deep enough,
             I'll pay it instantly with all my heart.

BASSANIO   Antonio, I am married to a wife
             Which is as dear to me as life itself,
             But life itself, my wife, and all the world
             Are not with me esteemed above thy life.
             I would lose all, aye sacrifice them all
             Here to this devil, to deliver you.

PORTIA   Your wife would give you little thanks for that
             If she were by to hear you make the offer.

GRATIANO   I have a wife who I protest I love;
             I would she were in heaven, so she could
             Entreat some power to charge this currish Jew.

NERISSA   'Tis well you offer behind her back,
             The wish would make else an unquiet house.

SHYLOCK   These be the Christian husbands! I have a daughter;
             Would any of the stock of Barabbas
             Had been her husband, rather than a Christian.
             We trifle time. I pray thee pursue sentence.

PORTIA   A pound of that same merchant's flesh is thine,
             The court awards it, and the law doth give it.

SHYLOCK   Most rightful judge!

PORTIA   And you must cut this flesh from off his breast,
             The law allows it, and the court awards it.

SHYLOCK   Most learned judge! A sentence! Come, prepare!

PORTIA	Tarry a little, there is something else.
	This bond doth give thee here no jot of blood;
	The words expressively are 'a pound of flesh'.
	Take then thy bond, take thou thy pound of flesh,
	But in cutting it if thou dost shed
	One drop of Christian blood, thy lands and goods
	Are by the laws of Venice confiscate
	Unto the state of Venice.

GRATIANO   O upright judge! Mark, Jew. O learned judge!

SHYLOCK   Is that the law?

PORTIA   Thyself shalt see the act,
            For, as thou urgest justice, be assured
            Thou shalt have justice more than thou desir'st.

GRATIANO   O learned judge! Mark, Jew. A learned judge!

SHYLOCK   I take this offer then. Pay the bond thrice
            And let the Christian go.

BASSANIO   Here is the money.

PORTIA   Soft!
            The Jew shall have all justice. Soft, no haste,
            He shall have nothing but the penalty.

GRATIANO   O Jew! An upright judge, a learned judge!

PORTIA   Therefore prepare thee to cut off the flesh.
            Shed no blood, nor cut thou less nor more
            But just a pound of flesh. If thou tak'st more
            Or less than just a pound, be it but so much
            As it makes it light or heavy in the substance
            Or the division of the twentieth part
            Of one poor scruple, nay, if the scale do turn
            But in the estimation of a hair,
            Thou diest, and all thy goods are confiscate.

GRATIANO   A second Daniel! A Daniel, Jew!
            Now, infidel, I have you on the hip!

PORTIA   Why doth the Jew pause? Take thy forfeiture.

SHYLOCK   Give me my principal, and let me go.

BASSANIO   I have it ready for thee; here it is.

PORTIA   He hath refused it in the open court.
            He shall have merely justice and his bond.

GRATIANO   A Daniel still say I, a second Daniel!
            I thank thee, Jew, for teaching me that word.

SHYLOCK	Shall I not have barely my principle?
PORTIA	Thou shalt have nothing but the forfeiture, To be so taken at thy peril, Jew.
SHYLOCK	Why, then the devil give him good of it I'll stay no longer question.
PORTIA	Tarry, Jew! The law hath yet another hold on you. It is enacted in the laws of Venice, If it be proved against an alien That by direct or indirect attempts He seek the life of any citizen, The party 'gainst the which he doth contrive Shall seize one half his goods, the other half Comes to the privvy coffer of the state, And the offender's life lies in the mercy Of the Duke only, 'gainst all other voice, In which predicament I say thou stand'st, For it appears by manifest proceeding That indirectly, and directly too, Thou has contrived against the very life Of the defendant, and thou has incurred The danger formerly by me rehearsed. Down therefore, and beg mercy of the Duke.
GRATIANO	Beg that thou mayst have leave to hang thyself, And yet, thy wealth being forfeit to the state, Thou hast not left the value of a cord, Therefore thou must be hanged at the state's charge.
DUKE	That thou shalt see the difference of our spirit, I pardon thee thy life before thou ask it. For half thy wealth, it is Antonio's, The other half comes to the general state, Which humbleness may drive unto a fine.
PORTIA	Aye, for the state, not for Antonio.
SHYLOCK	Nay, take my life and all! Pardon not that! You take my house when you do take the prop That doth sustain my house. You take my life When you do take the means whereby I live.
PORTIA	What mercy can you render him, Antonio?
GRATIANO	A halter gratis! Nothing else, for God's sake!
ANTONIO	So please my lord the Duke and all the court To quit the fine for one half of his goods, I am content, so he will let me have

                    The other half in use, to render it
                    Upon his death unto the gentleman
                    That lately stole his daughter.
                    Two things provided more: that for this favour
                    He presently become a Christian;
                    The other, that he do record a gift
                    Here in the court of all he dies possessed
                    Unto his son Lorenzo and his daughter.

DUKE   He shall do this, or else I do recant
                    The pardon that I late pronounced here.

PORTIA   Art thou contented, Jew? What dost thou say?

SHYLOCK   I am content.

PORTIA   Clerk, draw a deed of gift.

SHYLOCK   I pray you give me leave to go from hence,
                    I am not well; send the deed after me,
                    And I will sign it.

DUKE   Get thee gone, but do it.

GRATIANO   In christ'ning shalt thou have two godfathers,
                    Had I been judge, thou shouldst have had ten more,
                    To bring thee to the gallows, not to the font.

EXIT SHYLOCK

Questions:
1. Who was Daniel? Is Portia an advocate or a judge? If the former, whose advocate is she?

2. Is it unethical for someone like Portia, with personal interest in a case, to act as an advocate?

3. Describe Portia's tactics as an advocate. If the law in Venice, as she claims, made it an offence to plot to kill a citizen, should Portia have mentioned this earlier?

4. Was Portia a lawyer? Can non-lawyers be as effective advocates as lawyers? (For example, consider the operation of various tribunals where lawyers and non-lawyers are often acting as advocates against one another, and see pp. 221–5 below.)

5. Is the 'quality of mercy' relevant? Has mercy triumphed over justice in this scene? (See C Menkel-Meadow, Portia *Redux*: Another Look at Gender, Feminism and Legal Ethics', below.)

There is a considerable debate within feminist literary criticism as to whether Portia (who pretends to be a man since women were not allowed to be advocates in Venice then) is portraying a male or female style of advocacy. (See, more generally, J St Joan and A Bennington McElhiney, *Beyond Portia: Women, Law and Literature in the United States*, Boston, Northeastern University Press, 1997.)

Frances Heidensohn has suggested that Portia's style exemplifies one model of justice: F Heidensohn, 'Models of Justice: Portia or Persephone? Some thoughts on Equality, Fairness and Gender in the Field of Criminal Justice', *International Journal of the Sociology of Law* (1986), vol. 14, pp. 287–298 at p. 289.

The focus of the 'Portia' model is clearly male and a rational, clear-thinking, procedurally competent male at that. The means of achieving justice are through laws and courts, in the present system, and there is only one world-view which is ultimately valid, that of white middle-class males. The concept of justice is one of legal equity. Although feminist views have taken this rational-legal form . . . there are also deeper issues involved, a more profound 'hidden agenda' which we also need to explore. In both academic accounts and even more noticeably, in the views of women defendants and victims in the criminal justice system there is a sense of outrage greater than that which the violation of rational principles would justify.

C Menkel-Meadow, Portia *Redux*: Another Look at Gender, Feminism and Legal Ethics' in S Parker and C Sampford, *Legal Ethics and Legal Practice*, Oxford, Clarendon Press (1995), pp. 25–56, at pp. 52–3.

The extremes of the adversary system might be modified by a caring and empathetic concern for not only the other, but also for an effort to solve the conflict or problem that resulted in a dispute in the first place . . . This will not work in all cases. As I have stated in a variety of other contexts, situations requiring punishment in the criminal law or clear lines of tolerated and not tolerated behavior, in civil rights and some tort actions, may still require full blown advocacy. But I nevertheless believe that justice does not always require bipolar results and binary solutions to problems which would be better approached with more contextual and less oppositional consideration.

Asking students and lawyers to consider the effects of their work on others and on themselves, to consider the wear and tear of conventional adversary practice, and to work through legal ethical hypotheticals in groups is one of the ways that the conventional justice system, modelled on individual autonomy, could be affected by the voices of women and minorities in the law. Collective grappling with ethical problems as they unfold has always seemed far more enriching to me than resolving difficult problems through *a priori* rules that can then be argued to be inapplicable or capable of distinction. I know that we shall have to agree on some first principles for our legal communities, but it seems to me that, before we finalize our rules, we need to hear more conversations with more Portias and others who have new, if complex, suggestions as to how we should determine legal morality.

Questions:
1.   Are there any such gender differences in advocacy or in law teaching? For example, in attempting the mooting exercises below, does it make a difference whether the advocate is female or male?

2.   If such differences do exist, are they related to stereotypical notions of the ways in which women and men think?

3.   Do you agree with Menkel-Meadow that we should, in some cases, seek a solution which goes beyond the adversarial binary approach? How might ADR facilitate this? (See Chapter 5.)

   As with negotiation and many other legal and transferable skills, the most important way to develop them is to practise them either in seminars or outside the classroom with your fellow students. Throughout your legal education you should enjoy studying the skills of advocacy — whether or not you wish to become an advocate. In class you ought to have the opportunity to engage in role play from time to time and at least once in your undergraduate career, you should participate in a moot or mock trial. Develop a critical eye when watching 'legal' films or TV programmes. Always ask yourself (a) how an argument could be put more persuasively and (b) whether it is fair for good advocates to win cases simply through their advocacy. Watch how an experienced barrister lets an appellate judge articulate a point the barrister has raised in an inchoate way, so that the judge feels he or she 'owns' the point. Watch your colleagues in class and ask them to comment on *your* advocacy. Do you 'um' and 'er'? Do you sway on your feet? Do you mumble? Have you anticipated responses?

J Mortimer, *Clinging to the Wreckage op. cit.*, pp. 106–108.

   'The art of cross-examination,' my father told me, 'is not the art of examining crossly. It's the art of leading the witness through a line of propositions he agrees to until he's forced to agree to the *one fatal question*' . . .
   'Opinions vary as to whether you should ask your most devastating question first or save it up as a *bonne bouche* at the end.'
   'Do they?' . . .
   'My advice to you is to go in with your guns blazing. See if you can't knock the stuffing out of a witness in the first five minutes,' my father said . . .
   'I always ask a husband, or a wife, as the case may be,' my father told me, 'is there anything you have done in the course of your married life of which you are now thoroughly ashamed? The witness usually finds that a tricky one to answer.'
   'Why?' . . .
   'Well, if the husband, or wife, says "Yes" then he or she has made a damaging admission.'
   'But if he says "No"?'
   'He shows himself up as a self-satisfied hypocrite and has lost the sympathy of the Court . . ..'

Question:
1. To what extent is advocacy dependent on oratory skills and to what extent on clever strategy?

Try the following advocacy exercises:

ADVOCACY EXERCISE 1

One third of your seminar group should act as advocates for Mr Legras; one third should act as advocates for the surviving burglar and the widow of the one who died; while the remaining third should act as judges, both as to the outcome of the case and to pronounce on which member of your group was the best advocate. (This exercise is based on facts taken from a case reported in *The Times*, April 1978.)

> Lionel Legras, aged 50, is a respected garage owner and family man who spends his weekends at a cottage in the country. In his absences, the cottage was frequently broken into. Exasperated by the loss of property and damage to the cottage, Mr Legras issued a warning to the burglars: 'If they come again', he announced publicly, 'it will cost them dear'. He placed a sign outside the house which read: 'No trespassing: danger of death.'
>
> However, the burglars struck again, ignoring the warning. This time, the price was high. A transistor radio, which had been carefully booby-trapped, exploded as they tried to remove it from a locked cupboard. One burglar died instantly, the other suffered severe injuries, including the loss of an eye. The widow of the first burglar and the second burglar have both claimed damages from Mr Legras.

Question:
1. What criteria did you use in judging who was the best advocate in this case? Does your experience of judging your peers give any indication whether legal research, appeals to emotion or mercy, or oratory skills are the most important factor in making a good advocate?

ADVOCACY EXERCISE 2

Read the following factual situation and prepare to argue as either counsel for Ms A or for the health authority. (You may wish to break down along gender lines with female students acting as advocates for Ms A, and male students acting as advocates for the health authority or vice-versa.) To argue effectively for your client you will have to undertake some legal research. How will you begin? You may wish to start by doing some background reading in a health care law text book. Alternatively you may begin with a Lexis search or by using the Internet.

Having carried out the research, and briefed yourself fully on the relevant law, you should then prepare and practise a five minute speech making the case for your side. Think carefully about how much time you need to devote to legal research and how much to honing your presentation. Which is more important?

Ms A is 34 years of age. She is single and a physiotherapist and is nearing the end of her first pregnancy. In the 'birth plan', which she has agreed with her midwife, she has clearly stated that she wants a 'natural' birth, involving as little medical intervention as possible. Consequently she has made arrangements for a home birth, as she has disliked hospitals and surgical operations ever since she was admitted as a young child for an appendectomy. Her GP was very supportive of this plan.

However, complications develop towards the end of her pregnancy and it has now become apparent, with five days to go before her baby is expected, that the baby is in the breech position and that the birth is likely to be difficult. The health professionals involved, including her midwife and GP, have now formed the opinion that it is in the best interests of Ms A and her 'unborn child' that she should have a Caesarean section operation.

However Ms A is refusing her consent to the operation on the grounds that her younger sister had a Caesarean operation which Ms A believes was responsible for her sister's postnatal depression, consequent difficulties in bonding with her baby and the considerable soreness which she subsequently experienced.

Ms A claims that, having carefully considered the medical evidence and advice, she remains firmly of the opinion that it will be best for her and the child if she gives birth at home notwithstanding the risks. However, the Health Authority go to the High Court seeking a declaration that it would be lawful to perform the Caesarean operation on Ms A, even if she continues to withhold her consent.

Questions:
1.   Would female lawyers be better able to empathise with A's position, and would this make them better or worse advocates in this case? (Would having a female judge affect the outcome of the case?) Or is the advocate simply a 'hired gun', having no emotional or political investment in the case, using skills for whomsoever pays?

2.   On the 'hired gun' analogy, is the best advocate simply the one who wins most cases? If not, on what criteria would you judge advocates (as your teachers or peers will probably have to judge you in moots)?

3.   Which form of research did you find most productive? Was it easier to do the research on your own, or as part of a team? If you did work as part of a team, how did you break down the tasks, allocate roles etc?

ADVOCACY EXERCISE 3

As a final exercise, make a list of famous trials and advocates in fiction. Then take one of these topical or historical or fictional trials and try to improve on the advocacy in it. For instance, books on miscarriages of justice, such as those mentioned in Chapter 4, often carry extracts from trials, such as the trial of the Guildford Four. See, for example, R Kee, *Trial and Error*, London, Hamish Hamilton, 1986; C Mullin, *Error of Judgment*, 2nd edition, London, Chatto &

Windus, 1990; L Kennedy, *Ten Rillington Place*, London, Golancz, 1961. For more trials with literary themes, see H Montgomery Hyde *The Trials of Oscar Wilde*, New York, Denver Publications Inc. (1973).

Question:
1.   On whatever criteria you established for a good advocate, who is the best fictional advocate of all time (whether from a book, play, film, radio or television programme)?

THE POLITICS OF ADVOCACY

Having attempted one of the exercises above, or participated in your law school's undergraduate moot programme, consider the following criticism of moot classes which operate in US law schools:

M Morrison, 'May it Please Whose Court? How Moot Court Perpetuates Gender Bias in the 'Real World' of Practice', *UCLA Women's Law Journal* (1995) vol. 6, pp. 49–84, at pp. 52–6, 76–8 (footnotes omitted).

That gender bias exists in practice as well as in legal education is well-documented. This bias persists even though the number of women 'doing law' has increased to almost fifty per cent. Some lawyers, mostly those who have 'assimilated' to male standards, have achieved a level of professional success equal to their male counterparts. However, women, individually and as a group, do not possess what Mona Harrington calls 'Professional authority' — the power to influence and change law and law systems. Law school does not teach the skills needed to change the rules but instead teaches only how to work within existing hierarchies. The presence of women in the legal profession has not had the impact one might expect. While women are rewarded for becoming 'social males', men who possess traits traditionally associated with women may find themselves stigmatized as 'social females' . . .

At present, law schools use Moot Court solely as a training ground for the traditional legal version of the real world. By passively allowing its training goals to be shaped by the gender-biased world of practice, law schools perpetuate the existing system. Students are taught to excel in the traditional, linear, rational, dispassionate, and 'male' style of argument in which real life stories filled with detail and emotion give context to judges and juries.

However, there is a risk in using the alternative female style. To exercise such a style would be to move outside the mainstream and challenge the status quo in which male values are enshrined within the myth of neutral application of objective legal rules. The application of such a style would fly in the face of the one thing that traditional Moot Court programmes teach: 'how to play ball with the court' . . .

In order to survive professionally and to access justice for their clients, women lawyers are forced to develop the skill — call it flexibility or bilinguilism, double-consciousness or less positively, professional schizo-phrenia — of working both within the male-constructed legal paradigm and outside it. This kind of bilingualism has a long tradition in outsider groups pleading for outsider causes.

The skill of William Shakespeare's 'Portia' models the best in an outsider lawyer while highlighting the inequities of a system which requires advocates to develop bilingualism skills. In the play's most powerful speech, Portia, dressed as 'doctor of laws' Balthazar (a man), argues for mercy and justice rather than a strict construction of the law under which the merchant, Antonio, must pay a 'pound of flesh' according to agreement. In one of the most eloquent oral arguments in literature, Portia argues that '[t]he quality of mercy is not strain'd'. Mercy is not weakness but, instead, is 'mightiest in the mightiest'.

The properties of this fine argument, including appeals to kindness, flexibility, and emotion, are the kind that are traditionally associated with women. Unless employed by an extremely skilful female advocate today, a Moot Court judge might well take Portia to task for overemotionalism. Portia's plea for mercy is ignored in her time as well, perhaps because such unconventionality was outside the parameters of the accepted male argument style of that day.

When Portia/Balthazar's plea for mercy is ignored and the judge decides to apply the strict rule of law and enforce the words of the agreement so that Shylock gets his 'pound of flesh', Portia resorts to a strict legalistic argument. In so doing, she both wins for her client and highlights the ludicrous and inhumane nature of such rote applications of the law . . .

The story of Portia illustrates the problems inherent in a Moot Court which enshrines the characteristics of the social male and denigrates those of the social female. This is demonstrated in the fact that Portia, of necessity, employs two argument styles. Her first attempt is based on her 'female' values and the belief that the law should look to the whole person and that application of rules is a means to an end — justice. Her second attempt is based on the male thinking of the judge.

Such a strategy could easily be used with benefit by a man. But would it be? Perhaps if appeals to rights or appeals to mercy were seen as practical ones, rather than gender-related ones, the law profession as a whole would benefit.

Questions:
1.   From your experience of doing the advocacy exercises above, do you agree with Morrison's criticisms of moots?

2.   Does law school teach only the skills needed to work within rather than to challenge hierarchies (see also the barristers quoted by Scheingold below at pp. 220–1, and the extract from Duncan Kennedy in Chapter 1 at p. 26)? Should it teach skills which would challenge the decision? What would they be?

3.   Do moots, as Morrison suggests, socialise lawyers, especially female lawyers, in certain 'appropriate' ways of dressing and speaking? (See also M Thornton, *Dissonance and Distrust: Women in the Legal Profession*, Melbourne, Oxford University Press, 1996, Chapter 5.)

The extract from Morrison deals with gender issues in a moot court, which she suggests may perpetuate bias in actual legal practice. In the extract below,

Helena Kennedy deals with the issue of gender in the professional practice of law and advocacy:

H Kennedy, *Eve was Framed: Women and British Justice*, London, Chatto & Windus (1992), pp. 46–51.

The whole business of deciding who is any good as an advocate is fraught with value judgements. As in the theatre, styles change, and nowadays Marshall Hall would be considered a terrible old ham. Advocacy is about communicating and persuading, something women are not only as good at as men, but often in fact better — more down to earth and less pompous. It requires the marshalling of material, research, the ability to charge your argument with imagery. It involves an interplay of the cerebral and the emotional, with a shifting of emphasis between the two, depending on your recipients. You have to be quick on your feet and have a good memory.

The extraordinary thing about the Bar is that large numbers of practitioners rarely do the thing which most members of the public imagine must be their daily bread and butter — i.e. persuade a jury that someone is innocent or guilty. Many are civil practitioners, whose days are largely spent behind a desk working on a brief, advising in the capacity of consultant and only occasionally making a foray into court. Criminal advocacy is to my mind crucial work in the courts because the liberty of the subject is at stake, but there are parts of the Bar which are quite sniffy about crime, as though there is something unpleasantly contagious about the clientele.

Every barrister is asked regularly by perplexed laymen how they feel about representing someone they know to be guilty. I am told that each profession elicits a parallel classic enquiry: doctors are asked if they ever feel squeamish about blood; actors are quizzed about being able to learn their lines; dentists about being sadists. For my own part, representing clients who are probably guilty is rarely a problem; it is representing those you think are innocent which induces sleepless nights. However, the polite answer we all give is that it is not our role to judge guilt or innocence; we concentrate instead on evaluating and testing the evidence and putting our clients' cases as they would themselves if they were acting in person.

The reason, of course, for the question is the public feeling of distaste for the 'hired gun', the courtroom mercenary who will defend the indefensible — the challenge is invariably about representing terrorists, child abusers and rapists. What is misunderstood is the moral basis for advocacy; it is somehow assumed that representing those who are charged with terrible crimes is a mark of amorality. If every lawyer refused to act for those whose conduct is reprehensible, many unpopular people might go unrepresented or be represented by a limited section of the profession. But there is another important consideration. If a barrister was able to pick and choose his or her clients, endorsement would follow from having a certain counsel and, conversely, failing to secure eminent counsel would emit a damning message. The principle was expounded by Erskine when he represented Tom Paine on a charge of sedition in 1792.

If the advocate refuses to defend from what he may think of the charge or of the defence, he assumes the character of the judge; nay, he assumes it before the hour of judgement; and in proportion to his rank and reputation puts the heavy influence of perhaps a mistaken opinion into the scale against the accused.

Alternatively, if the 'cab rank' principle of taking all-comers did not exist, advocates might avoid a case for fear that acting for particular clients may identify them with the allegations. Even so, when Lord Hooson defended in the Moors Murders case some of the political opponents (not the candidates he hastened to add) tried to use it against him in an election campaign. Those of us who have acted in the Irish cases [see Chapter 4 at pp. 140–3] have always been subjected to allegations of being terrorist sympathisers.

The longer I practise the more whole heartedly committed I become to the cab-rank principle, not only because of its constitutional significance in protecting civil liberties, but because of the incoherence of any other course for criminal practitioners. Picking over the horrors of crime to settle for those which are least offensive is hardly a worthwhile pursuit. In any event it is by no means always possible to tell whether your client is indeed guilty. Often I read the papers in a case and think it sounds ridiculous until I meet the client, whose personal account is so compelling that my original view changes. And there are also occasions when I think a case is terrific — until ten minutes into the consultation.

The criminal courts also demand a rather different style, because here barristers are trying to persuade a jury rather than a judge. The pleasure of working with a jury is hard to describe, and for those who are addicted there is nothing like it . . .

But criminal advocacy can raise a particular problem for women in that it is the most adversarial arena in the court system. You have to enjoy the taste of blood and some men on the bench feel uncomfortable with assertive women, an ambivalence that becomes very clear when arguments are heated. If there is a woman on both sides, interventions of the 'Come now, ladies' variety are common, said in a tone which suggests that some kind of catfight is breaking out. Passivity is still the expected role; aggression is considered phallic, certainly unattractive in a woman. Those messages are in the air and undermining for young women struggling to feel comfortable as professionals. It is particularly hard on those whose femininity is still dependent on approval from male authority figures. The way we socialise girls means they are taught to avoid confrontation and encouraged to please. Both can be useful skills in advocacy, but in courtroom battles you also have to be bold, and having a cross Daddy figure up there on the bench can create a real identity problem.

Quite unjustly, women are still not rated highly as advocates. Johnson's old adage still holds: like performing dogs, the surprise is not that they might do it well but that they do it at all.

'Show me the woman barrister who can laugh a case out of court,' was the challenge made to me by one of the men at the Bar. I was pushed to think of one — but nor could I think of many men with the power and control to mock a whole state prosecution. That particular abandoned style is not available to most advocates, least of all to women.

Fortunately, women are becoming much less vulnerable to the criticism that only tough old boots survive in the criminal courts or that female criminal lawyers have to be as hard as nails. I am constantly told by my colleagues that the word amongst certain judges is that I am a terrible harridan who eats small boys for breakfast. Whoever this woman was that filled them with terror, she became particularly confusing when she became pregnant. The contradictory myths about women are profoundly in conflict when a woman advocate fighting her corner is also a symbol of fecundity. There is a tangible difference in atmosphere. Juries are bemused and interested; judges are benign, and worry about being seen to argue with you. I have been tempted to consider making it a permanent state in the interests of my clients.

Stereotypes are more likely to emerge when women are scarce than when they are common. For women lawyers they tend to eclipse demonstrations of competence and make it harder for them to show professional strength. To some extent the examples of stereotyping are trivial and have little to do with one's performance as a lawyer. But to the extent that women have to learn to ignore the comments they elicit, or to respond to them, or are made to feel trapped in uncomfortable roles, the prevailing images are handicaps which men do not share — unless they are black.

The casting of women as the protagonist lawyer in films of courtroom dramas has established a fashionable new persona: the message is that we can be tough, assertive and all-woman as well. A lawyer's womanliness is shown by giving her a sex-life, children and snazzy little suits nipped in at the waist, and she shows signs of being compassionate about her clients as well as passionate about winning. But never far behind is that terrible female give-away: over-identification with her clients. Women face this accusation much more frequently than men because explanations have to be found for why they fight so hard to win. Men performing with the same vigour are merely described as passionate advocates.

Over-identification is a charge rarely made of corporate lawyers: after all, it's hard to over-identify with a trust fund or the Credit Union. And while committed and zealous prosecutors do exist, I do not imagine that there are many who would be described as identifying too closely with the Queen. It is only ever said of defence lawyers who fight hard for their clients; and it is never a complaint from the customer. In my experience, professional distance is often used as an excuse for having no bedside manner. It is also a way of excluding women's values from notions of professionalism: caring is interpreted as partial; it is impartiality that is the male, legal, ideal.

It is however perfectly possible to feel for a client's anguish without losing the ability to judge the appropriate tactic. In fact the opposite — denial of the ways in which their cases affect them emotionally — is the problem with most male barristers and judges. You cannot remain unaffected in a criminal case involving child sexual abuse which goes on for several months, with detailed and repeated evidence from damaged children, in a courtroom awash with pornographic evidence. It may be that learning to acknowledge ways in which they are touched by different kinds of cases would enable lawyers to function more effectively as professionals.

Questions:

1. Do you think that women and male advocates are likely to have different styles? Is any gender difference apparent when you watch barristers in court?

2. Do you agree with Kennedy's argument that *everyone* deserves a fair trial? For example, did Nazi war criminals deserve a fair trial in the aftermath of the Second World War? Should Nazi war criminals be tried at all today (e.g. for crimes against humanity)?

3. If you think that everyone has a right to legal counsel, does it follow that every lawyer should be willing to represent any client? Would it be unethical for a lawyer to refuse to act as the advocate for a Nazi war criminal if asked?

S Scheingold, 'The contradictions of radical law practice', *op cit*, pp. 268, 269 (references omitted).

Radical lawyers in England are clearly uneasy with conventional restrictions on representation, because they distance lawyers from the broader interests of their clients. As a barrister well known for his criminal and public order work put it:

[A] sense of commitment. Now that is something that when I started I was told I shouldn't have. I don't mean professional commitment — being good at your job — because obviously they would say: professionals are good at the job. But what they frowned upon, and I was told in very clear terms, is don't identify with the client. Don't get involved with the client, or more particularly, don't get involved with the client's cause if there is one (19 January 1987).

As he sees things, effective lawyering entails a close involvement with clients and their causes:

And I always found that extraordinary advice, because it seemed to me that the only way I personally was going to operate is if I could get inside the shell of the person I was representing, or the issue that he or she represented, and understood what was going on . . . In order to have an understanding, I had to have, not only a sense of justice, but a sense of experience . . . I had to get inside it (19 January 1987).

And a minority barrister said roughly the same thing:

When the rules say you can't associate with your client: you don't feel; you are just there to defend. You are a barrister . . . that's the rule of etiquette — that you fight fearlessly but you don't get involved. Now that's wrong because if there's a riot in Bristol or in Brixton between black people and the police, now if you don't get involved, you are a *straight* barrister . . . You can't effectively defend them, because you must appreciate the issues and you must be bold enough. As far as my profession will allow me, I associate with them (24 December 1986).

Accordingly, radical lawyers reject the cab rank rule 'whereby a barrister is expected to accept any brief regardless of his or her commitment to the client'. They are equally uneasy with the prohibition against 'touting', which, among other things, has been interpreted to prohibit lawyers representing individual clients who are jointly charged from discussing common issues. The former limitation is objectionable because it seeks to prevent lawyers from consistent identification with causes. The latter is problematic because it inhibits concerted activity, which is a step towards making a private grievance into a public issue — or, more generally, towards a proactive search for meaningful cases.

Questions:
1.   Do you believe that lawyers should have a sense of commitment to their cases and the issues they raise? Or should lawyers maintain a distance from their cases and avoid emotional or political involvement?

2.   What precisely do you think accounts for public distaste for the concept of barrister as 'hired gun', to which Kennedy refers?

3.   How significant do you think the 'cab-rank' rule is in practice?

LAY ADVOCATES

In Chapter 9 we consider what lay involvement might add to the legal process. Here we consider the role of lay advocates (or litigants in person):

D Pannick, *Advocates, op cit*, pp. 190–3 (footnotes omitted).

Quintilianus explained in the first century AD that one of the central principles of good advocacy was to confine yourself to essential submissions: 'we must not always burden the judge with all the arguments we have discovered, since by so doing we shall at once bore him and render him less inclined to believe us'. Here, the interests of the client are entirely consistent with the interests of the judge, opposing counsel and the administration of justice, none of them benefitting from lengthy submissions from the advocate. As Lord Reid said in 1967, 'most experienced counsel would agree that the golden rule is — when in doubt stop. Lord Pearce agreed that 'one of the merits of great advocates has often been that . . . where ten possible points were available they would often ruthlessly select the best, sacrifice nine, and thereby win on the tenth' . . .
    Judges find it especially difficult to control the verbosity of litigants in person . . . In 1975, the Supreme Court of New South Wales complained in its judgment that the litigant in person had:

spent some time reading to the court disconnected statements as to the law from a series of cards, some of which statements it was impossible to understand and most of which had no significant relationship to the issues in the proceedings. Indications from individual members of the court that these readings were of no assistance in determining the appeal appeared to have no effect upon the manner of his conducting the proceedings.

In one recent burglary trial, in which the defendant represented himself, 'the manner in which the [defendant] chose to conduct his defence caused intense difficulty for the very experienced trial judge and grossly prolonged the proceedings . . . It is estimated that the evidence-in-chief given by the witnesses on behalf of the prosecution lasted little more than an hour, after an opening of the case for the prosecution which lasted six minutes. The trial, however, extended over 38 days.' The defendant was convicted. When he appealed to the Court of Appeal he submitted a 'notice of appeal [which] sets out 53 grounds and numerous sub-grounds of appeal and extends to 100 pages . . .' His appeal was dismissed . . .

Some professional advocates are almost as unwilling, or as unable, as amateurs to focus on the point at issue. Judges have therefore had cause to regret that the English legal system has proceeded on the generous assumption that advocates may occupy the court for as long as they can think of authorities to cite and submissions to make. When the aggravation becomes too intense, they may say, as did Mr Justice Harman in a 1954 tax case, 'this case has been an unconscionable time a-trying. I have listened with a patience which, I am afraid, has worn more thin as the hours succeeded one another, to a very nice exercise in dialectic by both counsel who have addressed me.'

More recently, courts have begun to appreciate that although the independent advocate has an important role, there is no principle of law or justice which entitles advocates, at great expense to the State and their clients, to take days to have their say.

Questions:
1. Are these arguments strong enough to outweigh the rights of advocates in person to represent themselves?

2. Will the introduction of the new procedures for case management by judges, as envisaged in *The Woolf Report* (see Chapters 5 and 9), facilitate an improvement in the way in which judges handle cases involving litigants in person?

The length of the burglary case mentioned in the Pannick extract pales into insignificance compared with what was to become known as the 'McLibel' trial. This case, in which McDonalds sued two environmental activists for libel after they distributed leaflets levelling a series of allegations at McDonalds, was to become the longest case in English legal history, lasting for 313 days. Since legal aid (see Chapter 9) is not available for libel cases the defendants, Helen Steel and David Morris, were forced to represent themselves. In the following extract John Vidal recounts the impact of representing oneself in such a major trial.

J Vidal, *McLibel: Burger, Culture on Trial*, London, Macmillan (1997), pp. 164–6, 169–71.

Sometimes the exhaustion gets to everyone. Tempers fray. The mindset of being a continual, professional adversary can drag people down. There are luminous days, OK days, angry, scratchy, tetchy days. And always day-to-day problems: how do you keep track of the mounting piles of transcripts, the legal points? Will it ever end? Is there life outside Court 35? Beyond McLibel? The early estimates of the length of the trial — first measured in days, then weeks — now seem from *Alice in Wonderland*. McLibel has been 'confidently' expected to end (a) by Christmas 1994, (b) March 1995, (c) summer 1995, (d) Christmas 1995 and now as late as (e) summer 1996. Some, more perceptively, say (f) even later.

And just as the possible finishing date stutters forward, so Steel and Morris 'um' and hesitate in their cross-examinations and falter with incomplete sentences. Sometimes they seem painfully slow, lost in the enormousness of their cause. Then the scale of their undertaking becomes apparent, and the slick, consummate skill of the professional advocate is seen.

Morris: 'I'm continuously aware of a hundred things that we should have done. We're just struggling each evening to keep up with the next day.'

Steel: 'The whole thing is stupid; having to spend days in court arguing whether for instance McDonald's wages are low. The law is basically there to protect business as usual.'

Morris: 'It's not so much David and Goliath as Prometheus. I feel chained to this rock that's trying to crush me.'

Steel: 'I feel fed up having to listen to their corporate propaganda and waffle. It's worse than a job, you can't get away.' . . .

McLibel has taken its toll. Morris has barely had a break in four years. 'It's just McDonald's, McDonald's, McDonald's,' he says. He describes it as 'exhausting and a nightmare; tedious and unfair, relentless, continuous, and very complicated'. It involves massive amounts of paperwork, and organization and legal research. Preparing questions for witnesses has been time-consuming. But he says, 'We're just driving ourselves on. The issues are so broad and the unknowns so huge that barristers have told us, "We just don't understand how you can do this — it's beyond all precedent," and it is.'

He doesn't think of it as sacrifice. 'If you want to achieve something you have to put work into it. If I have to work myself into the ground I'm going to do it in order to expose the truth.' The trial has, he says, helped him to see 'just how strong ordinary people can be if they're determined to achieve something and they stick by it whatever the consequences'. He concedes that the consequences, even the sacrifices, have been particularly hard for Charlie [his son]. 'We've lived in the shadow of the case for four years, and he's been very understanding, luckily for me. It's been very unfair on him and I'm angry with McDonald's about that — they've forced themselves into our life.'. . .

The case is devilish for the urbane Richard Rampton [counsel for McDonalds], too, even if there are compensations. He will have earned himself the better part of £1 million by the end, but he must negotiate professional elephant traps. Taking on 'litigants in person', people who represent themselves, is notoriously tricky, a bit like Newcastle United of British Football's Premier League taking on the amateurs of Kettering Town from the lowly Vauxhall Conference League. Mark Stephens, senior partner in law firm Stephens Innocent, says that a barrister in these cases must totally adjust their style to ensure they are not seen to be taking advantage of weaker foes. They should, he says, be doubly careful, triply polite. Moreover, the rhythm of a case can be lost; there must always be interruptions as the judge helps the amateurs through the legal points. It's easy to become overconfident and impatient, Richard Rampton does not seem naturally patient.

Nor can Rampton much further his career. For all his professionalism, his Dickensian interjections, his theatrical, staged gruffness and loud — but not too loud, mind — asides, Rampton is becalmed. This nightmare case against two legal beginners runs against his nature. Where he relishes the confrontational, the adversarial, and the banter of equal, well-trained legal minds, here he is pitted against people of passion; admirable enough: but Steel and Morris are people with a cause and not remotely to his taste politically, socially or intellectually. 'Is Rampton bored?' is a question frequently asked by observers of Court 35. Does the judge wear red?

Besides, at this rough mid-stage of the trial Rampton has everything to lose. He has the real legal advantage in that he has dealt with many of the points before in his career, but he cannot be seen by the public to genuinely win. He may score point after legal point, like a boxer jabbing away to the head, but even though the judge notices and may appreciate them, he is denied the public stage he loves. No one will stop him in the street and say well done this time.

And even if he and the well-oiled McDonald's corporate legal machine were to win 90 per cent or more of the verdict, few people are ever going to consider that it has been a level playing field, argues one of Britain's top QCs, Michael Mansfield. The public will say, he suggests, 'Ah yes, but there was such an imbalance between McDonald's' resources and Steel and Morris's that the inference will always be that Rampton won unfairly.'

Rampton has long made his name and will not be bothered, whatever he may feel personally about the use of the court, the way Steel and Morris have conducted their case or his own predicament. He will harrumph in public, be full of bonhomie in private, take a break and return to gobble up more libel cases as he always did; but questions will be raised if the defendants lose, such as what would have happened if Steel and Morris had had the money to track down all the relevant witnesses especially overseas, if they had had full-time professional back-up, if — imagine — Rampton had been arguing for the defence . . .

In July 1996, after six months' deliberation, Mr Justice Bell ruled that McDonald's had been libelled by various allegations, including claims that it causes food poisoning and was destructive of the environment. It was awarded £60,00 damages which it has not attempted to collect. However the judge also ruled that McDonald's did pay low wages, exploit children and were cruel to some animals. The defendants began an appeal against various aspects of the initial decision on 12 January 1999. (See J Vidal, 'McLibel 2: the dogged duo return with 63 objections' *The Guardian* 13 January 1999.)

In March 1999 the McLibel defendants were partially successful in their appeal against the findings of Bell J that they had libelled McDonalds. The Court of Appeal confirmed much of the original judgment, agreeing with Bell J that Morris and Steel had defamed McDonald's by claiming that its products were poisonous and increased the risk of cancer, and that the company contributed to starvation and deforestation in developing countries. However, the appellate level judges did rule that Morris and Steel were justified in claiming that regular customers faced a heightened risk of heart trouble, and that McDonald's employees were badly paid and subjected to poor working conditions. Accordingly, the level of damages awarded to McDonald's was reduced from £60,000 to £40,000.

Questions:
1.   Is it fair to criticise lay persons for being hesitant and faltering? Do you think that this would have had any impact on the outcome of the case? Would it be more or less likely to impact on a judge or a jury? (See Chapter 9 on this aspect of the case.)

2.   Is it just to refuse legal aid in such a case, given the disparity of resources between the parties?

3.   Are arguments against lay advocates a good reason to confine rights to a hearing in the higher courts to barristers, or is it a good idea to have solicitor advocates?

4.   What limits is it reasonable to impose on lay advocates? For instance, the Home Secretary has recently announced that defendants in rape trials will no longer be allowed to cross-examine the complainant. These proposals are now contained in the Youth Justice and Criminal Evidence Bill. Is this a reasonable restriction on the right of defendants to represent themselves? Can you think of any other cases in which it would be reasonable to take away the defendant's right to represent himself or herself?

5.   In cases which you observed in court have you seen any lay advocates? If so, how did they acquit themselves? Can you think of any reported cases where any of the parties have represented themselves? Have any of them been referred to in this text?

Chapter 7

Adjudication

THEORIES OF ADJUDICATION

In this chapter we consider a legal skill which may appear more pertinent to judges than to students — that of adjudication. Nevertheless, the skill of analysing adjudication — the process by which judges decide cases — is of immediate relevance to law students who seek to understand the whole legal reasoning process. This skill necessarily encompasses many of the skills we have already considered in the earlier chapters on finding facts, reading cases and interpreting statutes. In this chapter we will return to some of the more difficult issues concerning precedent and statutory interpretation, look at how judges decide 'hard' cases, and whether there are 'rules' to guide them in this process. This involves taking a more critical look at legal reasoning. Indeed, perhaps the fundamental question you should consider is whether there is a distinctively legal form of reasoning of a neutral and objective nature at all, or is it the case that law is the same as any other interpretive enterprise, such as literary or theological interpretation?

In Chapter 1 we introduced the notion that *law* can be considered from a variety of perspectives. This is equally true of the more specific process of *adjudication*. It too can be considered from a variety of viewpoints. Academics with varying shades of political opinion have constructed theories of adjudication to explain how judges do or ought to reason. Once again it is worth remembering that most of these theories contain some degree of plausibility, and consequently considering a variety of perspectives, even if you ultimately reject some or all of them, should ensure that you have a fuller picture of the process of legal reasoning with which the judge is engaged in deciding cases.

What we are in effect asking you to consider is: what factors most influence judges in deciding hard cases? Jot down a list of possible influences and then try to rank them in terms of plausibility.

For example, you might have listed: race, gender, class, zodiac birth sign, politics, previous cases, statutes, the advocacy in court, justice, economics.

Now try to rank those ten factors. You might be certain that previous cases have more impact than does the zodiac but (a) can you prove that and (b) can you similarly rank the impact of, say, justice and economics?

In this chapter we are returning to the ground covered in Chapters 2, 3 and 4, but this time asking you to look for deeper explanations of, and guidance on, the legal skills of interpretation and adjudication. If a legal academic were asked to jot down ten plausible theories of adjudication, they might list: black letter, interstitial legislator, consensus, principle, realism, politics, class, gender, original intent, economics. They might well reject the terms of the question altogether and will almost certainly claim that it is too complicated to reduce to a single, simple explanation.

Quite so. Hence, all we ask of you is to reflect on the following two cases, as well as the cases discussed in Chapters 2 and 3, and choose whichever of the following theories strikes you as (a) the best interpretation of how the judges decided and (b) the most desirable prescription of how they *should* have decided.

The first case of *R* v *Brown* concerned a group of gay men engaged in sado-masochistic acts which had been recorded on a video, which fell into police hands. The men were charged with assault occasioning actual bodily harm, contrary to s. 47 of the Offences Against the Person Act 1861, and unlawful wounding, contrary to s. 20 of the Act. They were convicted and appealed against their convictions, contending that a person could not be guilty of assault occasioning actual bodily harm or unlawful wounding in respect of acts carried out in private with the consent of the victim. The Court of Appeal dismissed their appeals which were then heard by the House of Lords, who gave the following judgment.

R v *Brown* [1993] 2 All ER 75, HL.

Lord Templeman

By the 1967 [Sexual Offences] Act Parliament recognised and accepted the practice of homosexuality. Subject to exceptions not here relevant, sexual activities conducted in private between not more than two consenting adults of the same sex or different sexes are now lawful. Homosexual activities performed in circumstances which do not fall within s. 1(1) of the 1967 Act remain unlawful. Subject to the respect for private life embodied in the 1967 Act, Parliament has retained criminal sanctions against the practice, dissemination and encouragement of homosexual activities.

My Lords, the authorities dealing with the intentional infliction of bodily harm do not establish that the courts have accepted that consent is a defence to a charge under the 1861 Offences against the Person Act. They establish that the courts have accepted that consent is a defence to the infliction of bodily harm in the course of some lawful activities. The question is whether the defence should be extended to the infliction of bodily harm in the course of sado-masochistic encounters. The Wolfenden Committee did not make any recommendations about sado-masochism and Parliament did not deal with violence in 1967. The 1967 Act is of no assistance for present purposes because the present problem was not under consideration.

The question whether the defence of consent should be extended to the consequences of sado-masochistic encounters can only be decided by consideration of policy and public interest. Parliament can call on the advice of doctors, psychiatrists, criminologists, sociologists and other experts and can also sound and take into account public opinion. But the question must at this stage be decided by this House in its judicial capacity in order to determine whether the convictions of the appellants should be upheld or quashed . . .

Counsel for the appellants argued that consent should provide a defence to charges under both ss. 20 and 47 because, it was said, every person has a right to deal with his body as he pleases. I do not consider that this slogan provides a sufficient guide to the policy decision which must now be made. It is an offence for a person to abuse his own body and mind by taking drugs. Although the law is often broken, the criminal law restrains a practice which is regarded as dangerous and injurious to individuals and which if allowed and extended is harmful to society generally. In any event the appellants in this case did not mutilate their own bodies. They inflicted bodily harm on willing victims. Suicide is no longer an offence but a person who assists another to commit suicide is guilty of murder or manslaughter.

The assertion was made on behalf of the appellants that the sexual appetites of sadists and masochists can only be satisfied by the infliction of bodily harm and that the law should not punish the consensual achievement of sexual satisfaction. There was no evidence to support the assertion that sado-masochistic activities are essential to the happiness of the appellants or any other participants but the argument would be acceptable if sado-masochism were only concerned with sex, as the appellants contend. In my opinion sado-masochism is not only concerned with sex. Sado-masochism is also concerned with violence. The evidence discloses that the practices of the appellants were unpredictably dangerous and degrading to body and mind and were developed with increasing barbarity and taught to persons whose consents were dubious or worthless.

A sadist draws pleasure from inflicting or watching cruelty. A masochist derives pleasure from his own pain or humiliation. The appellants are middle-aged men. The victims were youths some of whom were introduced to sado-masochism before they attained the age of 21. In his judgment in the Court of Appeal, Lord Lane CJ said that two members of the group of which the appellants formed part, namely one Cadman and the appellant Laskey —

'were responsible in part for the corruption of a youth "K" . . . It is some comfort at least to be told, as we were, that "K" has now it seems settled into a normal heterosexual relationship. Cadman had befriended "K" when the boy was 15 years old. He met him in a cafeteria and, so he says, found out that the boy was interested in homosexual activities. He introduced and encouraged "K" in "bondage" affairs. He was interested in viewing and recording on video tape "K" and other teenage boys in homosexual scenes . . . One cannot overlook the danger that the gravity of the assaults and injuries in this type of case may escalate to even more unacceptable heights.' (See 94 Cr App R 302 at 310.)

. . . The dangers involved in administering violence must have been appreciated by the appellants because, so it was said by their counsel, each victim was given a code word which he could pronounce when excessive harm or pain was caused. The efficiency of this precaution, when taken, depends on the circumstances and on the personalities involved. No one can feel the pain of another. The charges against the appellants were based on genital torture and violence to the buttocks, anus, penis, testicles and nipples. The victims were degraded and humiliated, sometimes beaten, sometimes wounded with instruments and sometimes branded. Bloodletting and the smearing of human blood produced excitement. There were obvious dangers of serious personal injury and blood infection. Prosecuting counsel informed the trial judge against the protests of defence counsel that, although the appellants had not contracted AIDS, two members of the group had died from AIDS and one other had contracted an HIV infection although not necessarily from the practices of the group. Some activities involved excrement. The assertion that the instruments employed by the sadists were clean and sterilised could not have removed the danger of infection, and the assertion that care was taken demonstrates the possibility of infection. Cruelty to human beings was on occasions supplemented by cruelty to animals in the form of bestiality. It is fortunate that there were no permanent injuries to a victim though no one knows the extent of harm inflicted in other cases. It is not surprising that a victim does not complain to the police when the complaint would involve him in giving details of acts in which he participated. Doctors of course are subject to a code of confidentiality.

In principle there is a difference between violence which is incidental and violence which is inflicted for the indulgence of cruelty. The violence of sado-masochistic encounters involves the indulgence of cruelty by sadists and the degradation of victims. Such violence is injurious to the participants and unpredictably dangerous. I am not prepared to invent a defence of consent for sado-masochistic encounters which breed and glorify cruelty and result in offences under ss. 47 and 20 of the 1861 Act.

. . .

Society is entitled and bound to protect itself against a cult of violence. Pleasure derived from the infliction of pain is an evil thing. Cruelty is uncivilised. I would dismiss the appeals of the appellants against conviction.

Lord Jauncey

Considerable emphasis was placed by the appellants on the well-ordered and secret manner in which their activities were conducted and upon the fact that these activities had resulted in no injuries which required medical attention. There was, it was said, no question of proselytising by the appellants. . . .

Be that as it may, in considering the public interest it would be wrong to look only at the activities of the appellants alone, there being no suggestion that they and their associates are the only practitioners of homosexual sado-masochism in England and Wales. This House must therefore consider the possibility that these activities are practised by others and by others who are not so controlled or responsible as the appellants are claimed to be.

Without going into details of all the rather curious activities in which the appellants engaged, it would appear to be good luck rather than good judgment which has prevented serious injury from occurring. Wounds can easily become septic if not properly treated, the free flow of blood from a person who is HIV positive or who has AIDS can infect another and an inflicter who is carried away by sexual excitement or by drink or drugs could very easily inflict pain and injury beyond the level to which the receiver had consented. Your Lordships have no information as to whether such situations have occurred in relation to other sado-masochistic practitioners. It was no doubt these dangers which caused Baroness Mallalieu [counsel for two appellants] to restrict her propositions in relation to the public interest to the actual rather than the potential result of the activity. In my view such a restriction is quite unjustified. When considering the public interest potential for harm is just as relevant as actual harm. As Mathew J said in *R* v *Coney* (1882) 8 QBD 534 at 547:

'There is, however, abundant authority for saying that no consent can render that innocent which is in fact dangerous.'

Furthermore, the possibility of proselytisation and corruption of young men is a real danger even in the case of these appellants and the taking of video-recordings of such activities suggests that secrecy may not be as strict as the appellants claimed to your Lordships. If the only purpose of the activity is the sexual gratification of one or both of the participants what then is the need of a video-recording?

My Lords I have no doubt that it would not be in the public interest that deliberate infliction of actual bodily harm during the course of homosexual sado-masochistic activities should be held to be lawful. In reaching this conclusion I have regard to the information available in these appeals and of such inferences as may be drawn therefrom. I appreciate that there may be a great deal of information relevant to these activities which is not available to your Lordships. When Parliament passed the Sexual Offences Act 1967 which made buggery and acts of gross indecency between consenting males lawful it had available the *Report of the Committee on Homosexual Offences and Prostitution* (the Wolfenden Report) (Cmnd 247 (1957)), which was the product of an exhaustive research into the problem. If it is to be decided that such activities as the nailing by A of B's foreskin or scrotum to a board or the insertion of hot wax into C's urethra followed by the burning of his penis with a candle or the incising of D's scrotum with a scalpel to the effusion of blood are injurious neither to B, C and D nor to the public interest then it is for Parliament with its accumulated wisdom and sources of information to declare them to be lawful. . . .

Lord Lowry

The appellant's main point is that, contrary to the view of the trial judge and the Court of Appeal, the consent of the victim, as I shall call the willing recipient of the sado-masochistic treatment, constitutes a defence to the charges of assault occasioning actual bodily harm contrary to s. 47 of the Offences against the Person Act 1861 and of wounding contrary to s. 20 of the 1861 Act (no more than actual bodily harm being occasioned) or, to put it another way, that, when the victim consents, no such offence of assault or wounding as I have described takes place . . . Everyone agrees that consent remains a complete defence to a charge of common assault and nearly everyone agrees that consent of the victim is not a defence to a charge of inflicting really serious personal injury (or 'grievous bodily harm'). The disagreement concerns offences which occasion actual bodily harm: the appellants contend that the consent of the victim is a defence to one charged with such an offence, while the respondent submits that consent is not a defence. I agree with the respondent's contention for reasons which I now explain.

The 1861 Act was one of several laudable but untidy Victorian attempts to codify different areas of law . . . It follows that the indications to be gathered from the 1861 Act are not precise. Nevertheless, I consider that it contains fairly clear signs that, with regard to the relevance of the victim's consent as a defence, assault occasioning actual bodily harm and wounding which results in actual bodily harm are not offences 'below the line', to be ranked with common assault as offences in connection with which the victim's consent provides a defence, but offences 'above the line', to be ranked with inflicting grievous bodily harm and the other more serious offences in connection with which the victim's consent does not provide a defence.

. . .

If, as I too, consider, the question of consent is immaterial, there are prima facie offences against ss. 20 and 47 and the next question is whether there is good reason to add sado-masochistic acts to the list of exceptions contemplated in *A-G's Reference*. In my opinion, the answer to that question is No.

In adopting this conclusion I follow closely my noble and learned friends Lord Templeman and Lord Jauncey. What the appellants are obliged to propose is that the deliberate and painful infliction of physical injury should be exempted from the operation of statutory provisions the object of which is to prevent or punish that very thing, the reason for the proposed exemption being that both those who will inflict and those who will suffer the injury wish to satisfy a perverted and depraved sexual desire. Sado-masochistic homosexual activity cannot be regarded as conducive to the enchancement or enjoyment of family life or conducive to the welfare of society. A relaxation of the prohibitions in ss. 20 and 47 can only encourage the practice of homosexual sado-masochism, with the physical cruelty that it must involve, (which can scarcely be regarded as a 'manly diversion') by withdrawing the legal penalty and giving the activity a judicial imprimatur. As well as all this, one cannot overlook the physical danger to those who may indulge in sado-masochism. In this connection, and also generally, it is idle for the appellants to claim that they are educated exponents of 'civilised cruelty'. A proposed general exemption is to be tested by considering the likely general effect. This must include the probability that some sado-masochistic activity, under the powerful influence of the sexual instinct, will get out of hand and result in serious physical damage to the participants and that some activity will involve a danger of infection such as these particular exponents do not contemplate for themselves. When considering the danger of infection, with its inevitable threat of AIDS, I am not impressed by the argument that this threat can be discounted on the ground that, as long ago as 1967, Parliament, subject to conditions, legalised buggery, now a well-known vehicle for the transmission of AIDS.

So far as I can see, the only counter-argument is that to place a restriction on sado-masochism is an unwarranted interference with the private life and activities of persons who are indulging in a lawful pursuit and are doing no harm to anyone except, possibly, themselves. This approach, which has characterised every submission put forward on behalf of the appellants, is derived from the fallacy that what is involved here is the restraint of a lawful activity as opposed to the refusal to relax existing prohibitions in the 1861 Act. If in the course of buggery, as authorised by the 1967 Act, one participant, either with the other participant's consent or not, deliberately causes actual bodily harm to that other, an offence against s. 47 has been committed. The 1967 Act provides no shield. The position is as simple as that, and there is *no legal right to cause actual bodily harm* in the course of sado-masochistic activity.

Lord Mustill

My Lords, this is a case about the criminal law of violence. In my opinion it should be a case about the criminal law of private sexual relations, if about anything at all. If the criminality of sexual deviation is the true ground of these proceedings, one would have expected that these above all would have been the subject of attack. Yet the picture is quite different. . . .

If repugnance to general public sentiments of morality and propriety were the test, one would have expected proceedings in respect of the most disgusting conduct to be prosecuted with the greater vigour. Yet the opposite is the case. Why is this so? Obviously because the prosecuting authorities could find no statutory prohibition apt to cover this conduct. Whereas the sexual conduct which underlies the present appeals, although less extreme, could at least arguably be brought within ss. 20 and 47 of the 1861 Act because it involved the breaking of skin and the infliction of more than trifling hurt.

I must confess that this distribution of the charges against the appellants at once sounds a note of warning. It suggests that the involvement of the 1861 Act was adventitious. This impression is reinforced when one considers the title of the statute under which the appellants are charged, 'Offences against the Person'. Conduct infringing ss. 18, 20 and 47 of the 1861 Act comes before the Crown Court every day. Typically it involves brutality, aggression and violence, of a kind far removed from the appellants' behaviour which, however worthy of censure, involved no animosity, no aggression, no personal rancour on the part of the person inflicting the hurt towards the recipient and no protest by the recipient. In fact, quite the reverse. Of course we must give effect to the statute if its words capture what the appellants have done, but in deciding whether this is really so it is in my opinion legitimate to assume that the choice of the the 1861 Act as the basis for the relevant counts in the indictment was made only because no other statute was found which could conceivably be brought to bear upon them.

In these circumstances I find it easy to share the opinion expressed by Wills J in *R* v *Clarence* (1888) 22 QBD 23 at 33, [1886–90] All ER Rep 133 at 137, a case where the accused had consensual intercourse with his wife, he knowing and she ignorant that he suffered from gonorrhoea, with the result that she was infected. . . .

'. . . such considerations lead one to pause on the threshold, and inquire whether the enactment under consideration could really have been intended to apply to circumstances so completely removed from those which are usually understood when an assault is spoken of, or to deal with matters of any kind involving the sexual relation or act.'

I too am led to pause on the threshold. Asking myself the same question, I cannot but give a negative answer. I therefore approach the appeal on the basis that the convictions on charges which seem to me so inapposite cannot be upheld unless the language of the statute or the logic of the decided cases positively so demand. Unfortunately, as the able arguments which we have heard so clearly demonstrate, the language of the statute is opaque, and the cases few and unhelpful . . .

I can understand why, in relation to homosexual conduct, Parliament has not yet thought fit to disturb the compromise embodied in the Sexual Offences Act 1967, but am quite unable to see any reason to carry a similar distinction into the interpretation of a statute passed a century earlier, and aimed at quite different evil. Since the point was not raised before the trial judge, and the House has properly not been burdened with all the committal papers, it is impossible to tell whether, if advanced, it might have affected the pleas offered and accepted at the Central Criminal Court, but its potential for creating anomalies in other cases seems undeniable.

I would therefore accede to this argument only if the decided cases so demanded. In my opinion they do not, for I can find nothing in them to suggest that the consensual infliction of hurt is transmuted into an offence of violence simply because it is chargeable as another offence.
. . .

I believe that the general tenor of the decisions of the European Court of Human Rights does furnish valuable guidance on the approach which the English courts should adopt, if free to do so, and I take heart from the fact that the European authorities, balancing the personal considerations invoked by art 8(1) against the public interest consideration called up by art 8(2) [see Chapter 3 at p. 75] clearly favour the right of the appellants to conduct their private lives undisturbed by the criminal law: a conclusion at which I have independently arrived for reasons which I must now state.
. . .

The purpose of this long discussion has been to suggest that the decks are clear for the House to tackle completely anew the question whether the public interest requires 47 of the 1861 Act to be interpreted as penalising an infliction of harm which is at the level of actual bodily harm, but not grievous bodily harm; which is inflicted in private (by which I mean that it is exposed to the view only of those who have chosen to view it); which takes place not only with the consent of the recipient but with his willing and glad co-operation; which is inflicted for the gratification of sexual desire, and not in a spirit of animosity or rage; and which is not engaged in for profit.

My Lords, I have stated the issue in these terms to stress two considerations of cardinal importance. Lawyers will need no reminding of the first, but since this prosecution has been widely noticed it must be emphasised that the issue before the House is not whether the appellants' conduct is morally right, but whether it is properly charged under the 1861 Act. When proposing that the conduct is not rightly so charged I do not invite your Lordships' House to indorse it as morally acceptable. Nor do I pronounce in favour of a libertarian doctrine specifically related to sexual matters. Nor in the least do I suggest that ethical pronouncements are meaningless, that there is no difference between right and wrong, that sadism is praiseworthy, or that new opinions on sexual morality are necessarily superior to the old, or anything else of the same kind. What I do say is that these are questions of private morality; that the standards by which they fall to be judged are not those of the criminal law; and that if these standards are to be upheld the individual must enforce them upon himself according to his own moral standards, or have them enforced against him by moral pressures exerted by whatever religious or other community to whose ethical ideals he responds. . . .

This point leads directly to the second. As I have ventured to formulate the crucial question, it asks whether there is good reason to impress upon s. 47 an interpretation which penalises the relevant level of harm irrespective of consent: i e to recognise sado-masochistic activities as falling into a special category of acts, such as duelling and prize-fighting, which 'the law says shall not be done'. This is very important, for if the question were differently stated it might well yield a different answer. In particular, if it were to be held that as a matter of law all infliction of bodily harm above the level of common assault is incapable of being legitimated by consent, except in special circumstances, then we would have to consider whether the public interest required the recognition of private sexual activities as being in a specially exempt category. This would be an altogether more difficult question and one which I would not be prepared to answer in favour of the appellants, not because I do not have my own opinions upon it but because I regard the task as one which the courts are not suited to perform, and which should be carried out, if at all, by Parliament after a thorough review of all the medical, social, moral and political issues . . .

Let it be assumed however that we should embark upon this question. I ask myself, not whether as a result of the decision in this appeal, activities such as those of the appellants should cease to be criminal, but rather whether the 1861 Act (a statute which I venture to repeat once again was clearly intended to penalise conduct of a quite different nature) should in this new situation be interpreted so as to make it criminal. Why should this step be taken?

Leaving aside repugnance and moral objections, both of which are entirely natural but neither of which are in my opinion grounds upon which the court could properly create a new crime, I can visualise only the following reasons.

(1) Some of the practices obviously created a risk of genito-urinary infection, and others of septicaemia. These might indeed have been grave in former times, but the risk of serious harm must surely have been greatly reduced by modern medical science.

(2) The possibility that matters might get out of hand, with grave results. It has been acknowledged throughout the present proceedings that the appellants' activities were performed as a prearranged ritual, which at the same time enhanced their excitement and minimised the risk that the infliction of injury would go too far. Of course things might go wrong and really serious injury or death might ensue. If this happened, those responsible would be punished according to the ordinary law, in the same way as those who kill or injure in the course of more ordinary sexual activities are regularly punished. But to penalise the appellants' conduct even if the extreme consequences do not ensue, just because they might have done so, would require an assessment of the degree of risk, and the balancing of this risk against the interests of individual freedom. Such a balancing is in my opinion for Parliament, not the courts; and even if your Lordships' House were to embark upon it the attempt must in my opinion fail at the outset for there is no evidence at all of the seriousness of the hazards to which sado-masochistic conduct of this kind gives rise. . . .

(3) I would give the same answer to the suggestion that these activities involved a risk of accelerating the spread of auto-immune deficiency syndrome (AIDS), and that they should be brought within the 1861 Act in the interests of public health. The consequence would be strange, since what is currently the principal cause for the transmission of this scourge, namely consenting buggery between males, is now legal. Nevertheless, I would have been compelled to give this proposition the most anxious consideration if there had been any evidence to support it. But there is none, since the case for the Crown was advanced on an entirely different ground.

(4) There remains an argument to which I have given much greater weight. As the evidence in the present case has shown, there is a risk that strangers (and especially young strangers) may be drawn into these activities at an early age and will then become established in them for life. This is indeed a disturbing prospect, but I have come to the conclusion that it is not a sufficient ground for declaring these activities to be criminal under the 1861 Act. The element of the corruption of youth is already catered for by the existing legislation; and if there is a gap in it which needs to be filled the remedy surely lies in the hands of Parliament, not in the application of a statute which is aimed at other forms of wrongdoing. . . .

Leaving aside the logic of this answer, which seems to me impregnable, plain humanity demands that a court addressing the criminality of conduct such as that of the present should recognise and respond to the profound dismay which all members of the community share about the apparent increase of cruel and senseless crimes against the defenceless. Whilst doing so I must repeat for the last time that in the answer which I propose I do not advocate the decriminalisation of conduct which has hitherto been a crime; nor do I rebut a submission that a new crime should be created, penalising this conduct, for Mr Purnell has rightly not invited the House to take this course. The only question is whether these consensual private acts are offences against the existing law of violence. To this question I return a negative response. . . .

Accordingly I would allow these appeals and quash such of the convictions as are now before the House.

Lord Slynn

Three propositions seem to me to be clear. It is '. . . inherent in the conception of assault and battery that the victim does not consent' (see Glanville Williams 'Consent and Public Policy' [1962] Crim LR 74 at 75). Secondly, consent must be full and free and must be as to the actual level of force used or pain inflicted. Thirdly, there exist areas where the law disregards the victim's consent even where that consent is freely and fully given. These areas may relate to the person (eg a child); they may relate to the place (eg in public); they may relate to the nature of the harm done. It is the latter which is in issue in the present case.

I accept that consent cannot be said simply to be a defence to any act which one person does to another. A line has to be drawn as to what can and as to what cannot be the subject of consent.
. . .

If a line has to be drawn, as I think it must, to be workable it cannot be allowed to fluctuate within particular charges and in the interests of legal certainty it has to be accepted that consent can be given to acts which are said to constitute actual bodily harm and wounding. Grievous bodily harm I accept to be different by analogy with and as an extension of the old cases on maiming. Accordingly, I accept that, other than for cases of grievous bodily harm or death, consent can be a defence. This in no way means that the acts done are approved of or encouraged. It means no more than that the acts do not constitute an assault within the meaning of these two specific sections of the Offences against the Person Act 1861.

None of the convictions in the present cases have been on the basis that grievous bodily harm was caused. Whether some of the acts done in these cases might have fallen within that category does not seem to me to be relevant for present purposes.
. . .

I agree that in the end it is a matter of policy. It is a matter of policy in an area where social and moral factors are extremely important and where attitudes can change. In my opinion it is a matter of policy for the legislature to decide. If society takes the view that this kind of behaviour, even though sought after and done in private, is either so new or so extensive or so undesirable that it should be brought now for the first time within the criminal law, then it is for the legislature to decide. It is not for the courts in the interests of 'paternalism', . . . or in order to protect people from themselves, to introduce, into existing statutory crimes relating to offences *against* the person, concepts which do not properly fit there. If Parliament considers that the behaviour revealed here should be made specifically criminal, then the Offences against the Person Act 1861 or, perhaps more appropriately, the Sexual Offences Act 1967 can be amended specifically to define it. Alternatively, if it is intended that this sort of conduct should be lawful as between two persons but not between more than two persons as falling within the offence of gross indecency, then the limitation period for prosecution can be extended and the penalties increased where sado-masochistic acts are involved. That is obviously a possible course; whether it is a desirable way of changing the law is a different question.

Note that the defendants in the *Brown* case took the United Kingdom government to the European Court of Human Rights, alleging that their rights under the Convention were infringed (see Chapter 10 at pp. 282–3).

We have already looked at the case of *R* v *R* in Chapter 2 at pp. 69–70, where we considered the Court of Appeal judgment for the purposes of precedent. Below are extracts from the House of Lords decision.

R v *R (rape: marital exemption)* [1992] 1 AC 599 (HL).

Lord Keith of Kinkel

. . . The appeal arises out of the appellant's conviction . . . upon his pleas of guilty, of attempted rape and assault occasioning actual bodily harm. The alleged victim in respect of each offence was the appellant's wife . . . On 21 October 1989 the wife left the matrimonial home with the son and went to live with her parents. She had previously consulted solicitors about matrimonial problems, and she left at the matrimonial home a letter for the appellant informing him that she intended to petition for divorce. On 23 October the appellant spoke to his wife on the telephone indicating that it was his intention also to see about a divorce. No divorce proceedings had, however, been instituted before the events which gave rise to the charges against appellant. About 9 pm on 12 December 1989 the appellant forced his way into the house of his wife's parents, who were out at the time, and attempted to have sexual intercourse with her against her will. In the course of doing so he assaulted her by squeezing her neck with both hands. The appellant was arrested and interviewed by police officers. He admitted responsibility for what had happened. On 3 May 1990 a decree nisi of divorce was made absolute.

The appellant was charged on an indictment containing two counts, the first being rape and the second being assault occasioning actual bodily harm. When he appeared before Owen J in the Crown Court at Leicester on 30 July 1990 it was submitted to the judge on his behalf that a husband could not in law be guilty as a principal of the offence of raping his own wife . . .

Sir Matthew Hale in his *History of the Pleas of the Crown* wrote (1 Hale PC (1736) 629):

'But the husband cannot be guilty of a rape committed by himself upon his
lawful wife, for by their mutual matrimonial consent and contract the wife
hath given herself up in this kind unto her husband which she cannot
retract' . . .

It may be taken that the proposition was generally regarded as an accurate
statement of the common law of England. The common law is, however,
capable of evolving in the light of changing social, economic and cultural
developments. Hale's proposition reflected the state of affairs in these
respects at the time it was enunciated. Since then the status of women, and
particularly of married women, has changed out of all recognition in various
ways which are very familiar . . . Apart from property matters and the
availability of matrimonial remedies, one of the most important changes is
that marriage is in modern times regarded as a partnership of equals, and no
longer one in which the wife must be the subservient chattel of the husband.
Hale's proposition involves that by marriage a wife gives her irrevocable
consent to sexual intercourse with her husband under all circumstances and
irrespective of the state of her health or how she happens to be feeling at the
time. In modern times any reasonable person must regard that conception as
quite unacceptable . . .

[Lord Keith proceeded to discuss a number of Scottish and English cases]

The position then is that that part of Hale's proposition which asserts that a
wife cannot retract the consent to sexual intercourse which she gives on
marriage has been departed from in a series of decided cases. On grounds of
principle there is no good reason why the whole proposition should not be
held inapplicable in modern times. The only question is whether s. 1(1) of
the 1976 [Sexual Offences] Act presents an insuperable obstacle to that
sensible course. The argument is that 'unlawful' in the subsection means
outside the bond of marriage. That is not the most natural meaning of the
word, which normally describes something which is contrary to some law or
enactment or is done without lawful justification or excuse. Certainly in
modern times sexual intercourse outside marriage would not ordinarily be
described as unlawful. If the subsection proceeds on the basis that a woman
on marriage gives a general consent to sexual intercourse, there can never be
any question of intercourse with her by her husband being without her
consent. There would thus be no point in enacting that only intercourse
without consent outside marriage is to constitute rape . . .
    The fact is that it is clearly unlawful to have sexual intercourse with any
woman without her consent, and that the use of the word in the subsection
adds nothing. In my opinion there are no rational grounds for putting the
suggested gloss on the word, and it should be treated as being mere
surplusage in this enactment . . .
    I am therefore of the opinion that s. 1(1) of the 1976 Act presents no
obstacle to this House declaring that in modern times the supposed marital
exception in rape forms no part of the law of England. The Court of Appeal,

Criminal Division took a similar view. Towards the end of the judgment of that court Lord Lane CJ said ([1991] 2 All ER 257 at 266, [1991] 2 WLR 1065 at 1074):

'The remaining and no less difficult question is whether, despite that view, this is an area where the court should step aside to leave the matter to the parliamentary process. This is not the creation of a new offence, it is the removal of a common law fiction which has become anachronistic and offensive and we consider that it is our duty having reached that conclusion to act upon it.'

I respectfully agree.

The defendant in the *R* case above took his case to Europe and you can find out for yourself what happened at, *SW* v *United Kingdom, CR* v *United Kingdom* (1995) 21 EHHR 363.

1 BLACK LETTER (OR FORMALISM)

This is the theory (which few admit to holding) that there is a distinctively legal mode of reasoning that determines 'correct' rules, facts and results in particular cases, i.e. law is presented as a closed logical system. On this view the answers to all legal queries are contained in books — legal reasoning is simply a matter of looking up the rules of law (in statutes and case-books), applying them to the facts of the problem (which can be uncontroversially ascertained) and by this process arriving at the 'right' result.

The following extract comes from an article on the *R* case, which exemplifies a black-letter approach to law (or a traditional perspective on law — see Chapter 1 at pp. 9–11):

G Williams, 'Rape is rape', *New Law Journal* (1992), vol. 142, pp. 11–13.

So, with the decision in *R*, Hale's law on marital rights has gone, and we can all be unfeignedly pleased about that, even though some of us are uncomfortable about the manner of its going and the unconsidered consequences of its precipitous demise. Of course, the Lords had authority, so far as the doctrine of precedent went, to overrule such decisions as there were on the marital exemption; but this was not the whole of the matter. There were also questions of constitutional doctrine and human rights.

Dicey told us that in Britain the 'rule of law' was supreme. More than two centuries before Dicey, Hobbes had proclaimed that 'No law, made after a fact done, can make it a crime . . . For before the law, there is no transgression of the law.' Two principles endeavour to carry out this idea: *nullum crimen sine lege* (no crime unless by law) and *nulla poena sine lege* (no punishment unless by law). For both maxims, 'law' means a pre-ordained law: a retrospective law was not law at the time to which it is applied. Parliament accepts these principles: penal statutes are not made retrospective, and when permitted punishments are increased, the increase applied only to crimes committed after the statute. The courts play a supporting role, applying a strong presumption against applying penal legislation retrospectively.

But when one comes to 'judicial legislation' the picture changes. In 'declaring' the common law and in 'interpreting' statutes, neither the populace at large nor the judges of this country see any objection to punishing retrospectively, and the decision in *R* again repudiates *nulla poena*.

Naturally the courts do not assert that reasons of policy alone are enough to justify a retrospective extension of penal law. They know their place better than that. The traditional idea of the judges' function is to *say* the law not to give it (*jus dicere, non jus dare*). But in purporting to say, they can give. In *R* they got their result by conjuring with the phrase 'unlawful sexual intercourse' in the statutory definition of rape . . . They held that in the context of rape, with the changed status of women, 'the use of the word ["unlawful"] in the sub-section adds nothing'. This was high-handed judicial action taken for a praiseworthy purpose and differences of opinion have been expressed on whether the praiseworthiness redeemed the high-handedness.

Lord Lane CJ in the court below, after a careful examination of the authorities, summed up his opinion by saying that 'a rapist remains a rapist subject to the criminal law, irrespective of his relationship with his victim'. This immediately passed into popular currency in the form 'rape means rape', a good battle-cry but a none too subtle way of begging the question. Will the courts now decide that 'murder means murder', with the consequence that judicial action can be taken to abolish the defence of provocation? Of course not . . .

Lord Keith, in the leading speech in the Lords, quoted with approval another remark of Lord Lane in the court below. The Chief Justice justified the decision as being, 'not the creation of a new offence, it is the removal of a common law fiction which has become anachronistic and offensive'. This is utterly implausible. (1) A legal fiction is only a way (even though it may be an objectionable way) of stating a legal rule. Judges may eliminate the fiction from their speech, but ought not under cover of that, to change the law. And (2) the constitutional objection to the judicial creation of new crimes applies with equal force to the judicial enlargement of old ones.

The practical result of the decision in *R* was that the Crown Prosecution Service reopened its files and started to prosecute a backlog of charges dating from before the decision. Some of the cases concerned outrageous attacks upon the woman, involving the infliction of actual bodily harm, and in my view the CPS was at fault in not prosecuting such cases immediately they occurred, under OAPA, ss. 20 or 47; the rest could have been charged as common assaults . . .

It will be interesting to see what happens if one of these backlog cases gets to the European Commission and Court of Human Rights. To abolish the rape exemption would in itself be a praiseworthy extension of human rights, but to abolish it retrospectively is another matter. If Parliament had passed a statute retrospectively abolishing the marital exemption there would be a distinct possibility of its being held to offend against Art 7 of the Convention on Human Rights, in which case the Government would have to set aside all convictions and pay compensation to those convicted and punished. The only possible defence would be under Art 7(2):

'This article shall not prejudice the trial and punishment of any person for any act or omission which, at the time when it was committed, was criminal according to the general principles of law recognised by civilised nations.'

The provision was inserted in order to avoid impugning the validity of the Nuremberg trials after the war and I believe that the Strasbourg court has not had occasion to consider its application to ordinary municipal law. Rape is criminal in all civilised nations, but what about husband rape? Many countries, including all common law jurisdictions and some closely associated with them, started with the marital exemption, but most (not all) of these (most per head of population, anyway) have abolished it by legislation. It would be surprising if the human rights court held that legislation passed in other countries, passed on such terms as seemed proper to them, gave the British Parliament *carte blanche* to extend our criminal law *retrospectively*. If, as seems likely, Art 7(2) does not validate retrospective penal legislation, how can it validate retrospective judicial action having like effect? . . .

My own opinion . . . is that the sentencing of a cohabitee (even of an ex-cohabitee) for a first rape on a scale roughly the same as for a stranger (one, for instance, who rapes a woman in an alley-way, or who breaks into a woman's bedroom), is too harsh.

There are four powerful reasons for distinguishing rejected husbands and other co-habitees from strangers.

First and foremost, other things being equal, rape by a cohabitee or ex-cohabitee, though horrible, as all rape is, cannot be *so* horrible and terrifying as rape by a stranger. I speak with the handicap of being a male, but a male can empathise with the female victims of crime, and anyway I take courage from the support of some women (including the woman most important to me), even though they are not the vociferous ones.

Secondly, the stranger who pounces, perhaps wearing a mask, is a greater menace to society and a greater terror to women than the known attacker who acts in pursuance of what he misguidedly thinks of as his rights, or who is suffering from an unbearable sense of loss of his partner by separation (he may even, stupidly, think that by forcing himself upon her he may regain her affection).

Thirdly, the husband, if distraught by what he regards as the unfaithfulness of his wife, deserves some consideration of his account. He should receive this consideration, just as we make some allowance (often a large allowance) for a man or woman who kills a spouse under provocation of unfaithfulness. 'Men are as they are made.' Do the feminists, who demand full retribution against the deserted husband who rapes, demand equally full retribution against the deserted wife who kills?

Fourthly, the victim herself, though generally wanting protection against her former lover is unlikely to want the same fate to befall him as if he were a stranger. (Sometimes she is sufficiently ambivalent to want the possibility of a reconciliation kept open.) There are instances . . . where a woman, having made a charge against her mate, bitterly regrets it when he is sentenced to a long spell in prison; whereas when she succeeds in putting a stranger-rapist behind bars she probably regards it as a good job well done.

Questions:

1. Does Glanville Williams base his criticism of *R* v *R* entirely on black letter law analysis?

2. If you try to put yourself in the shoes of a woman who has been raped by her husband, do you think that it necessarily follows that rape by a stranger is always worse than rape by someone with whom you have had consensual sex in the past?

3. Do you imagine that a man who actually does rape his wife is concerned at the time he commits the offence with whether what he is doing is technically classified as rape in law? If not, does it matter that law applies retroactively to his actions? Does this application of the law really amount to a breach of his human rights?

4. Williams proposes that the CPS could have processed marital rape cases under the same provisions of the Offences Against the Person Act at issue in *Brown*. In what way(s), if any, do you think his proposal is problematic?

5. In reaching their decision in the *Brown* case the Law Lords devote much of their judgment to the meaning of various provisions of the Offences Against the Person Act 1861. Does it follow that the outcome of the case was determined purely on the basis of their analysis of the law? To what extent was the outcome of the *R* case determined by the pre-existing legal rules?

6. In the light of your experience of law so far, is the 'black letter law' account of adjudication plausible? If you regard the theory as tenable, how do you account for the differences in the opinions delivered in *Brown*? Are any law courses which you are taking taught on a black-letter basis? Do any of the other cases we have considered so far undermine this theory?

In evaluating the black letter view it is important to consider what we mean by a legal rule. Twining and Miers suggest that a rule is 'a general norm mandating or guiding conduct or action in a given type of situation'. They suggest that a rule has four aspects:

W Twining and D Miers, *How To Do Things With Rules*, London, Weidenfeld and Nicolson (1991), 3rd edn, p. 131.

(a) A rule is normative or *prescriptive*, that is, it is concerned with ought (not), may (not) or can (not), in relation to behaviour, rather than with factual *description* of behaviour.

(b)   A rule is *general* in that it is concerned with *types* of behaviour in *types* of situation or circumstances; a prescription governing a unique event is not a rule.

(c)   Rules both guide and serve as standards for *behaviour*, that is to say activities, acts or omissions. In the present context we are concerned solely with *human* behaviour.

(d)   Rules provide one kind of *justifying* reason for decision or action. When asked, 'Why did you do this?', the actor may justify the action by reference to a rule, for example, 'Because I was required/permitted/empowered to do so under Regulation . . .'.

It is also important to consider how judges 'find' legal rules, which, as we have seen, usually involves interpretation of statutes or cases.

Twining and Miers, *op. cit.*, pp. 173–4.

The word 'interpretation' has various shades of meaning; in respect of rules, 'to interpret' is generally used in the sense of 'to clarify the scope of' or 'to attribute a meaning to' a rule or part thereof. In some contexts it can be treated as being synonymous with such words as 'elucidate', 'explain' or 'construe', all of which suggest that the subject-matter has an established or settled meaning which it is the role of the interpreter to search for, discover and bring to light, as in a hunt for buried treasure. But often the word 'interpret' is used to suggest a wider role for the interpreter, one that involves an element of elaboration or choice or even of creation. Typically it calls for exercise of the elusive quality of 'judgment'. Thus the buried treasure analogy is inappropriate in the context of Olivier's interpretation of Hamlet or Brendel's interpretation of a Beethoven sonata, or a Muslim theologian's 'free' interpretation of the Koran. In such contexts it would seem odd to treat interpretation as solely a matter of explanation or discovery; the interpreter is working with material that offers a greater or lesser degree of scope for choice and intervention on his part.

The scope for choice and creativity in interpretation depends in part on the malleability of the raw material to be interpreted, in part on the interpreter's situation and conception of his role, and in part on a variety of other factors.

Questions:
1.   In *Brown* and *R*, how far were the judges creative in searching for legislative intent? Is it a sensible or worthwhile exercise for judges to seek to have regard to the intent of a Parliament sitting over a century ago?

2.   In reaching the decision they did in the *Brown* case, the judges purportedly differed only on the interpretation of the Offences Against the Person Act 1861. But was the decision really just about the scope of legal rules or how statutes should be interpreted? (Also refer to cases in Chapter 3 — compare and contrast the approaches of the Court of Appeal and House of Lords to statutory interpretation in *Mandla* v *Lee*.)

3. Which do you think is more important in influencing the judge's decision — the legal text (in these cases the 1861 Act and the Sexual Offences Act 1976) — or the context of the type of activity to which this legislation was to be applied?

4. What impact do you think the Human Rights Act 1998 will have on such decisions by British courts in the future (see Chapter 3 at pp. 103–10).

5. Were *Brown* and *R* 'hard' cases? How would you define a hard case?

2   INTERSTITIAL LEGISLATOR

It should now be clear that the black-letter approach which treats the judge simply as a legal technician, and underplays the role of choice in interpretation, will fail to explain adjudication adequately in hard cases. Some cases may be 'hard' because there are simply no applicable legal rules (see, for example, *Re B* in Chapter 2) or because the rules have run out, or conflict, or can be interpreted in various ways. In such cases the judge's role is more akin to that of a legislator. Hence the judge operates as what John Bell has called an 'interstitial legislator' — meaning simply that where the legislator leaves gaps in the law the judge makes law to fill those gaps (see J Bell, *Policy Arguments in Judicial Decisions*, Oxford, Oxford University Press (1983)). This was an idea of judicial interpretation expounded most famously by legal philosopher H L A Hart in his book *The Concept of Law* (2nd ed), Oxford University Press (1994).

Questions:
1. In the *R* case, do you think that the Law Lords should have waited for Parliament to reform the Sexual Offences Act (as it later did in the Criminal Justice and Public Order Act 1994)? What are the advantages and disadvantages of leaving it to Parliament to act?

2. As the law didn't seem to supply a clear answer in *Brown*, do you think that the majority judges were effectively operating as deputy legislators? Were they in *Re B*   (See Chapter 2.)

3. Given Lord Mustill's comment in *Brown* that he 'regard[ed] the task as one which the courts are not suited to perform, and which should be carried out, if at all, by Parliament after a thorough review of all the medical, social, moral and political issues', does it follow that the majority judges were usurping Parliament's power? Or should judges act where there is a moral/legal vacuum? Will your answer to this question depend on the subject matter of the case? For example, were the House of Lords right to abolish the marital rape exemption in *R* v *R*?

4. What accounts for the difference in role between judge and legislator?

5. Why do/should judges feel more constrained than legislators about effectively making law? Is there anything which *legally* so constrains them?

3   LEGAL REALISM

Once it is acknowledged that there are gaps in the law, and that judges have a certain amount of discretion to fill those gaps, the edifice of law as a system of rules begins to crumble. It was particularly attacked by the American Legal Realist scholars in the 1920s and 1930s. The Legal Realists claimed that a realistic view of law is one which not only accepts that rules can and do run out but questions whether law really consists of rules at all, and whether legal rules are ever binding. Hence, on this view of adjudication judges have a virtually unfettered discretion to decide cases as they please. Whilst it is difficult accurately to capture the essence of such a diverse movement, the essential claims of most Realists were that as the real law-creating power lay with the interpreter all law is effectively judge-made. They drew on the insight of Bishop Hoadley that 'whoever hath an absolute authority to interpret any . . . laws, it is he who is truly the law giver to all intents and purposes, and not the person who first wrote . . . them'.

The Realists emphasised behaviouralism, i.e. a concentration on what judges actually do — the decisions they make — rather than the reasoning with which they cloak their decisions. Hence in K Llewellyn's words (*The Bramble Bush*, New York, Oceana Publications (1951), p. 12) 'What officials do about disputes is the law itself'.

According to one of the forerunners of the Realists the most important perspective from which to view law is from the point of view of the 'bad man', who is concerned solely with prophesying how the courts will treat him if he is caught: O W Holmes, *The Path of Law*, (1897).

In the words of Karl Llewellyn, the most famous Realist:

'There is no school of realists. There is no likelihood that there will be such a school. There is no group with an official or accepted, or even with an emerging creed . . . There is, however, a *movement* in thought and work about law.' (K Llewellyn, *Some Realism about Realism* (1931)).

Nevertheless, the Realist movement has had important implications for legal reasoning in raising awareness of the following issues:

(a)   That what judges do is more important than the reasoning with which they justify their decisions.
(b)   That there is more to law than rules.
(c)   That legal reasoning is indeterminate.

Thus the Realists particularly attacked precedent. As no two cases are exactly identical, they claimed that there is no 'rule' laid down in an earlier case which *must* be simply applied in a later case. Instead the judge has a choice as to whether or not he or she is bound by the earlier case. If he/she chooses not to be bound she/he can always assert some factual difference, since the other major contribution of certain Realists (like Jerome Frank) was to problematise the process of fact-finding (see Chapter 4).

Questions:
1. Were the judges in *Brown* and *R* totally unconstrained by legal rules or precedents? Did the judgments merely reflect the whim of the judges? In general, how persuasive do you find the view that judges have more power than legislators?

2. Do you agree with the Realists about the extent of discretion which judges possess? Does this apply only to more difficult cases like *Brown* and *R* which are decided by the higher level appellate courts, or do judges at first instance also have this broad discretion? (See p. 256 below)

4   THE POLITICS OF THE JUDICIARY

Through time many of the insights of the American Legal Realists have been absorbed by mainstream legal theory with the result that the movement itself, which originated as a reaction against formalism, fizzled out. However, John Griffith has drawn on Realist insights and applied them in a contemporary British context. He concurs with the Realist contention that judges have a wide discretion, but draws on another Realist insight which suggests that such unfettered discretion does not necessarily lead to uncertainty and unpredictability in the adjudication process. This is so because there are also a number of 'steadying factors' contained in the law which combine to make the outcome of cases predictable. Such factors include the homogeneous background and shared education of most judges. Drawing on this strand of sociological enquiry and finding, unsurprisingly, that judges are overwhelmingly white, male, middle or upper class, and public-school and Oxbridge-educated, Griffith injects politics into his theory of adjudication. He argues that judges use their discretion (though not necessarily consciously) to maintain the status quo, and that this furthers their own position as members of the ruling oligarchy. In making political choices which they claim will further the 'public interest', judges in fact, according to Griffith's thesis, equate the public interest with the preservation of the status quo. Hence judges' views of the public interest are necessarily coloured by their privileged position in society. Therefore whilst Dworkin (see below) argues that freedom from the pressure of pursuing electorally-popular policies means that judges are particularly well placed to protect unpopular minority rights, Griffith contends that judges necessarily prefer their own interests to those of the disadvantaged minorities.

J A G Griffith, *The Politics of the Judiciary*, 5th edn, London, Fontana (1997) pp. 7–8, 21–22.

When people like the members of the judiciary, broadly homogeneous in character, are faced with [politically contentious] situations, they act in broadly similar ways. It will be part of my argument to suggest that behind these actions lies a unifying attitude of mind, a political position, which is primarily concerned to protect and conserve certain values and institutions. This does not mean that the judiciary invariably supports what governments do or even what Conservative governments do. Individually, judges may support the Conservative or Labour or the Liberal parties. Collectively, in their function and by their nature, they are neither Tories nor Socialists nor Liberals. They are protectors and conservators of what has been, of the relationship and interests on which, *in their view,* our society is founded. They do not regard their role as radical or even reformist, only (on occasion) corrective . . .

In January 1994 the average age, the number of women, and those from the ethnic minorities were:

	Average age	Women	Ethnic minorities	Total number
Law Lords	66.5	0	0	10
Heads of Division	63.0	0	0	4
Lords Justices	63.0	1	0	29
High Court judges	57.6	6	0	95
				138

Of 514 Circuit judges in post on 1 December 1994, 29 were women, and 4 were of ethnic minority origin. In 1996 there were 7 female judges on the High Court bench.

In summary, 80 per cent of the senior judiciary are products of public schools and of Oxford or Cambridge, with an average age of about sixty; 5.1 per cent are women; 100 per cent are white. Some explanation of the gross disproportions in gender and colour can no doubt be found in the structure of the legal profession, in the financial and other difficulties facing those wishing to qualify as barristers, and then needing to support themselves in the early years of practice. Another part of the explanation is sexual and racial discrimination within the profession.

The process of appointment to the judiciary and of promotion rests broadly, as we have seen, on consultation by the Lord Chancellor and his department. But the decisions are all his or the Prime Minister's after consultation with him. In 1995 the Lord Chancellor said that he encouraged greater numbers of women and ethnic minority practitioners to apply to become judges but that he had no plans to reconstitute the professional judiciary to reflect the composition of society as a whole. Little comfort is to be obtained from the official view of the Lord Chancellor's Department who told the Home Affairs Committee in 1995.

This is not to say that the Lord Chancellor does not appreciate the value of the judiciary more closely reflecting the make-up of society as a whole. Other things being equal, that should tend over time to result from ensuring the fullest possible equality of opportunity for persons in all sections of society who wish to enter the legal profession and who aspire to sit judicially. This implies equality of opportunity at all levels of the educational system and the legal profession as well as in the appointments system itself.

These are weasel words indeed from which all meaning has been extracted. The gross imbalance in the representation of women and those from the ethnic minority is to await the day when they are treated equally by society as a whole. Judges are appointed and promoted by the most senior judge, advised by other senior judges. The system is self-perpetuating and it would be remarkable if the products were not homogeneous.

Questions:
1.   Given our stress on the significance of different standpoints and perspectives in Chapter 1, how important is it that our judiciary are representative?

2.   Do the decisions in *Brown* and *R* support Griffith's thesis? How far do you think it was influential in the majority's decision in *Brown* that the participants in the sado-masochistic activity were *homosexual*? Would the outcome have been different if a married heterosexual couple engaged in such activity? (In this regard see the subsequent Court of Appeal decision in *R* v *Wilson* [1996] 3 WLR 125.) Was *Brown* really a case where the outcome depended on the majority's distaste for gay, sado-masochistic activity, or their concern to preserve the white, male, heterosexual establishment? Do you think an openly gay judge would have decided the case differently?

3.   Are the differing judgments in the *Brown* case really about differing opinions held by the Law Lords on the relationship between law and morality (see Chapter 8)? Were any of the judges prepared to *morally* tolerate homosexual sado-masochistic conduct? (For discussion of *Brown* and other cases raising moral issues, see Chapter 7 of the 1997 edition of Griffith's book.)

4.   We have already queried whether the process of adjudication is a purely legal one. But is it any more insightful to argue that it is a purely political one? How do you explain cases which do not seem to preserve the status quo, or operate *against* powerful vested interests? Consider *Stevens* v *Avery* [1988] 2 WLR 1280, *Duport Steel* v *Sirs* [1980] 1 All ER 529, *Bromley* v *GLC* [1983] 1 AC 768, *R* v *Liverpool City Council, ex parte Ferguson, The Times*, 20 November 1985.

5   LAW AS INTEGRITY

From a completely different standpoint, one concerned to justify the role of judges in a democracy, Ronald Dworkin has propounded a 'principled' theory of adjudication, which argues that law consists of a 'seamless' web, and that the 'right answer', even in a hard case, is always implicit in existing law, so that the judge never has an unfettered discretion to decide cases. Whilst he accepts that legal rules do run out, he contends that law does not simply consist of rules, but also contains principles and policies which underlie the legal rules and provide a justification for them. He distinguishes principles and policies by suggesting that policy arguments are those which 'justify a political decision by showing that the decision advances or protects some collective goal of the community as a whole', whereas 'arguments of principle justify a political decision by showing that the decision respects or secures some individual or group rights'. (R Dworkin, *Taking Rights Seriously*, London, Duckworths (1977), p. 82). As Cotterrell points out, Dworkin's claim seems to be that 'law is *more fundamental* than rules and that rules are incomplete and problematic expressions of the content of law' (R Cotterrell, *The Politics of Jurisprudence*, London, Butterworths (1989)). Therefore, even if rules conflict, run out or are inconclusive there are other factors to guide judges. However, on Dworkin's account the roles of judge and legislator are sharply differentiated and judges should refrain from making policy decisions on three grounds:

(a) the argument from democracy;
(b) the argument from retroactivity;
(c) the argument from consistency.

Questions:
1.   What do you think the above three arguments mean?

2.   Are there valid objections to judges making decisions based on policy? Even if there are, can judges avoid making policy decisions? Were either the *Brown* or *R* decisions based on policy? If so, what was that policy?

3.   Does the whole principle/policy distinction stand up:

(a) in legal theory?
(b) in judicial decision-making?

Even Dworkin himself appears to concede the difficulties in distinguishing between the two concepts. He asks rhetorically: 'How shall we tell as a matter of history, whether a particular political decision has been taken on grounds of principle or policy? *It may not be a simple matter*, the appeal to consequences is not decisive' (emphasis added) (*Taking Rights Seriously, op. cit.*, p. 297).

Similarly, many of the judiciary appear uncertain about the precise distinction. For example, Lord Scarman has said in *McLoughlin* v *O'Brian* [1982] 2 All ER 298 that: 'The distinguishing feature of the common law is this judicial development and formulation of principle. Policy considerations will have to be weighed; but the objective of the judges is the formulation of principle.'

4.   Would you agree with Bell, *op. cit.*, that: 'The fundamental objection to Dworkin's thesis is that his political division of power is unsuited to many countries . . . it does not work for countries like Britain, where the achievement of individual fulfilment is considered to be tied more closely to the development of the community as a whole'?

The importance of principled and consistent decision-making are essential features of Dworkin's conception of 'law as integrity' which is elaborated in his later work.

R Dworkin, *Law's Empire*, London, Fontana (1986), p. 96.

> Law as integrity 'argues that rights and responsibilities flow from past
> decisions and so count as legal, not just when they are explicit in those
> decisions but also when they follow from the principles of personal and
> political morality the explicit decisions presuppose by way of justification'.

R Dworkin, *op. cit.*, pp. 243–5.

> Law as integrity asks judges to assume, so far as this is possible, that the law
> is structured by a coherent set of principles about justice and fairness and
> procedural due process, and it asks them to enforce these in the fresh cases
> that come before them so that each person's situation is fair and just
> according to the same standards. That style of adjudication respects the
> ambition integrity assumes, the ambition to be a community of principle . . .
> [It] requires a judge to test his interpretation of any part of the great network
> of political structures and decisions of his community by asking whether it
> could form part of a coherent theory, justifying the network as a whole.

More recently, Dworkin has neatly summarised the concept of law as
integrity as follows:

R Dworkin, *Life's Dominion: An Argument about Abortion and Euthanasia*,
London, Harper Collins (1993), p. 146.

> Integrity in law has several dimensions. First, it insists that judicial decision
> be a matter of principle, not compromise or strategy or political accommo-
> dation . . . Second . . . integrity holds vertically, a judge who claims that a
> particular liberty is fundamental must show that his claim is consistent with
> principles embedded in Supreme Court precedent and with the main struc-
> tures of our constitutional arrangement. Third, integrity holds horizontally: a
> judge who adopts a principle in one case must give full weight to it in other
> cases he decides or endorses, even in apparently unrelated fields of law.

Hence, although the judge's function is not legislative, it is creative. Dworkin
claims that a judge's role in deciding a case and thus creating new law, is
analogous to that of a writer engaged in the enterprise of writing a chain novel,
in that both are constrained by what has happened in earlier cases or chapters,
and by the dimension of 'fit'; but are also adding creatively to that history.

Questions:
1. How apt is the analogy with a chain novel? Are later judges more
constrained than earlier judges in the chain? For instance, is this true of judges
deciding cases subsequent to *Re B* on treatment of disabled neonates? (See
Chapter 2.) Can you think of any better analogies than that of the chain novel
to describe the judge's function?

2. Do you think that it was arguments of legal principle which determined the decisions in *Brown* and *R*? If so, what was that principle? How can Dworkin's theory explain the difference in the majority and minority opinions in the House of Lords in *Brown*?

3. Given that principles do seem to be more fundamental than law, and that judges must test their interpretation of law according to whether it coheres with the framework of political structures and decisions in their community, it would appear that there must be some consensus about fundamental moral values in the community. But does such consensus exist to guide the judges in a case like *Brown*? If such consensus is lacking, does that undermine Dworkin's thesis? Even if there is some consensus on an issue, how can judges ascertain what it is? Are legislators well placed to decide whether there is a consensus in society about important moral issues like sexual behaviour, abortion, euthanasia or pornography (see Chapter 8)?

4. HLA Hart has claimed that Dworkin's vision of law is simply a 'noble dream' and contrasted it with the 'nightmare' vision of law portrayed by Legal Realism (H Hart, 'American Jurisprudence through English Eyes: The Nightmare and the Noble Dream', in *Essays in Jurisprudence and Philosophy*, Oxford, Clarendon Press (1983)). Do you agree with these characterisations?

6   ECONOMIC ANALYSIS OF LAW

In the wake of the havoc wreaked by Legal Realism and its debunking of formalism, the history of American legal thought this century can be read as an attempt to demonstrate that whilst formalism was too simplistic, nonetheless law is not completely indeterminate. Dworkin's theory of law is one response to the charge of indeterminacy; and another has come from the more right-wing standpoint of economic theorists of law who suggest that all judicial decisions can be reduced to or evaluated on the basis of how efficient they are in economic terms. It contends that judges do and should decide cases with the objective of efficiency in mind. In this context efficiency means that resources end up where they are most valued. The aim and function of law, and the judge's role in deciding cases is to promote the most efficient allocation of resources. We will consider this theory more fully in the next chapter.

Questions:
1. Can all the myriad factors which may influence the outcome of judges really be reduced to the single factor of efficiency?

2. Even if considerations of efficiency may dictate the outcome of particular areas of law, such as tort or contract, could considerations of efficiency influence judicial thinking in a case like *Brown* or *R*? What about a case like *Mandla* v *Lee* (see Chapter 3)?

7   CRITICAL LEGAL STUDIES

In contrast to the efforts of both Dworkin and economic theorists (albeit from different perspectives) to assert some sort of determinacy in legal doctrine, the

Critical Legal Studies movement, which originated in the United States in the 1970s, emphasises the indeterminacy of legal doctrine. It draws on Legal Realism, Marxism and Feminism, amongst other diverse influences such as Semiotics, post-modern and critical theory. It differs from Legal Realism in that it is much more theoretical and orientated to the legal academy, rather than the more empirical Realist movement which was concerned with producing better lawyers. CLS is also much more politically motivated, attacking not only liberal legal theories but the whole structure of liberal society. It is however crucially concerned with the judges' role and how judges reason, but unlike Dworkin or the adherents of economic analysis of law, who are concerned to justify the role of judges in a democracy, they are concerned to expose the judges' role.

A Hutchinson and P Monaghan, 'Law, Politics and the Critical Legal Scholars. The Unfolding Drama of American Legal Thought', *Stanford Law Review* (1984), Vol. 36, pp. 199–245 at p. 206.

> Like traditional jurists, the critical scholars are obsessed with the judicial function and its alleged central importance for an understanding of law in society. Yet while they share this infatuation, they adopt a radically different view of the judicial process: all the critical scholars unite in denying the rational determinacy of legal reasoning. Their basic credo is that no distinctive mode of legal reasoning exists to be contrasted with political dialogue. Law is simply politics dressed in different garb.

Thus legal reasoning, like political reasoning, is wholly indeterminate and cannot generate determinate results. Consequently legal doctrine can be manipulated by judges to reach any decision at all.

According to critical legal theory, both law and the process of legal reasoning serve to 'legitimate' the existing order:

R W Gordon, 'New Developments in Legal Theory' in D Kairys (ed.), *The Politics of Law,* New York, Pantheon Books (1990) pp. 418–20 (references omitted).

> Law, like religion and television images, is one of those clusters of belief — and it ties in with a lot of other non legal but similar clusters — that convince people that all the many hierarchical relations in which they live and work are natural and necessary . . . This process of allowing the structures we ourselves have built to mediate relations among us so as to make us see ourselves as performing abstract roles in a play that is produced by no human agency is what is usually called (following Marx and such modern writers as Sartre and Lukács) reification. It is a way people have of manufacturing necessity: they build structures, then act as if (and genuinely come to believe that) the structures they have built are determined by history, human nature, economic, law.

Hence critical legal scholars contend that there is a need to 'deconstruct' legal doctrine to expose the reality of judicial decision-making.

One of the main challenges which the CLS movement has faced is whether it can or should move beyond deconstruction to a more positive programme.

(On this issue see R Unger, *The Critical Legal Studies Movement,* Cambridge, Massachusetts, Harvard University Press, 1987.)

The following are two contrasting summaries of the CLS movement to date:

D Nelken, 'What's so Special About Criminal Law?' in P Fitzpatrick and A Hunt (eds), *Critical Legal Studies,* Oxford, Blackwell (1987).

CLS is a 'left leaning, unorthodox form of legal scholarship which challenges what is taken to be the mainstream liberal consensus concerning the nature and purpose of law. To do this it draws on diverse strands of modernist social, political and literary theory. Amongst its targets are the ideas that law is to be explained in terms of the functional and instrumental purposes it serves, the attempt to present law as rational and coherent, and the effort to separate legal discourse from moral and political argumentation'.

Dworkin, *Law's Empire, op. cit.* at p. 272.

Save in its self conscious leftist posture and its particular choice of other disciplines to celebrate critical legal studies resembles the older movement of American legal realism, and it is too early to decide whether it is more than an anachronistic attempt to make that dated movement reflower.

Questions:
1. Which of these two summations do you regard as the more accurate?

2. Can people really be 'duped' into believing (wrongly) that their lives are determined by factors over which they have no control?

3. Do you agree that there is no difference between legal and political reasoning? If so, what consequences does this have for the role of the judge in our society?

4. Could the judges have manipulated the law and facts in *Brown* to reach any result they wanted? Was this equally true of the case of *R*? Do you think they decided on the result they wanted to achieve and then used legal arguments as a justification for that decision?

5. If the outcome of legal cases is never/rarely determined by purely legal considerations, does it follow that a lay person could have adjudicated on *Brown* or *R* with as much authority as the Law Lords who did decide those cases? What consequences would this have for law and legal education?

8 FEMINISM

Although the critical legal studies movement now seems to have spent much of its critical force, one of its effects has been to create space for women and minority scholars to make their own distinctive contribution to legal theory. Most feminist legal scholars would agree with critical scholars that law is political, but would focus on how this is manifested in decisions which (perhaps again unconsciously) favour men. (Consider for example recent decisions on provocation such as *Thornton* and *Ahluwalia*, Chapter 4 at pp. 159–67.) They may also dispute with male critical scholars the possibility of devising an alternative structuring of society which would command consensus, and argue instead for a society which acknowledges the reality of difference (see N Duxbury, 'Pessimism of the Intellect, Optimism of the Will', Chapter 6 in *Patterns of American Justice*, Oxford, Oxford University Press (1995)). However, due to the increasing influence of postmodernism (see below), feminist legal scholars have become aware that law may uphold a particular type of masculinity, thus favouring only certain men, for example, those of a particular class or race:

N Naffine, *Law & The Sexes: Explorations in Feminist Jurisprudence*, London, Allen & Unwin (1990), pp. 115–16.

. . . one can discern in law a certain male style but . . . it does not represent the style of all men or even of the majority. Law . . . embodies a middle-class style of masculinity. The man of law is a middle-class man whose masculinity assumes a middle-class form. He is therefore at some remove from his earthier, working-class brother who, as a consequence, may well find the law an alien institution . . . He is aware that the public sphere is a battleground and that only the best man will win. The man of law competes, pushes his own suit and succeeds . . . But there is also another side to the man of law which complements his rugged image of masculinity and demonstrates his cultural superiority. This is the man of reason: the prudent maker of contracts, advancing his own interests with rational calculation. His is a high-brow, cultivated form of masculinity which depends on an ability to think and act intelligently, not with brute force.

Questions:
1.   On what grounds do you think a feminist legal scholar might (a) applaud the *R* decision and (b) criticise the *Brown* decision?

2.   Do you think that it was implicit in the judgments in *Brown* that the judges held a particular vision of masculinity — the 'rugged image of masculinity' embodied in law — as evidenced by their references to normality, normal relationships and behaviour, and their conception of what were manly sports or forms of behaviour?

3.   Lord Templeman (at p. 228 above) states: 'In my opinion sado-masochism is not only concerned with sex. Sado-masochism is also concerned with violence.' Do you think that the judges apply the same reasoning to cases on rape?

9   POSTMODERNISM

Feminist and critical legal studies theories of adjudication have been heavily influenced by postmodern thinking. We have already discussed the influence of postmodernism in Chapter 1 (see pp. 23–5). In many respects formulating a postmodern theory of adjudication is a contradiction in terms, since the emphasis on indeterminacy and fragmentation in postmodern theory, and its distrust of meta narratives makes it difficult to formulate reductionist accounts of how judges decide hard cases. However the following extract offers some insight to the process of adjudication. In it the authors challenge the fundamental tenet of much legal scholarship, that legal texts can be authoritatively interpreted and that law is bounded from other institutions:

C Douzinas and R Warrington, 'A Well-Founded Fear of Justice: Law and Ethics in Postmodernity', *Law and Critique* (1991), vol. II, pp. 115–16 (references omitted).

Legal judgments are both statements and deeds. They both interpret the law and act on the world. A conviction and sentence at the end of a criminal trial is the outcome of the judicial act of legal interpretation. But it is also the authorisation and beginning of a variety of violent acts. The defendant is taken away to a place of imprisonment or of execution, acts immediately related to, indeed flowing from judicial pronouncement. Again, as a result of civil judgments people lose their homes, their children, their property or they may be sent to a place of persecution and torture.

The recent turn of jurisprudence to hermeneutics, semiotics and literary theory has focused on the word of the judge and forgotten its force. The meaning seeking and meaning imposing component of judging is analysed as reasoned or capricious, principled or discretionary, predictable or contingent, shared, shareable, or open-ended, according to the political standpoint of the analyst. But as Cover has reminded us, in our obsession with hermeneutics we forget that 'legal interpretation takes place in a field of pain and death'. The main if not exclusive function of many judgments is to legitimise and trigger off past or future acts of violence. The word and the deed, the proposition and the sentence, the costative and performative are intimately linked.

Legal interpretations and judgments cannot be understood independently of this inescapable imbrication with — often violent — action. In this sense legal interpretation is a practical activity, -other -oriented and designed to lead to effective threats and — often violent — death. The architecture of the courtroom and choreography of the trial process converge to restrain and physically subdue the body of the defendant. From the latter's perspective, the common but fragile facade of civility of the legal process expresses a recognition 'of the overwhelming array of violence ranged against him and of the hopelessness of resistance or outcry'. But for the judge too, legal interpretation is never free of the need to maintain links with the effective official behaviour that will en-*force* the statement of the law. Indeed the expression 'the law is enforced' recognises that force and its application lies at the heart of the judicial act. Legal sentences are both propositions of law and acts of sentencing. Judges whatever else they do, they deal in fear and pain and death. If this is the case any aspiration to coherent and shared legal meaning will founder on the inescapable and tragic line that distinguishes those who mete out violence from those who receive it.

Questions:

1. To what extent are judicial pronouncements in the various cases in this book really about violence?

2. Compare this view of adjudication with Dworkin's view that the process of adjudication is comparable to that of writing a chain novel. Does this extract point to the crucial difference between legal and literary interpretation? (See further Chapter 10 at pp. 409–11.)

10 SUMMARY

S Lee, *Judging Judges*, London, Faber and Faber (1989), pp. 201–203.

My thesis is that judicial decisions are, and should be, influenced by many factors which can be usefully analysed under three main headings: first, the judges' view of the past law (statutes, precedents and principles); second, the judges' evaluation of the consequences of the options before them; third, the judges' view of their own role. I claim that these factors are not always acknowledged by judges, who often prefer to squeeze them into the first issue, but that they are always at work and that if judges were to be more candid, this would help the quality of their law-making. I insist, contrary to some commentators and some judges, that judges *are* entitled to take account of the consequences of their decisions. I insist, contrary to most commentators and some judges, that different views of the judicial role are legitimate, even within the same court at the same time. With more support, perhaps I may remind readers that the judicial roles will vary even more as we move from time to time, court to court, and topic to topic.

It is only realistic to accept that judges *do* disagree on their proper role. I would go further and say that there *should* be a diversity of role perceptions.

In particular, it seems to me that judges' creativity ought to vary according to four factors:

1. Does the case involve statutes or common law (the latter allowing more freedom)?
2. Where is the judge in the courts' hierarchy (the higher up, the more creativity is suitable)?
3. Is the subject matter such that certainty or justice is more important?
4. What is the likelihood of other institutions of government correcting any injustice?

Thus a first instance judge in a commercial court should not allow his notions of justice to overtake his commitment to precedent. He might be interpreting a statute, he is not an appellate judge, his area is one in which both parties will have been professionally advised and will have planned their businesses on the basis of the past law. But a Law Lord in the *Spycatcher* case should rightly regard himself as having much more freedom of action to do whatever he thinks is right.

More controversially, I believe that different Law Lords will legitimately differ on the degree of flexibility which they allow themselves. The line between proper and improper judicial roles is constantly in need of being redrawn as circumstances change (such as the comparative legitimacy and willingness of other branches of government to develop the law). It is therefore healthy to have competing views jostling for acceptance within the judiciary. The task of judging judges is a dynamic, not a static, one. Each generation will need to rewrite the rules of the game. But the rules allow a variety of tactics by which judges can score goals, although I should hasten to add that some moves should be ruled offside by the referees, who in this case are other judges, commentators and the public.

The negative side of my thesis is that I disagree with anyone who maintains that judicial decisions should ignore 'policy', if by policy they mean consequences and the values by which we declare the consequences desirable or disastrous, and that I disagree with those who say that the whole truth, or even very much of the truth, can be discerned by looking at the judges' background.

Questions:

1.   Do any of the judges in *R* or *Brown* make reference to the consequences of their decisions? What consequences do you think will follow from these decisions?

2.   Why do judges not openly acknowledge that they evaluate the consequences of their decision, and are influenced by their own perception of their role?

3.   Why is it important that there should be a dialogue between judges and society?

Finally, having now considered the above theories of adjudication, how many of them would you reject totally as being as meaningless as the judge's zodiac sign? Do these theories contain all the factors which influence the result of a case?

If, in Chapter 6, you thought that advocacy made a difference to the outcome of a case, how come in Chapter 7 you don't think it is as relevant as factors such as judicial bias, past cases, or economics?

Chapter 8

Critical Skills

In this chapter we focus on skills which enable you to assess laws critically. This should help you to argue more logically and persuasively, and to present your arguments more clearly. Laws can be evaluated as to both their intrinsic and instrumental value according to a number of different criteria. We have selected three concepts which can be used as standards by which to criticise law — efficiency, morality and justice. We have chosen these three because the commonest complaints you are likely to hear about a law is that it is inefficient, immoral or unjust. Can you think of any laws which you have studied, or come across recently in the media, which you would criticise on one of these grounds? What does it mean to criticise laws in one of these ways?

An understanding of such critical concepts will:

(a)   ensure that you are better informed; and
(b)   enable you to avoid the mistake of using bad and irrelevant lines of argument,

both of which will make you a better advocate and negotiator.

1   EFFICIENCY

In the last chapter, when looking at theories of adjudication, we briefly considered Economic Analysis of Law — the theory that judges decide cases so as to produce the most efficient outcome. Hence efficiency is a relevant criterion which we can use to evaluate law — a particular judgment or statute can be judged according to how efficient are the results which it produces. Indeed whole legal systems can be judged on the basis of their efficiency.

First, however, we need to consider in more detail what efficiency means:

D Harris, *Remedies in Tort and Contract,* London, Weidenfeld and Nicolson (1988), pp. 6–8.

> Lawyers do not need a sophisticated knowledge of economics in order to gain a useful external view of the law, which may lead to a deeper understanding of legal rules and a new perspective from which to appraise them. An economic concept often helps the lawyer to perceive more clearly an issue of which he was previously only vaguely aware. The economic approach should not be expected to solve all legal problems, but rather to clarify the issues. Legal rules often need to go beyond some of the assumptions made by economists, e.g. the assumption that the existing distributions of wealth and incomes should be accepted as the starting point. The law cannot avoid using ethical standards like justice and fairness in many rules but even here the lawyers should recognise whether the rule is allowing economic 'efficiency' to be overridden by a concept such as 'distributive justice'.
>
> The economist's concept of efficiency is quite consistent with the everyday use of the term, which tends to emphasise the avoidance of waste. Because resources are scarce relative to people's wants, it is seen as wasteful to ignore potentially rewarding opportunities for exchange. Any exchange of goods or resources which increases the well being of at least one person without reducing the well being of another is said to improve social welfare. When a position has been reached in which it is impossible to exchange goods and services further without somebody becoming worse off, the resulting allocation of goods and services is said to be *'Pareto-efficient'.* Obviously there may be obstacles to the free exchange of goods and services and a crucial function of the law from this perspective is said by economists to be the creation of enforceable 'property rights' to facilitate exchange, as well as the reduction in 'transaction costs' which limit exchange. A Pareto-efficient allocation, in which the potential for mutually beneficial trade has been exhausted is clearly dependent upon the relative wealth of the parties to the transaction. Those with the greatest wealth will be allocated the most goods, because their *willingness to pay* in the process of exchange is conditioned by their ability to pay. Hence there will be a separate Pareto-efficient allocation associated with each distribution of wealth. Correspondingly, economists often attempt to separate analysis of the efficiency effects of the law from the distributive, or equity, effects.
>
> Efficiency in the Pareto sense is consequently concerned with achieving maximum gains through voluntary agreement. In most contractual contexts, where the transacting parties are known to each other, this is clearly a valid and justifiable way of evaluating the law. A good rule is one which achieves what would have been mutually agreed between contracting parties. However, the law is frequently concerned with influencing behaviour in the wider community, in which case general rules may be devised to apply to many individual disputes. Because of this, the prospect of differential outcomes arises: a rule which benefits most people may nevertheless impose a cost on

some. This causes fundamental problems for the concept of efficiency: according to the Pareto criterion, we cannot say whether such a rule is efficient, because at least one person is worse off. Various alternative criteria have been suggested. Essentially these come down to devising ways of evaluating 'welfare gains and losses' in terms of some common numeraire, so that an aggregate measure of the change in social welfare can be produced. 'Efficiency' in this sense (sometimes referred to as 'Hicks-Kaldor efficiency') means the maximisation of this measure of social welfare. It is this definition of efficiency which underpins the cost-benefit analysis of legal rules. While it would appear that this approach offers more flexibility with respect to equity (because it permits 'efficient' distributional changes) it does so at the cost of a somewhat arbitrary means of comparing individual gains and losses. Using aggregate willingness to pay as a criterion for social welfare improvement implicitly assumes that a pound is worth the same to everyone — which is not a widely acceptable value judgment. Again, the conflict between efficiency and equity objectives is apparent.

The social cost-benefit calculation introduces the concept of an 'externality'. This is a benefit or detriment (cost) to third parties which arises from the behaviour of a given individual or transaction between particular individuals but which will not be taken into account by them when deciding whether to behave in that way or to enter that transaction. The standard example is where the inhabitants of a residential area suffer from a polluting factory. In this situation, there is a divergence between the social cost of the factory, and the private costs which the factory-owner will take into account in his planning. The law may impose liability — in this case under the tort of nuisance — to force the factory-owner to take the externality into account when choosing the method and volume of production. Thus, the object of many legal rules is to give an incentive to actors to take into account the effects of their actions on the benefits and costs of others.

C Veljanovski, *The Economics of Law*, London, Institute of Economic Affairs (1992) (references omitted).

Increasingly, economics is being extended beyond its traditional precincts of the market-place and the economy to sociology, political science, philosophy and law. One endeavour which is gaining momentum and respectability is the economic analysis of law. This development is yet another example of the phenomenon Kenneth Boulding has called economic imperialism: 'the attempt on the part of economics to take over the other social sciences'.

Most of this interest in the economic analysis of law has been shown not by economists but by lawyers mainly in North America. 'Conversational literacy in neo-classical welfare economics', observes Coleman, 'is an apparent prerequisite to gainful employment in American law schools'. While this overstates the situation, it nonetheless indicates the importance that the subject has attained in North America.

In marked contrast, the study of the law in the UK is exceptionally narrow. 'The English lawyer', Ogus and Richardson comment, 'has been notoriously unwilling to admit the relevance of social science to his discipline.' Similarly, UK economists have seriously lagged behind their North American counterparts. Campbell and Wiles conclude in their survey:

'in comparison with the position in America, economists in Britain have virtually ignored studies of law or the relevance of legal regulation to economic development'.

There exists an unnecessary and positively harmful disciplinary divide between law and economics which has practical consequences. Both disciplines suffer from what Veblen called 'trained incapacity'. Lawyers and policy-makers are economically illiterate and frequently innumerate. The English legal fraternity is wary of theory, contemptuous of experts and academics, and reluctant to accept the idea that other disciplines have something valuable to say about 'law'. The situation is precisely captured by Professor Patrick Atiyah:

'Most English judges are emphatically neither intellectuals nor theorists; few are ever given to doubting their own first principles, at least in public, and most are deeply sceptical of the value of theory . . . Very few have more than the faintest glimmering of the vast jurisprudential literature concerning the nature of the judicial process. Most would pride themselves on being pragmatists, and not theorists.'

To the economist, the approach of lawyers is excessively descriptive and legalistic. On the occasions that they do venture to comment on legal reform, their conclusions appear *ad hoc* rationalisations, ethical and moralistic value-judgments, or simply assertions based on dubious casual empiricism. The economics editor of the Australian *Sydney Morning Herald* captured the lawyers' approach in his blunt attack on a proposal by the Law Reform Commission to permit class actions as:

'. . . a highly interventionist remedy, typical of the legal mind. It ignores many of the economic issues involved and falls back on the lawyer's conviction that all of the world's problems can be solved if only we had the right laws. Finding a lawyer who understands and respects market forces is as hard as finding a baby-wear manufacturer who understands and respects celibacy. *The legally trained mind cannot grasp that it is never possible to defeat market forces, only to distort them so they pop up in unexpected ways.*'

Economists, too, must shoulder considerable criticism. The general inclination, particularly, though not exclusively, of British economists, is to treat the law as datum. Professor Karl Llewellyn touched on this many years ago in a comment which still accurately describes the attitude of most economists:

'. . . the economist takes . . . [the law] for granted. Law exists. If it serves economic life well, he has ignored it; if ill, he has pithily cursed it and its devotees, without too great an effort to understand the reason of disservice'.

This is now changing. In the academic climate of the 1970s it was difficult to present economic views of law principally because the idea appeared irrelevant, seen as largely imported from the United States where market and free-enterprise values are more acceptable and accepted. The 1980s has seen free-market economic thinking move to the centre of government policy in Europe and many other parts of the world. The supply-side policies of the Thatcher Government have given an intellectual impetus to the economic analysis of laws and regulation. Privatisation and the regulation of utility industries, such as gas, water, and electricity, have brought into prominence the economic dimension of different laws. But even though economics has, and will increasingly, become central to the control of industry as we move from nationalisation to regulation, the basis of the new regulatory approach has not exhibited a deep concern for sound economic principles. In the UK the rhetoric of economic rationalism may have been adopted to justify the growth of regulation, but the reality is an *ad hoc* assembly of laws and decisions cemented together by the greatest of all expedients — political compromise implemented through bureaucratic discretion.

. . . The economics of law can be defined rather crudely as the application of economic theory, mostly price theory, and statistical methods to examine the formation, structure, processes and impact of the law and legal institutions. It consists of a dispersed and unsystematic literature written by economists and lawyers. No consensus has yet emerged, nor do economists possess a coherent explanatory theory of law. Nevertheless, in the last decade it has developed into a distinct field of study with its own specialist scholars, journals and texts, with every indication that interest in the field is growing.

The economics of law is not confined to those areas of law that directly affect markets or economic activity. It goes well beyond these areas to examine fundamental legal institutions. The subject can be arbitrarily separated into 'old' and 'new' parts. The old law-and-economics is concerned with laws that affect the operation of the economy and markets. It examines the effects the law has on competition, the performance of markets, industries and firms, and economic variables such as prices, investment, profits, income distribution and resource allocation generally. It includes competition law, industry regulation (the regulation of the privatised utilities and nationalised industries, quotas and price controls), and tax and trade laws. This application is witnessing a resurgence in the UK and Europe as the supply-side reforms of privatisation and liberalisation paradoxically thrust government regulation of industry to the forefront.

The most innovative extension of economics in recent years has been the 'new' law-and-economics which takes as its subject-matter the entire legal and regulatory systems irrespective of whether or not the law controls economic relationships. In recent years contract, tort (the area of the common law which deals with unintentional harms such as accidents and nuisance), family law, criminal law and legal procedure have all been subjected to economic analysis.

Questions:

1. Do you think that judges are ever guided by considerations of efficiency in reaching decisions?

2. How important do you think that efficiency is as a criterion for evaluating law? Is it becoming more important as we move towards the millennium?

3. Is the most efficient result likely to be the one that does justice between the parties to a dispute? Which is more important?

4. Can you think of any cases which you have studied (e.g. in courses such as Contract and Tort) where judges appear to take considerations of efficiency into account?

5. What about particular laws:

    (a)   Is the law prohibiting a market in babies (or parental rights) efficient?
    (b)   Is the law precluding criminal liability for omissions efficient?

6. If you apply economic analysis to specific subjects of law:

    (a)   is our criminal law efficient?
    (b)   is our tort system efficient?

7. What are the limitations of the economic approach to law? What criticisms would you make of it?

Posner considers the following criticisms:

R A Posner, 'The Economic Approach to Law'; in A Ogus and C E Veljanovski, *Readings in the Economics of Law and Regulation,* Oxford, Clarendon Press (1984), pp. 43–6.

Because economics is an incomplete and imperfect science, it is easy to poke fun at, just as it is easy to poke fun at medicine for the same reason. But it is as foolish to write off economics as it would be to write off medicine.

    A closely related criticism of the economic approach to law is that since economics has its limitations — for example, there is no widely accepted economic theory of the optimum distribution of income and wealth — the lawyer can ignore or even reject the approach until these limitations are overcome. This is tantamount, however, to the absurd proposition that unless a method of analysis is at once universal and unquestioned it is unimportant. A variant of this criticism is made by some legal philosophers who argue that since the philosophical basis of economics is utilitarianism, which they consider discredited, economics has no foundation and must collapse, carrying the economic approach to law with it. Admittedly, economics does not provide a basis for unconditional normative statements of the form, 'because the most efficient method of controlling crime would be to cut off the ears and nose of a convicted felon and brand him on the forehead, society should adopt these penalties'. What the economist might be able to say, by way of normative analysis, is that a policy such as mutilation of felons increases efficiency and should therefore be adopted, unless its adoption would impair some more important social value. The economist's ability to make conditional suggestions of this sort is not endangered by the debate over the merits of utilitarianism, unless the challenge to utilitarianism is a challenge to ascribing *any* value to promoting economic efficiency. Even more clearly, the economist's ability to enlarge our understanding of how the legal system actually operates is not undermined by the attacks on utilitarianism. If the participants in the legal process act as rational maximisers of their satisfactions, or if the legal process itself has been shaped by a concern with maximising economic efficiency, the economist has a rich field of study whether or not a society in which people behave in such a way or institutions are shaped by such concerns can be described as 'good'.

Another common criticism of the economic approach to law is that the attempt to explain the behaviour of legal institutions, and of the people operating or affected by them, on economic grounds must fail because, surely, much more than rational maximising is involved in such behaviour. The motivations of the violent criminal cannot be reduced to income maximisation nor the goals of the criminal justice system to minimising the costs of crime and its control. This criticism reflects a fundamental misunderstanding of the nature of scientific inquiry. A scientific theory necessarily abstracts from the welter of experience that it is trying to explain, and is therefore necessarily 'unrealistic' when compared directly to actual conditions. Newton's law of falling bodies is 'unrealistic' in assuming that bodies fall in a vacuum, but it is still a useful theory because it correctly predicts the behaviour of a wide variety of falling bodies in the real world. Similarly, an economic theory of law is certain not to capture the full complexity, richness, and confusion of the phenomena — criminal activity or whatever — that it seeks to illuminate. That lack of realism does not invalidate the theory; it is, indeed, the essential precondition of a theory . . .

Still another common criticism of the 'new' law and economics is that it manifests a strongly conservative political bias. Its practitioners have found, for example, that capital punishment has a deterrent effect and that legislation designed to protect the consumer frequently ends up hurting him. Findings such as these provide ammunition to the supporters of capital punishment and the opponents of consumerist legislation. The oddest thing about this criticism is that economic research that provides support for liberal positions is rarely acknowledged, at least by liberals, as manifesting political bias. The theory of public goods, for example, could be viewed as one of the ideological underpinnings of the welfare state, but it is not so viewed . . .

Another criticism levelled against the economic approach is that it ignores 'justice', which in these critics' view is and should be the central concern of the legal system and of the people who study it. In evaluating this criticism, it is necessary to distinguish different senses in which the word justice is used in reference to the legal system. It is sometimes used to mean 'distributive justice', which can be defined very crudely as the 'proper' degree of economic inequality. Although economists cannot tell you what that degree is, they have much to say that is extremely relevant to the debate over inequality — about the actual amounts of inequality in different societies and in different periods, the difference between real economic inequality and inequalities in pecuniary income that merely compensate for cost differences or reflect different positions in the life cycle, and the costs of achieving greater real or nominal equality . . .

A second meaning of 'justice', and the most common I would argue, is simply 'efficiency'. When we describe as 'unjust' convicting a person without a trial, taking property without just compensation, or failing to require a negligent automobile driver to answer in damages to the victim of his carelessness, we can be interpreted as meaning simply that the conduct or practice in question wastes resources. It is no surprise that in a world of scarce resources, waste is regarded as immoral. There may be, however, more to notions of justice than a concern with efficiency, for many types of conduct widely condemned as unjust may well be efficient . . . I doubt, however, that . . . [our] views are completely impervious to what an economic study might show. For example, would the objection to medical experimentation on convicts remain unshaken if it were shown persuasively that the social benefits of such experiments greatly exceeded the costs? Would the objections to capital punishment survive a convincing demonstration that capital punishment had a significantly greater deterrent effect than life imprisonment? All of these are studiable issues, and since no rational society can ignore the costs of its public policies, they are issues to which economics has great relevance. The demand for justice is not independent of its price.

Questions:
1.   Do you think that Posner has succeeded in rebutting the criticisms of the economic approach to law which he outlines? To what extent is efficiency synonomous with justice?

2.   Can you think of any other criticism of this approach?

2 MORALITY

The issue of the relationship between law and morality has been one of the main concerns of jurisprudential debate; and one of the most vexed questions for legislators, judges and lawyers is the role law should play in dealing with moral issues. That law must engage with such issues is already apparent from our consideration of cases involving disabled neonates and sado-masochism. Of particular interest is how far law, and particularly the criminal law, should be allowed to interfere with individual liberty. For instance, should law circumscribe the liberty of men to consume pornography, of women to have abortions, of consenting adults to commit incest, of scientists to experiment on embryos? From the point of view of developing legal skills the crucial ability is to be able to argue in an informed manner, avoiding 'bad' arguments. Obviously everyone will have differing viewpoints on such issues but the lawyers' contribution, whatever perspective he or she adopts, should be rational and informed.

S Lee, 'Crucial Battle for the Moral High Ground', *The Independent,* 13
October 1989.

After a 5-year delay, the Government is finally bringing forward for
legislation the 1984 Warnock Report's agenda on human embryo experimentation (subsequently implemented in the Human Fertilization and Embryology Act 1990). The coming parliamentary session will provide a momentous
opportunity for public debate on a matter of deep moral significance.

The debate will centre on alternative clauses: one outlawing all experiments on embryos from the moment of conception, the other (the Warnock
majority's view) allowing them for the first 14 days.

The Bill will be a special one in that the political parties are allowing their
members in both Houses a free vote because the issue is deemed to be one
of conscience.

But the likelihood is that bad arguments will dominate the discussions. On
all known form, campaigners, opinion-formers, and politicians themselves
will engage in polarising rhetoric rather than genuine debate, particularly
since amendments by pro-life campaigners will seek to yoke the issue of
abortion to the question of embryo experimentation.

What a beneficial change it would be if instead it was acknowledged that
these issues present tragic choices between compelling arguments which are
held on both sides in good faith.

There are five bad lines of approach which should be banished from the
debate — and from all discussions of law and morals. The first line of attack
is often name-calling: 'You would say that, wouldn't you, because you're a
Catholic/a man/fertile/infertile/a doctor/a research scientist'.

A second bad approach is seeking to win the debate by definitions. On the
one hand, there are scientists who are only too willing to call a spade a
pre-spade. The term 'pre-embryo', for example, is now used by some
researchers. It attracts support for the Warnock majority proposal by implying
that the pre-14 day embryo has an inferior moral worth to the post-14 day
embryo. These embryologists, who do not call themselves pre-embryologists,
never used that before the Warnock committee drew that line.

All language is morally loaded (one campaigner's unborn child is another's
clump of cells) but those who would trick the public by the term 'pre-embryo'
should be prepared to concentrate on the moral status of the early embryo,
not on dreaming up a new vocabulary.

On the other side, we hear the accusation that scientists are 'playing God'.
But what exactly does this mean? This is a linguistic smoke-screen which
obscures an absence of reasoning. Surely it is not the scientists who are guilty
of hubris here but their accusers, in implying that humans *could* play God.

A third approach is to pray in aid the so-called slippery slope. Pro-lifers
will claim that if we allow experiments up to 14 days, then next year it will
be a month, then three months. Meanwhile, pro-choicers argue that if we
restrict abortion to 18 weeks, then next year it will be 15 then 12. The reality
is that it is extraordinarily difficult to get any change in these kinds of laws
— as the last 30 years of procedural mugging by both sides shows in relation

to abortion, and the five year gestation period of this Bill shows with regard to experimenting.

Too often we are faced with clambering *up* the slippery slopes to the law more than sliding down them. We have to accept that the reality is that we are always already on the slope, holding a position.

A fourth bad approach is to claim that the law cannot stop research or whatever is under discussion, so why try? This is usually expressed in terms of pushing an activity underground (e.g. pornography) or into the backstreets (e.g. abortion) or abroad (e.g. experiments on embryos). But the law does not stop all murder, yet most of us are grateful that it tries.

A fifth mistaken approach is the facile assertion that opponents are being inconsistent. There are two lines of rebuttal. One is to say that there are subtle differences which explain alleged inconsistencies, as for example between banning experiments altogether or after 14 days yet allowing later abortions. Some people believe that the different intentions of the experimenter and the abortionist, or the different location of the embryo in a petri dish or in a woman's womb, are morally relevant factors. It behoves the sceptics among us to listen and argue rather than to whoop with delight at the superficial difficulties.

The other plausible strategy is to admit an inconsistency but to accept that the law should not necessarily be consistent across the range of tragic choices. Indeed, the only way in which a society can come to terms with its conflicting values is to prefer one value in some circumstances and another in different conditions. It is difficult enough for an individual to be consistent, let alone a society. Are all pro-lifers anti-capital punishment, anti-nuclear weapons and anti-cars?

Supposing that we did turn away from the cheap arguments, where could we find a better way? Sadly, the Warnock majority is confused as to its basic philosophical arguments, condemning utilitarianism in its foreword but relying on it in justifying its crucial recommendation to allow experiments up to 14 days, only to reject it again in opposing the routine testing of drugs on human embryos at any stage from conception.

The Government has wisely allowed legislators to choose between this approach and one of the Warnock minority alternatives. But how should we decide between them?

Help is at hand in the more constructive approach of the Glover Report on Fertility and the Family, compiled for the European Commission and now published by Fourth Estate. Chaired by the distinguished philosopher Jonathan Glover, a small committee of experts recognised that the issue is a classic test of our deepest moral views. What matters is not just *what* Parliament decides but how it decides. In what is heralded as a vote of conscience, any conscience ought to be deeply troubled by the agonising choice between respecting human embryos from their earliest moments and responding to the plight of infertile couples.

The issue represents the ultimate test — and perhaps the convergence — of two opposing moral theories. Recognition of that and an agreement to forgo the linguistic tricks and the cheap jibes would help convince all sides that their arguments have been listened to with respect. It would also help convince them that politicians have decided not on the basis of the best orchestrated campaign but by seeking to occupy the high moral ground, wherever it might be found.

Questions:
1. We have considered in other Chapters the possibility that that women and men do in fact reason in different ways. In the light of this, is it not valid to claim 'you would say that, wouldn't you, because you're a man'?

2. Are 'slippery slope' arguments *always* invalid? What part did such arguments play in *R* v *Brown* (Chapter 7)?

3. Regardless of your moral beliefs regarding abortion, is it not a valid point that it should be legalised to avoid the horrors of backstreet abortions?

4. Compare UK law on embryo research (the Human Fertilisation and Embryology Act 1990) with the provisions on the status of the embryo contained in the Council of Europe's Convention of Human Rights and Biomedicine (see Chapter 10 at p. 388).

Even if you agree that some of these standard arguments are 'bad', or at least less than convincing, you need to develop good arguments. Once again it is worthwhile considering various perspectives on the problem and how the classical legal theorists have argued. The classic debate in the field of law and morals has been waged between Lord Devlin and Professor H L A Hart:

P Devlin, *The Enforcement of Morals,* Oxford, Oxford University Press (1965), pp. 7–18.

I think it is clear that the criminal law as we know it is based upon moral principle. In a number of crimes its function is simply to enforce a moral principle and nothing else. The law, both criminal and civil, claims to be able to speak about morality and immorality generally. Where does it get its authority to do this and how does it settle the moral principles which it enforces? Undoubtedly, as a matter of history, it derived both from Christian teaching. But I think that the strict logician is right when he says that the law can no longer rely on doctrines in which citizens are entitled to disbelieve. It is necessary therefore to look for some other source . . .

This view — that there is such a thing as public morality — can be justified by *a priori* argument. What makes a society of any sort is a community of ideas; not only political ideas but also ideas about the way its members should behave and govern their lives: these latter ideas are its morals. Every society has a moral structure as well as a political one: or rather, since that might suggest two independent systems, I should say that the structure of every society is made up both of politics and morals . . .

[I]f society has the right to make a judgment and has it on the basis that a recognised morality is as necessary to society as, say, a recognised government, then society may use the law to preserve morality in the same way as it uses it to safeguard anything else that is essential to its existence. If therefore the first proposition is securely established with all its implications, society has a prima facie right to legislate against immorality as such.

I think, therefore, that it is not possible to set theoretical limits to the power of the State to legislate against immorality. It is not possible to settle in advance exceptions to the *general* rule or define inflexibly areas of morality into which the law is in no circumstances to be allowed to enter. Society is entitled by means of its law to protect itself from dangers, whether from within or without. The suppression of vice is as much the law's business as the suppression of subversive activities; it is no more possible to define a sphere of private morality than it is to define one of private subversive activity. There are no theoretical limits to the power of the State to legislate against treason and sedition, and likewise I think there can be no theoretical limits to legislation against immorality. You may argue that if a man's sins affect only himself it cannot be the concern of society. If he chooses to get drunk every night in the privacy of his own home, is any one except himself the worse for it? But suppose a quarter of or a half of the population got drunk every night, what sort of society would it be? You cannot set a theoretical limit to the number of people who can get drunk before society is entitled to legislate against drunkenness. The same may be said of gambling . . .

How are the moral judgments of society to be ascertained? . . . It is surely not enough that they should be reached by the opinion of the majority; it would be too much to require the individual assent of every citizen. English law has evolved and regularly uses a standard which does not depend on the counting of heads. It is that of *the reasonable man* . . . For my purpose I should like to call him the man in the jury box, for the moral judgment of society must be something about which any twelve men or women drawn at random might after discussion be expected to be unanimous . . .

It is not nearly enough to say that a majority dislikes a practice; there must be a real feeling of reprobation . . . No society can do without intolerance, indignation, and disgust, they are the forces behind the moral law, and indeed it can be argued that if they or something like them are not present, the feelings of society cannot be weighty enough to deprive the individual of freedom of choice . . . [B]efore a society can put a practice beyond the limits of tolerance there must be a deliberate judgment that the practice is injurious to society. In matters of morals the limits of tolerance shift. Laws, especially those which are based on morals, are less easily moved. It follows as another good working principle that in any new matter of morals the law should be slow to act . . .

A further elastic principle must be advanced more tentatively. It is that as far as possible privacy should be respected. This is not an idea that has ever been made explicit in the criminal law. Acts or words done or said in public or in private are all brought within its scope without distinction in principle. But there goes with this a strong reluctance on the part of judges and legislators to sanction invasions of privacy in the detection of crime.

The last and the biggest thing to be remembered is that the law is concerned with the minimum and not with the maximum; there is much in the Sermon on the Mount that would be out of place in the Ten

Commandments. We all recognise the gap between the moral law and the law of the land.

H L A Hart, *Law, Liberty and Morality,* Oxford, Oxford University Press (1963), pp. 4–5, 31–32, 44–48.

Is the fact that certain conduct is by common standards immoral sufficient to justify making that conduct punishable by law? Is it morally permissible to enforce morality as such? Ought immorality as such to be a crime?

To this question John Stuart Mill gave an emphatic negative answer in his essay *On Liberty* . . . He said, 'the only purpose for which power can rightfully be exercised over any member of a civilised community against his will is to prevent harm to others.' And to identify the many different things which he intended to exclude, he added, 'His own good either physical or moral is not a sufficient warrant. He cannot rightfully be compelled to do or forbear because it will be better for him to do so, because it will make him happier, because in the opinions of others, to do so would be wise or even right . . . '

This doctrine, Mill tells us, is to apply to human beings only 'in the maturity of their faculties': it is not to apply to children or to backward societies. . . . I wish to enter a *caveat;* I do not propose to defend all that Mill said; for I myself think there may be grounds justifying the legal coercion of the individual other than the prevention of harm to others. But on the narrower issue relevant to the enforcement of morality Mill seems to me to be right . . .

Paternalism — the protection of people against themselves — is a perfectly coherent policy. The supply of drugs or narcotics, even to adults, except under medical prescription is punishable by the criminal law . . . If, as seems obvious, paternalism is a possible explanation of such laws, it is also possible in the case of the rule excluding the consent of the victim as a defence to a charge of assault. In neither case are we forced to conclude with Lord Devlin that the law's 'function' is 'to enforce a moral principle and nothing else.'. . .

In sexual matters a line generally divides the punishment of immorality from the punishment of indecency . . .

The distinction is both clear and important. Sexual intercourse between husband and wife is not immoral, but if it takes place in public it is an affront to public decency. Homosexual intercourse between consenting adults in private is immoral according to conventional morality, but not an affront to public decency, though it would be both if it took place in public. But the fact that the same act, if done in public, could be regarded both as immoral and as an affront to public decency must not blind us to the difference between two aspects of conduct and to the different principles on which the justification of their punishment must rest. The recent English law relating to prostitution attends to this difference . . .

It may no doubt be objected that too much has been made in this discussion of the distinction between what is done in public and what is done in private. For offence to feelings, it may be said, is given not only when immoral

activities or their commercial preliminaries are thrust upon unwilling eyewit-
nesses, but also when those who strongly condemn certain sexual practices
as immoral learn that others indulge in them in private. But a right to be
protected from the distress which is inseparable from the bare knowledge that
others are acting in ways you think wrong, cannot be acknowledged by
anyone who recognises individual liberty as a value. For the extension of the
utilitarian principle that coercion may be used to protect men from harm, so
as to include their protection from this form of distress, cannot stop there. If
distress incident to the belief that others are doing wrong is harm, so also is
the distress incident to the belief that others are doing what you do not want
them to do. To punish people for causing this form of distress would be
tantamount to punishing them simply because others object to what they do;
and the only liberty that could coexist with this extension of the utilitarian
principle is liberty to do those things to which no one seriously objects. Such
liberty plainly is quite nugatory. Recognition of individual liberty as a value
involves as a minimum, acceptance of the principle that the individual may
do what he wants, even if others are distressed when they learn what it is that
he does — unless, of course, there are other good grounds for forbidding it.
No social order which accords to individual liberty any value could also
accord the right to be protected from distress thus occasioned.

Protection from shock or offence to feelings caused by some public display
is, as most legal systems recognise, another matter. The distinction may
sometimes be a fine one. Nonetheless the use of punishment to protect those
made vulnerable to the public display by their own beliefs leaves the offender
at liberty to do the same thing in private, if he can. It is not tantamount to
punishing men simply because others object to what they do.

S Lee, *Law and Morals,* Oxford, Oxford University Press (1986), pp. 22–3.

Mill's harm-to-others principle seems simple, but it gives rise to many
problems. Firstly, what is harm? Secondly, who counts as others? Thirdly,
given that Mill says that the prevention of harm to others *can* be the reason
for restrictions, he presumably thinks that there is still a question as to
whether we *should* restrain conduct even if it causes harm to others. The only
reason for which power *can* be exercised over citizens against their will is to
prevent harm to others, but Mill does not say power *must* be used to prevent
harm to others. Harm to others is a necessary but not a sufficient condition.
We may have to calculate the harm caused by intervention and weigh it
against the harm caused by the initial action. A fourth issue is, why should
we accept the harm-to-others principle as the exclusive justification for
intervention? Why not allow society to be paternalistic, preventing people
from harming themselves?

Mill clearly intended harm to include physical harm, but what about
mental, moral, emotional and spiritual harm? The criminal law's control over
pornography, for instance, would depend partly on whether one counts any
moral harm as sufficient reason for intervention. Or, to take another example,
adultery does not physically harm participants, but surely it does cause

emotional harm to others. But once Mill's principle is enlarged to include non-physical harm it can be extended to the point at which it allows intervention in practically all circumstances.

Business life, for instance, is all about competing and therefore, in a sense, 'harming' competitors by succeeding. . . . Who counts as 'others' is obviously at the centre of disputes over abortion and experimenting on embryos. There is no doubt that abortion causes physical harm to the foetus. There is no doubt that experiments harm the embryo. But the debate over these issues concerns the question whether the embryo or foetus is a person or potential person who deserves society's protection. Just as the harm-to-others principle does not help us define harm, so it does not help us to define others since we can see that many important legislative tussles hinge precisely on what is harm and who are others. Bandying Mill's phrase around is far from conclusive.

Even if we establish harm-to-others, much work remains to be done. Many debates over law and morality are not about whether or not harm-to-others is caused, but revolve around whether the harm is sufficiently serious for the State to intervene and whether the State's intervention will cause more problems than it solves.

Our final problem is that paternalism (preventing someone from 'harming' himself) is excluded by the harm-to-others principle. But why shouldn't society be concerned to protect individuals from their own folly? Whether it concerns alcohol — or drug-addiction or under age sexual activity, parents and friends *are* paternalistic in practice.

Questions:

1. Which of the theories on the relationship of law and morals do you prefer? Is Hart's theory or Devlin's most in vogue today?

2. How is the prevailing morality of a society to be ascertained?

3. Are there spheres of activity within which it would be wrong for the law to interfere?

4. Legislation frequently seems to represent a political compromise on complex social, moral and economic issues. The Human Fertilisation and Embryology Act 1990 is a classic example of this. Is law therefore more flexible than moral judgments are?

5. Can the law change a society's moral attitudes? If not, what is the importance of law?

6. Why do you think that the law and morals debate has mainly revolved around the role of the criminal law and control of sexual behaviour? Is it important to move beyond such issues? (See S Lee, *Law and Morals, op. cit.,* pp. 1–8, 31–35.)

7. Was the case of *R* v *Brown* (see Chapter 7) an example of paternalistic judicial decision-making? If so, do you regard paternalism as justifiable in that case?

8. How is the civil law based on morality? Can you think of examples?

The classical liberal way of viewing the world has been to see it as divided into separate public and private spheres, but this notion has been attacked not only by conservative moralists such as Lord Devlin, but also by feminist theorists. Essentially they criticise the public/private dichotomy on two grounds arguing:

(a) that the division of society into a public sphere (corresponding variously to the workplace, market, civil society), and a private/domestic sphere (the home/family) which is largely unregulated by law, may have adverse consequences for women who tend to be assigned to the private sphere; and

(b) that in any event the distinction is malleable and much depends upon how we define state regulation.

K O'Donovan, *Family Law Matters*, London, Pluto (1993), pp. 22–23.

[T]he distinction between the public and private . . . refer[s] to two distinct social realms constituted within liberal social philosophy, divided from one another by legal regulation. The public realm is presented as that of state, market and politics, and is the world of men; the private realm, associated primarily with women, is the world of the family. The values prevalent in the former are those of individualism; in the latter self-sacrifice and altruism are idealised. This picture of a dichotomised world contains a scene in which subordinated family members lack legal power. Law's respect for the privacy of the family leaves women and children unequal to men. Male power is not only divorced from structures external to the family, from the public world, but it is reinforced by ideologies of family privacy, and exercised within the family.

M Thornton, 'The Public/Private Dichotomy: Gendered and Discriminatory', *International Journal of the Sociology of Law* (1991), vol. 18, pp. 448–463 at pp. 448, 449.

'[T]he malleability of the public/private dichotomy within liberal discourse is deployed by the state in order to mediate polarized interests. Even though anti-discrimination legislation does challenge the assignation of women to the private and men to the public spheres, the centrality of the dichotomy ensures that any changes which occur in the relations between men and women do not threaten the immunity accorded domestic life, the primary site of inequality for women . . . Classical liberal theory accepts the division between public and private as the reason for the existence of state regulation. Thus, that sphere designated as public constitutes the appropriate terrain of regulation, whereas that designated as private is treated as beyond the purview of the state. While the family has been conceptualized as private and the affairs of government as public, the sphere of the market and economic activity has become increasingly difficult to categorize, particularly as the state has become more interventionist . . . Even the family, viewed as quintessentially private within classical liberal theory is not necessarily so in practice. Matrimonial matters, child welfare and incest are well-established subjects of state intervention, although the state continues to be ambivalent about the criminalization of "domestic" violence. However, we should not ignore the fact that the state shapes the territoriality of public and private. The legislative and administrative activity involved in constituting the private sphere in the character of the family is clearly *public* action. For example, by continuing to permit taxation rebates for "dependent spouses" the state seeks to entrench the norm of women's economic dependency on men. The endorsement by the state of the idea of the husband as the head of the household, even if only in an indirect sense, conduces to the blurred line of demarcation between public and private in addition to signalling a potential conflict with the application of the non-discrimination principle . . . The political malleability of the public/private line of demarcation ensures that domestic labour remains cordoned off because the repercussions of regulation would be devastatingly destabilizing. Just imagine a regime of formal equality, let alone a substantively equal regime, operating within the home, given that women are presently expected to care not just for children, the aged and the sick but also for adult men — husbands, lovers, fathers and grown-up sons — that is, those who are perfectly capable of caring for themselves! Like justice, the equality prescript of anti-discrimination legislation operates only within the public sphere of the liberal paradigm.

Questions:
1. Was *R v Brown* (see Chapter 7) an example of law intervening in the private sphere? Is this always a bad thing? Consider in this regard the case of *R* v *R* (also extracted in Chapter 7.)

2. Taking housework, abortion, prostitution, pornography, and 'domestic' violence as examples, how does confining these issues to the private sphere contributes to the oppression of women?

3   JUSTICE

One of the most frequent reactions of law students to particular laws or legal practices is to complain that they are unjust or unfair; and the language of justice certainly seems inextricably linked with that of law. It is therefore important for lawyers to have some understanding of what the concept of justice means before engaging in such arguments. Tom Campbell (*Justice*, London, Macmillan (1988) p. 1) has claimed that: 'There is some basis for the belief that it is the sense of injustice or grievance that is at the core of our ideas about justice and explains its powerful emotive force'. Certainly it is often easier to recognise instinctively what is unjust than it is to define what is just.

Perhaps the only factor that everyone can agree on is the value of *procedural or formal* justice i.e. of treating like cases alike. Yet this in itself poses problems — what exactly is a like case?

A Hutchinson, *Dwelling on the Threshold,* Toronto, Carswell (1988), p. 23.

A year or so ago, a swimming meet took place at the University of Toronto. Most of the races proceeded as planned. But, at the end of one race, there was a challenge to the winner of the race. The appropriate group of officials convened. The deliberations were lengthy and tense. After much argument and poring over the rules, a decision was announced: the winner had been disqualified and the second swimmer was acclaimed the victor. The Referee took the unusual course of offering a brief justification of the committee's decision, 'the rules were clear (The winner is the first swimmer to touch the side of the pool with both hands) and, if this regrettable outcome is to be avoided in the future, it will be necessary to change the rules'. The winning swimmer had only one arm.

Question:
1. If you had to adjudicate on the outcome of this race how would you decide in order to do justice to all competitors?

The notion of procedural justice is at the core of one of the justifications of the system of precedent. Yet, the system of precedent which claims to place a high value on fairness can itself produce injustice. What if the earlier case was wrongly decided? To follow a bad precedent in a later case would itself be substantively unjust, as Radcliffe-Richards demonstrates.

J Radcliffe-Richards, *The Sceptical Feminist,* London, Routledge & Kegan Paul (1980), pp. 91–2.

Suppose that there is in a society a system of laws which are substantially unjust. Where this happens, and these unfair laws are consistently and impartially applied (that is, where there is formal justice) it must follow that people are going to be treated unjustly. It must, therefore, also follow that where the laws are unjust it must be *substantially* just to disregard them in certain ways, and so perpetrate formal injustice. For instance at the time when children were always legally the property of the husband, a judge who gave custody to a responsible and ill-treated wife would have been treating the husband with formal injustice (he would have been breaking the law to benefit the wife), but we would certainly say that he had acted with substantial justice. The fact is that formal injustice sometimes is and sometimes is not unjust.

Questions:
1. Do you think that the society in which you live is substantially unjust?

2. Can law do anything to change this?

3. Is inequality necessarily a bad thing?

4. What types of inequality should the law seek to remedy?

T Nagel, *What Does It All Mean?*, Oxford, Oxford University Press (1987),
pp. 76–80.

The world is full of inequalities — within countries, and from one country to
another. Some children are born into comfortable, prosperous homes, and
grow up well fed and well educated. Others are born poor, don't get enough
to eat, and never have access to much education or medical care. Clearly, this
is a matter of luck: we are not responsible for the social or economic class
or country into which we are born. The question is, how bad are inequalities
which are not the fault of the people who suffer from them? Should
governments use their power to try to reduce inequalities of this kind, for
which the victims are not responsible?

Some inequalities are deliberately imposed. Racial discrimination, for
example, deliberately excludes people of one race from jobs, housing and
education which are available to people of another race. Or women may be
kept out of jobs or denied privileges available only to men. This is not merely
a matter of bad luck. Racial and sexual discrimination are clearly unfair: they
are forms of inequality caused by factors that should be open to those who
are qualified, and it is clearly a good thing when governments try to enforce
such equality of opportunity.

But it is harder to know what to say about inequalities that arise in the
ordinary course of events, without deliberate racial or sexual discrimination.
Because even if there is equality of opportunity, and any qualified person can go
to a university or get a job or buy a house or run for office — regardless of race,
religion, sex or national origin — there will still be plenty of inequalities left.
People from wealthier backgrounds will usually have better training and more
resources, and they will then be better able to compete for good jobs. Even in a
system of equality of opportunity, some people will have a head start and will
end up with greater benefits than others whose native talents are the same.

Not only that, but differences in native talent will produce big differences
in the resulting benefits, in a competitive system. Those who have abilities
that are in high demand will be able to earn much more than those without
any special skills or talents. These differences too are partly a matter of luck.
Though people have to develop and use their abilities, no amount of effort
would enable most people to act like Meryl Streep, paint like Picasso, or
manufacture automobiles like Henry Ford. Something similar is true of lesser
accomplishments. The luck of both natural talent and family and class
background are important factors in determining one's income and position
in a competitive society. Equal opportunity produces unequal results.

These inequalities, unlike the results of racial and sexual discrimination are
produced by choices and actions that don't seem wrong in themselves. People
try to provide for their children and give them a good education, and some have
more money to use for this purpose than others. People pay for the products,
services and performances they want, and some performers or manufacturers
get richer than others because what they have to offer is wanted by more
people. Businesses and organisations of all kinds try to hire employees who
will do the job well, and pay higher salaries for those with unusual skills . . .

We have to think about both the inequality itself, and the remedy that would be needed to reduce or get rid of it. The main question about the inequalities themselves is: What kinds of *causes* of inequality are wrong? The main question about remedies is: What *methods* of interfering with the inequality are right?

Obviously if we start from a position of injustice it is difficult to change the situation simply through the use of law. Some theorists have therefore proposed that we must in effect step out of our present unjust world, wipe the slate clean, and begin again to construct principles of justice to govern our society, commencing from a starting point which is itself just. The most famous of such strategies is that devised by John Rawls, who suggests a fair procedure for choosing principles of justice, whereby we imagine ourselves to be drawing up these principles in what he calls an '*original position*', in which we are stripped of all knowledge of ourselves and of what our eventual position in society will be.

J Rawls, *A Theory of Justice,* Oxford, Oxford University Press (1971), pp. 136–37.

The idea of the original position is to set up a fair procedure so that any principles agreed to will be just. The aim is to use the notion of pure procedural justice as a basis of theory. Somehow we must nullify the effects of specific contingencies which put men at odds and tempt them to exploit social and natural circumstances to their own advantage. Now in order to do this I assume that the parties are situated behind a veil of ignorance. They do not know how the various alternatives will affect their own particular case and they are obliged to evaluate principles solely on the basis of general considerations.

It is assumed, then, that the parties do not know certain kinds of particular facts. First of all, no one knows his place in society, his class position or social status; nor does he know his fortune in the distribution of natural assets and abilities, his intelligence and strength and the like. Nor, again does anyone know his conception of the good, the particulars of his rational plan of life or even the special features of his psychology such as his aversion to risk or liability to optimism or pessimism. More than this, I assume that the parties do not know the particular circumstances of their own society. That is, they do not know its economic or political situation, or the level of civilisation and culture it has been able to achieve. The persons in the original position have no information as to which generation they belong . . . They must choose principles the consequences of which they are prepared to live with whatever generation they turn out to belong to.

As far as possible, then the only particular facts which the parties know is that their society is subject to the circumstances of justice and whatever this implies. It is taken for granted, however, that they know the general facts about human society. They understand political affairs and the principles of economic theory; they know the basis of social organisation and the laws of human psychology. Indeed, the parties are presumed to know whatever general facts affect the choice of the principles of justice.

Questions:
1.   Imagine that you are a person in Rawls's original position. What principles of justice would *you* devise to govern society? For example, would you want a society in which everyone was treated equally? Would you want a society in which everyone had as much liberty as possible? Would you want a society in which individuals were allowed to acquire privately-owned property?

2.   Now imagine that you are a disabled black woman in the original position. Would you still be happy to live in a society governed by the principles of justice that you chose? Do you think that knowledge of such factors as colour and gender affect the principles that you would choose in the original position? Are the principles you would choose universal principles?

3.   Imagine that you are a non-human animal in the original position. Would you choose different principles of justice from a human being? Would you want to live in a society that would allow meat-eating/the wearing of fur or leather/animal-testing/xenotransplantation/hunting? Is it important that we treat animals justly? (See Chapter 10 at pp. 390–400.)

4.   Rawls has suggested that 'a just society would be the one you would design if you know that your enemy was to assign you your place in it'. Do you think everyone would necessarily adopt such a pessimistic outlook? (Note that Rawls said that a person in the original position does not know 'the special features of his psychology such as his . . . liability to optimism or pessimism'. But are not all persons in the original position unduly pessimistic?)

5.   Is Rawls's enterprise a plausible or worthwhile one? Can we successfully strip ourselves of our prejudices and biases and imagine ourselves in an original situation wherein we could devise objectively fair principles of justice?

In his later work, Rawls attempts to deal with criticisms of his 'original position' by arguing that it has been misunderstood, and wrongly taken to be more than simply a representational device:

J Rawls, *Political Liberalism*, New York, Columbia University Press (1993), pp. 26–28.

As a device of representation the idea of the original position serves as a means of public reflection and self-clarification. It helps us work out what we now think, once we are able to take a clear and uncluttered view of what justice requires when society is conceived as a scheme of cooperation between free and equal citizens from one generation to the next. The original position serves as a mediating idea by which all our considered convictions, whatever their level of generality — whether they concern fair conditions for situating the parties or reasonable constraints on reasons, or first principles and precepts, or judgments about particular institutions and actions — can be brought to bear on one another. This enables us to establish greater coherence among all our judgments; and with this deeper self-understanding we can attain wider agreement among one another.

We introduce an idea like that of the original position because there seems no better way to elaborate a political conception of justice for the basic structure from the fundamental idea of society as an ongoing and fair system of cooperation between citizens regarded as free and equal. This seems particularly evident once we think of society as extending over generations and as inheriting its public culture and existing political and social institutions (along with its real capital and stock of natural resources) from those who have gone before. There are, however, certain dangers in using this idea. As a device of representation its abstractness invites misunderstanding. In particular, the description of the parties may seem to presuppose a particular metaphysical conception of the person; for example, that the essential nature of persons is independent of and prior to their contingent attributes, including their final ends and attachments, and indeed their conception of the good and character as a whole.

I believe this to be an illusion caused by not seeing the original position as a device of representation. The veil of ignorance, to mention one prominent feature of that position, has no specific metaphysical implications concerning the nature of the self; it does not imply that the self is ontologically prior to the facts about persons that the parties are excluded from knowing. We can, as it were, enter this position at any time simply by reasoning for principles of justice in accordance with the enumerated restrictions on information. When, in this way, we simulate being in the original position, our reasoning no more commits us to a particular metaphysical doctrine about the nature of the self than our acting a part in a play, say of Macbeth or Lady Macbeth, commits us to thinking that we are really a king or a queen engaged in a desperate struggle for political power. Much the same holds for role playing generally. We must keep in mind that we are trying to show how the idea of society as a fair system of social cooperation can be unfolded so as to find principles specifying the basic rights and liberties and the forms of equality most appropriate to those cooperating, once they are regarded as citizens, as free and equal persons.

Having surveyed the idea of the original position, I add the following to avoid misunderstanding. It is important to distinguish three points of view: that of the parties in the original position, that of citizens in a well-ordered society, and finally, that of ourselves — of you and me who are elaborating justice as fairness and examining it as a political conception of justice.

The first two points of view belong to the conception of justice as fairness and are specified by reference to its fundamental ideas. But whereas the conceptions of a well-ordered society and of citizens as free and equal might conceivably be realized in our social world, the parties as rational representatives who specify the fair terms of social cooperation by agreeing to principles of justice are simply parts of the original position. This position is set up by you and me in working out justice as fairness, and so the nature of the parties is up to us: they are merely the artificial creatures inhabiting our device of representation. Justice as fairness is badly misunderstood if the deliberations of the parties, and the motives we attribute to them, are mistaken for an account of the moral psychology, either of actual persons or of citizens in a well-ordered society. Rational autonomy must not be confused with full autonomy. The latter is a political ideal and part of the more complete ideal of a well-ordered society. Rational autonomy is not, as such, an ideal at all, but a way to model the idea of the rational (versus the reasonable) in the original position.

The third point of view — that of you and me — is that from which justice as fairness, and indeed any other political conception, is to be assessed. Here the test is that of reflective equilibrium: how well the view as a whole articulates our more firm considered convictions of political justice, at all levels of generality, after due examination, once all adjustments and revisions that seem compelling have been made. A conception of justice that meets this criterion is the conception that, so far as we can now ascertain, is the one most reasonable for us.

Question:
1.   Does this clarification avoid the problems with the original position?

The following are the principles of justice which Rawls suggests any rational person would agree upon:

J Rawls, *A Theory of Justice, op. cit.,* pp. 60–63.

I shall now state in a provisional form the two principles of justice that I believe would be chosen in the original position . . .

First: each person is to have an equal right to the most extensive basic liberty compatible with a similar liberty for others.
Second: social and economic inequalities are to be arranged so that they are both (a) reasonably expected to be to everyone's advantage, and (b) attached to positions and offices open to all . . .

By way of general comment, these principles primarily apply, as I have said, to the basic structure of society. They are to govern the assignment of rights and duties and to regulate the distribution of social and economic advantages. As their formulation suggests, these principles presuppose that the social structure can be divided into two more or less distinct parts, the first principle applying to the one, the second to the other. They distinguish between those aspects of the social system that define and secure the equal liberties of citizenship and those that specify and establish social and economic inequalities. The basic liberties of citizens are, roughly speaking, political liberty (the right to vote and to be eligible for public office) together with freedom of speech and assembly; liberty of conscience and freedom of thought; freedom of the person along with the right to hold (personal) property; and freedom from arbitrary arrest and seizure as defined by the concept of the rule of law. These liberties are all required to be equal by the first principle, since citizens of a just society are to have the same basic rights.

The second principle applies to the distribution of income and wealth and to the design of organisations that make use of differences in authority and responsibility, or chains of command. While the distribution of wealth and income need not be equal, it must be to everyone's advantage and at the same time positions of authority and offices of command must be accessible to all. One applies the second principle by holding positions open, and then, subject to this constraint, arranges social and economic inequalities so that everyone benefits.

These principles are to be arranged in a serial order with the first principle prior to the second. This ordering means that a departure from the institutions of equal liberty required by the first principle cannot be justified, or compensated for, by greater social and economic advantages. The distribution of wealth and income and the hierarchies of authority must be consistent with both the liberties of equal citizenship and equality of opportunity.

. . . [The] two principles are a special case of a more general conception of justice that can be expressed as follows:

> All social values — liberty and opportunity, income and wealth, and the bases of self-respect — are to be distributed equally unless an unequal distribution of any, or all, of these values is to everyone's advantage.

Injustice, then is simply inequalities that are not to the benefit of all . . .

As a first step, suppose that the basic structure of society distributes certain primary goods, that is things that every rational man is presumed to want. These goods normally have a use whatever a person's rational plan of life. For simplicity, assume that the chief primary goods at the disposition of society are rights and liberties, powers and opportunities, income and wealth. (Later on . . . the primary good of self-respect has a central place). These are the social primary goods. Other primary goods such as health and vigour, intelligence and imagination, are natural goods; although their possession is influenced by the basic structure, they are not so directly under its control. Imagine, then, a hypothetical initial arrangement in which all the social primary goods are equally distributed; everyone has similar rights and duties, and income and wealth are evenly shared. This state of affairs provides a benchmark for judging improvements. If certain inequalities of wealth and organisational powers would make everyone better off than in this hypothetical starting situation, then they accord with the general conception.

Now it is possible, at least theoretically, that by giving up some of their fundamental liberties men are sufficiently compensated by the resulting social and economic gains. The general conception of justice imposes no restrictions on what sort of inequalities are permissible; it only requires that everyone's position be improved. We need not suppose anything so drastic as consenting to a condition of slavery. Imagine instead that men forgo certain political rights when the economic returns are significant and their capacity to influence the course of policy by the exercise of these rights would be marginal in any case. It is this kind of exchange which the two principles rule out; being arranged in serial order they do not permit exchanges between basic liberties and economic and social gains. The serial ordering of principles expresses an underlying preference among primary social goods. When this preference is rational so likewise is the choice of these principles in this order.

Questions:
1.   Did Rawls's principles accord with those which you selected?

2.   Would you agree with Rawls that basic liberties, such as freedom of speech, are the most important primary social goals? Would people give up their liberty to speak freely in order for gains in material wealth? Does wealth enhance freedom of speech? For example, does a wealthy media magnate like Rupert Murdoch have more freedom to speak than you do?

3.   What do we mean by equality? Does justice necessarily entail equality? Why does Rawls reject the principle of equality?

4.   In striving for justice should we take into account only the interests of the *presently* existing members of a given society, or must we take into account future generations of human beings as well?

5.   What about non-human animals — are there significant moral questions to be raised about our use of animals? Or are all non-humans beyond the moral pale? (See Chapter 10 at pp. 390–400.)

Subsequently, Rawls has slightly modified his principles of justice.

J Rawls

Political Liberalism, op. cit., p. 56:

The two principles of justice . . . are as follows:

   a.   Each person has an equal claim to a fully adequate scheme of equal basic rights and liberties, which scheme is compatible with the same scheme for all; and in this scheme the equal political liberties, and only those liberties, are to be guaranteed their fair value.

   b.   Social and economic inequalities are to satisfy two conditions: first, they are to be attached to positions and offices open to all under conditions of fair equality of opportunity; and second, they are to be to the greatest benefit of the least advantaged members of society.

Questions:
1.   Does this modification of the principles involve significant change?

2.   Are justice and liberty compatible? How does Rawls deal with this issue?

3.   Robert Nozick has objected to Rawls's theory on the grounds that it allows the state to play too great a role and involves unwarranted interference with individual liberty. Does the maintenance of a state of equality or fairness necessarily involve a great deal of state regulation?

Nozick proposes instead what he calls an 'entitlement' theory of justice. He argues that the state should have no role to play in distributing resources.

R Nozick, *Anarchy State and Utopia,* Oxford, Basil Blackwell (1974), pp. 150–53.

There is no *central* distribution, no person or group entitled to control all the resources, jointly deciding how they are to be doled out. What each person gets, he gets from others who give to him in exchange for something, or as a gift. In a free society, diverse persons control different resources, and new holdings arise out of the voluntary exchanges and actions of persons. There is no more a distributing or distribution of shares than there is a distributing of mates in a society in which persons choose whom they should marry. The total result is the product of many individual decisions which the different individuals involved are entitled to make . . .

If the world were wholly just, the following inductive definition would exhaustively cover the subject of justice in holdings.

1. A person who acquires a holding in accordance with the principle of justice in acquisition is entitled to that holding.
2. A person who acquires a holding in accordance with the principle of justice in transfer, from someone else entitled to the holding, is entitled to the holding.
3. No one is entitled to a holding except by (repeated) applications of 1 and 2.

The complete principle of distributive justice would say simply that a distribution is just if everyone is entitled to the holdings they possess under the distribution . . . Not all actual situations are generated in accordance with the . . . principle of justice in acquisition and the principle of justice in transfer. Some people steal from others, or defraud them, or enslave them, seizing their product and preventing them from living as they choose or forcibly excluding others from competing in exchanges. None of these are permissible modes of transition from one situation to another. And some persons acquire holdings by means not sanctioned by the principle of justice in acquisition. The existence of past injustice (previous violations of the first two principles of justice in holdings) raises the third major topic under justice in holdings: the rectification of injustice in holdings. If past injustice has shaped present holdings in various ways, some identifiable, some not, what now, if anything, ought to be done to rectify these injustices? . . .

How far back must one go in wiping clean the historical slate of injustices? Idealising greatly, let us suppose theoretical investigation will produce a principle of rectification. This principle uses historical information about previous situations and injustices done in them (as defined by the first two principles of justice and rights against interference), and information about the actual course of events that flowed from these injustices, until the present, and it yields a description (or descriptions) of holdings in the society.

The general outlines of the theory of justice in holdings are that the holdings of a person are just if he is entitled to them by the principles of justice in acquisition and transfer, or by the principle of rectification of injustice (as specified by the first two principles). If each person's holdings are just, then the total set (distribution) of holdings is just.

Questions:
1.   Do you think that holdings are ever justly acquired in accordance with Nozick's principle of justice in acquisition? What of the Marxist dogma that all property is theft?

2.   Since North America historically belonged to the Indians, from whom it was appropriated by European settlers, does Nozick's principle of rectification of injustice in holdings logically entail that the land should be restored to the American Indians?

3.   Consider the consequences of Nozick's entitlement theory of justice: does it mean that all taxation, or at least that portion of taxation which is spent on providing state services such as education or healthcare is unjust, and as he claims equivalent to forced labour?

In this book we have been concerned with looking at different perspectives on law, theories of adjudication etc. What consequences do you think follow from the fact that these theories of justice have been constructed by males of either conservative or liberal persuasion? (See below, T Campbell, *Justice*, for an illustration of the extent to which the writing on justice has been dominated by such perspectives.)

However Campbell has argued that a socialist conception of justice can be built upon the idea of need:

T Campbell, *Justice,* London, Macmillan (1988), pp. 180–210.

(R)ecent debate on Marx and justice takes up the question of whether there might be — at a deeper level of analysis — distinctively socialist normative conceptions of rights and justice which capture at least some of the values which can be realised only in a socialist society. This approach draws on Marx's clear abhorrence of the miseries engendered by capitalism and his allegations that capitalism, as a form of theft perpetrated against the workers, fails to match up to even its own moral ideals.

More particularly, it is argued that socialist societies will at least approximate to, if not directly aim at, the genuinely socialist principle of distribution 'from each according to their ability, to each according to their needs', a maxim which Marx himself endorses. The communal egalitarianism implied by such a principle could be said to embody an aspect of socialism's moral superiority over other forms of political philosophy which is particularly relevant to justice. In brief, the socialist conception of justice can be regarded as distribution according to need. The fact that there will be no scarcity of resources in an actual communist society may render justice less problematic than it is in other societies, but this does not mean that socialist societies are not, in their own distinctive sense, just. Nor does it negate the claim that socialist justice is — in its proper historical context — to be preferred to other conceptions of justice . . .

The function of justice in socialist society will not be a matter of distributing the spoils of the division of labour in an incentive-based market economy. Socialist justice has to do with non-monetary ways of recognising the worth of the different efforts made by individuals and groups towards the realisation of a socialist society in which the full satisfaction of genuine human needs is the corporate *telos* . . .

Socialist justice has to do with more than the rectification of injurious interpersonal behaviour, the struggle to make competitive economic systems more 'fair', and the provision of a safety net for the sick, the old and the disabled. Rather it enters into the organising principles of all social activities, which will be directed at the satisfaction of 'needs' in a sense broad enough to take in all the creative and community aspirations of the fully developed individual.

Within the liberal tradition from which socialist theory has emerged it is more natural to present such a goal in terms of liberty than in the language of justice or equality, for liberty, when conceived of in positive terms as involving the power to realise capacities as well as the absence of the constraints of oppressive laws and social conventions, more readily captures the flavour of the contrast between socialism and capitalism. Yet it is misleading to present this as a contrast between liberty and justice, for it is assumed that the genuine interests of all members of a socialist society will have equal weight and it is denied that the tensions between these two norms, which is manifested in liberal societies, will be a problem in socialist ones.

Questions:
1.   Is a socialist conception of justice as valid as any other conception?

2.   As with Marxism there is no fully developed *feminist* theory of justice. In view of the fact that 'being born a woman is likely to mean being poorer, less well-educated, having a more routine job, carrying a double burden of work in and out of the home; above all having far less autonomy and far fewer real choices in life than being born to manhood' (F Heidensohn, 'Models of Justice: Portia or Persephone? Some Thoughts on Equality, Fairness and Gender in the Field of Criminal Justice', *International Journal of the Sociology of Law* (1976) vol. 14, pp. 287–98 at p. 290) do you think that there is a need for a specifically feminist theory of justice?

Radcliffe-Richards has claimed that principles of sexual justice can be derived from Rawls's conception of justice as fairness. She modifies Rawls's first principle to read: 'the most important purpose of society is to improve the well-being of sentient things, which should all be as well off as possible' (*The Sceptical Feminist, op. cit.* at p. 93), but preserves the 'difference principle' because she claims that 'justice . . . does not entail equality on average between men and women.'

Do you agree?

Rawls has been criticised by other feminists for ignoring women in the construction of his theory. Carol Pateman has claimed:

C Pateman, *The Disorder of Women,* Oxford, Basil Blackwell (1989), p. 46.

In the most recent rewriting of the liberal contract story . . . Rawls claims that his parties in their original position know none of the essential facts about themselves. Thus it might seem that Rawls' parties are truly universal and that the original choices include a choice between the two bodies (sexes) of humankind. The fact that Rawls ignores this possibility and writes that the parties can be seen as heads of families (p128) shows how deeply entrenched are patriarchal assumptions about the proper characteristics of the 'individual'. Moreover the attributes of the parties and their original position illustrates the fact that Rawls stands at the logical conclusion of the fraternal contract tradition. The original position and its choices are explicitly hypothetical (logical) and the parties are nothing more than the disembodied entities of reason; otherwise they could not help but know the natural facts about themselves, inseparable from their bodies' such as the facts of sex, age and colour.

Susie Gibson agrees, and has contended that a feminist theory of justice cannot be abstract and universal:

S Gibson, 'The Structure of the Veil' (1989), 52 *Modern Law Review,* pp. 420–40 at pp. 436–7.

The first rather crude feminist point is that this classically decontextualised reasoning relies upon two evidently social constructions: the rational self-interest of the individual, and concomitantly, a notion of social commitment based upon 'rights to' rather than 'responsibilities for' priorities. The first assumption, that human beings in an 'original position' (whatever that might be) would think like mid-twentieth century man, is questionable but obviously unverifiable. The second assumption, that all human beings would sensibly privilege the ethical value of rights over the ethical value of care, meets a vigorous challenge in Carol Gilligan's work on the sexual difference of moral discourse. The 'feminine' ethic of care which Gilligan identifies is founded on *contextualised* ethical decision making, in which 'equal rights' are as an overarching principle, an irrelevance, and equality meaningless. It might be argued then that by decontextualising the discussion the moral principles are, merely determined as 'masculinist' at the outset. The bald feminist point is that Rawls' attempt to ground a notion of 'justice as fairness' simply does so by further perpetrating a particular perspective on how fairness is found out.

There is further scope for feminist criticism of the project . . . appropriated from feminist analyses of the public/private dichotomy. All of these analyses argue that the valorisation of masculine activity in the public sphere, the privileging of the private as women's sphere, and the invisibility of private sphere exploitation contribute in some way to women's 'inequality'. Conversely, private sphere ethical values have, some feminists argue, been undervalued. The immediate criticism, then, of Rawls is precisely that he visualises the 'public' as the appropriate sphere for his exercise in egalitarian reasoning.

Question:
1. In the introduction to *Political Liberalism*, p. xxix, Rawls states that he *does* assume that in some form the family is just, and that much criticism of his *Theory of Justice* 'holds that the kind of liberalism it represents is intrinsically faulty because it relies on an abstract notion of the person and uses an individualist, nonsocial, idea of human nature; or else that it employs an unworkable distinction between the public and the private that renders it unable to deal with the problems of gender and the family. I believe that much of the objection to the conception of the person and the idea of human nature springs from not seeing the idea of the original position as a device of representation'. But, does the extract from *Political Liberalism* quoted above at pp. 278–80 fully answer these feminist criticisms?

No feminist writer has yet developed a fully fledged feminist theory of justice to rival that of the liberal theorists, but again the foundations for such a theory have been laid:

K O'Donovan, 'Engendering Justice: Women's Perspectives and the Rule of Law' (1989), 39 *University of Toronto Law Journal,* pp. 127–48 at p. 141.

The theory of justice that takes account of different perspectives and voices is the theory that allows for competing versions of reality. It is a 'no right answer' approach that defines justice as being dependent on strife. Absolutes are rejected. The struggle over meaning is out in the open. It is for all members of a society to influence content. Putting forward one's viewpoint in an attempt to convince others is presented as an essential activity. This is an invitation to participation despite barriers; an invitation to expression despite difficulties; an invitation to hope rather than despair. It does presuppose an open, listening judiciary, and a legal method that helps rather than hinders the expression of competing viewpoints.

Questions:
1. If women and men are granted an equal platform from which to speak, do you think they will have an equal chance of making themselves heard? If, at present, women are generally less confident, assertive and well-educated than men, will they lack the power to speak equally?

2. Is it more important that our legal system and law are moral, just or efficient? Are the three concepts compatible?

3. Is the present situation where some couples can have healthy babies, whilst others cannot, just? Would it be more efficient simply to allow a free market in babies, or at least in parental rights? Would such a free market be immoral?

Chapter 9

Law for All?

In this chapter, we hope you will reflect on the skills we have considered throughout this book in a *procedural* context, looking at two of the issues which face any legal system. First, to whom should legal skills be available and how should they be delivered? Second, what can non-lawyers contribute to the administration of justice: what scope is there for lay participation, such as the jury, lay advocates or lay assessors, or lay magistrates in the legal process?

ACCESS TO JUSTICE

Turning first to the matter of accessibility, the critical concepts of justice and efficiency must be brought to bear on such questions as unmet legal need and antiquated procedures. In considering the provisions governing state-funded legal services we discuss in this Chapter, you should ask yourselves whether they promote justice and whether they are efficient?

The ideal that everyone should have equal access to the law has been enshrined for centuries in the ideology of our legal system. As long ago as 1215 the Magna Carta declared 'To no-one will we sell, to no-one will we refuse or delay right or justice'. It was such ideology which prompted the establishment of the Legal Aid Scheme in 1949 (it was extended to Northern Ireland in 1965). The twin aims of the scheme were stated by the Lord Chancellor's Department, which is responsible for administering the scheme, as being:

> to provide legal advice for those of slender means and resources so that no one will be financially unable to prosecute a just and reasonable claim or defend a legal right, and to allow counsel and solicitors to be remunerated for their services.

The current law governing the provision of legal aid is the Legal Aid Act 1988, although we shall see this law is in the process of being substantially revised.

Until 1988 legal aid was administered on a daily basis by the Law Society, but the 1988 Act transferred responsibility for all but criminal legal aid to a newly-created, semi-autonomous agency — the Legal Aid Board. Under s. 4 it was given wide powers to do anything it considered necessary or desirable to provide or secure the provision of advice, assistance and representation under the Act, or which is calculated to facilitate or is incidental to or conducive to the discharge of its functions.

There are currently four separate legal aid schemes:

(1) Civil legal aid covers the provision of legal services up to and including representation in court by a solicitor, plus representation by a barrister if necessary. The applicant for this type of legal aid must satisfy a means test, based upon their levels of disposable income and capital, and a merits test. The application of the latter test involves two questions — firstly, are there sufficient prospects of the applicant being successful, and secondly, a reasonableness test — would a reasonable solicitor advise a reasonable client who *had* the means to spend their own money on the case. If the legally aided person wins the case, any legal costs which are recovered from the losing party go to the Legal Aid Fund. If those costs, plus any contribution the applicant may have had to make, are insufficient to repay the actual costs to the Legal Aid Fund, the Legal Aid Board has a *statutory charge* or entitlement to any damages which the legally aided party receives.

(2) Legal Advice and Assistance (The Green Form Scheme). This was introduced in 1973, and provides that anyone who qualifies under a simple means test, based upon their levels of disposable income and capital, can seek preliminary advice and assistance from a solicitor on any matter of law. It is intended to cover matters such as writing letters, conducting negotiations, making applications for civil or criminal legal aid, and doing preparatory work for tribunals.

(3) Advice by way of representation is an adjunct to the Green Form scheme introduced in 1979. Under s. 8(2) Legal Aid Act 1988 the Lord Chancellor is empowered to prescribe certain proceedings in respect of which representation at tribunals may be available under the Green Form scheme. Eligibility is again dependent upon a means test, and the same merits test as for Civil legal aid.

(4) Criminal legal aid covers advice and representation in criminal trials. Applications are directed to the magistrates or Crown Court rather than the Legal Aid Board. It is also merits and means tested, though because of the consequences of a criminal trial both tests are more flexible. In four situations the defendant *must* be granted criminal legal aid (see s. 21 Legal Aid Act 1988) including where the charge is murder. In other situations the applicant must satisfy the court that 'it is desirable in the interests of justice' that she be given legal aid — a test which grants enormous discretion to the clerk of the court

who normally deals with applications. Section 22, Legal Aid Act 1988 lays down statutory criteria to guide the decision, but the wide fluctuations in the granting of legal aid in various parts of the country remain a cause for concern.

Seton Pollock has claimed that the original 1949 scheme was:

a development in the legal systems of the world which has been brought about through the underlying spirit of the law which has always tended, though often almost imperceptibly, to move in the direction of equality. The introduction of all forms of legal aid is a response to this requirement of equality and springs from the spirit of justice that ultimately informs the law.

(See *Legal Aid — The First Twenty-Five Years,* London, Oyez Publishing (1975), p. 129.)

Hence the issue of access to legal help is often seen as intrinsically linked to justice — access to legal help is frequently equated with access to justice. For example Michael Zander states:

The concept of justice has been central to civilisation from time immemorial. But it is only in this century that the concept of universal access to justice has been taken seriously . . . Today the problem of access to justice is seen to consist of a variety of issues — the extent of the use and non-use of lawyers, the scope of the legal aid scheme, the availability of other systems for financial assistance to those who need the services of lawyers, and alternative systems for providing legal services through non-lawyers and for avoiding the need for legal services through the use of alternative techniques.

(See *A Matter of Justice,* Oxford, Oxford University Press (1989), p. 45.)

It is patently clear that despite an increasing amount of state money being poured into the legal aid system there is a vast area of 'unmet legal need'.

O Hanson, 'A Future for Legal Aid?', in P Thomas (ed), *Tomorrow's Lawyers,* Oxford, Blackwell (1992), pp. 88–90.

From 1949, and until very recently, all governments accepted that measuring the proportion of the population which was eligible was a valid test of the effectiveness of the legal aid scheme. In 1950, when the scheme was introduced, it covered over 80 per cent of the population on income alone. However, by 1973, only 40 per cent of the population was eligible . . .
    At the same time, the position of people outside the scheme had become worse than it was in 1950 because the cost of civil litigation had risen faster than earnings. In 1974 the legal aid limits and allowances were pegged to supplementary benefit levels and as a result were increased annually in line with average earnings . . . Michael Murphy has calculated that eleven million

adults lost eligibility for civil legal aid between 1979 and 1990. In personal injury cases, because of higher income limits introduced in 1990, nine million had lost eligibility. In percentage terms 79 per cent of the population was eligible in 1979. By 1990 that had dropped to 47 per cent generally and 52 per cent in personal injury cases . . .

Between January 1980 and January 1988, average earnings rose by 107 per cent but the legal aid limits increased by only 37 per cent. In April 1986, as a result of the crisis that year over the legal aid estimates, Lord Hailsham became the first Lord Chancellor to actively reduce eligibility: dependants' allowances were cut from 50 per cent to 25 per cent above supplementary rates. This had the greatest effect on families with children.

Questions:
1. From what you have already learnt of justice (Chapter 8) do you think access to the law can be equated with access to justice? See R Smith, *Justice: Redressing the Balance*, London, Legal Action Group (1997).

2. Should *every* citizen have a *right* to legal aid? i.e. even if the notions of access to the law and access to justice can be equated, should our legal system aim at providing 'justice for all'? Do the current provisions for state-funded legal services in the UK accord with Article 6 of the ECHR (see Chapter 3 pp. 75–6).

3. If the Government simply poured more money into the existing legal aid system would that solve the problem of 'unmet legal need'? Would that be an efficient solution (see Chapter 8)?

4. What other reasons, apart from lack of finance, might prevent persons from going to a lawyer for help with their problems?

M Partington, 'Great Britain', in F Zemans (ed), *Perspectives on Legal Aid*, London, Frances Pinter (1979), pp. 166–8, 171.

Present defects in legal aid
Such defects may be divided into two categories: remediable defects and structural defects:

(a) *Remediable defects*

Remediable defects are those which, with more government money and comparatively little alteration of the statutory framework, might be easily remedied. They include the following:

    (i) the means-test limits are too low
    (ii) the contribution levels are too high
    (iii) the statutory charge on damages awarded is crippling, particularly for those who wish to bring small claims
    (iv) the 'merits' test is too restricted and leads to inconsistencies in the granting of legal aid

(v)   levels of remuneration for lawyers are too low, especially for legal advice and assistance short of litigation

(vi)   costs for the successful opponents of legally aided litigants are not awarded frequently enough

(vii) there is no legal aid for representation before most tribunals

(viii) there can be practical difficulties in applying for legal aid; the forms to be completed are long and complex; and there are unnecessary delays

(ix)   criminal legal aid is granted too haphazardly

(x)   the administration of legal aid is confusing and irrational. Further, this means that there is no clear responsibility for the scheme.

(b) *Structural defects*

Even if all the defects just listed were eradicated, however, the problem remains of whether the legal aid scheme would even then be able to provide an effective legal service for all members of the community. It may help to state some of the structural defects which are argued to exist:

(i)   Location of solicitors

The siting of solicitors' firms in most towns is totally inimical to the development of comprehensive legal services since they are predominantly situated in city centres and are far from conveniently placed.

(ii)   Psychological barriers

Abel-Smith, Brooke and Zander discovered that many people, almost as a matter of principle, refuse to go to solicitors. They simply would not conceive of so doing. Many more do not go for fear of the expense.

(iii) Ignorance of legal rights

Many people do not understand the law or how it might help them. They may not even appreciate that they have problems which could be classified as 'legal'.

(iv)   Education and background of lawyers

Many lawyers just do not understand the problems of the poor in Britain, or how the law might be used to protect them. Further, most legal education is not designed to develop insight into these matters.

(v)   Community issues

It is often argued that existing legal education and practice encourages lawyers too much to see their cases as battles between individuals and to ignore wider implications. One of the important contributions of law centres is that they have sought ways to see some of the problems that come to them not merely as individual problems but also as community problems. This is a perspective on their work which private practitioners do not have.

(vi)   Control of legal services

Stemming from the above points there is also a frequently stated view that legal services would be more comprehensively developed if responsibility were taken away from the Law Society and placed in the hands of a more independent agency.

Questions:
1. Do you agree that all of the above defects remain barriers to legal help?

2. Why are people reluctant to consult lawyers about legal problems when they readily consult doctors about health problems? Can a valid analogy be drawn between the medical and legal professions, and the services (health care and legal help) that they offer? Are the services offered by the two professions of equal value to the community?

3. What would be the advantages and disadvantages of establishing a nationalised 'public legal service' on the same basis as the national health service? (For discussion of this issue see pp. 183–5 of the first edition of this book). Would this solve the structural defects with legal aid listed by Partington?

The following extract sets out the proposals on legal aid by the current Lord Chancellor a few years ago, when he was in opposition:
Lord Irvine of Lairg QC, Shadow Lord Chancellor, 'The Legal System and Law Reform under Labour' in D Bean (ed) *Law Reform for All*, London, Blackstone Press (1996), pp. 4–29, at pp. 4–5, 6, 7, 8, 10, 14–15.

Access to justice is an issue which stands high on the political agenda today. The claims that our justice system, and provision for legal aid securing access to that system, were the best in the world, were fashionable in earlier decades. They had some considerable plausibility in 1979, when Labour lost power. Then 72 per cent of households were eligible for legal aid. That proportion, however, has been reduced to 50 per cent by the recent eligibility cuts.

There is now a widespread agreement . . . that a crisis affects access to justice. Even the Lord Chancellor has been constrained to acknowledge that he does not regard as desirable any further reductions in eligibility.

Also there has always been a gap, which cannot rationally be justified, in the provision of legal aid. It is not available for representation before industrial, social security or immigration tribunals, or for coroners' inquests. A frequent excuse is that these tribunals apply simple and easily understood law in informal settings. Both these propositions are false . . .

The fact is, however, that no one, including the Labour Party, has any quick fix for the crisis besetting legal aid. Labour will have no new money to throw at problems whose solution calls for structural change. The figures are well known — in 1987/88 legal aid totalled £426 million. By 1993/94 it had risen to £1,020 million, of which £350 million went on civil proceedings. By 1996/97 the cost of legal aid is estimated to become £1,633 million, of which £685 million will go on civil legal aid. All lawyers are only too conscious of the sharp rise in recent years of the cost of legal proceedings.

The ambition of any Labour Lord Chancellor must be to restore legal aid to the status of a public social service which is so highly regarded for its economy and efficiency in securing access to justice that, with the support of the public, it can compete for scarce resources with the most highly regarded services such as health . . .

There is a major point which separates Labour's policy from that of the present Conservative government. Labour does not see the reform of legal aid as a distinct issue, hermetically sealed from the reform of the civil justice system itself. The best way to save money is not to exclude people from access to justice, but to cut the cost of litigation. The unacceptable cost of justice must be tackled at its source. So the reform of legal aid, and of the civil justice system, must go hand in hand. They are intimately bound up together. It is highly significant that Lord Woolf's remit for [his interim report — see p. 317 below] included no examination of the legal aid system, nor of the funding of civil litigation in general. It is bizarre that preparation of the 1995 Green Paper on legal aid and Lord Woolf's inquiries should have been conducted side by side yet entirely separately. The question of access to justice cannot be divorced from the question of funding . . .

What is required is prompt action to reduce the delays, the cost and, above all, the undue length of civil legal process: what is emphatically not required now is rationing of legal aid by cost capping . . .

Capping signified an abandonment of an entitlement basis for the grant of legal aid, based on merits. Legal aid will cease to be a benefit to which the individual who qualifies is entitled. It will in practice become a discretionary benefit, available at bureaucratic disposal — a benefit which will have to be disallowed when the money runs out, or when another category of cases has been given funding preference . . .

Labour favours *block franchising*, but opposes *compulsory competitive tendering*. Labour is against it because of the inevitable tendency to favour low-price against higher-quality bidders. Franchising will play a key role in developing the Community Legal Service that Labour proposes to develop. Compulsory competitive tendering, however, would be likely to undermine the whole franchising project, driving some firms away from the scheme and encouraging others to emphasise cost control, at the expense of quality assurance for the client.

Labour favours the delivery of publicly funded civil legal services on the basis of block franchises. It will, however, reform and improve the Legal Aid Board's franchising scheme by placing much greater emphasis on the quality of service and advice provided to clients. Quality control does not merely require transaction criteria to assess how well a case has been taken through a standardised procedure. Labour favours the introduction of more stringent and sophisticated quality control standards, together with improved assessment and compliance mechanisms . . .

A major plank in Labour's policy is the development of a Community Legal Service, within the existing legal aid budget. What is envisaged is a scheme much more broadly based than one which merely provides public money to purchase from individuals private commercial legal services. A scheme so limited cannot require solicitors to provide the full range of services that individuals require.

Labour intends to promote the rationalisation and revitalisation of the voluntary sector by deploying a much greater proportion of publicly funded services through CABs, law centres and the advice agencies. This could only proceed with the consent of the voluntary sector after the fullest consultation. The aim would be to secure a geographically fair network of CABs, advice centres and law centres across the country.

The Government's proposals for the provision of publicly-funded legal services have now been published in the following White Paper. (Note that the full text of this White Paper, and most of the other papers referred to in this section, is published on the Lord Chancellor's Department website: www.open.gov.uk/lcd. The proposals are given effect in the Access to Justice Bill, which is also available on the following website — www.parliament.the-station/ld199899/ldbills/004/1999004.htm).

Modernising Justice: The Government's plans for reforming legal services and the courts, Lord Chancellor's Department, London, (December 1998) Cm 4155

1. The Government's Objectives

1.1 This White Paper describes the Government's comprehensive programme for modernising the justice system in England and Wales . . . We are committed to more coherent, or 'joined up', government, in policy-making and working practices. So we have avoided the fragmented and piecemeal approach often taken in the past . . .

1.9 [T]he Government's twin aims are to:
- bring about a significant increase in access to justice.
- obtain the best value for the taxpayers' money spent on legal services and the courts.
  We will publish targets and measures of success, so that the public can see whether we have achieved our aims.

1.10 'Access to justice' means that, when people do need help, there are effective solutions that are proportionate to the issues at stake. In some circumstances, this will involve going to court, but in others, that will not be necessary. Someone charged with a criminal offence should have access to proper legal advice and representation, when the interests of justice require it. But in civil matters, for most people, most of the time, going to court is, and should be, the last resort. It is in no-one's interests to create a litigious society. People must make responsible choices about whether a case is worth pursuing; whether to process by negotiation, court action, or in some other way; and how far to take a relatively minor issue . . .

1.13 The Government will extend the provision of basic information and advice about avoiding or resolving legal problems, so it is available on the widest possible scale. We will do this through a new Community Legal Service, which will co-ordinate the way in which the services of advice agencies are planned and funded and by using new information technology. Reform of civil court procedures will mean that, in the great majority of cases, people will know from day one how long it will take to resolve their case. Conditional fees, fixed trial costs in 'fast track' cases, and fixed-price legal aid contracts, will all lead to greater certainty about what cases are likely to cost . . .

1.23   When these changes are complete:
- there will be a Community Legal Service. This will improve access to information advice and assistance, by working with other funders to identify local needs and co-ordinate funding. It will also manage a fund (which will replace civil legal aid), and use it to provide services in the most important cases. These will be the cases judged to have priority, in terms of: the importance of the issue to the person bringing the case; their prospects of success; the availability of alternative financing; and the public interest.
- there will be a Criminal Defence Service, which will provide criminal defence services of high quality to people who need them.
- the legal profession will be challenged to become more flexible and more innovative, while maintaining high standards. For example, greater use will be made of mediation where it is appropriate; and conditional fee arrangements will open up for many the realistic prospect of a successful resolution of cases which they would not have been able to afford.
- the courts will provide a system in which procedures and costs are proportionate to the importance of the issues going before them.
- court structures and the enforcement of penalties will underpin our efforts to tackle crime.

This will be a system in which every citizen feels confident to assert his or her rights, and which both the citizen and the taxpayer can afford . . .

2. Legal Services

COMMUNITY LEGAL SERVICE

2.6   As promised in our Manifesto, the Government intends to establish a Community Legal Service. We will do this both by tackling the current lack of planning and co-ordination in the advice sector; and by fundamentally reforming civil legal aid. Our longer-term aim is to ensure that every community has access to a comprehensive network of legal service providers of consistently good quality, so that people with actual or potential legal problems are able to find the information and help they need.

2.7   At present the fragmented and unplanned nature of the advice sector prevents the various funders and providers of services from working together to achieve the maximum value and effect overall. In most parts of England and Wales, people can seek information, advice and assistance from several different sources . . .

2.9   The Government believes that the solution lies in two key developments:
- there should be common systems, developed centrally and agreed by all funders, for defining and assessing needs and priorities, and for setting and monitoring appropriate standards of service.
- there should be a system for co-ordinating the plans of the various funders, so that the resources available to them are put to the best effect overall . . .

2.11 The Government intends to set up a new body, the Legal Services Commission (LSC), to take the lead in establishing the Community Legal Service. The LSC will be funded by central Government, but managed independently by a board of directors. Its responsibilities will be to:
- develop, in co-operation with local funders and other interested bodies, local, regional and national plans to match the provision of legal services to identified needs and priorities.
- report annually to the Lord Chancellor on how effectively planning and expenditure has been co-ordinated at local level, and the impact of this on the delivery of legal services to meet need.
- manage the Community Legal Service fund, which will replace legal aid in civil and family cases. As a funder of services in its own right, LSC will be able to make contracts with providers of all types of legal service. As well as funding traditional legal aid services, the LSC will use this power to fund other types of provider, and pioneer new ways of delivering information and legal services . . .

2.13 The Government intends to change the law in order to set up the LSC. Meanwhile, we will be preparing for the start of the Community Legal Service in three ways, by:
- pioneering different systems for assessing need and planning provision.
- developing a set of core quality criteria, to form the basis of a common 'kitemark' recognised by all funders.
- setting up a website on the Internet, to provide a new source of information and advice about legal problems . . .

2.17 [T]he LSC will take on responsibility for maintaining and developing the new quality system; and integrating it with the Legal Aid Board's existing franchising scheme . . .

SPECIALIST HELP FROM LAWYERS

2.21   . . . The Government is committed to safeguarding a strong and independent legal profession. Lawyers should not fear to defend unpopular causes or people, or act against popular and powerful ones . . .

2.26   In June 1998, the Government published proposals for a more effective system. We intend to sweep away the unjustified restrictive practice that prevents most qualified lawyers from appearing before the higher courts; and establish an efficient and streamlined procedure for promoting and regulating the future development of lawyers' services in England and Wales. As a result:

- firms, Government departments, and others who employ lawyers will no longer be required to pay a private lawyer to represent them in the higher courts. This will help, in particular, the Crown Prosecution Service to provide a more efficient and effective service to the taxpayer and the law-abiding public.
- people will not be required to pay for two lawyers, when one would do.
- a wider choice of legal service providers will develop over time, subject only to those training and other requirements that are in the public interest. Wider choice and more competition should lead to lower prices.

2.27   In future, all barristers and solicitors will, in principle, be qualified to appear in any court. Full rights of audience will extend to Crown Prosecutors as well as other employed lawyers . . .

Questions:
1.   Is it clear from the above proposals what sort of structural change to legal services provision the Lord Chancellor has in mind?

2.   Do you agree with the Lord Chancellor that more use should be made of advice agencies in the voluntary sector, or is this simply a way of dispensing justice on the cheap?

3.   Do you think the Government's proposals will really safeguard a strong and independent legal profession? (See R Smith, *Justice: Redressing the Balance*, London, Legal Action Group, (1997), Chapter 7.)

In addition to the general objectives of reform, the White Paper contains specific proposals on reform of the various legal aid schemes outlined above:

Modernising Justice: The Government's plans for reforming legal services and the courts, op.cit.

3. Reform of Civil Legal Aid

3.4   The Government is committed to tackling social exclusion. An effective justice system contributes to this aim by enabling people to uphold their rights and defend their interests when they need to do so . . .

3.6   The Government . . . believes that any system for funding legal services in civil and family cases should meet the following objectives. It should:
- direct the available resources to where they are most needed, to reflect clearly defined priorities.
- ensure, so far as possible, that disputes are resolved in a manner which is fair to both sides.
- provide high quality services that achieve the best possible value for money.
- have a budget which is affordable to the tax payer; and can be kept under control.

3.7   With these objectives in mind, we believe the following areas should have greater priority:
- social welfare cases, which help people to avoid, or climb out of, social exclusion; for example, cases about people's basic entitlements like a roof over their heads and the correct social security benefits.
- other cases of fundamental importance to the people affected. This covers cases involving major issues in children's lives (like care and adoption proceedings); and cases concerned with protecting people from violence.
- cases involving a wider public interest. This category includes two types of case: those likely to produce real benefits for a significant number of other people, or which raise an important new legal issue; and those challenging the actions, or failure to act, of public bodies (including cases under the Human Rights Act), or alleging that public servants have abused their position or power . . .

3.9   The new Community Legal Service fund will be capable of meeting the Government's objectives and priorities, listed in paragraphs 3.6 and 3.7. It will operate under a controlled budget — with finite resources, there should be no expectation of an unqualified entitlement to public funding. But the new scheme will be more flexible and adaptable than legal aid . . .

Contracting
3.17   The LSC will use the CLS fund to procure services for the public under contracts (or through conditional grants). This means that the LSC will decide what services to buy, and who to buy them from. This

is a fundamental change from the existing legal aid scheme, under
which any lawyer can take a case and submit a bill to the Legal Aid
Board for payment. In future, lawyers and other providers will only be
able to work under the scheme when they have a contract with, or a
grant from, the LSC. The Government has already announced that all
advice and assistance, and representation in family litigation, will be
provided under contract from the end of 1999.

3.18   Contracting is the key to meeting the Government's objectives:
- by purchasing specified services in specified categories of case,
  contracts give effect to priorities on the ground.
- contracts will enable the LSC to control its budgets, because they
  will usually determine expenditure in advance.
- contracting will help to ensure the quality of service consumers
  receive; only those lawyers who meet prescribed quality standards
  will be able to obtain contracts, and their performance will be
  monitored.
- contracting will promote better value for money, by providing the
  basis for competition; and by fixing prices in a way that encourages greater efficiency.
- by fixing the price, and the timing of payments, contracts can
  provide greater certainty about cost and cash flow. This is good
  for providers, because it lets them plan and manage their businesses more efficiently. It is also good for both parties in a case,
  because it should be possible to tell them at the outset, how much
  they might have to pay in contributions or costs . . .

3.20   All contracts will include quality standards, and the work that
providers do will be monitored . . .

The new Funding Assessment
3.24   The new, more focused funding assessment, which will replace the
existing merits test, will ensure that the available resources are spent
on the cases that most need help. The assessment will be more or less
strict, depending on the priority of the category of case concerned. It
will be possible to vary the way in which the assessment is made to
particular categories, to reflect changing demands and priorities.

3.25   The funding assessment will consider three key questions:
- would another type of service be a better way of dealing with the
  case? For example, in some types of family case, it will be
  necessary to show that the case is unsuitable for mediation, in
  order to qualify for representation by a lawyer.
- could the applicant fund the case in some other way? Unlike now,
  the assessment will consider whether the case is of a kind suitable
  for a conditional fee [see below].

- do the merits of the case itself, in the context of the Government's priorities and available resources, justify public funding? The general test will be whether a reasonable person able to fund the case with his or her own money would be prepared to pursue it. The strictness of this general test would be varied if other factors applied — for example if there were a wider public interest involved. The priorities and resources context is important. It cannot be assumed that any case necessarily has an automatic right to public funding because of its intrinsic merits. This is not possible where resources are finite.

3.26 To answer the third of these questions, cases will be assessed against four criteria (which may also be relevant when deciding if the case is suitable for a conditional fee). The criteria will be:
- the legal strength of the case and the prospects of a successful outcome.
- the importance and potential benefit to the assisted person, and the likely cost.
- the wider public interest (as defined in Paragraph 3.7 above).
- the availability of resources and the likely demands on those resources . . .

Financial eligibility, contributions, and costs
3.29 These rules are designed to target resources on the people most in need of help; ensure that, when they can, people contribute towards the cost of their case; and prevent people from being put off unreasonably by the fear of being left facing large legal bills. The existing rules are frequently criticised as unfair to the opponents of people with legal aid, because they do not sufficiently encourage legally-aided people to assess the risk of a case as if they were paying for it themselves. The Government intends to make two broad adjustments to strike a better balance:
- We intend to increase the number of people potentially eligible for advice and assistance under the scheme, to bring it back into line with that for representation in litigation. People brought within the scope of the scheme as a result will pay a contribution. This change reflects our intention to give priority to social welfare issues, and removes an anomaly by which people may be driven by the different eligibility limits to seek a more substantial service than their case warrants. At the same time, we intend to tighten the rules for those who are eligible but can afford to contribute something.
- For the most part, we will retain the existing system of costs protection, which requires the court to consider the means and conduct of both parties, before ordering an unsuccessful litigation on legal aid to pay his or her opponent's costs. Most people on legal aid would be unable to pay costs, even if they were unable to do so.

Earlier versions of the proposals in the White Paper, which had been outlined in various speeches by the Lord Chancellor, have attracted academic criticism, particularly from Professor Michael Zander:

M Zander, 'The Government's Plans on Legal Aid and Conditional Fees', *Modern Law Review* (1998), vol. 61, pp. 538–550, at pp. 538–546 (footnotes omitted).

In his Cardiff speech [to the Law Society's annual conference in Cardiff on 18 October 1997] Lord Irvine began by making a number of general statements. First, he asserted that there had been 'a collapse of public confidence in legal aid'. It has to be said that although statements of this kind were repeatedly made by Lord Mackay [then Lord Chancellor] as well, there is no worthwhile evidence to support this contention. Second, legal aid expenditure had risen dramatically and well ahead of inflation. There is no dispute about this proposition — and also no convincing explanation as to the reasons. Third, 90 per cent of the legal aid bill went on lawyers' fees. In fact the proportion is a good deal less than 90 per cent after allowance is made for fees paid to expert witnesses, court fees, VAT and other disbursements, but since the main purpose of legal aid is to provide lawyers it is hardly surprising that a high proportion of the bill is for lawyers' fees. Fourth, Lord Irvine said, legal aid had to be re-focused: 'It must be made a tool to promote access to justice for the needy — not be seen by the public as basically a means for keeping lawyers in business.' This proposition was plainly phrased in a tendentious way and is typical of remarks hostile to the legal aid system and to legal aid lawyers quite frequently made by both the Lord Chancellor and his House of Commons representative Geoffrey Hoon. The whole point of the legal aid system is that in order to give the needy access to justice the state pays for the legal services they require. Obviously, the needy will not get the legal services they require unless the lawyers can do the work on a basis that enables them to remain in business. There is therefore no conflict between paying lawyers properly and providing the poor what they need to get access to justice.

Lord Irvine's fifth general proposition was by far the most important. The resources available for legal aid, the Lord Chancellor, were finite. The days of 'free-flowing legal aid' were gone forever. 'No Government could tolerate an ever-growing, demand-led budget that just cannot be controlled.' The fact is that every Government since the inception of the scheme in 1949 has tolerated an ever growing, demand-led budget for legal aid. This, it might be said, has been one of the chief glories of the English system — that the use of the scheme was determined by the numbers of eligible citizens with proper cases who came forward to use it. Lord Mackay was the first Lord Chancellor to adopt the Treasury view that this was no longer to be tolerated. In his speech on 18 October 1997 Lord Irvine accepted Lord Mackay's conclusion. A way had to be found to control legal aid expenditure. Lord Mackay's proposed method was an overall cap on expenditure. The principal route identified by Lord Irvine was through block contracting for both civil and criminal legal aid:

The future lies in contracting for services, in both criminal and civil cases. The way ahead is contracts that will specify in advance what services are being bought and at exactly what price. It is only through contracting that Government can hope to gain sufficient control over the shape of the legal aid scheme to ensure that resources are targeted on the needy. To stop cases going on for too long. To cut waste and duplication. To trim costs and expense. And to focus this vital fund on the people who need it.

Contracting at fixed prices, agreed in advance, Lord Irvine said at Cardiff, would give the Government control over the legal aid budget. 'It will enable choices to be made. It will allow us to set priorities, and to shape the budget to fit the country's needs and circumstances.' Whether there is a difference between Lord Mackay's cap and Lord Irvine's control through contracting remains to be seen. In all probability it will turn out to be largely a matter of semantics. Of many regrettable aspects of the new system perhaps the worst is that the Government and its agencies will take over from citizens with legal problems the allocation of legal aid resources and the selection of lawyers able to do the work.

Immense difficulties (not to speak of cost) will be created by the need for the Legal Aid Board to select providers and to manage thousands of contracts. Block contracting will quickly involve compulsory competitive tendering with all its obvious dangers of cost-cutting and reduction of quality. It will set practitioner against practitioner . . .

To the extent that any proposed redirection of resources takes place, on what basis is it to be done, and how will one know whether it results in more help for the needy? The Lord Chancellor says that the allocation of resources by the Legal Aid Board will be guided by regional Legal Services Committees 'which will match services to the needs of a particular area and determine how they can best be delivered'. The only way decisions regarding allocation of resources responding to need can be soundly based is if they are based on research . . .

In his speech in Cardiff Lord Irvine went on to say that legal aid would in time be restricted to providers who had a contract with the Legal Aid Board. Providers would be franchised by the Board. Franchising would be broadened by the addition of a new dimension to permit monitoring of quality of the work done. One way of measuring quality would be to test firms' success in predicting the outcome of cases! The restriction of legal aid to franchised providers with contracts will drastically reduce the number of access points for members of the public seeking legally aided services. At present legal aid payments are made to over 10,000 firms of solicitors of which some 1,350 are franchised. The Legal Aid Board has suggested that there may eventually be some 3,000 firms with franchises. The withdrawal of such a huge number of legal aid access points will have serious consequences for the public in terms not simply of convenience but of getting legal services at all . . .

Another change announced by the Lord Chancellor in his Cardiff speech was that the merits test for civil legal aid would be tightened . . .

In his speech, Lord Irvine conceded that there would be some cases that would not meet the merits test and where the cost would be disproportionate to the likely benefit to the individual litigant, where it was nevertheless in the public interest that the case be brought. He agreed with Middleton [who chaired a government review of civil justice and legal aid] that special arrangements should be made for such cases. The concept of a special fund for public interest cases is potentially useful, though the extent of its value will obviously depend on its terms of reference, how and by whom it is to be administered and what kinds of cases will be supported. In particular, will the special fund be restricted to test cases or will it be available to bring ordinary cases in the excepted categories? Is the size of the fund to be subject to a cap? A sobering note was the warning given by Lord Irvine in his Cardiff speech that, 'It would be difficult to establish a separate budget for public interest cases until the cost of civil legal aid overall has been brought under control' . . .

One of the few things said in his speech by Lord Irvine on legal aid that was welcomed was his rejection of the proposal made by both Lord Mackay and Sir Peter Middleton that every applicant for civil legal aid should be required to make a contribution. (Middleton suggested it should be £5 or £10 and that it should be paid even by those on Income Support.) Lord Irvine said that he could not accept that the poorest in society should be expected to pay a flat rate charge as a ticket of admission to legal aid.

Potentially the most positive part of Lord Irvine's plan for legal aid is the plan for a Community Legal Service. This had already been trailed in the Labour Party's Election Manifesto: 'We will develop local, regional and national plans for the development of Legal Aid according to the needs and priorities of regions and area'. In his Cardiff speech Lord Irvine said that the principal aim of a Community Legal Service would be to help people decide if their problem is really a legal one and to point them in the right direction. This would involve the coordination of Citizens' Advice Bureaux and other information and advice centres in a coherent scheme. 'Local communities should have a strong say in the development of information and advice services which meet their needs.' But in the House of Lords debate Lord Irvine painted a broader and more exciting role for the proposed Community Legal Service: 'The service could provide telephone helplines; education in rights and obligations; legal advice on the Internet; referrals to alternative dispute resolution; legal representation in tribunals; even interactive kiosks in every high street or supermarket dispensing basic information about the law and the legal system.' Middleton saw the centrepiece of the Community Legal Service as 'a network of small local offices, providing basic information and diagnostic advice'. These might be co-located with advice agencies or based on the premises of county or magistrates' courts, council offices or libraries.

Questions:
1. Should reforms to legal aid, such as those currently proposed by the Lord Chancellor, be introduced without primary legislation and thus without full parliamentary debate?

2. Do you agree with the categories of legal actions which have been temporarily excluded from the plans to abolish civil legal aid? (see pp. 349–52 for some indication of the impact of the fact that legal aid has never extended to libel actions.)

3.   In view of the Lord Chancellor's subsequent depiction of 'fat cat' lawyers earning huge fees for legal aid work, is it disingenuous for Professor Zander to claim that legal aid payments are simply enough to keep lawyers in business?

4.   Do you agree with Professor Zander's assessment of the worst aspects of the Government's proposals?

5.   Do you think that the merits test does need to be tightened up? (For the current merits test, see p. 289 above.) If so, do you agree with the Government's proposals for so doing?

6.   How do you think a Community Legal Service could supplement the work of the existing law centres (see p. 329 below)?

R Moorhead, 'Legal Aid in the Eye of a Storm: Rationing, Contracting and a New Institutionalism', *Journal of Law and Society* (1998) vol. 25, pp. 365–387, at pp. 365–8, 383–4, 387.

> '. . . [T]he role of legal aid should be to ensure that less well off people have access to justice on a broadly equal basis to everyone else, but that this objective should be set against the background of limited resources . . . The issue is not *whether* to limit expenditure, but *how* to devise a legal aid scheme under which decisions about resources, priorities and targeting are taken in a transparent and accountable way' [Sir Peter Middleton, *Review of Civil Justice and Legal Aid: Report to the Lord Chancellor* (1997) 35.]
>
> Rising legal aid expenditure has driven the debate on structural reform of the legal aid system for several years. Allied to the concern for fiscal restraint is a concern about the nature and impact of current legal aid provision. The appropriateness of particular methods of service delivery (courts, mediation, Alternative Dispute Resolution, and public legal education) and particular forms of legal service organization (private practice, non-profit making agencies, and law centres) has moved towards the centre of public policy debates from their more radical origins. At the same time, new institutional tools have begun to be introduced for organizing provision: contracts, competition and 'contestability' are all making their way into legal services . . . [Recent] publications point to the tension between the current demand led system of funding and the political desire to restrain costs and facilitate greater planning and prioritization . . .
>
> Readers of recent government proposals on legal aid will be perplexed if they seek a developed and clearly articulated view of the purpose of a reformed legal aid scheme. The overwhelming focus of language and ideas promotes ideas of efficiency and managing scarce resources. In part, the current economic orthodoxy justifies such an approach: scarcity of resources is a political fact which legal aid policy must address. Yet the *purpose* of any legal aid scheme requires careful and detailed analysis and explanation if efficiency and effectiveness are to achieve any meaningful end beyond minimal cost.

The Middleton report begins with a conventional formulation: 'the role of legal aid should be to ensure that less well off people have access to justice on a broadly equal basis to everyone else.' Even a superficial understanding of the legal services market suggest the unreality of such a phrase as meaningful guide to policy formulation. There is no 'everyone else'. Different sections of society have very different needs for legal services which cannot be measured in simple terms of equality . . .

The Rushcliffe committee's recommendations, as selectively implemented by the then Labour administration, formed the bedrock of the existing legal aid scheme. For current purposes, these can be summarised as:

(a) Legal aid should be available for those types of cases where lawyers normally represented private individual clients.

(b) Legal aid should include coverage for people regarded as poor, but also those of small or moderate means . . .

[R]ising costs and the resulting cuts in financial eligibility, have led to a significant erosion of one of the Rushcliffe principles: it is very difficult to argue that legal aid is still available to those of moderate, or even limited means. Legal aid is now a service predominantly for the poor: women, children and those accused of crime. This has altered the nature of services provided under legal aid and undermined the extent to which legal aid funds cases where lawyers normally represent private clients. There has also been a marked increase in the amount of social welfare law being conducted under the green form scheme. It now accounts for a considerable proportion of expenditure on civil certificates. In relation to such work, Rushcliffe's principles provide little relevant guidance: housing disrepair, welfare-benefit problems, and so on, are simply not problems where access can be meaningfully compared to normal private paying clients.

Furthermore, the future of some of the larger areas of traditional work where some comparison with levels of access to private-paying clients may be more apt now look far less secure. The Lord Chancellor's Department has proposed that conditional fee arrangements (CFAs) [see below] be available for all money claims coupled with the removal of legal aid funding of many such cases. Putting family and criminal work to one side, this raises the possibility of removing almost all areas of 'traditional' private provision of civil law from the legal aid sphere altogether.

The result is that the Rushcliffe principles, and the Middleton equivalent, are increasingly irrelevant, as a description of, or guiding principle for, the legal aid scheme. A re-definition of the conceptual basis for publicly funded legal services is implicit in the shift towards social-welfare provision. There is a need to consider from first principles the purpose of public legal services . . .

The place of entitlement at the centre of legal aid policy is clearly being questioned. Middleton speaks of making merits tests dependent on the availability of resources with legal aid operating within capped budgets. The merits test may also be adapted to give graded priority to certain types of cases. This suggests a more administrative approach to planning and resource allocation, with supplier discretion being weakened by bureaucratic control. Also, given pressure on resources, a harder look at the priorities of the current legal aid scheme is inevitable . . .

Similarly, a more sophisticated analysis of legal 'need' and the benefits and limitations of legal services is required.

It is important, however, to recognise the significant difficulties in defining needs and priorities in any objective sense. In health, the definition and articulation of 'needs' appear as a negotiated process where the views of patients, doctors, and administrators compete for influence and control against a plurality of theoretical paradigms such as the balancing of outcome against process values. Similar difficulties will be faced by a formulation of proper understandings of legal need and the 'equality' of citizenship that the system promotes. Any definition of priorities and service levels will be a dynamic, negotiated process. It remains to be seen whether this process will take place at a national or regional level and to what extent interested parties will play a role in influencing priority setting. The current negotiations on the exclusion of civil damages claims from legal aid suggest a relatively piecemeal approach to particular substantive areas of legal services.

Attempts to evaluate the effectiveness of legal service approaches are essential if informed rationing decisions are to be taken. Comparatively little research seeks to quantify the *benefits* of legal services in a way that would enable better judgments about cost-benefit to be reached. Whilst there is an understandable reluctance to state some legal aid work is less useful than other work, without this, policy makers will be required to indulge pragmatic adjudication of competing claims: entitlement will be relativized on the basis of conjecture and anecdote and strongly driven by the one quantitative indicator which is always present: cost.

In a climate of financial restraint, frameworks of entitlement negotiated annually at the macro-legal and more frequently at the micro-level are likely to be the mechanisms by which services are rationed. Developing indicators, such as the quality of life scale used in health planning, is no panacea, but it suggests the possibility of a more rigorous framework for analysing legal services. This requires a well researched analysis of the costs and benefits (economic and social) of the legal process, particularly its impact on the would-be client, but also on the broader regulatory systems governing such decision, the overall costs to the system and the effect on the quality of the outcome which results . . .

This complexity suggests that a more sophisticated analysis of legal services is needed, as are mechanisms of control and administration which are more complex and responsive than the simple hierarchical system of rules embodied in current approaches to eligibility. A negotiation of the legal aid systems norms and methods will take place at both a national level and also a local level (where individual contracts are being negotiated). Such complexity poses its own problem: models of provision will be difficult to produce, monitor and adapt in a way that is genuinely accountable. The definition of legal service needs and accompanying decisions on service provision are political decisions, to be taken in the light of competing priorities. The role of regional legal service committees, designed to monitor, consult and advise on legal strategy, is likely to be crucial. Currently the membership base of these committees is narrow and the regional determination of expenditure appears to be minimal. Decisions over resources will be taken in a negotiated environment mediated mainly by nationally set priorities, formal contracting behaviour, and informal cultural behaviour in particular organizations. The development of independent and clear systems for evaluating such provision will be critical to ensuring the proper administration of this 'storm' of values.

Questions:

1. Can you track down, in your University library, or on the Internet, the various Consultation documents and proposals on legal aid provision referred to in the above articles?

2. Should standards and priorities for legal service provision be set? If so who should be involved in such standard and priority-setting?

3. Imagine that the Government decides to appoint a Royal Commission to address the issue of effectively delivering publicly-funded legal services. Write a submission outlining how you would reform the current system, and what priorities you would set in rationing services.

The reforms and alternatives to legal aid currently being canvassed are market-based solutions, particularly the introduction of franchising of legal aid firms and conditional fee arrangements.

The last Government claimed that the introduction of a franchising system, whereby firms which carry out large amounts of legal aid are licensed to do such work, would improve the efficency of legal aid and the quality of service delivered. In the initial stages at least, other firms would still be free to carry out legal aid work. As is apparent from the extracts above, the current Lord Chancellor appears to share the view of his predecessor that concentrating state-funded legal services in the hands of fewer firms will allow more scope for training staff, specialising and securing economies of scale. Currently, franchises are granted to those firms complying with 'transaction criteria' adopted by the Legal Aid Board. Initially franchises are granted for a period of five years, with the possibility of renewal for another three.

Modernising Justice: The Government's plans for reforming legal services and the courts, op.cit.

How lawyers are paid

2.34 . . . The Government intends to make legal bills more affordable and predictable, by:

● working with the insurance industry to develop less expensive legal insurance.

● ensuring that lawyers provide full and clear information to their clients about the likely cost of taking a case; and, where

appropriate, regulating the costs which lawyers can charge their
own client or recover from the other side.
- extending and improving conditional fees . . .

Insurance
2.36 Insurance cover against the cost of becoming involved in a future legal
action is one way in which people can solve the problem of unafford-
able and uncertain lawyers' bills. Policies attached to other insurance
policies have been available for over 20 years. The premiums, often
between £4 and £20, are so small that most people do not realise they
have cover in the event that they need to go to law. Some 17 million
people are already covered by one of these policies. The Government
will be discussing with the insurance industry how more people could
be encouraged to take out legal expenses insurance.

Controlling lawyers' fees in litigation
2.37 In the past, lawyers would simply present a bill at the end of the case,
often having given little or no indication of how much it would be.
This practice is no longer acceptable in a modern society . . .

2.38 In future, the Government expects to see lawyers give clear and firm
estimates of the likely costs of cases, so clients can make informed
decisions about whether to proceed. The circumstances in which an
estimate might have to be changed, and how any change would be
calculated, should also be explained clearly at the outset. We recognise
however, that this can be difficult at present, because the way litigation
is conducted leaves too much that the lawyer cannot control or predict.
This will change when we implement the [civil justice] reforms . . .

2.40 As a first step, the Government has decided to set a sliding scale of
fixed costs to cover the cost of advocacy at a trial in the fast track [see
below], up to a maximum figure of £750. This will be introduced in
April 1999 at the same time as the fast track itself. Later this year, we
will consult about further possible controls, which we would seek to
implement at the same time. We propose to require solicitors to:
- tell their clients at the start of court proceedings what their full
  charging rate is (replacing the current practice of adding a substantial
  mark-up to the nominal charging rate at the end of the case).
- provide their clients and the court, at an early stage in all civil
  proceedings, with a statement of the costs incurred to date and an
  estimate of the further costs likely to be incurred in taking the
  case to trial.
- provide, at a later stage in fast track cases (which will be defined
  in court rules) a firm estimate of the full cost of taking the case
  to trial. This estimate will then become the maximum amount that
  the solicitor can charge his or her client, or seek to recover from
  the opponent as costs between the parties . . .

Conditional fees

2.42 The last Government introduced conditional fees for certain types of civil case, most importantly personal injury cases. Under a conditional fee agreement, the lawyer agrees not to charge a fee if the case is lost, in return for a higher fee than normal if it is won. The client or the lawyer can take out insurance to cover the risk of losing and having to pay the other side's costs. In a successful case, the other party will usually be ordered to pay most of the lawyer's normal fee. The client currently has to find the additional 'success fee' out of whatever damages he or she has won. The success for which cannot be more than 100% of the normal fee; and most solicitors have agreed not to take more than 25% of the damages recovered in a personal injury case.

2.43 Where they are allowed, conditional fees have already greatly extended access to justice. With conditional fees, people can take good cases, in the certain knowledge that will not be left out of pocket if they lose (except by the amount of any insurance premium). In July 1998, following consultation, the Government extended the benefits of conditional fees to all types of civil case, except family proceedings. This was a far as we could go under the present law. In future, we intend to allow conditional fees in some types of family case as well. Conditional fees are not appropriate in cases about the care of children or domestic violence. On the other hand, they offer a potentially attractive option in cases about the division of matrimonial property. We see no reason to prevent people from choosing to fund those cases by a conditional fee, rather than having to pay their lawyer win or lose.

2.44 . . . [I]n future, we intend to make it possible for the winning party to recover the success fee, and any insurance premium, from the losing party — the person or organisation that has committed the legal wrong. This will make conditional fees more attractive and fairer, and allow defendants and claimants whose case is not about money to use them. This will be a further radical expansion of access to justice . . .

Question:
1. Do you think that the Government is being unduly optimistic about the contribution private insurance can make to legal costs? What sort of cases would insurance be likely to cover?

Consider the following response to the earlier proposals on franchising in Legal Aid Board's document, *Franchising: The Next Steps* (1993):

S Webster, 'Kentucky Fried Law?', *Solicitor's Journal*, 5 February 1993, p. 86.

The basic philosophy of the publication is that the legal process can be industrialised. Lawyers are, interestingly, referred to as 'suppliers' in the document. Clients are presumably to be regarded as recipients of services; and the main concern of the paper seems to be process. Most lawyers involved with dealing with individual clients do not view themselves as suppliers engaged in the delivery of a process, but that will change in many respects, if franchises are to be applied for successfully and retained. The LAB's [Legal Aid Board's] insistence with regard to management is that systems are in place. Those wishing to be franchisees will not be able to practise on an ad hoc or one-off basis. The beauty of systems, so far as the board is concerned, is that they can be checked by audit. Idiosyncrasy will disappear and the assembly line will rule.

. . .

The board's obsession with systems continues into the area of case management. There must be written procedures for taking instructions, case-planning and closing. Written procedures for showing the lawyers responsible for materials and documents provided by the clients are a novel twist, as is a written policy for the selection of barristers, solicitor agents and expert witnesses. There has to be a plan for regular internal audits of case files, which will presumably be supplemented by the board's own audit. A passive audit is not sufficient, and there must be a means of assessing its outcome and the effectiveness of any corrective action taken as a result . . . A cost-control system must be in place, to allocate all expenses to particular areas of work and/or fee earners.

. . .

A great dilemma will be faced by the practice which does a proportion of legal aid work only. The firm which is exclusively involved in legal aid, or where legal aid provides the majority of the fee income, will have little alternative but to apply for a franchise. How do you mix a legal aid and a private practice when satisfying the board's requirements will be such an onerous activity? The answer, probably, is to split off the legal aid part of the practice into a separate firm. There has always been a considerable dichotomy between legally aided and private practice. The grant of a franchise will accentuate that situation and the stresses and strains between the two types of practice, especially if there are non-legal aid partners as against legal aid partners within the same firm, will become almost intolerable.

Questions:
1. Is it desirable that lawyers should regard themselves as 'suppliers engaged in the delivery of a process'? Why/why not? Can law be treated and regulated like an industry?

2. Do you think that franchising will broaden or restrict access to legal services? Will it effectively result in a two-tier legal system — one for the rich and another for the poor?

The idea of conditional fees is based on the contingency fee system which operates in the United States, under which the client either pays nothing or something less than the full fee if the case is lost. If the case is won, the lawyer takes a fee out of the damages, and it will normally be assessed as a percentage of those damages. Section 58 of the Courts and Legal Services Act 1990 provided for the introduction of conditional fees to this jurisdiction. The scheme differs from the North American one in that the fee will not be a percentage of damages, but the usual hourly or fixed fee uplifted by a maximum of 100% to compensate lawyers for the risk of receiving no fee if the case is lost. As we have seen above, the government now proposes a significant extension of such arrangements.

For a viewpoint from the United States on how conditional fee systems operate, consider the following:

D de Keiffer, 'Contingent Justice', *New Law Journal*, 20 August 1993, pp. 1223–4.

> . . . [T]he Lord Chancellor is going to allow solicitors and barristers to receive conditional fees for some types of cases. Although the system envisaged by Lord Mackay is somewhat different than that normally used in the United States, our experience might be instructive both to the profession and the consuming — or consumed — public . . . [A]ttorneys in the UK will now be allowed to charge double their usual hourly rates if successful in prosecution of personal injury cases. Aside from the fact that this plan could result in legal fees which far exceed any recovery, it raises some nice questions of the perception of the legal profession. As most readers will be aware, lawyers in the United States are regarded with an esteem which is the rough equivalent to that of swamp leeches . . . One need look no further than the *Yellow Pages* of our nation's capital (or turn on the television) to understand what is going on. While I recognise that Attorney advertising is not what the Lord Chancellor had in mind in permitting conditional fees, the slope, shall we say, has been greased . . . The ads almost uniformly tout: 'No fee if no recovery.' This is the major selling point for law firms which specialise in contingent fee personal injuries. Whatever formula one uses — 'conditional fees' or 'contingent fees', the principle is the same — 'Get justice FREE (12″ colour TV for first 20 people responding)'.
>
> . . . Attorneys who accept contingent — or conditional — fee cases do not do so for altruistic motives. They do it because they believe the cases are so strong there is little chance that they will *not* be paid. And if the case is *that* strong, why not take the case at twice the fee? Some altruism . . . What almost always happens is that the parties reach a negotiated settlement either before or during the trial. It is unknown (and unknowable) whether victims would have been better off by accepting a lower initial offer from an insurance carrier early in the game, or taking a higher amount later — which is then offset by the attorney's fee. What is knowable is that the attorneys personally profit — a lot — from this arrangement.

I am sure that lawyers in the United Kingdom will be SHOCKED by the above scenario, and note that *your* new system is designed to avoid these scandalous situations. Well, we have 'conditional fees' as well as 'contingent fees' in this country. The following is an (almost) verbatim transcript of a discussion with counsel:

> Client: 'Mr Lupus, we have received a very generous offer from the insurance company for my injuries. I think we should accept.'
>
> Counsel Lupus: 'As your attorney, I strongly advise against that course of action. Not only is the amount not enough, but I am honour bound as an attorney to fight this matter to the ends of the Earth and beyond.'

Client: 'Um, Uh, I'm terribly sorry sir, but I don't understand. The amount offered is more than I ever expected and if you keep working on this case, I will have to pay you double your regular hourly rates. Why are you bound to continue this case when I am satisfied with the result I could get today?'

Counsel Lupus: 'It is quite clear, my dear man, that you do *not* understand the ethical imperatives of the law. Since we are operating under a "conditional fee" arrangement, I cannot in good conscience allow you to settle this case for anything less than the National Debt of Nicaragua, a large portion of which, of course, will accrue to myself and my elderly mother. To satisfy my solemn duty as an officer of the court I simply *must* litigate this case until we reach the end of all appeal. This, of course, will require the expenditure of at least 24.7 hours/day of my time for the next 13 years. I am sure you are grateful for the opportunity to be a foot soldier in the service of the law. Now, please leave me so that I may prepare the Surrejoinder to the Defendant's Second Rebuttal Brief to the Motion to Dismiss (twice removed).'

Client: 'But I want an *end* to this litigation. I want my money!'

Counsel Lupus: 'Sir, I rarely advise my clients to stop whining, but this is one of those times. As you may know, if we are successful in this case, *you* may not have to pay one shekel of my fees. Those greedy bastards on the other side will have to ante up the modest amounts I would otherwise charge you. Slight delays in your receiving your due and tying the court system in knots for years is a small price indeed to pay for justice. Besides, if we *lose* it is possible that those bad people against whom I am struggling will ask *you* to pay *their* counsel's fees. You wouldn't want *that*, would you?'

Client: 'Heavens no — that's the reason I'd like to settle now and be done with it.'

Counsel Lupus: 'I'm very sorry, but as I patiently explained to you, a settlement on any terms which do not guarantee the greatest pain to the miscreants in terms of paying my fees is simply unethical. I cannot do otherwise. I could never face my colleagues again. They would drum me out of the club!'

Given these scenarios, which are true beyond peradventure, what is the problem? Essentially none if the legal profession did not attempt to deceive the public and itself that it represents much more than an attempt by attorneys to maximise their client base (and not, incidentally, their income). Although there may be some worthy cases which would go wanting for counsel if 'conditional' or 'contingent' fees were not available, these are generally the exceptions which demonstrate the rule.

For an alternative view consider the following:

D Luban, 'Speculating on Justice: The Ethics and Jurisprudence of Contingency Fees', in M Cain (ed) *Lawyers in a Postmodern World*, Buckingham, Open University Press (1995) (references omitted).

In Kafka's famous parable *Before the Law*, a door-keeper bars a simple country man from entering the Courts of Justice, until the dying man learns in his final moments that the door before which he has waited vainly for years was meant for him and him alone. In the real world of law, it is attorneys' fees that are the door-keeper. My principal focus will be the contingency fee which — though it is viewed with suspicion by all the world except the United States and a few Canadian Provinces — is one of the two most effective routes around the obstructive door-keeper . . .

The fundamental argument on behalf of the contingency fee is completely straightforward. Contingency fee arrangements allow individuals who might otherwise be unable to afford legal vindication of their rights to gain access to justice. Such fee arrangements aid in fulfilling the fundamental ideal of equality before the law. Proponents of the contingency fee argue that — in the words of the Commonwealth Senate report on contingency fees — 'it would widen access to the legal profession and the courts and, therefore, to justice', adding, 'it is impossible to oppose the proposition that all members of the community should posses the ability to have their legal rights enforced'. Opponents reply that 'much of this increased volume [of litigation] would comprise opportunistic and vexatious claims'. Both arguments plainly have a point, though the empirical case is unclear on each side, but it would be a mistake to view the argument as a standoff. The proponents' argument should carry the day, for the following reason. Everyone is in favour of aggrieved parties having their legal rights enforced — as the Commonwealth Senate report notes, echoing the Law Institute of Victoria, 'access to justice is a 'motherhood' issue'. Likewise, everyone is against opportunistic and vexatious claims. The trick, clearly, is to determine which is which, and society has evolved the institution of adjudication expressly to make that determination.

The standoff itself is therefore an argument for subjecting contested claims of legal rights to adjudication; that is, it is an argument on the proponents' side, representing the conservative alternative of settling a vexed question by the time-honoured social mechanism devised for that purpose. The opposing argument, by contrast, amounts to suggesting that one should make it difficult for plaintiffs to utilize the accepted social mechanism for separating legitimate claims from opportunistic and vexatious ones, simply on the opponents' assurances that too many claims would opportunistic and vexatious. It is hard to take such an argument, with its patent contempt for the adjudicatory process, seriously . . .

Many writers assert that the contingency fee is a mechanism whereby clients of limited means borrow litigation expenses from their lawyer, using the value of their claim to secure the loan; the fee uplift built into contingency contracts represents (on this analysis) the lawyer's interest for the loan. Though it is possible to view contingency fees in this way, the loan theory does not adequately distinguish contingency fees from any other fee arrangement. After all, nothing prevents a lawyer working under any fee arrangement from waiting until after the conclusion of a case to submit her bill. It may be objected that few lawyers would accept such an arrangement, since if the case is lost the clients may have insufficient resources and incentive to pay their legal bills. But this does not put the lawyer in a worse situation than she

would be under a contingency fee contract, where she will likewise collect
nothing if the case is lost.

In my view, the essence of the contingency fee is that it represents a kind
of litigation insurance . . .

The crucial point with both conditional and percentage contingency fee
arrangements is that successful clients will pay their lawyers more that they
would under alternative fee arrangements, while unsuccessful clients pay
their lawyers nothing. In effect, then, the lawyer — like an insurance
company — subsidizes unsuccessful litigants out of premium revenues
collected from successful clients. The extra emoluments paid by successful
litigants amount to insurance premiums, insuring them against the possibility
of failure. The contingency fee is at bottom a risk-spreading device . . .
[T]here is no question of the legal system imposing mandatory insurance on
consumers who may prefer to take their chances on lower-priced but
uninsured commodities. Nobody is proposing mandatory contingency fees;
rather, the current prohibition on contingency fees takes the opposite tack,
forbidding willing consumers from purchasing litigation insurance which may
represent the only alternative safe enough to permit them to enforce their
legal rights.

Viewing contingency fees as a form of litigation insurance can help to
determine what type and magnitude of contingency fee is fair . . .

Marc Galanter . . . demonstrated — in one of the most oft-cited papers in
the American literature on litigation — a systematic structural imbalance in
litigation, favouring repeat players (such as insurance companies or governmental agencies) over one-shot players (such as accident victims). Repeat
players enjoy numerous advantages, including (1) a superior understanding of
enforcement practices allowing them to concentrate resources on the subset
of adjudicatory decisions that really matter; (2) various economies of scale;
(3) superior resources that permit the repeat player to tolerate lengthy delays,
as compared with one-shotters who may often need money quickly and
therefore be compelled to accept lower settlement than the merits of their
cases warrant; and (4) the all-important ability to play the odds in a
risk-neutral fashion, whereas one-shotters are typically compelled to be
highly risk-adverse.

This latter point in particular confers a potent bargaining endowment on
the repeat player, allowing him or her to bargain hard against a one-shot
plaintiff who simply cannot risk losing everything by holding out for a fairer
settlement. (Recall that insurers make a substantial number of strategically
low offers.) It is here that the contingency fee can play an important role in
evening the balance in bargaining. As Gross and Syverud explain:

'[contingency fee] attorneys — unlike plaintiffs — are likely to be
(comparatively) risk neutral with respect to such costs, both because they
have greater resources and because they are repeat players. They can afford
to finance their clients' cases, and they can gamble on the chance of
winning an occasional big judgment even if in the process they have to
invest in several losing trials. The position of the plaintiffs' attorneys limits

the strategic bargaining power of the defendants personal injury cases, and restores some balance to pretrial negotiations . . .

The American legal profession is highly stratified, so much so that it is something of a deception to refer to it as a single profession. A partner in a major Wall Street law firm, practising company law and earning over one million dollars a year, has very little in common with a personal injury lawyer practising out of a suburban shopping-mall office in an ethnic neighbourhood. In the United States, where law schools are stratified in a rather rigid pecking order, the class and status differences between these two lawyers will usually manifest itself in the fact that the Wall Street partner will have graduated from Harvard or Yale or Columbia, while the suburban personal injury lawyer will have graduated from a relatively undistinguished state or local law school . . .

These differences in turn reflect differences in class origin (as indicated, for example, by the occupation and ethnicity of a lawyer's parents). In the United States, the contingency fee is used almost exclusively in tort actions, by plaintiffs of limited resources, and frequently in personal injury cases. There is thus a rough correlation between the contingency fee and the social class of lawyers: contingency fee lawyers come from more modest and marginal class origins than their uptown brethren . . .

By permitting lawyers to offer clients of modest means an otherwise unavailable service, the contingency fee not only improves access to the law for non-elite clients, it also creates new markets for legal services and thereby improves access to the legal profession for non-elite lawyers. The two egalitarian arguments for the contingency fee — enhancing access to lawyers for non-elite clients and enhancing access to clients for non-elite lawyers (thereby opening up the Bar) represent two sides of the same coin. Both strike me as considerations of profound significance to increasingly multicultural and multi-ethnic countries . . .

Questions:
1.   Which of these competing evaluations of contingency fees do you find most persuasive and why?

2.   To what extent do you think conditional fees will improve access to legal services? Is the government now in effect proposing mandatory contingency fees?

3.   Are such innovations in legal services likely to prove both more efficient, and also guarantee a better quality of service? Are these two ideals reconcilable? Will the accountability of the legal profession improve as a result of the introduction of franchising and conditional fee arrangements as the government suggests?

4.   Is it a good argument in favour of contingency fees that they create additional markets for non-elite lawyers as Luban suggests?

As noted at the beginning of the White Paper the Government took the view that it was crucial to address the issue of legal costs in the context of access to justice. Following a review chaired by Sir Peter Middleton the Government endorsed most of the key recommendations contained in Lord Woolf's Final Report on *Access to Justice* (London, HMSO, 1996). The full report is available on the following website: www.law.warwick.ac.uk/Woolf/report/html. The following extract from the White Paper summarises the key aspects of that report which are relevant to securing access to justice:

Modernising Justice: The Government's plans for reforming legal services and the courts, op.cit.

4.   The Civil Courts

4.1   This chapter describes the Government's comprehensive programme to reform the jurisdiction and procedures of the civil and family courts. These reforms are designed to eliminate unnecessary cost, delay and complexity; and to ensure that cases are dealt with at a cost that is proportionate to the value and importance of the issue at stake . . .

4.3   The key elements of the reform package are:
- **a unified code of procedural rules**, written in plain English, to replace the existing separate sets of High Court and county court rules. The overriding objective of the new Rules is to enable the courts to deal with cases justly. This includes the court taking a more active case management role than now, to ensure that cases are dealt with in a way which is proportionate to their value, complexity and importance.
- pre-action protocols setting standards and timetables for the conduct of cases before court proceedings are started. These will require more exchange of information and fuller investigation of claims at an earlier stage. People will therefore be in a better position to make a realistic assessment of the merits of a case far earlier than now. This will encourage them to settle disputes without recourse to litigation. Where litigation is unavoidable, cases coming before the court will be better prepared than now. Judges will be expected to apply the protocols strictly, and impose sanctions on those breaching them.
- **a system of 3 tracks** to which disputed claims will be assigned by a judge. These are:
  - the **small claims** procedure, which enables people to pursue small, straightforward claims themselves, without fear of incurring large legal bills. Cases are dealt with at an informal hearing before a district judge. The district judge can award certain limited costs only. At present, this procedure generally applies to claims worth less than £3,000, except for personal injury cases where the limit is £1,000. The Government intends to raise the £3,000 limit to £5,000, but retain the £1,000 limit for personal injury cases; reduce the limit to

£1,000 for housing disrepair cases; and exclude unlawful eviction and harassment cases from the small claims procedure altogether.

- a **fast track** for claims between the relevant small claims limit and £15,000. These cases will be subject to a fixed timetable, which will usually require a hearing within 30 weeks of allocation to the fast track. The court will monitor the progress of each case to ensure that the parties adhere to the timetable. At the trial the amount of oral evidence will be strictly limited. Paragraphs 2.36–41 explained our proposals for developing a system for controlling legal costs, especially in fast track cases.

- a **multi-track** for cases worth over £15,000 or lower value claims of unusual complexity. This track will offer a higher level of judicial intervention, tailored to the specific features of each dispute. The legal work conducted by both sides will be directed and controlled by a judge, who will monitor the procedures adopted, and the costs incurred, to ensure that they are proportionate to the value and complexity of the claim.

4.4   The judges will have a key role in ensuring that the new procedures deliver the objectives of reducing cost, delay and complexity. The judges will manage cases to ensure that litigants and their representatives keep to the timetable, and will be able to penalise unnecessary work . . .

4.6   As part of the reform programme, the court services are introducing new information technology to support the work of judges and staff in the civil courts . . .

Appeal in civil cases
4.17   The Government's guiding principles are that someone who wishes to appeal should be required to show reasonable grounds; and that, in normal circumstances, more than one appeal cannot be justified. In a well-functioning justice system, the emphasis should be on assuming that the court of first instance has reached the right decision; so there should not be an automatic right to appeal. But the parties to a case should have the right to ask a higher court to determine whether or not there are grounds for an appeal to proceed. Excluding groundless appeals will increase the time available for hearing meritorious ones, and so reduce delay.

Questions:
1.   Why do you think the Woolf proposals have been broadly accepted by two governments of different political complexions?

2. Do you agree with Lord Woolf that it was necessary to change the landscape of civil litigation? If so, why?

3. Do you think that three hours in court is an adequate period of time to allocate for most cases? Is it a good idea to stop expert witnesses from giving oral evidence in court?

4. Why do you think the Woolf report was so keen on encouraging alternative dispute resolution as opposed to litigation? (See also Chapter 5)

Notwithstanding the broad welcome given to the Woolf proposals, some criticisms have been made. (These apply to Chapter 4 of *Modernising Justice*.) The most vociferous critic of the Woolf Report has been Professor Michael Zander:

M Zander, 'The Woolf Report: Forwards or Backwards for the New Lord Chancellor?', *Civil Justice Quarterly* (1997), vol. 16, pp. 208–227, at pp. 208–211, 213–18, 221, 223 (footnotes omitted).

[I]mplementation of the Woolf project appears to have almost universal support including, so far as one can tell, that of the senior judiciary, the Bar Council and the Law Society as well as both the lay and the legal press.

Nevertheless, my intention here is to present the case for second thoughts even at this 59th minute of the 11th hour. My thesis is that implementation of Woolf will disrupt valuable elements of our traditional system, that the hoped-for compensating benefits will not materialise and that implementation will actually make things worse rather than better. I take the view that the widespread belief in those hoped-for benefits is based mainly on wish fulfilment.

I do not think it will be easy to get many to listen. My experience of the debate over the past two or so years is that the feeling that 'something must be done' about what is understandably thought to be a serious problem is so strong that there seems to be remarkably little interest in awkward facts and analysis that suggest that this emperor is wearing no clothes.

The basic thesis of Lord Woolf's Report was set out at the beginning of the Interim Report:

'The key problems facing civil justice today are cost, delay and complexity.' (p. 7, para. 1)

There is no agreement as to what constitutes undue cost, undue delay or undue complexity, but I will assume that we are agreed that cost, delay and complexity of litigation are real and serious problems with which it is important to grapple and that solutions should, if possible, be found. Lord Woolf said that:

'[T]he three are interrelated and stem from the uncontrolled nature of the litigation process. In particular, there is no clear judicial responsibility for managing individual cases or for the overall administration of the civil courts.' (*ibid.*)

The solution suggested was judicial case management:

'I believe there is now no alternative to a fundamental shift in the responsibility for the management of civil litigation from litigants and their legal advisers to the courts.' (*ibid.*, p. 18, para. 2)

Lord Woolf made it clear that he seeks a fundamental change in our legal culture:

'A change of this nature will involve not only a change in the way that cases are progressed within the system. It will require a radical change of culture for all concerned.' (*ibid.*, para. 4)

The Interim Report said:

'By tradition the conduct of civil litigation in England and Wales, as in other common law jurisdictions is adversarial . . . [T]he main responsibility for the initiation and conduct of proceedings rests with the parties to each individual case.' (*ibid.*, p. 7, para. 3)

But without effective judicial control, it went on:

'. . . the adversarial process is likely to encourage an adversarial culture and degenerate into an environment in which the litigation process is too often seen as a battlefield where no rules apply.' (*ibid.*, para.4)

The consequence was that 'expense is often excessive, disproportionate and unpredictable; and delay is frequently unreasonable'. This arose because 'the conduct, pace and extent of litigation are left almost exclusively to the parties' and that there 'is no effective control of their worst excesses' (*ibid.*, para. 5). Thus for instance, in regard to delay, Lord Woolf opined that:

'In the majority of cases the reasons for delay arise from failure [by the lawyers] to progress the case efficiently, wasting time on peripheral issues or procedural skirmishing to wear down an opponent or to excuse failure to get on with the case'. (*ibid.*, p. 13, para. 36).

The conclusion was that the excesses of the adversarial system in the operation of the civil justice system were so great that only a transfer of control to the judges could put matters right. There was no alternative . . .

If, as Lord Woolf suggests, undue delay in civil litigation is common and, the prime cause of delay in the system is the way the lawyers operate the adversary system, then attempts to tackle that problem by wholesale reform are at least understandable. If, however, as Cantley suggested [Report of the

Personal Injuries Litigation Procedure Working Party, Cmnd 7476 (1979), chaired by Cantley J], the way the lawyers operate the system is a very minor aspect of undue delay, wholesale reform can obviously do little to deal with the problem — which may, moreover, not be such a great problem anyway . . .

Neither Lord Woolf nor Heilbron-Hodge [an independent Working Party set up in 1992 jointly by the General Council of the Bar and the Law Society] conducted research on the matter. For what it is worth I incline to the view taken by the Cantley Committee. But the fact is that we have no solid basis for any statement about the proportion of cases in which there is undue delay nor do we have much knowledge of the reasons for the delay.

In the absence of hard evidence it behoves those who make reform proposals to be very careful about their analysis of the problems and their recommendations. The more radical the proposals, the greater the need for care. To base radical reform proposals, as Lord Woolf did, largely on unsubstantiated opinions is a recipe for getting things radically wrong . . .

The second reason for believing Lord Woolf's approach to be fundamentally misconceived is that it inevitably leads to the application of wholly disproportionate sanctions. Recognising the truth that it is difficult to get lawyers to keep to procedural time-limits, Lord Woolf (like Heilbron-Hodge before him) urges the need for extraordinary sanctions. In the passage just cited, the appropriate sanction, it is said, should normally be 'automatic' . . .

The philosophy is misconceived, thirdly, because it is based, I believe, on a fundamentally wrong-headed view of the nature of procedural rules. Sir Jack Jacob, truly a master of civil procedure, and wiser in these matter than any of us, said this of procedural rules and sanctions in his Note of Reservation to the Report of the Winn Committee [Report of the Committee on Personal Injuries Litigation, Cmnd 3691 (1968)]:

'The admonition by Lord Justice Bowen that "courts do not exist for the sake of discipline" should be reflected in the principle that rules of court should not be framed on the basis of imposing penalties or producing automatic consequences for non-compliance with the rules or orders of the court. The function of rules of court is to provide guide-lines not trip wires and they fulfil their function most where they intrude least in the course of litigation.'

The edifice based on a series of elaborately time-tabled procedural steps by sanctions for non-compliance which is central to Lord Woolf's scheme is founded on sand and is doomed to go the way of all sand-castles. Even if insistence on compliance leads to the imposition of inappropriately Draconian penalties, the sanctions do not work. Non-compliance goes on anyway. Sooner or later that policy breaks down. Breaches of the rules are condoned, at which point the threat of the sanction evaporates . . .

The attempt to strictly enforce procedural time-limits sounds sensible and even laudable, but in practice it is unworkable and therefore ultimately creates more problems than it solves.

Let me now turn to Lord Woolf's chief substantive proposal, that judges should take over from the lawyers responsibility for the progressing of cases — what is known as judicial case management (or sometimes, differential case management). The idea that judicial case management is the answer to the twin evils of cost and delay in civil litigation has in recent years taken hold not just here, but in other common law countries including in particular Australia, Canada and above all the United States . . .

The proposal that we should go over to judicial case management raises many different issues and problems. Let me mention a few:

(1)   English judges have not previously engaged in case management of the kind contemplated here. This therefore is a new skill to be learned. But it is much more than a skill. It is a whole philosophy without which there will not be the radical change of culture called for by Lord Woolf. Profound changes of culture are extremely difficult to achieve and changes of legal culture perhaps especially so. Reform attempts based on a call for a fundamental change of culture are apt to fail. Notwithstanding lip service paid to the Woolf reforms (sometimes one suspects out of political correctness), not all judges will want to learn . . .

(2)   Quite apart from varying attitudes, judges will also vary in their aptitude for case management. Thus, for instance, some will use their new I.T. equipment effectively; others will not.

(3)   In the United States, each trial judge has a docket of cases allocated to him and he is personally responsible, and accountable, for progress in those cases. In this country the judge does not have a docket and even Lord Woolf does not propose it. Instead he suggests that cases should be assigned to teams of judges. It would be very surprising if those worked efficiently.

(4)   Case management means, by definition, a vast increase in judicial discretion. Over and over again in the Woolf Report one reads, 'the judge will decide', 'the judge will direct', 'the judge will have a discretion', 'the judge will have the power to . . .'.

In some contexts, such as sentencing, judicial discretion is inevitable and even, on balance, and within limits, desirable. In others, it is less desirable. Discretionary power in regard to the progressing of civil cases is, I would say, in the category of less desirable. Case management decisions will often be of great importance. I do not regard it as an improvement in the system if similar procedural issues are routinely decided by different judges in different ways.

Lord Woolf admits that inconsistency in the application of judicial discretion in case management needs to be addressed. The answer he suggests is training. But how can training touch this problem? The discretion is the discretion to judge . . .

(5)   The proposal that the judge should be in charge of the progress of all cases is based on the belief that the judge knows better than the lawyers what is in the best interests of the case. In my view, this proposition is

questionable. The lawyers know their clients; they live with the case. The judge comes into it briefly and inevitably with less knowledge. For every case where now the lawyers drag it out unnecessarily, there will I fear be many where the judge through misjudgment makes case management decisions which are inappropriate.

(6)   Case management involves many additional functions for the courts which will have to be performed — some by judges, some by court clerks . . . I regard it as exceedingly improbable that the Lord Chancellor will get the money from the Treasury for the additional person power required . . .

(7)   Whether or not the necessary number of new judges are appointed, many of the proposed new judicial functions are absolutely certain greatly to increase delays and costs in the system — the opposite of what Lord Woolf intends. Let me give just a couple of examples. Lord Woolf proposes that in all cases where there is a defence, both on the Fast Track and on the Multi-Track, the court should vet the pleadings to see whether they conform to the new principle that where the facts are disputed there should be clear statements of case by both claimant and defendant . . .

Or take Lord Woolf's proposal that at the end of a case the judge should allocate costs on the basis of whether the parties have comported themselves reasonably or unreasonably not only during the litigation but even in the pre-action stage. The amount of time that would be absorbed by such an enquiry would obviously be very great . . .

(8)   If judicial management will tend to increase rather than reduce cost, will it at least reduce delay? The answer is that it may. The RAND study [the product of US research published in 1997] tells us that early case management can cut time to disposition. It also reports that the most effective device to achieve that result is the simple one of giving the parties a trial date from a very early stage and then adhering to that date, as Lord Woolf proposed. RAND also reports that having the lay client present at settlement conference speeds disposition — another Woolf proposal. The Australian data also suggest that delay can be cut by case management — though the effect may only be temporary.

But then the question arises by how much could delay be cut and what would be lost in the process? . . .

(9)   This leads to what ought to be our main focus — justice for the litigant. An earlier study by RAND found that, contrary to what one might think, litigants are not primarily concerned about cost and delay. What they are primarily concerned about is a fair process. One aspect of a sense of fair process is having one's day in court, feeling that one has been able to present one's story. Lord Woolf's Fast Track abbreviated procedure is consciously designed to inhibit the client's opportunities to tell his story. Thus, in particular, the evidence at trial is generally to be restricted to three hours for both sides together and experts will not be allowed to testify orally at all. This may make sense in terms of economy but for the litigants, perhaps the litigants on both sides, it may provoke a sense of frustration. Claims

involving sums of £3,000 to £10,000 may seem like relatively small beer for practising lawyers and judges — justifying somewhat summary procedures. But £3,000 to £10,000 is not small beer for most ordinary citizens and I am not sure that they will appreciate being fobbed off with what is bound to be thought of as a restricted, second-class service — neither cheap nor cheerful.

I am therefore concerned that Lord Woolf's Fast Track may turn out to be more of a minus than a plus. A rushed pre-trial stage is to culminate in a rushed trial. I am sceptical as to whether litigants will regard that as better or even adequate justice. The same issue will occur equally in Multi-Track cases when the court's case management decisions appear unreasonable to the litigants.

Questions:
1. Do you agree with Professor Zander about the difficulty of changing cultures, and particularly legal cultures? Is this a sufficiently compelling reason not to try?

2. Is Zander unduly pessimistic about the skills and abilities of judges?

3. In practice do you think that implementation of the Woolf proposals will really increase the amount of discretion which judges wield? (See M Zander, 'The Govenment's Plans on Civil Justice', *Modern Law Review* (1998) vol. 61 pp. 382.)

The following extract contains Lord Woolf's response to Professor Zander's criticisms:

The Rt. Hon. Lord Woolf MR, 'Medics, Lawyers and the Courts', *Civil Justice Quarterly* (1997) vol. 16, pp. 302–317, at pp. 302, 307–11.

In this lecture I intend to say something about the recommendations I have made and about criticisms that have been made about some of them, notably by Professor Michael Zander . . .
    If you heard [Professor Zander's] lecture you would no doubt be impressed by his eloquence but you should not have been impressed by the content. It was not based on any relevant practical experience. He is a distinguished academic and contributions from academics can be important. However he has not suggested that the views that he holds are based on any research which he has conducted himself into the workings of the civil courts in recent time.
    By contrast, although I of course accept that this does not mean that my recommendations have any validity, they were produced after an intense two year consultation process conducted with the assistance of assessors with a wide ranging experience of the subject with which my report deals. I was also helped by expert working parties of highly experienced practitioners and academic consultants of distinction whose findings supported my conclusions.

Those findings were that the civil justice system has become excessively adversarial, slow, complex and expensive and that this is especially true of litigation over alleged medical negligence in the delivery of health care whether by doctors, nurses or other health carers. For example, there are five respects in which medical negligence actions conspicuously failed to meet the needs of litigants:

1. The relationship between the costs of the litigation and the amount involved was particularly disproportionate. The costs were peculiarly excessive, especially in low value cases.
2. Delay; the period which regularly elapsed before claims are resolved is more often unacceptable in the case of medical negligence claims than other classes of proceedings.
3. Unmeritorious cases are pursued and clear-cut claims defended for longer than happened in other areas of litigation.
4. The success rate is also lower than in other personal injury litigation.
5. Finally the lack of co-operation between the parties to the litigation and the mutual suspicion as to the motives of the opposing party is frequently more intense than in other classes of litigation . . .

I was convinced that a way had to be found for breaking down the barriers which divided the patient from his carers so that wherever possible litigation could be avoided. This could only help everyone involved. It would save on costs. It could result in those patients who deserve to be compensated receiving proportionate compensation voluntarily, and in an atmosphere which did not poison relations between the patients and those who had been treating them. Often, where things have gone wrong the need for treatment is at its greatest and the breakdown results in the professional feeling frustrated in not being able to provide that treatment.

The opposition of Professor Zander to my recommendations is based on his unwillingness to accept that the civil justice system has these serious faults. Faults that I and virtually all commentators are agreed the system suffers from, and his unwillingness to accept that, if the faults do exist, my recommendations will improve the situation. Let me therefore deal with these points in turn . . .

Professor Zander . . . suggests that I am being 'Canute like' and defying reality in suggesting something can and should be done about this instead of recognising that 'the enterprise is hopeless'. He also categorises the failures of lawyers in this area as 'minor failures' . . .

However, I certainly dissent from his conclusion as to what should be the response. Professor Zander suggests we should accept and I quote:

'there is really nothing that can be done about the problem other than the application of sanctions that are ridiculously out of proportion to the offence, a policy which, sooner or later has to be abandoned because it is manifestly unjust' . . .

What then should be done? First, the lesson should be learnt that there will be a substantial number of the cases, in which contrary to Professor Zander's views, if the lawyers for the Plaintiffs are left to their own devices they will delay taking even the most elementary steps in the interests of their clients.

Secondly, it must be accepted that in the interests of justice, as no one else can take the responsibility, the court must take the responsibility for seeing this does not happen.

Thirdly, it must be recognised that the solution is not to impose Draconian sanctions except as a last resort but to achieve a situation where sanctions of this sort are not necessary because (a) the court does not allow the situation to deteriorate to the extent that they become necessary, and (b) the court has the wider range of alternative sanctions I propose. Unfortunately this will only be possible when the technology I have recommended is in place . . .

Professor Zander's criticism to date as far as I am aware is only as to two important elements of the package of reforms that have been recommended. They are the related subjects of the fast track and case management. However, the merits of those two recommendations can only be appreciated in the context of the recommendations as a whole. Among the most important of these recommendations are the reorganisation of the civil courts, the creation of a single Rule Committee for the civil justice system as a whole and the creation of the Civil Justice Council and the greater involvement of litigants in their own litigation. These recommendations are intended to provide the structure in which a radically reformed system can operate and to then enable that system to be kept under review.

Among the more specific recommendations are those as to protocols and expert evidence in the case of both of which my recommendations are designed to establish an agreed best practice.

The protocols are a wholly novel concept designed:

1.   to focus the attention of litigants on the desirability of resolving disputes without litigation;
2.   to enable them to obtain the information they need to settle the action or to make an offer to settle; and
3.   if settlement is not possible to enable the ground to be prepared for the action to proceed expeditiously . . .

Questions:
1.   Is it fair of Lord Woolf to criticise Professor Zander's proposals on the grounds that his academic opinions are not based on 'any relevant practical experience'?

2.   Should Lord Woolf have paid more attention to relevant experience in the United States, Australia and elsewhere, as Professor Zander suggests? (See BC Cairns 'Lord Woolf's Report on Access to Justice: an Australian Perspective', *Civil Justice Quarters* (1997) vol. 16. pp. 98–301.)

To date, less attention has been devoted to the Government's plans for reforming Criminal Legal Aid, which involve the establishment of a new Criminal Defence Service, comprised of state-approved lawyers:

Modernising Justice: The Government's plans for reforming legal services and the courts, op.cit.

5. Criminal Justice

5.2   ... [W]e are embarking on a comprehensive programme for modernising the criminal justice system, and ensuring it is planned and managed in a more coherent and co-ordinated way... [It includes] plans to reduce delay in criminal cases, and modernise the structure and organisation of Magistrates' Courts Service, and the way in which the Crown Court works . . .

6. Criminal Defence Service

6.1   ... For a criminal justice system to be fair, as well as efficient, people accused of crimes must receive appropriate legal representation, and a robust and competent defence, when the interests of justice require it . . . [T]he Government will ensure this, by setting up a new Criminal Defence Service to replace the current criminal legal aid system . . .

Fundamental reform
6.10   The Government intends to replace the existing criminal legal aid scheme with a new Criminal Defence Service (CDS). The CDS will be a separate scheme from the Community Legal Service (CLS) described in Chapters 2 and 3, and its budget will not form part of the Community Legal Service fund. Separating the two schemes in this way reflects the fact that they are responsible for providing different types of service in very different types of case; and that each scheme has its own distinct objectives and priorities. For this reason, there may be advantages in the longer term in establishing two completely separate and clearly-focused bodies to administer the two schemes. For the foreseeable future, however, both the CDS and the CLS will be run by the Legal Services Commission (paragraph 2.11). This will ensure a smooth transition from the old legal aid scheme, and make the best use of the existing expertise and infrastructure of the Legal Aid Board.

6.11   The new CDS scheme will cover all the main services currently provided by criminal legal aid, including representation in court when this is in the interests of justice, and advice and assistance for suspects being questioned by the police. Change will focus on securing better quality and value for money, by developing more efficient ways of procuring services — contracting and directly employed by lawyers — and by streamlining the arrangements for granting representation.

Contracting

6.12 In future, most publicly-funded criminal defence services will be provided by lawyers in private practice under contracts . . . Contracts can be designed to include the quality standards and financial incentives that best suit the type of case concerned.

6.13 Wherever possible, contract prices should be fixed in advance. Fixed prices create an incentive to keep delay to a minimum. They reward efficient practitioners, and allow quick and certain payment.

6.14 So far as possible, contracts with solicitors' firms should cover the full range of criminal defence services, from advice at the police station, to representation in the magistrates' courts and, if necessary, the Crown Court. This will eliminate the fragmentation that bedevils the current scheme . . .

6.15 Very expensive cases — those where the trial is expected to last 25 days or more — will fall outside the scope of contracts designed to cover ordinary cases. Instead, a separate contract will be negotiated for each individual case. A defendant's choice of solicitor will be restricted to firms on a specialist panel. The firm selected by the defendant will be expected to negotiate prices for discrete stages of the with the CDS, on the basis of a plan for managing the case . . . If the CDS and the chosen firm cannot agree on acceptable terms, the defendant may be required to choose a different firm from the panel. This approach will enable the CDS to negotiate contracts that keep a tight rein on the cost of potentially long, complex and expensive criminal cases; rather than handing over a blank cheque, as the current legal aid arrangements effectively do . . .

Salaried defenders

6.18 The Government believes that, in addition to contracting for the services of lawyers in private practice, the CDS should be able to employ lawyers directly as salaried defenders. Evidence from other countries suggests that properly funded salaried defenders can be more cost-effective and provide a better service than lawyers in private practice . . .

6.19 The Government believes that, in the longer term, the best approach will prove to be a mixed system, combining both private and staff lawyers. This will produce better value for money for the taxpayer; because the two systems will, in effect, both complement and compete against one another. The cost of the salaried service will provide a benchmark, which the CDS can use to assess whether the prices charged by private lawyers are reasonable. Staff lawyers will also give the CDS flexibility to fill gaps in the system, for example where too few local solicitors' firms and barristers' chambers participate . . .

6.22   In order to maintain an element of choice, the government intends to ensure that most firms which undertake a significant amount of criminal work and which meet quality standards, remain part of the CDS scheme. At the same time, in order to secure better value for taxpayer's money, firms should have to compete for work under the scheme . . .

Granting representation and defendants' costs
6.25   Under the new scheme, the courts will, as now, be responsible for deciding whether a defendant should be represented at public expense.

6.27   . . . [W]e intend to replace the existing system with a new, better-targeted one . . . In future, a judge in the Crown Court will be able to order a convicted defendant to pay some or all of the costs of his or her defence. Sometimes it will have emerged before or during the trial that the defendant, perhaps a fraudster or drug trafficker; has substantial assets. The judge will then be able to make an order when passing sentence. In other cases, the judge will be able to ask the CDS to investigate the defendant's means, and make an order later. Leaving this decision to the end of the case will stop time being wasted on means-testing defendants whose contributions are later returned when they are acquitted. But some rich criminals will pay much more than now, because costs orders will be able to take account of assets that were frozen, or only came to light, during the case . . .

Questions:
1.   As the White Paper acknowledged (para 6.20), the Government's proposals in relation to criminal cases entail restrictions on the unfettered choice of lawyer. Is this justifiable or desirable?

2.   Do you think that expenditure of £733m on Criminal Legal Aid in 1997–8 is the real driving force behind these proposed reforms?

3.   Will the element of competition to win contracts to do state-funded criminal defence work act as a disincentive to take on controversial cases, such as those involving miscarriages of justice?

The issue of nationalising legal services provoked a lively debate throughout the 1970s. In the present political climate it would seem that, quite apart from ideological objections, a nationalised legal service is a non-starter for purely practical and financial reasons. In July 1998, as Chair of the Campaign for a National Legal Service backbench Labour MP Austen Mitchell unsuccessfully introduced a private members' Bill, with the aim of introducing a salaried legal service. The Campaign argues that legal aid through private practice has failed and a salaried legal service with a fixed budget should be introduced in direct competition with private legal firms. A less radical alternative to a nationalised service was the introduction of law centres:

K Marcus, 'The Politics of Legal Aid', in I Grigg–Spall and P Ireland (eds), *The Critical Lawyers' Handbook*, London, Pluto (1992), pp. 187–189.

In the last 20 years and more, a wide variety of methods of work has been developed by law centres. Since the first law centre in 1970, they have sprung up in many, mainly inner-city, areas of the country, initiated by local community activists and lawyers as a result of perceived local needs for adequate legal services which private practice was failing to meet. Law centres have become popular and much in demand.

Despite the diverse nature of their services, there are common threads running through all law centres:

1.   Their services are usually free, thus overcoming many of the problems associated with the means-testing of legal aid or the Law Society charge.

2.   Law centres are run by locally elected management committees, which employ the staff of the centres. The management committee decides on the centre's policies and priorities, ensuring that as far as possible each centre responds to local demands and is accountable to their users.

3.   The traditional hierarchical structures of solicitors' offices serve to deny access to lawyers. Law centres have, in various ways, found alternative structures.

4.   Law centres do not employ lawyers alone. Because of the wide range of services they offer, and their innovative methods of working, they rely on diverse resources. Apart from the lawyers, there are specialists in various aspects of community work, and those with expertise ranging from local government administration to trade unionism, education and housing. Many centres offer a range of languages appropriate to their locality.

5.   There are no predetermined limits on their work (other than professional limits) so law centres can work creatively and innovatively in a wide range of issues thus exposing need that would not otherwise be apparent. It was mainly through law centres' prioritising immigration and nationality case-work that that area became one of growth and resulted in the establishment of local agencies around the country providing specialist immigration and nationality advice and representation services.

6.   They aim to direct their resources to best effect, providing the most needed and popular service for the community in which they operate. This often involves determining priorities and setting criteria by which work is or is not undertaken.

7.   Law centres encourage self-help, and aim to provide people with sufficient information to deal themselves with actual or potential legal problems without unnecessary dependence on lawyers. They produce leaflets, posters and other publications that are easy to understand and often in languages other than English. They give talks, explaining to people what their rights are and how they can enforce or defend them. They work with local groups and organisations, providing them with the necessary information and support so they can put forward their own views and demands to their local authority, employer or landlord.

8. They deliberately set out to attract and encourage users who would not normally approach lawyers in private practice. Generally they are in shop-front, high-street premises or other offices designed to attract such people. However, the more important aspect of the law centre approach is the way in which they target the working-class, disadvantaged or vulnerable people in their areas, providing them with information and encouraging them to exercise their rights. The centres will often have to make a commitment to give quite long-term support to growing organisations and campaigns to achieve this.

9. Law centres have also found that needs for legal services are often concealed and need to be deliberately searched out. So in an area with no agency providing advice on schools and education, very few problems of that nature will come to the attention of local lawyers. Parents, teachers and pupils become more frustrated with the inadequacies of the local education scheme and respond in a haphazard and individualistic way — for instance, parents may remove their children from the school, which in turn results in further degeneration of the abandoned schools. However, the provision of specialist advice on education issues will result in a growth of awareness of the real problems and possible means of tackling them. In many areas where law centres have recently begun to provide such advice, parents have organised themselves for the first time into effective groups which make unique and valuable contributions to the development of their local education systems.

10. The function of law centres is therefore very different to that of Citizens' Advice Bureaux and other generalist advice agencies, which tend to offer an open door to all requiring advice and operate on an individual case-by-case level. Law centres have developed close working relationships with these other agencies at a local level, referring cases to each other, often jointly identifying and tackling issues, and pressing for further advice and legal services in areas of still unmet need.

Questions:
1. Do you think that the Community Legal Service which the Lord Chancellor proposes to develop will revitalise the law centre movement.

2. Can you think of any alternative means of providing legal services for those currently not receiving them?

3. Are such alternative proposals more efficient than the present legal aid schemes?

So far we have focused on the idea of 'bringing law to the poor' or providing financial aid to middle income persons. However, for a totally different perspective consider the following analysis from a self-proclaimed Marxist standpoint:

Z Bankowski and G Mungham, *Images of Law*, London, Routledge & Kegan Paul (1976), pp. 68–70.

In this final section we examine this notion of 'bringing law to the people'. What does that mean? What ideologies underpin it? In the last few years we have seen the emergence of community law centres, duty solicitor schemes and the like. These developments are being accompanied by changes in the education and training programmes of many law students — where the current vogue is for 'clinical legal education'. Indeed, so widespread is the enthusiasm for innovations of this particular kind that we can talk in terms of a minor social movement in some quarters of the legal profession designed to expand these new services even further, even faster. For the supporters of these innovations the problem is the small effect the law has on people's lives; the task is seen as one of legitimating law and authority by making communication and access to the law easier and by granting people a greater measure of participation in the law making process. The question as to whether people should have control is never asked because it is already assumed that this can never be — there must always be law-givers on the one hand, and law-breakers on the other.

By this light, law is still seen as a benevolent institution to which people might have greater or lesser access, but ultimately no control. The indifference that people have to the law is interpreted as showing lack of publicity, the force of other social norms, bad law, etc. — but it is never taken as an attack on domination and as an attempt by people to run their own lives. It is assumed that law dominates and, if it does, the problem is seen as one of how to ameliorate the situation by providing greater access and participation in order to make the domination 'fairer'.

The duty solicitor scheme is, we think, a good example of how attempts to 'bring law and lawyers to the people' has the effect of increasing the domination of law over people's lives. As we showed, many local solicitors saw the scheme as a good way of 'helping' people. Part of their concern was increasing people's knowledge of available legal services. But this highly partial notion of 'sharing' is only aimed at securing a better distribution of existing knowledge. No interest is shown, or credence given, to any attempt people might make to construct different kinds of knowledge — and through this, different ways of acting upon the world. The obsession is with 'spreading law around', pushing it into the furthest corners of hearth and home. This taking of law to the people is finally justified in terms of the importance of defining and meeting 'needs'; 'needs', that is, that only the professional can meet. In this way, 'satisfying needs' becomes linked with an extension and consolidation of professional control. Seen another way, the end result of the ideology and practice of 'helping' is merely to confirm again the supremacy and domination of law'

The idea of 'help' in this context is only help in choosing a lawyer. As one solicitor observed:

'The choice is effectively that of a solicitor who has represented you before, or the duty solicitor — the man in front of you. But you don't get any other alternatives'.

If we return to the notion of 'choice' in the context of legal representation, it should be clear that one kind of choice is altogether absent, and neither is it encouraged, namely, the freedom of the defendant to represent himself, either alone, or with the help of a friend.

Question:
1. For Bankowski and Mungham the legal profession helps people to have access to the law only to reinforce its own domination and control, whereas extra-legal self-help methods may more effectively solve a person's problem. Would you agree?

For Philip Lewis the crucial issue is the process whereby problems come to be defined as *legal* problems.

P Lewis, 'Unmet Legal Needs', in P Morris, R White and P Lewis, *Social Needs and Legal Action,* London, Martin Robertson (1973), pp. 78–79, 87–88.

> People often speak as if to say that someone has a legal problem is to make a statement of fact about his situation; once one has appreciated that situation, one can realise that it falls within the class of situations which raise a legal problem, and any lawyer can say what situations are contained in that class, just as he can say what the statute book has to say on some given point. A closely related way of speaking is to treat the judgment that someone has a legal problem as a judgment which is typically a clear one, admitting of no doubt; people either do or do not have a legal problem. It is this clarity which makes it possible to come to the judgment that people with a legal problem 'need' a lawyer, just as no-one would suppose that an engineering problem could be solved by anyone else than an engineer . . .
>
> It seems likely then that when someone says that a person has a legal problem or says that a particular problem under discussion is a legal one he is offering a suggestion about the action that the person should take or the method which should be adopted to solve the problem. The typical suggestion is that action should be taken before some court or similar institution or that the services of a lawyer should be employed. Very broadly, the point I should like to make in this paper is that if certain problems are spoken of as legal ones and official support is given to legal methods of solving them, that is to take a particular attitude to problems of that kind, problems which may be capable of solution in some other way, and which may be seen by those most closely concerned as best solved in that other way. For instance, if a tenant in a flat has a leaking roof he may be regarded as having a legal problem; does his lease provide that the landlord should do the repairs, and is the mechanism of the courts adequate to ensure quick action? But he may choose to get a ladder and not a lawyer, and we can argue whether it is better that people should be made to fulfil their legal duties or that they should be encouraged to take practical steps to avoid material damage regardless of their legal responsibilities . . .
>
> To look at a problem as a legal one is particularly appropriate in this country if one has a narrow view of the extent to which existing laws, regulations, or institutions can be changed, or if someone's need for action is so urgent that any likely change will be too late. The positive aspect of this is that legal action may provide some definite step to take within the existing framework; the negative aspect is that the legal profession in this country, as opposed to some parts of that in the United States, is not geared to bringing

about change in laws or institutions. There may be situations in which people's interests are better served by regarding them as having a political problem, either in the narrow sense of needing, if they are to be satisfied, to have some general public policy changed or in some wider sense, of needing to persuade some part of the machinery of government, seen perhaps as a bureaucracy with its own priorities and methods, to change a practice or decision. They may best be served by a public campaign, of the kind run by the Child Poverty Action Group, or by a new form of organisation such as the Golborne Community Council; neither of these seem to me to be particularly novel in conception, though it may only be recently that their particular constituencies have been represented in this way. If someone's problem is seen as a political problem, the possible solutions are wider than the mere enforcement of a right which may do little to help. But since a solution will affect other people the individual will probably have to combine with others to have a chance of success.

Z Bankowski and G Mungham, *Images of Law, op. cit.,* p. 76.

To begin with, helping people pays and it also serves to create a whole new job-opportunity structure for lawyers, especially young lawyers. Thus law centres, like duty solicitor schemes, give work and profits to many more lawyers than those actually working on these projects. It is now clear . . . that these legal innovations have had the result of generating more work for lawyers . . . Thus the greater the input of lawyers and schemes for law reform, the greater becomes the number of legal problems for lawyers to solve. To take the example of law centres again, many of them may be seen to serve — though quite unintentionally — as 'touters' for the orthodox law firm. Located as they usually are, in down-town or inner-city areas, law centres frequently find themselves having to send a steady stream of clients up-town to the ordinary law office. In this way the problems of the poor become the vehicle for a larger and more affluent legal profession, even though — and this is the important point — law centre workers themselves may be unhappy about such an outcome.

Questions:
1. Do you think Bankowski and Mungham's somewhat cynical view of the extension of legal services still holds true in the 1990s, with widespread concern over low rates of remuneration for those lawyers undertaking legal aid work?

2. How, if at all, do you think that the Government's plans for reforming access to justice meet the criticisms made by radical commentators like Bankowski and Mungham?

LAY PARTICIPATION IN THE LEGAL PROCESS

As noted above, Bankowski and Mungham have suggested that one of the effects of the extension of state-funded legal services and consequent increase in the number of lawyers has been to eliminate the possibility of self-representation — the dispute is effectively relinquished to professionals — yet, as they point out, much advocacy demands a comparatively low level of expertise and experience. However, even tribunals have become characterised, as they predicted, by an increased level of lawyer participation and consequent professionalisation. Hence one alternative to providing legal services is to allow people to manage their own disputes.

Less radical reformers like Partington have also suggested that an important reform of legal services provision would be to allow greater participation by ordinary members of the public, for example, to run the provision of legal aid and other legal services. As he also points out in *Perspectives on Legal Aid op. cit.* at p. 171:

> there are increasing calls for more lay participation in the legal process with simpler procedures and different types of court structure (e.g., small claims courts, family courts, housing courts) to encourage people to take advantage of their legal rights by using their own skills.

This leads us into the issue of what skills lawyers and lay people actually possess, and whether there is a significant difference in such skills.

In Chapter 6 on advocacy, we discussed the role of lay advocates, particularly in the context of the 'McLibel' trial (see pp. 221–5.) This case brings together issues concerning lay participation in the legal system, access to justice (legal aid has never been available for libel actions) and the right to trial by jury. In the following extracts, taken from the opening speeches by the defendants — Helen Steel and David Morris — who described themselves as unwaged environmentalists, and were respectively a former gardener and postman with no legal experience, some sense of the difficulties of self-representation, plus the importance of legal aid and trial by jury is conveyed.

You can read the trial transcripts in full for yourself on the Internet at www.mcspotlight.org/cgi-bi...e/trial.transcripts/940629/01.htm. The following extracts are taken from that website at pp. 3, 7, 8, 9, 12, 13–14, 16, 17, 25:

[Morris]
In this case on one side we have McDonald's Corporation with an annual turnover of 24 billion dollars every year. On the other side we have two unwaged individuals, members of the public. Not only on their side is us, but also the people they exploit; they exploit consumers, they exploit staff workers, they exploit children with their advertising, they exploit animals and they exploit the environment. Their only interest is maximising their profits from exploitation.

In this case, there is no jury. We are asking you, the judge, obviously, and the public as a whole to be our jury. We believe we have a right to be tried by our peers and the peers are the members of the public of which we are a part . . .

Why did McDonald's bring this case? Just to run through some of the issues regarding this case, we believe McDonald's have brought this case as a form of censorship and intimidation. We believe it is an abuse of the laws of this country. We believe they are continuing this case because they want to turn it into a show trial and propaganda platform against two unresourced, unwaged individuals and then use that throughout the world as an example of how they have been exonerated — if they win . . .

Despite our exhaustion after three years of pretrial hearings, it is our determination to stand up for our principles that has carried us thus far and, hopefully, will carry us throughout the long and further exhausting trial. There is an enormous imbalance in this case which has been described by one commentator; he could not think of a case where 'the cards had been so spectacularly stacked against one party'. That was Marcel Berlins . . .

We believe that they never expected us to be able to fight this case. In the first couple of years after the writs were served, the process was long and drawn out. Then suddenly it speeded up when McDonald's realised we were determined to stand up for our rights. They did not believe that we could personally or financially or legally overcome all the obstacles that have been placed in our path to bring this case to its conclusion . . .

We believe it is not only the public's right but also their duty to criticise those with wealth and power in society. I am not over familiar with libel laws in other countries. It has taken me a long time to get familiar with the libel laws in this country, but I know that in the United States this case probably could never have been brought because of the constitutional guarantees on rights of expression . . .

We have been denied legal aid, as always under the libel laws, and we made an application to Europe to try to challenge the rights of libel defendants to have access to legal aid, which is pretty essential, or to suggest that the British libel laws should be changed so that they are more accessible or accessible in any way to members of the public in defending themselves.

That application was lost in Europe on the grounds that 'we put in a tenacious defence and therefore could not claim we were being denied access to libel justice'. A more ridiculous Catch 22 situation I have never been in. If we had given up the ghost, we might have won in Europe.

We have no jury which we think is going to seriously affect, not only the approach to the evidence and the judgment on the evidence, but also the conduct of the trial. It is going to be extremely difficult for us to maintain our concentration when all the public and press have given up in this long trial. So we hope the court bears that in mind. Because it does sharpen you up when you are actually speaking to members of the public in trying to explain and put your case in the best possible way . . .

I propose to start going through that fact sheet, as Mr Rampton did yesterday. Please bear with me because this is quite difficult for us. Mr Rampton is very well experienced in this kind of thing, but we have not had that much time to prepare — I was up in the middle of the night doing this . . .

Clearly these extract can only give you a flavour of the defendants' opening speech. You should see the website for the full text and compare it with Mr Rampton's opening speech, which took place on the previous day.

Questions:
1. Should this case have ever been brought?

2. What do you think the 'McLibel' case demonstrates about the power of law?

3. Do you think it is worthwhile for individual citizens to take on the corporate might of organisations like McDonald's?

4. At the beginning of the book we suggested a list of legal skills. Are such skills peculiar to lawyers? From reading the transcripts on the 'McLibel' website, how adequately do you think the defendants coped with representing themselves?

5. Are these skills necessary to present a case before a court or tribunal, or could a lay person be entrusted with conducting their own case?

6. Apart from advocacy, in what other ways do lay persons participate in the legal process? Is such lay participation a good thing? Why/why not?

7. What do these cases reveal about access to justice? Was it a denial of the defendants' human rights to refuse them legal representation in this case?

8. The jury is probably the most obvious manifestation of the lay role in the legal process, albeit one which has come under increasing attack in recent years. Should the 'McLibel' case have been heard by a jury? Why/why not? What are the advantages of having a jury involved in the trial process?

Simon Lee, 'Judging the Jury', *The Listener*, 9 January 1986.

[The] jury provides a non-legal input to the administration of our legal system. This has several advantages. First, it means that lawyers are forced to explain the law in language which lay people can understand. Without that constraint, the law would become even more complex and inaccessible to the people whose behaviour it is meant to guide.

Secondly, the criminal law is not allowed to stray beyond the people's levels of tolerance. An unduly harsh law or penalty is ameliorated by the reluctance of juries to convict in such circumstances. The Official Secrets Act and the notorious direction to the jury in Clive Ponting's trial failed to secure a 'guilty' verdict in a case where the judge sitting alone clearly would have found Ponting guilty.

A third strength of the jury concerns its fact-finding ability. There is no reason to suppose that one bewigged judicial head is better than 12 punk juror heads (I assume here that blue rinses will be peremptorily challenged but orange rinses allowed to stay) in assessing the credibility of witnesses. The judge has the advantage of experience in court, but the jury has the advantage of wider experience in the outside world.

But the most important trump card possessed by the jury is that, by and large, it has retained the confidence of the public from which it is drawn.
. . .

Z Bankowski, 'The Jury and Reality', in M Findlay and P Duff (eds), *The Jury Under Trial,* London, Butterworths (1988), pp. 8–26 at pp. 18–22.

What were Frank's specific criticisms of the jury? Briefly, they were that he saw the jury as an obstacle to the establishment of legal certainty. Time and time again he attacks the jury system, recording jurors' biases, their inability to absorb and remember the mass of evidence in the trial and the inadequacy of the secret and collective deliberation process (1930). Given all this why have juries? What is wrong with trained officials such as judges with scientific training?

Much jury research has gone along this way, implicitly sanctifying the legal expert . . . The main trend then, has been to verify the accuracy of the jury by the opinion of experts, usually lawyers . . . The point of the jury is to guard against this stylised fight, to inject a 'lay acid' into the system which helps to ensure that the 'fight' does not always go its pre-ordained way. It prevents the closed shop of the legal expert. The jury is an element of lay participation in the system, standing both within and without the law. It forces some demystification of law because lawyers have to address lay people, it is no longer just expert speaking unto expert. Though jurors learn how to be jurors from their experience in the court, their views and actions will also be affected by their experience outside the courtroom. If the juror experiences the world outside the jurybox not as the calm, consensual and just one portrayed by liberal ideology, but as one which is full of conflict and injustice, then that experience is also brought into the court where it can counter the orderly legal consensual view of things and lay bare the contest as real and not stylised. It is here that one can see the ideological significance of the jury research discussed above. The implication of the methodology of using, in the main, legal 'experts' to show whether acquittal rates are too high or too low, is that the good juror is one who is as good as a lawyer, 'one who accepts the prevailing courtroom norms of legal rationality and who is willingly incorporated into the social order of the courtroom and the trial' (Mungham and Bankowski, 1976). By this method of verification of the truth or falsity of a jury's verdict these studies serve to reconstitute the juror in a legal and sometimes scientific mode. By doing so they tend to exclude his or her function of being a surrogate for society, in Devlin's (1956) words, 'a little parliament'. What this means is that the jury has a role to play in the formulation of new norms for society and does not just judge upon existing ones. Michael Freeman (1981) enumerates this function well and goes through, with characteristic thoroughness, the various ways in which this function is expressed and some of the theories behind it. He shows how the jury mediates between the law and the people and how, right up to the present time, it has acted in defiance of established norms, exercising the right of jury 'nullification':

' . . . juries may and do infuse 'non-legal values' into the trial process. They are the conscience of the community; they represent current ethical conventions. They are a constraint on legalism, arbitrariness and bureaucracy.'

. . . [On one view], lay participation, such as that of lay magistrates, juries and the like, is anomalous since it disturbs the basis for objectivity and predictability. These groups do not possess the skills required, nor the necessary socialisation and so decisions stemming from them will tend to be uncertain and unpredictable . . .

Here we can see the contradiction in a liberal democracy instantiated in the rule of law. For in order that the main moral imperative of that society, 'the government of laws and not men', flourish, another important value, that of participation must, in part, be negated. One can see this in the tension between efficiency and democracy where efficiency, in the shape of speed, reliability and constancy, is seen as continually subverted by the demands of democratic, and therefore inefficient participation. It is institutions like the jury which manage this tension in our society, by providing participation within the framework of the 'rule of law' and thus not damaging the main moral imperative of the system. This is how in practice the rule of law works and what a system of organisation based on it means — the tension between the 'efficiency' of the legal experts and the 'democracy' of lay people. Looking at it in this way we can also see the ideological dangers of some of the jury studies. They celebrate the idea of the expert, of efficiency as against democracy.'

Questions:

1.   Do you think that jurors reason in a different way from judges and lawyers? I.e., is there a peculiarly *legal* form of reasoning, different from that employed by lay people or politicians?

2.   A problem with answering that question is the difficulty in conducting research on jury performance as a result of the Contempt of Court Act 1981 which prohibits juries from disclosing their deliberations. Is such a rule justifiable?

The OJ Simpson case was one real-life trial where the jury came under attack for its verdict (see also the Louise Woodward case discussed in Chapter 4). It was variously alleged that the jurors misunderstood the facts or acquitted OJ Simpson on the basis of non-legal factors, such as racial prejudice. In the following extract one of Simpson's defence attorneys, Alan Dershowitz, offers a defence of the jury's unanimous, not guilty verdict:

A Dershowitz, *Reasonable Doubts: The Criminal Justice System and the O.J. Simpson Case*, New York: Touchstone (1996), pp. 69–71, 86–9, 90, 93–4. (footnotes omitted)

Most Americans — certainly most white Americans — believe that O.J. Simpson killed Nicole Brown and Ronald Goldman. They also believe that no reasonable jury could have found otherwise. According to a *Washington Post* poll conducted within days after the verdict, 70 per cent of white Americans thought Simpson was guilty, and 63 per cent thought the jury was biased in his favour. Of the nation as a whole, 60 per cent thought Simpson was guilty, 56 per cent '[d]isagreed with the verdict', and 51 per cent thought that the jury was biased in favour of Simpson. Many Americans view the jury's verdict of acquittal, therefore, as 'racist', 'obscene', 'irrational' and 'stupid'. But in order to convict, the jurors in the Simpson case had to be convinced of his guilt 'beyond a reasonable doubt'. Perhaps, then, they had decided that this exacting legal standard had not been met and that it was not their job to solve a whodunnit but rather to apply the legal standard about which Judge Ito had instructed them. The question still remains: Were the juror's doubts in this case 'reasonable', as that word is defined in law? . . .

The problem with 'reasonable doubt', however, is that juries do not necessarily know it when they see it because legislatures and the courts have been utterly unwilling to tell them what it is, beyond a few unhelpful cliches . . .

In the Simpson case, Judge Ito did define reasonable doubt in the following way:

> It is not a mere possible doubt because everything relating to human affairs is open to some possible or imaginary doubt. It is that state of the case, which after the entire comparison and consideration of all the evidence, leaves the minds of the jurors in that condition that they cannot say they feel an abiding conviction about the truth of the charge.

Were the jurors' doubts in the Simpson case 'reasonable' or 'unreasonable' under this instruction? We can never know with certainty, of course, because we do not have access to the mental processes of each of the jurors. But consider the following line of reasoning that could have been — and, according to several juror interviews, probably was — employed by jurors in this case . . .

There are several possible ways a jury could deal with the remaining evidence after concluding (or having a reasonable doubt) that some of it was corrupted. First, the jury could simply act as if the corrupted evidence had never been introduced. Many commentators stated that this is precisely what any reasonable juror should do. They argue that the remaining evidence, standing alone, proved Simpson's guilt beyond a reasonable doubt, and they point to incriminating evidence found at the crime scene, including Simpson's blood, a hat bearing hair consistent with Simpson's, shoe prints the same size as Simpson's, and a left glove that resembled one Simpson was seen wearing on tapes of a football game. This crime scene evidence — standing alone, without any of the questionable evidence found at the Simpson estate — would establish Simpson's guilt, according to these observers. In addition, there was other evidence, such as Simpson's blood drops at his estate, which could not have been corrupted by the police, as well as the blood found in the Bronco, which included Simpson's, Goldman's, and Brown's. Then there was the time line, which established opportunity. Finally, there was the history of spousal discord, which established motive. The commentators who argue that the uncorrupted evidence should have been independently considered, without taking the arguably corrupted evidence into account, point to the above items standing alone as enough to establish Simpson's guilt.

The fallacy in their reasoning is that this evidence *did not stand alone*. No reasonable juror could totally ignore the fact that *this* evidence was gathered by the same police department that might have tampered with the other evidence, and that it was presented by the same prosecutor's office that might knowingly have presented perjured testimony in support of the search of the Simpson estate. Any reasonable juror who believed that several police officers might have lied to them about *some* of their actions and tampered with *some* evidence could not simply ignore those beliefs in assessing the rest of the evidence. *All* the police evidence and testimony would now come before the jurors bearing a presumption or at the very least a suspicion, that it had been corrupted. Perhaps the prosecutors could have overcome that presumption or suspicion, but it would not have been easy. After all, policemen who are deemed willing to lie and tamper with respect to some evidence should not be deemed unwilling to lie and tamper with respect to other evidence.

Moreover, some of the prosecution's evidence, even standing alone, did not present all that compelling a circumstantial case. The hair found in the hat was consistent with the hair of a great many black men, and the fibres were inconclusive. The defence argued that hair and fibre are 'weak association' evidence — they do not 'match' an individual as narrowly as blood evidence. But even if the hair and fibres were Simpson's, it was not surprising. Simpson was a frequent visitor to the Bundy residence; strands of his hair and fibres from his clothing were all over the place. They could have been spread around the crime scene and onto the victims by Nicole Brown's dog, or by blankets from the house that were used to cover the crime scene. Or they could have been mixed together when crime evidence was stored in the same box during the investigation.

Simpson's shoe size is shared by millions of men. The defence noted that this, too, is 'weak association' evidence, consistent with any large man. The prosecution never established that Simpson owned or wore the type of shoe that matched the print.

The presence of Simpson's degraded and discoloured blood near a residence where he spent a great deal of time playing with kids, dogs, bikes, and so on, would seem consistent with his earlier, innocent presence there. The defence also argued that investigator Dennis Fung had left this blood in a hot car for four hours, 'cooking' it and degrading the DNA. When the blood finally got to the lab, Yamauchi handled the swatches at the same time as he did a reference tube of Simpson's blood, not following the proper procedure of changing gloves and washing down between handling separate samples. Thus, the swatches could have been cross-contaminated in the lab, creating a false positive match with Simpson. In addition, the swatches were never sent for the EDTA preservative testing which might have indicated whether they were planted from laboratory samples. A few blood drops near Simpson's own house would hardly be enough to convict, since it is quite natural that traces of someone's own blood should appear around his house as a result of minor cuts and scrapes. Moreover, Simpson told the police — before he knew about the prosecution's evidence — that he had cut his finger while retrieving his cellular phone from the Bronco.

And the glove didn't fit.

The strength of the prosecution's case was that *so many* pieces of evidence — any of which independently would be consistent with innocence — *all* failed *to exclude* Simpson. Quantity thus mattered, along with quality. To the extent that the quantity of the prosecution's evidence was lessened by the quality of the evidence believed corrupted, the prosecution's circumstantial case was weakened considerably. For example, the jury may have discounted the blood found in the Bronco, suspecting that it could have been placed there — deliberately or accidentally — by Fuhrman or another officer who had first stepped in the blood at the crime scene and then entered the Bronco to search or move it . . .

Nor, apparently, was the jury helped much by the prosecution's evidence of opportunity and motive. The time line, which purported to show that Simpson *could have* committed the murders in the time available, was, at best, ambiguous. The defence made a powerful showing that Simpson could not have committed two brutal and bloody murders, cleaned himself up, and gotten back home in the time between the wails of the dog and the three bangs on the air conditioner . . .

As to the motive, the jurors were apparently not impressed with the prosecution's domestic discord evidence. Men who abuse rarely kill (although men who kill have often abused), and these jurors were not persuaded that a single episode of violence five years earlier — the only such evidence the jury heard — and several other nasty incidents proved that O.J. Simpson murdered Nicole Brown and Ronald Goldman . . .

Jury nullification 'occurs when a jury — based on its own sense of justice or fairness — refuses to follow the law and convict in a particular case even though the facts seem to allow no other conclusion but guilt.'. The Honorable Jack B. Weinstein, United States district judge for the Eastern District of New York, has argued:

> 'The legitimacy of the jury process demands respect for its outcomes, whatever they may be. Attempting to distinguish between a "right" outcome — a verdict following the letter of the law — and a "wrong" one — a "nullification" verdict — can be dangerous, and this endeavour depends largely on personal bias. Nullification is but one legitimate result in an appropriate constitutional process safeguarded by judges and the judicial system. When juries refuse to convict on the basis of what they think are unjust laws, they are performing their duty as jurors.'

Jury nullification has both deep roots and a vibrant history in American jurisprudence. In 1895, the Supreme Court recognised the jury's power to nullify. It ruled that judges could not overrule acquittals even if they appeared to have been reached in the face of overwhelming evidence of guilt . . .

The form of jury nullification that may have been employed by some jurors in the Simpson case — the refusal to convict a defendant who they believed guilty but who had also been 'framed' by the police — draws some support, as well, from judicial authority. This form of nullification is related to the exclusionary rule, the 'shock the conscience' test, and the 'outrageous governmental misconduct' defence, all of which require the release of guilty defendants in order to send an important message to the police.

Questions:

1.   Are you convinced by Dershowitz's argument that it was reasonable for the jury to acquit, even given what some observers thought was overwhelming evidence of Simpson's guilt?

2.   Is jury nullification an argument for or against retention of the jury system?

3.   Can jurors leave their prejudices and biases outside the courtroom? Are they likely to be more or less successful at this than judges? Should black defendants be tried by black jurors? Should women-only juries try rape cases?

Runciman Commission, The Royal Commission on Criminal Justice (1993), Cm 2263.

Juries

. . .

61.   Although the initial summoning of persons from the electoral rolls is done on a random basis, several factors may affect that randomness by the time a jury is selected. The rules on eligibility and disqualification are relevant factors, as are the various reasons that people may advance for wishing to be excused jury service on a discretionary basis. It may for example be that some women find it more difficult to serve as jurors on account of domestic commitments. The Crown Court Study did in fact find that women were slightly underrepresented on juries compared with what might have been expected. Comparison with the 1991 census, however, indicates that on a national basis ethnic minority groups were not seriously underrepresented. Non-white jurors made up 5% of jurors as compared with 5.9% of the total population.

62.   We are reluctant to interfere with the principle of random selection of juries. We are, however, anxious that everything possible should be done to ensure that people from the ethnic minority communities are represented on juries in relation to their numbers in the local community. The pool from which juries are randomly selected would be more representative if all eligible members of ethnic communities were included on the electoral roll. Even if this were to be achieved, however, there would statistically still be instances where there would not be a multi-racial jury in a case where one seemed appropriate. The Court of Appeal in *Ford* [[1989] 3 All ER 445] held that race should not be taken into account in selecting juries. Although we agree with the court's position in regard to most cases, we believe that there are some exceptional cases where race should be taken into account.

63.   We have therefore found very relevant a proposal made to us by the Commission for Racial Equality (CRE) for a specific procedure to be

available where the case is believed to have a racial dimension which results in a defendant from an ethnic minority community believing that he or she is unlikely to receive a fair trial from an all-white jury. The CRE would also like to see the prosecution on behalf of the victim be able to argue that a racial dimension to the case points to the need for a multi-racial jury. In such cases the CRE propose that it should be possible for either the prosecution or the defence to apply to the judge before the trial for the selection of a jury containing up to three people from ethnic minority communities. If the judge grants the application, it would be for the jury bailiff to continue to draw names randomly selected from the available pool until three such people were drawn. We believe that, in the exceptional case where compelling reasons can be advanced, this option, in addition to the existing power to order that the case be transferred to another court centre, should be available and we so recommend. However, we do not envisage that the new procedure should apply (as proposed by the CRE) simply because the defendant thinks that he or she cannot get a fair trial from an all-white jury. The defendant would have to persuade the judge that such a belief was reasonable because of the unusual and special features of the case. Thus, a black defendant charged with burglary would be unlikely to succeed in such an application. But black people accused of violence against a member of an extremist organisation who they said had been making racial taunts against them and their friends might well succeed.

64.   The CRE considered whether the judge should have power to order that the three jurors from the ethnic minority communities should come from the same ethnic minority as the defendant or victim. They concluded, however, that this would be impracticable. While this may be so, we believe that it should be open to the defence or prosecution to argue the point and to the judge to be able to order in appropriate cases that one or more of the three jurors should come from the same ethnic minority as the defendant or the victim. We so recommend.

Questions:

1.   Do you agree that some interference with the principle of random selection of juries is permissible? Why/why not?

2.   Is the CRE's proposal sufficiently radical? Why not draw 50 per cent or 100 per cent of the jury from the same ethnic background as the defendant?

3.   Are there any other types of cases, aside from those with a racial dimension, where it might be justifiable to interfere with the random selection principle?

One area where it has been possible to some extent to measure the cost of wholly dispensing with the jury is in the trial of 'scheduled' criminal offences in Northern Ireland (i.e. those offences listed in Schedule 4 to the Northern Ireland (Emergency Provisions) Act 1978) which are deemed to be the ones most commonly committed by paramilitaries in Northern Ireland. In 1973 a Commission to consider legal procedures to deal with terrorist activities in Northern Ireland, chaired by Lord Diplock, recommended the abrogation of the right to trial by jury, on the twin grounds of alleged intimidation of jurors and alleged perverse acquittals of paramilitaries by biased juries.

Since the institution of the single judge Diplock courts there is fairly clear evidence that the acquittal rate has declined.

S Greer and A White, 'Restoring Jury Trial to Terrorist Offences in Northern Ireland', in M Findlay and P Duff (eds), *The Jury Under Attack,* London, Butterworths (1988), pp. 173–89 at p. 178.

> Independent research has shown that the effective acquittal rate in the Diplock courts has declined progressively, from 57 per cent in 1973 to 33 per cent in 1981, while the acquittal rate in jury trials in Northern Ireland (i.e., in cases involving non-scheduled offences) has risen in the same period, from 38 per cent in 1974 to 61 per cent in 1977, falling slightly to 59 per cent in 1978 and 1979. The figures cited by Baker in his review [of the working of the emergency procedures], which were drawn from a different data base and exclude refusals to recognise the jurisdiction of the court, show a decline in the acquittal rate in Diplock cases from 38 per cent in 1973 to a fairly constant 20 per cent for the next ten years with the exception of 1981 and 1982 when it rose to 34 per cent and 35 per cent respectively. Partly on the basis of these two atypical years Baker feels able to reject the case-hardening hypothesis. (He suggests that any fall in the acquittal rate 'must be' due to better selection and preparation of cases by the prosecuting authorities.) It is hard to find this dismissal convincing, based as it is on the two years which support it rather than on the eight which do not.

Drawing on the widespread concern and lack of faith in the Northern Ireland legal system Greer and White suggest that the criminal justice system cannot function properly without this lay element for a variety of procedural and substantive reasons, and have concluded that the Diplock courts should be abolished. Other commentators have suggested that the following lessons can be learned from a study of the Diplock system:

J Jackson and S Doran, *Judge Without Jury: Diplock Trials in the Adversary System*, Oxford, Oxford University Press (1995), pp. 292–5.

> The cardinal lesson to be drawn from the study of the Diplock system is that the absence of the jury does not lead ineluctably to the abandonment by triers of fact of the traditional umpireal role and the adoption of an active case management approach which substantially increases the guilty plea and conviction rate. Much depends on the context in which the professional trial operates and a number of factors seem to be relevant to the issue of whether the trial will uphold the due process values associated with traditional jury trial. First of all, there is a question of whether trial by judge alone is considered of equal importance to jury trial. Diplock proceedings involve the most serious offences and they must therefore attempt to match the standards of jury proceedings. Other kinds of professional trial, of course, may

determine less serious cases. Secondly, ideological considerations, together with societal and institutional pressures, motivate judges and counsel to adopt a particular stance. In the Diplock context we have seen that judges have to perform their fact-finding functions in the full glare of publicity, and this extra pressure has made them particularly anxious to be seen to uphold the 'rule of law' and the principle of proof beyond reasonable doubt. However, the temptation to pursue policies which are less advantageous to the accused might be much stronger in a regime which is under less constant scrutiny. Judges are, of course, required to be independent, but they can never be totally independent of the environment in which they work and any pressure to increase quantitative output at the expense of qualitative output could work to the disadvantage of defendants. Another important consideration here is the degree to which practitioners are steeped in a jury culture. When practitioners appear regularly in both jury and non-jury proceedings, the influences of jury trial are reinforced in their day-to-day practice. A third factor derives from the institutional practices which have taken hold in the working environment of the criminal courts. As we have noted, the intimacy of the Northern Ireland jurisdiction promotes the evolution of informal working practices among judges and counsel which would not be possible in a larger jurisdiction. Moveover, when judges are permitted to read the prosecution papers before trial they can get a feel of the case before it is formally presented in court. Finally, there are the personalities of the individual actors and working relationships between them. A dominant judge may be inclined to adopt an inquisitorial approach, particularly before inexperienced counsel. Conversely, experienced practitioners may dominate proceedings before a relatively passive judge.

All these factors show that there is room for significant variation in the way in which non-jury proceedings are conducted. Whatever attempts are made, however, to base such proceedings on the model of the jury trial, the accused necessarily suffers an 'adversarial deficit' when tried in a totally professional environment. In Chapter Three we discussed various meanings of adversariness. The first definition associated adversariness with a liberal ideology in which the individual is entitled to have the case against him or her proved. This has tended to be associated with Anglo-American procedures, although we noted that many of the features identified as adversarial are found in European procedures. Although adversariness is often associated with giving primacy to individual rights, there has been considerable imprecision about what 'adversial rights' are. One way of clarifying 'adversariness' is to view it as a set of processual characteristics which enable individuals both to invoke legal procedures to uphold their legal rights and interests and also to participate in any procedures which affect their rights and interests, in order that they may influence the outcome of the proceedings.

It is our argument that even when constraints are placed on judges to adopt an umpireal role in proceedings where they are charged with the task of determining guilt, the defendant suffers an adversial deficit in at least two respects. The first concerns the nature of the fact-finding function which the tribunal is required to discharge. On one view, when judicial triers assume fact-finding responsibilities their role is no different from that of jurors. Essentially this role is to determine whether the prosecution has proved the guilt of the accused. On a different view, guilt is not the only issue to be decided. Criminal proceedings are taken on behalf of the community and decisions must therefore be taken either by the community or by persons acting on its behalf. When lay triers are the decision-makers they act *as* the community and they can afford to take a more wide-ranging view of both the merits of the proceedings and the merits of convicting the defendant as charged. Professional triers cannot take such a wide-ranging view of the case. They are accountable first to the legal system and ultimately to the community for their decisions and this requires them to apply the criminal law to the accused strictly on the basis of the evidence relevant to the specific charge brought. The nature of the proceedings therefore shift away from the resolution of a dispute between the state and the individual towards a more tightly controlled forum for determining the defendant's guilt. The chief reason why defence counsel seemed to prefer jury to Diplock proceedings was that the former gave them more freedom to develop their case. Although professional proceedings may remain adversarial in form, the parties themselves are granted less scope to determine the ambit of the dispute.

The second respect in which the accused suffers an adversarial deficit is derived from the position occupied by the professional trier in the proceedings. Whatever stance individual professional triers assume, we have seen that they exercise a more pervasive influence over the proceedings than lay triers could ever achieve. It could not, of course, be argued that the parties to *any* type of dispute would thereby necessarily suffer an adversarial deficit. In civil proceedings, for example, the parties decide on the ambit of the dispute, and they are put on an equal procedural footing to influence the professional trier deciding the case. In criminal proceedings, however, the parties are not in a position of equality. The prosecution is invariably in a much stronger position than the defence and procedures have to be designed to protect the accused. Where procedural control of the action is vested in the parties, as in the common law world, this requires that high evidentiary barriers be erected to enable the defendant to confront and challenge the prosecution case at trial where all admissible evidence is presented freshly before a tribunal unversed in the details of the case.

One problem with this, however, is that it is easier to keep information away from lay triers than from professional triers, and there are greater opportunities for a professional tribunal to reach conclusions about the case which are not based strictly on admissible evidence adduced at trial. Juries generally come to the trial ignorant about the details of the case whereas professional triers may have some inside information. This need not always follow, of course. Jurors may have some knowledge of cases which have provoked widespread media attention and, conversely, judges may on occasions be unable to read any papers in advance of the trial and therefore have little idea of what the case is about. Once the case starts, however, professionals are much better placed than lay triers to pick up background about the case which may not be apparent to lay minds . . . [F]or example, judges can very quickly work out whether a defendant is of good or bad character. Apart from this, judges can easily become privy to inadmissible evidence during the trial. It may be that judges are better placed than lay triers to prevent themselves being influenced by this inadmissible evidence. This is not because they are endowed with a superhuman ability to exclude such evidence from their minds, but rather because the judicial fact-finder must confine the scope of his or her inquiries within legal boundaries. Nevertheless . . . there are several ways in which inadmissible evidence may affect the judge's fact-finding inquiries.

A further problem is that proceedings which are structured to enable the defence to mount a full contest to the prosecution case may become skewed by the intrusion of a professional trier, who inevitably exercises a greater influence over the conduct of the case than a lay tribunal. The result is that counsel may be less contest-oriented in their approach to the case. Professional triers have an opportunity to make their views known even before the contest has begun. Once the case has started they can indicate, either explicitly or implicitly, how they view it. Of course, counsel may resist such signals, but there is little point in doing so if it is clear that the judge's mind is veering in a particular direction. Moreover, counsel must maintain a working relationship with the judge which is likely to last beyond the individual case at hand. The point is not just that judges may consciously try to influence counsel's approach to the case, but that judges and counsel may with time get to know each other so well that counsel has a very clear idea how the case will be received, which may in turn influence his or her conduct of the case. It is not likely that a jury's reaction can be gauged so readily. Jurors are less able to communicate their views to counsel during the trial and even if this opportunity were given, since the jury consists of twelve individuals, they are unlikely to speak with one voice. This may suggest that a collegiate bench would be preferable to trial by a single judge because it may be less easy for a collegiate bench to come to a view about a case at an early stage of the proceedings. Much, however, would depend on the composition of such a bench, as less experienced judges might find it difficult to withstand the forcefully expressed views of their more senior colleagues.

Questions:

1.   Is it now realistic to restore jury trials in Northern Ireland? Could jury trials ever be as *efficient* as Diplock trials? Does it matter whether trial processes are efficient?

2.   Do juries really inspire public confidence? Can you think of other cases where trial by jury is problematic? For example, in Chapter 4 on fact-finding, do you think that juries could really understand evidence on probability theory in DNA cases?

3.   Can juries decide fairly cases involving high-profile defendants like Mike Tyson, William Kennedy-Smith and OJ Simpson?

4.   In the light of this chapter, how important do you think it is to:

(a)   make legal expertise accessible to everyone?

(b)   preserve an element of lay participation in the legal process?

5.   Is legal expertise more valuable than other types of expertise in the legal process? What other types of expertise are important in our legal system?

6.   Does the preservation of an element of lay participation in the legal process help to ensure that it is accessible?

7.   Does an awareness of the problems of ensuring accessibility and an element of lay participation in the legal system equip you to be a better lawyer? How?

8.   In the light of proposals to reduce further the right to jury trial in England and Wales, by removing the right to trial by jury in fraud cases because of their length and complexity (see Home Office, *Juries in Serious Fraud Trials: A Consultation Document*, February 1998) and by removing the right of defendants to elect for trial of certain criminal offences in the Crown Court (see Home Office, *Review of Delay in the Criminal Justice System: A Report*, July 1998; available at www.homeoffice.gov.uk/crimerev1.htm), what relevant insights can a study of the Diplock courts system offer?

9.   Given Jackson and Doran's arguments about the adversarial deficit, is it a good idea to further reduce numbers of jury trials?

As a summary of the issues addressed in this chapter, consider the following statement by the defendants in the 'McLibel' case:

J Vidal, *McLibel: Burger Culture on Trial*, London, Macmillan (1997), at pp. 322–4; 339–41.

We're exhilarated by what we, and the campaign, have been able to achieve over the last few years. By standing up to the company's bullying we turned the tables on them and all their dirty laundry was aired in public, exposing the reality behind the glossy image. The case was transformed into what may have been the first ever public tribunal on the business practices of a multinational corporation. And of course leaflets are circulating worldwide in ever greater numbers.

We're convinced that the only reason we didn't win on all points was due to technicalities — controversial legalistic and semantic interpretations of the meaning of the 'What's Wrong With McDonald's' Factsheet, which therefore increased the burden of what we were expected to prove. The judge adopted virtually all McDonald's extreme arguments about this. And his failure to find for us over our counter-claim [alleging that McDonald's had libelled them on the grounds that they were said to be distributing information they knew to be false] was probably the biggest scandal of them all.

However, despite being up against oppressive and unfair laws stacked in favour of the plaintiff, the denial of legal aid, a huge imbalance in the resources of the two sides, and the denial of our right to a jury trial, we won on the issues that go to the very core of McDonald's' business. The corporation must be devastated to have been found guilty of 'exploiting children', of deceptively promoting their food as 'nutritious' and putting the health of their most regular, long-term customers at risk, of paying 'low wages' and of being 'culpably responsible' for cruelty to animals.

One thing the case has clearly shown is how inappropriate it is for a single judge to be deciding what issues can be debated in the public arena. Issues such as whether consumers should worry about pesticides and their diet, whether working conditions and pay are bad, whether advertising is exploitative and who is responsible for environmental damage should be freely debated, without fear of litigation. Such fears prevent open, uninhibited debate which is necessary for progress to be made.

We don't believe that multinationals should have the right to sue for libel over public interest issues which affect people's everyday lives, but while they do, cases should at minimum be tried by a jury, who, as ordinary people, may be less ready to swallow the line of establishment organizations and those in power.

Having been denied a jury, the judge has in the main chosen to prefer the evidence of those representing the establishment or status quo. But, based on our experience at pre-trial hearings, we had expected this to happen and so from the start of the trial we adopted a strategy of gaining admissions from McDonald's' witnesses, so that it thereby became not just 'their word against their own'. Having to break down the slick PR speak to gain these admissions lengthened the trial considerably, but it meant that most of the findings of fact went in our favour (it was the *interpretation* of the Factsheet that we 'lost' on). And it ensured that the truth could not be brushed under the carpet . . .

Few people have any idea of the nature of libel laws and the way in which they are used. It was the same for us when we first got the writs. Despite not being the authors of the London Greenpeace Factsheet we found the burden of proof was put on us, that there was no legal aid, that we could not rely on previous reports, no matter how authoritative, and that there was no protection of freedom of speech whatsoever.

Most people (including us) generally believe what they read or are told *unless* they have some reason not to believe it. When we read the Factsheet and other subsequent leaflets about McDonald's we had every reason to believe their contents. They were exactly the kind of thing we'd read in any number of places before, including statements made by those most prominent in the respective fields. Yet now it was down to us to prove it all true.

Imagine (you may not need to) that a factory in your neighbourhood is pumping out pollution which is affecting people's health. You decide you want to stop this, and you get together with neighbours to start a campaign. A leaflet is produced which repeats information reported in newspapers and scientific journals about the relevant chemicals or substances being released in the environment, and the effect that it's had or may have on people's health. The company slaps a writ on you claiming it has been libelled. You may or may not have helped with writing the leaflet, but it's now your responsibility to prove to the satisfaction of the English libel courts that those chemicals or substances do have those effects, and even if you can prove that, that it's actually had that effect in your neighbourhood.

What do you know about how to file a defence to a libel claim? Probably nothing. How many libel lawyers do you know? Probably none. If you're lucky you may have access to a library with a good stock of law books, and you might just be able to puzzle out how to file that defence.

But even if you can get as far as filing a defence, think, as an ordinary person, how difficult it is to prove something true. Particularly on matters of health. How do you actually *prove* that the pollution has made or may make somebody ill? First you have to find some eminent scientists in the field — the courts won't take notice even of scientific reports without an 'expert' in court to back them. But how many eminent scientists do you know? And even if you can get hold of one, you're entirely reliant on their goodwill, you couldn't afford to pay their fees to produce a report for you. Meanwhile the company concerned has plenty of money with which to pay for reports saying that the amount of chemicals released are negligible or that there are no ill effects. There's always at least one scientist whose point of view coincides with the company.

We were fortunate that when we got writs we were put in touch with a barrister, Keir Starmer, who had experience in the field of libel law (most lawyers don't). Without him, it's unlikely we would ever have got our defence off the ground, because the laws and procedures are so complex. We were fortunate that some experts did step forward to give evidence on our behalf without the standard fee for preparing a report and testifying. And that so many ex-employees too found the time to come to court. We were also fortunate that people sent in enough money to enable us to pay photocopying and phone bills, and for our witnesses' fares to court. But it could have been different.

It should be different. Companies which have such power and influence over the lives of ordinary people should not be able to use libel laws against their critics. It is of vital public importance that matters which affect people's lives and health are areas of free, uninhibited public debate. Even the House of Lords recently admitted that the threat of a libel writ had a 'chilling effect on freedom of speech' and therefore ruled that it was in the public interest that governmental bodies would no longer be allowed to sue for libel. So why should multinational corporations? They are often more powerful than local or national governments, and even less accountable.

In the USA companies and public figures have to show that the critics *knew* what s/he was saying was false before they can even begin an action for libel — if adopted here that would be a start. Then at least campaigners who produced leaflets based on information reported in newspapers and/or scientific journals could not be sued.

When we got beyond the initial panic of trying to file a defence it became apparent that it was important to fight the case not just as a battle with McDonald's but as a fight against this country's oppressive libel laws. We became aware of the widespread unseen censorship going on. Most libel cases don't even make it to court because defendants face years of long, drawn-out, unfair, complex and archaic proceedings and there's no legal aid available, so generally a humiliating apology or settlement is made to avoid the massive costs of a case. These settlements inevitably include an undertaking not to repeat the criticism, and on top of that the fake 'apologies' are paraded around as if they vindicate the reputation of the plaintiffs. The result is mass censorship, and no one knows what's really going on behind the scenes. [Note that the claims made at the beginning of this extract were partially vindicated by the appellate court's ruling on this case. See p. 225 above.]

Chapter 10

Putting It All Together

Studying law is not simply a question of acquiring certain knowledge (which would, in any event, rapidly become outdated), nor is it a process of learning discrete skills. While particular weeks of a course might focus on precedent or statutory interpretation or whatever, the student will have to put skills together to analyse problems in the wider world. The law itself will need to be seen in context, from a variety of perspectives. So this chapter invites students to round off their introduction to law by beginning the process of 'putting it all together'. Paradoxically, sometimes, putting it all together, first requires pulling it all apart!

RETHINKING CATEGORIES

Many of the chapters in this book have suggested different ways of looking at, or categorising law. In the first chapter we examined different perspectives on law, and thought about what skills lawyers should have. In Chapters 2 and 3 we looked at legal reasoning and the doctrines of statutory interpretation and precedent, and how different approaches lead to different results. In Chapter 4, we addressed some of the factors underlying the construction of 'fact finding' in law, the categorisation of what is legally significant or relevant, and the process of defining issues as 'factual' or 'legal', in the first place. The negotiation and advocacy chapters looked at different approaches to problem solving, some of which prevent problems from being defined as 'legal' in the first place. In Chapter 7 on adjudication we considered some theories which try to explain what the judge is (and should be) doing when he or she decides cases. Again, various legal theorists espoused different approaches. In critical skills we explored some of the arguments (efficiency, morality and justice) which are often interwoven with and inseparable from legal argument. In Chapter 9, 'Law for All?', we explored access to justice, and the extent to which the door of the law is open to all.

If you glance at your future law syllabus, you will see other ways of categorising law — criminal law, family law, tort (or torts), contract law, commercial law, human rights law, civil liberties, law and literature, health care law. Yet when you are a practising lawyer, a client will come with a problem which they feel is legal, and which they want solved. They are unlikely to tell you which of your subject areas it falls into, and indeed as an innovative lawyer, you may well approach the problem from several categories at once. A problem may be a tort problem and a contract problem and a land law problem all at once. The problem may be overlaid with a rights issue, or even several conflicting rights issues. The same problem may be able to be addressed at domestic and then at regional or even international levels.

This final chapter draws on themes and areas of law which you have already come across throughout the book. By probing a few of these themes in depth we can examine further what it means to 'think like a lawyer'.

We address four main themes: discrimination, informed consent, bioethics and legal cultures. When approaching the first three sections you should keep in mind the following questions (some will have more relevance to some of the themes than others):

1.   What legal concepts are used to address the issue?
2.   What are the connections between law and morals? Does the moral position affect the law? Does the legal position affect the moral one? How do we decide between competing moralities?
3.   How are different legal systems and areas of law used to address the same problem using different legal tools and concepts?
4.   How does categorisation used in law and by lawyers match with categorisation used in every day life?

In the final section we re-consider issues of globalisation and interdisciplinary studies, and return to the role of legal culture and legal education in shaping legal practice.

DISCRIMINATION

The first category of law we shall consider is discrimination. Discrimination law provides an interesting example from which to learn legal skills. Equality is often taken to be an accepted value in society (see Chapter 8). Anti-discrimination law is seen as one way of achieving equality. What other ways are there?

In the following extract we return to Martha Minnow's examination (see Chapter 1 at p. 6) of how legal analysis itself involves categorising. In effect she suggests that this is a form of 'discriminating' in both a non-pejorative and a pejorative sense. She argues that legal analysis itself in many cases hides essentially political, and often problematic choices.

M Minnow, *Making All the Difference: Inclusion, Exclusion and American Law*, New York, Cornell University Press (1990), pp. 3–4.

Except for its specialized vocabulary, legal analysis looks a lot like other kinds of analysis — as the comparison with the *Sesame Street* song should suggest. When we analyze, we simplify. We break complicated perceptions into discrete items or traits. We identify the items and call them chair, table, cat, and bed. We sort them into categories that already exist: furniture and animal. It sounds familiar. It also sounds harmless. I do not think it is.

I believe we make a mistake when we assume that the categories we use for analysis just exist and simply sort our experiences, perceptions, and problems through them. When we identify one thing as like the others, we are not merely classifying the world; we are investing particular classifications with consequences and positioning ourselves in relation to those meanings. When we identify one thing as unlike the others, we are dividing the world; we use our language to exclude, to distinguish — to discriminate. This last word may be the one that most recognizably raises the issues about which I worry. Sometimes, classifications express and implement prejudice, racism, sexism, anti-Semitism, intolerance for difference. Of course, there are 'real differences' in the world; each person differs in countless ways from each other person. But when we simplify and sort, we focus on some traits rather than others, and we assign consequences to the presence and absence of the traits we make significant. We ask, 'What's the new baby?' — and we expect as an answer, boy or girl. That answer, for most of history, has spelled consequences for the roles and opportunities available to that individual. And when we respond to persons' traits rather than their conduct, we may treat a given trait as a justification for excluding someone we think is 'different'. We feel no need for further justification: we attribute the consequences to the differences we see. We neglect the other traits that may be shared. And we neglect how each of us, too, may be 'different'.

Presuming real differences between people, differences that we all know and recognise, presumes that we all perceive the world the same way and that we are unaffected by our being situated in it. This presumption also ignores the power of our language, which embeds unstated points of comparison inside categories that falsely imply a natural fit with the world. The very term 'working mother' reveals that the general term 'mother' carries some unstated common definition — that is, a woman who cares for her children full time without pay. Even if unintended, such unstated meanings must be expressly modified if the speaker means something else. Labels of difference often are assigned by some to describe others in ways they would not describe themselves, and in ways that carry baggage that may be difficult to unload.

If you have ever felt wronged by a label of difference assigned to you, you may know what I mean. People often feel unrecognized, excluded, or degraded 'because' of their gender, religion, race, ethnicity, nationality, age, height, weight, family membership, sexual orientation, or health status. The expansiveness of this list does not trivialize the issue, even though it does suggest that there are many more differences that people make significant than any of us may note self-consciously. Organizing perceptions along some lines is essential, but which lines will we use — and come to use unthinkingly? Human beings use labels to describe and sort their perceptions of the world. The particular labels often chosen in America culture can carry social and moral consequences while burying the choices and responsibility for those consequences. The labels point to conclusions about where an item, or an individual, belongs without opening for debate the purposes for which the label will be used. This is what worries me about any mode of analysis that asks, 'which one of these is not like the others?'.

Questions
1. What labels have been applied to you in your life? How have you felt about these labels?

2. On what grounds do we discriminate against people? Are all these forms of discrimination equally illegitimate?

3. Is the word 'discrimination' always a pejorative word? In what other ways might it be used?

While anti-discrimination law deals with preventing abuses on grounds of race, sex, religion or disability (note s. 1(1)(a), Sex Discrimination Act 1975 'A person discriminates . . . on the ground of her sex if he treats her less favourably than he treats or would treat a man'). Paradoxically it must first be decided what race, sex, religion or disability means. We also consider why certain factors are protected by legislation and others (e.g. religion in Britain, or age in the UK) are not. For the purposes of 'putting it all together', the following materials focus initially on the *grounds* on which discrimination is prohibited and how those grounds are developed (should it be by judicial discretion or statutory intervention?).

First, then, we return to *Mandla* v *Lee* (1983) (see Chapter 3), a case in which the Law Lords have, for a decade, been commended by many students for their 'generous' approach to defining 'ethnic group' so as to bring a religious group, Sikhs, within the compass of the race relations legislation. Would it have been better, however, for the Court of Appeal's more literal approach to have been upheld and the matter resolved by Parliament extending the race relations legislation so that all religious groups were clearly and equally protected? The Law Lords, no doubt unwittingly, contributed to a climate in which Muslims felt aggrieved within British society — Jews and Sikhs were protected but not Muslims. A Muslim submission to a Home Office review of the Race Relations Act argues for a change.

Muslims and the law in multi-faith Britain. Need for Reform. UKACIA (1993).

The CRE in its Second Review of the RRA 76 has proposed that the Act be amended in several respects so that it is a more effective tool in fighting race discrimination. As regards Muslims, the CRE in the afore-mentioned document states:

'. . . the Race Relations Act does not give protection against religious discrimination as such, and the Muslim communities have been understandably disappointed that the Commission has been unable to translate its concerns for their interest into effective law enforcement. We believe that the government should now give consideration to introducing legislation with enforcement machinery to combat religious discrimination. We do not believe, however, that this would be best achieved by extending the scope of the Race Relations Act or the powers of the Commission.'

This judgment is welcomed not least because it is the view of many Muslims that the CRE and the race relations legislation and policies have been of little help to Muslims and, indeed, have exacerbated our problems.

In the case of Jews and Sikhs the Courts have dealt with the absence of religious discrimination laws by accepting them as ethnic groups under the Act. In *Mandla* v *Dowell Lee* [1983] IRLR 209 the House of Lords brought in elements of religion into the definition of 'ethnic group' so as to bring discrimination against Sikhs (in that particular case) within the ambit of direct race discrimination. In the case of Jews the Courts accepted that it would be unthinkable for race relations legislation not to have sought to protect Jews. We do not disagree that the social problems in this country made it imperative to protect these religious minorities under the protective umbrella of the Act. Indeed there was much confusion during the Parliamentary debate on the 1965 Bill as to whether it was unlawful to discriminate against Jews given the omission of religion. According to Parliamentary records the words ethnic origins were used 'by the Home Secretary (at that time James Callaghan), or at any rate, the Parliamentary Draftsman, on the basis of including religion. Furthermore, that was the message communicated to the leaders of the Jewish community on repeated occasions'.

The inclusion of Jews and Sikhs (and Gypsies for that matter) as ethnic groups involved a purposive interpretation of the Act and was motivated by considerations of public policy. There was a pressing social need to outlaw the discrimination suffered by Jews and Sikhs and the RRA 76 was the only means by which this could be engineered. Whilst that was a morally and socially just course to pursue Muslims appear not to come within this category of oppressed minorities requiring protection.

The position of Muslims under the Act is that they are not deemed to constitute an ethnic group and so cannot claim direct discrimination. In the words of the Tribunal Chairman in Commission for Racial Equality v Precision Manufacturing Limited (1991):

'. . . to discriminate against Muslims, appalling and inexcusable though it may be, therefore is not to discriminate on racial grounds'.

The Courts, however, have held that discrimination against a Muslim could amount to indirect discrimination if the complainant is a member of a racial group in which 'Islam' is the dominant faith. In other words if the victim's ethnic or national origins are from a geographical location which has an association with Islam. The ability to claim indirect discrimination offers some remedy under the Act. However, it is far from satisfactory as the following makes clear:

In the absence of legislation to eliminate discrimination on grounds of religion, the prejudice against Muslims will, therefore, continue to flourish. In the case of other religious minorities the lack of legislation appears not to have hindered the judiciary in interpreting the Act in such a way as to provide them with legal redress. Leaving aside the case of Muslims, the judiciary has attempted to perform the functions ascribed to them of 'protecting the minorities and providing leadership in the solution of social problems requiring the use of law'. However, the English judiciary has displayed a marked insensitivity to the discrimination suffered by Muslims (which may be merely a reflection of the perception of Muslims by the majority community). It was precisely a corresponding reluctance by the Courts to outlaw racial discrimination that led to the enactment of the first Race Relations Act in 1965; it is time for the Government to propose remedies against the discrimination directed at Muslims and other minorities. It is in this vein that the recent West Yorkshire Multifaith conference on Inner Cities convened by the Government-sponsored Inner Cities Religious Council in Huddersfield on 27 October 1992 passed a resolution 'support(ing) the call for all major religions in this country to be recognised under national law and ask(ing) that legislation should be enacted to make discrimination on the grounds of religion unlawful'.

The Commission for Racial Equality (CRE), in its contribution to the same review, endorses this approach.

Review of the Race Relations Act, Commission for Racial Equality (1992) at p. 80.

By bringing in elements of religion into the definition of 'ethnic group' in the Race Relations Act 1976, the House of Lords in *Mandla* v *Dowell Lee* [1983] IRLR 209 has, to an extent, made it possible to get round the lack of a ban on religious discrimination as such. Much discrimination against Jews and Sikhs can be dealt with as discrimination against them as members of those ethnic groups. And much religious discrimination is caught by the law on indirect racial discrimination, at least where the exercise of a religion has a particular association with the country of origin. A case of discrimination against Muslims was held by a Sheffield tribunal to be indirect racial discrimination. But, as the law currently stands, compensation would only become payable if intention was proved. Improvements in the general law of indirect racial discrimination, in particular permitting compensation in all cases as we advocate elsewhere in this review, could remove much difficulty.

Even so, a new statutory prohibition on religious discrimination might be better than trying to stretch the Race Relations Act to cover all cases of religious discrimination. Stretching the Act might not work where the religious practice at issue is that of a minority group in the country of origin and that group is not recognised as an ethnic group under the 1976 Act.

It is anomalous that protection against religious discrimination exists in Northern Ireland, but not in the rest of the UK. But we doubt whether it would be appropriate merely to tack onto the Race Relations Act a prohibition on religious discrimination for this Commission to enforce. The whole subject has ramifications going well beyond the area of good race relations.

For that reason, we are keen to see the debate widened and would hope that Government would listen carefully to the views expressed. We can envisage that the principled conclusion might well be to make religious discrimination unlawful, and, if so, it would reflect the considerable measure of public support in our own consultation.

The CRE's annual report for 1993–4 gives two illustrations of subsequent decisions where Muslims have been able to succeed on the ground of indirect discrimination.

Annual report, CRE, 1993–4.

Mr M Yassin v Northwest Homecare Ltd

The Liverpool Industrial Tribunal awarded £3,000 compensation for injury to feelings and loss of potential earnings after Mr Yassin was dropped from a sales representative training course. Mr Yassin had sought to be able to attend Friday prayers at the Mosque but the training manager said he had to 'choose between work and the Mosque'.

The Tribunal said: 'The respondents demanded a type and degree of commitment from the applicant that amounted to discrimination . . . The requirement not to attend Mosque . . . seems to us to be wholly unreasonable. In a working day of 12 or 13 hours there had to be breaks of refreshment and rest. The working day was not strictly defined. One hour a week to visit the Mosque (and the hour included travelling time) could easily be accommodated, even when a high commitment to the job was required.'

Mr Mohammed Azam and 16 others v JH Walker Ltd

The applicants had been working for the Dewsbury textile firm for an average of 10 years when management announced a change to holiday and work arrangements. For 20 years Muslim employees had been allowed to take Eid as holiday or unpaid leave. They made up any loss of output for the firm in extra hours on other days. The applicants were only able to give three days notice of Eid and were then told not to take it. When they did take it they were then given a final, written warning. This was, the Tribunal found, indirect discrimination against the complainants.

If, in the light of all these developments there were now to be a case along the lines of *Mandla* v *Lee* but with a Muslim girl, rather than a Sikh boy, would you, as a member of the Judicial Committee of the House of Lords extend the definition of ethnic group so as to protect Muslims under the *existing* legislation? Would you expect to be supported, or criticised, for that decision by Muslims?

As in the case of race, it might have been thought that discrimination 'on the grounds of sex' was a relatively straightforward matter. However, in Chapter 3

we considered the case of *Chessington* (Chapter 3 p. 110) where the court
grappled with whether discrimination against a transsexual constituted sex
discrimination? *Chessington* was used to illustrate the effect on statutory
interpretation of a ruling of a European Court of Justice decision in the case of *P*
v *S and Cornwall County Council* (C-13/94) [1996] IRLR 347. Below we extract
the opinion of the Advocate-General in *P* v *S*, who identifies the legal issues and
suggests a ruling to the ECJ. The ECJ ruled in favour of the applicant.

Transsexuality and Law

First, what is transsexuality? Far be it from me to venture into territory
requiring quite different knowledge and learning. I consider it preferable to
recall the definition given in a recommendation of the Council of Europe
which states that 'transsexualism is a syndrome characterised by a dual
personality, one physical, the other psychological, together with such a
profound conviction of belonging to the other sex that the transsexual person
is prompted to ask for the corresponding bodily "correction" to be made.'.

The applicant has produced a great number of learned articles which claim
that the causes of the condition are to be found in biological dysfunctions
which are therefore present already at birth, or else in psychological disorders
linked to environment. The effect is, however, the same: biological sex and
sexual identity fail to coincide. Let it suffice here, however, to note the facts
that studies relating to transsexuality have produced highly interesting results,
in any event such as to refute entirely groundless old taboos and prejudices,
by turning attention away from the *moral* dimension of the question, which
is entirely reductive and at times misleading, to the strictly medical and
scientific.

What I am concerned to emphasise is that the phenomenon of transsexuality, even though it is not of great significance in statistical terms, constitutes
a reality today which has been discussed in various bodies, not only scientific
but also legal, in particular from the point of view of fundamental human
rights. Consequently, the law is faced with that reality — and is destined to
come up against it to an increasing degree. This is inevitable. In society as it
is today, in which customs and morals are changing rapidly, citizens are
guaranteed ever wider and deeper protection of their freedoms, and social and
legal studies are increasingly taking on present-day — and, for that very
reason, real — values on the principle that it is effective to do so, it would
be unjustifiable to reject out of hand the problem of transsexuality — which
certainly can still be assessed quite independently in moral terms — or simply
to condemn it and consider it contrary to the law.

To my mind, the law cannot cut itself off from society as it actually is, and
must not fail to adjust to it as quickly as possible. Otherwise it risks imposing
outdated views and taking on a static role. In so far as the law seeks to
regulate relations in society, it must on the contrary keep up with social
change, and must therefore be capable of regulating new situations brought
to light by social change and advances in science. From that point of view,
there is no doubt that for present purposes the principle of the alleged
immutability of civil status has been overtaken by events. This is so in so far

as and from the time that the fact that one cannot change one's sex for bureaucratic and administrative purposes no longer corresponds to the true situation, if only on account of the scientific advances made in the field of gender reassignment.

A swift glance at the situation in the various Member States of the Community reveals a clear tendency, especially since the early 1980s, towards ever wider recognition of transsexuality, both by legislation and by judicial decision . . .

Answers to the questions

The national court asks the Court to determine whether, in the light of the purpose of the Directive, as set out in Article 1, the dismissal of a transsexual on account of a sex change constitutes discrimination prohibited by the Directive, and, more generally, whether Article 3(1) must be interpreted as also encompassing, with regard to working conditions, discrimination against transsexuals.

The national court starts from the premiss that the Directive, in particular Article 3(1) in so far as it prescribes that 'there shall be no discrimination whatsoever on grounds of sex', does not mean, or at least does not necessarily mean, that discrimination can exist only as between a male and a female, but may be interpreted as covering discrimination against transsexuals as well.

First of all, I would observe that the provisions relevant to this case are rather Article 2(1), which lays down in general terms the prohibition of discrimination on grounds of sex, and Article 5(1) of the Directive, which more specifically prohibits discrimination on grounds of sex with regard to the conditions governing dismissal. The question referred must therefore be reformulated to that effect.

Having said that, it is necessary in any event to establish whether the dismissal of a transsexual because of her change of sex falls within the field of application of Community law, more specifically of the Directive concerning equal treatment for men and women.

While it is quite true that the Directive prohibits any discrimination whatsoever on grounds of sex, it is equally indisputable that the wording of the principle of equal treatment which it lays down refers to the traditional man/woman dichotomy.

In order to ascertain whether the Directive can, as the industrial tribunal suggests, be so interpreted as to cover discrimination against transsexuals too, it must, in any event, be determined in the first place whether the unfavourable treatment of transsexuals constitutes discrimination on grounds of sex. It will then be necessary to decide whether it is only discrimination between men and women which is covered by the expression 'discrimination on grounds of sex' or, more generally, all unfavourable treatment connected with sex.

I shall start by calling to mind the proposition, which has ever stronger support in medical and scientific circles, that it is necessary to go beyond the traditional classification and recognise that, in addition to the man/woman dichotomy, there is a range of characteristics, behaviour and roles shared by men and women, so that sex *itself* ought rather to be thought of as a continuum. From that point of view, it is clear that it would not be right to continue to treat as unlawful solely acts of discrimination on grounds of sex which are referrable to men and women in the traditional sense of those terms, while refusing to protect those who are also treated unfavourably precisely because of their sex and/or sexual identity.

The argument just put forward, attractive as it is, requires a redefinition of sex which merits deeper consideration in more appropriate circles; consequently, this is not the path that I propose that the Court should follow. I fully realise that from time immemorial a person's sex has merely been ascertained, without need of the law to define it. The law dislikes ambiguities, and it is certainly simpler to think in terms of Adam and Eve.

Having said that, I regard as obsolete the idea that the law should take into consideration, and protect, a woman who has suffered discrimination in comparison with a man, or vice versa, but denies that protection to those who are also *discriminated against*, again by reason of sex, merely because they fall outside the traditional man/woman classification.

The objection is taken too much for granted, and has been raised on several occasions in these proceedings, that the factor of sex discrimination is missing, on the grounds that 'female transsexuals' are not treated differently from 'male transsexuals'. In short, both are treated unfavourably, hence there can be no discrimination at all. A survey of the relevant case law confirms that point of view, albeit with some exceptions.

I am not convinced by that view. It is quite true that even if P had been in the opposite situation, that is to say changing from female to male, it is possible that she would have been dismissed anyway. One fact, however, is not just possible, but certain: P would not have been dismissed if she had remained a man.

So how can it be claimed that discrimination on grounds of sex was not involved? How can it be denied that the cause of discrimination was precisely, and solely, sex? To my mind, where unfavourable treatment of a transsexual is related to (or rather is caused by) a change of sex, there is discrimination by reason of sex or on grounds of sex, if that is preferred.

On this subject I cannot do other than recall that the prohibition of discrimination on grounds of sex is an aspect of the principle of equality, a principle which requires no account to be taken of discriminatory factors, principally sex, race, language and religion. What matters is that, in like situations, individuals should be treated alike . . .

I must add that, for the purposes of this case, sex is important as a convention, a social parameter. The discrimination of which women are frequently the victims is not of course due to their physical characteristics, but rather to their role, to the image which society has of women. Hence the rationale for less favourable treatment is the social role which women are supposed to play and certainly not their physical characteristics. In the same way it must be recognised that the unfavourable treatment suffered by transsexuals is most often linked to a negative image, a moral judgment which has nothing to do with their abilities in the sphere of employment.

Such a situation is still less acceptable when the social change and scientific advances made in this area in recent years are taken into consideration. Whilst it is true, as I have already said, that transsexuals are in fact not very significant in statistical terms, it is equally true that for that very reason it is vital that they should have at least a minimum of protection. On this view, to maintain that the unfavourable treatment suffered by P was not on grounds of sex because it was due to her change of sex or else because in such a case it is not possible to speak of discrimination between the two sexes would be a quibbling formalistic interpretation and a betrayal of the true essence of that fundamental and inalienable value which is equality.

It remains to be determined whether a Directive whose purpose, according to its wording, is to ensure the elimination of discrimination between men and women may also cover unfavourable treatment afforded to transsexuals. In other words, in the absence of specific legislation which expressly takes transsexuals into consideration, must it be concluded that transsexuals — once they have suffered discrimination — are deprived of any legal protection whatsoever? . . .

I note that the Directive is nothing if not an expression of a general principle and a fundamental right. Here I would point out that respect for fundamental rights is one of the general principles of Community law, the observance of which the Court has a duty to ensure; and that 'there can be no doubt that the *elimination of discrimination based on sex* forms part of those fundamental rights'.

When the problem is expressed in those terms, it seems to me only too clear that the Directive, which dates from 1976, took account of what may be defined as 'normal' reality at the time of its adoption. It is quite natural that it should not have expressly taken into account a question and a reality that were only just beginning to be 'discovered' at that time. However, as the expression of a more general principle, on the basis of which sex should be irrelevant to the treatment everyone receives, the Directive should be construed in a broader perspective, including therefore all situations in which sex appears as a discriminatory factor . . .

Finally, I am well aware that I am asking the Court to make a 'courageous' decision. I am asking it to do so, however, in the profound conviction that what is at stake is a universal fundamental value, indelibly etched in modern legal traditions and in the constitutions of the more advanced countries: *the irrelevance of a person's sex with regard to the rules regulating relations in society*. Whosoever believes in that value cannot accept the idea that a law should permit a person to be dismissed because she is a woman, or because he is a man, or because he or she changes from one of the two sexes (whichever it may be) to the other by means of an operation which — according to current medical knowledge — is the only remedy capable of bringing body and mind into harmony. Any other solution would sound like a moral condemnation — a condemnation, moreover, out of step with the times — of transsexuality, precisely when scientific advances and social change in this area are opening a perspective on the problem which certainly transcends the moral one.

I am quite clear, I repeat, that in Community law there is no precise provision *specifically* and literally intended to regulate the problem; but such a provision can readily and clearly be inferred from the principles and objectives of Community social law, the statement of reasons for the Directive underlining 'the harmonisation of living and working conditions while maintaining their improvement', and also the case law of the Court itself, which is ever alert and to the fore in ensuring that disadvantaged persons are protected. Consequently, I consider that it would be a pity to miss this opportunity of leaving a mark of undeniable civil substance, by taking a decision which is bold but fair and legally correct, inasmuch it is undeniably based on and consonant with the great value of equality.

Finally, I would point out in the words of Advocate-General Trabucchi in an Opinion now 20 years old, that 'if we want Community law to be more than a mere mechanical system of economics and to constitute instead a system commensurate with the society which it has to govern, if we wish it to be a legal system corresponding to the concept of social justice and European integration, not only of the economy but of the people, we cannot disappoint the [national] court's expectations, which are more than those of legal form.

Questions:

1.   The Advocate-General states: 'To my mind, the law cannot cut itself off from society as it actually is, and must not fail to adjust to it as quickly as possible. Otherwise it risks imposing outdated views and taking on a static role. In so far as the law seeks to regulate relations in society, it must on the contrary keep up with social change, and must therefore be capable of regulating new situations brought to light by social change and advances in science.' Do you agree with this?

2.   Are scientific advances a good reason for changing the law through interpretation? How are they to be balanced with considerations of morality? (Recall the debate over the relationship of law and morality in Chapter 8.)

3.   Does our notion of what a man or woman is depend on: law, society, or science?

4.   What type of statutory interpretation is the Advocate-General using?

5.   To what extent does the Advocate-General employ 'legal' analysis to support the outcome he reaches, and to what extent does he use a call to principles? What are these principles: equality, justice, courage? Does his use of principle exemplify Dworkin's theory of adjudication? (See Chapter 7.)

The European Court of Human Rights' cases cited in the *P* v *S* opinion were not centrally concerned with discrimination and jobs, rather they concerned alleged violations of privacy and family life when transsexuals were denied treatment as a member of the gender they claimed for themselves. In the recent case of *X, Y & Z* v *UK* the ECHR considered whether a transsexual, his partner and their child (conceived through donor insemination (AID)) had their rights to privacy and family life violated when the transsexual parent was refused registration as the father on the birth certificate. The Registrar General's view was that only a biological man could be regarded as a father for the purposes of the registration. The case indicates how the issue can be raised as a rights based one, and provides an interesting comparison with *P* v *S*, in terms of the legal analysis used.

European Court of Human Rights Case of X, Y and Z v *The United Kingdom* (75/1995/581/667), (1997) 24 EHRR 143, (ECHR).

I.   ALLEGED VIOLATION OF ARTICLE 8 OF THE CONVENTION

32.   The applicants, with whom the Commission agreed, submitted that the lack of legal recognition of the relationship between X and Z amounted to a violation of Article 8 of the Convention, which provides:

> '1.   Everyone has the right to respect for his private and family life, his home and his correspondence.
> 2.   There shall be no interference by a public authority with the exercise of this right except such as is in accordance with the law and is necessary in a democratic society in the interests of national security, public safety or the economic well-being of the country, for the prevention of disorder or crime, for the protection of health or morals, or for the protection of the rights and freedoms of others.'

The Government denied that Article 8 was applicable and, in the alternative, claimed that there had been no violation . . .

2.   The Court's general approach
41.   The Court reiterates that, although the essential object of Article 8 is to protect the individual against arbitrary interferences by the public authorities, there may in addition be positive obligations inherent in an effective respect for private or family life. The boundaries between the State's positive and negative obligations under this provision do not always lend themselves to precise definition; nonetheless, the applicable principles are similar. In both contexts, regard must be had to the fair balance that has to be struck between the competing interests of the individual and of the community as a whole, and in both cases the State enjoys a certain margin of appreciation (citations omitted).

42.   The present case is distinguishable from the previous cases concerning transsexuals which have been brought before the Court (see . . . *Rees* judgment, the . . . *Cossey* judgment and the *B* v *France* judgment of 25 March 1992, Series A no. 232-C), because here the applicants' complaint is not that the domestic law makes no provision for the recognition of the transsexual's change of identity, but rather that it is not possible for such a person to be registered as the father of a child; indeed, it is for this reason that the Court is examining this case in relation to family, rather than private, life.

43.   It is true that the Court has held in the past that where the existence of a family tie with a child has been established, the State must act in a manner calculated to enable that tie to be developed and legal safeguards must be established that render possible, from the moment of birth or as soon as practicable thereafter, the child's integration in his family. However, hitherto in this context it has been called upon to consider only family ties existing between biological parents and their offspring. The present case raises different issues, since Z was conceived by AID and is not related, in the biological sense, to X, who is a transsexual.

44.   The Court observes that there is no common European standard with regard to the granting of parental rights to transsexuals. In addition, it has not been established before the Court that there exists any generally shared approach amongst the High Contracting Parties with regard to the manner in which the social relationship between a child conceived by AID and the person who performs the role of father should be reflected in law. Indeed, according to the information available to the Court, although the technology of medically assisted procreation has been available in Europe for several decades, many of the issues to which it gives rise, particularly with regard to the question of filiation, remain the subject of debate. For example, there is no consensus amongst the member States of the Council of Europe on the question whether the interests of a child conceived in such a way are best served by preserving the anonymity of the donor of the sperm or whether the child should have the right to know the donor's identity.

   Since the issues in the case, therefore, touch on areas where there is little common ground amongst the member States of the Council of Europe and, generally speaking, the law appears to be in a transitional stage, the respondent State must be afforded a wide margin of appreciation . . .

51.   It is impossible to predict the extent to which the absence of a legal connection between X and Z will affect the latter's development. As previously mentioned, at the present time there is uncertainty with regard to how the interests of children in Z's position can best be protected (see paragraph 44 above) and the Court should not adopt or impose any single viewpoint.

52.   In conclusion, given that transsexuality raises complex scientific, legal, moral and social issues, in respect of which there is no generally shared approach among the Contracting States, the Court is of the opinion that Article 8 cannot, in this context, be taken to imply an obligation for the respondent State formally to recognise as the father of a child a person who is not the biological father. That being so, the fact that the law of the United Kingdom does not allow special legal recognition of the relationship between X and Z does not amount to a failure to respect family life within the meaning of that provision.

   It follows that there has been no violation of Article 8 of the Convention.

Questions:
1.   In what way(s) does the legal analysis in this case differ from that used in *P v S*? Were you surprised by the Court's reasoning in this case? If so, why?

2. Do you think it was a good idea, strategically, for the applicant in this case to stress the impact on his children of the Court's decision?

In their commentary written shortly after the *P* v *S* case, Campbell and Lardy state '[i]f tolerating discrimination against a transsexual person would be a "failure to respect the dignity and freedom to which he or she is entitled", then to permit discrimination against someone on the grounds that he or she is gay or lesbian must surely also represent such a failure of respect.'.

Imagine a case where a female employee whose contract of employment entitles her to travel concessions for herself and her 'spouse and dependants'. Regulations state that 'spouse' includes unmarried couples 'subject to a statutory declaration being made that a meaningful relationship has existed for a period of two years or more'. The women applies for travel concessions for her female partner, with whom she declares she has had a 'meaningful relationship' for over two years. The employer refuses to allow the travel pass to her partner. Try making a legal argument based on *P* v *S*, that discrimination on grounds of sexual orientation violates the equal treatment directive. Now read the following case extract, which involved the above facts (and which is famous not just for its legal content, but because Cherie Booth was the barrister).

Grant v *South-West Trains Ltd* (C-249/96) [1998] ICR 449, at pp. 478–480 ECJ.

37. Finally, the applicant submits that it follows from *P* v *S* (Case C-13/94) [1996] ICR 795 that differences of treatment based on sexual orientation are included in the 'discrimination based on sex' prohibited by article 119 of the EC Treaty.

38. In *P* v *S* the court was asked whether a dismissal based on the change of sex of the worker concerned was to be regarded as 'discrimination on grounds of sex' within the meaning of Directive (76/207/EEC).

39. The national court was uncertain whether the scope of that Directive was wider than that of the Sex Discrimination Act 1975, which it had to apply and which in its view applied only to discrimination based on the worker's belonging to one or other of the sexes.

40. In their observations to the court the United Kingdom Government and the Commission submitted that the Directive prohibited only discrimination based on the fact that the worker concerned belonged to one sex or the other, not discrimination based on the worker's gender reassignment.

41. In reply to that argument, the court stated that the provisions of the Directive prohibiting discrimination between men and women were simply the expression, in their limited field of application, of the principle of equality, which is one of the fundamental principles of Community law. It considered that that circumstance argued against a restrictive interpretation of the scope of those provisions and in favour of applying them to discrimination based on the worker's gender reassignment.

42. The court considered that such discrimination was in fact based, essentially if not exclusively, on the sex of the person concerned. That

reasoning, which leads to the conclusion that such discrimination is to be prohibited just as is discrimination based on the fact that a person belongs to a particular sex, is limited to the case of a worker's gender reassignment and does not therefore apply to differences of treatment based on a person's sexual orientation.

43.   The applicant submits, however, that, like certain provisions of national law or of international conventions, the Community provisions on equal treatment of men and women should be interpreted as covering discrimination based on sexual orientation. She refers in particular to the International Covenant on Civil and Political Rights of 19 December 1966 (United Nations Treaty Series, vol. 999, p. 171), in which, in the view of the Human Rights Committee established under article 28 of the Covenant, the term 'sex' is to be taken as including sexual orientation (see communication No. 488/1992, *Toonen* v *Australia* (1994) 1–3 HRR 97, point 8.7).

44.   The Covenant is one of the international instruments relating to the protection of human rights of which the court takes account in applying the fundamental principles of Community law: see, for example, *Orken* v *Commission of the European Communities* (Case 374/87) [1989] ECR 3283, 3351, para. 31, and *Dzodzi* v *Belgian State* (Cases C-297/88 and C-197/89) [1990] ECR I-3763, 3800, para. 68.

45.   However, although respect for the fundamental rights which form an integral part of those general principles of law is a condition of the legality of Community acts, those rights cannot in themselves have the effect of extending the scope of the EC Treaty provisions beyond the competences of the Community: see, inter alia, on the scope of article 235 of the EC Treaty as regards respect for human rights, *Opinion No. 2/94* [1996] ECR I-1759, 1789, paras. 34 and 35.

46.   Furthermore, in the communication referred to by the applicant, the Human Rights Committee, which is not a judicial institution and whose findings have no binding force in law, confined itself, as it stated itself without giving specific reasons, to 'noting . . . that in its view the reference to "sex" in articles 2, paragraph 1, and 26 is to be taken as including sexual orientation.'

47.   Such an observation, which does not in any event appear to reflect the interpretation so far generally accepted of the concept of discrimination based on sex which appears in various international instruments concerning the protection of fundamental rights, cannot in any case constitute a basis for the court to extend the scope of article 119 of the EC Treaty. That being so, the scope of that article, as of any provision of Community law, is to be determined only by having regard to its wording and purpose, its place in the scheme of the treaty and its legal context. It follows from the considerations set out above that Community law as it stands at present does not cover discrimination based on sexual orientation, such as that in issue in the main proceedings.

48.   It should be observed, however, that the Treaty of Amsterdam amending the Treaty on European Union, the Treaties establishing the European Communities and certain related acts, signed on 2 October 1997, provides for the insertion in the EC Treaty of an article 6a which, once the Treaty of

Amsterdam has entered into force, will allow the Council under certain conditions (a unanimous vote on a proposal from the Commission after consulting the European Parliament) to take appropriate action to eliminate various forms of discrimination, including discrimination based on sexual orientation.

49. Finally, in the light of the foregoing, there is no need to consider the applicant's argument that a refusal such as that which she encountered is not objectively justified.

50. Accordingly, the answer to the national tribunal must be that the refusal by an employer to allow travel concessions to the person of the same sex with whom a worker has a stable relationship, where such concessions are allowed to a worker's spouse or to the person of the opposite sex with whom a worker has a stable relationship outside marriage, does not constitute discrimination prohibited by article 119 of the EC Treaty or Directive (75/117/EEC).

Questions:

1. What sources of law are used in this case? What weight is accorded to them?

2. What reasons can you give for the different outcome in this case compared with that of *P* v *S*? What reasons did the Court give for distinguishing the two?

3. As a matter of legal strategy do you think it was advisable to base an important issue of legal principle on a matter which may be regarded as comparatively trivial, such as the use of train passes?

Throughout this book and so far in this chapter you have examined how categories which you might have thought were fixed — race, gender, religious belief or political opinion — have posed difficulties for statute drafters, judges interpreting statutes, and individuals. The issue of disability discrimination raises this issue more explicitly. If you were drafting disability discrimination legislation, would you attempt to define 'disability' or leave it up to judges? What are the advantages and disadvantages of each approach? If you would seek to define it, what terms would you use? What is a 'disability'? Is it ever justifiable to discriminate against a person on grounds of disability? Often efficiency arguments, such as those we explored in Chapter 8, are used to argue against measures (such as access to buildings) which are necessary for equal treatment of those with disabilities.

The much criticised Disability Discrimination Act 1995 has provided the following definition of 'disability'; consider it in the light of your Chapter 3 skills of Statutory Interpretation:

Disability Discrimination Act 1995, s. 1.

(1) Subject to the provisions of Schedule 1, a person has a disability for the purposes of this Act if he has a physical or mental impairment which has a substantial and long-term adverse effect on his ability to carry out normal day-to-day activities.

(2) In this Act 'disabled person' means a person who has a disability.

Question:
1. What problems can you foresee with this definition?

A schedule to the Act expands and explains the definition.

Disability Discrimination Act 1995, Schedule 1.

PROVISIONS SUPPLEMENTING SECTION 1

Impairment

1.—(1) 'Mental impairment' includes an impairment resulting from or consisting of a mental illness only if the illness is a clinically well-recognised illness.

[What is a clinically well-recognised illness? Who decides if an illness is clinically well-recognised? What happens if doctors and other experts disagree on this?]

Long-term effects

2.—(1)   The effect of an impairment is a long-term effect if—
   (a)   it has lasted at least 12 months;'
   (b)   the period for which it lasts is likely to be at least 12 months; or
   (c)   it is likely to last for the rest of the life of the person affected.
   (2)   Where an impairment ceases to have a substantial adverse effect on a person's ability to carry out normal day-to-day activities, it is to be treated as continuing to have that effect if that effect is likely to recur . . .

Severe disfigurement

3.—(1)   An impairment which consists of a severe disfigurement is to be treated as having a substantial adverse effect on the ability of the person concerned to carry out normal day-to-day activities . . .

[Why do you think 'severe disfigurement' was expressly included? Would it fit in the above general definition without this section?]

Normal day-to-day activities

4.—(1)   An impairment is to be taken to affect the ability of the person concerned to carry out normal day-to-day activities only if it affects one of the following—
   (a)   mobility;
   (b)   manual dexterity;
   (c)   physical co-ordination;
   (d)   continence;
   (e)   ability to lift, carry or otherwise move everyday objects;
   (f)   speech, hearing or eyesight;
   (g)   memory or ability to concentrate, learn or understand; or
   (h)   perception of the risk of physical danger . . .

[What about the ability to work? Why do you think it was not included?]

Effect of medical treatment

6.—(1)   An impairment which would be likely to have a substantial adverse effect on the ability of the person concerned to carry out normal day-to-day activities, but for the fact that measures are being taken to treat or correct it, is to be treated as having that effect.

(2)   In sub-paragraph (1) 'measures' includes, in particular, medical treatment and the use of a prosthesis or other aid.

(3)   Sub-paragraph (1) does not apply—

(a)   in relation to the impairment of a person's sight, to the extent that the impairment is, in his case, correctable by spectacles or contact lenses or in such other ways as may be prescribed; or

(b)   in relation to such other impairments as may be prescribed, in such circumstances as may be prescribed.

. . .

Definition Regulations produced under the Act ('secondary legislation') have provided that certain conditions are to be regarded as not amounting to impairments for the purposes of the Act. These are:

- addiction to or dependency on alcohol, nicotine, or any other substance (other than as a result of the substance being medically prescribed);
- seasonal allergic rhinitis (e.g. hayfever), except where it aggravates the effect of another impairment;
- tendency to set fires;
- tendency to steal;
- tendency to physical or sexual abuse of other persons;
- exhibitionism;
- voyeurism.

Also, disfigurements which consist of a tattoo (which has not been removed), non-medical body piercing, or something attached through such piercing, are to be treated as not having a substantial adverse effect on the person's ability to carry out normal day-to-day activities.

[Why should these not amount to a 'disability'?]

The Act has been much criticised, particularly for its definition of disability. One of the main criticisms is that the definition is medical and physical, while disabilities are also related to the conditions of the social environment. For example, if ramps were used instead of steps into buildings, wheel chair users would not experience a disability in accessing buildings. Just as glasses can make poor sight less relevant (a factor which the statutory definition accounts for), so other changes in society can make other disabilities less relevant. A recent United Nations study into disability discussed what the elements of a definition should be, and opted for one which would also reflect the societal and environmental factors which make a disability a disability.

Despouy (1993) 'Human Rights and Disabled Persons', *UN Human Rights Study Series*, No. 6 (UN, New York).

100.   In defining a disabled person, domestic laws use different criteria, characteristics or classifications. For example, some include total and partial impairment of senses, and physical and intellectual capacities. Others refer to a handicap or deviation of a social nature, injury or illness, or incapacity to accomplish physiological functions or to obtain and keep employment. Some definitions refer to age as a factor of disability. These definitions usually also reflect the consequences for the individual — cultural, social, economic and environmental — that stem from the disability. Of these the following may be mentioned: inability to function normally in certain areas of social life, and restricted possibilities of education, rehabilitation and employment . . .

101.   . . . The Special Rapporteur considers that it will be sufficient to restrict himself to outlining some basic criteria which the failure definition should contain so that it will encompass, in addition to the medical and clinical aspects of disability, the social and cultural factors attendant on disability. It may be recalled here that the members of the Sub-Commission at its fortieth session agreed with the proposal to formulate a definition, the essential criterion of which would be the existence of specific long-term problems affecting the person or behaviour of the disabled person and constituting major long-term obstacles to the enjoyment of human rights, to equality of opportunity and treatment, to social participation and to independent living.

102.   . . . The balance which was required in the definition involved both clinical and socio-cultural aspects. Too broad or too vague a formula from the clinical point of view ran the risk of undermining its primary objective, which was to protect the human rights of persons who really needed protection, in other words, those who suffered from some type of disability and were therefore in a situation of genuine disadvantage. It was this that justified, or rather required, special attention (regulation). On the other hand, a narrow definition from the socio-cultural point of view meant that a large number of persons who obviously needed protection might be cut off from it. In other words, where this aspect was concerned, the definition needed to be capable of a broad interpretation in order to be compatible with concepts applicable to human rights and to serve as a universal reference . . .

104.   While the Special Rapporteur makes no claim to formulate a universally valid definition — the drafting of which should be the responsibility of the Ad Hoc open-ended working group of government experts to elaborate standard rules on the equalization of opportunities for disabled persons — he considers that the conjunction of these clinical and socio-cultural elements, on which there is a clear consensus, enables a disabled person to be defined as follows: 'Any person suffering from a permanent or prolonged functional disorder, whether physical or mental, which having regard to his age and social environment entails considerable disadvantages for the purpose of his family, social, educational or occupational integration, and for the effective

enjoyment of his human rights, shall be considered disabled'. This formula, it should be reiterated, not only takes clinical aspects into account, but also the specific issues which affect disabled persons and create certain obstacles to the enjoyment of their human rights, to equality of opportunities and treatment, to their participation in society and to their independence.

Question:
1. Do you prefer the definition offered by the British legislation or by the UN study? Why? What is the difference between the two?

INFORMED CONSENT

In considering the issue of transsexualism in the first section of this Chapter our concern was with the issue of discrimination against the post-operative trans-sexual. However, a prior question is whether transsexuals should be permitted, on policy grounds, to consent to such radical and invasive surgery. It seems now to be generally accepted that gender reassignment surgery is lawful. This may be contrasted with the case of *R v Brown* (extracted in Chapter 7) in which a majority of the House of Lords was prepared to use criminal law to enforce certain limitations on those activities to which adults may consent in the privacy of their homes, even if any resulting injuries are trivial. Indeed the issue of consent has been a recurring theme in this book. The case of *R v R* (again extracted in Chapter 7) also concerned the issue of consent — in this case whether a wife could revoke her consent to sexual intercourse with her husband, which was presumed upon marriage. Similarly the line of cases on disabled neonates and children considered at the beginning of Chapter 2 addressed the issue of who, if anyone, could consent or refuse their consent to medical treatment of infants who lacked capacity. In this chapter we attempt to bring together these various themes in a move towards 'A Jurisprudence of Consent'.

S Lee, 'Towards a Jurisprudence of Consent' in J Eekelaar and J Bell (eds), *Oxford Essays in Jurisprudence (3rd series)*, Oxford University Press (1987) pp. 199–220, at pp. 199–200, 202, 216, 219.

The concept of consent features throughout the law . . .
Given the wide range of legal contexts in which consent appears, it seems unlikely that we can discover some 'real essence' in the concept. Lawyers manipulate the notion of consent. There are undoubtedly some limits to what could plausibly count as consent but there are undoubtedly many plausible interpretations within those limits. The questions for debate are not about the abstract 'meaning' of consent but what does the law use consent to represent and what content would we prefer the law to attribute to it? . . .
We need to decide when and under what conditions a person is capable of autonomous decision-making, and when we should override exercises of autonomy. This requires consideration of at least the following issues:

(1) Does the person concerned have the capacity to consent?

(2)   If not, who is in the best position to act as proxy and on what criteria should the proxy decide?
(3)   Is the 'consent' voluntary?
(4)   Is the 'consent' based on information as to the risks of the course of conduct?
(5)   Is the 'consent' based on information as to the alternative courses of action?
(6)   Even if the above conditions are satisfied, is there any overriding reason to invalidate the consent? . . .

I suspect that medical law and ethics is getting ahead of the field. There is tremendous interest in the concept of consent as it applies to medicine, but the rest of our lives may not match the ideal of informed consent. This is clearly something to consider in a variety of contexts. Decisions on a range of major and minor matters (marriage, career, university, degree subject) may seem relatively uninformed. Who next, once the law has forced the powerful doctors towards informed consent? I have little doubt that *Sidaway* will come to be seen as a significant expansion of the ambit of informed consent. Medical negligence cases seem to take years to come to court, but I imagine that ever since *Sidaway* plaintiffs have been tacking on to claims of negligent treatment a claim that they were not in a position to give an informed consent [*Sidaway* v *Bethlem* 1985 1 All ER 643, in which the House of Lords ruled that while the doctrine of consent did not form part of English law, nevertheless certain risks accompanying medical treatment did have to be disclosed to the patient.]. Once those cases come to court, if not before, medical   practice will alter to cover against such actions in the future. But there is still much work to be done on the detail of what information is necessary for informed consent . . .
If we accept that consent is a concept which lawyers and others can shape, then we need to consider from where the shapers derive their ideas. Lord Scarman's *Sidaway* judgment included an expansive appreciation of academic influences. The American landmark case of *Canterbury* v *Spence*, said Lord Scarman, is:

discussed learnedly and lucidly in an article published in the Law Quarterly Review, upon which I have drawn extensively in reaching my opinion in this appeal. I wish to put on record my deep appreciation of the help I have derived from the article, the author of which is Mr Gerald Robertson, 'Informed Consent to Medical Treatment' (1987) 97 L.Q.R. 102. The author deals so comprehensively with the American, Canadian and other countries' case law that I find it unnecessary to refer to any of the cases to which our attention has been drawn, interesting and instructive though they are, other than *Canterbury* v *Spence* [(1972) 464 F. 2d 772] and *Reibl* v *Hughes* (1980) 114 D.L.R. (3d) I, in which the judgment of the Supreme Court of Canada came too late to be considered by Mr. Robertson in his article. I have also been greatly assisted by the note on the present case by Professor Ian Kennedy in the *Modern Law Review* (1984) 47 M.L.R. 454.

This influence is not to be underrated. Nor should one ignore the imaginative move of the DHSS in *Gillick* to engage as junior counsel for the appeal to the House of Lords the leading academic in the field, the aforementioned Ian Kennedy. [*Gillick* v *West Norfolk & Wisbech Area Health Authority* [1985] 3 All ER 402, famously addressed the issue of whether adolescent children possessed capacity to consent to medical treatment. A majority of the Law Lords enunciated the test of the 'mature minor', declaring that an adolescent under 16 of sufficient maturity and understanding could consent to contraceptive treatment.] With this kind of interaction between legal theory and practice, one can only hope that legal philosophers will be encouraged to contribute towards the emerging jurisprudence of consent.

Questions:
1.   From other law courses you have studied, can you give examples of how the concept of consent is deployed?

2.   From the various cases you have already studied on consent, do you agree that the doctrine of consent can be manipulated to reflect our own (or a judge's) values and interpretations of the facts?

3.   In contexts other than health care law do you agree that the issue of informed consent is underdeveloped? Is that now changing, as Lee predicted it would?

4.   Have the cases led to any consistent articulation of the concept of consent?

5.   Is it common for judges to refer to academic articles in their judgments or speeches? Do you think that judges should do so? Why/why not?

6.   How common is it in the cases you read for judges to draw on decisions in other jurisdictions? (On different legal cultures see p. 400 below.)

Following the controversy generated by the House of Lords' decision in *R* v *Brown* (see Chapter 7 p. 227 above), the Law Commission issued two consultation papers on the issue of consent in the criminal law and is still working on this issue. In the following extracts from the second paper are outlined first the general principles which underpin its law reform proposals and then its position in relation to sado-masochism:

Law Commission, *Consent in the Criminal Law: A Consultation Paper* (No. 139, London, HMSO 1995).

2.17   In this Paper we have been concerned to look very carefully at all the different problem areas that have been illuminated by this study and the comments and factual contributions it has elicited, even though our critics may maintain that our provisional conclusions still show too much evidence of a broadbrush approach that does not do justice to the sophistication of the subject matter . . . We have endeavoured to follow what we perceive to be the prevailing attitude in Parliament to questions of criminalisation, and this may lead us into what our critics may believe to be attitudes on related issues that are mutually inconsistent in a philosophical sense. It will be an important part of this consultation exercise to identify such inconsistencies and to seek ways of remedying them that do not cut across the prevailing Parliamentary culture, although we recognise that in the last resort we may simply have to live with them.

2.18   It is for these reasons that we have decided to propose on a provisional basis a law reform strategy that recognises people's entitlement to make choices for themselves but has the following distinctive features:

(1)   We shall start by identifying the rules that will be needed in order to ensure, as far as practicable, that non-voluntary consents are treated as ineffective.

(2)   The exercise will involve making special rules for the young and the disabled: in certain circumstances the state will be entitled to dictate that there is an age below which no consent shall be valid, but this must be determined on a case by case basis.

(3)   Next, we will take into account a person's interests in his or her own physical health and vigour, the integrity and normal functioning of his or her body, the absence of absorbing pain and suffering or grotesque disfigurement.

(4)   As a consequence of the concern expressed in (3), if seriously disabling injury results, we will take the view that a person who consents to it has made a mistake and that to be really disabled is against his or her interests.

(5)   On the other hand, we will not take the view that if consent is given in the context of an activity that is widely regarded as beneficial and for which the state is satisfied that the risks are properly controllable and containable (for example, surgery and risky sports).

(6)   We are also unwilling to decriminalise the consensual infliction of seriously disabling injury in other circumstances because, in the absence of effective regulation, we cannot be sure that the consent will be entirely voluntary.

(7)   In certain cases we will not permit the causing of injuries to others, even with a completely voluntary consent, because we are concerned to prevent the increased likelihood of harm to others. It is for this reason that we will be provisionally proposing that the criminalisation of causing injury in the course of casual fighting should remain in place . . .

Intentional causing of seriously disabling injury
4.47   We provisionally propose that the intentional causing of seriously disabling injury (as defined in paragraph 4.51 below) to another person should continue to be criminal, even if the person injured consents to such injury or the risk of such injury.

Reckless causing of seriously disabling injury
4.48   We provisionally propose that—

(1)   the reckless causing of seriously disabling injury (as defined in paragraph 4.51 below) should continue to be criminal, even if the injured person consents to such injury or to the risk of such injury; but

(2)   a person causing seriously disabling injury to another person should not be regarded as having caused it recklessly unless—

(a)   he or she was, at the time of the act or omission causing it, aware of a risk that such injury would result, and

(b)   it was at that time contrary to the best interests of the other person, having regards to the circumstances known to the person causing the injury (including, if known to him or her, the fact that the other person consented to such injury or to the risk of it), to take that risk.

Intentional causing of other injuries
4.49   We provisionally propose that the intentional causing of any injury to another person other than seriously disabling injury as defined in paragraph 4.52 below (whether or not amounting to 'grievous bodily harm' within the meaning of the Offences Against the Person Act 1861 or to 'serious injury' within the meaning of the Criminal Law Bill) should not be criminal if, at the time of the act or omission causing the injury, the other person consented to the type of injury caused.

Reckless causing of other injuries
4.50   We provisionally propose that the reckless causing of any injury to another person other than the seriously disabling injury as defined at paragraph 4.52 below (whether or not amounting to 'grievous bodily harm' within the meaning of the Offences Against the Person Act 1861 or to 'serious injury' within the meaning of the Criminal Law Bill) should not be criminal if, at the time of the act or omission causing the injury, the other person consented to injury of the type caused, to the risk of such injury or to the act or omission causing the injury.

Definition of seriously disabling injury.
4.51   We provisionally propose that for the purpose of paragraphs 4.47–4.50 above 'seriously disabling injury' should be taken to refer to an injury or injuries which—

(1)   cause serious distress, and

(2)   involve the loss of a bodily member or organ or permanent injury or permanent functional impairment, or serious or permanent disfigurement, or severe and prolonged pain, or serious impairment of mental health, or prolonged unconsciousness;

and in determining whether an effect is permanent, no account should be taken of the fact that it may be remediable by surgery.

Meaning of consent
4.52   We provisionally propose that for the purposes of the above proposals:

(1)   'consent' should mean a valid subsisting consent to an injury or to the risk of an injury of the type caused, and consent may be express or implied;

(2)   a person should be regarded as consenting to an injury of the type caused if he or she consents to an act or omission which he or she knows or believes to involve a risk of injury to him or her of the type caused.

Burden of proof on the issue of consent
4.53   We invite views on whether, if the proposals in paragraphs 4.49–4.50 were accepted—
(a)   it should be for the defence to prove, on the balance of probabilities, that the person injured consented to injury of the type caused, or (in the case of injury recklessly caused) to the risk of such injury or to the act or omission causing the injury; or
(b)   it should be for the prosecution to prove, beyond reasonable doubt, that the person did not so consent . . .

Questions:
1.   Critically assess the drafting of these provisions.

2.   If the Law Commission's proposals as outlined here were enacted, do you think that a case involving the same facts as *Brown* would be prosecuted?

In Chapter 10 of the paper the Law Commission addressed the issue of sado-masochism.

10.17   If the primary motivation for inflicting pain, by consent, is not religious but sexual, English law treats the person who inflicts that pain as a criminal if any resulting injury is more than 'transient or trifling'. The majority of the House of Lords in *Brown* held that it was not in the public interest that a person should wound or cause actual bodily harm to another for no good reason, that in the absence of such a reason, the victim's consent afforded no defence to a charge under sections 20 or 47 of the Offences Against the Person Act 1861, and that the satisfaction of sado-masochistic desires did not constitute such a good reason. Lord Templeman said in his speech in *Brown* that the question whether the defence of consent should be extended to the consequences of sado-masochistic encounters could only be decided by consideration of policy and public interest. He contrasted the position of Parliament, which could call on the advice of doctors, psychiatrists, criminologists, sociologists and other experts, and also take into account public opinion, with the position of the House of Lords in its judicial capacity which was being called upon to decide a point of law without recourse to such materials . . .

10.18   We received a wealth of evidence on consultation from people of both sexes who indulged in sado-masochistic activities to enhance sexual pleasure . . .

10.28   [T]hey submitted that sado-masochism was part of the spectrum of human sexual response, and that it should not be treated as analogous to activities like killing or mutilation. The subjective experience of the active party who is engaged, for example, in flagellation, can, they said, combine pride in the exercise of skill, a sense of care and service towards the passive partner, and sexual excitement at the exercise of power over that person. Active and passive roles are commonly exchanged, and many contributors in their evidence made it clear that the power they enjoy exercising is the power to give the submissive partner what they want and so excite them that they achieve the maximum pleasure of which they are capable . . .

10.30 'Countdown on Spanner' is a mixed sexuality campaign group which was formed . . . by about 200 people determined to support the defendants in the case of *Brown* in their appeal to the House of Lords. They told us that their campaign had produced the following working definition of sado-masochistic sex:

SM sex is obtaining pleasure from and exchange of power and/or pain in consensual sex play or sexual fantasy.
SM sex is, by definition, consensual. Non-consensual sex is an abuse of power and is therefore sexual violence, not SM sex.
There are no pre-determined roles in SM sex. Power relations are determined by choice.

10.31 These three points figured frequently in the evidence received from individual respondents. An academic respondent who has made a study of the subject said that SM sex is essentially a theatrical activity in which the sadists and masochists act out roles of symbolic dominance and submission, of shaming and being shamed. Their aim is not pain *per se*, which they fear as much as anyone else, but pleasurable excitation which is linked, or becomes switched to, sexual pleasure. They may suffer some degree of injury, but they view this much as a sports player views the risk of injury which is inevitably found in most games . . .

10.33 [Two] factors, that SM sex is consensual and that roles may readily be reversed, were repeatedly stressed by respondents who had personal experience of the practice . . .

10.35 [Another] group, SM Gays, was founded 13 years ago as a social and support group for gay men interested in consensual SM sex . . . They told us that human sexuality does not fall easily into compartments. It is a spectrum along which people travel from day to day or from one relationship or sexual encounter to another . . .

10.38 The importance of proper attention to safety and the need for dissemination of advice about safety measures was stressed not only by this group but by other respondents . . .

10.39 Another point that was made by a number of respondents was that the effect of the publicity given to the *Brown* case was that people who practised SM sex were very frightened about giving evidence to the police when they were investigating serious crime. They were afraid that this might lead to their own prosecution for taking part in illegal activities . . .

10.40 Illegality drives a wedge between the minority community and the police making people less willing to give information regarding the genuinely dangerous in case they are prosecuted themselves.

10.41   The final point made by SM Gays in their evidence was that the wide diversity of SM activities which might cause any degree of injury posed problems for those who might attempt a legal definition. No list of such activities would ever be complete, and no definition which concentrated on the physical activities separated from issues of consent and the personal power dynamics of domination and submission could be guaranteed to separate a sexual SM scene from a real assault . . .

10.46   Professor Feldman expressed the opinion that to classify sado-masochism as being about violence, and therefore as having no redeeming social value, but to accept that boxing or rough and undisciplined play do have social value, is to turn reality on its head. In his view the interest (whether public or private) in allowing people to express their sexuality, which forms a fundamental part of a person's personality, is no less important than the interest in allowing people to pursue sports. Sports is fun, but sex for so many people is more than fun: it is a form of self expression.

10.47   For many people, he said, violence and sex are not separate. There are overwhelming reasons for preventing people from making others the unwilling vehicles of their sexual gratification, but there is no more — and arguably, in his opinion, less — reason for preventing people from consenting to bodily harm in the pursuit of sexual pleasure than there is for preventing people from consenting to it in the pursuit of sporting pleasure . . .

10.49   We were reminded that Professor Hart, in his defence of the Wolfenden Committee's proposals, observed that laws restricting (consenting) sexual behaviour 'may create misery of quite special degree. [For fuller discussion of Professor Hart's views, see Chapter 8 at p. 270.] For both the difficulties involved in the repression of sexual impulses and the consequences of repression are quite different from "ordinary" crime'. Sexual impulses, Professor Hart observed, form a strong part of each person's day to day life, so that their suppression can affect 'the development or balance of the individual's emotional life, happiness and personality . . .'

10.51   The SPTL [Society of Public Teachers of Law], more briefly, submitted that the divide between sexual offences and offences of violence was not clear, and it was essential that there should be consistency in the meaning of consent in each area. 'Assault merges into indecent assault, which merges into attempted rape and rape.' A number of women's organisations stressed that the issue of consent was central. Feminists against Censorship and the English Collective of Prostitutes both emphasised this in their responses, and another women's group, without referring to sado-masochistic sex, said that 'consenting sex should not be the business of the law', while urging us most strongly to review the law of consent in the context of sexual offences.

LAW REFORM PROPOSALS

10.52   We envisage that appropriate protection will be given to the activities described in this Part, insofar as they would otherwise amount to offences against the person, by the terms of the provisional proposals we have made at the end of part IV above [the extracts at pp. 375–8 above]. The circumstances in which such acts should be permitted is a matter for legislation relating to public morality and decency, and not for the present project, which is concerned solely with the question whether such acts should in themselves constitute criminal offences even if a valid consent is given to them. In other words, nobody may give a valid consent to seriously disabling injury, but subject to this limitation the law ought not to prevent people from consenting to injuries caused for religious or sexual purposes. We see no value in circumscribing the law by reference to any specific limitation of purpose. This proposed policy is consistent with the third, fourth and sixth principles in our suggested law reform strategy . . .

10.54   For the present consultation process we propose that the same age limit should apply to activities involving the infliction of pain-creating injury for the purposes of religious mortification or for spiritual motives as to similar activities for the purposes of sexual gratification, and we would be interested to hear from any respondent who believes that a different age limit should apply in these cases, and if so why. In making these two proposals we are giving effect to the second principle contained in our suggested law reform strategy.

Questions:
1.   In the light of your consideration of the relationship between law and morality in Chapter 8, critically evaluate the general principles outlined by the Law Commission. Does it matter whether they are consistent or not?

2.   Do you agree with the analogy, repeatedly drawn in this debate between sado-masochism and contact sports? Why/why not?

3.   Many of the submissions received by the Law Commission came from pressure groups representing those who practice sado-masochism. Other submissions mentioned in the above extract were made by law professors or groups like the Society of Public Teacher of Law. Do you think the latter are likely to carry more weight with a body like the Law Commission? Should they?

4.   Compare Professor Feldman's analysis of the relationship between sex and violence, with that in the speech by Lord Lowry at Chapter 7 p. 230 above.

5.   Imagine that you are asked to draft a submission to the Law Commission on reform of the law in relation to sado-masochism. Write a submission outlining your views which does not exceed one page of A4. Law Commission consultation papers are now published on the Internet. For an update on the law reform issues with which it is currently engaged check its website on www.open.gov.uk/lawcomm/homepage.htm.

The following extract indicates how the ECHR actually dealt with the issue when the defendants in the *Brown* case alleged that the UK violated their rights to privacy under Article 8 of the Convention:

Laskey, Jaggard and Brown v *United Kingdom* (1997) 24 EHRR 39, at 57, 58–60.

. . .

37.   The applicants maintained that the interference at issue could not be regarded as 'necessary in a democratic society'. This submission was contested by the Government and by a majority of the Commission . . .

42.   According to the Court's established case law, the notion of necessity implies that the interference corresponds to a pressing social need and, in particular, that it is proportionate to the legitimate aim pursued: in determining whether an interference is 'necessary in a democratic society', the Court will take into account that a margin of appreciation is left to the national authorities, whose decision remains subject to review by the Court for conformity with the requirements of the Convention.

The scope of this margin of appreciation is not identical in each case and will vary according to the context. Relevant factors include the nature of the Convention right at issue; its importance for the individual and the nature of the activities concerned.

43.   The Court considers that one of the roles which the State is unquestionably entitled to undertake is to seek to regulate, through the operation of the criminal law, activities which involve the infliction of physical harm. This is so whether the activities in question occur in the course of sexual conduct or otherwise.

44.   The determination of the level of harm that should be tolerated by the law in situations where the victim consents is in the first instance a matter for the State concerned since what is at stake is related, on the one hand, to public health considerations and to the general deterrent effect of the criminal law, and, on the other, to the personal autonomy of the individual.

45.   The applicants have contended that, in the circumstances of the case, the behaviour in question formed part of private morality which is not the State's business to regulate. In their submission the matters for which they were prosecuted and convicted concerned only private sexual behaviour.

The Court is not persuaded by this submission. It is evident from the facts established by the national courts that the applicants' sado-masochistic activities involved a significant degree of injury or wounding which could not be characterised as trifling or transient. This, in itself, suffices to distinguish the present case from those applications which have previously been examined by the Court concerning consensual homosexual behaviour in private between adults where no such feature was present.

46.   Nor does the Court accept the applicants' submission that no prosecution should have been brought against them since their injuries were not severe and since no medical treatment had been required.

In deciding whether or not to prosecute, the State authorities were entitled to have regard not only to the actual seriousness of the harm caused — which as noted above was considered to be significant — but also, as stated by Lord Jauncey of Tullichettle, to the potential for harm inherent in the acts in question. In this respect it is recalled that the activities were considered by Lord Templeman to be 'unpredictably dangerous'.

47. The applicants have further submitted that they were singled out partly because of the authorities' bias against homosexuals. They referred to the recent judgment in the *Wilson* case, where, in their view, similar behaviour in the context of a heterosexual couple was not considered to deserve criminal punishment.

The Court finds no evidence in support of the applicants' allegations in either the conduct of the proceedings against them or the judgment of the House of Lords. In this respect it recalls the remark of the trial judge when passing sentence that 'the unlawful conduct now before the court would be dealt with equally in the prosecution of heterosexuals or bisexuals if carried out by them'.

Moreover, it is clear from the judgment of the House of Lords that the opinions of the majority were based on the extreme nature of the practices involved and not the sexual proclivities of the applicants.

In any event, like the Court of Appeal, the Court does not consider that the facts in the *Wilson* case were at all comparable in seriousness to those in the present case.

48. Accordingly, the Court considers that the reasons given by the national authorities for the measures taken in the respect of the applicants were relevant and sufficient for the purposes of Article 8(2).

49. It remains to be ascertained whether these measures were proportionate to the legitimate aim or aims pursued.

The Court notes that the charges of assault were numerous and referred to illegal activities which had taken place over more than 10 years. However, only a few charges were selected for inclusion in the prosecution case. It further notes that, in recognition of the fact that the applicants did not appreciate their actions to be criminal, reduced sentences were imposed on appeal. In these circumstances, bearing in mind the degree of organisation involved in the offences, the measures taken against the applicants cannot be regarded as disproportionate.

50. In sum, the Court finds that the national authorities were entitled to consider that the prosecution and conviction of the applicants were necessary in a democratic society for the protection of health within the meaning of Article 8(2) of the Convention.

51. In view of this conclusion the Court, like the Commission, does not find it necessary to determine whether the interference with the applicants' right to respect for private life could also be justified on the ground of the protection of morals. This finding, however, should not be understood as calling into question the prerogative of the State on moral grounds to seek to deter acts of the kind in question.

Questions:

1.   Were you surprised at the conclusions reached by the European Court of Human Rights, especially in the light of the Law Commission's deliberations extracted above?

2.   Can you track down the Court of Appeal decision in the case of *Wilson* referred to in the judgment? Do you agree that it was distinguishable from the decision in *Brown*?

3.   Having read the classic debate about the relationship between law and morality in Chapter 8, do you think the State should retain the prerogative to deter such acts on moral grounds?

4.   The European Court of Human Rights in this case is explicit that one factor which will influence the Court in reaching a judgment regarding the margin of appreciation left open to Member States is the nature of the Convention right at issue. How highly would you rank the right to privacy in any scale of 'fundamental values'?

Brown is categorised as a criminal law case. However, *Brown* may also be regarded as a case about civil liberties or human rights, and as Lord Mustill noted (at Chapter 7 p. 232 above) one of the problems with *Brown* is that it was conceptualised (because of time limitations) as a matter of Offences Against the Person rather than 'a case about the criminal law of private sexual relations, if about anything at all'. Issues of categorisation are also raised by *Re B* and the subsequent cases concerning decisions made on behalf of children and neonates. Potentially the professionals involved in such cases are policed by the criminal law; they certainly raise family law issues about the locus of decision-making power and they are also defined as falling within the field of health care law, which itself transgresses the boundaries of criminal law, tort, contract, family law and public law. In the following extract Katherine O'Donovan assesses the issue of consent in health care law, and how it relates to the way in which consent is employed in other legal contexts:

K O'Donovan, 'Is the Patient Position Inevitably Female?' in S Sheldon and M Thomson (eds) *Feminist Perspectives on Health Care Law*, London, Cavendish (1998) pp. ix–x.

Consent is placed as central to law and ethics in the treatment of patients. This is a reflection of the creation of the patient as a rational, choosing person, capable of choices and decisions. Consent is a paradigmatic aspect of autonomy. Yet brief thought reveals it to be placed in an ambivalent relationship to 'the best interests of the patient', also upheld as one ethical part of the doctor's duty. The ideals of the classical mode of doctoring thus become confused with respect for individual patients' decisions.

Feminist analyses of the concept of consent in areas of criminal and family law throw the limitations of the concept as deployed in the discourse of law and medical ethics into relief. Yet such analogies have not been heard as part of legal arguments regarding medical consent. Exclusionary reasons of boundary maintenance have been given as reasons for excluding such comparisons. Perhaps the underlying reason, however, is the instability of the concept, as revealed in feminist analysis.

When the concept of consent, as it has been elucidated within commercial law, is compared with consent in tort, criminal, family and health care law, we find many varieties of legal consent. In criminal rape cases consent is gendered and is surrounded by stereotyped assumptions. The discourse of consent in family law concerns voluntary unions in which consent is eternal and is gendered in so far as one partner consents to give up her autonomy, and therefore her future ability to consent. The reality is somewhat different, given the power relationships involved. In any case the courts have their own version of this, which omits the word 'informed'. Commercial law, in which the paradigmatic economic rational chooser reigns, offers opportunities to the legal subject to change his mind after giving consent. Paradoxically, commercial consent is permissive about hesitation containing 'cooling-off' periods. The conclusion is that the concept of consent has to be understood in the context of the figures that are constructed in the history and landscape of particular legal areas. [For instance] [c]onsent in health care law must be understood in the context of assumptions about trust and healing.

Questions:
1.   Are reasons of boundary maintenance adequate reasons to exclude analogies drawn in other areas of law?

2.   In the cases concerning withdrawal of treatment from disabled children and neonates, considered in Chapter 2, did the judges draw on analogies from other areas of law? Did they do this in the cases concerning marital rape and sado-masochism?

3.   Does it surprise you that concepts such as consent are differentially employed across different subject boundaries in law? How does this square with Dworkin's notion of 'law as integrity' in which law is visualised as a seamless web (see Chapter 7)?

BIOETHICS: A BRAVE NEW LEGAL WORLD?

The two previous sections in this chapter, namely 'Discrimination' and 'Informed Consent', have been concerned to identify themes running throughout various of the cases and statutes which we have considered in earlier chapters in this book. Many of these cases involved new challenges for lawyers and policy makers. As we have seen in both this chapter and Chapter 3, a particular problem for legislators is the difficulty of anticipating new developments or innovations and of foreseeing their legal consequences. In this regard one of the greatest challenges is posed by innovations in biomedicine. The development of new technologies such as genetic screening, *in vitro* fertilisation, cloning and xenotransplantation have raised crucial issues, with which law is increasingly having to grapple. One potentially important new source of law is the adoption by the Council of Ministers of the Council of Europe of a convention for the protection of human rights and dignity of the human being with regard to the application of biology and medicine (hereafter 'The Convention on Human Rights and Biomedicine') on 19 November 1996. This will not have legal effect until it has been ratified by the governments of the various member states of the Council of Europe, but it does offer some indication of the bioethical problems which have to be dealt with at a supranational level. It also contains significant provisions pertaining to consent to medical treatment and research:

Council of Europe, *Convention for the Protection of Human Rights and Dignity of the Human Being with regard to the Application of Biology and Medicine.*

Preamble
The Member States of the Council of Europe, the other States and the European Community signatories hereto . . .
Considering that the aim of the Council of Europe is the achievement of a greater unity between its members and that one of the methods by which that aim is to be pursued is the maintenance and further realisation of human rights and fundamental freedoms;
Conscious of the accelerating developments in biology and medicine;
Convinced of the need to respect the human being both as an individual and as a member of the human species and recognising the importance of ensuring the dignity of the human being;
Conscious that the misuse of biology and medicine may lead to acts endangering human dignity;
Affirming that progress in biology and medicine should be used for the benefit of present and future generations;
Stressing the need for international co-operation so that all humanity may enjoy the benefits of biology and medicine;
Recognising the importance of promoting a public debate on the questions posed by the application of biology and medicine and the responses to be given thereto;

CHAPTER I
General Provisions
Article 1. (Purpose and object)
Parties to this Convention shall protect the dignity and identity of all human beings and guarantee everyone, without discrimination, respect for their integrity and other rights and fundamental freedoms with regard to the application of biology and medicine.
    Each Party shall take in its internal law the necessary measures to give effect to the provision of this Convention.

Article 2. (Primacy of the human being)
The interests and welfare of the human being shall prevail over the sole interest of society or science.

CHAPTER II
Consent
Article 5. (General rule)

An intervention in the health field may only be carried out after the person concerned has given free and informed consent to it.

This person shall beforehand be given appropriate information as to the purpose and nature of the intervention as well as of its consequences and risks.

The person concerned may freely withdraw consent at any time.

Article 6. (Protection of persons not able to consent)

1.   Subject to Articles 17 and 20 below, an intervention may only be carried out on a person who does not have the capacity to consent, for his or her direct benefit.

2.   Where, according to law, a minor does not have the capacity to consent to an intervention, the intervention may only be carried out with the authorisation of his or her representative or an authority or a person or body provided for by law.

The opinion of the minor shall be taken into consideration as an increasingly determining factor in proportion to his or her age and degree of maturity.

3.   Where, according to law, an adult does not have the capacity to consent to an intervention because of a mental disability, a disease or for similar reasons, the intervention may only be carried out with the authorisation of his or her representative or an authority or a person or body provided for by law.

The individual concerned shall as far as possible take part in the authorisation procedure.

4.   The representative, the authority, the person or the body mentioned in paragraphs 2 and 3 above shall be given, under the same conditions, the information referred to in Article 5.

5.   The authorisation referred to in paragraphs 2 and 3 above may be withdrawn at any time in the best interests of the person concerned . . .

Article 9. (Previously expressed wishes)

The previously expressed wishes relating to a medical intervention by a patient who is not, at the time of the intervention, in a state to express his or her wishes shall be taken into account . . .

CHAPTER V
Scientific research
Article 15. (General rule)

Scientific research in the field of biology and medicine shall be carried out freely, subject to the provisions of this Convention and the other legal provisions ensuring the protection of the human being.

Article 16. (Protection of persons undergoing research)

Research on a person may only be undertaken if all the following conditions are met:

i)   there is no alternative of comparable effectiveness to research on humans;

ii)   the risks which may be incurred by that person are not disproportionate to the potential benefits of the research;

iii)   the research project has been approved by the competent body after an independent examination of its scientific merit, including the importance of the aim of the research, and ethical acceptability;

iv)   the persons undergoing research have been informed of their rights and the safeguards prescribed by law for their protection;

v)   the necessary consent as provided for under Article 5 has been given expressly, specifically and is documented. Such consent may be freely withdrawn at any time.

Article 17. (Protection of persons not able to consent to research)

1.   Research on a person without the capacity to consent as stipulated in Article 5 may be undertaken only if all the following conditions are met:

i)   the conditions laid down in Article 16, sub-paragraph (i) to (iv) are fulfilled;

ii)   the results of the research have the potential to produce direct benefit to his or her health;

iii)   research of comparable effectiveness cannot be carried out on individuals capable of giving consent;

iv)   the necessary authorisation provided for under Article 6 has been given specifically and in writing, and

v)   the person concerned does not object.

2.   Exceptionally and under the protective conditions prescribed by law, where the research has not the potential to produce results of direct benefit to the health of the person concerned, such research may be authorised subject to the conditions laid down in paragraph 1, sub-paragraphs (i), (iii), (iv) and (v) above, and to the following additional conditions:

i)   the research has the aim of contributing, through significant improvements in the scientific understanding of the individual's condition, disease or disorder, to the ultimate attainment of results capable of conferring benefit to the person concerned or to other persons in the same age category or afflicted with the same disease or disorder or having the same condition.

ii)   the research entails only minimal risk and minimal burden for the individual concerned.

Article 18. (Research on embryos in vitro)

1.   Where the law allows research on embryos in vitro, it shall ensure adequate protection of the embryo.

2.   The creation of human embryos for research purposes is prohibited.

CHAPTER VI

Organ and tissue removal from living donors for transplantation purposes

Article 19. (General rule)

1.   Removal of organs or tissue from a living person for transplantation purposes may be carried out solely for the therapeutic benefit of the recipient

and where there is no suitable organ or tissue available from a deceased person and no other alternative therapeutic method of comparable effectiveness.

2. The necessary consent as provided for under Article 5 must have been given expressly and specifically either in written form or before an official body.

Article 20. (Protection of persons not able to consent to organ removal)

1. No organ or tissue removal may be carried out on a person who does not have the capacity to consent under Article 5.

2. Exceptionally and under the protective conditions prescribed by law, the removal of regenerative tissue from a person who does not have the capacity to consent may be authorised provided the following conditions are met:

i) there is no compatible donor available who has the capacity to consent;
ii) the recipient is a brother or sister of the donor;
iii) the donation must have the potential to be life-saving for the recipient;
iv) the authorisation provided for under paragraphs 2 and 3 of Article 6 has been given specifically and in writing, in accordance with the law and with the approval of the competent body;
v) the potential donor concerned does not object.

CHAPTER VII
Prohibition of financial gain and disposal of a part of the human body
Article 28. (Public debate)

Parties to this Convention shall see to it that the fundamental questions raised by the developments of biology and medicine are the subject of appropriate public discussion in the light, in particular, of relevant medical, social, economic, ethical and legal implications, and that their possible application is made the subject of appropriate consultation.

Questions:

1. How adequately do you think this Convention defines and deals with the issue of consent, given our earlier discussion of the contested nature of consent? Does this Convention support Lee's contention (at p. 374 above) that consideration of the concept of consent is most developed in the field of health care law?

2. Does the Convention contain adequate protection for human beings?

3. Should the Convention have excluded from the ambit of moral and legal concern the question of research on animals? Is it (a) consistent and (b) ethically justifiable to grant special protection to embryos (in Article 18 which was one of the most fiercely contested articles of the Convention), but not to animals?

4. A protocol has been added to this Convention, Additional Protocol on the Prohibition of Cloning Human Beings (ETS No. 168). Is cloning a human rights issue?

Earlier in this Chapter we saw that how transsexuals are categorised poses some problems for law, given the nature of legal method and its search for defined categories. The barrier between the species is another boundary now being called into question. In part, this is due to genetic developments which reveal the similarities between human beings and primates:

J Diamond, 'The Third Chimpanzee' in P Cavalieri and P Singer (eds) *The Great Ape Project: Equality beyond Humanity*, London, Fourth Estate (1993), pp. 88–101, pg 95.

> DNA studies have now revealed that humans share 98.4 per cent of our DNA with common chimps and pygmy chimps. Gorillas differ somewhat more, by about 2.3 per cent from us and both types of chimp. The genetic distance (1.6%) separating us from pygmy or common chimps is barely double that separating pygmy from common chimps (0.7%); it is less than that between the two species of gibbons (2.2%) and significantly less than the difference of 3.6% which separates orang-utan DNA from that of humans, chimps and gorilla; or the 7% difference which separates monkey from humans and apes.

Such figures remain contested; however, challenges to the species barrier stem not only from scientific developments, but also from opposition to the universalising claims of human rights discourse. As Diana Fuss claims, in the following extract, traditional conceptions of 'the human' which stem from the eighteenth century Enlightenment are dramatically challenged by debates over issues such as genetic surgery, virtual reality, reproductive technologies and artificial intelligence:

D Fuss, 'Introduction' in *Human. All Too Human*, New York, Routledge (1996) pp. 1–3.

> A sign whose history has rarely been examined, the human is a linguistic, cultural and sociopolitical construct of comparatively recent date. That the human has a history comes as no surprise to those subjects so routinely and so violently excluded from its ideological terrain. In the past the human has functioned as a powerful juridical trope to disenfranchise slaves, immigrants, women, children and the poor. Some of the most ferocious and unthinkable events of our century — mass extermination in Europe, genocide in Armenia, apartheid in South Africa, repression in Latin America, ethnic cleansing in Bosnia — have all been waged passionately in the name of *humanitas*. In America, the human continues to be deployed as a weapon of potent ideological force, its unstable boundaries perpetually challenged and redrawn to exclude entire groups of socially disempowered subjects: the homeless, mothers on welfare, blacks in prison, people with HIV/AIDS, illegal 'aliens'. The human is not, and never has been, an all inclusive category . . .
> The human has always been a politically charged referent with a complicated and difficult social history. Just who counts as human, and why, underwrites a long saga of contentious debate within humanist discourse, a discourse mired from the start in the amalgamated histories of imperial expansion, scientific experimentation, and industrial revolution. The human may, in fact, be one of our most elastic fictions. As the dividing lines between

humans and 'nonhumans' have been historically redrafted to accommodate new systems of classification and new discourses of knowledge, the human has proceeded to mutate many times over . . .

Any re-examination of the human places us immediately inside an ever-widening field of alterity: animate and inanimate, natural and artificial, living and dead, organic and mechanistic . . . The vigilance with which the demarcations between humans and animals, humans and things, and humans and children are watched over and safeguarded tells us much about the assailability of what they seek to preserve: an abstract notion of the human as a unified, autonomous, and unmodified subject. It is as if the alieness of these borderlanders lies not in their distance from the human, but in their proximity. Sameness, not difference, provokes our greatest anxiety (and our greatest fascination) with the 'almost human'. Indeed, whenever we are called to become 'more human' we are reminded that the human is never adequate to itself, and may be defined more by its likeness to these alien others than by its unlikeness.

Questions:
1. What role does law play in shaping our notions of the 'human'?

2. If you now reread the provisions of the Convention on Human Rights and Biomedicine extracted above, what do you think it reveals about our cultural anxieties concerning what it means to be human?

The possibility of xenotransplantation — the transplanting of animal organs and tissues to human beings to relieve organ shortages — has now become a possibility and pigs are being genetically engineered for this purpose. This contributes to a further blurring of the division between human and non-human animals. The issue was addressed in the following report, chaired by law professor Ian Kennedy, for the Department of Health (hereafter 'the Kennedy Report'):

A Report by the Advisory Group on the Ethics of Xenotransplantation, London, Department of Health (1997).

THE PRINCIPAL QUESTION: THE USE OF ANIMALS
4.4 Religious and secular traditions of ethical thinking in the west have tended to give animals a low status. The Bible sets the tone in the very first chapter of Genesis when God places human beings above animals. Religious thinkers have followed this lead. For example, Aquinas holds that we have no duty of charity towards animals as such, although we should not be cruel to them in case this develops habits of cruelty which might carry over into our dealings with human beings. Some secular thinkers such as Descartes take the line that animals are like machines which might move and emit sounds but have no feelings. Kant finds supreme ethical worth in the exercise of the autonomous or purely rational will. Human beings have the capacity for autonomous action and are on that account 'ends in themselves'. Animals do not have that capacity so their value is simply to be a means to human ends.

Like Aquinas, Kant holds that the only reason we should be kind to animals
is to train ourselves in kindness, which can then be shown to human beings.
In essence, the Judaeo-Christian religious tradition excluded animals from
ethical consideration because they were thought to lack souls, and the secular
tradition rejected them because they lacked reason, or some reason-dependent
ability such as the ability to use language.

4.5   During the last few decades, the situation has changed dramatically.
There has been an explosion of popular interest in the natural world including
animals, as evidenced, for example, by the appearance of the 'green movement', the spread of vegetarianism and the commercial success of products
'not tested on animals'. Basically there are two distinct but overlapping
movements. The 'animal rights' movement, which opposes any exploitation
of animals for human ends; and the environmental movement, which opposes
the exploitation of the natural environment, including animal species, for
human ends. The environmental movement is divided in to 'shallow'
environmentalists and 'deep' environmentalists. The 'shallow' environmentalists oppose the exploitation of the planet because this will eventually harm
human beings; the 'deep' environmentalists think that the present, what they
view as reckless, exploitation of the environment is wrong in itself. These
popular and political movements have significant theoretical underpinning.
Any review of xenotransplantation must take account of these various
arguments and recognise the fact that, whatever view we take here, there will
be a responsible body of opinion which will oppose it.

4.6   There are a range of arguments against the use of animals for xenotransplantation: the religious, those based on consideration of what is 'natural'
and 'unnatural', and those based on the assertion of animal rights.

THE RELIGIOUS ARGUMENT
4.7   One kind of religious argument is to the effect that every living thing is
sacred, and therefore it would be wrong to kill an animal for human benefit.
A second sort of religious argument is that animals, or some animals
including pigs, are unclean and therefore their organs ought not to be
transplanted into human beings. These arguments depend on beliefs which
not everyone shares and which cannot be established beyond doubt.

NATURALNESS AND UNNATURALNESS
4.8   Some people might argue that animal transplants are unethical because
they are 'unnatural'; that it is 'contrary to nature' that a human being should
be given, for example, an animal heart or kidney.

4.9   As we have seen, the animal most likely to be used for xenotransplantation is the pig. There would appear to be a simple argument in favour of
using the pig. It begins by reminding us that there is a consensus moral
position that the pig's right to life is outweighed by the benefits its carcase
will bring to human beings as food . . . Now, the argument goes, if there is
a consensus that it is ethically justifiable to eat pigs, what can be wrong with

using their organs or tissue for the purpose of transplant? Indeed, some who regard it as wrong to use pigs and other animals as food (because other foods are available) may admit that animal parts can legitimately be used for human therapeutic purposes, if there is no non-animal substitute . . .

ANIMAL RIGHTS

4.12 The third set of arguments which may suggest that xenotransplantation is ethically unacceptable from the outset are the arguments falling under the general heading of 'animal rights' . . . In general, rights safeguard interests. Human animals certainly have more, and more complex, interests than non-human animals; but all animals, human and non-human, share certain interests, such as in avoiding suffering and leading a life. These fundamental rights have been called natural or inalienable rights. It can be maintained that, if there is a human natural right to life, or to be safeguarded against unmerited suffering, there must in logic be similar rights for animals, for they too have these vital interests . . .

4.15 In order to understand the potentially confusing contemporary proliferation of rights it is necessary to draw some distinctions.

(a) The rights which emerged from the ancient tradition of natural law can be called universal rights. They are 'moral' in the sense that they are thought to exist whether or not a given legal jurisdiction recognises them, and they are 'universal' in that they belong to all human beings.

(b) The rights which are recognised or created by a given jurisdiction are legal rights. There is always pressure to convert natural or human rights into legal rights, although there are of course many legal rights which have nothing to do with human rights.

(c) There are also many specific moral rights which are not human rights. For example if A borrows a book from B on the understanding that it will be returned on Tuesday then B has a moral right to its return. But this is not a human right — it is not universal or of paramount importance to human life.

4.16 Rights, legal and moral, have also been classified by the jurist Wesley Hohfeld as claims, powers, liberties and immunities. A claim is a right (say) to have a sum of money paid back, or to have a job application considered; a power is a right (say) to enter and search a property; a liberty is a right (say) of adults over the age of 18 to vote; and immunity is a right (say) of a student in full-time education not to pay National Insurance. In all cases there is the implication that another person, a state, or people in general have a reciprocal duty to observe the right.

4.17 What follows from the general overview is that if animals are to be said to have rights it can only be in the sense of claims (as distinct from powers, liberties or immunities). The essential claim will be to have their interests considered. If this position is accepted we are granting or recognising in animals moral rights (although of course these moral rights may become legal rights if they are recognised by a system of law). Presumably, the animal interests which rights would principally protect would be that of protecting and preserving animal life and having animal suffering minimised.

4.24   Objections to our view may take two opposing forms. Some would argue that our minimal view of the rights of animals is claiming *too little*. While we argue for the position that animals have a right to be considered in the total calculus of harm and benefit, some would maintain that because animals are the *subject of a life* they have rights in a much stronger sense. For those who hold this position any use of animals which involves their death or suffering for human benefit will be ruled out. This position must be respected, but it is not our position.

4.25   Other philosophers, and many members of the public, might maintain that our minimal position on animal rights is claiming *too much*. For it follows from our position that not every use of animals for human benefit is justifiable. For example, it would follow (say) that the considerable cruelty involved in bull fighting cannot be justified in terms of the minor gratification of the spectators. Presumably the manufacturers who advertise their products as 'not tested on animals' are reflecting what we see as a growing consensus that not every human use of animals can be justified.

OUR POSITION

4.26   Notwithstanding these objections, we hold to our position: that animals do have rights in this minimal sense. This means that while there is no fundamental right not to be used for xenotransplantation, animals may not be so used in circumstances which violate unjustifiably the minimum rights they may have.

4.27   Their interests must, therefore, be considered in any assessment of the benefits and harms arising from the introduction of xenotransplantation . . .

4.28   As a first step, we have already indicated that animals vary a great deal in their complexity and presumably in their capacity for suffering. Primates, including chimpanzees and baboons, are at the higher end of this scale, and have close affinities with humans. We consider that these animals can be distinguished from the other animals not least by virtue of their greater self-awareness, particularly given the conditions under which source animals would be kept in order to ensure proper controls (e.g. biosecure and isolated accommodation). To use them for xenotransplantation would therefore, in our view, constitute too great an infringement of their right to be free from suffering.

We therefore conclude that it would be ethically unacceptable to use primates as source animals for xenotransplantation, not least because they would be exposed to too much suffering.

4.29   We reach this view quite apart from the fact that there may also be other reasons for ruling them out, such as the difficulty of rearing them in captivity, slowness of breeding and greater liability for causing cross-species infection. Primates are also involved in the research being carried out into xenotransplantation, primarily as recipients of tissue transplanted from pigs.

Can this use in research be justified? A primate used for research purposes may (indirectly) provide benefit for a large number of humans, due to the information generated from the research. Thus, the ratio of benefit to humans against harm to the primate may provide an ethical basis for the use of primates in research. By contrast, a primate used as a source animal could only benefit one or at best a very small number of humans. Further, the conditions which would prevail for primates to be used in research would not be those which prevail for source animals. We recognise the case for such research to take place and note that such research is currently permitted under the provisions of the Animals (Scientific Procedures) Act [1986] and thus:

We conclude that it would be ethically acceptable to use primates in research into xenotransplantation, but only where no alternative method of obtaining information exists and this use should be limited so far as is possible.

4.30 Our next step is to ask whether the arguments which rule out primates also rule out the use of the pig. We conclude that they do not. While the pig may be exposed to harm, we do not regard it as so unjustifiable as to make the use of the pig unacceptable in principle. Instead, as regards the pig, the issue is one of balancing the rights of the pig to be free from harm, as we understand them, against the rights of the human who, as we have seen, could benefit from xenotransplantation. The ethical acceptability of the use of the pig then becomes a matter of balancing the potential benefits, which we have already outlined, against the harm involved, particularly, in using the pig, and reaching a view.

Questions:
1. Would the publication of a document like the Kennedy Report fulfil the obligation on signatories to the Convention on Human Rights and Bioethics to have full and informed public debate (see p. 389 above)? If not, what would you interpret this Article of the Convention as requiring?

2. Is the Kennedy Report's classification of humans, primates and pigs morally or rationally defensible?

3. Should UK law allow someone to consent to be a recipient of a pig organ? For that consent to be fully informed, what sort of information do you think the recipient should be given? In the light of our earlier discussion of the legal concept of consent, and in particular the question of *who* can consent, do you think that any persons aside from the recipient should be consulted or required to consent?

4. What would treating animals justly require in the context of xenotransplantation? (Refer to Chapter 8, and q. 3 on p. 278).

The following report was issued by a pressure group opposed to xenotransplantation, following the publication of the Kennedy Report:

S Beddard and D Lyons, *The Science and Ethics of Xenotransplantation: A Report by Uncaged Campaigns*, Sheffield (1996).

Introduction
The fundamental position that Uncaged Campaigns takes is that public policy should be based on what is ethical.

Ethics as fairness
Ethical inquiry should be a rigorous and critical affair. It is not simply about recording what people do, and collecting information about their attitudes. That approach would beg the question of whether social attitudes and practices are ethical, and would . . . commit the naturalistic fallacy by implying that what 'is', in terms of existing attitudes and practices, is what ought to be.

Thus we take issue with the approach of the [Kennedy Report]. The report attempts to justify speciesism (defined as a prejudice in favour of one species over another) thus:

> Our natural emotional response to, and concern for, members of our own species is clearly built deeply into our nature and it is not clear that the option of responding to members of other species, with the same concern in every case, is open to us.

This justification is flawed in two significant ways. First of all, it is far from obvious that the suggestion put forward by the [Kennedy Report] — of a natural prejudice in favour of our own species — is universally true. On the one hand, an 'emotional response to' or 'concern for' other members of our own species varies to a huge extent, both culturally and individually. Therefore, it seems unlikely that there is such a thing as a 'natural' attitude towards other human beings. On the other hand, it is clear that many humans build up very strong emotional relationships with other animals. On a moral level, more and more human beings appear to be embracing the case for the equal consideration of the interests of nonhuman animals, as witnessed by the impressive philosophical theory advocating an enhanced moral status for animals, and the popularity of the social movement for the recognition of the rights of animals.

Secondly, even if the [Kennedy Report] is correct in its ascription of human emotional responses, it still cannot serve as a justification for speciesist attitudes. Any 'natural' favouritism towards those with whom we most closely identify is 'quite independent of issues of rights and justice'. And the logical implications of this approach to ethics are very worrying. As Ted Benton points out in the introduction to his book 'Natural Relations', '. . . we are on very thin ice. What if we shift from humans and animals . . . to adults of different races, or of different cultures? . . . radical preferential dispositions are certainly widespread, but we would certainly want to censure them on moral grounds'.

In concluding that the use of pigs for the routine supply of organs for xenotransplantation is ethically acceptable, the [Kennedy Report] once again falls back on its structurally-flawed argument: 'It is difficult to see how, in a society in which the breeding of pigs for food and clothing is accepted, their use for life-saving medical procedures such as xenotransplantation could be unacceptable.'.

But there is neither logic nor morality in these arguments put forward in the [earlier] Nuffield Report. It is a morally conservative position based on the reprehensible notion that two wrongs *do* make a right. Just because most people eat pigs doesn't mean that it's right to do so. For a start, the growing number of vegetarians show that killing pigs for the sake of the taste of their flesh is becoming less socially acceptable. Furthermore, it would be reasonable to suggest that the vast majority of people who persist in eating meat do not do so as a result of having carefully weighed up the moral arguments for and against the killing of animals for food. Indeed, many meat-eaters may acknowledge the moral case for vegetarianism, yet continue to eat meat through force of habit and/or downright selfishness.

As mentioned earlier, morality ought to be a critical and rigorous affair — rigour implies *consistency*. In fact, the issue of consistency is crucial in ethics. The notion of *consistency* is very closely linked to that of *fairness*. Fairness plays an absolutely fundamental role in our thinking about what is 'food' or 'just'. So when the [Kennedy Report] states: 'We should consider therefore what our treatment of nonhuman animals should be in its own terms, rather than in terms of *consistency* with our treatment of human beings' (our emphasis), we must reply that to follow this advice is not to think ethically at all. In a similarly unfair manner, the [Nuffield Report] employs different methods of ethical reasoning when talking about nonhuman animals, especially non-primates, compared to humans and non-human primates.

So, let us come to a fair, consistent and unbiased assessment of the ethics of our treatment of animals. Both the [Kennedy Report] and the [Nuffield Report] take the human condition as the paradigm of moral value. Thus, according to their reckoning, nonhuman animals deserve moral consideration to the extent that they resemble human beings in certain ways — particularly in terms of self-awareness and rationality. But is this justifiable?

The moral value of reason
Human beings have often been given supreme moral status on account of their faculty of reason. The first point to be made here is that not all human beings are more self-aware, or rational, than all nonhuman animals. So the rationality criteria cannot justify universally preferential treatment for all human beings in relation to nonhumans.

Anyhow, further attention to this issue reveals that the assertion that rationality endows an individual with unique and supreme moral value is an arbitrary and inconsistent criterion for moral considerability. To begin with, society does not measure the moral value of individual humans in terms of intelligence. In theory at least, we are all moral equals, geniuses or not.

But the deeper point, and one that was made by the Epicureans in ancient Greece, is that reason is good for us because it *serves* our good. We don't live in order to reason well, but reason in order to live well. Reason is a tool,

an instrument — not an end-in-itself. We can use our reason for good or evil
— the value of reason is to be found in both its motivation and its
consequences for the well-being of all, ie in its morality. Thus Hitler or Pol
Pot's reasoning abilities did not endow them with unique moral value,
according to the argument proposed here. It seems unreasonable to think that
a genocidal dictator has more value than a cat, or a rat even.

In addition to these problems with the notion of reason as an intrinsic moral
value, the very definition of reason seems profoundly unclear. It may have
been an incredible feat of technology and instrumental reason but, on the
whole, was the invention of the atom bomb a reasonable thing to do?

It is hoped that these arguments provoke thought about how we think about
'rationality', and successfully demonstrate the illegitimacy of employing
'rationality' as the criteria for moral considerability.

Interests, self-realisation and rights

If not rationality, then what is it that endows us with intrinsic moral
significance, if anything? And is it something that human beings share with
other animals? The concept of (vital) interests and well-being plays an
important role in ethical thinking. A capacity for well-being is something that
at least most other animals share. Human well-being probably consists of
different things from the well-being of pigs, but it is merely self-serving to
assume that human interests are therefore more important than pigs'.

Let's take the morally crucial interest in avoiding pain as an example. Our
supposedly greater capacity for reason does not affect our interest in not
feeling pain, relative to the pig, just as the ability to feel pain in the human
sphere is not a function of our IQ. It is thought that the subcortex is the area
of the brain that experiences pain, and this area of the brain is roughly
comparable between humans and many other animals. Nonhumans are not
only susceptible to physical suffering. The denial of other vital needs, such as
adequate space and other conditions necessary for the flourishing of animals
causes psychological pain. The lack of comprehension of their situation could
just as easily exacerbate the suffering of animals as ameliorate it.

The vital interest in avoiding suffering and living a life which enables a
being to flourish is a common feature of all animals, human or nonhuman.
So how do we protect these interests? The notion of rights plays an important
role morally, politically and legally in the protection of the individual, from
the 17th and 18th Century theories of natural rights through to the UN
Declaration of Human Rights in 1948. Although the [Kennedy Report] claims
that 'rights . . . remain controversial', this underestimates both the rhetorical
and the philosophical force of the rights discourse . . .

Rights are designed to protect such intrinsically valuable individuals from
being used merely as instruments for the good of others. In other words,
according to the rights view, it is wrong to treat a being who is an
end-in-itself as merely a means to an end. The rights view fits in with our
moral intuition that it is wrong to harm the innocent for the benefit of others.
Thus there is a significant moral difference between suffering which occurs
spontaneously through no fault of anyone (eg many instances of illness and

naturally-caused death), and deliberately inflicted violence (eg the breeding and killing of pigs to provide organs).

On the other hand, the utilitarian approach gives us morally repugnant outcomes. The fundamental aim of utilitarianism is to increase the overall amount of happiness, and minimise the overall amount of harm. This may seem like a laudable goal. But the problem arises because individuals have no intrinsic value in this theory — they are merely receptacles of the 'good'. Therefore, the well-being of innocent individuals can be sacrificed for the good of others. As Tom Regan explains, utilitarianism can sanction successful secret killings (of humans, never mind other animals) if it brings about the optimal balance of pleasure and pain for those affected by its outcome.

The cost benefit analysis employed by the [Kennedy Report], the [Nuffield Report] and the Animals (Scientific Procedures) Act 1986 is the practical upshot of this morally repugnant theory which sanctions the active oppression of innocent individuals. Although this theory has been shown to be seriously counter-intuitive because of its implications for human beings, the foregoing discussions demonstrate that in all fairness, we must apply the same reasoning to other animals. And in addition to this demand of consistency, the application of cost-benefit analysis to intrinsically valuable entities, who are ends-in-themselves, is morally wrong. Cost-benefit analysis turns living beings with all their qualitative values into numerical, quantitive values. Thus it distorts what it purports to examine and attempts to compare incommensurable values.

There are additional problems with cost-benefit analysis which are particularly relevant to the question of xenotransplantation. The many uncertainties involved with xenotransplantation mean that a reasonably accurate cost-benefit analysis is impossible to carry out. On a deeper level, there is an inescapable arbitrariness in trying to quantify the interests of living beings. Given these uncertainties and judgements, there is a very real danger that those who are unable to articulate and defend their interests, pigs and primates in this case, will find their interests are overridden and devalued in favour of the interests of the more powerful group — human beings and in particular the commercial organisations with a financial interest in the realisation of xenotransplantation.

Finally, the whole notion of cost-benefit analysis presupposes a view of reality that sees the flourishing of some as in some way dependent on the suffering of others. This competitive, antagonistic worldview prevents human beings working together in order to achieve true progress through a more civilised and humane culture. Similarly, the attempt to dominate nature, be it the whole biosphere or individual animals, gives us the illusion of progress when in fact we are sowing the seeds of our own downfall. The issue of xenotransplantation provides a clear example of the folly of cost-benefit analysis, both fundamentally, and in its own terms . . .

The notion of animal rights is based on an extension of the notion of human rights, it does not supersede them. Indeed the philosophical basis of animal rights is a human-nonhuman animal continuum, so animal rights, by necessity, include human rights. **The bottom line is that violence is wrong, whoever suffers it, be they black, white, man, woman, homosexual, heterosexual, nonhuman or human.**

Questions:
1.   Compare and contrast the Kennedy and Uncaged reports. Which do you find more persuasive, and why?

2.   How should a potential law-maker adjudicate upon the relative merits of the reports by the Department of Health and a pressure group? Should one carry more weight than the other?

LEGAL CULTURES

Throughout this book and particularly in this chapter you have seen the use of both national and international sources of law; you have examined different categories of law; you have examined the categorisations with which law deals. In this final section we look, first, at the extent to which law and your legal studies are contingent on the culture (legal and otherwise) in which you are learning. This is particularly important given international, European and other comparative law systems' impact on our own. Here we examine how specific our legal cultures are, which links back to the introduction where we examined different perspectives on law. We also think again about what law is, and to what extent values should and can be made part of legal education. The following extract by William Twining discusses the effects on law, and in particular, legal theory, of globalisation:

W Twining, 'Globalisation and Legal Theory: Some Local Implications', (1996) vol. 49 *Current Legal Problems* at pp. 1–42 at pp. 1, 7–13.

Jeremy Bentham sometimes referred to himself as a citizen of the world. In his later writings he recognized the tension between his universal ethics and his theory of sovereignty, and he wrestled with it not very successfully. I was born in Uganda of an English father and a mother of Welsh-Huguenot descent. I had a colonial childhood, a neo-colonial adolescence and a post-colonial start to my career. I married an Irish wife. My daughter was born in Khartoum and my son in Dublin. I have just returned from India. I seem to have far better credentials than Bentham to claim to be a citizen of the world. Yet in style, residence, outlook, accent, and prejudices, I am irredeemably English. At best I am, in Bruce Ackerman's phrase, a rooted cosmopolitan. And it is as a cosmopolitan, rooted in London and Oxford, that I want to share with you some thoughts about the local implications of globalization for Jurisprudence as a subject and for the institutionalized discipline of law in this country.

Three Challenges to Legal Theory
Globalization has stimulated major rethinkings in several fields. I propose to argue that jurisprudence has so far responded only patchily to these challenges, but that the prospects for a sustained response are better than might appear on the surface. The processes of globalization are extremely complex and their impact is already pervasive. In the course of a single lecture, one has to be highly selective. I shall focus on three themes which seemingly present fundamental challenges to legal theory.

First, globalization and interdependence challenge 'black box theories' that treat nation-states or societies or legal systems as discrete, impervious entities that can be studied in isolation either internally or externally. This challenge operates in two main ways: municipal law can no longer be treated in isolation from outside influences, legal or otherwise. To take a familiar example: witness the daily impact of European Law, the European Convention on Human Rights, GATT, and transnational religious laws on our internal legal relations between local citizens, the state, and other legal persons. Conversely, the twin doctrines of national sovereignty and non-interference in internal affairs of independent states is being steadily challenged, most prominently, but not exclusively, by international humanitarian and human rights law and regional legal orders, such as the EU. In so far as our stock of theories of law assumes that municipal legal systems are self-contained or that public international law is concerned solely with external relations between states, such theories just do not fit the modern facts.

Secondly, mainstream Anglo-American legal theory has traditionally focused on only two types of legal order: municipal state law and public international law. Today a picture of law in the world must deal with a much more complex picture involving established, resurgent, developing, nascent, and potential forms of legal ordering. At the global level, there is a need for new orderings, especially in respect of communications, the environment, and natural resources on this and other planets. What are the prospects for a genuine *ius humanitatis* dealing with the common heritage of mankind? And what will be its philosophical or political base? Can public international law, as traditionally conceived, cope adequately with such problems as environment, international crime, and basic human needs or rights at the global level? At the transnational level, are we seeing the development of a new *ius mercatoria* — a system of largely private regulation within the capitalist world economy with institutions such as international arbitration playing an increasingly significant role? Also at the transnational level, what is general jurisprudence to make of, for example, the revival of Islamic Law in which the theological–juridical schools transcend national boundaries, and in many countries are part of the opposition to the government of the day? Even in officially Islamic states, those in power may represent only one point of view in ongoing juristic debates.

At the regional level, new legal orders are developing rapidly. The EU is the most salient from our vantage-point, but it is not the only one. Only relatively recently have fundamental questions begun to be asked in a sustained way about the juridicial nature of European Union Law. Does it fit any of our standard stock of theories of law and, conversely, which, if any, of the theories can provide any useful guidance to its development? Public International Law, I have already suggested, has already expanded and diversified in so many ways that it no longer fits old simple models of external relations between states. But further questions arise as to whether Public International Law, in which the nation-state still plays by far the dominant role, provides a suitable framework for conceptualizing transnational relations, both in obvious areas such as humanitarian and human rights law, but also in less obvious ones such as labour and domestic relations. One clear example of any uneasy fit is the artificial distinction between problems of international refugees, which fall largely under public international law, and the problems of internally displaced persons (now a more numerous group), who by and large are treated as the responsibility of their own states, which are often at least partly the cause of the problem.

One theme that links the emergence or re-emergence of these new kinds of legal order is the disengagement of law and state. A *ius humanitatis*, a transnational *lex mercatoria*, Islamic Law, transnational humanitarian and human rights law, and, in a different way, some new regional orderings, and even parts of Public International Law itself are all arguably more or less clear examples of the amorphous category 'non-state law' . . . an account of the phenomenon of law in the contemporary world would for most purposes be incomplete if it did not treat of legal families and legal cultures. Nation-states have, of course, played a major role in the diffusion and imposition of law in modern times, but so have immigration, informal networking, and the globalization of communication. One suspects, for example, that most of the younger generation in Continental Europe have obtained their picture of courts and trials and lawyers from American films and soap operas and, recently, from such live dramas as the O J Simpson case on CNN. One suspects also that orthodox accounts of reception and diffusion of law, at least in modern times, have been unduly influenced by formalist, state-oriented conceptions of law, which tend to downplay or overlook the other, often more elusive, elements that go to make up a legal culture.

The third challenge of globalization to legal theory that I wish to highlight is rather less fashionable. This is the matter of conceptual clarification, more particularly the construction of a conceptual framework and meta-languages that can transcend legal cultures. During the nineteenth century this was a central concern of both analytical and historical jurists . . . Theorizing can help us construct and clarify conceptual frameworks, models, ideal types, and other thinking tools — this might be called the conceptual or analytical function. Constructing general concepts, principles, taxonomies, and hypothesis can also save repetition and be economical — one might call this the simplifying function.

The division of intellectual labour into more or less self-contained institutionalized specialisms tends to create artificial boundaries between disciplines and discourses; these boundaries tend to disappear or fade as one moves up ladders of abstraction. Theories of justice for example, are as much the concern of lawyers, economists, and political theorists as they are of moral philosophers. Similarly, basic problems of evidence are to a greater or lesser extent shared with historians, social scientists, physical scientists, statisticians, and logicians . . . This transcending of boundaries between institutionalized fields of learning might be called the cross-disciplinary function. Jurisprudence is also involved in other tasks, such as the history of legal thought, the construction of working theories for participants (for example, prescriptive theories of legislation, adjudication, mediation, or advocacy) and . . . in the development of legal technology — that is the invention or creation of concepts, devices, institutions, and procedures as solutions to practical problems.

However, the most important theoretical function of all is the sustained teasing out, articulation, and critical examination of the general assumptions and presuppositions underlying the discourse of any discipline at a given moment in history.

Questions:

1. Returning to the questions we posed in Chapter 1, what are your own cultural influences? How did they influence your study of law?

2. Why did you choose law as a subject? What do you like about studying law? What do you dislike? How does law relate to subjects you have studied before?

3. Do you see theorising about legal concepts as important?

The issue of cultural relativism is particularly important in human rights law, which makes claims to universal acceptance and application across a number of countries. You will have noted how the cases of *P* v *S* and *X, Y & Z* v *UK* examined the law of different European countries on the issue of transsexualism as an important benchmark of acceptance. You may also have noticed reference in the earlier European Court of Human Rights decisions to the doctrine of the 'margin of appreciation'. We mentioned this briefly in Chapter 3, as a doctrine whereby states are given some leeway as regards application of rights, in matters which are of moral significance in their culture. So human rights law itself contains some recognition that different countries have different values (although this doctrine is often criticised as weakening protection of rights).

We examined in the first chapter various different perspectives on law. One other standpoint, raised in the first section of this chapter, is a Muslim one. As we saw, one source of grievance felt by some Muslim groups in Britain is precisely that their perspective is excluded in British law. The following writer deals with issues of conflicts between Muslim law and human rights law. The next extracts deal with conflict between human rights and Asian law.

Abdullah Ahmed An-Na'im, 'Human Rights in the Muslim World', *Harvard Human Rights Journal*, vol. 3 (1990) 13, as cited in H Steiner & P Alston, *International Human Rights in Context: Law, Politics, Morals,* Oxford, Clarendon (1996) pp. 210–213.

Historical formulations of Islamic religious law, commonly known as Shari'a, include a universal system of law and ethics and purport to regulate every aspect of public and private life. The power of Shari'a to regulate the behaviour of Muslims derives from its moral and religious authority as well as the formal enforcement of its legal norms. As such, Shari'a influences individual and collective behaviour in Muslim countries through its role in the socialization processes of such nations regardless of its status in their formal legal systems. For example, the status and rights of women in the Muslim world have always been significantly influenced by Shari'a, regardless of the degree of Islamization in public life. Of course, Shari'a is not the sole determinant of human behaviour nor the only formative force behind social and political institutions in Muslim countries . . .

I conclude that human rights advocates in the Muslim world must work within the framework of Islam to be effective. They need not be confined, however, to the particular historical interpretations of Islam known as Shari'a. Muslims are obliged, as a matter of faith, to conduct their private and public affairs in accordance with the dictates of Islam, but there is room for legitimate disagreement over the precise nature of these dictates in the modern context. Religious texts, like all other texts, are open to a variety of interpretations. Human rights advocates in the Muslim world should struggle to have their interpretations of the relevant texts adopted as the new Islamic scriptural imperatives for the contemporary world.

A.   Cultural Legitimacy for Human Rights

The basic premise of my approach is that human rights violations reflect the lack or weakness of cultural legitimacy of international standards in a society. Insofar as these standards are perceived to be alien to or at variance with the values and institutions of a people, they are unlikely to elicit commitment or compliance. While cultural legitimacy may not be the sole or even primary determinant of compliance with human rights standards, it is, in my view, an extremely significant one. Thus, the underlying causes of any lack or weakness of legitimacy of human rights standards must be addressed in order to enhance the promotion and protection of human rights in that society . . .

This cultural illegitimacy, it is argued, derives from the historical conditions surrounding the creation of the particular human rights instruments. Most African and Asian countries did not participate in the formulation of the Universal Declaration of Human Rights because, as victims of colonization, they were not members of the United Nations. When they did participate in the formulation of subsequent instruments, they did so on the basis of an established framework and philosophical assumptions adopted in their absence. For example, the preexisting framework and assumptions favoured individual civil and political rights over collective solidarity rights, such as a right to development, an outcome which remains problematic today. Some authors have gone so far as to argue that inherent differences exist between the Western notion of human rights as reflected in the international instruments and non-Western notions of human dignity. In the Muslim world, for instance, there are obvious conflicts between Shari'a and certain human rights, especially of women and non-Muslims . . .

In this discussion, I focus on the principles of legal equality and nondiscrimination contained in many human rights instruments. These principles relating to gender and religion are particularly problematic in the Muslim world . . .

II   ISLAM, SHARI'A AND HUMAN RIGHTS

A.   The Development and Current Application of Shari'a

To the over nine hundred million Muslims of the world, the Qur'an is the literal and final word of God and Muhammad is the final Prophet. During his mission, from 610 A.D. to his death in 632 A.D., the Prophet elaborated on the meaning of the Qur'an and supplemented its rulings through his statements and actions. This body of information came to be known as Sunna. He also established the first Islamic state in Medina around 622 A.D. which emerged later as the ideal model of an Islamic state . . .

Shari'a is not a formally enacted legal code. It consists of a vast body of jurisprudence in which individual jurists express their views on the meaning of the Qur'an and Sunna and the legal implications of those views. Although most Muslims believe Shari'a to be a single logical whole, there is significant diversity of opinion not only among the various schools of thought, but also among the different jurists of a particular school . . .

Furthermore, Muslim jurists were primarily concerned with the formulation of principles of Shari'a in terms of moral duties sanctioned by religious consequences rather than with legal obligations and rights and specific temporal remedies. They categorized all fields of human activity as permissible or impermissible and recommended or reprehensible. In other words, Shari'a addresses the conscience of the individual Muslim, whether in a private, or public and official, capacity, and not the institutions and corporate entities of society and the state . . .

Whatever may have been the historical status of Shari'a as the legal system of Muslim countries, the scope of its application in the public domain has diminished significantly since the middle of the nineteenth century. Due to both internal factors and external influence, Shari'a principles had been replaced by European law governing commercial, criminal, and constitutional matters in almost all Muslim countries. Only family law and inheritance continued to be governed by Shari'a . . .

Recently, many Muslims have challenged the gradual weakening of Shari'a as the basis for their formal legal systems. Most Muslim countries have experienced mounting demands for the immediate application of Shari'a as the sole, or at least primary, legal system of the land. These movements have either succeeded in gaining complete control, as in Iran, or achieved significant success in having aspects of Shari'a introduced into the legal system, as in Pakistan and the Sudan. Governments of Muslim countries generally find it difficult to resist these demands out of fear being condemned by their own populations as anti-Islamic. Therefore, it is likely that this so-called Islamic fundamentalism will achieve further successes in other Muslim countries.

The possibility of further Islamization may convince more people of the urgency of understanding and discussing the relationship between Shari'a and human rights, because Shari'a would have a direct impact on a wider range of human rights issues if it became the formal legal system of any country . . .

I believe that a modern version of Islamic law can and should be developed. Such a modern 'Shari'a' could be, in my view, entirely consistent with current standards of human rights. These views, however, are appreciated by only a tiny minority of contemporary Muslims. To the overwhelming majority of Muslims today, Shari'a is the sole valid interpretation of Islam, and as such *ought* to prevail over any human law or policy.

Y Ghai, 'Human Rights and Governance: The Asia Debate', *Australian Year Book of International Law* (1994), vol. 15, 1, p. 5, as cited in Steiner & Alston, *op. cit.*, pp 236–238.

. . . It is easy to believe that there is a distinct Asian approach to human rights because some government leaders speak as if they represent the whole continent when they make their pronouncements on human rights. This view is reinforced because they claim that their views are based on perspectives which emerge from the Asian culture or religion or Asian realities. The gist of their position is that human rights as propounded in the West are founded on individualism and therefore have no relevance to Asia which is based on the primacy of the community. It is also sometimes argued that economic underdevelopment renders most of the political and civil rights (emphasised in the West) irrelevant in Asia. Indeed, it is sometimes alleged that such rights are dangerous in view of fragmented nationalism and fragile Statehood.

It would be surprising if there were indeed one Asian perspective, since neither Asian culture nor Asian realities are homogenous throughout the continent. All the world's major religions are represented in Asia, and are in one place or another State religions (or enjoy a comparable status: Christianity in the Philippines, Islam in Malaysia, Hinduism in Nepal and Buddhism in Sri Lanka and Thailand). To this list we may add political ideologies like socialism, democracy or feudalism which animate peoples and governments of the region. Even apart from religious differences, there are other factors which have produced a rich diversity of cultures. A culture, moreover, is not static and many accounts given of Asian culture are probably true of an age long ago. Nor are the economic circumstances of all the Asian countries similar. Japan, Singapore and Hong Kong are among the world's most prosperous countries, while there is grinding poverty in Bangladesh, India and the Philippines. The economic and political systems in Asia likewise show a remarkable diversity, ranging from semi-feudal kingdoms in Kuwait and Saudi Arabia, through military dictatorships in Burma and formerly Cambodia, effectively one party regimes in Singapore and Indonesia, communist regimes in China and Vietnam, ambiguous democracies in Malaysia and Sri Lanka, to well established democracies like India. There are similarly differences in their economic systems, ranging from tribal subsistence economies in parts of Indonesia through highly developed market economies of Singapore, Hong Kong and Taiwan and the mixed economy model of India to the planned economies of China and Vietnam. Perceptions of human rights are undoubtedly reflective of these conditions, and suggest that they would vary from country to country.

Perceptions of human rights are reflective of social and class positions in society. What conveys an apparent picture of a uniform Asian perspective on human rights is that it is the perspective of a particular group, that of the ruling elites, which gets international attention. What unites these elites is their notion of governance and the expediency of their rule. For the most part, the political systems they represent are not open or democratic, and their publicly expressed views on human rights are an emanation of these systems, of the need to justify authoritarianism and occasional repression. It is their views which are given wide publicity domestically and internationally . . .

[S]ome Asian governments claim that their societies place a higher value on the community than in the West, that individuals find fulfilment in their participation in communal life and community tasks, and that this factor constitutes a primary distinction in the approach to human rights . . . This argument is advanced as an instance of the general proposition that rights are culture specific.

The 'communitarian' argument is Janus-faced. It is used against the claim of universal human rights to distinguish the allegedly Western, individual-oriented approaches to rights from the community centred values of the East. Yet it is also used to deny the claims and assertions of communities in the name of 'national unity and stability'. It suffers from at least two further weaknesses. First, it overstates the 'individualism' of Western society and traditions of thought . . .

Secondly, Asian governments . . . fall into the easy but wrong assumption that they or the State are the 'community' . . . Nothing can be more destructive of the community than this conflation. The community and State are different institutions and to some extent in a contrary juxtaposition. The community, for the most part, depends on popular norms developed through forms of consensus and enforced through mediation and persuasion. The State is an imposition on society, and unless humanised and democratised (as it has not been in most of Asia), it relies on edicts, the military, coercion and sanctions. It is the tension between them which has elsewhere underpinned human rights. In the name of the community, most Asian governments have stifled social and political initiatives of private groups . . . Governments have destroyed many communities in the name of the development of State stability . . .

Questions:

1. Is interpreting religious texts such as the Qur'an or the Bible, comparable to interpreting legal texts?

2. Are human rights a Western notion, or do they have universal claims to validity?

3. Is it justifiable for western legal systems to respond to practices such as female circumcision by outlawing them (in the Prohibition of Female Circumcision Act 1985), when such practices are integral to how women are perceived in certain other cultures? (For the Law Commission's consideration of this issue, see Chapter 9 of its Consultation Paper on Consent in the Criminal Law, extracted above at p. 375. Generally see J Bridgeman and S Millns, *Feminist Perspectives on Law*, London, Sweet & Maxwell, 1998, Chapter 10.)

It is hoped that while you have understood more about law through learning legal skills, you have also begun to question the whole idea of what law is, and what legal skills are. In 'putting it all together' we have found that at times arguments based on morality, efficiency and justice are just as important as arguments based on the text of statutes and case law. This then brings us back to some of the questions we raised at the start of this book as to what makes a good lawyer. Is it someone with particular skills? Is it someone who 'knows the law'? Is it a moral person?

If being a good lawyer means being a good person, can this be taught? What should be the main thrust of legal education? American law schools are famous for the 'Socratic method' of teaching whereby teachers ask a series of questions to probe a point, a method originally attributed to Socrates. In part, we have used this method in this book. The following extract from Plato's Dialogues provides a dialogue (probably fictional) between Socrates and a student, Meno, on whether virtue can be taught. After a lengthy series of questions on the nature of virtue, Socrates concludes that it is in the gift of the gods:

The Dialogues of Plato, Vol. 1, trans. B Jowett, Oxford, Clarendon Press (1953) pp. 265–266, 300–301.

Meno. Can you tell me, Socrates, whether virtue is acquired by teaching or by practice; or if neither by teaching nor by practice, then whether it comes to man by nature, or in what other way?

Socrates. Here at Athens there is a dearth of the commodity, and all wisdom seems to have emigrated from us to you. I am certain that if you were to ask any Athenian whether virtue was natural or acquired, he would laugh in your face, and say: 'Stranger, you have far too good an opinion of me, if you think that I can answer your question. For I literally do not know what virtue is, and much less whether it is acquired by teaching or not'. And I myself, Meno, living as I do in this region of poverty am as poor as the rest of the world; and I confess with shame that I know literally nothing about virtue; and when I do not know the 'quid' of anything how can I know the 'quale'? How, if I knew nothing at all of Meno, could I tell if he was handsome, or the opposite; rich and noble, or the reverse of rich and noble? Do you think that I could?

Men. No, indeed. But are you in earnest, Socrates, in saying that you do not know what virtue is? And am I to carry back this report of you to Thessaly?

Soc. Not only that, my dear boy, but you may say further that I have never come across anyone else who did, in my judgment . . .

Soc. But if virtue is not taught, neither is virtue knowledge.

Men. Clearly not . . .

Soc. To sum up our inquiry — the result seems to be, if we are at all right in our line of argument, that virtue is neither natural nor imparted by teaching, but an instinct given by God to those to whom it is given. Nor is the instinct accompanied by reason, unless there may be supposed to be among statesmen someone who is capable of educating statemen. And if there be such a one, he may be said to be among the living what Homer says that Tiresias was among the dead, 'he alone has understanding, but the rest are flitting shades'; in point of virtue he will be in like manner a reality among shadows.

Men. That is excellent, Socrates.

Soc. Then, Meno, the conclusion is that virtue comes by the gift of God to those to whom it does come. But we shall never know the certain truth until, before asking how virtue is given, we set ourselves to inquire into the essential nature of virtue . . .

Some lawyers have suggested that education for lawyers needs to be much broader than the study of legal texts. Note the comments of Felix Frankfurter, US Supreme Court judge in the middle of this century.

Letter from Felix Frankfurter, Associate Justice, US Supreme Court, to M Paul Claussen, Jr (May, 1954) in *The World of Law: The Law as Literature* 725 (Ephraim London edn, 1960), cited in J Fischer, 'Reading Literature/Reading Law: Is There a Literary Jurisprudence?', *Texas Law Review*, vol. 22 (1993) 135–160, p. 135.

No one can be a truly competent lawyer unless he is a cultivated man . . . The best way to prepare for the law is to come to the study of the law as a well-read person. Thus alone can one acquire the capacity to use the English language on paper and in speech and with the habits of clear thinking which only a truly liberal education can give. No less important for a lawyer is the cultivation of the imaginative faculties by reading poetry, seeing great paintings . . . and listening to great music. Stock your mind with the deposit of much good reading, and widen and deepen your feelings by experiencing vicariously as much as possible the wonderful mysteries of the universe, and forget all about your future career.

Recently, a movement known as the 'law and literature' movement has used literature in the teaching of law. The following extract both uses literature to make points of law, and questions whether the study of literature for lawyers can generate empathy with particular predicaments, in other words whether literature can 'teach virtue' to lawyers.

K O'Donovan, 'Identification with Whom?' in C Bell and J Morison (ed), *Tall Stories? Reading Law and Literature*, Aldershot, Dartmouth (1996) pp. 39–56, at pp. 39–41, 42–45.

The argument that literature can enable imaginative leaps and empathy, thus developing a sense of justice, has not been put forward in a sustained way by writers on law and literature. There have been such suggestions. The case in favour posits that by allowing the reader to enter into the experiences of characters in drama or novel, in biography or autobiography, literature can broaden and deepen feelings of empathy. Arguments for the development of empathy in education are various. They include ethical arguments about deepening imaginative experience, sharing the feelings of others, understanding others, finding expression of one's own and others' experiences and emotions, foreshadowing and anticipating future experience of life. There are also arguments about improving legal skills and the lawyering function.

Identification

Sympathetic identification with others is a basis of ethical experience, but
there is no law of reading which states that readers must identify with one
character rather than another. So it is also in life. Peter van Daan in his
wartime attic hiding-place confides to Anne Frank his uneasiness in being a
Jew and how he would have found it much easier if he had been a Christian,
and if he could he would be one after the war. His hope for the future is to go
to the Dutch East Indies and live on a plantation. One interpretation of this
desire for the future is that Peter hopes to find in colonial life an independence
and power he cannot have as a Jew in Europe. This interpretation is not
intended as a criticism of Peter. Given his miserable existence in hiding, and
the threat to his life, it is hardly surprising that he dreams of another existence.
Given the social stigmatization of his identity, it is not surprising that he seeks
a different identity. But my interpretation is intended to illustrate the point
that choice of identification is possible. Because of their stigmatization and
victimization some identities are subordinate, or possibly dangerous. Such
identities may not be identified with, even by those categorised by others as
having such identities. So we may choose who we identify with and whether
or not to identify with the victimized or the stigmatized. One of the more
powerful arguments for reading imaginative literature is that it gives voices to
those often not heard. It is in the pages of literature that we find the excluded.

It must also be acknowledged that the phenomenon of unreflective empathy
exists, in which we identify with those persons or characters whom we
perceive as being like ourselves. This has been recognised by decision-
makers, such as judges, as limiting their neutrality or objectivity. It is not just
that such understanding is so automatic that it goes unnoticed by the
empathiser, but that literature offers opportunities for contested readings.
How one reads may relate to one's own values.

A caveat must be entered to the theory that understanding always leads to
morality and justice. For example, understanding the feelings of another may
increase cruelty, manipulation and sadism. The bully may use his knowledge
of his victims' vulnerability to inflict pain more successfully. Bernard
Williams makes this point:

> But one thing that must be true is that the insightful understanding of
> others' feelings possessed by the sympathetic person is possessed in much
> the same form by the sadistic or cruel person; that is one way in which the
> cruel are distinguished from the brutal or the indifferent.

However, this is not an argument against empathy, but rather a caution; for
as Williams says elsewhere, 'sympathetic identification with others . . . [is]
basic to ethical experience'. Such experience may be lacking in law students
at the beginnings of their working lives, who may nevertheless arrive at some
understanding through reading.

Our identities

Working out who and what we are is a major preoccupation in most lives.
Some aspects might seem to be given: our genes, our bodies, sex, colour,

appearance. Yet doubt has been cast on the extent to which such material aspects of the self are fixed. Geneticists, whilst positing that genes can be mapped and located for physical and mental traits, including criminality, also propose that DNA will enable the elimination of 'undesirable' genes. In other words some scientists argue that the fixedness of genetic inheritance can be changed through science. Significant academic writers also argue fluidity and even plasticity of the self. The relevance of this new 'fluid identity' is that it appears to deny the limitations of our actual identities — limitations to cognition of difference — limitations to empathetic identification with others. The agenda of choice presented includes not only our outward and inward selves, but also the very material, DNA, of which we are made.

I have argued elsewhere that this is a mistaken agenda. Firstly, most people have little or no choice about their genes. Secondly, parental choices about the genetic make-up of their children are largely negative choices. These are choices *not* to reproduce with a particular partner, or at all. Thirdly, the idea of changing genes, because of alleged criminality, for example, pre-supposes current beliefs in genetic essentialism. A debate about change starts from a premise of fixedness. An alternative method of analysis, I suggest, should start from the social interpretations placed on embodiment and external appearances. For the purposes of this paper we must consider how such interpretations construct and limit the possibilities of what a person can be. It may be that empathy, or imaginative sympathy, developed through reading and discussion, can challenge social interpretations which stigmatize and victimize. Whether this is expressed in terms of the 'neighbour principle' or of Kantian universalisability, is of lesser significance. At present, external interpretation allied with internal self-identity limits the possibilities of empathy for, or identification with, others.

I have already suggested that empathy requires a stepping-aside from our own self-interest, emotions, and immediate concerns. This does not necessarily involve leaving our own identities behind; for it is possible to build into our identities a capacity for empathy. I am deliberately presenting this as a social trait, a social choice, rather than as an inherent or genetic trait.

The stepping-aside under discussion here is intended to deal with a different scenario from the mind experiments involved in the Rawlsian social contract. Rawls argues that his principles of justice will be chosen under a veil of ignorance because no-one will want to risk ending up poor or oppressed. In a sense, Rawls assumes self-interest, albeit in a highly theoretical scene. This chapter addresses the practicalities of the education of real people who already exist in a world of identities.

Questions:

1. Do you agree with Justice Frankfurter's view that one cannot be a competent lawyer unless one is a civilised person?

2. Can you think of any instance where reading a novel or watching a film or play altered your perception of a legal issue?

3. Can you think of a novel, play or film which sparked different and opposite reactions from people?

Finally, it is often at graduation that role models are presented to student lawyers or that students are given some indication of what roles they might seek to model for themselves. We conclude with one of the most striking of these addresses from an American judge:

A L Higginbotham, 'The Life of the Law: Values, Commitment and Craftman-ship', *Harvard Law Review* (1990), Vol. 100, pp. 795–816 at pp. 814–16.

I wish to question more broadly the role of today's lawyer in assuring the attainment of justice in America. In my opinion, lawyers must be the visionaries in our society. We must be the nation's legal architects who renovate the palace of justice and redesign the landscape of opportunity in our nation . . .

When it comes to moral values and ethical commitments, lawyers have been found on all sides of every major issue. Some lawyers have ruthlessly exploited the helpless while others have tirelessly aided the weak, the poor and the dispossessed.

. . . Poverty, hatred, malnutrition, inadequate health care and housing, corruption in government, and the failure of our public school system continue to haunt us today because those in power often have lacked personal morality or have failed to make real the values that they have professed to hold in the abstract. To paraphrase Justice Holmes, the life of the law must not be mere logic; it must also be values. Each lawyer — whether judge or political, professor or entrepreneur — must make personal judgments. Those critical moral and human values cannot be acquired by even the most meticulous reading of opinions or statutes. Each lawyer must consciously and constantly assess his or her values and goals in forging rules of law for the future.

. . . It is especially appropriate for lawyers to evaluate how successful we have been as a profession in moving towards the goal of social and legal justice for all.

. . . Where will each of you stand? Will you be aligned with those forces that expand the horizons of opportunity for the weak, the poor, the powerless, and the many who have not had our options? Or will you become members of the indulgent new majority in our society who seem to feel that the quality of morality in our nation's public life is unimportant as long as they have good salaries and comfortable suburban homes or luxurious condominiums in the city? Will you as a lawyer merely become a technical expert, detached and indifferent? Will you be concerned solely with obtaining the highest fees for the least amount of effort, untroubled by the quality of life in our nation or world? Or will you care enough to make a difference?

These goals and challenges that I offer are not pipe dreams. They are real possibilities, and whether we strive to achieve them as lawyers will depend upon the moral philosophies that guide our daily lives. I am confident that most law students are capable of becoming good legal technicians. But our world today needs more than mere craftsmen and craftswomen. I welcome today's students into the life in this world by committing themselves to pursuing their moral visions.